PACIFISM IN THE
TWENTIETH CENT

To Hugh and
Sivkha in coop. you will
and respect for and
peaceworld for you
gratitude for this Louise
kindness
cousin
Nigel

Leaflet for the Belligerents (1939)

PACIFISM IN THE TWENTIETH CENTURY

by
PETER BROCK and NIGEL YOUNG

Distributed by
SYRACUSE UNIVERSITY PRESS
1600 Jamesville Avenue
Syracuse
New York 13244-5160

© Peter Brock and Nigel Young

ISBN: 0-8156-8125-9

First published in February 1999

Printed by
UNIVERSITY OF TORONTO PRESS INCORPORATED

Let us pray that all living beings realize that they are all brothers and sisters, all nourished from the same source of life.

Let us pray that we ourselves cease to be the cause of suffering to each other.

Let us plead with ourselves to live in a way which will not deprive other living beings of air, water, food, shelter, or the chance to live.

With humility, with awareness of the existence of life and of the sufferings that are going on around us, let us pray for the establishment of peace in our hearts and on earth.

—From "A Buddhist Litany for Peace" by the Venerable Thich Nhât Hanh in 1976; George Appleton, ed., *The Oxford Book of Prayer* (Oxford: Oxford University Press), p. 306.

Contents

Preface

In 1970, Peter Brock published his *Twentieth-Century Pacifism* (Van Nostrand Reinhold Company), a survey of pacifism from roughly 1914 to the early 1960s. The work became something of a minor classic on the subject. However, the history of pacifism has continued and evolved in the following three decades, and further scholarship has thrown new light on the earlier periods. In 1994, I approached Peter Brock with the idea of bringing the book up to date and including chapters on the 1970s, 1980s and early 1990s, as well as the new strands of pacifism – and fresh debates since the 1960s. I also urged him to include illustrations in a new edition so as to make the book more attractive to students as well as to the general reader. The bulk of the revised work remains Peter Brock's. But we have rewritten sections on the 1950s and 1960s, while I am largely responsible for the second chapter on the Cold War. He has added fresh chapters on the "new" conscientious objection, the historic peace churches since 1945, and religious pacifist outreach since 1945. Some of the earlier chapters have been reorganized and reused; the bibliography has been replaced, while the conclusion is mainly mine. Almost all the illustrations were selected by Peter Brock.

By pacifism, the authors mean a pacifism that rejects involvement in war. The book centers on an analysis of the movement which has grown up in our century, combining advocacy of personal nonparticipation in war of any kind or in violent revolution with an endeavor to find nonviolent means of resolving conflict.

On the European continent, "pacifism" (a term first used in 1901) usually includes all efforts to achieve international peace and understanding. But in Anglo-American usage, the term is normally limited to the definition given above; of course the adjectives "absolute" or "integral" might well be used for the type of pacifism with which we are mainly concerned in this book. Even inside these narrower limits, however, it is sometimes impossible to divide the pacifists from the nonpacifists. Within the twentieth-century pacifist community itself, a wide spectrum of opinion has existed on the subject of war as well as on other political, religious, and moral problems. Pacifist ideals range from rigid vegetarianism, which recoils from killing any sentient being, to war resistance or conscientious objection which is usually confined to fighting in national wars and does not include taking human life in self-defense or in defense of an accepted system of international law – or for the internal maintenance of a democratically elected government.

December 1996   Nigel Young

Acknowledgements

For assistance in various ways we would like to thank William C. Berman, Philip L. Borkholder, Wendy E. Chmielewski, Richard B. Deats, Nándor F. Dreisziger, Donald F. Durnbaugh, William B. Edgerton, Cecil R. Evans, J. William Frost, Larry Gara, Kathleeen Hertzberg, Charles F. Howlett, Milton Israel, Lawrence Klippenstein, Malcolm Saunders, Gerald W. Schlabach, Jane Oakley Sweet and Jo Vellacott.

With regard to the illustration credits we have endeavored to obtain permission to reprint if copyright was involved. In a few cases, however, we did not succeed in our attempts to contact a possible copyright holder. We hope in such instances that our intention will be taken in good spirit.

Trudy King typed a large part of the text. We are grateful for the care with which she did this as well as for her patience with the numerous changes we made in the course of her labors.

We owe a special debt of gratitude to Antonia Young and to Colgate University's Peace Studies program and staff as well as to its division of University Studies and Social Sciences for their assistance – physical, material, and moral – during the preparation of this book. We are greatly indebted, too, to Cynthia Maude-Gembler who, as Executive Editor of Syracuse University Press, gave continuous support to our project.

Thomas P. Socknat kindly undertook the compilation of the index, despite the pressures of a heavy teaching load. Jim Paterson of the Printing Division of the University of Toronto Press skillfully guided our book through the final stages of production.

P.B.
N.Y.

Authors' Note

The manuscript of this volume was ready at the end of 1996. But a series of unforeseen vicissitudes delayed publication; so that it has been possible to take into consideration only a few items appearing after that year.

During the autumn of 1968 Carmen Brock typed almost the whole manuscript of the original book. We dedicate the present volume to her memory. She would have been happy to see it appear in print at last.

In many areas of twentieth-century pacifist history, both scholarly studies and accounts for the general reader continue to appear as well as biographies and autobiographies of leading pacifists and memoirs by former conscientious objectors, especially C.Os. in the United States. We may note, as an example, one item in the last category, which is scheduled for publication by the Kent State University Press (Kent, OH) in March 1999: Larry Gara and Lenna Mae Gara, eds., *A Few Small Candles: War Resisters of World War II tell Their Stories*. The essays in this volume describe the experiences of ten young Americans imprisoned "because of their convictions against kiling," and how today these men, all of them now septuagenarians at least, feel about the time they spent in prison in their youth.

P.B.
N.Y.

Illustration Credits

Page xxiii. From the files of Nigel Young.

Page xxiv. Top: From *The Tribunal* (No. 126, 26 September 1918). *Bottom:* A prison cell – from W.J. Chamberlain, *Fighting for Peace: The Story of the War Resistance Movement* (London: No More War Movement, n.d.).

Page xxv. From Harold Studley Gray, *Character "Bad": The Story of a Conscientious Objector* (New York and London: Harper & Brothers, 1934).

Page xxvi. From Carl Zigrosser, ed., *Prints and Drawings of Käte Kollwitz* (New York: Dover Publications, 1969).

Page xxvii. Still from *All Quiet on the Western Front.* Copyright © 1998 by Universal Studios, Inc. Courtesy of Universal Studios, Universal City, CA. Publishing Rights. All Rights Reserved.

Page xxviii. From V. Brittain, *The Rebel Passion ...*

Page xxix. Top: H.R.L. Sheppard – from the files of Nigel Young. John Middleton Murry – from a selection of his essays, *Looking before and after* (London: Sheppard Press, 1948). *Bottom:* PPU deputation – from Albert Beale, *Against All War: Fifty Years of Peace News 1936–1986* (London: Peace News, 1986).

Page xxx. From Thomas P. Socknat, *Witness against War: Pacifism in Canada 1900–1945* (Toronto: University of Toronto Press, 1987).

Page xxxi. Top: From *L.N. Tolstoi: Dokumenty, fotografii, rukopisi* (Moscow: Planeta, 1995). *Bottom:* Photograph of Bart de Ligt courtesy of Herman Noordegraaf.

Page xxxii. From William Axling, *Kagawa* (New York and London: Harper & Brothers, 1932).

Page xxxiii. From Daniel Anet, *Pierre Ceresole: Passionate Peacemaker* (abridged translation of the edition in French, Delhi: The Macmillan Company of India Limited, 1974). © Ethelwyn Best.

Page xxxiv. From Denis Hayes, *Challenge of Conscience: The Story of the Conscientious Objectors of 1939–1949* (London, 1949), published for the Central Board for Conscientious Objectors.

Page xxxv. Top: From file #30, Brethren Historical Library and Archives, Elgin, IL. *Bottom:* From Susan Hoeppner photo file in the archives of the Mennonite Heritage Centre, Winnipeg, MB.

Page xxxvi. Top: From H. Martin Lidbetter, *The Friends Ambulance Unit 1939– 1943: Three and Three Quarter Years ...* (York, U.K.: Sessions Book Trust, 1993). Photograph courtesy of Eva M. Lidbetter Sessions. *Bottom:* From D. Hayes, *Challenge of Conscience ...*

Page xxxvii. From George Lang, Raymond L. Collins, and Gerard F. White, eds., *Medal of Honor Recipients 1863–1994* (New York: Facts on File, Inc., 1995), vol. II.

Page xxxviii. From *Pacifica Views,* vol. I, no. 13 (3 December 1943). Drawing from Lowell Naeve, *A Field of Broken Stones* (Glen Gardner, NJ: Libertarian Press, 1960).

Page xxxix. Hermann Stöhr – from Eberhard Röhm, *Sterben für den Frieden-Spurensicherung: Hermann Stöhr (1898–1940) und die ökumenische Friedensbewegung* (Stuttgart: Calwer Verlag, 1985). Max Josef Metzger, André Trocmé, and Philippe Vernier – from V. Brittain, *The Rebel Passion ...*

Page xl. From Bruce Kent, *Franz Jägerstätter (The Man who said 'No' to Hitler).* London: Incorporated Catholic Truth Society, n.d.

Page xli. From the archives of the American Friends Service Committee (Philadelphia).

Page xlii. From A. Ruth Fry, *A Quaker Adventure: The Story of Nine Years' Relief and Reconstruction* (London: Nisbet & Co. Ltd., 1926).

Page xliii. Top: From Roger C. Wilson, *Quaker Relief: An Account of the Relief Work of the Society of Friends 1940–1948* (London: George Allen & Unwin Ltd., 1952). *Bottom:* From Madeleine Yaude Stephenson and Edwin "Red" Stephenson, *Journey of the Wild Geese: A Quaker Romance in War-Torn Europe* (Pasadena, CA: International Productions, 1999). Photographs courtesy of Edwin Stephenson and the American Friends Service Committee.

Page xliv. Top: From Albert Beale, *Against All War ... Bottom:* From Peggy Duff, *Left, Left, Left: A Personal Account of Six Protest Campaigns of 1945–65* (London: Allison & Busby Ltd., 1971).

Page xlv. From Lanza del Vasto, *Gandhi to Vinoba: The New Pilgrimage* (New York: Schocken Brooks, 1974).

Page xlvi. From R. Cooney and H. Michalowski, eds., *The Power of the People ...*

Page xlvii. Top: From Jervis Anderson, *Bayard Rustin: Troubles I've seen – A Biography* (New York: HarperCollins, 1997). *Bottom:* From Barbara Deming, *Prisons that could not hold* (San Francisco: Spinsters Ink, 1985). Photograph © by Joan E. Biren.

Page xlviii. From Bronson P. Clark, *Not by Might: A Viet Nam Memoir* (Glastonbury, CT: Chapel Rock Publishers, 1997). Photographs courtesy of the American Friends Service Committee.

Page xlix. From R. Cooney and H. Michalowski, eds., *The Power of the People ...*

Page l. Top: Photograph of Dorothy Day by Fritz Kaeser, 1958. Courtesy of the Marquette University Archives and Mildred T. Kaeser. *Bottom:* From Daniel

Berrigan, *To dwell in Peace: An Autobiography* (San Francisco: Harper & Row, 1987).

Page li. From Bradford Lyttle, *You come with Naked Hands: The Story of the San Francisco to Moscow March for Peace* (Canton, ME: Greenleaf Books, n.d.).

Page lii. From the files of Nigel Young.

Page liii. Top: From *Grundgesetz für die Bundesrepublik Deutschland* (Basic Law of the Federal Republic of Germany): "Die Grundrechte." *Bottom:* Photo KEM / MOC. From *Peace News*, no. 2433 (January 1999), by permission of the editors.

Page liv. From the *Toronto Globe and Mail*, 24 December 1998.

Pages 422–4. From Fritz Eichenberg, *Works of Mercy,* ed. Robert Ellsberg (Maryknoll, NY: Orbis Books, 1992). © Fritz Eichenberg Trust / VIS-ART, Montreal / VAGA, New York.

LEV (LEO) TOLSTOY (1828–1910), with his wife Sofia; photograph taken six weeks before his death

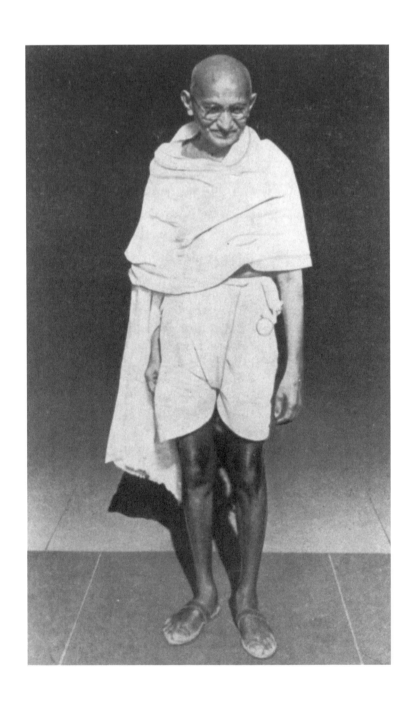

MOHANDAS KARAMCHAND GANDHI (1869–1948)

THE GANDHIAN WAY (*GANDHI MARG*)

गांधी-मार्ग

Gandhi walking through the villages of East Bengal in 1947 to help quell Hindu-Muslin violence

There is no way to peace. Peace is the way.

Mahatma Gandhi
Walking in Noakhali (Bengal), 1946

MATHILDA WREDE
(1864–1928)

ELEANOR MAY MOORE
(1875–1949)

JESSIE WALLACE HUGHAN
(1875–1955)

JEANNETTE RANKIN
(1880–1973)

MURIEL LESTER
(1883–1968)

VERA BRITTAIN
(1893–1970)

PAT ARROWSMITH
(b. 1930)

HILDEGARD GOSS-MAYR
(b. 1930)

CLIFFORD ALLEN
(1899–1939)
Chairman of the No-Conscription
Fellowship after his release from
prison

CATHERINE E. MARSHALL (1880–1961)
Honorary Secretary of the No-Conscription
Fellowship

Leading members of the No-Conscription Fellowship at its National
Convention in London, November 1915

THE C·O·'S HANSARD

RETROSPECTIVE SERIES No. 6

A WEEKLY REPRINT FROM THE OFFICIAL
PARLIAMENTARY REPORTS · · PUBLISHED
BY THE NO·CONSCRIPTION FELLOWSHIP
5, YORK BUILDINGS, ADELPHI, W.C.

OCTOBER 12, 1916   ONE PENNY   COVERING THE PERIOD FROM

MAY 11 TO MAY 15, 1916

	Page		Page
Alternative Civil Service	61	Limitation of Exemption	69
Appeal Tribunals, The···	68	Order for Alternative	
C.O.'s Sent to France ···	61	Service··· ··· ··· ···	69
Exemption by Statutory		Second Military Service	
Declaration··· ··· ···	68	Act, The ··· ···	61

HOUSE OF COMMONS
C.O.'S SENT TO FRANCE
Thursday, 11th May, 1916

Mr. TENNANT, in reply to Mr. Rowntree, said Rendal Wyatt, a
conscientious objector, went to France on May 8 with No. 2 Non-Combatant Corps.

The

-- TRIBUNAL --

No. 126.	Thursday, September 26, 1918.	One Penny

MANIFESTO

OF THE ABSOLUTISTS AT WAKEFIELD

It is not generally known that there are to-day over 1,500 Conscientious Objectors in prison. Of these nearly 700 have served sentences amounting to two years' hard labour. The Government is now transferring these long sentence men to Wakefield prison, and instead of granting them the absolute exemption which is their right, is trying to induce them to administer their own punishment by working a scheme of Industrial Conscription. In the following Manifesto the men set forth clearly their reasons for refusing to surrender the principle for which they have already suffered two years' imprisonment.

H.M. Prison, Wakefield,
Sept. 14, 1918.

In view of the grave misunderstanding and misrepresentation concerning the principles of the Absolutist Conscientious Objectors, we issue the following brief statement :—

1. Our vital principle as Absolutists is not a refusal to serve the community. It is that we cannot accept either Military Service or any compulsory work, organised to facilitate the prosecution of the war.

2. Therefore we cannot accept any scheme of work, involving our actual or implied consent to the carrying out of any such purpose.

3. We are faced with a situation, submission to which may involve the complete denial of our principles, by implicitly introducing an element of voluntary or semi-voluntary co-operation on our part.

4. It appears that the Government still misunderstand our principles, in that they take for granted that any safe or easy conditions can meet the imperative demands of our conscience. No offer of schemes or concessions can do this. We stand for the inviolable rights of conscience in the affairs of life. We ask for liberty to serve, and if necessary to suffer for the community and its well-being. As long as the Government deny us this right, we can only take with cheerfulness and unmistakable determination whatever penalties are imposed upon us.

We want no concessions. We desire only the liberty to serve.

Signed on behalf of the Absolutists in Wakefield Prison :

WALTER H. AYLES, Chairman.
P. T. DAVIES, General Secretary.
W. H. THOMPSON
E. P. SOUTHALL } Members of the Advisory Committee
HENRY SARA
J. SCOTT DUCKERS
GEO. HORWILL

A PRISON CELL, LOOKING TOWARDS THE HEAVILY-BARRED WINDOW.

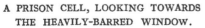

Drawing by E. M. Wilson.

A PRISON CELL, SHOWING IRON DOOR, WITH SPY HOLE.

Drawing by E. M. Wilson.

Dishonorable Discharge from the Army of the United States

TO ALL WHOM IT MAY CONCERN:

This is to Certify, That *Harold S Gray* *Private 1st Battalion Conscientious Objector National Army* is hereby **Dishonorably Discharged** from the military service of the United States by reason of the sentence of a General Court-Martial *#92 Hqrs Camp Funston* dated *November 14th 1918*

Said *Harold S Gray* was born in *Detroit*, in the State of *Michigan* When enlisted he was *24* years of age and by occupation a *Student* He had *Brown* eyes, *Brown* hair, *Ruddy* complexion, and was *5* feet *9½* inches in height.

Given under my hand at *Alcatraz California* this *5th* day of *Sept*, one thousand nine hundred and *Nineteen*

Geo. Ganard

Colonel. U.S.A. Retired.
Commanding.

FORM No. 371, A. G. O.

FIRST PAGE OF ARMY DISCHARGE HANDED TO HAROLD S. GRAY AT ALCATRAZ, SEPTEMBER 5, 1919

Knowledge of any vocation: *Student*

Wounds received in service: *None*

Physical condition when discharged: *Good*

Typhoid prophylaxis completed *May 18th 1918*

Paratyphoid prophylaxis completed *May 18th 1918*

Married or single: *Single*

Remarks: *Character "Bad"*

A SECTION OF THE REVERSE PAGE OF DISCHARGE

One objector's experience: From college to Alcatraz

"Killed in Action" (*Gefallen*), 1921, a lithograph by KÄTHE KOLLWITZ
(1867–1945)

LEW AYRES (1908–1996) as Paul Baumer in *All Quiet on the Western Front* (1930): the film shot showing Baumer alone in a trench at night with the "enemy" soldier he has killed

JOHN HAYNES HOLMES
(1879–1964)

JOHN NEVIN SAYRE
(1884–1977)

A.J. MUSTE
(1885–1967)

KIRBY PAGE
(1890–1957)

H.R.L. ("Dick") SHEPPARD
(1880–1937)

JOHN MIDDLETON MURRY
(1889–1957)
Editor of *Peace News*, 1940–1946

A deputation from the Peace Pledge Union to the Prime Minister, Neville
Chamberlain, in 1938: left to right — GEORGE LANSBURY (1859–1940), AL-
FRED SALTER (1873–1945), Canon CHARLES RAVEN (1885–1964), LAURENCE
HOUSMAN (1865–1959), VERA BRITTAIN, and Canon STUART MORRIS
(1890–1967)

RICHARD ROBERTS
(1874–1945)

ROBERT EDIS FAIRBAIRN
(1879–1953)

J. LAVELL SMITH
(1892–1973)

CARLYLE KING
(1907–1988)

Leaders of the Canadian Fellowship of Reconciliation

VLADIMIR CHERTKOV (1854–1936) and TOLSTOY at Yasnaya Polanya, 1909

BART DE LIGT (1883–1938) and the title pages of his path breaking two-volume history of pacifist thought and action

KAGAWA TOYOHIKO
(1888–1960)

CERESOLE at SCI work camp, Feldis (Switzerland)

PIERRE CERESOLE (1879–1945)
Founder of SCI

SCI work site at Brynmawr (Wales)

NEWS CHRONICLE   THE FIRST TRIBUNAL SINCE 1919

THE TRIBUNALS—INFORMAL AND FORMAL

PLANET NEWS   ONE OF THE FIRST WOMEN'S TRIBUNALS

Planting trees at Church of the Brethren CPS "Camp Walhalla," Michigan

Canadian conscientious objectors (primarily Mennonites) on work break at a C.O. camp

The first FAU party assigned for Red Cross work during the Russo-Finnish War with their ambulances in London, January 1940

Digging for bombs with the Non-Combatant Corps

DOSS, DESMOND THOMAS

Rank: Private First Class (highest rank: Corporal)
Service: U.S. Army
Birthday: 7 February 1919
Place of Birth: Lynchburg, Lynchburg County, Virginia
Entered Service at: Lynchburg, Lynchburg County, Virginia
Unit: 307th Infantry, Medical Detachment, 77th Infantry Division
Served as: Medical Aidman
Battle or Place of Action: Urasoe-Mura, Okinawa, Ryukyu Islands
Date of Action: 29 April-21 May 1945
G.O. Number, Date: 97, 1 November 1945
Date of Presentation: 12 October 1945
Place of Presentation: The White House, presented by Pres. Harry S. Truman
Citation: He was a company aidman when the 1st Battalion assaulted a jagged escarpment 400 feet high. As our troops gained the summit, a heavy concentration of artillery, mortar, and machine-gun fire crashed into them, inflicting approximately 75 casualties and driving the others back. Pfc. Doss refused to seek cover and remained in the fire-swept area with the many stricken, carrying them one by one to the edge of the escarpment and there lowering them on a rope-supported litter down the face of a cliff to friendly hands. On 2 May, he exposed himself to heavy rifle and mortar fire in rescuing a wounded man 200 yards forward of the lines on the same escarpment; and two days later he treated four men who had been cut down while assaulting a strongly defended cave, advancing through a shower of grenades to within eight yards of enemy forces in a cave's mouth, where he dressed his comrades' wounds before making four separate trips under fire to evacuate them to safety. On 5 May, he unhesitatingly braved enemy shelling and small-arms fire to assist an artillery officer. He applied bandages, moved his patient to a spot that offered protection from small-arms fire, and, while artillery and mortar shells fell close by, painstakingly administered plasma. Later that day, when an American was severely wounded by fire from a cave, Pfc. Doss crawled to him where he had fallen 25 feet from the enemy position, rendered aid, and carried him 100 yards to safety while continually exposed to enemy fire. On 21 May, in a night attack on high ground near Shuri, he remained in exposed territory while the rest of his company took cover, fearlessly risking the chance that he would be mistaken for an infiltrating Japanese and giving aid to the injured until he was himself seriously wounded in the legs by the explosion of a grenade. Rather than call another aidman from cover, he cared for his own injuries and waited five hours before litter bearers reached him and started carrying him to cover. The trio was caught in an enemy tank attack and Pfc. Doss, seeing a more critically wounded man nearby, crawled off the litter and directied the bearers to give their first attention to the other man. Awaiting the litter bearers' return, he was again struck, this time suffering a compound fracture of one arm. With magnificent fortitude he bound a rifle stock to his shattered arm as a splint and then crawled 300 yards over rough terrain to the aid station. Through his outstanding bravery and unflinching determination in the face of desperately dangerous conditions Pfc. Doss saved the lives of many soldiers. His name became a symbol throughout the 77th Infantry Division for outstanding gallantry far above and beyond the call of duty.

The Congressional Medal of Honor for a Seventh-day Adventist

PACIFICA VIEWS
Edited and Published Weekly By
PACIFICA ASSOCIATES
P. O. Box 65
GLENDORA, CALIFORNIA
Yearly Subscription $2   Single Copy 5 Cents

Murphy and Taylor

In October, 1942, Stanley Murphy and Louis Taylor walked out of the Big Flats, N. Y., CPS Camp in protest against conscription and the administration of the c.o. provisions of the Selective Service Act. Imprisoned as violators of the Act, they refused to work in prison and went on a hunger strike lasting 82 days.

When promised by a Federal prison official that better treatment and work would be given to parolees, they stopped fasting, but refused for themselves paroles to jobs in the West with only $2.50 a month "allowance" as pay. Both men were then transferred from the prison at Danbury, Conn., to the Federal Prison Hospital at Springfield, Mo., where, for some time at least, they were placed in "strip cells"—bare cells with a hole in the floor as a toilet—in which, it is said, men are left without any clothing.

Following is part of a written statement passed by Stanley Murphy to his mother when she succeeded in seeing him on Aug. 14:

> As you know, I have from the beginning made clear the position I took and still hold on the matter of work. It was known to the men in charge of 10-B (Note: the section containing the strip cells), and Dr. Cox (the Warden), etc. None the less, on Tuesday (Aug. 3) two attendants opened the door of the strip cell and threw in a pair of pajamas which I put on, and they took me to the shower and told me to emory-paper

the shower stall. I replied that I was not able to do so. They then summoned another attendant from the outside and said they would make me do it. With the arrival of the outside attendant, the business started. The first blow to the jaw must have dazed me, for the next thing I knew, one man had both his arms around my neck, choking and dragging me along the floor, while another kept kicking me in the stomach. After a while they let me up and said to throw me back into the cell and let me rot there. During this time, Lou had been removed to L-1-East, and one attendant told me it was the practice there to beat men three times a day. Later an inmate managed to tell me that Lou asked him to tell me that they had beaten him badly. I have not been able to see Lou nor get direct word to or of him, but I have reason to believe he has resumed the hunger strike and is not being forcibly fed.

Letters protesting this inhuman treatment, by no means limited to the conscientious objectors, should be addressed to Attorney General Francis J. Biddle, and to James V. Bennett, Director, Federal Bureau of Prisons, Washington, D. C.

Funds are needed to fight the cause of Murphy and Taylor, and should be sent to Dr. Evan Thomas, who has published Murphy's letter, at the War Registers League, 2 Stone St., New York, 4, N. Y.

Contributions
Articles and letters to PACIFICA VIEWS should be brief. Use only one side of the paper, and, if possible, type the contribution—with double spacing. The Editors reserve the right to cut articles to fit available space. Only manuscripts accompanied by a self-addressed, stamped envelope will be returned.

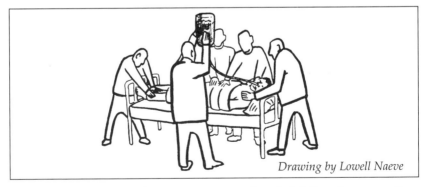

Drawing by Lowell Naeve

An artist's depiction of the forcible feeding of a jailed C.O. on hunger strike
(Naeve suffered such tube-feeding himself in May 1943)

HERMANN STÖHR
(1898–1940)

MAX JOSEF METZGER
(1887–1944)

— Both men were executed in wartime Germany —

ANDRÉ TROCMÉ
(1901–1971)

PHILIPPE VERNIER
(1909–1985)

Franz Jägerstätter

The man who said 'No' to Hitler

The 36-year-old Austrian farmer, who was beheaded on 9 August 1943 for refusing on grounds of conscience to serve in the German army

MARGARET BACKHOUSE (1887–1977) representings Friends Service Council, who is shaking hands with King Haakon VII of Norway, and HENRY J. CADBURY (1883–1974), representing American Friends Service Committee, in Oslo for the presentation of the 1947 Nobel Peace Prize to the Quakers

Quaker relief in the district of Buzuluk during the Russian Famine of 1921–22

Quaker relief in post-1918 Germany

Quaker transport team (*Secours Quaker*) in Caen at the end of World War II

British member of the Anglo-American Quaker Relief in Poland talking to a family in front of their bunker-home

American member of the transport team of the Quakers' Relief Mission in Poland

"Operation Gandhi": pacifists sitting down outside the War Office in Whitehall, January 1951

Head of the Campaign for Nuclear Disarmament on march from London to Aldermaston, March 1962, with Canon JOHN COLLINS (1905–1982) in clerical dress at the front

VINOBA BHAVE (1895–1982) on his "long march" of over 100,000 miles, with LANZA DEL VASTO (1901–1981) on his left

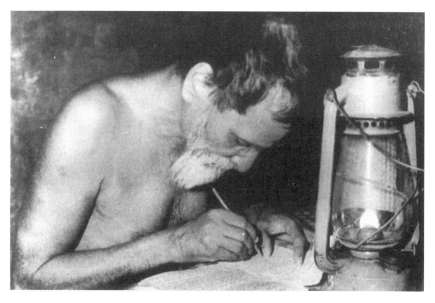

VINOBA writing by oil-lantern light

A.J. MUSTE climbing the fence surrounding Mead Missile Base (Nebraska) on 1 July 1959

Five young pacifists burning their draft cards at a noon rally in Union Square, New York City, on 6 November 1965, with MUSTE looking on

MARTIN LUTHER KING (1929–1968) marching with BAYARD RUSTIN (1912–1987) during the Montgomery bus boycott of 1956

BARBARA DEMING (1917–1984) at one of the all-women peace circles at the Seneca Women's Encampment for a Future of Peace and Justice (New York), 1983

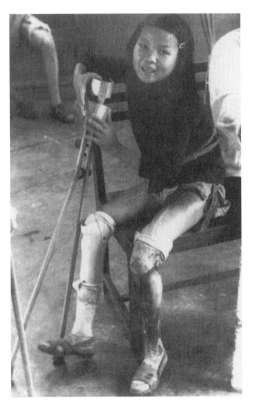 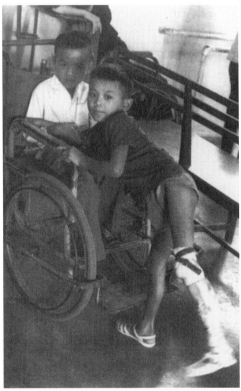

From the American Quakers' war victims relief program

Buddhist monk protesting against the war in Vietnam through self-immolation by fire on the market square of Saigon, 5 October 1963

(Quang Duc's suicide depicted here was, we should note, his personal decision, respected indeed but not endorsed – still less adopted – by most of his fellow monks and other antiwar Buddhists in Vietnam.)

DOROTHY DAY
(1897–1980)

"A decade after Vietnam, [my brother] Philip and I [Daniel] are in no wise rehabilitated. In Morristown, Pennsylvania, on February 23, 1981, we are in court again. Our crime: bashing unarmed nuclear warheads and pouring our blood. Verdict: guilty. Sentence: three to ten years." DANIEL BERRIGAN (b. 1921) on the left of the photograph and PHILIP BERRIGAN (b. 1923) on the right

1

San Francisco to Moscow peace marchers in Red Square, October 1961

Winners of the 1976 Nobel Peace Prize, MAIREAD CORRIGAN [MAGUIRE] (b. 1944) on the right and BETTY WILLIAMS [PERKINS] (b. 1943) in the middle, with the American pacifist folksinger, JOAN BAEZ (b. 1941), on the left of the photograph

GRUNDGESETZ

für die Bundesrepublik Deutschland

I. Die Grundrechte

Artikel 4

[Glaubens-, Gewissens- und Bekenntnisfreiheit]

(1) Die Freiheit des Glaubens, des Gewissens und die Freiheit des religiösen und weltanschaulichen Bekenntnisses sind unverletzlich.

(2) Die ungestörte Religionsausübung wird gewährleistet.

(3) Niemand darf gegen sein Gewissen zum Kriegsdienst mit der Waffe gezwungen werden. Das Nähere regelt ein Bundesgesetz.

Article 4, section 3 ("Basic Rights") of the Basic Law of the Federal Republic of Germany, promulgated on 23 May 1949: no one to be forced against their conscience to perform military service involving armed combat (*Kriegsdienst mit der Waffe*)

"Cover yourself with paint to avoid being conscripted (Basque total resisters demonstrate the technique!)"

AND ON EARTH PEACE, GOOD WILL ...

A message to:

Prime Minister Chrétien and Foreign Affairs Minister Axworthy:

Tomorrow Christians around the world celebrate the birth of the Prince of Peace, but for many, the joy that accompanies Christmas has been mixed with sorrow and anger because of last week's bombing of Iraq.

This is the most recent violent episode in a conflict that has caused the deaths of hundreds of thousands of children, women and men in Iraq. We are deeply saddened that Canada chose to support the bombings, and continues to support the economic sanctions.

Eight years of military intervention and punishing sanctions have failed to resolve the Iraqi dilemma. Other ways must be found to build a just peace, to support Iraq's civil society, and bring Iraq back into the family of nations.

In a few days Canada will begin a two year term on the UN Security Council. We urge the Canadian government to use this role to seek new approaches to peacebuilding and human security in Iraq. We know that there are no easy solutions, but we also know that the peacebuilding values that Canada has promoted in other contexts are critical to the resolution of this conflict.

Announcing the birth of Christ, angels proclaimed peace and good will to all. We believe Canada can provide significant leadership in the struggle for peace, and we pledge our support to that end.

Signed,
The Right Reverend Bill Phipps
Moderator, United Church of Canada

Walter Pitman, Chair
Project Ploughshares

Harry Kits, Executive Director
Citizens for Public Justice

George Richert, Chairperson
Mennonite Central Committee Canada

Gale Wills, clerk
Canadian Yearly Meeting
Religious Society of Friends

Carol Dixon, clerk
Canadian Friends Service Committee

Dale Hildebrand, Executive Director
Inter-Church Action for Development, Relief and Justice

For further information, please contact Mennonite Central Committee Canada (204) 261-6381.

A Canadian Mennonite initiative for peace in the world's festering Iraqi crisis (Christmas 1998)

PACIFISM
in the
TWENTIETH CENTURY

I. Varieties of Pacifism at the Outset of the Twentieth Century

At the outset of the twentieth century the prospects for a continuing world peace looked promising. Yet there were dark shadows – increasing armaments, hardening alliances, overseas imperialist rivalries, economic unrest in the industrialized countries, and rising nationalist passions in many areas of the world. The scale of destruction by weapons of war had multiplied many times during the previous century. Most public figures in the West, from semi-absolutist tsars to expansionist presidents, paid lip-service to international peace. Their actions, however, were often more expressive of the *Realpolitik*, of which they accused their nations' opponents, than of the pacifistic international morality on which they prided themselves. Not only did statesmen succumb to nationalist ambitions, but large sections of the population in most advanced countries were also carried away by chauvinist slogans and imperialist designs.

Throughout the European continent, still the center of world civilization, universal military service had long been the rule. Britain and the United States, on the other hand, retained the voluntary system for military recruitment. Peace organizations and pacifist sentiments flourished, especially among the middle classes, more vigorously in the latter two countries than in lands where long-term conscription faced the male population. However, the socialist and labor movement in Europe was as strongly influenced by antiwar as by anticapitalist ideology.

Despite signs of an approaching clash between the great powers, few persons could have envisaged that within the first half of the twentieth century the world would be rocked by two successive wars of catastrophic dimensions, or that, by the second half of the century, men would be seriously contemplating the eventuality of universal destruction as a result of the new weaponry. Instead, in the early 1900s Norman Angell in England demonstrated that in modern war conquest would never pay economically. Therefore war, he implied, was not likely to take place if men saw where their real material interests lay. Although he never claimed that war and conquest could not actually occur in the future, his arguments illustrate the optimistic outlook of many peace workers at that time.

Pacifism *sensu stricto* emerged as a political factor only after the outbreak of war in 1914, mainly in Britain and the United States. Post-1914 pacifism had its roots, however, in previous developments. There are five sources of twentieth-century pacifism which we consider most important for its understanding: (1) the doctrine of nonresistance as developed by the Anabaptists and Mennonites of the Reformation era; (2) the peace testimony – dating back to the Commonwealth period in English history – of the Quakers, who were to contribute substantially to the creation of an organized Anglo-American peace movement in the nineteenth century; (3) the emerging conscientious objection of the Bible Students/Jehovah's Witnesses; (4) the institutional approach to the problem of war evolved by these peace societies; and (5) the socialist antimilitarism which emerged, along with the organized labor movement, in the half century before 1914.

Mennonite Nonresistance

In twentieth-century United States the Mennonites have produced the largest percentage of conscientious objectors. The Mennonite denomination was founded by Menno Simons from Frisia in the Netherlands, who died in 1561. He, in turn, had derived his faith from the Anabaptists, who originated in Zürich in 1525 in opposition to the Protestant reformer Zwingli. They soon spread from Switzerland to Germany and Holland. Persecuted almost everywhere by the authorities, Protestant as well as Catholic, for their institution of adult baptism as a sign of separation from the established church, Anabaptists also attempted to separate from the life of the contemporary state. Their object, like that of certain medieval sects before them (e.g., the Waldenses or the early Czech Brethren), was to restore the fellowship of the primitive Christians and to practise the kind of discipleship depicted in the New Testament.

Thus, from the beginning the Anabaptists regarded government as incompatible with true Christian discipleship. Though ordained by God to protect the good and punish the wicked, this was, however, a punishment of the more wicked by the less wicked. Politics was not work for the regenerate or baptized believers. Had not Christ told his followers: "Resist not evil"? How then could they, as soldiers did, slaughter their fellow human beings in war or, like magistrates, inflict harsh punishment and even death on malefactors? As their first confession of faith stated in 1527: within their own community "only the ban is used for a warning ... – simply the warning and the command to sin no more."[1] An Anabaptist must never resist wrong by violence. Instead, he must suffer whatever evil befalls him, for his reward will come in the life after death.

Yet, an apocalyptic, even violent, strain in early Anabaptism broke out in the mid-1530s in the German city of Münster, where Anabaptists undertook by force to achieve the Kingdom of God here on earth. By no means did all Anabaptists participate. After it was over pacifist elements rallied under the leadership of Menno Simons and returned speedily to the previous pessimistic view of the impossibility of Christian believers achieving anything good by political action. All desire to change the world disappeared rapidly. The "post-revolutionary"[2] phase of Anabaptism had begun.

For the next 400 years Mennonites (as the Anabaptists were now known) developed in two different directions. First in Holland, and later in Germany, they began to integrate slowly with the rest of the community, eventually abandoning their nonresistant principles along with other peculiarities of dress and habit. This was accompanied by decreasing spiritual impetus and a continuing fall in numbers. On the other hand, in Switzerland (where the sect always remained very small) as well as in Russia, the United States and Canada, where the Mennonites emigrated in considerable numbers in search of land and religious freedom, they remained withdrawn from the world up into the twentieth century. A people apart, they carefully nurtured their pacifism and their hostility to the state, along with many old inherited customs like their German speech from the sixteenth century. And in the New World they were joined by several similar nonresistant groups from Germany, the most important of which were the German Baptist Brethren or Dunkers (today known as the Church of the Brethren).

Among the Baptists, today one of the largest Free Churches in the world, a tenuous thread of pacifism can be traced back to the denomination's founder, the Englishman John Smyth, who had accepted Anabaptist–Mennonite nonresistance shortly before his death in 1612. Subsequently, pacifist views emerged sporadically among Baptists; this, however, scarcely constituted a tradition such as we find among the "historic peace churches," for Baptists have only exceptionally condemned war on principle, at any rate before the twentieth century. But during the American Revolution, for instance, James Childs, a Baptist minister in North Carolina, stated publicly that he and his congregation believed it wrong to bear arms even "defensively." For this stand Childs was soon thrown into jail. And there were Baptist pacifists, both pastors and laity, who after 1815 played an active part in the Anglo-American peace movement. At the end of the century a prominent Baptist minister, George Dana Boardman, vigorously opposed the Spanish-American War, pleading for the adoption of the Sermon on the Mount as "the supreme constitution for mankind."[3] In Sweden, from the later nineteenth century the rural Free Baptist sect rejected military service and, if conscripted, its members refused to enter the army, meekly suffering repeated imprisonment for their unwillingness to serve.

A more militant version of Christian nonresistance was propounded at the end of the nineteenth century by the great Russian novelist, Lev Tolstoy, although he was not directly influenced by Mennonite doctrine. The sources of his pacifism were twofold: a literal acceptance of the perfectionist teachings of the New Testament, and an angry rejection of contemporary Western society, of which war and the state appeared to him essential aspects. To speak of the early Anabaptists and Mennonites as anarchists would be anachronistic; indeed their religion tended at times to be excessively legalistic, with Christ's new law of love taking on the character of a legal code, while lacking earthly sanctions for its enforcement. Tolstoy, on the other hand, was truly a Christian anarchist – a man who took the inward spirit alone as his guide. His idea of nonresistance to evil was designed as a powerful spiritual weapon for undermining the foundations of the modern Moloch erected by the essentially militaristic state. The state, in his view, must be dismantled entirely and replaced by a voluntarist society before nonviolence could be fully effective.

In many countries of Europe, as well as in North America, his disciples founded Tolstoyan groups. They were small and uninfluential, however. The influence exerted by Tolstoy on the thinking of individuals was ultimately more important. In the United States, for instance, persons as diverse as the politician William Jennings Bryan, or the labor lawyer Clarence Darrow, or the social reformer Jane Addams, came under the spell of Tolstoyan nonresistance – without, however, ever accepting it in full. Tolstoy had followers in the Anglo-American Quaker community, especially among those concerned with radical politics or social reform. But the most seminal influence of Tolstoyism, which will emerge later in this book, was exercised on the Indian nationalist leader, M.K. Gandhi.

The Quaker Peace Testimony

Mennonites urged a politics of withdrawal from the world. At the very beginning, Quakers, or the Society of Friends, sought, a little differently, to transform the world so as to establish a realm of the "saints." Later, after early millenarian or perfectionist hopes had been abandoned, they strove rather to reform society than to effect a total change. They aimed at Christianizing politics, for they did not favor relegating the political realm to the unregenerate, as did the Mennonites.

Quakerism first arose in Cromwell's England in the early 1650s. Its founder was a simple shoemaker, George Fox. In contrast to the legalistic emphasis of the Anabaptist-Mennonite tradition, Fox and early Friends stressed the Inner Light and inward experience, in addition to scriptural revelation, as the guide for the spiritual life. After some hesitation and uncertainty Quakers concluded that war and violence, even when employed by the "saints," contradicted the Inner Light of Christ within us. Thus in their declaration to King Charles II in January 1661, which represents the first clear statement of the Quaker peace testimony, they point to "the Spirit of Christ which leads us into all truth"[4] as the basis of their repudiation of war, and not to any biblical text or earlier church teaching. By the nineteenth century, a change had come about. Due to evangelical influence on large sections of the Society of Friends, their pacifism became more Bible-centered for a time. "War unlawful for Christians" now figured in the titles of Quaker antiwar literature as it did in the works of other pacifist authors. In the twentieth century there emerged among those Friends who still cleaved to their Society's peace testimony a renewed vision of pacifism based primarily on the Inner Light and an intuitional view of the wrongness of war.

Quakers in the seventeenth and eighteenth centuries, especially those who migrated to the American continent, were in trouble more often than Mennonites were as a result of their refusal to do military service. Whereas the Mennonites did not balk at paying a fine in lieu of service where the state was prepared to offer exemption on these terms (for they regarded it simply as rendering unto Caesar what was justly his), Quaker conscientious objectors demanded unconditional exemption when called upon to serve in the militia. The Society considered that the state had no right to demand money in return from a man who was only acting according to his conscience. Therefore, they suffered distraint of goods and occasional imprisonment for refusing to pay commutation. Those Quakers, who did not follow their Society's discipline in such matters, were liable to be disowned. In addition to being conscientious objectors to military service, a few Quaker radicals also refused to pay not only direct war taxes, which Quakers usually withheld, but also those "in the mixture," i.e., where only an undefined part of the tax went toward war. From the mid-nineteenth century, however, in contrast to the Mennonites in Europe who had to contend with the rising claims of universal military service, the Quaker communities of the British Isles and North America, along with other pacifists there, were no longer faced – except briefly in the American Civil War – with a system of national conscription, for Britain and the United States, as we have noted, now maintained the voluntary system for their armed forces.

Although some early Quakers, like the Mennonites, felt uncertain if government could ever be conducted without a recourse to the sword and if, therefore, true Christians could rightly participate, Quakerism eventually came to regard the magistrate's office as compatible with a pacifist stance. When not excluded by legal restrictions on dissenters, they participated actively in political life. From 1682 until 1756 they actually ruled Pennsylvania, dominating both the provincial assembly and the lower magistracy. This "Holy Experiment" was not altogether successful and eventually led Quaker politicians to sacrifice their pacifism for political power. Pennsylvania's dependence on the home government provided a complicating factor, since its Quaker rulers were never free from the restraints of British imperial policy.

The Mennonites, at least until they assimilated into society as in Holland, had lived physically as citizens of their country but spiritually they were denizens of another world. They were mostly humble people, farmers or craftsmen, who in their European homeland entertained no wish to participate in the political life of the ruling class. They brought this apolitical ethos with them to America. Quakers, on the other hand, soon developed an intense interest in politics. Originally recruited chiefly from the lower strata of the community, Quakerism subsequently became to some degree middle-class and affluent. Moreover, at home and also as members of the new and more democratic society across the Atlantic, Quakers prided themselves on being free-born Englishmen and were ready to resist (nonviolently) any attempt by authority to encroach on these rights. Even Proprietor William Penn, himself a Whig by conviction, had difficulty sometimes in controlling his ebullient Friends, who were the subjects of his province of Pennsylvania. It is no wonder, therefore, that – disregarding the apolitical and quietistic trend which gained predominance for a time during the eighteenth century – Quaker pacifism, in contrast to the inward-looking Mennonite tradition of nonresistance, became an outreaching creed and sought to find expression in both domestic politics and international relations.

Thus, quite early in the history of the Society of Friends we find English Quakers, like William Penn or John Bellers, propounding schemes for establishing peace between the nations without, at the same time, requiring their statesmen and citizens to become converts to the unconditional pacifism of the Friends. In nineteenth-century Britain, Quakers were among the earliest promoters of the new peace movement (as well as of a number of other contemporary reform endeavors). In the United States, though they were much less active at first, the inspiration of their example was an important factor in developing the peace movement there. Indeed so close was the identification, in the popular mind, of Quakerism with pacifism that in both England and North America a pacifist from another nonpacifist denomination (almost all pacifism at that time was religious) would often, in explanation of his position, say simply: "I hold Quaker views on war."

Bible Students/Jehovah's Witnesses

Before we leave the sectarian component of pre-1914 pacifism something should be said about the Jehovah's Witnesses (JWs, known before 1931 as International Bible Students). The Witnesses do not call themselves pacifists. But they have steadfastly refused to bear arms when conscripted. Indeed "Witness men and women have suffered more than the members of any religion in this century for their refusal to perform military service or certain forms of compulsory civilian alternative service.[5] This has happened not only under totalitarian and authoritarian régimes, which have sometimes executed JWs for their refusal to serve in the army, but also in democracies like Britain and the United States. Though not rejecting self-defense and, like some Christian pacifists too, believing Israel's wars in the Old Testament sometimes justified, JWs regard warfare since that time as the work of Satan.

The sect originated in the United States during the 1870s under the influence of the millenarianism that swept the country periodically. Its founder, Charles Russell (1852–1916) was a largely self-educated theologian and self-designated pastor, whose "divine plan" for humanity based on a rather peculiar interpretation of Bible prophecy included the destruction of the wicked by God's avenging angels at the future battle of Armageddon, with the righteous as passive onlookers. The dating of these apocalyptic events, however, Russell and his successors in the sect's leadership have repeatedly had to postpone.

For his antimilitarism Russell seems to have been indebted chiefly to the small Advent Christian Church, which had adopted a pacifist position during the Civil War, through his contacts with one of its ministers.[6] Russell later set out his views on war in the last part of a large-scale work, many times reprinted, which he entitled *Studies in the Scriptures*; rather grandiloquently he described its six volumes as "practically the Bible topically arranged."[7] At any rate, members of the rapidly expanding sect accepted what he wrote there as authoritative, attempting to follow what he taught in an increasingly violent world.

Adopt "the position of aliens," Russell told his followers; they must be law abiding and pay all lawfully imposed taxes but not participate in politics or voting. He praised those governments which had "exempted from military duty ... some who, like ourselves, believe war to be unrighteous; viz, the Friends or Quakers." If Bible Students were, after all, required to perform military service, Russell gave them somewhat impractical advice. "In such event," he wrote, "we would consider it not amiss to make a partial explanation to the proper officers, and request a transference to the medical or hospital department, where our services could be used with the full consent of our consciences; – but even if compelled to serve in the ranks and to fire our guns we need not feel compelled to shoot a fellow-creature."[8] In fact, especially after Russell's death, the position of Bible Students/Jehovah's Witnesses toward the draft became much more radical than their founder had recommended.

For a long time JWs were to derive almost exclusively from the economically and educationally underprivileged: factory workers, artisans and petty shopkeepers, and agricultural laborers. Some writers, therefore, have argued that newcomers were drawn to the sect from "a sense of deprivation." But a generalization of this kind, though substantially correct, should not be accepted without qualification; latterly, for instance, professionals found a somewhat uneasy place among the Witnesses.[9]

The Institutional Approach of the Peace Societies

The peace societies, the oldest of which date back to the end of the Napoleonic wars, formed part of a vast movement of reform which included in its sweep such causes as temperance, antislavery, penal reform, women's rights, etc., and embraced Britain and North America as well as large parts of the European continent. "The promotion of permanent and universal peace" was the avowed object of these societies. Often, their members shared this concern with a number of other interests; in each country the membership lists of the various reform societies overlapped to some extent.

The London Peace Society opposed all war, though it accepted into associate membership those unable to go quite that far. The American Peace Society, after a long and at times acrid controversy between the supporters and opponents of "defensive" war, decided to remain neutral and receive into full membership all who wished to work to eliminate war from the community of civilized nations. On the European continent, where the peace movement was for many decades less flourishing than in Britain or the United States, pacifism in the Anglo-American meaning of the word was virtually nonexistent until the advent of Tolstoyism at the end of the century.[10]

A radical wing eventually developed within the peace movement in the United States. Its leader was William Lloyd Garrison, the abolitionist who founded the New England Non-Resistance Society in 1838. Its creed was a kind of Tolstoyism before Tolstoy (as Tolstoy himself recognized when he first read this Society's "Declaration of Sentiments"), repudiating not only war but the whole machinery of government as incompatible with a consistent Christianity. A few members even experimented with nonviolent techniques of resistance – an area that remained virtually unexplored, indeed almost totally neglected, by the peace movement into the twentieth century. The Non-Resistance Society, however, soon showed signs of declining vigor as its most active members became absorbed in the antislavery struggle. Some finally lost confidence in a peaceful solution and, even before the firing at Fort Sumter, were ready to urge a holy war against the slaveholding South.

The quasi-millenarian hopes of the New England nonresistants were perhaps closer to those entertained during the first decade of Anabaptism over three centuries earlier than to the thinking of the sober clergymen and merchants who made up the backbone of the more moderate Anglo-American peace societies. Such hopes were even more remote from peace workers on the European continent. Moderates of all kinds were repelled by the nonresistants' attacks on the institution of government. What above all they strove to achieve by patient effort was the establishment of machinery for preventing international war and not any radical transformation in the political system.

"The [peace] schemes of the nineteenth century all centered on five fundamentals: arbitration, arbitration treaties and clauses in treaties, an International Authority or Tribunal or Congress, the codification of International Law, and [simultaneous and proportional] disarmament. These five essentials were regarded as interrelated and interdependent; it was held to be extremely doubtful whether, for lack of one of them, any of the others (except arbitration) could be secured."[11] At various periods the emphasis in the peace societies' propaganda was placed on one or another aspect of this program, but the combined goal was never lost sight of altogether. Especially in England, the peace cause was intimately bound up, too, with the struggle for free trade. The removal of tariff barriers appeared to be an essential step toward world peace. The peace societies in the various countries kept in touch with each other by means of periodic conferences and later by establishing coordinating bodies which transcended the national boundaries. True, disagreement concerning the inclusion of military sanctions in proposals for international organization continued to divide the Anglo-American societies, which opposed them, from many of their European counterparts, which considered such sanctions to be essential for effective world government. Yet amicable relations prevailed on the whole between peace workers.

The impulse behind this organized peace movement was derived in part – at least in Protestant countries – from the powerful evangelical movement, which also underlay many of the other reform movements of the age. (The Mennonites kept entirely aloof from the peace movement, regarding its attempt to create a warless world among the unregenerate as a utopian dream.) A second source, and perhaps a more fundamental one, lay in the thought of the Enlightenment. Christian pacifists had from the beginning condemned war as sin. The men of the Enlightenment attacked war as both inhumane and irrational, following in the footsteps of Renaissance predecessors like the Christian humanist, Desiderius Erasmus. They denounced war, too, as in total contradiction to their ideal of human brotherhood and unity. Here were the roots of a secular case against war; a pacifism that might be absolute or conditional, but in any case drawing its strength primarily from reason and humanitarian considerations instead of from religion. During the Enlightenment some of the major schemes for universal peace were devised. The Abbé de Saint-Pierre and Jean-Jacques Rousseau, Jeremy Bentham and Immanuel Kant were among those who then turned their pens to this purpose.

The institutional approach of the nineteenth-century peace movement had much to its credit both in countering (in its publications and its organized activities) the age-long glorification of war, and in pressing the material and moral case against the continuance of international war in a supposedly civilized community of nations. The movement's proposals for introducing international organization and a measure of world government in place of the international anarchy that had prevailed hitherto were to be commended. Indeed they have served as a model in many ways for twentieth-century efforts in this area. Yet in one important respect the vision of the "bourgeois" peace movement before 1914 failed. It did not often penetrate the relationship between war and the economic order nor did it detect the hidden seeds of war in the exploitation of labor. True, the peace movement vehemently denounced war for the material destruction it caused, but the movement failed to pursue the matter deeply into the structure of contemporary society. Its protagonists were mainly respectable, middle-class folk, often "do-gooders" whose consciences prompted them to be active in social reform. They were rarely connected with the emergent labor movement and they scarcely ever entertained sympathy for any far-reaching schemes of social reconstruction. This was especially true of the movements in Britain and the United States; it constituted in fact a major obstacle to renewal in their activities, not to mention expansion.

Socialist Antimilitarism

By the beginning of the twentieth century organized labor with its political expression in the socialist movement formed a force of considerable importance in the life of many European countries as well as the Americas. Wherever industry developed, there labor eventually strove to exert pressure so as to extract from its rulers better working conditions and a greater say in the affairs of the state. The cause of labor also attracted the support of a small number of persons from the middle and upper classes, who often acquired a position of political and intellectual leadership in the movement.

No socialist or labor party adopted a completely pacifist stand. Marxist parties rejected pacifism categorically. Whereas the left wing regarded it as a bourgeois deviation, the revisionists reserved the right of national defense. In a country like France where the majority of the socialist movement did not claim to be Marxist, the party leader, Jean Jaurès, looking back to the French Revolution with its *levée-en-masse*, urged the creation of a citizen army as the sole viable alternative to a professional service dominated by militarists. Only in Britain's Independent Labour Party (ILP) were avowed pacifists to be found in any numbers, though there were a few isolated pacifists in the socialist parties of the European continent and in the American labor movement.

Many socialists, especially on the left, favored the class war – at least in theory. Even reformist socialists and trade unionists tended to doubt if the capitalist order would disappear without a final struggle and few among them thought that the workers could carry on a struggle of this kind by nonviolent means. Yet in regard to international war the position of the socialist movement sometimes bordered on pacifism. Socialism at its best expressed an ideal of human brotherhood which transcended frontiers and united races. Until the guns of August 1914 shattered this ideal along with so many others, the international socialist movement condemned war between capitalist governments. War, most socialists believed, resulted from the inevitable clash of economic rivalries. Under the capitalist system every war was inevitably in some measure an imperialist war. And in wars the workers suffered, but not the capitalists who fomented them. Since, at that time, in advanced countries power rested exclusively in the hands of capitalist politicians and their allies, this condemnation, if its logic were observed in practise, should have sufficed to prevent socialist or labor support in any future war conducted between capitalist governments.

Actually there was no unanimity among socialists concerning the most efficacious means to prevent war if it threatened to break out. The socialist parties were all willing to stage antimilitaristic demonstrations; however, their leaders were less ready to agree on a strategy to combat war. Ardent antimilitarists like the British ILP leader, Keir Hardie, advocated the proclamation of a general strike as did the anti-parliamentarian anarchists and anarcho-syndicalists on the European continent. Other prominent socialists opposed the idea as being either impractical or positively harmful since it might benefit the aggressor. In 1914, as it turned out, the major socialist parties in the countries involved in war backed their respective governments; the workers fought against each other in the ranks of their national armies. Only in countries which shared the Anglo-American pacifist tradition did a comparatively small number of socialists (by no means all complete pacifists) take the conscientious objector stand. A few anarcho-syndicalists adopted it, too, in states like the Netherlands where conscription was not as onerous as in the rest of the European continent. On 6 August, shortly before his death, Keir Hardie wrote: "Ten million Socialist and Labour voters in Europe, without a trace or vestige of power to prevent war! ... Our demonstrations and speeches and resolutions are all alike futile. We have no means of hitting the warmongers. We simply do not count."[12]

Socialist antimilitarism failed to stop war. It failed even to prevent the working classes in the belligerent countries from becoming infected with chauvinistic passions and hatred of the enemy. Yet from 1914 onward the new pacifism that was generated in the course of the struggle came to possess a social concern that had not been present in the peace movement earlier. Neither Mennonite nonresistants nor

Quakers nor the members of the various nineteenth-century peace societies saw at all clearly the connection between the evil of war and the ills of the economic system. There were exceptions, of course, like the eighteenth-century American Quaker, John Woolman, or Tolstoy and his disciples. In the postwar world, however, most pacifists, along with large sections of the wider peace movement, were to become acutely aware of the need for social change in effecting the elimination of war and violence from the world. The exploration of this fresh dimension grew into one of the major tasks facing them.

Notes

1 William R. Estep, Jr., ed., *Anabaptist Beginnings 1523–1533: A Source Book* (Nieuwkoop: B. de Graaf, 1976), p. 103.

2 This definition is borrowed from David A. Martin, *Pacifism: An Historical and Sociological Study* (London: Routledge & Kegan Paul, 1965), p. 69.

3 Paul R. Dekar, *For the Healing of the Nations: Baptist Peacemakers* (Macon, GA: Smyth & Helwys Publishing, 1993), pp. 21, 22, 30–54, 57–60; Reid S. Trulson, "Baptist Pacifism: A Heritage of Nonviolence," *American Baptist Quarterly* (Valley Forge, PA), vol. 10, no. 3 (September, 1991), pp. 199–210, 212–16. That an American Baptist minister, Henry Holcombe, in his *Primitive Theology, in a Series of Lectures* (Philadelphia: published privately, 1822), lectures XIV–XVI, had composed a pioneering defense of Christian pacifism, was forgotten by his coreligionists long before the end of the century.

4 Quoted in Howard H. Brinton, *Sources of the Quaker Peace Testimony* (Wallingford, PA: Pendle Hill Historical Studies, [1941]), p. 16.

5 M. James Penton, *Apocalypse Delayed: The Story of Jehovah's Witnesses* (Toronto: University of Toronto Press, 1985), p. 142.

6 *Ibid.*, pp. 15, 17, 309, 310.

7 *Ibid.*, p. 32.

8 Charles Taze Russell, *The New Creation* (Brooklyn, NY: International Bible Students Association, 1912), pp. 593–5. The volume was first published in 1904.

9 Penton, *op. cit.*, pp. 253–6.

10 See Sandi E. Cooper, *Patriotic Pacifism: Waging War on War in Europe 1815–1914* (New York: Oxford University Press, 1991), also Verdiana Grossi, *Le pacifisme européen 1889–1914* (Brussels: Bruylant, 1994), and F.S.L. Lyons, *Internationalism in Europe 1815–1914* (Leiden A.W. Sythoff, 1963), pp. 309–61. Even the indefatigable Austrian peace advocate, Bertha (Baroness) von Suttner, who died on the eve of World War I, while personally regarding all

types of soldiering as immoral never publicly supported conscientious objection.

11 A.C.F. Beales, *The History of Peace* (London: G. Bell & Sons Ltd., 1931), pp. 8, 14.

12 Quoted in David Boulton, *Objection Overruled* (London: Macgibbon & Kee, 1967), p. 42.

II. The Pattern of Conscientious Objection: World War I

With the outbreak of war in Europe in August 1914 a new epoch in world history began. In the history of the peace movement, too, this date marks the symbolic beginning of a new stage in development. Hitherto, historic pacifism, in the sense of a thoroughgoing renunciation of at least international war and a personal refusal to participate in military service, had been very largely religious in motivation. At the outset of the twentieth century, pacifism of this kind was confined – apart from a few small isolated groups – to the English-speaking world. In fact it had secure roots only in Britain and the United States. For many persons in these two countries, pacifism was equated with Quakerism on account of the Society of Friends' long witness for peace. Tolerated as the peculiarity of a small sect, war renunciation took on a new character in the popular mind and in the eyes of national leaders when it was found – even if thinly spread – in other churches as well as among the unchurched.

In Britain and the United States conscription became the harsh midwife of twentieth-century pacifism. The authorities in these countries had resorted in previous centuries to compulsion to fill the ranks of their peace time militias and wartime armies. But service was usually selective. In addition, the possibility of commutation offered a way of escape, at least for those with means to pay. Commutation, indeed, was practiced not only in Britain and America but on the European continent up into the nineteenth century. Whereas in countries like France, Germany, and Russia universal military service was established in the second half of the nineteenth century, Britain after 1860 and the United States after the Civil War went over entirely to the voluntary system. Their imposition in World War I of compulsory military service for all adult able-bodied males, the introduction of which earlier on the European continent had acted as a deterrent to the growth of pacifism, now served instead to reactive pacifism in the differing political environment of these two English-speaking countries.

The Framework of Conscription

Britain

Britain entered the war under a Liberal government, many of whose members and followers regarded the idea of military conscription with abhorrence. Before 1914 the call for national service had been a Conservative slogan. During the early months of the war the army had some difficulty in absorbing the volunteers who crowded the recruiting stations to enlist, for the British people greeted the outbreak of war in an upsurge of national feeling and an idealistic enthusiasm for the wronged Belgians. Pressure to introduce a measure of conscription came from the Conservative opposition in parliament and from a widespread sentiment in the country that only by compulsion would "slackers" be forced to take their fair share in the defense of their native land. In July 1915 the government, in an attempt to assuage the growing demands for conscription, introduced national registration. But this did not prove enough. In January 1916, therefore, the first Military Service Act became law. It affected only unmarried men between the ages of 18 and 41. A second act was passed in May of the same year introducing the principle of universal conscription of all able-bodied males, and, in fact, by the beginning of 1918 the upper age limit of those liable to conscription had been raised to 56.

In the debates on the first conscription bill, government spokesmen recognized the right of those holding a conscientious objection to military service to have their scruples respected. This was considered a part of the English heritage of religious and civil liberties. Therefore, conscientious objectors (C.Os.) were to be exempted, along with men employed in work of national importance or those supporting dependents. Local and Appeal Tribunals were to be set up to hear applications for exemption on one or another of these grounds. In regard to conscientious objectors, provision was made for unconditional (or "absolute") exemption, or for exemption on condition that the applicant undertake noncombatant service in the armed services or that he engage in work which the tribunal considered to be "of national importance." The legislation did not specify that the conscientious objection must be based on religious belief. Although efforts were made in April 1918, during the German advance on the Western front, to get parliament to withdraw all previously granted exemptions, including those given to conscientious objectors, the attempt was not successful.

On paper, at any rate, this legislative provision for conscientious objection was remarkably liberal. If liberally interpreted, it would surely provide satisfaction for even the most sensitive conscience – except perhaps for any who might object to the very act of registration as in itself a compromise with the evil of military conscription. The test of the act's liberality, of course, lay in the spirit in which its clauses were interpreted. A country which believed it was fighting for its existence – and, as many thought, for the salvation of civilization as well – might be inclined to give short shrift to a dissident minority, even when its claims were in theory given legislative backing.

Alternative service, where the tribunal decided to grant the applicant conditional exemption, might, according to the letter of the law, be any activity that the tribunal deemed fit to allocate, even including the applicant's present occupation. But in fact the conditions most frequently granted were consignment to the Non-Combatant Corps or to "work of national importance."

The Non-Combatant Corps (NCC), which was set up in March 1916, formed part of the regular army, from which its officers were drawn. Conscientious objectors who were allocated to it had the status of army privates. They wore army uniforms and were subject to army discipline. They were not required to carry weapons, however, or to take part in combat. But their duties included forms of labor closely associated with the functioning of the military. Most conscientious objectors considered that service in the NCC, as well as in the Royal Army Medical Corps to which conscientious objectors were less frequently assigned, signified becoming part of "the military machine," and they chose prison rather than compliance if there were no other alternative. Some compromised and accepted noncombatant service, though unwillingly. But for members of certain religious sects, such as the Plymouth Brethren or the Seventh-day Adventists, whose objection was based on a simple and literalist repudiation of killing as unchristian, the NCC appeared as an acceptable alternative. An element of risk, where present, may have sometimes proved attractive. For instance, when drafted, the ninth Earl De La Warr, a young socialist aristocrat with pacifist convictions, volunteered for hazardous work on a minesweeper, which he obviously regarded as a noncombatant occupation despite its close connection with naval operations. The Earl eventually became a Conservative; his entry in *Who's Who* describes him discreetly as having "served as a sailor during the War." His duties at sea, while certainly more exhilarating, cannot always have proved more satisfying to a convinced pacifist than many of the tasks performed by members of the NCC.

Work of national importance was a somewhat elastic concept. Usually it meant employment in agriculture or forestry, the food processing industries, the merchant navy or shipbuilding, transport, mining, education, hospital or sanitary services or other public utilities. Unlike the NCC, the work was under civilian control; and the conscientious objector was legally bound to undertake such work until the end of the war emergency – unless his tribunal released him from this particular condition. While some objectors argued that acceptance of work of this kind was (though less directly) as much an abetment of the military system as service in the NCC, many felt that refusal would be carrying logic to undesirable lengths. In fact, only the comparatively small band of "absolutists" held out for unconditional exemption.

The United States

America entered the war against the Central Powers in April 1917. The following month Congress passed a Selective Service Act requiring all males between the ages of 21 and 30 to register for military service. The law exempted from combatant service those who were *bona fide* members of existing pacifist sects (the names of the bodies qualifying as such were not specified, however). On paper, at any rate, neither religious objectors unaffiliated to a pacifist denomination nor nonreligious objectors were eligible for exemption. Thus, American legislative provision for conscientious objection proved considerably less liberal than the British, despite the fact that Secretary of War Newton D. Baker had once had the reputation of being a peace man and that conscription in Britain had already been functioning for over a year. Even though leading pacifists and liberals, who could refer both to the advantages of the British legislation and the shortcomings in its practical implementation, pointed out to Baker that his proposed legislation failed to provide either for those who objected to noncombatant as well as combatant service or for genuine objectors outside the peace sects, the Secretary of War refused to extend the range of exemption.

On June 5 registration was held. Most conscientious objectors, as their counterparts in Britain had done, complied while stating their unwillingness to undertake military service. The local boards which were set up to administer selective service were empowered to give noncombatant status only within a narrow frame of reference. In fact they did not always recognize even those who were entitled to this classification. Many conscientious objectors, even though classified as such, were unwilling to accept noncombatant service. As it turned out, in practice almost all conscientious objectors (apart from nonregistrants) found themselves, whether recognized or rejected by their local boards, in one or another of the army camps which had been set up throughout the country. What to do with these recalcitrant conscripts after their arrival within the army's jurisdiction was soon to prove a minor headache to the military authorities and to demand the attention once again of the administration in Washington. But before we describe the confrontation of these objectors with the American military machine, along with the experiences of their British confrères in facing the working of conscription in England, we must discuss the character of the pacifist movement in both countries and the categories of objectors who made up its most active following.

Pacifist Organization

Britain

In nineteenth-century Britain the peace movement had been represented by several rather sedate bodies – eminently respectable, predominantly middle-class, and somewhat limited in their range of interests. The oldest of these bodies was the London Peace Society, founded in 1816 under Quaker auspices. It was the only one which had written unqualified pacifism into its statutes, though it admitted to membership all who wished to work for the establishment of a warless world.

By 1914 these organizations were all rather moribund. In theory they continued to maintain an antiwar stand; in practice many of their members supported the war. They took little part in the antiwar movement and after the conclusion of hostilities their activities dwindled away. At the outbreak of war the Peace Society had as it president the Right Honourable Joseph Pease, President of the Board of Education in Asquith's Liberal cabinet and a member of the Society of Friends. Pease approved the declaration of war as the only possible reply to German aggression; when war began he relinquished his presidency of the Peace Society. On the other hand, the Society's general secretary, the Rev. W. Evans Darby, was a convinced religious pacifist who had served the peace movement devotedly for over quarter of a century. He was then suffering from ill health, however, and resigned his post at the end of 1915. During the war, writes a historian of the international peace movement, "the Peace Society remained passive. It never once wavered in its principles, but its existence ... can be traced only in it annual meetings. The *Herald of Peace* [the Society's organ] virtually died."[1]

The old-time peace associations, thus, were in a state of decline at the beginning of the twentieth century. On the other hand, the Quaker Society of Friends, which since the third quarter of the seventeenth century represented the nucleus of religious pacifism in Britain, had begun toward the end of the nineteenth century to undergo a renewal. In particular, some of its younger and more active members were attempting to deepen the Society's long-standing interest in philanthropy by a concern for social and political problems. Although some Quakers supported the war (perhaps almost as many as a third of the Society's members eligible for military service served in the armed forces), the majority continued to adhere to its peace testimony even in wartime and the Society's official utterances were without exception in support of the pacifist stand. In earlier times – on both sides of the Atlantic – Quakers who joined up were usually disowned by the Society. This no longer happened in the world wars of this century. But at least in Britain in the 1914–18 war, conscientious objection was as much the stance expected by the Society of younger Friends as military service was expected of active members of most other churches.[2] Quakerism had its peace militants among older members, too. In May 1918 three highly respected Quakers were sent to jail for circulating a leaflet entitled *A Challenge to Militarism*, which they had signed as officers of the Friends' Service Committee.[3] Quaker pacifism, however, was often granted grudging recognition; it seemed to many somehow part of the English tradition for which the war was (allegedly) being fought.

In addition, the Quaker stress on positive peacemaking, on the relief of war's victims, provided a meeting point with those who differed on the subject of the justifiability of war. At first, it was the enemy aliens stranded in Britain by the outbreak of war who demanded the Quakers' attention: a work of mercy that showed courage in those years of "Hun-hating." Later, their War Victims Relief Committee extended their activities to the war-ravaged lands of Europe. The Quaker star, the badge worn by Quaker field workers and imprinted on the consignments they distributed, became known not only in France but in Russia and Serbia and, in the immediate postwar years, in Germany, Austria and Poland.[4] As a result of Quaker relief work, a picture was created in the popular mind of kindly and mild men and women dressed in gray, handing out food and clothes to starving and ragged thousands. Like the legendary "good Quaker" in eighteenth-century

France who fired the imagination of Voltaire, this picture was a mixture of fact and fancy. In subsequent years it certainly helped Friends in many areas in their work of political conciliation. It also drew a comparatively small number of people to Quakerism and to pacifism in countries where these had been virtually unknown before. In the long run, however, this twentieth-century legend may have proved to some extent a disadvantage in the Quaker quest for a solution to the problem of war, for, if indubitably it has added to Friends' reputation in the contemporary world, it has also served to largely isolate them in the world's opinion from serious consideration in the realm of politics. With quasi-sainthood bestowed on the Quakers it has not proved too difficult to reject their proposals as the fruits of excessive religious idealism. Thus, Quakers have sometimes been known to wish – at least in theory – a return to the days of George Fox, when the world held them in scorn and misused them and they themselves looked forward not to the quiet life of an apolitical sect, which in the next century they did indeed become, but to the reordering of the whole world according to their peaceable principles.

Whereas before 1914 articulate pacifism had been confined (apart, that is, from labor antimilitarism and the pacifistic internationalism of many liberals) to the Quakers and a sprinkling of clergy and laymen in the nonpacifist denominations, World War I saw the emergence of pacifism in a number of Protestant churches. The pacifists, of course, remained a small minority there, but they were to become increasingly vocal. In politics the Christian pacifist was more often than not a socialist: the war had gravely shaken the long association of liberalism with the peace cause. The saintly Dr. Alfred Salter (later a Labour member of parliament) is an example of the Christian pacifist-socialist alliance. Soon after war broke out he published in the Independent Labour Party's organ, *Labour Leader*, an article entitled "The Religion of a C.O.," which was soon translated into many other languages and circulated in as many as half a million copies.[5] The tone was emotional. The appeal, as in the case of much early socialist propaganda, was to the heart rather than the head: "Look! Christ in khaki; out in France thrusting His bayonet into the body of a German workman ... Hark! The Man of Sorrows in a cavalry charge, cutting, hacking, thrusting, crushing, cheering. No! No! That picture is an impossible one, *and we all know it*. That settles the matter for me." Salter called on all Christians, all socialists, to refuse war service and to urge their comrades to take a similar stand.

In December 1914 a group of Christian pacifists "profoundly dissatisfied with the confused utterance of the Christian churches concerning the War"[6] had gathered in Cambridge – from their deliberations the Fellowship of Reconciliation (FOR) emerged. The idea of founding such a fellowship had originated in the immediate prewar initiative of an English Quaker and ex-missionary, Henry T. Hodgkin, and an influential German Lutheran clergyman, Friedrich Siegmund-Schültze, who was a prime mover in the emerging ecumenical movement among Protestants temporarily suspended by the outbreak of hostilities and was himself already a convinced pacifist. The British Fellowship, which sought to unite the efforts not only of Quakers but of all who based their pacifism on Christian grounds, did not aspire to exercise pressure on public opinion or on government. Its members did not enter into controversy as to the rights and wrongs of the war. Their goal of "a world order based on love" was to be reached, they hoped, by a gradual leavening of society. They were, in a way, revolutionaries – at least their call for "the enthronement of love in personal, social, commercial life" was surely a summons to revolution – but they were quiet revolutionaries, as distant from the political scene as were the first Christians gathered in an upper room.

Political opposition to the war, however, was not lacking. While some of its opponents might be practising churchmen, except in the case of the four Quaker members of parliament it was not from religion but from economics and recent diplomatic history that the antiwar forces drew their ammunition to blast the war establishment. Inside the House of Commons the peace "party" numbered about forty M.P.s. They formed a somewhat amorphous group with no formal organization and with no clearly defined membership. There were the five ILP-ers, led by Ramsay Macdonald and Philip Snowden, and a sprinkling of Labour Party members, as well as some twenty-five independent liberals among whom the most vocal and cogent critics of the war were representatives of the Union of Democratic Control (UDC) such as Arthur Ponsonby and Charles P. Trevelyan.

The UDC, like the ILP, was not a pacifist body. Many pacifists, however, supported it and themselves drew support form its denunciations of prewar diplomacy, the "secret diplomacy" of the European powers including Britain, which in the UDC's view had dragged the country unknowingly into war. Its spokesmen, of whom perhaps the ablest and most industrious was the journalist E.D. Morel, roundly condemned prewar British foreign policy for its commitments to France and Russia and for involving the country in war over Belgium. The war, they believed, was an unnecessary war. They demanded parliamentary control of foreign policy in the future and the establishment of an international organization after the war was ended. Meanwhile they called for a negotiated peace and, while condemning Prussian militarism along with the military establishments of the Allied powers, they argued against any attempt to penalize the vanquished if the Western allies succeeded in pursuing the war to a successful conclusion. Denounced as "pro-German" by much of the wartime press, the UDC came to exercise a significant influence on British left-wing opinion in the decade or so after the armistice.

The conscientious objectors, too, were often branded as traitors and spokesmen of Prussian militarism. As one of the doughtiest champions of the pacifist cause wrote from prison:

I do not anticipate that public opinion is likely to show any appreciable acceptance of the conscientious objector's point of view during the panic of war. We must not, therefore, exaggerate the effect of our efforts on the immediate issue of peace and war. But I am convinced that wise action and persistent propaganda now will assist in creating an opinion which will be eagerly embraced as soon as men and women are freed from the terror of war in their midst.[7]

"Persistent propaganda" was certainly the keynote of the chief pacifist organization in World War I Britain, the No-Conscription Fellowship (NCF),[8] of which the author of this letter, Clifford Allen, was chairman. The NCF was in many ways a remarkable body. It drew together under one umbrella devout religious pacifists like Dr. Alfred Salter, the Congregationalist minister Leyton Richards, or the Quaker Edward Grubb who became its treasurer; agnostics like Bertrand Russell the philosopher[9]; a wide variety of socialists of varying degrees of militancy from idealistic ILPers to fiery Tynesiders and members of small Marxist sects. It also had more than its fair share of individualist antimilitarists as well as a sprinkling of syndicalists and anarchists. It was indeed a lively organization whose members, when they were not in jail, were constantly debating with each other the issues of war and peace, and striving to convince an unreceptive public of the evils of conscription and of an international system that bred wars like the present one.

Moreover – and this is probably its most remarkable feature – the NCF, unlike many radical bodies, functioned with great efficiency. Its Record Department under the able guidance of an ex-suffragette, Catherine E. Marshall, who as a woman was not liable to military service, kept a reliable register of the status, experiences and whereabouts of almost all conscientious objectors (with a duplicate file hidden away in case of seizure of the original by the police). The information was used not only to help the men concerned directly, but also to supply information for pamphlets and newspaper articles in defense of the conscientious objectors' stand and for the use of sympathetic members of parliament in their speeches and questions in the House concerning the antiwar movement. Once, even the War Office had occasion to apply to the NCF for information on a conscientious objector whose whereabouts they could not trace in their own records.

The Fellowship's other departments were no less active than its records section. The Press Department kept newspapers and periodicals informed concerning the NCF's activities and about conscientious objectors in general. (It may have regretted sometimes what the press did with this information.) The Literature Department produced over a million copies of pamphlets and leaflets: from March 1916 it issued a weekly journal, *The Tribunal*, sales of which at one period reached the considerable figure of 10,000 copies. A Campaign Department organized petitions asking for the release of imprisoned conscientious objectors, with signatures gathered from persons prominent in public life who were usually unconnected with pacifism. A Political Department acted as a liaison between the NCF and the peace "party" in parliament, organized delegations to government, and publicized the NCF's position in regard to existing and proposed legislation which touched the interests of conscientious objectors. Finally, two departments were directly concerned with the conscientious objectors' welfare: Visitation, which kept in contact with those in prison, army camps or guardroom, and Maintenance, which (under the chairmanship of Ramsay Macdonald, though he was himself neither a pacifist nor an NCF member) raised money to help their dependents if in need.

This elaborate organization had not sprung up unprepared upon the introduction of conscription at the beginning of 1916. The idea originated with a young socialist journalist Fenner Brockway, editor of the *Labour Leader*. On 12 November 1914 he had published in its columns an appeal asking for the names and addresses of persons between the ages of 18 and 38 who would refuse combatant service if conscription were imposed. The response was good; Brockway and his associates at once went to work and within a month the NCF had come into being. Its members were drawn mainly from men of military age but sympathizers among older men as well as among women were welcome in its ranks, too. Membership eventually reached nearly 10,000; around 6,000 members belonged to the ILP with Quakers as the next largest element.

The primary object of the Fellowship was to challenge the right of government to impose military conscription, even in wartime. This was defense of libertarian rather than pacifist principle. The NCF did, in fact, accept as members all who "from conscientious motives" refused to bear arms. But it also wrote into its "Statement of Faith,"[10] in an attempt to satisfy the complete pacifist point of view within the Fellowship, a clause implying that absolute pacifism was a basic article of this faith: members, it was there stated, objected to fighting "because they consider human life to be sacred." This confusion of thought, covered over during the period when all efforts were being concentrated on the struggle against the conscription acts, began to cause dissension as the war neared an end and as the effect of the Russian Revolution began to be felt in Britain.

Even earlier the NCF had not been free of controversy. In the first place, there was the question whether the Fellowship should stand out against all proffered alternatives to combatant service. Many of its leaders, including Allen, Brockway, and some Quakers, believed it should oppose at least noncombatant service in the army. There was also some support among the rank and file for a rejection of alternative service of any kind, even when it was of a civilian character, and a conference resolution to this effect was eventually passed by a small majority. However, except perhaps among the more rigid "absolutists," there was a strong feeling in the Fellowship that the question should be left open and each individual member should decide according to his conscience. And, in fact, this remained the policy of the NCF.

A second debate revolved around the objectives of the Fellowship. Should it concentrate on a campaign against conscription as an institution inimical to freedom and in conflict with the British tradition of liberty? Or should it continue as a primarily antiwar and pacifist body? The leadership was split on the issue: as a result the emphasis swung somewhat uneasily between an anticonscriptionist and a pure pacifist line.

The tactics to be adopted by the Fellowship provided a third topic for heated debate. Should it try to recruit conscientious objectors actively in an effort to defeat the working of the conscription system or was its function merely to act as a self-help organization for conscientious objectors who had already reached their position independently? While the Fellowship did its best to publicize the ideas of the movement, it never attempted any kind of mass resistance to wartime conscription – an action which would undoubtedly have led to its suppression.

As it was, the NCF from 1916 on had its hands full in coping with harassment from the government. There were constant clashes with the authorities. The London police frequently raided the Fellowship's offices, and provincial police raided the houses of district officers and broke up, sometimes with the assistance of unruly mobs of outraged "patriots," public meetings organized by local branches of the NCF. There were prosecutions of members under the notorious wartime Defence of the Realm Acts (D.O.R.A.). Bertrand Russell, for instance, was prosecuted for writing a leaflet published by the NCF, which gave an account of the tribunal hearing and eventual imprisonment of a young socialist conscientious objector. "It is not only I that am in the dock," Russell told the court, "it is the whole tradition of British liberty which our forefathers built up with great trouble and with great sacrifice." He spoke out in favor of "the invincible power of that better way of passive resistance, which pacifists believe to be stronger than all the armies and navies in the world."[11] Earlier in the same year, 1916, five members of the NCF's committee, charged with attempting to hinder army recruiting by the publication of a leaflet entitled *Repeal the Act*, had each received a 61-day prison sentence. (The *Tribunal* on this occasion inquired ironically if the government would also consider the Sermon on the Mount a hindrance to recruiting and its author liable to prosecution on that count.)

The NCF, as the threat from the authorities mounted, went partly underground. Vital documents were hidden or duplicated; its departments were located separately and the most important of these, Records, was made into an independent organization; nominal officers substituted for those really responsible in order to prevent the latter's arrest. By early 1918 almost all the leaders of military age had been jailed as conscientious objectors. Leadership was then taken over by the women and older men or by men like Bertrand Russell, who for one reason or another were not liable for call-up. The climax came in the spring of 1918 when the Home Office, worried by signs in the country of increasing radicalism and war weariness, attempted to stop publication of the *Tribunal*. But the police failed to discover who really was the responsible editor. They did succeed in destroying the press on which the paper was being printed. But to their surprise it appeared the following week as usual, though in a smaller format and with a much reduced circulation: the paper continued to be produced on a small hand-press located in a private house.

Thus the NCF weathered the storm of war. It wound up its activities in late November 1919, for with the coming of peace and the ending of conscription it had lost its *raison d'être*. A new organizational framework had to be constructed to meet the needs of the pacifist movement in the years ahead. The NCF drew its strength and some of its weaknesses (for instance, a sectarian smugness, that could occasionally approach arrogance, and a readiness to understand the enemy's point of view that sometimes fell over into its justification) from the British tradition of radical dissent. It expressed, too, the English dissenting conscience, which once more, as often in the past, stood in close relationship to political radicalism. The treatment meted out to it by the authorities was frequently deplorable. Yet, it must still be said, the No-Conscription Fellowship could only have functioned in wartime in a country where, at least to some extent, the claim of conscience was still understood, nonconformity tolerated, and radicalism given a respected place in the national tradition.

The United States

"In America," wrote Norman Thomas, "the defense of the conscientious objector was left almost wholly to religious sects such as Quakers and Mennonites, and to political radicals and pacifists."[12] This was in contrast to Britain where prominent nonpacifists (including some of unimpeachable Conservative principles) – Lord Hugh Cecil, Lord Parmoor, Professor Gilbert Murray, Bernard Shaw, Arnold Bennett, to cite only a few names – were prepared to speak and write on behalf of the conscientious objectors, even of those who took the absolutist position. In the United States, not only was unconditional exemption unrecognized in law but the "absolutist" found little understanding among nonpacifist liberals and churchmen. Here the popular feeling ran even stronger against the conscientious objector and all who opposed the war than in Britain. The ex-Tolstoyan nonresistant turned ardent patriot, Clarence Darrow, could write: "The pacifist speaks with the German accent. Even if his words are not against America, the import of all he says is to aid Germany against America and its allies in the war."[13] If a pro-war radical could talk like this, little wonder if the ordinary patriotic citizen should equate pacifism with treason and feel sometimes that the proper place for opponents of the war was swinging from a lamp-post. In addition, the rising Bolshevik scare from the end of 1917 onward served to increase the unpopularity of the antiwar movement. Were not the Bolsheviks against the war and were there not many "Reds" among the conscientious objectors and the antimilitarists?

The weakness of the pacifist movement in the United States in comparison with its counterpart in Britain (where its position in the country could scarcely be described as strong) derived from several factors. In the first place it lacked the support in the legislature that British pacifists enjoyed. Politicians who were sympathetic to pacifists, like Senator Robert M. La Follette of Wisconsin, were a mere handful. Secondly,

the labor movement, which in Britain contained a powerful antimilitarist wing, was in the United States a much less influential element in
the life of the nation. The frequent and ruthless suppression of trade
unions and labor organization in America at this period is a well
known story. The labor movement here could not serve to cushion the
blows directed by the authorities against pacifists and antimilitarists,
as was the case in Britain to some extent. In the third place, it would
seem that American society, as it had crystallized in the course of the
nineteenth century, while it was certainly far more egalitarian than
British society, was at the same time less inclined to tolerate social dissenters. True, a Boston "brahmin" decades earlier might defy with
impunity the mores of his social caste and fling himself without suffering too severe a social ostracism into such radical causes as nonresistance, abolitionism or communitarianism. But now in wartime
America the drive to conformity swept dissent angrily aside.

No body with the vigor and dimension of the No-Conscription Fellowship emerged on the American wartime scene. Before the United
States entered the war there was considerable opposition to the struggle raging across the Atlantic. The millionaire industrialist, Henry
Ford, financed a "peace ship," which set sail for Europe in December
1915. Some pacifists participated; yet it was not, properly speaking, a
pacifist venture. The Woman's Peace Party, founded in 1915 and
including both pacifist and nonpacifist antiwar activists, formed the
first "gender-exclusive" American women's peace organization. Transforming itself, when the war ended, into the American section of the
Women's International League for Peace and Freedom, it became the
precursor of a number of women's peace groups which sprang up in
the United States after 1918. Yet its impact at first was small. In addition, a number of ephemeral groups had been formed to canvas for
conscientious objection in case war came, but these "mushroom
leagues or fellowships" mostly dissolved after America became
directly involved in hostilities. "To one who heard the vehemence of
their professions," wrote Norman Thomas, "it still remains somewhat
surprising, not that they disappeared, but that they vanished so easily,
completely, and finally, before the government had time to take really
aggressive action against them."[14]

The Socialist Jessie W. Hughan, for instance, had collected from
recruits to the Anti-Enlistment League, which she had started up in the
spring of 1915, some 3,500 declarations of membership stating: "I,
being over 18 years of age, hereby pledge myself against enlistment as
a volunteer for any military or naval service in international war, offensive or defensive, and against giving my approval to such enlistment

on the part of others." And on the very eve of war we find the veteran worker for peace, Mrs. J. Sergeant Cram, and her "World Patriots" gathering signatures to the following pledge: "I will not kill, nor help kill my fellowmen."[15] In November 1915, as a result of the visit to America of the founder of the British FOR, the Quaker Henry Hodgkin, an American Fellowship of Reconciliation had been established. It provided a focal point for the thinking and activities of Christian pacifists; but, like the British branch, in wartime it did not agitate politically, but placed its emphasis on the personal conscience. Some of its members, like the YMCA leader John R. Mott, left the organization after the United States became involved in war. Only in the interwar years did the FOR emerge as the major element in the pacifist movement and a factor not without importance in the development of American political thought.

The old-time peace organizations switched over to support of the war immediately after their country's entry. The American Peace Society, which already had experience of this type of operation at the time of the Civil War, after proclaiming in 1916 "that Jesus Christ was a pacifist," declared in May 1917 its belief that war was unavoidable and its backing of the administration.[16] Even among the Quakers, "many distinguished Friends" publicly proclaimed their "loyalty to the Cause of Civilization, and to the President of the United States" in pursuit of military victory.[17] We find, for instance, a group of prominent Hicksite (i.e., liberal) Friends declaring in a paroxysm of war fever: "We do not agree with those who would utter sentimental platitudes while a mad dog is running amuck biting women and children [or] with those who would stand by idly quoting some isolated passage of scripture while an insane man murdered him, ravished his wife, bayoneted his babies or crucified his friends ... We will not equivocate with honor or compromise with wickedness." Swarthmore College (Hicksite) established a military training unit for its students, while Haverford College (Orthodox) forced one of its instructors, Henry J. Cadbury (later to gain renown as a New Testament scholar), to resign on account of his openly expressed antiwar views. Indeed, only the still largely rural Conservative (Wilburite) Quakers remained united behind their traditional pacifism. In general, the story of wartime Quakerism is that "of a small but admired religious group struggling to reconcile their feelings of loyalty to the United States" with their inherited, and in many cases still fervently held, peace testimony.[18]

Officially of course the Quakers, along with the Mennonites, the Church of the Brethren, and a number of smaller denominations, continued – albeit sometimes somewhat cautiously – to support their historical peace testimonies and to regard the conscientious objector as acting in conformity with his sect's traditional stand. Ironically, with such groups it was often the conformist, and not the rebel, who became a conscientious objector to the draft. Outside these bodies, the clergy (Protestant, Catholic, and Jewish) were usually hostile both to pacifism and to conscientious objectors. A careful student of the subject has calculated that the total number of pacifist ministers was in the whole country scarcely above seventy (including three Jewish rabbis). Some of these men lost their pulpits (even among the Unitarians whose principles were founded on free religion) and the only Bishop in the company, the Episcopalian Paul Jones of Utah, was forced to resign his office. Whereas the Mennonites, because of their German speech and ancestry, were sometimes threatened with mob violence or neighborly boycotts, and the leaders of the Church of the Brethren were at one point threatened with prosecution for impeding the draft if they did not order the immediate withdrawal from circulation of a pamphlet advising members against acceptance of noncombatant service, Quaker pacifism was usually tolerated as an inherited peculiarity of a group that had nevertheless contributed much in the past to creating the American way of life.

No account of American pacifism in World War I would be complete without at least brief mention of the stand of the Socialist Party. Socialism in the United States had not succeeded in gaining as secure a foothold in political life as the socialist movement had in Great Britain. The American party's wartime stand, however, was as decidedly antiwar as was the British ILP's. As in the case of the British ILP, American socialists, however, were free to reach their own decision whether to obey the call-up or to take their stand as conscientious objectors. At the same time veteran socialist party leaders, like Eugene V. Debs, for instance, a man who professed the profoundest revulsion at the thought of killing a fellow human for whatever cause, found themselves behind bars with sentences often ranging between ten and twenty years. In some cases, terms of imprisonment went even higher. "One who remembers our war-time sentences," to quote Norman Thomas again, "must conclude that life imprisonment would have been the mildest punishment the resourceful leaders of the [British] No-Conscription Fellowship could have expected in the United States."[19]

H.C. Peterson and Gilbert C. Fite have meticulously documented in their study of the *Opponents of War 1917–1918* (1957) the whole dismal story: not only the imprisonment of antiwar leaders and rank-and-file left-wingers but the tarring and feathering of antiwar agitators by infuriated mobs, the breaking up of meetings by the police, the lashings and beatings perpetrated by vigilante groups, and the less virulent but even more frequent minor harrying to which the antiwar minority was subject during these years. "Conservative people who displayed an intemperance that would do credit to the wildest of radicals" and "an extensive picture of intolerance and the demand for conformity" were the phrases used by Peterson and Fite in the foreword to their book in describing the atmosphere of that time. The wartime anti-Red scare merged into the postwar Red panic, and the last of the political opponents of the war were not released from prison until December 1923.

It was not merely popular opinion that was swept by war fever. The intellectual leaders with few exceptions supported the war effort enthusiastically. "To those of us who still retain an irreconcilable animus against war," wrote Randolph Bourne in his now famous essay on "The War and the Intellectuals" first published in June 1917, "it has been a bitter experience to see the unanimity with which the American intellectuals have thrown their support to the use of war-technique in the crisis in which America found herself." In this essay he expressed his amazement at the gullibility with which the educated sections of the American community had followed in the footsteps of their European colleagues and swallowed whole the idea of their country's being engaged in a holy war for democracy and a new international order. "The American intellectuals," he lamented, "seem to have forgotten that the real enemy is War rather than imperial Germany." There appeared to be no alternative but to conform. "Dissenters are already excommunicated." Nonetheless, it was, in Bourne's opinion, still worth proclaiming that nothing could justify the evil of modern international conflict. He cried out in frustrated fury, "There must be some irreconcilables left who will not accept the war with walrus tears."[20]

Types of Objectors

In the United States and Britain, at least, Bourne's irreconcilable remnant was represented in most tangible form among the objectors to military service. We must turn now to consider the main types of conscientious objection to be found in these countries.

The two most convenient categories into which objectors may be divided are the religious and the political. This division, however, can be made only with the proviso that it represents an oversimplification. Many religious objectors, especially in Britain, regarded the existing social system as evil and war as merely the most flagrant example of a way of life opposed to Christian social justice. On the other hand, many nonreligious objectors looked on human life as something sacred and war in all its forms as the negation of the socialist or libertarian order they sought to create. They, no less than their colleagues who based their convictions on the Christian gospel, drew their strength to resist from the tradition of moral protest fostered in the course of religious dissent in their countries. Even those who did not reject war in all circumstances but foresaw the possibility of a justifiable war, either in defense of a socialist commonwealth or to enforce the decisions of a world government, had taken their stand as conscientious objectors, instead of entering the war as their comrades on the continent had done and attempting to act as antimilitarists in uniform. They acted not merely in that way because such an alternative was open to them whereas it was closed to socialists and libertarians elsewhere, but also because, if often only obscurely, they felt that individual protest was meaningful and that assertion of moral principle had value in itself. As a Quaker wrote of this kind of "selective" objector: "He stands ... for freedom of conscience in matters of life and death. This ... is a position entitled to all respect."[21] Even those "Bloomsbury" quasi-pacifists, described by Martin Ceadel as representing a type of "pacifist elitism" (because they derived their unwillingness to be conscripted into the armed forces, at any rate in part, from a belief in the priority of their vocation as artists or writers over all other considerations), had indeed displayed a certain courage in swimming against the tide of wartime public opinion. Lytton Strachey, for instance, who later gained fame for his biography of Queen Victoria, could easily have obtained exemption from military service on the grounds of his poor health. Instead, he chose to appear before a tribunal. And if he had not done this, we may add, the world would have lost his classic reply to the question what he would do if one of the enemy attempted to rape his sister: "I should try and come between them."[22]

No completely reliable figures are available as to the religious or political affiliations of objectors in World War I. In the United States the religious objectors predominated (they numbered almost 90% of the total), whereas there were a substantial number of nonreligious objectors of one kind or another in Britain. There it was the Society of Friends that provided the core of religious objection to military service, though many other denominations contributed their quota of objectors. Indeed certain apocalyptic sects probably produced more C.Os. than any other single source, including of course the Quakers. In the United States the Mennonites and Church of the Brethren provided numerically the largest contingent. In both countries, there were certain sects of a fundamentalist or chiliastic character whose members were forbidden combatant service but recommended to accept non-combatant duties in the army. This was true of the rapidly increasing Seventh-day Adventists and the small body of inward-looking Plymouth Brethren. On the other hand, the Christadelphians disfellowshipped members who entered the army even in a noncombatant capacity. And the International Bible Students (today known as Jehovah's Witnesses), whose militant opposition to the war brought twenty-year sentences for Judge Joseph T. Rutherford and six other leading American Witnesses on the pretext that they were hindering the draft, in most cases claimed a right to unconditional exemption, most frequently without success. Major Kellogg, chairman of the U.S. President's Board of Inquiry, described the Witnesses who appeared before him as follows: "These objectors were of all nationalities. Italians, whose testimony had to be taken through an interpreter, had read "Pastor" Russell [the sect's founder] in the Italian just as Greeks, who knew no English, had read him in the Greek. His pacifism permeates a dozen languages: the immigrant may absorb it in his native tongue before ever he comes to our shores."[23] The Witnesses, in fact, along with the socialists and the adherents of some of the smaller religious sects, represented a proletarian element within the community of conscientious objectors, which in Britain was predominantly middle-class and in America had a strong rural, farming admixture. It should also be noted that in World War I religious pacifism was confined almost exclusively to the Protestant denominations.[24]

Kellogg, despite strong disagreement with his political views, pays grudging tribute to the socialist objector. "He commonly made," writes the Major, "an unequivocal statement of his case with no apparent concern whether his asserted scruples fell within or without the provisions of the Executive Order ... The frankness of the Socialists was impressive."[25] For many socialist objectors, whether in Britain or the United States, their stand was not the result of political calculation or a tactical move in the class war but an ethical imperative, an act of obedience to a secular version of the Sermon on the Mount. We find, for instance, the Englishman Herbert Morrison, a future Labour wartime cabinet minister, telling his Tribunal: "I belong to the I.L.P. and Socialism is my religion."[26] This creed was intensely individualistic. Its proponents were socialists because in their view the capitalist system stultified the free development of the individual; they were pacifists and conscientious objectors because they saw war and conscription as the destroyers of both personal liberty and the spiritual and material welfare of the citizen. Though they usually professed to be agnostics or atheists, these men spoke of "the sacredness of human life" with as much conviction as any birthright Quaker. They often preached nonresistance to evil as fervently as any Mennonite. And even if they did not think in terms of the Fatherhood of God, they had made a religion of the Brotherhood of Man.

In the course of 1917, events were to occur on the far side of Europe that were to bring to the surface the hitherto partly concealed distinction among Britain and America's conscientious objectors – between those who opposed war in all circumstances and those who rejected bloodshed only when carried out on behalf of a capitalist government. In the United States, where the objectors had no independent organization of their own, the clash of opinions did not take place within an institutional framework. But in Britain both viewpoints had been represented inside the No-Conscription Fellowship: their adherents were united for the time being in the fight against the military service acts and in opposition to the war then in progress. The Bolshevik Revolution in Russia of October 1917, which followed hard in the footsteps of the liberal revolution of the previous February, brought to the fore the question whether continued alliance was possible between those who actively supported violent revolution and those who believed in nonviolent means, even if they might in many instances share the same enthusiasm for the ultimate goal of a classless society.

In April 1917, Bertrand Russell acting in the name of the NCF's National Committee sent a message of fraternal greetings to the new Provisional Government in Russia on the overthrow of the centuries-long tyranny, in the course of which he expressed the Fellowship's refusal to participate in war.[27] It was, however, not the Provisional Government but the Bolsheviks who took Russia out of the war. Sympathy for the transformation of society taking place in Russia was felt in varying degrees of intensity by many members of the NCF. But could a revolution ever be achieved without violence? Should pacifists and antimilitarists support revolution, if social change seemed imperative, even though the revolutionaries resorted to arms to gain their ends? Debate began toward the end of the war and continued into the months after the armistice when the conscientious objectors were being released from prison or alternative service, and men everywhere were turning their thoughts earnestly toward the shaping of the postwar world.

In the middle of 1919 Dr. Alfred Salter wrote: "I have been staggered at the number of discharged prisoners who have told me that they are prepared to take up arms on behalf of the social revolution." He doubted "if one-third of our people are pacifist in the sense that they believe *all* war to be wrong and that *all* methods involving the use of violence to attain a desired end are futile in the long run." He felt sure that the extreme left within the NCF would not oppose conscription if it were imposed by a revolutionary proletarian government.[28] At the other extreme, even among the most uncompromising pacifists there were probably few who went as far as the NCF's first organizing secretary, Aylmer Rose. Expressing "a conscientious objection to the works and methods of Bolshevists, Spartacists, ... and all others engaged in driving out the old devils of militarism and capitalism by the strangely new devils of civil war, proscription and confiscation," Rose considered that "Bolshevism and Militarism are one and the same thing, only differing in the ends for which violence is proposed ... Killing is killing even when you kill a capitalist." "Anti-Bolshevist propaganda seems to me to be an essential part of our work," he forthrightly stated.[29]

From the ranks of the conscientious objectors were to come some of the founding members and early apostles of the British Communist Party. Most leftist objectors, however, remained in the ILP or became affiliated with the rising Labour Party. Whatever their ultimate affiliation, they were now increasingly troubled by the question whether perhaps capitalism and militarism could only be defeated by their own weapons. As one of them wrote soon after release from prison: "To some people, fighting is so evil in itself that no cause could justify it. There are others, and I must confess I am one, who feel bound to investigate whether or not society can be renovated – failing other methods – by those of the soldier, much as I dislike them."[30]

Growing disillusionment on the left with the increasingly authoritarian trend of the Soviet experiment certainly affected pacifists, too. Nevertheless, a clear-cut line between pacifism and the communist-sponsored peace movement was not to be finally drawn until the 1930s, and even thereafter it was occasionally to become blurred again.

"The [war] resister desires a new internationalism," the doyen of British wartime objectors had written, "by which States are concerned less as embodiments of power and more as instruments of social administration."[31] Indeed democratic decentralization, and not centralized democracy, has been the most usual political expression of twentieth-century pacifism. It is not surprising, therefore, that the Soviet behemoth, with its inflated bureaucracy, its suppression of all libertarian tendencies and its ruthless pursuit of power politics, soon began to lose its attraction for believers in nonviolence, even if they strove to dissociate themselves from the virulent forms of anti-Bolshevism fostered by supporters of the old order in Russia and only too often promoted in the interests of the Soviet Union's rivals on the international scene. Bertrand Russell, who took a prominent part in the work of the NCF and continued active in the pacifist movement after the war was over, well illustrates this point. From the beginning he took up a critical stand toward the Soviet Union while remaining an exacting critic of the policies of the noncommunist world.

Russell, although a socialist, had opposed the war on rationalist and humanitarian grounds rather than because, like some of his NCF colleagues, he wished to stand aside from a struggle which was of concern only to capitalists. It should be stressed at this point that among the nonreligious objectors in Britain and America there was a sizeable minority who refused to perform military service, not on account of any political or economic theory, but primarily because war contravened their personal ethic, because the bloodshed then going on over the waters seemed neither reasonable nor worthy of an enlightened human being. In this category there were men who forswore all violence as firmly as the religious pacifists; there were others who rejected violence under the present conditions of "international anarchy" but approved its harnessing behind an international authority, the creation of which in the future they saw as the major task before men of goodwill; there were still others who, disapproving of the present conflict as being simply a matter of "prestige," considered – balancing the good produced against the evil – that certain wars were justified in the past, whether to settle the empty spaces of the earth or in defense against the encroachments of an inferior level of civilization or for some grand principle.

Of the latter group, Russell was the most cogent spokesman. Yet it was Russell who provided the most eloquent exposition of the efficacy of nonviolence in the contemporary world in his essay on "War and Non-Resistance," which he published in the American *Atlantic Monthly* in August 1915.[32] He argues his case on strictly utilitarian grounds: his premise for the successful application of nonviolent resistance was, basically, that the conflict should be one between civilized nations observing the rule of law in their own communities, yet at the same time lacking any impartial authority to which to appeal for action "in the general interest and not primarily in the interest of one of the parties to the quarrel." In such circumstances (they were those of contemporary Europe), unilateral disarmament, followed by "passive non-obedience" in case of subsequent invasion by a hostile power, appeared to Russell the most expedient policy for England or any other civilized country. Disarmament would remove any "pretext for invasion" – and with the growing power of public opinion this, Russell believed, was now an important factor. But should any power be tempted, nevertheless, to embark on aggression against a disarmed state, with "fortitude and discipline" on the part of the invaded people a policy of noncooperation would win in the end. As in war, there would be some casualties: some high officials might even be shot by the occupiers – Russell is speaking specifically of the Germans and the English – but all functionaries could scarcely be killed or imprisoned, for this would make the administration of the occupied country impossible. In England's case the Germans might take away the colonies, but their loss, in the view of Russell, the anti-imperialist, would be no tragedy. They might possibly exact tribute by threatening to deprive the country of its food supplies. But would not the consequent lowering of living standards still be preferable to the material and moral destruction of modern war? German militarism could only be permanently undermined by tangible proof that its opponents were themselves ready to do without war.

Russell's essay, though not quite the earliest attempt to envisage the consequences of civil disobedience directed against a foreign occupation, foreshadows the later interest in this problem in the West that was to arise from the Gandhian experiments in nonviolence. It represents an extension of pacifist thinking from a perhaps excessive concern for problems of moral conscience into the realm of international relations. Undoubtedly Russell's discussion has an air of unreality; it is merely a sketch with the details to be filled in later. Moreover, the author vacillates uncertainly between the view that nonviolence is a morally superior method of resistance with the implication, therefore, that it possesses permanent political validity (Gandhi's standpoint), and the opinion that it is merely an expedient technique in the existing state of civilization poised hesitantly between the jungle world of pre-civilization and a coming world order where violence would be employed solely to enforce the rule of law between the nations. But Russell's rational protest against war was shared by many at that time.

Among the fighting men, too, there were a number who felt a growing disenchantment with war. The postwar pacifist movement drew many of its most devoted adherents from veterans of 1914–18, like Lieutenant Mark Plowman whom we find in February 1918 writing to his brother: "Bless my soul one need not be a Quaker to think the present war a bit of a failure or object to sticking steel in human flesh."[33] But "Max" Plowman was an exceptional man – at that moment he was awaiting courtmartial for refusing continued service in the army. A more restrained antimilitarism is displayed, for instance, in the letters of another subaltern, Wilfred Owen, the most outstanding of England's war poets, who was killed in action shortly before the armistice. In May 1917 he wrote home from a military hospital in France:

I am more and more Christian as I walk the unchristian ways of Christendom. Already I have comprehended a light which never will filter into the dogma of any national church: namely that one of Christ's essential commands was: Passivity at any price! Suffer dishonour and disgrace; but never resort to arms. Be bullied, be outraged, be killed; but do not kill. It may be a chimerical and an ignominious principle, but there it is. It can only be ignored; and I think pulpit professionals are ignoring it very skilfully and successfully indeed ... Thus you see how pure Christianity will not fit in with pure patriotism.

"And am I not myself a conscientious objector with a very seared conscience," he finally bursts out.[34]

With Lieutenant Wilfred Owen, the "conscientious objector with a very seared conscience," we conclude our survey of the types of objectors in the Britain and America of World War I.

The Experiences of the Objectors

In Britain (that is, excluding Ireland where the government did not risk the introduction of conscription on account of the country's increasingly militant nationalism) there were some 16,000 conscientious objectors; in the United States, according to the War Department, the figure did not quite reach 4,000. Numerically, this represented a very small percentage of the total number of men drafted for military service: in the United States, for instance, nearly three million men were inducted into the armed forces.

The objectors were divided, we have seen, as to the proper stand to adopt in face of conscription between those who were ready to accept some form of alternative service (many, though, rejected noncombatant duties in the armed services) and those who held out for unconditional exemption. The "absolutists" were stronger in Britain than in the United States. They drew their inspiration from the long English libertarian tradition, which had earlier found expression in political radicalism and in religious dissent. Their way of thinking appealed strongly to ethical socialists of the ILP variety as well as to the more socially minded among the younger generation of British Quakers. Indeed, in past centuries the Society of Friends on both sides of the Atlantic had forbidden its members to purchase exemption from service in the militia by paying the small fine which the authorities demanded for this privilege. The state had no right, said Friends, to require anything in exchange for doing what conscience told a man was right. The twentieth-century absolutists were as opposed to military conscription as to war and regarded their noncooperation with the military service acts as a struggle waged for liberty in the tradition of their forefathers.

If Clifford Allen incarnated the position of the British unconditionalists, Roger N. Baldwin, who then served as director of the National Civil Liberties Bureau, may be taken as a typical representative of American absolutism. In a declaration made in 1918 explaining why he was refusing to register for the draft (a logical conclusion to which, however, most absolutists were unwilling to carry their argument), Baldwin stated:

The compelling motive for refusing to comply with the draft act is my uncompromising opposition to the principle of conscription of life by the state for any purpose whatever, in time of war or peace. I not only refuse to obey the present conscription law, but I would in future refuse to obey any similar statute which attempts to direct my choice of service and ideals. I regard the principle of conscription of life as a flat contradiction of all our cherished ideals of individual freedom, democratic liberty and Christian teaching.[35]

The absolutists felt that to accept any alternative to military service was to become an accomplice in the working of conscription for war. And military conscription demanded, too, that a man sacrifice his life even in a cause in which he did not believe. Like the old-time Quakers they denied that a government had the right to ask from one of its citizens any service in exchange for doing what he thought was right. Thus the state was not entitled to require alternative service from the conscientious objector to the evil of war: the demand was inimical to civil liberty as well as a denial of the rights of the individual. Though mostly socialists by conviction – many of them were active in the labor and trade union movements of their respective countries – they contested the arguments put forward by socialists on the European continent in favor of a citizen militia. The Anglo-American absolutists rejected impatiently the view that compulsory service, at least when it was for a democratically organized army, not only constituted the most egalitarian system but would act as a school for the inculcation of civic virtue in the young male citizenry. In the first place, of course, if they were complete pacifists (as many of them were), the absolutists disapproved of arms even to defend a people's state. They also considered the spirit of militarism, against the Prussian form of which the Western allies claimed to be waging war, as an inevitable concomitant of compulsory military service in any form. Thus conscription, instead of promoting freedom, would shackle the development of any country that adopted it. The best service they could render their native land, argued the absolutists, was to make no compromise with conscription. In addition, in wartime the acceptance of alternative service would release someone else for the fighting line, who might otherwise be spared from the clutches of the military: perhaps some unfortunate youth who scarcely had had time or opportunity to make up his mind on the question of war.

The alternativists, while they were no less opposed than the absolutists to the principle of peacetime military conscription, felt nevertheless that in times of national emergency, like a war, the state had the right to demand some kind of service from its citizens. By making provision in law for conscientious objection, the government had shown respect for their scruples, for which they were grateful. They might contrast their privileged position with the fate of the handful of objectors on the European continent where noncombatant service was the only alternative – and one that was only rarely offered – to prison or the firing squad. Unlike their absolutist brethren, the alternativists regarded the carrying on of work under civilian control, even if it were at the behest of a tribunal, as a means whereby they could witness to their pacifist convictions rather than as a tribute extracted from them unwillingly by Moloch. To exist at all in a modern state at war was to contribute indirectly to the military effort, argued the alternativists. They pointed out that even with an unconditional exemption a man could not find release from this dilemma. They doubted if the possibility that acceptance of alternative service might lead in some cases to the call-up of men who were not conscientiously opposed to the war, should deter them from undertaking such work. They were not out primarily, as the absolutists were, to smash the conscription system – they wanted rather to prove that, in time of need, antimilitarism was consistent with good citizenship and that pacifists were prepared to help their country in any way that they conscientiously could.

Thus ran the debate on theory. In practice the alternativists, among whom were represented many fine distinctions of outlook, not infrequently had their cases dismissed and found themselves in army camps or prison along with the more refractory absolutists. Even the most conciliatory group – the noncombatants – on occasion clashed with the military authorities. We must now turn, therefore, to the experiences of the objectors as they took shape separately in Britain and the United States.

Britain

In Britain the main stumbling block to the equitable treatment of conscientious objectors lay not in inadequate legislation but in inadequate staffing of the tribunals set up to administer the legislation relating to exemption from military service, whether on conscientious or other grounds. True, the deportment of some objectors was aggressive and rude; others, especially the young and less well educated, were tongue-tied and had difficulty in articulating their objections to military service; a few would have nothing to do with the tribunals and could not easily have been accommodated under any system of conscription. Even so, while in a few cases the tribunals attempted to be scrupulously fair, the majority only too often displayed misunderstanding of the applicants' viewpoint, petty bullying, and even crass stupidity. The chief concern of most tribunal members was not to assess sincerity and to satisfy conscience but, especially as the manpower shortage grew, to provide recruits for the armed forces. Therefore, when they were not rejecting applications outright, the tribunals were frequently attempting to press noncombatant service in the army on the objector – even against his better judgment.

Quakers usually fared better than the other religious objectors. Nonreligious objectors, especially if they held radical or socialist (not to speak of anarchist) views, were less likely to gain the type of exemption they sought than those who took their stand on Christian grounds, especially if they were church members in good standing. Some tribunals found it hard to believe that boys in their teens or young men in their early twenties could have reached independently a decision to stand as a conscientious objector (although they saw nothing abnormal in the state making up their minds for them and sending them willy-nilly into military service). Many tribunal members displayed by their utterances a conviction that conscientious objectors were cowards or shirkers or even sympathizers with the German cause. Objectors might be told: "Yours is a case of an unhealthy mind in an unwholesome body," or even "You are nothing but a shivering mass of unwholesome fat."[36] The regional tribunals had been filled with local civic dignitaries, many of them active in the established political parties. Doubtless ordinarily exemplars of the middle-class virtues, they had come briefly to hold authority over the destiny of other men; their sense of fair play had become clouded by the wartime jingoism that swept the country. In the gutter press, a campaign was soon under way to stir up public opinion (including tribunal members) against the objectors. Moreover, few tribunal members had had previous experience in the workings of a court. The presence of a "military representative" at each tribunal sometimes exercised, too, undue influence on its decisions.

The Local Government Board, when setting up the tribunals in February 1916, had issued instructions (for the most part in vain) concerning the conscientious objectors who would appear before them:

> While care must be taken that the man who shirks his duty to his country does not find unworthy shelter behind this provision, every consideration should be given to the man whose objection generally rests on religious or moral convictions. Whatever may be the views of members of the Tribunal, they must interpret the Act in an impartial and tolerant spirit. Difference of convictions must not bias judgment ... Men who apply on this ground should be able to feel that they are being judged by a Tribunal that will deal fairly with their cases. The exemption should be the minimum required to meet the conscientious scruples of the applicant.[37]

Even though the Board pointed out clearly that whenever a tribunal had reason to believe that only unconditional exemption would satisfy the conscience of the applicant this should in fact be given, some tribunals continued to assert that they were not entitled to grant complete exemption to any objector – even in cases where they frankly admitted the sincerity of the applicant. Still more tribunals frequently interpreted the only exemption which the objector deserved as an exemption from merely combatant duties, regardless of the fact that this would mean the consignment to prison not simply of the absolutists but also of men eager to undertake some form of civilian alternative service.

In April 1919, after the war was over, the War Office – perhaps in an effort to deflect criticism from deficiencies in army policy toward the objectors who had come under military command – issued a revealing statement concerning the effect of so many tribunals' failure to carry out the legislators' intentions. A London liberal newspaper summarized the War Office's findings thus:

> As a matter of fact the Army authorities themselves recognize that the lot of the conscientious objector is a hard one. They recognize that he has been the victim of ineptitude. Their view is that many hundreds of men have been thrust into the Army whom the House of Commons never intended should become soldiers. The Tribunals, they consider, rejected the applications of hundreds of these men whose consciences were sincere, and to protect whom the conscience clause was expressly framed by the House of Commons.[38]

To judge another man's conscience is admittedly an almost impossible task. The difficulties of the tribunals were confounded by the fact that many of them were genuinely confused as to exactly which categories of objectors were entitled to what kind of exemption. The antiwar movement – at least its more radical section – was for the most part inclined to regard as a *conscientious* objector any man who sincerely objected to taking part in the present war. This distinction would include, for instance, a radical Irish nationalist Sinn Feiner, whose residence in England had made him liable to the call-up – he could scarcely be described as an adherent of nonviolence.[39] One may also sympathize with a harassed tribunal chairman when faced with a member of the International Bible Students Association, whose witness for Jehovah included, it is true, abstention now from the wars of this world but might not exclude at least passive support in fiery apocalyptic conflicts to come. The Central Tribunal, whose decisions were circulated by the Local Government Board for the guidance of the Local and Appeal Tribunals, recommended finally that members of the Association be exempted only from combatant duties (whether with the knowledge that almost all the Witnesses would refuse to accept this classification and end up in jail is not clear). And what should be done with socialists who, while not always willing to commit themselves to a wholesale condemnation of violence in all circumstances, based their antiwar stand not on any accepted religious creed but upon a quasi-religious belief in the brotherhood of man or in the international solidarity of the working class? In actual practice no consistent policy in regard to such cases was ever laid down from above: each tribunal proceeded as it thought fit.

Opinions have differed greatly as to how well the tribunals carried out their task of assessing conscience. In his detailed study of government policy toward the C.Os. of World War I, John Rae writes:

It was a measure of the tribunals' success that they were able to grant a form of exemption to so many conscientious objectors; it was a measure of their failure that there were nevertheless a large number of cases in which they were unable to match the form of exemption to the objection of the applicant. Both the success and the failure have to be seen in the context of the tribunals' difficulties. The tribunals' role in the military recruiting organization, the uncompromising policy advocated by the N.C.F., the pressures of time, and the limitations of the Government's provisions, all made it hard for the members to avoid coming to decisions that were unacceptable to some applicants.[40]

It would not be easy to quarrel with this judicious conclusion.

It was indeed the absolutists who received most attention at the time – in parliament, in the press and with the general public. On the whole they were condemned, or at best regarded as stubborn and misguided fanatics. In July 1916 Lloyd George, then Secretary of State for

War (in the Boer War he had been a political opponent of war), expressed to the House of Commons his complete lack of sympathy for the absolutist objectors who, in his view, deserved no consideration, and he promised the House that he would make their path as hard as he could.[41] Nevertheless, a few applicants – mostly birthright Quakers, whose cases could more easily be judged by rule of thumb – did receive unconditional exemption either at the local or appellate level. As neither rough handling (even brutal treatment), first in army camps and then in detention barracks, nor subsequent repeated sentencing to civil prisons for essentially the same offense – the notorious "cat-and-mouse" treatment which derived its name from its application to English suffragettes prior to the war – succeeded in breaking the will of the absolutists,[42] voices began to be raised fairly soon in their defense, not only within the pacifist community but among enlightened sections of pro-war opinion.

Attempts by the army authorities in May and June 1916 to covertly ship a number of absolutists to France, where they would be subject to the most severe penalties of military law for continued refusal to fight (34 were actually condemned to death, though the sentences were not carried out) were foiled by the intervention of a group of Liberals led by Gilbert Murray. The Prime Minister, Asquith, who had not previously known of the army's intentions, was genuinely shocked by Murray's revelations, and eventually the army authorities gave up their endeavors to impose this kind of radical solution to the absolutist problem. As accounts of the army's actions were published in the liberal sections of the press and as information concerning the harsh treatment of objectors in barracks and civilian jails percolated through to the public, the government, along with the military, stood accused, by no means without cause, of attempting to browbeat the absolutists into submission, a design, moreover, which was only rarely proving successful.

In the interwar years the tide of opinion began to turn still more in favor of the absolutists. Their stand acquired a posthumous reputation (not at all undeserved) among the growing number of persons who were becoming disillusioned with the outcome of the war. The absolutist objectors had stood firm against the allmighty modern state: their challenge had a completeness, a consistency that was less apparent in the position of the more conciliatory alternativists. This shift in opinion was foreshadowed by some pacifists earlier. In the spring of 1919 in an article summing up "What the conscientious objector had achieved," Bertrand Russell wrote: "The absolutists have won in the contest of endurance: they have shown that the will to resistance is stronger than the community's will to persecution."[43] The absolutists indeed represent the liberal tradition carried to its extremity: their successful defiance of conscription, however, could only have been achieved in a community which, even in wartime, had not entirely abandoned its respect for this tradition.

To move, as we shall now do, from the roughly 1,700 absolutist objectors to the 3,400 men who accepted noncombatant service in the armed forces is to swing the discussion from one end of the pacifist spectrum to the other. The difference between the two stands was by no means necessarily a question of varying firmness in pacifist conviction or contrasting temperament. When, for instance, members of the NCC were ordered to do work they considered an infringement of their noncombatant status, or when Seventh-day Adventists were required to perform duties on their Saturday Sabbath, they endured – if more briefly – similar treatment to that meted out to the absolutist objector. It was chiefly by their ideological background that the men who served in the NCC (or in the Royal Army Medical Corps with noncombatant status) were distinguished from their colleagues who would accept only civilian work or no condition for exemption at all. For the sects which strove, with a fine disregard of anything but a literalist interpretation of the Ten Commandments, to fulfill the Biblical injunction, "Thou shalt not kill," noncombatancy of this sort provided a quite acceptable minimum which their adherents could conscientiously accept.

A curious anomaly in a twentieth-century Europe at war has been the Friends' Ambulance Unit (FAU), which was set up in the early months of the war by a group of young Quakers. The FAU had no official connection with the Society of Friends. Some Quakers disapproved of its close connection with the army. Although its 1,200 members remained civilians and subject only to their own internal discipline, the Unit worked in uniform alongside the regular forces. Its commander overseas held an honorary captaincy and there was an unwritten agreement that its members would not engage in peace activities while in the FAU. As a former member expressed it, the FAU in fact was "a strange hybrid of pacifism and militarism." "Its personnel consisted mostly of Quakers, but not entirely ... Some were ardent Christian pacifists ... Some based their pacifism on broader grounds. Some were in the 'Unit' out of deference to their Quaker upbringing. Some [at first] were simply men in a hurry to take part in the war without the tedium of military training." Permitted to act as pacifists at war by the British military authorities, members of the FAU were regarded by the French Army, to which some of them were attached for ambulance duties, "as amiable and efficient cranks." "Our pacifism was put down to some eccentricity of religion. We discussed it freely, and were treated with respect, sympathy and almost complete incomprehension."[44]

For those objectors in whom the impulse to render humanitarian service prevailed over the desire to protest the war (and who were fortunate enough to get accepted by the Unit) the FAU appeared to provide an excellent outlet for their energies. However, after the introduction of conscription early in 1916, a crisis occurred. Apprehension grew that the FAU was becoming simply part of the military machine. The Unit's adjutant, himself now convinced "that the Unit is no longer a place for the strong peace man" and about to move over to an absolutist stand, reported: "A good many of my boys are getting restless, being afraid that C.O.'s will be forced either into the N.C.C. or into prison, and that if so they must resign [from] the F.A.U. and take their share of the hardships."[45] Opinions differ as to the contribution made by the Unit's work in World War I. Did it prove that, in a liberal democracy, pacifists even in wartime could still find a place inside the military framework and yet preserve their peculiar witness intact? Or did it, instead, show that modern war demanded a more radical protest from its opponents than the patching up of the wounds inflicted by the opposed military machines? The argument, as we shall see, was reopened again with the coming of World War II.

Apart from men assigned to the FAU or confirmed by a tribunal in their membership in the Unit, over 5,000 objectors were given exemption from combatant service on condition that they undertook civilian work of national importance. Job allocation was mostly carried out under the auspices of the Pelham Committee (so called from the name of its first chairman). In addition, in the early summer of 1916, under pressure of liberal opinion in the country which was becoming increasingly scandalized by official treatment of the conscientious objector, the Home Office set up a scheme for reviewing cases of imprisoned objectors and releasing those considered genuine "on their undertaking to perform work of national importance under civil control." It became apparent thereafter that among the over 6,250 men who refused to abide by their tribunal's decision, only a minority were thoroughgoing absolutists. Roughly 3,750 accepted work under the auspices of the Home Office Scheme. To some pacifists this was a disappointment. Bertrand Russell, for instance, wrote around this time: "Odd things give me a sense of failure – for instance the way the C.O.'s all take alternative service, except a handful."[46] Fervent, occasionally bitter, debate took place within the NCF concerning the merits and disadvantages of the Scheme. Although Clifford Allen and many other influential NCF members, including the whole National Committee, opposed it as an unjustifiable compromise with militarism and an attempt to split the united front of those engaged in fighting conscription, the feeling among imprisoned objectors and in the organization at large continued to run in favor of accepting the Scheme (though, of course, with the proviso that full support should still be given to the men who wished to resist conscription *à l'outrance*). Moderates, like the Quaker M.P., T. Edmund Harvey, felt that the Scheme had positive value. Not merely did it demonstrate the government's goodwill and desire to avoid the persecution of genuine conscience, it would also serve to show, in Harvey's view, that the imprisoned objectors were prepared to shoulder the burdens of citizenship by hard and, at the same time, useful work.

English prisons of the early twentieth century still retained in their regimen much of the harshness of the nineteenth-century system – in particular, the silence rule, bizarre – and humiliating – prison garb, and a sense of complete isolation oppressed the wartime prisoners of conscience. The system's "silent inhumanity ... scarcely dreamt of in proper society"[47] made outstanding exponents of penal reform in the postwar years out of some absolutist objectors, like the socialist Fenner Brockway and the Quaker Stephen Hobhouse. At the time these rigorous conditions, the after-effects of which in a few cases are known to have resulted in death, undoubtedly led objectors not infrequently to a reconsideration of their absolutist stand and to a readiness to exchange prison for civilian work, especially if they felt their health and sanity threatened by prolonged incarceration. However, most of the "schemers," as they were called, were men who had landed in jail not because they refused to accept any alternative to military service, but as a result of their tribunal's failure to recognize the sincerity of their objection to army service. They, therefore, welcomed the Home Office Scheme as an attempt by the government to rectify the tribunal's mistaken judgment.

Yet many of them were soon to lose their enthusiasm. In the first place, labor was of a semi-penal character and carried out in conditions not vastly different from those the men had left behind in jail. Nevertheless, the gutter press repeatedly reported that the Scheme was pampering and coddling its "conchies" (as objectors were derisively called in Britain). Sometimes work centers were actually located in prisons; asylums and workhouses were also used for this purpose. Men who accepted the Scheme were required to undertake whatever work was allotted them by the committee which administered the Scheme. This Committee framed the regulations which governed daily activities, including a ban on all peace activities. Remuneration and conditions of labor were not subject to collective bargaining in any form, which particularly riled the many socialist objectors among the schemers. Discipline in cases of disobedience was enforced by the threat of return to prison for completion of sentence and subsequent army call-up. In fact, some schemers preferred to go back voluntarily to jail rather than to continue to work under conditions they considered intolerable. After all, prison had its compensations. For the saintly Welsh pacifist George Davies, for instance, his time in the "Scrubs," i.e., London's Wormwood Scrubs Prison, provided "an experience for which," he told his brother later, "I shall always be grateful. It showed how love and faith overcome the unkindness and brutality of human punishments."[48]

Revolutionary events in Russia and the approaching end of the war led to unrest among imprisoned objectors as well as among those in Home Office camps. The signing of the armistice increased these feelings of dissatisfaction still further. In jail, political activists like Clifford Allen as early as mid-1917 had refused to work as a form of protest against prolonged imprisonment – contrary to the advice, however, of Dr. Alfred Salter and other religious pacifists, who felt that the men were endangering their health and sanity in an empty gesture of defiance. Early in 1919 militants resorted to even more radical forms of protest including the hunger strike (a weapon of resistance used also by militant suffragettes and by Sinn Feiners) in an effort to gain release. The prison authorities answered this at first by forcible feeding, bringing on death in one instance on account of the roughness with which the operation was conducted. The NCF did not officially approve these prison strikes. Instead, it concentrated on mobilizing liberal public opinion behind the demand for freeing the objectors who remained in prison: in November 1918 there were still some 1,500 of them. The NCF had been unable to prevent parliament in the Representation of the People Act of June 1918, which gave the vote to women over the age of 30, from disqualifying all conscientious objectors from exercising the franchise for a period of five years, and there was continued postwar discrimination against conscientious objectors in municipal and government employment. But with the war over, feeling against the objectors began to subside gradually.

The release of imprisoned objectors, however, commenced in earnest only in April 1919: it was completed by the following August. In November of the same year, after some discussion, the NCF, believing that its work was done and that a new organizational framework was needed for the tasks of the pacifist movement that lay ahead, decided to dissolve. The wartime objectors in Britain had represented a small and outcast minority. While the fighting raged their fellow citizens had given scant attention to their views; insofar as they noticed them at all, they, for the most part, regarded them with a mixture of apprehension and contempt. "The question seemed trivial at the time; it had great effect later."[49]

The United States

The administrative pattern of conscientious objection in the United States differed considerably from that which prevailed in Britain. For one thing there was nothing equivalent to the British system of tribunals, which required every applicant for exemption to present a statement of his belief. Neither the American local selective service boards nor other bodies dealing with conscientious objectors, whether army court-martials or the War Department's Board of Inquiry, permitted this procedure. Organizations like the leftist American Union against Militarism or the Emergency Peace Federation or the National Civil Liberties Bureau, which fought against conscription and for the rights of the conscientious objector, did not provide the latter with a forum for airing his views in the same way as the NCF was doing for his British counterpart. Newspapers rarely gave space to letters from opponents of the war. Little wonder, then, that Norman Thomas in his book on American conscientious objectors in World War I complains that "their dialectic skill was confined to controversies with officers, judges and jailers, and left little record."[50]

A second major distinction between the two patterns lies in the fact that in the United States, as we have seen, the law granted exemption only from combatant service (and that solely for religious objectors). Therefore, the experiences of the American conscientious objectors are set, at least at first, almost entirely within the framework of the army camps to which they were required to report along with their fellow draftees.

Of the 64,693 men who had registered a claim to a noncombatant classification, the local boards recognized 56,830 as sincere. Since the authorities were not anxious to touch those who could be deferred on nonconscientious grounds, only 20,783 were actually inducted into the army in the period before the Armistice. But of that number – and this is a surprising fact – considerably less than 4,000, which is less than a fifth of the total, made use after induction of their "Certificate of Exemption from Combatant Service" issued to them by their local selective service board; for it must be remembered that in the War Department's total figure for conscientious objectors of 3,989 were

included some whose applications for objector status had been rejected
by their local boards. We can only guess at the reasons for the small
number which stuck by its original determination not to fight. A genuine change of hear – as, for instance, in the case of the later war hero,
Sergeant Alvin C. York – or the growing pressures of war feeling in the
country or uncertainty and isolation probably all contributed to this
rapid shrinking of the community of objectors.

Once in camp the conscientious objectors presented the military
authorities with an awkward problem – except for those religious
objectors who were willing to accept noncombatant service in the
armed forces. The latter were assigned to the Medical Corps, the Quar-
termaster Corps and the Engineer Service, even though this last assignment included construction of fortifications and defenses as well as
work on camouflage. The Seventh-day Adventists, as in Britain, were
occasionally in trouble over their refusal to work on Saturdays. They
and other noncombatants were sometimes put in detention, too, for
refusing orders to carry rifles (still others were ready to accept rifles
when issued but would not produce them for drill). Eventually noncombatant soldiers were provided with certificates guaranteeing their
immunity from transfer to combatant units without their consent –
which had occasionally been attempted earlier – and were expressly
exempted from carrying sidearms. It later became the administration's
policy to exert pressure on all objectors in camp – whether acknowledged sincere by local boards or not – to accept noncombatant service.
Altogether around 1,300 men accepted this status.

At first the army authorities were at a loss to know exactly what to
do with the remaining objectors: doubtless, they had many more
urgent tasks requiring their attention. As a result, treatment of objectors varied greatly from camp to camp. In some places religious objectors belonging to churches generally known to be pacifist were shown
more consideration than other objectors. Isolated objectors were more
likely to meet rough and sometimes cruel treatment than those held in
large cantonments; similarly those, like the Russian-speaking Molokans or the German-speaking Hutterites, who combined imperfect
mastery of the English language with what was regarded as eccentricity in dress or personal appearance. The War Department, indeed,
deplored any manhandling of objectors, and instances where this did
occur were usually the result of overzealous junior officers acting on
their own initiative. Though the army did not cease its endeavors to
persuade objectors to accept some sort of service, in the large camps at
any rate it soon stopped any attempt to impose drill or military duties.
In the end the only work usually required of them was performance of

camp chores such as cooking and tidying up. This regimen, which was finally confirmed by the War Department, but not until June 1918, was indeed monotonous but gave plenty of opportunity for reading and study – and for endless discussions among a motley community, which included college educated urban Quakers, militant and agnostic socialists and anarchists, pious ploughboys from Mennonite farms of the rural mid-West, members of pentecostal groups like the recently formed Assemblies of God, as well as illiterate black sectaries from the deep South and long-haired devotees of the esoteric House of David.

If the army was puzzled to know how to proceed with the objectors, many of the objectors, young men in their twenties often away from home for the first time, were equally uncertain as to the right behavior in the circumstances. "You apparently, when you reached camp, did not know what you could and could not conscientiously do and have been floundering ever since," an official of the American Friends Service Committee told a young Quaker. The AFSC advised Quaker objectors to think out the implications of their position carefully beforehand. Without forethought it was very easy to slide unthinkingly into acceptance against one's true inclinations of at least noncombatant duties.[51] The AFSC gave objectors, who were unwilling to become noncombatant soldiers, three pieces of advice: first, refuse to wear a uniform as this may be misunderstood as readiness to accept service in the army; secondly, do not take army pay since to do so is really inconsistent with your stand; thirdly, do not obey military orders, even when seemingly unconnected with war. "Planting flowers around the hospital grounds," wrote another AFSC worker, "sounds like an innocent kind of work but you have seen the principle involved: as this work is under the military and therefore as you cannot, in accordance with the principles of the Society of Friends, conscientiously perform work under military [command], you cannot conscientiously do this work."[52]

As early as September 1917 the Secretary of War had directed the army, in regard to Mennonite objectors, not on any account to employ force to make them wear uniforms "as the question of raiment is one of the tenets of the faith." Eventually, this ruling was also extended to most other objectors. In the following month the Secretary of War issued instructions that objectors be segregated within the camps from other draftees and placed under specially selected officers, who were to treat them tactfully. He expressed a hope that in this way what browbeating and coercion had failed to achieve milder methods would accomplish – namely, the renunciation by many of their objector status. At once a problem arose in relation to men who claimed to be conscientious objectors but had not been recognized as such by their local boards. (In practice camp commanders hitherto had usually solved the problem by treating as legitimate objectors all who continued obdurate in refusing army service after varying degrees of harassment.) In December the Secretary of War issued a further directive: until further notice all claimants to that status should be segregated as conscientious objectors. The War Department still appeared to be hesitant concerning the best policy to be adopted. Therefore, it continued to drift along uncertainly.

The position, however, was becoming increasingly unsatisfactory. Since the army regarded an objector as a soldier subject to military discipline, minor infractions of regulations caused either by the objector's defiance of authority or by his conscientious scruples – or by a mixture of both – could lead to his trial by court-martial and sentencing to a stiff term of detention in a military prison. The inflamed state of public opinion made it difficult for Congress to extend the existing terms of exemption for conscientious objectors. Many persons then agreed with ex-President Theodore Roosevelt in considering objectors as either slackers (at best) or plain traitors; if the men were black, like the members of the pentecostal Church of God in Christ, racial prejudice intensified the feeling that here lay a danger to the country's security.

But in March 1918 a law was passed allowing the furloughing of draftees to civilian work if deemed in the national interest. The way was now open for the War Department to rid the army of its remaining refractory objectors, including those who had been rejected earlier by the local boards. The process of sifting the "sincere" objectors from the "insincere" began in earnest at the beginning of June with the setting up of a Board of Inquiry consisting of two judges and the dean of Columbia University's Law School. Objectors deemed "sincere" after appearing before the Board and unwilling to accept noncombatant service were usually directed to undertake agricultural work or in a few cases employment in industry. Prior to the Armistice about 1,200 men had been furloughed in this way. In addition 99 men were permitted to join the Friends Reconstruction Unit in France – naturally they were mostly members of the Society of Friends but a few non-Quakers were included in this group. A court-martial was the fate of men considered "insincere" by the Board (under this designation were included most of the political objectors who held a selective objection to the current war) and those who refused the proffered furloughing or "whose attitude in camp [in the words of an order of the Secretary of War, dated 27 April 1918] is sullen and defiant" or who engaged in political propaganda. Altogether some 450 objectors were sent to military prisons. Finally, at the time of the Armistice 940 objectors (of whom 225 sought noncombatant status only) still remained in camp awaiting assignment by the Board of Inquiry.

The three members of the Board seem to have made every effort to be scrupulously fair to the men who appeared before them. But it was often difficult for highly trained lawyers to comprehend, in particular, the motives and values of rural religious sects, from which many of the objectors came. It was hard, too, for these respectable members of bourgeois society to appreciate the antiwar militancy of working-class agitators, whose passion for building a new social order, after they had destroyed the old, sometimes reached an almost religious fervor. The Board's chairman, Major Walter G. Kellogg, for instance, found the Quaker objectors from middle-class homes nice boys (his Board usually exempted them without more ado) and he admired at least the dialectical skill of the socialists who argued the case against capitalist wars. But for the Mennonites, mostly farming folk with little formal education and sometimes an imperfect mastery of the English tongue, he had little but a contemptuous pity. "Civilization," he writes, "apparently has passed them by ... They remain a curious and alien survival of an old-world people, an anachronism amid the life of today."[53] What is perhaps more curious is the fact that the major for all his learning appears to have been utterly unaware of the sociological transformation and the currents of intellectual and spiritual renewal that were already at work in the American Mennonite community.[54]

The men who were furloughed on the Board of Inquiry's recommendation to work in agriculture were technically still regarded by the army as soldiers. But this was largely a formality. They were given work on private farms and the farmers paid them current wage rates – with the proviso that anything above $30 per month, i.e., the pay of a private soldier, should be forwarded to the Red Cross. The men were not permitted to leave their employment without permission, and they were not allowed to take a job in the area of their home (a ruling that was designed to prevent ill feeling on the part of those whose sons had had to leave home for the army). In fact, most furloughed objectors were assigned employment in the vicinity of the camp in which they had previously been held. In some cases local "patriots" attempted to whip up resentment in their local community against the assignees. When this happened, however, the army intervened at once: these men were soldiers, it explained, and were engaged on work of national importance and any attempt to harass them would not be tolerated. After the war was over, objectors on furlough from the army were demobilized along with the regiments to which they had been nominally assigned. On leaving service each man received a certificate stating: "This is a conscientious objector who has done no military duty whatsoever and who refused to wear a uniform."[55]

Thus we find that the American military authorities' policy for dealing with objectors who were prepared to undertake alternative civilian service but would not accept noncombatant status in the army compares not unfavorably with that devised by the British government. But it had been long delayed owing to political hindrances, which held up the application of a satisfactory solution to the problem. The War Department was circumscribed, too, by the legal framework of exemption which, on paper at any rate, permitted conscientious objector status only on religious grounds. Though the furlough system allowed the objector rather less freedom of choice and movement than the conditional exemption which tribunals in Britain were entitled to grant applicants, it was considerably more generous than the British Home Office Scheme. However, the American system of dealing with conscientious objection had, apart from the fact that it was much more closely controlled by the military than its British counterpart, a further major shortcoming: Congress omitted from the legislation any provision for the absolutists who would be satisfied only with unconditional exemption. True, unconditionalists were much less numerous in America than in Britain, but for those who did take that stand there was no alternative but jail.

The best that may be said of American military prisons of World War I (known officially as disciplinary barracks) is that they were perhaps no worse than those in Britain. Concerning the fate of the American prisoners of conscience, whether absolutists or political objectors, who were incarcerated in them, Norman Thomas has written: "Most of [their] experiences ... can be paralleled by cases of the maltreatment of ordinary military prisoners, though it was less frequently that the latter were so persecuted."[56] Overcrowding and subjection to a savage discipline framed to break the will of recalcitrant soldiers were the common lot of all inmates, conscientious and otherwise. The objectors, however, since many of them refused to work under a military régime, received more than their share of solitary confinement and punishment diet. Some were shackled for hours on end to the bars of their cells. Therefore, following the public protest which stemmed from publicity in the press, the War Department in December 1919 forbade altogether the manacling of military prisoners. Two Hutterites, the Hofer brothers, died in jail from the results of ill treatment experienced in Alcatraz and Fort Leavenworth (Kansas). Alarm at these kinds of incidents led around a thousand Hutterites and some 600–800 Mennonites of draft age to leave, illegally, for Canada in search of a more tolerant environment there than the wartime United States had proved to be. These "draft-evaders" came mainly from the mid-West and were drawn from families which had emigrated from Russia in the 1870s in response to the introduction of a universal military service law in that country. Such people were evidently used to the idea of migrating when conditions at home appeared to become intolerable, for Mennonites in past centuries had done this, too.[57]

At their court-martials objectors had usually received inordinately lengthy sentences, though not longer, it must be said, than were normally meted out to military offenders. Seventeen objectors got commuted death sentences (one objector who was somehow sent overseas indeed narrowly escaped execution, his reprieve being due only to his volunteering to fetch the wounded from No Man's Land); 142 were given life sentences. Sentences of 20 to 25 years can be regarded as average; they were not cut down on review. However, no objector was kept in jail for much more than three years, since the release of the last group took place toward the end of November 1920. As in Britain, after the conclusion of the Armistice, work strikes were organized by the political radicals in protest both against their continued incarceration and the inhuman conditions prevailing in the jails. In several instances the objectors succeeded in extending the strike so as to include the other military prisoners; many of these were not really criminals so much as offenders against military discipline, who felt indignant at the thought of being held captive for long years after the war was ended.

In World War I the prison community of conscientious objectors in America was indeed small, especially if one remembers that, according to the War Department's figures, there were as many as 171,000 draft-evaders who escaped service. Those objectors sentenced by court-martial amounted to less than one eighth of the total number of objectors. Several hundred nonregistrants and objectors to undergoing the army medical examination were tried in the ordinary courts where they received relatively short terms in civil prisons. On release, however, they were automatically registered for military service and thereby became liable for forcible induction into the army if they failed to present themselves voluntarily in camp. As thoroughgoing absolutists, most of them eventually found their way to the court-martial chamber. American pacifism of this period certainly had its radical wing. But whereas in Britain the typical objector (at least in the public image) was the absolutist, who shunned so far as he was able all association with the military machine, most American objectors sought a viable compromise with the state at war, which would leave them free to serve their country according to the dictates of their conscience.

Conscientious Objection Outside Great Britain
and the United States

In the countries of the British Empire where conscription was introduced, the pattern followed in dealing with conscientious objectors
was roughly the same as in the motherland. The percentage of draftees
who applied for conscientious objector status was, however, lower
than in Britain and the objectors were drawn almost exclusively from
pacifist sects. In Canada, for instance, Quakers, Mennonites, and Brethren in Christ possessed a hereditary claim in law to exemption at least
from bearing arms. Of these three peace sects the Mennonites, divided
into a number of subsects as in the USA, were by far the largest; they
provided a large proportion of Canadian C.Os.[58] The turbulent Dukhobors of British Columbia, a sect of Russian origin whom Tolstoy had
aided at the beginning of the century in their emigration to Canada,
were rarely touched after conscription had been introduced in 1917
(over the opposition, it may be noted, of the French Canadians). The
scruples of religious objectors prepared to accept noncombatant service or farm work were given consideration by the government. But
for the nonreligious there was even less organizational support for
their stand than in the neighboring United States. Some of them
endured imprisonment and maltreatment.[59] In general, pacifists in
Canada suffered from a more extreme sense of isolation than their fellows did in Britain or the United States.

On the other side of the globe both Australia and New Zealand had
introduced compulsory military service for teenage boys in 1910.
When youngsters began to be jailed for refusing to drill – among them
a handful of Quakers and children of pacifist parents – there was a
public outcry which was unsuccessful, however, in putting an end to
the scandal for the time being.[60] Wartime conscription after all was not
imposed, however, in Australia, except for a few weeks during October and November 1916; then in two successive referenda the people
rejected compulsion. Even so, some cases of imprisonment of COs
occurred despite the brief period during which a draft was imposed. In
New Zealand the draft came into operation in June 1916, despite lively
opposition, inside parliament and out, from the small Labour Party,
whose activists continued thereafter to agitate against conscription and
to carry on antiwar propaganda. Some of them were arrested and
imprisoned for sedition. The New Zealand government interpreted
conscientious objection very narrowly. Only members of prewar pacifist denominations (this meant mainly Quakers and Christadelphians,
both very small groups) were granted exemption and this exemption

was only from combatant duties. Since both Quakers and Christadelphians were conscientiously opposed to service within the armed forces, the act's exemption clause was virtually of no effect. Though "for the scruples of ... the Quakers," at any rate, "widespread sympathy" existed among the general public, most Quakers who were liable to military service spent time in jail.[61] Eventually the government did set up a farm camp scheme for those willing to accept alternative service of a civilian character – but not before the imprisonment of nearly 300 objectors, a small party of whom were even shipped by the military overseas to the Western front in France.[62]

Respect for conscientious scruples in regard to military service was not confined to countries where English was spoken. Yet outside the British Empire and the United States recognition of the right to exemption on this account was usually minimal. Where it did exist it most often applied solely to birthright members of certain nonresistant sects, who were usually excused only from combatant duties. In Tsarist Russia, however, Mennonites, who lived in what is today Ukraine, could apply either for assignment to the civilian forestry service, an alternative dating back to 1875, or to army hospital work.[63] Their brethren in Germany, on the other hand, where Mennonitism had steadily dwindled throughout the nineteenth century and nonresistance was largely abandoned by those remaining in the church, could obtain only noncombatant duties in the army; most young Mennonites now accepted full military service.

Under the Tsar, wartime objectors from non-Mennonite Russian sects as well as Tolstoyans were usually jailed for periods of four to six years: the February Revolution of 1917 brought them release and the prospect of gaining recognition from the government. The Bolshevik government, after it came to power in October, was eventually persuaded (but not until January 1919) to confirm the assignment of *bona fide* religious objectors to civilian work, an arrangement which was already in practice informally, and even to grant unconditional exemption in certain exceptional cases. In 1918, however, while the grip of the central government on the country was not yet firm, cases had occurred not only of the imprisonment but also of the shooting of conscientious objectors. Treatment of C.Os. at that time was mainly a question of the disposition of the local authorities.

A remarkable wartime case of conscientious objection, recently revealed by the Russian Quaker historian Tatiana Pavlova, occurred in 1916. When the well known poet and artist, Maksimilian Voloshin, was called up in that year, he informed the military authorities of his conviction that it was morally preferable to be killed than to kill. The poet declared that, as a believer in the harmony of all creation, he refused "to become a soldier ... I cannot participate in ... war undertaken for whatever purpose." Fortunately for Voloshin the army rejected him for medical reasons. Thus he survived to continue his witness for reconciliation during the troubled period that ensued after the Revolution.

Before the war the Nazarenes in Hungary, where the sect had adherents especially among the South Slav peasantry, were allowed to serve in the Medical Corps. After the outbreak of hostilities, however, many members of the sect were imprisoned – and some may even have been executed – for their pacifist stand.[64] A long term of imprisonment, too, was the best the occasional Tolstoyan or anarchist objector could hope for from the military authorities of the Central Powers, who also resorted to putting objectors – including the handful who opposed the war on socialist grounds – into the lunatic asylum. In Germany, Seventh-day Adventists mostly consented to bear arms; only the small breakaway Reformation movement refused to do so; despite their readiness to do noncombatant service in the army, the latter sometimes ended up in jail.[65] In France and Belgium, no provision at all existed for exemption on grounds of conscientious objection. But in France, where a lonely intellectual like Romain Rolland might attempt to stand "above the battle" (the title he gave to his book: *Au-dessus de la mêlée* [1915]), a vigorous antiwar campaign did eventually emerge. This movement though, understandably enough, did not advocate conscientious objection.

The situation of the French Mennonite communities was complex. Despite willingness to make extensive compromises, French Mennonites had suffered for adhering to their peace witness during the Napoleonic Wars. But by 1850 they had accepted the idea of full military service for all conscripts. Most forgot the old doctrine of *Wehrlosigkeit*, the nonresistance professed by their ancestors; they now took pride in serving in the French army and gloried in their readiness to fight for their country. Yet there remained a few who continued to feel that actually to kill was contrary to their religion. If young Mennonites conscripts of this kind found they were unable to obtain assignment to a noncombatant branch of the forces, then they took satisfaction that, at any rate in time of war, they could avoid using their rifles – or at least avoid aiming at an enemy soldier.

There were no French Mennonite objectors in either world wars. But in the first global conflict one of the church's leaders, Pierre Kennel, took a defiantly pacifist stand by emigrating to Switzerland where, because of his Bernese ancestry, he could claim Swiss citizenship and thus avoid the combatant service to which he would have been liable if he had remained in the country of his birth. The church was profoundly shocked by his action; he became an embarrassment to his coreligionists and was made to feel no longer welcome in the Mennonite fellowship. Kennel, who held a doctorate in science, was one of their few intellectuals; he had played hitherto an important part in the Mennonite *Réveil*, the evangelical revival of the early years of the present century.[66] All this perhaps compounded his offense. "The Mennonite congregations," wrote the sociologist of religion, Jean Séguy, in the early seventies, "do not like to recall the memory of Pierre Kennel's stance. Fifty years afterwords their veterans of 1914–18 still condemn passionately his act of conscientious objection. That shows to what a point the 'Anabaptist vision' has become blurred among the French brethren."[67]

Lastly among the belligerents we may mention Italy, where hitherto no pacifist tradition of any kind existed. There only three C.O. cases are known: a Tolstoyan, a humanist, and a Bible Student (as the Jehovah's Witness was then called).[68] Each received a long term of imprisonment with the further threat of incarceration in a lunatic asylum.

The outlook for the conscientious objector was rather better in some neutral countries of the European continent. Before the war only Norway had exempted at least religious objectors from army service. But in 1917 Denmark instituted an alternative civilian service system for which no explicitly religious test was required. In the Netherlands, where during World War I there were several hundred syndicalist and anarchist objectors, the most the government would concede them unofficially was noncombatant army service, which was usually unacceptable. Christian socialist pastors, like Bart de Ligt – the future theoretician of anarchopacifism – and Annee R. de Jong and J. Sevenster, supported war resistance and were among the signatories of the manifesto, issued in September 1915, in favor of conscientious objection to military service even in a defensive war. Fines or brief terms of imprisonment resulted from this act of defiance, which the Dutch authorities viewed with a considerable degree of apprehension.

Pacifism of the type that postulated a personal stand against war possessed two powerful institutional bases in the English-speaking world that were absent on the European continent: the nonconformist conscience, incarnated in its most sensitive form in the Quaker Society of Friends, and the radical political individualism which found expression within the labor movement in such bodies as the British ILP. European socialists of the left abhorred war as fervently as their British or American comrades, but they did not become conscientious objectors. There were almost no Quakers on the continent at this date; the Protestant churches represented the establishment and were anything but nonconformist in relation to the demands of the state. Only in Russia was there a powerful indigenous sectarian movement but there the sects' often wild and apocalyptic messianism failed to move a religious Orthodoxy that remained the strongest bulwark of the Tsarist régime.

In Britain a lingering tradition of aristocratic liberalism and in the United States a retreating, but not quite vanished, frontier democracy still retained sufficient strength in the community at large to cushion the shock of a failure to conform in wartime to the mores of society. Over large areas of the European continent, on the other hand, even leftwingers either succumbed to the spell of *la gloire* or abandoned international solidarity in favor of the defense of the Fatherland. Those who continued to oppose war either remained secluded intellectuals isolated in their studies from any form of action or pursued international peace by entering the ranks of their national armies and working there, if they could, for the social revolution, which would destroy the roots of war along with capitalism. Conscientious objection was the path chosen only by a few obscure and harmless religious sectaries and a handful of eccentric radicals.

In Britain and the United States, the conscientious objectors of World War I belonged in the tradition that stretched back at least to the seventeenth century, to the English Revolution and its Puritan antecedents. Of this ancestry were not only the Quakers and other religious objectors of Protestant background but the agnostic socialists and *enragé* libertarians, who opposed conscription not necessarily from a repugnance to all violence but always in the belief that a personal witness against war held value. By their stance they proved their right, too, to this genealogy. A young Englishman of the post-1918 generation, who fell in the Spanish Civil War fighting on the side of the Loyalists, wrote not long before his death of the conscientious objectors of the 1914–18 war: "We look [back] with respect and gratitude" to them for their "personal integrity and intellectual courage."[69]

Notes

1 A.C.F. Beales, *The History of Peace* (London: G. Bell & Sons Ltd., 1931), p. 283. Evans Darby was succeeded as secretary by the Rev. Herbert Dunnico, subsequently a Labour member of parliament. In World War II, ironically, Dunnico – still secretary of the now almost defunct Peace Society – was a supporter of the extreme anti-Germanism of Sir Robert (later Lord) Vansittart.

2 To the indignation of some prowar Quakers, who objected in particular to the eighth of the "queries" the Society continued periodically to address to its members. This ran as follows: "Are you faithful in maintaining our Christian testimony against all war, as inconsistent with the precepts and spirit of the Gospel?" H. Sefton Jones, for instance, in "The Eighth Query," *Friends' Quarterly Examiner* (London), no. 202 (April, 1917), pp. 226, 227, protested vigorously against those he considered "extremists in the Yearly Meeting," who had "been able to commit that body to a dogmatic pronouncement on the subject of War which goes beyond anything asserted by the Society in its original teaching, and which ... assumes a Scriptural prohibition which does not exist [and] ... is ignored in practice by most Friends."

3 Leigh Tucker, "English Friends and Censorship, World War I." *Quaker History* (Haverford, PA), vol. 71, no. 2 (Fall, 1982), pp. 120–24. The three Quakers involved were Harrison Barrow, Edith M. Ellis, and Arthur Watts.

4 See A. Ruth Fry, *A Quaker Adventure: The Story of Nine Years' Relief and Reconstruction* (London: Nisbet & Co. Ltd., 1926).

5 Reprinted in John W. Graham, *Conscription and Conscience: A History 1916–1919* (London: George Allen & Unwin Ltd., 1922), pp. 46–50. Italics in the original.

6 From a leaflet entitled *The Order of Reconciliation: Draft* [ca. 1915], in Archives, Swarthmore College Peace Collection: Great Britain, FOR. We may note most Christian pacifists in Britain were nonconformists. Alan Wilkinson in his study, *The Church of England and the First World War* (London: SPCK, 1978), could discover only two pacifists among the Anglican parochial clergy; see pp. 53, 54. There were of course more Anglican pacifist lay persons, including an ordinand (Philip Carrington) who later became Archbishop of Quebec.

7 Letter dated December 14, 1916 in Arthur Marwick, *Clifford Allen: The Open Conspirator* (Edinburgh and London: Oliver & Boyd, 1964), p. 37.

8 There is an excellent monogaph on the NCF: Thomas C. Kennedy, *The Hound of Conscience: A History of the No-Conscription Fellowship 1914–1919* (Fayetteville: The University of Arkansas Press, 1981).

9 Jo Vellacott, *Bertrand Russell and the Pacifists in the First World War* (Brighton, U.K.: The Harvester Press Limited, 1980), covers in detail Russell's role in the wartime anticonscriptionist movement.

10 Printed in Graham, *op. cit.*, p. 174.

11 Quoted in Boulton, *Objection Overruled* (London: Macgibbon & Kee Ltd., 1967), pp. 183, 184.

12 Norman Thomas, *Is Conscience a Crime?* (New York: Vanguard Press, 1927), p. 261. This volume was originally published as *The Conscientious Objector in America* (New York: B.W. Heutsch, Inc., 1923).

13 Clarence Darrow, *The War* (New York: National Security League, 1917), pp. 13, 14.

14 Thomas, *op. cit.*, p. 69.

15 Jessie Wallace Hughan, *Three Decades of War Resistance* (New York: The War Resisters League, 1942 ed.), pp. 8, 9.

16 *Advocate of Peace* (Washington, D.C.), 78 (November, 1916), p. 288; 79 (May, 1917), pp. 134, 135.

17 See, for instance, the leaflet *Some Particular Advices for Friends & A Statement of Loyalty for Others* (Philadelphia and Baltimore, 1918), signed by 120 prominent Quakers. It was reprinted in the *Advocate of Peace*, 80 (May, 1918), pp. 146, 147.

18 Allan Kohrman, "Respectable Pacifists: Quaker Response to World War I," *Quaker History*, vol. 75, no. 1 (Spring, 1986), pp. 39, 40, 46–53. The first quotation is from the *Particular Advices* cited in the previous note.

19 Thomas, *op. cit.*, p. 70.

20 Randolph S. Bourne, *War and the Intellectuals: Collected Essays, 1915–1918* (New York: Harper Torchbooks, 1964), pp. 3, 13, 14. In his posthumously published essay on "The State" (pp. 65–104), Bourne developed his quasi-anarchist critique of the modern state as an instrument of power inseparable from the waging of war. "War is the health of the state" (p. 71). However, despite some of his wartime utterances he was not an absolute pacifist: he approved of certain spontaneous manifestations of armed resistance exemplified in his view in the French people's resistance to invasion in 1792 – a position not very different from Bertrand Russell's.

21 Edward Grubb in *The Tribunal* (London), No. 171 (21 August 1919), p. 1.

22 Martin Ceadel, *Pacifism in Britain 1914–1945: The Defining of a Faith* (Oxford: The Clarendon Press, 1980), pp. 44–46. Most of these "elitist" objectors had strong moral or humanitarian objections to war in addition to their "vocationalism."

23 Walter Guest Kellogg, *The Conscientious Objector* (New York: Boni and Liversight, 1919), p. 52. In fact, the Witnesses' "pacifism" does not preclude support for God's side in a future Armageddon; most Witnesses, though, believe such support would be passive, and not active combatancy.

24 Apart from a handful of Catholics and Jews.

25 Kellogg, *op. cit.*, pp. 173, 174.

26 Quoted in Fenner Brockway, *Bermondsey Story* (London: George Allen & Unwin Ltd., 1949), p. 65.

27 For Russell,'s evolving attitude to the Russian Revolutions of 1917, see Vellacott, *op, cit.*, pp. 152–71, 219, 224, 230, 248, 249.

28 *The Tribunal*, No. 167 (14 July 1919), p. 1. Italics in the original.

29 *Ibid.*, No. 156 (8 May 1919), p. 4; No. 166 (17 July 1919), p. 1. Earlier the NCF had greeted with enthusiasm the German Spartacist Karl Liebknecht's

antiwar stand; while before the Russian Revolution the future Soviet Commissar for Foreign Affairs, Georgii Tchitcherin, then a Menshevik refugee in England, had been one of the organizers of an NCF branch recruited from opponents of the war among the exiled Russian revolutionaries.

30 H.P. Adams, "Problems of Revolution," *ibid*., No. 160 (5 June 1919), p. 1.

31 Clifford Allen, Preface to Graham, *op. cit*., p. 23.

32 Republished in *Justice in War Time* (London: George Allen & Unwin Ltd., 1924 ed.), pp. 38–57. See also pp. 19, 27, for discussion of what Russell considered were justified or unjustified wars in the past. Russell's wartime writings on pacifism and conscientious objection are now available in their entirety in the superbly produced *Collected Papers of Betrand Russell*, ed. Richard A. Rempel *et al*., vol. XIII (1988): *Prophecy and Dissent, 1914–16* (London: Unwin Hyman) and vol. XIV (1995): *Pacifism and Revolution, 1916–18* (London and New York: Routledge). These two massive volumes contain over 1300 pages. Even if few people will wish to read them from cover to cover, students may usefully consult them – despite their bulk – as a supplement to Vellacott's monograph on the subject, cited above in note 9.

33 Dorothy L. Plowman, ed., *Bridge into the Future: Letters of Max Plowman* (London: Andrew Dakers Limited, 1944), p. 99. See *The Faith Called Pacifism* (London: J.M. Dent and Sons Ltd., 1936), for his fully matured standpoint.

34 Harold Owen and John Bell, eds., *Wilfred Owen: Collected Letters* (London: Oxford University Press, 1967), p. 461.

35 Quoted in Thomas, *op. cit*., p. 27.

36 Graham, *op. cit*., p. 71.

37 Quoted in *ibid*., p. 67.

38 Quoted in *ibid*., pp. 326, 327, from the *Daily News*, 7 April 1919.

39 To my knowledge only one radical Irish nationalist of any prominence was also a complete pacifist: Francis Sheehy Skeffington. During Easter Week 1916, the English repaid him for this irregularity in conduct by shooting him.

40 John Rae, *Conscience and Politics: The British Government and the Conscientious Objector to Military Service 1916–1919* (London: Oxford University Press, 1970), pp. 132, 133.

41 Cf. A.J.P. Taylor, *English History 1914–1945* (Oxford: The Clarendon Press, 1965), p. 73, n. 4: "Lloyd George lacked physical courage. The air raids of the first war, and still more those of the second, terrified him, and he rarely spent a night in London."

42 Mrs. Henry Hobhouse, *"I appeal unto Caesar": The Case of the Conscientious Objector* (London: George Allen & Unwin Ltd., n.d.) is an important source for the treatment of the absolutists. In fact Bertrand Russell was author of most of the booklet; see Vellacott, *op. cit*., p. 210.

43 *The Tribunal*, No. 154 (24 April 1919), p. 2.

44 Olaf Stapledon, "Experiences in the Friends' Ambulance Unit," in Julian Bell, ed., *We did not Fight* (London: Cobden-Sanderson, 1935), pp. 363, 364, 367. Cf. the pioneer peace researcher and birthright Quaker L.F. Richardson's explanation of why he joined the FAU: "In August 1914 1 was torn between an intense curiosity to see war at close quarters, an intense objection to killing people, both mixed with ideas of public duty, and doubt as to whether I could endure danger." Quoted in G.D. Hess, "An Introduction to Lewis Fry Richardson and His Mathematical Theory of War and Peace," *Conflict Management and Peace Science* (Binghampton, NY), vol. 14, no. 1 (Spring, 1995), p. 78.

45 T. Corder Catchpool, *On Two Fronts* (London: Headley Bros., 1918), pp. 105, 107–110.

46 Letter to Lady Ottoline Morrell, September, 1916, in *The Autobiography of Bertrand Russell*, vol. II (London: George Allen and Unwin Ltd., 1968), p. 74.

47 Kennedy, *op. cit.*, p. 283. From his time spent as a C.O. in Wormwood Scrubs and Wandsworth prisons, architect and Anglican pacifist Tom Attlee recalled most vividly the diet. "In the monotony and hunger of a long imprisonment," he wrote in his memoirs, "how the acquisition of an extra potato or a second bit of bread created a feeling of satisfaction out of all proportion to its normal value." "My hunger in the Scrubs was largely ... due to having little to occupy one's mind: hence intense preoccupation with the next meal!" Quoted from Peggy Attlee, *With a Quiet Conscience: Thomas Simons Attlee 1880–1960* (London: Dove & Chough Press, 1995), pp. 58–61. Tom was older brother of Clement Attlee, the Labour Party leader who became Britain's Prime Minister in 1945.

48 E.H. Griffiths, *Heddychwr mawr Cymru* (Caernavon: Llyfrfa'r Methodistiaid Calfinaidd), vol. I (1967), p. 89. Cf. vol. II ("*Seraff yr Efengyl Seml*," 1968), pp. 188, 189.

49 Taylor, *op. cit.*, p. 54.

50 Thomas, *op. cit.*, p. 23.

51 In fact, the overwhelming majority of drafted Quakers accepted combatant service. Lester M. Jones has blamed the "pre-war unpreparedness" of American Friends with regard to the possibility of their country becoming involved in world war for this situation; *Quakers in Action: Recent Humanitarian and Reform Activities of the American Quakers* (New York: The Macmillan Company, 1929), pp. 14–17. Another factor here was, of course, the virtual disappearance of pacifism by this date among many evangelical and fundamentalist Friends, especially in the West. But some liberal Quaker meetings in the East were also rather shaky on this issue!

52 Arle Brooks and Robert J. Leach, eds., *Help Wanted: The Experiences of Some Quaker Conscientious Objectors* (Philadelphia and Wallingford, PA: AFSC and Pendle Hill, 1940), pp. 133, 227–29, 231. For the relief activities of

American Quakers during and after World War I, see J. William Frost, " 'Our Deeds carry Our Message': The Early History of the American Friends Service Committee," *Quaker History*, vol. 81, no. 1 (Spring, 1992), pp. 1–51.

53 Kellogg, *op. cit.*, pp. 37–42, 66–69.

54 See Gerlof D. Homan, *American Mennonites and the Great War 1914–1918* (Scottdale, PA and Waterloo, Ontario: Herald Press, 1994), esp. chaps. V and VI.

55 Quoted in Thomas. *op. cit.*, p. 119.

56 *Ibid.*, pp. 146, 147.

57 Allan Teichroew, "World War I and the Mennonite Migration to Canada to avoid the Draft," *The Mennonite Quarterly Review* (Goshen, IN), vol. 45, no. 3 (July, 1971), pp. 245, 246.

58 See Adolf Ens, *Subjects or Citizens? The Mennonite Experience in Canada, 1870–1925.* (Ottawa: University of Ottawa Press, 1994), chap. V ("The War Issues"). Appendix 6 (p. 244) reproduces a Mennonite Identification Certificate issued under the Military Service Act, 1917, to descendants "of one of those Mennonites who came to Canada from Russia" in the 1870s and had received a *Privilegium* of exemption from military service to induce them to settle in the new dominion. Mennonites who had moved up from the United States, beginning in the 1790s, had also been exempted from bearing arms, along with Quakers and Brethren in Christ, by the legislature of Upper Canada. Though they encountered some difficulties, C.Os. from these three sects on the whole received the kind of exemption that satisfied them. (The Dukhobors, whose response to World War I was more negative than that of the other recognized peace sects, had also been assured of military exemption when they settled in Canada at the end of the last century.) For the Canadian Quaker peace testimony, see Lise Hansen, "Friends and Peace: Quaker Pacifist Influence in Ontario to the Early Twentieth Century," *Canadian Quaker History Journal* (Toronto), no. 55 (Summer, 1994), pp. 8–15.

59 William Janzen. *Limits on Liberty: The Experience of Mennonite, Hutterite, and Doukhobor Communities in Canada* (Toronto: University of Toronto Press, 1990), pp. 167–97.

60 See Peter Brock, *The Quaker Peace Testimony 1660 to 1914* (York, U.K.: Sessions Book Trust. 1990), pp. 277–84; William N. Oats, "The Campaign against Conscription in Australia – 1911 to 1914," *The Journal of the Friends' Historical Society* (London), vol. 55, no. 7 (1989), pp. 205–19.

61 P.S. O'Connor, "The Awkward Ones – Dealing with Conscience, 1916–1918," *The New Zealand Journal of History* (Auckland), vol. 8, no. 2 (October, 1974), pp. 119, 120, 123–6; Paul Baker, *King and Country Call: New Zealanders, Conscription and the Great War* (Auckland: Auckland University Press, 1988), pp. 73–78, 170–78, 243. Many Maoris, particularly those belonging to the

Waikato tribe, refused to serve if conscripted. Their objection to joining the army included, besides land grievances and a sense of alienation, a vague pacifism compounded of Christianity and injunctions of their own religious leaders. See Baker, *op. cit.* pp. 213–22.

62 See H.E. Holland, *Armageddon or Calgary: The Conscientious Objectors of New Zealand and "the Process of Their Conversion"* (Wellington, N.Z.: The Maoriland Worker Printing and Publishing Co. Ltd., 1919); Baker, *op. cit.*, pp. 178–201; also Archibald Baxter, *We will not cease* (London: Victor Gollancz Ltd., 1939) for an account of his experiences en route to, and at, the Western front.

63 *Journal of Mennonite Studies* (Winnipeg), vol. 11 (1993): Al Reimer, "*Sanitätsdienst and Selbstschutz*: Russian-Mennonite Nonresistance in World War I and Its Aftermath," pp. 134–48, and David G. Rempel, "Mennonite Medics in Russia during World War I," pp. 149–61. We should note, however, that a perceptible erosion of Mennonite nonresistance had already begun several decades before the outbreak of war, e.g., hiring armed Cossacks to protect property. See *JMS*: Helmut-Harry Loewen and James Urry, "Protecting Mammon: Some Dilemmas of Mennonite Non-resistance in Late Imperial Russia and the Origins of the *Selbstschutz*," vol. 9 (1991), pp. 34–53, and Jacob A. Loewen and Wesley J. Prieb, "The Abuse of Power among Mennonites in South Russia 1789–1919," vol. 14 (1996), p. 36; also Terry Martin, "The Terekers' Dilemma: A Prelude to the *Selbstschutz*," *Mennonite Historian* (Winnipeg), vol. 17, no. 4 (December 1991), pp. 1, 2. The Terek Mennonite colony in the foothills of the Caucasus Mountains existed precariously in a frontier "no-man's land" from 1901 to February 1918 when the colonists were at last driven out by hostile mountaineers. Such developments foreshadow the creation of the Mennonite *Selbstschutz* at the end of the war, which marked a – temporary – abandonment of nonresistance.

64 Jenő Szigeti (with László Kardos as co-author), *Boldog emberek közössége: A magyarországi nazarénusok* (Budapest-Magvető Könyvkiadó, 1988), pp. 272, 274, cites cases of military courts sentencing Nazarene consciprts to three or four years – sometimes longer – in prison for refusing to carry weapons or take the military oath. On the other hand, according to Szigeti, there were a few Nazarene draftees whom the army assigned immediately to noncombatant duties. Several of these men were later decorated for bravery in the battle zone or became prisoners of war. (A similarly mixed treatment marked the experience of Nazarene conscripts in Hungary during the Second World War; see *ibid.*, pp. 288–93.) We may note that among Hungary's leftwing intellectuals there was considerable antiwar feeling of various degrees of intensity; the feminist leader Rosika Schwimmer, for instance, was, like Olive Schreiner in England, a convinced pacifist who worked indefatigably for peace throughout the years of conflict. Several members

of the prewar radical and antimilitarist Galileo Circle (*A Galilei Kör*) "refused military service on ... principle, and were sentenced to 15 years' imprisonment"; other Galileans were imprisoned for antimilitarist propaganda among soldiers and munition workers, especially in 1917. See War Resisters' International *Bulletin* (Enfield, Middlesex), No. III (December, 1923), p. 7. The Galileo Circle left it to each individual member how to respond to the war and the military call-up.

65 Recalcitrant Jehovah's Witnesses, too were imprisoned – or placed in psychiatric clinics for the rest of the war, like some other German C.Os. The most detailed account of conscientious objection in Germany and Austria during World War I is given in a pamphlet by Martha Steinitz, Olga Misar and Helene Stöcker, *Kriegsdienstverweigerer in Deutschland und Österreich* (Berlin: "Die neue Generation," 1923). See Markus Mattmüller, *Leonhard Ragaz und der religiöse Sozialismus*, vol. II (Zürich: EVZ-Verlag, 1968), chap. VI (B) and (F), for wartime conscientious objection in neutral Switzerland and the stand of one of its foremost defenders. Though Ragaz himself was never an absolute pacifist, his disciple, the socialist pastor Willi Kobe, was. Kobe after 1945 played a prominent role in the Swiss antinuclear movement. Swiss World War I C.Os. included Plymouth Brethren, Seventh-day Adventists, and *Antonianer* (members of an indigenous sect centered around Bern) as well as nonsectarian Christian pacifists like the primary schoolteacher, John Baudraz, or the young Protestant pastor, Jules Humbert-Droz, and socialist objectors whose religion was human brotherhood. They were given short prison terms, usually repeated at the next annual call-up for military training. The number of C.Os. remained very small, however; most Swiss regarded conscription for military service as both democratic and patriotic. But the law allowed young Mennonites, the spiritual descendants of the anabaptist Swiss Brethren of 1525, to perform their conscript service in the army medical corps; and a similar concession was sometimes granted, too, to other sectarian objectors if they were willing. Neutral Switzerland, like belligerent Germany, also sent C.Os. to psychiatric clinics for observation, at any rate if their objections were of a somewhat primitive or bizarre kind that could be branded as "psychopathic" or "schizophrenic." See J.B. Jörger, "Über Dienstverweigerer und Friedensapostel," *Zeitschrift für die gesamte Neurologie und Psychiatrie* (Berlin): *Originalien*, vol. 43 (1918), pp. 117–33.

66 Jean Séguy, *Les assemblées anabaptistes-mennonites de France* (Paris and The Hague: Mouton, 1977), pp. 558–60, 783, 784. According to Michel Auvray, *Objecteurs, insoumis, déserteurs: Histoire des réfractaires en France* (Paris: Stock, 1983), pp. 160, 161, there were a small number of isolated Christian – and humanist – pacifists who, on being drafted, accepted military service but then at some stage refused to become combatants on the grounds that they

believed it wrong to take human life. Auvray mentions four of these men by name: Jean Paganon and Lucien Gross who were sentenced to life imprisonment, and Emile Bonnet and pastor Guitton, who were incarcerated in a mental hospital.

67 Séguy, *op. cit.*, p. 604 n. 69. See also p. 786. We may note that the Alsatian congregations, which came under German rule from 1871 to 1918, opted for the noncombatant service permitted Mennonite conscripts by imperial law; they did so even during World War I. After Germany lost Alsace their young men became subject once more to combatant service in the French army, which they may have resented but understandably did not attempt to resist. And as time passed, the Mennonites of Alsace tended increasingly to accept the views of their francophone brethren on war and army service.

68 Sergio Albesano, *Storia dell'obiezione di coscienza in Italia* (Treviso: Editrice Santi Quaranta, 1993), pp. 21, 22.

69 Bell, ed., *op. cit.*, intro., p. xv.

III. Gandhi as a Pacifist

In the autumn of 1914 an Indian lawyer in his middle forties, who had recently stopped off in England on his way back to his native land after a prolonged residence in South Africa, began to recruit volunteers among Indian students for an ambulance corps, which he hoped would serve with the British armed forces. This was roughly at the same time that British pacifists were taking the first steps to launch their campaign against the threat of conscription. It is unlikely that the Indian lawyer, whose name was Mohandas Karamchand Gandhi (1869–1948),[1] then met any of the men who were to lead the conscientious objector movement in Great Britain. Their purposes scarcely coincided. The Indian wished to prove his compatriots' devotion to the British Crown, the British pacifists hoped successfully to defy their government's efforts to make them fight for King and country. Gandhi, however, was soon to become the greatest exponent of the philosophy of nonviolence that the world had hitherto known.

In South Africa Gandhi had led a partly successful campaign of non-violent resistance by members of the country's Indian colony against the legal discrimination to which they, along with all other non-white groups, were subjected by the ruling minority. What was at that date unique about Gandhi's leadership was that he not only deliberately rejected violence to gain the just rights of his countrymen, he had also begun to evolve a technique of extra-legal action to achieve this goal. It was neither the way of parliamentary government, for Indians in South Africa were deprived of most democratic rights, nor, of course, was this kind of civil disobedience a rebellion or civil war, for at its very center stood the principle of nonviolence.

Gandhi called this sort of nonviolent action *satyagraha* (truth-force): a term he derived from Sanskrit via his Gujarati mother tongue. He was to apply this technique in order to gain his country's freedom, with results that shook the British Empire to its foundations and sent ripples round the globe. A new method of winning political independence and social injustice, of transforming society, and potentially even of defending a country against outside aggression, without the use of violence now made its appearance. Before moving on to examine the theory and practice of Gandhi's nonviolence, both as a "weapon" against internal oppression and as a "defense" against external attack and a substitute for war (the two aspects are in fact closely interlinked), we should first enquire whence Gandhi derived the intellectual inspiration to launch nonviolence on a surprised world. Were its origins basically in the Hindu religious tradition in which Gandhi himself was reared? Or should we rather seek its roots above all in the thought of the West to which, by his education, Gandhi had been exposed?

The Roots of Gandhi's Nonviolence

Gandhi himself admitted that neither his beloved *Bhagavad-Gita*, nor the other Hindu religious classics, nor contemporary Hindu practice condemned war directly or preached the need for nonviolence in group relations. But all living religions are in a state of evolution; what he in fact achieved was the transformation of traditional Hindu ideas into something new. In many cases the terminology remained the same, and thereby acceptable even to conservative Indian minds, while the meaning given bore a revolutionary significance. Thus he poured the new wine of Western thinking into the old bottles of Hindu tradition; out of the resulting fusion he created a novel ethic and a dynamic political technique.

The idea of *ahimsa*, for instance, of non-injury to any living creature, went back deep into the Indian past. "Hinduism, especially in Gandhi's home region of Gujarat, had inherited [this idea] from Buddhism and Jainism."[2] Gandhi completely remolded the concept and made a politico-social obligation from what had been primarily a personal duty. The same thing occurred with his search for *satya*, the ultimate and elusive Truth, which Hinduism posited as the paramount goal of religion. Here Gandhi created a gospel of social action where before there had been only an individual quest. Or take *tapasya*, the ascetic ideal of self-restraint and self-sacrifice which the holy men of India expressed in its most austere form – Gandhi strove to harness such self-discipline to social ends. To him the true goal of *tapasya* was not withdrawal to the caves but return to the market place.

His Indian background, therefore, supplied Gandhi with the vocabulary and the symbols of his nonviolent philosophy.[3] The set of values he affixed to them he derived from a different source. As a young student in London he had come upon the New Testament. In the Sermon on the Mount he read the injunctions to love enemies and not to resist evil by violent means. From two other favorite authors, Ruskin and Emerson, he took over the idea of utilizing military heroism and discipline for peaceful goals and of directing warlike instincts into creative, instead of destructive, channels. There should be a new chivalry of peace which would incorporate all the moral virtues formerly contained in war. Thoreau's famous essay on civil disobedience to unjust acts of government he first read in 1907 when he had already been conducting his own campaign against racial discrimination, at first legal and then finally illegal, for nearly fourteen years, indeed almost from his first arrival in Natal in 1893. But the essay provided him with confirmation, and an eloquent apologia, for the line of action he was pursuing, as well as an impulse to further extend its range to meet new injustices.[4]

The most seminal Western influence on Gandhi, however, was undoubtedly that of Tolstoy. He read the latter's *Kingdom of God Is Within You* in 1894, soon after its first publication, and was immensely impressed by it. Tolstoy's bold denunciation of modern civilization with its latent violence and essential falsity, and his call to a simple life, struck an answering chord in the Hindu, whose religion taught him non-injury, asceticism and the illusoriness of the visible world. Tolstoy's search for the truth in all the world's religions matched Gandhi's syncretic approach to spiritual problems, which he inherited from his Indian background. Yet in Gandhi the sharp edges of Tolstoy's philosophy are softened: with the former, existing society must be transformed by the spirit of love rather than rejected in a passion of hatred. To Gandhi the political arena and not an apolitical society was the most direct way to reach a nonviolent world. Tolstoy was an avowed cosmopolitan, Gandhi an ardent Indian nationalist. But Tolstoy, when shortly before his death he heard of Gandhi's campaign in South Africa, at once recognized their basic spiritual affinity; and he clearly foresaw the tremendous impact that Gandhi's actions (and thus indirectly his own ideas) would make on the humankind.

Scholars have argued concerning the primacy in Gandhi's development of Western or Eastern influences. Did he merely seek confirmation in Christianity and in the writings of secular Western thinkers of concepts that already lay buried deep in his own mind? Or did he go back to the Indian scriptures and traditions only to seek confirmation there of truths he had learned elsewhere? In fact the final result of Gandhi's explorations was a synthesis of several traditions. Without his Indian background the shape of his political and social philosophy, including his views on nonviolence, would have been very different. If he had remained without contact with Western ideas, on the other hand, it is extremely doubtful if he could have evolved a revolutionary technique of political action on the basis alone of the Hindu tradition combined with his special talent for social action.

The Practice of *Satyagraha*

Pursuit of truth (*satya*), non-injury (*ahimsa*), and readiness to suffer (*tapasya*): these were the principles which Gandhi believed should guide the follower of nonviolence. In bridging the gap, however imperfectly, between ethic and practice lay the heart of Gandhi's genius and the essence of his contribution to the twentieth-century world.

Nonviolence, Gandhi emphasized constantly, must never be employed frivolously, without just cause. A *satyagraha* campaign should crystallize around some truth – or rather, it must embody some aspect, admittedly partial, of universal Truth. In South Africa the struggle had been against legal discrimination of the Indian minority on grounds of race. After Gandhi's return to India, he embarked on a series of struggles, either led by himself or by one of his deputies, which were directed not solely against the British authorities but sometimes also against Indian wielders of religious or economic power.

In the Vykom Temple Road *Satyagraha* (1924–25), for instance, the object was to vindicate "the right of every human individual to pass along a public road without discrimination on the basis of caste," for here the untouchables had been forbidden to use the highways around the temple. In the Bardoli campaign of 1928, "the granting of an impartial enquiry into the enhanced assessment of land" was the demand for which the *satyagrahis* undertook action: the provincial government had arbitrarily raised the taxation imposed on the local peasantry, who now sought relief from this injustice. Sometimes a labor dispute, such as occurred in 1918 at Ahmedabad between laborers and textile-mill owners, provided the occasion for the exercise of *satyagraha*. It was "the social justice underlying the demand for increased pay" – a 35 percent increase for the workers to cover a steep rise in cost of living over recent years – that embodied the truth for those who engaged in this campaign. Those campaigns that were directed against the foreign occupying power aroused the most controversy, since "truth' was matched here not against a group, however powerful, of private citizens but employed against the British in order to bring about a change in the law of the land or even a totally new regime. Near the beginning of his political career in India, Gandhi had launched a struggle of this nature: the unsuccessful nationwide *satyagraha* in 1919 against the obnoxious Rowlatt Acts, which *inter alia* allowed preventive detention for political offenses. The famous Salt *Satyagraha* of 1930–31, the largest-scale effort ever mounted by Gandhi, was directed overtly toward political goals: at first "the removal of laws [creating a government monopoly of salt manufacture] which worked a hardship upon the poor" and broadening later to resistance against "the subjugation of India by a foreign power," whose continued presence in the country appeared contrary to the interests of its inhabitants.[5]

The Truth embodied in a campaign of *satyagraha* was not open in Gandhi's view to negotiation. Only a conviction as to their inconsistency with what was really true should lead *satyagrahis* to alter or abandon their avowed objectives. Yet essentially what Gandhi strove for was agreement and conciliation between the conflicting parties – provided this did not involve a compromise concerning what was right. The victory, at least in theory, should not mean the triumph of either contestant; it should signify the victory of Truth in itself.

Techniques

"For Gandhi ... nonviolence was more than just a tactic, it was a creed."[6] Nevertheless, *satyagraha* is not merely a philosophy of nonviolence; it is also a technique for the creative resolution of conflict. It does not aim at the elimination of conflict from human relationships. Conflict is admitted as a built-in element of the human situation. But conflict, Gandhi claimed, may be directed into creative, nonviolent channels with a proper understanding of the means necessary for this purpose. Thus *satyagraha* is not a perfectionist ethic or a counsel of withdrawal, but a tool for the collective achievement of practical objectives.

There are two major types of *satyagraha* in action, both of which were employed on different occasions by Gandhi: noncooperation and civil disobedience. Noncooperation does not normally involve the breaking of any human law (though of course in certain circumstances it may do so). It can be directed either against the state or against some private group in the community. A *satyagraha* movement of noncooperation, if concerned with fighting against an economic wrong, might take the form of a strike, walk-out or sit-in or of a boycott of goods; one aimed at political injustice could involve, for instance, the resignation of civil servants from their posts or the renunciation of official titles and honors or the boycott of some educational or cultural institution. The second type of *satyagraha*, the best known and the more widely practised – civil disobedience – involves by its very nature the breaking of laws in the name of a higher than human law expressing Truth. Nonpayment of taxes, refusal of compulsory military service, or the manufacture of some prohibited article (here the breaking of the state monopoly by making salt practised by Gandhi and his followers in 1930 is the best known instance) are examples of such principled disobedience. For successful *satyagraha*, nonviolent suffering of the penalties of disobedience – manhandling, imprisonment or even death – is absolutely essential. In rare cases Gandhi or a chosen follower fasted as a form of individual *satyagraha*. However, he warned repeatedly against the dangers this action might entail.[7]

A supplement to *satyagraha* – but a very important one – is the positive program of constructive work, which should always accompany the more negative forms of nonviolent struggle, whether noncooperation or civil disobedience. Only with such a program would it normally be possible, thought Gandhi, to find a creative solution to a conflict situation, for a program of this kind pointed the way to achieve a just society, which would embrace "the welfare of all (*sarvodaya*)." Gandhi centered his constructive program in the village and its needs, but this, of course, was conditioned by the Indian situation and was by no means an essential characteristic. In fact the idea is an old one: "He shall know them by their fruits" [Matt. 7:16]. Under Gandhi's leadership *satyagrahis* engaged in such activities as communal reconciliation, the fight against untouchability and for equal rights for the *harijans*, the promotion of village industries and handicrafts, basic education, the improvement of sanitation and health services, and the cultural development of the country's backward tribes.

In choosing the target of the *satyagraha* campaign, the symbolic element was extremely important for Gandhi. When he embarked on his famous Salt March to the sea at Dandi, his efforts were not directed primarily against the salt monopoly. It was the oppression of the poor deprived in this way of cheap salt, one of the basic constituents in their daily fare, against which nonviolent struggle was to be waged. And from social injustice the campaign eventually turned to direct its efforts toward the winning of national independence, *swaraj*. Gandhi always insisted on the need for extreme care in choosing the right symbol on which to focus a *satyagraha* movement. The inner meaning of the symbol must be clear to all; the truth which it sought to express

(Gandhi saw this as an aspect of universal Truth) should shine forth so that even the simplest soul might understand what was at stake. To gain this truth men and women followed Gandhi. In winning them for the truth there was need for a kind of divine expediency.

In Gandhi's strategy, however, resort to civil disobedience or noncooperation should come only after every effort has been made to reach an acceptable solution. Even after the lines are drawn and some form of nonviolent coercion is employed (for attempts by some Gandhians to deny the presence of a coercive element appear disingenuous), the door should always be left open for renewed talks and negotiations and an agreed settlement. "If ... the nonviolent struggle itself [brings] to light relevant facts which the *satyagrahis* failed to take into account when drawing up their proposals for a settlement, these proposals will be amended."[8] So long as there is no agreement – despite genuine efforts to reach one on the part of the *satyagrahis* – the strength of their movement and its effectiveness, Gandhi believed, lay above all in the moral quality of those participating. The campaigners' behavior should always be in consonance with their nonviolent principles: they must refrain from reacting violently to any injury suffered, submitting peacefully to arrest or confiscation of property while at the same time refusing to obey unjust orders whatever the consequences. They must never utter angry words whatever the provocation. Willingness to abide by the decisions of the campaign leaders was likewise basic to *satyagraha's* success: if a campaigner experienced a fundamental disagreement with its direction, he should withdraw altogether. The *satyagrahi* was a soldier, but a volunteer not a conscript. Gandhi stressed four essential qualities in a perfect *satyagrahi*: courage, patience, self-reliance, freedom from covetousness.

Is *satyagraha*, then, a technique only for those near to attaining perfection? Are only saints, a small band of elect spirits, ripe for engaging in such nonviolent confrontation with evil? Should its use be confined to specially selected groups, a kind of nonviolent order of chivalry? Gandhi stoutly denied that nonviolence was a prerogative of a spiritual élite. It was a weapon that could be wielded by ordinary men and women, one that would serve to elevate as well as defend them. Nonviolence, Gandhi believed, could be practised by everyone, and not merely by holy men and saints. Indeed it was the latent capacity for nonviolence that distinguished humans from animals.

Satyagraha was capable of becoming a mass movement. But Gandhi fairly soon came to realize that training for nonviolence was essential if it was to be conducted on a wide scale. Where, as in the Vykom Temple Road *Satyagraha*, specially selected volunteers of high moral caliber were alone involved, the maintenance of a nonviolent stance was comparatively simple even over a long period of time. In campaigns where large numbers were involved, the danger of a lapse into violence, of destructive outbreaks against the opposing forces, was a serious one. When this happened, Gandhi at once put an end to the campaign. "I had called on the people to launch upon civil disobedience before they had ... qualified themselves for it," he wrote later of such a lapse into violence on the part of some of his followers, "and this mistake seemed to me of Himalayan magnitude."[9]

Whereas the successful employment of *satyagraha* demanded dedicated leadership committed to the principle of nonviolence and, if possible, some degree of previous instruction in nonviolent ideas and techniques for all participants, the rank and file did not need to share in full the rigorous moral and physical discipline that Gandhi imposed on himself. He took all who volunteered and were willing to abide by the rules. He never demanded that all those who joined him on a campaign cease to eat meat or become celibates or give up their worldly possessions. He did not even ask them to pledge themselves to be nonviolent for the rest of their lives, though he did expect of them unqualified nonviolence for as long as they were part of a *satyagraha* movement. And he hoped, of course, that their experiences as *satyagrahis* would eventually make them convinced adherents of *ahimsa*.

Apart from preliminary instruction of those taking part in a *satyagraha* movement, including the training of specially chosen volunteers to deal with large crowds, Gandhi devised certain methods for averting violence or containing it once it had erupted. Most important in this respect were his efforts to decentralize leadership by strengthening what Joan Bondurant has called "secondary leadership" and to see that those responsible for organizing a campaign were well known in their own district and aware of its needs and problems, and able, thereby, both to enjoy the confidence of the people and to control the local *satyagraha* movement. The creation of a chain of leadership stretching downwards was designed to help remove some of the disadvantages that could result from large-scale arrests at the top. Even after the campaign commanders had disappeared into jail, the movement might continue to function – and to function nonviolently, which was even more vital to its success – if it was firmly rooted in the community.

A problem faced by Gandhi in many of his campaigns was that of maintaining the morale of his followers after the first enthusiasm had worn off. He stressed the need for retaining the initiative on the side of the *satyagrahis*. Thus in the Salt *Satyagraha* as the excitement generated by this march to the sea began to wane and there was a danger of the campaign petering out in anticlimax, he inaugurated a series of nonviolent raids on the government salt depot at Dharsana. Successive parties of volunteers advanced against the cordon of police, who kicked and beat them mercilessly without evoking a violent response. Meanwhile, throughout the length and breadth of India the illegal manufacture of salt, sometimes only in symbolic quantity, proceeded. The jails filled, but the participation of the masses in the movement was kept up for twelve months until negotiations, which finally led to Indian nationalist participation in the Round Table Conference in London, were initiated between the Indian National Congress, on whose behalf Gandhi was directing the campaign, and the British authorities.

The Nonviolence of the Weak

In speaking of "the nonviolence of the weak," Gandhi meant two different things.[10] He might be referring to the practice of nonviolence by those who had adopted it simply because they were too cowardly to resist by arms, although they had no objections in principle. This attitude Gandhi condemned (though he seems to have felt voluntary exile [*hijrat*] might be permissible for those who lacked either sufficient courage to undertake violent resistance or sufficient conviction to initiate nonviolent action). "I would rather have India resort to arms in order to defend her honour," he told his countrymen, "than that she would, in a cowardly manner, become or remain a helpless witness to her own dishonour."[11] But he might also mean by the term a more honorable and a not necessarily ineffective stance. He could be referring to those who adopted nonviolent techniques of resisting wrong not from cowardice, or from a principled objection to all violence, but from expediency – from a belief that use of violence in the given circumstances would be self-defeating and ineffectual. Many of Gandhi's most respected colleagues in the Indian nationalist movement – Jawaharlal Nehru, to cite just one name – belonged to this category. Accepting Gandhi's leadership (until his temporary retirement from active politics in 1934), they were also prepared to accept the discipline of *satyagraha*, because arms were not available to the Indian people and military superiority was overwhelmingly on the side of the British raj. But they did not disavow resorting to arms if conditions changed.

Gandhi believed, as they did, that nonviolent resistance to injustice was possible for a nation forcibly deprived of weapons. He also believed, as they did not, that it remained morally the preferable, and ultimately the more effective, method of resistance even if military success were attainable.

But this did not mean that, in his view, *satyagraha* was not open to debasement either through abuse as to the occasion of its use or through the lack of a truly nonviolent spirit behind the campaign. For nonviolent action of this latter kind Gandhi used the term *duragraha* (stubborn persistence). "Forms of passive resistance are usually forms of *duragraha*," writes Bondurant.[12] Most strikes, boycotts and demonstrations come within this category; though obviously preferable to armed clashes over the issues in dispute, they usually fall short of those qualities – produced only as a result of conscious will to reconciliation – which provided the dynamic of Gandhi's nonviolence.

Gandhi's civil disobedience was conducted in countries such as South Africa and British India where, however circumscribed, certain freedoms did exist and where the rule of law prevailed within a restricted area. Moreover, in Britain where the ultimate policy decisions were taken, public opinion had considerable weight in directing government action and this opinion was to some extent colored by liberal and humanitarian thought. Many of Gandhi's opponents, too, were men of high personal rectitude (General Smuts, for instance, or Lord Irwin) – persons with whom meaningful and creative dialogue could be carried on. Would this be possible, it has often been asked, with the ruthless thugs who often initiate and execute the policies of totalitarian régimes? Moreover, would the moral appeal of nonviolent resistance operate in regard to men who consider their opponents as racially inferior?

To these questions no certain answer can be given for, as Bondurant has remarked, "we do not have any direct empirical evidence."[13] Certainly Gandhi expressed confidence in the ability of nonviolence to overcome, even within a totalitarian setting. He pleaded with the Jews in Germany to adopt nonviolence, though he never claimed that nonviolent resistance under such circumstances did not involve great risk or would not, almost inevitably, lead to considerable loss of life. He contemplated stoically (some might say with an Oriental calm) the possibility of thousands dying in the course of a *satyagraha* movement. This attitude, as he explained, did not stem from his holding life cheap or regarding it as a kind of nonviolent cannon fodder; it flowed from his belief that nonviolence would prove ultimately the method of resistance least wasteful of human life and resources, and one, too, that was more ennobling and morally sound than insurrection or war. To the famous Jewish philosopher Martin Buber, *satyagraha* such as Gandhi envisaged against the Nazis appeared to augur no more than "a martyrdom cast to the winds."[14] But, for Gandhi nonviolence could not fail in the long run for it represented the law of the universe.

Satyagraha and War

The techniques of *satyagraha* were applied by the Mahatma exclusively to group relations within the state. International relations were a branch of politics on which Indians under British rule could make little impact. Foreign policy decisions affecting India were made in London and not at home. Gandhi, therefore, "had no occasion to show how this non-violent strategy could work in the face of an invading army."[15] Nevertheless, he stressed that violence within the state and violence between states formed an organically interrelated. problem. He insisted, too, on the relevance of nonviolence as an instrument for obtaining and maintaining peace and justice in the relations between states. It is of course these last aspects of nonviolence that became of primary concern to the pacifist movement in the West.

In 1939, on the occasion of Gandhi's seventieth birthday, a Western admirer greeted him as "the greatest living exponent of successful pacifism."[16] Yet, as the reader has already seen from the opening paragraph of this chapter, his career reveals a certain ambiguity on the issue of war. It is certainly true that he preferred violent resistance in the face of injustice and tyranny to a cowardly, if formally nonviolent, submission. He appreciated martial valor. But he never failed to point out that, in his opinion, nonviolent resistance was the best way. Again, he did not object to military conscription in a free country (such as he hoped India would become) for those who had not accepted the principle of nonviolence: an attitude, of course, that was repugnant to most libertarian pacifists in Europe and America. As a protagonist of Indian freedom, he resented their British rulers' depriving his countrymen of the right to carry arms: he saw in it a mark of inferiority and enforced cowardice rather than a sign of nonviolence. And he wholeheartedly supported conscientious objectors in the West in their refusal of military service and contemplated sympathetically the proposal that pacifists refrain from paying taxes for war purposes. However, he considered that military service was only a symptom: the disease went much deeper. Therefore, conscientious objection, like patriotism, was not enough: state and society must be remolded in the spirit of nonviolence.

More controversial, and more difficult for Westerners to comprehend, was Gandhi's seeming support of the British war effort on several occasions. In South Africa, during the Boer War and in the Zulu rebellion in Natal in 1906, and then again in World War I, he rallied to Britain's cause, helping to recruit Indians for ambulance duties at the front and himself participating actively in such work. Indeed, in 1918 he went further and urged his countrymen to enlist for combatant service.[17] "How could you do that, Gandhi, you who stand for fraternity and moral resistance?" a Dutch pacifist once asked him indignantly.[18]

The explanations Gandhi gave of his wartime actions testify to his honesty and to the sincerity of his basic devotion to nonviolence, if not always to the strength of his logic. He admitted that his wartime stance could not be justified from the viewpoint of a rigid adherent of *ahimsa*. At the time, however, he had believed that only if Indians showed their willingness to back Britain's war effort to the hilt would the mother country be ready to acknowledge their right to self-government and equality within the Empire. Since only a handful of Indians at that period accepted Gandhi's teaching on nonviolence, and since in these circumstances creative action against war did not appear possible, loyalty to the British Empire seemed to be the only attitude he could honestly recommend to his countrymen. Even so, objectively he had to acknowledge there was little difference between combatant service and the type of Red Cross work in which he participated. Yet, he went on to argue, "so long as I lived under a system of government based on force and voluntarily partook of the many facilities and privileges it created for me, I was bound to help that Government to the extent of my ability when it was engaged in a war, unless I non-cooperated with that Government and renounced to the utmost of my capacity the privileges it offered me."[19]

Gandhi developed a more militant stand against war only after Indian loyalty had failed to evoke the expected reward from Great Britain and he had begun to reassess his earlier stance. "If another war were declared tomorrow," he stated in 1928, "I could not, with my personal views about the present Government, assist it in any shape or form; on the contrary I should exert myself to the utmost to induce others to withhold their assistance and to do everything possible and consistent with ahimsa to bring about its defeat."[20]

Nonviolent Resistance to Aggression

Gandhi's approach to international relations assumed the existence of the sovereign state. Like Mazzini and the liberal nationalists of nineteenth-century Europe, Gandhi, however, conceived of a natural, God-willed harmony between the political entities into which the world was divided. He shared with Mazzini, too, the idea of national mission. For Gandhi the mission of his India, however apostate, was to show the world, under his tutelage, the way to nonviolence, to a new universalism subsuming but not eliminating the separate national states. "My patriotism," he wrote, "includes the good of mankind in general. Therefore my service [to] India includes the service of humanity."[21] He did not appear interested in the finer problems of nationalist theory or in the dilemmas of self-determination as revealed with special acuteness, for example, in the interwar experience of East Central Europe. But he assumed that the state was normally the expression of a national consensus.

Righteousness, not peace, was for Gandhi the primary aim of society, not only in its internal relations but as reflected in the international society of "nation-states." Nonviolence was a means toward achieving this goal, a method of adjusting human relations on a higher ethical plane than civil violence or war.

With the contemporary peace movement in the West, Gandhi shared many practical proposals for avoiding war. While remaining, it is true, somewhat suspicious of institutional machinery for settling disputes (the League of Nations or the United Nations, for instance) he did give his support at one time or another to such measures as informal third-party arbitration, disarmament, world government and an impartially administered international police force. He viewed them as means to avoid war and achieve justice in a world that had not yet embarked on the higher path of nonviolence. But nonviolence with Gandhi was far from being a doctrine of nonintervention or an instrument for upholding the international (or domestic) *status quo*, for justice might sometimes require alterations in the existing order.

In regard to the employment of nonviolent resistance against aggression, in the practice of which he hoped (though later with decreasing optimism) that an independent India would lead the way, he was already being questioned on this subject as early as 1920. What, asked his critics, would India do if the British withdrew and left the country to the mercies of the wild mountain tribesmen, who coveted the riches of the Indian plains? "If India returns to her spirituality," Gandhi answered, "it will react upon the neighbouring tribes; she will interest herself in the welfare of these hard, but poor people, and even support them, if necessary, not out of fear but as a matter of neighbourly duty."[22] Thus here, at any rate in theory, we already see Gandhi applying the techniques of domestic *satyagraha* to an external situation. The power of nonviolence, if combined with a constructive program to remedy grievances, would prevail. He pleaded, in addition, for India to become self-sufficient in respect to the basic necessities of life: food, clothing, etc. In this way, it would form a less tempting prey for an invader.

His success in converting the hitherto bellicose Pathans to nonviolence in considerable numbers showed at least that it could touch the hearts of so called backward peoples.[23] Could *satyagraha* be applied with success with regard to the kind of aggression that led to World War II? Gandhi believed that it could. He spoke on one occasion of the need to re-enact the battle of Thermopylae, to present "a living wall of men and women and children"[24] in an effort to block an invading army or an army in transit to invade another country. From what he had seen of the behavior of his *satyagrahis* in the recent civil disobedience campaign – ordinary human beings transformed by a cause – he felt confident that such heroism and such discipline did not require super-men or saints. And although he never expanded the idea, he did advocate the creation of a nonviolent army should a country adopt this method of defending itself.

To the victims of fascist aggression in the 1930s – China, Abyssinia, Spain, Czechoslovakia, and Poland – he recommended (though scarcely with any hope of his advice being followed) the practise of nonviolent resistance. Unlike some Western pacifists, he condemned the Munich settlement root and branch. And he accused England and France of cowardice for not backing Czechoslovakia by arms against German threats.

At the same time Gandhi refused to admit that even Hitler and Mussolini[25] were "beyond redemption," since "belief in nonviolence is based on the assumption that human nature in its essence is one and therefore unfailingly responds to the advances of love." "The hardest metal yields to sufficient heat." Yet the efficacy of nonviolence did not stem from the essential goodwill of the opponent, "for a successful non-violent resister depends upon the unfailing assistance of God which sustains him throughout difficulties which would otherwise be insurmountable. His faith makes him indomitable."[26]

We can see from the above that, unlike some Western pacifists of his time, Gandhi did not consider that in modern war there could be no real aggressor (though he did share many of their reservations concerning the 1918 peace settlement). He believed that it was usually possible to assess relative blame in international disputes. He told the British in 1939, for instance, that his sympathies were wholly on the side of the Allies. And indeed throughout his career he had rarely remained neutral in international conflicts. Was not *satyagraha* itself based on the idea of the justice of one's own side over the opponent's? Gandhi held that the strength of nonviolent resistance lay not merely in the ethical character of the means but in the righteousness of the *satyagrahi's* cause. Should some imperfection be found in their case, then what was wrong, he felt, must at once be righted before the campaign could be permitted to continue.

In World War II Gandhi called upon the British to free India but at the same time he was prepared to approve a liberated India's support of Britain's war effort (preferably by nonviolence). The *satyagraha* he launched in October 1940 in the person of the saintly ascetic, Vinoba Bhave, with other individuals also selected by the Mahatma following him a little later, was intended more as a symbolic act than a serious threat to the country's rulers. But what he regarded as British intransigence on the issue of Indian independence led him later to support Congress in launching its massive civil disobedience campaign in August 1942 under the slogan "Quit India."

Shortly before the initiation of the campaign, Gandhi had felt compelled to write as follows:

I always thought that I would have to wait till the country was ready for a non-violent struggle. But my attitude has undergone a change. I feel that if I continue to wait I might have to wait till doomsday. For the preparation that I have prayed and worked for may never come, and in the meantime I may be enveloped and overwhelmed by the flames of violence that are spreading all around. We have to take the risk of violence to shake off the great calamity of slavery. But even for resort to violence one requires the unflinching faith of a non-violent man. There cannot be any trace of violence either in my plans or in my thoughts ... How can a man who has consciously pursued ahimsa for the last fifty years change all of a sudden? So it is not that I have become violent ... [But] the people do not have my ahimsa. And therefore I have to take a risk, if I cannot curb their violence. I cannot remain inactive. I will certainly launch a non-violent movement. But if people do not understand it and there is violence, how can I stop it? I ... prefer anarchy to the present system of administration because this ordered anarchy is worse than real anarchy ... We have to take the risk of anarchy if God wills it. However, we shall try our best to prevent violence. If in spite of that there is violence then it is His wish. I am not responsible for that. But if I ... remain inactive and unconcerned ... I will be proved guilty. My ahimsa will not be effective at all then ... I will be ashamed of such ahimsa.[27]

Though now ready to risk violence rather than see his countrymen remain passive in the face of a gross injustice, Gandhi was shocked when he learnt of the tempest which had swept India after his arrest and that of the other Congress leaders. For the "Quit India" movement, almost from the outset, had degenerated in some areas into – unsuccessful – guerilla warfare. There is no evidence whatsoever that Gandhi gave even qualified approval to such activities. But they did show, as the bloody communal disturbances of 1946 and 1947 were to do even more clearly, that his people remained generally unprepared to adopt nonviolence in the sense the Mahatma understood it. The knowledge that this was so cast a shadow over his final years.

The arrival of the atom bomb seemed to Gandhi (as well as to some who had previously felt his doctrine to be too otherworldly) to confirm his belief that the world's future lay in the development of nonviolent resistance. The only alternative might now be mankind's eventual suicide. True, the time for nonviolent Thermopylaes seemed to have passed, along with more conventional military techniques, but in the nuclear age, when war threatened universal annihilation in the process of repelling aggression, nonviolence appeared to offer, if governments as well as individuals could be persuaded to adopt it, a viable technique for achieving at least a measure of justice between states.

Gandhi's Nonviolence and Independent India

Gandhi's last years were clouded not only by the menace of nuclear warfare but by the fratricidal conflict between Hindus and Muslims, which accompanied the birth of an independent India and Pakistan. In his attitude toward India's freshly emergent neighbor, Gandhi unwittingly illustrates some of the difficulties involved in the relationship between nonviolence and international justice. The Mahatma had steadfastly opposed the creation of Pakistan, regarding a Pakistani nation as a fiction (at that date perhaps not an altogether unjustified conclusion). When the Muslim League under Jinnah's leadership had finally come out in favor of an independent state of Pakistan, Gandhi wrote: "As a man of non-violence I cannot forcibly resist the partition if the Muslims of India really insist upon it. But I can never be a willing party to the vivesection. I would employ every non-violent means to prevent it. For it means the undoing of centuries of work done by numberless Hindus and Muslims to work together as one nation. Partition means a patent untruth."[28] And a little later he told a Muslim supporter of the Pakistan idea, who was also a believer in nonviolence:

As I understand Pakistan I do not regard it as a worthy ideal. But since you consider it to be a worthy end, you can certainly carry on a non-violent movement on its behalf. This means that you will always strive to convert your opponents by patient reasoning. You will impress everybody by your selfless devotion to your ideal. You will give a respectful hearing to what your opponents might have to say, and respectfully point out to them their mistake if they are in the wrong. Finally, if you feel that the people do not listen to you out of sheer bigotry and prejudice, although your cause is absolutely just, you can non-violently non-cooperate with the obstructionists. But you may not injure or seek to injure anybody and must, on your part, patiently endure any injury that might be done to you. All this you will be able to do if objectively your cause can be considered a just one.[29]

Gandhi did not swerve from his viewpoint; it emerges later in several dialogues he had with Jinnah. For instance, writing to the Viceroy, Lord Mountbatten, he reported as follows on a conversation with the Muslim leader: "I told him that my opposition to Pakistan persisted as before and suggested that in view of his [recent] declaration of faith in non-violence he should try to convert his opponents by reasoning with them and not by show of force."[30] When Gandhi failed to carry the majority of the Congress leaders with him in his desire to oppose non-violently, i.e., through organizing a *satyagraha* movement, the creation of a separate Muslim state and partition became a reality in mid-August 1947, Gandhi accepted this as a *fait accompli* and worked for conciliation between the two successor states of the British raj. Still, a little later he did conditionally approve of India's taking armed action against Pakistan by occupying Kashmir. Nehru and his government, Gandhi felt, were justified in doing this since they were not committed, like he was, to nonviolence on principle.

Three years before his assassination on 30 January 1948, the Mahatma had declared: "Non-violence, translated 'love', is the supreme law for human beings ... I have tried ... to live by that law and hope to die in that state."[31] His rejection of violence included war between states as much as it did the employment of violence to win political and social justice and national independence. Nevertheless, in both cases, he believed men and women must choose between nonviolent resistance or taking up arms to prevent the Truth from being overthrown. If nonviolence were not adopted, then Gandhi did not hesitate to condemn a failure to resist by other means.[32]

Notes

1 Good one-volume biographies are Louis Fischer, *The Life of Mahatma Gandhi* (New York: Harper & Brothers, 1950); B.R. Nanda, *Mahatma: A Biography* (Beacon Press, 1958); Geoffrey Ashe, *Gandhi A Study in Revolution* (London: Heinemann, 1968); and, above all, Judith M. Brown, *Gandhi: Prisoner of Hope* (New Haven and London: Yale University Press, 1989). Excellent brief biographies include George Woodcock, *Mohandas Gandhi* (New York: The Viking Press, 1971) and Antony Copley, *Gandhi: Against the Tide* (Oxford:

Basil Blackwell, 1987). There is abundant material on nonviolence in the eight-volume life of Gandhi by D.G. Tendulkar, *Mahatma* (2nd edn., Delhi: Government of India, 1960–63). Much of the vast literature on Gandhi, appearing in many languages, deals of course with his nonviolence; and the *Collected Writings of Mahatma Gandhi* (1958–1984), published by the Government of India, contains almost all he wrote and much that he said on that subject. The core collection (cited below as *CWMG*) is now complete in ninety volumes and a (not entirely satisfactory) subject index volume (1988); supplementary volumes are in process of publication (1989ff.). The English language journal *Gandhi Marg* (New Delhi, 1957ff.) is devoted to Gandhian and related studies. Useful compilations of his writings on nonviolence include M.K. Gandhi, *Satyagraha (Non-violent Resistance)* (Ahmedabad, Navajivan Publishing House, 1951), and *Non-violence in Peace and War* (3rd edn., 2 vols., Ahmedabad: Navajivan, 1948–49); Ronald Duncan, ed., *Selected Writings of Mahatma Gandhi* (London: Faber and Faber Limited, 1951), esp. pp. 35–108; Nirmal Kumar Bose, *Selections from Gandhi* (2nd edn., Ahmedabad: Navajivan, 1957), pp. 149–89, 198–253; Thomas Merton, *Gandhi on Non-violence* (New York: New Directions Paperbook, 1965); Raghavan Iyer, ed., *The Moral and Political Writings of Mahatma Gandhi* (Oxford: Clarendon Press), vol. II (1986), pts. 5 and 6, vol. III (1987), pt. 2. Though she has her critics, Joan Bondurant in her *Conquest of Violence* (rev. edn., Berkeley and Los Angeles: University of California Press, 1965) provides a most valuable tool for understanding "the Gandhian philosophy of nonviolence." Among a number of other studies concerned with Gandhi's nonviolence we can mention only a few: Krishnalal Shridharani, *War without Violence* (Bombay: Bharatiya Vidya Bhavan, 1962); Iyer, *The Moral and Political Thought of Mahatma Gandhi* (New York: Oxford University Press, 1973), chaps. VII–XI; William Borman, *Gandhi and Non-violence* (Albany: State University of New York Press, 1986); Dennis Dalton, *Mahatma Gandhi: Nonviolent Power in Action* (New York: Columbia University Press, 1993). See also Rashmi-Sudha Puri, *Gandhi on War and Peace* (New York: Praeger, 1987), and two essays in K.P. Misra and. S.C. Gangal, eds., *Gandhi and the Contemporary World: Studies in Peace and War* (Delhi: Chanakya Publications, 1981): Pyarelal, "Gandhian Analysis of the Causes of International Tension and War" (pp. 101–10) and I.N. Tewary, "Gandhi's Attitude to War" (pp. 144–50).

2 Hugh F. Owen, *Gandhi* (St. Lucia: University of Queensland Press – Leaders of Asia Series, 1984), p. 17.

3 See Indira Rothermund, *The Philosophy of Restraint: Mahatma Gandhi's Strategy and Indian Politics* (Bombay: Popular Prakashan, 1963), chap. III: "Gandhiji and the Hindu Tradition."

4 Thoreau, like Emerson (or Ruskin), was never an absolute pacifist or

believer in unconditional nonviolence. See Daniel Walker Howe, *Henry David Thoreau on the Duty of Civil Disobedience* (Oxford: Clarendon Press, 1990), pp. 3, 10–12, 28, 29.

5 Bondurant, *op. cit.*, pp. 50, 61, 71, 83, 100. The best treatment of the Salt *Satyagraha* is in Dalton, *op. cit.*, chap. IV.

6 Dalton, *op. cit.*, p. 96.

7 See the pamphlet compiled by R.K. Prabhu and Ravindra Kalelkar from Gandhi's writings on the subject, *Fasting in Satyagraha (Its Use and Abuse)* (Ahmedabad: Navajivan Publishing House, 1965). In a study of Gandhi and conflict resolution, the Norwegian Johan Galtung (along with Theodor Ebert and Gene Sharp, one of the most prominent post-1945 theorists of nonviolence) has described the fast or hunger-strike as a "much disputed form of *satyagraha* where it is questionable whether more compulsion than persuasion is not involved." From his *Der Weg ist das Ziel* (Wuppertal and Lunen: Peter Hammer Verlag, 1987), p. 156. Dalton, *op. cit.*, chap. V, contains a perceptive account of Gandhi's successful Calcutta fast, undertaken in September 1947 to put a stop to Hindu-Muslim violence in that city and restore communal harmony there.

8 H.J.N. Horsburgh, *Non-violence and Aggression: A Study of Gandhi's Moral Equivalent of War* (London: Oxford University Press, 1968), p. 22.

9 M.K. Gandhi, *An Autobiography: The Story of My Experiments with Truth*, translated from the Gujarati (London: Phoenix Press, 1949), p. 392; in *CWMG*, vol. 39, p. 374.

10 See Horsburgh, *op. cit.*, p. 64.

11 *Young India* (11 August 1920); in *CWMG*, vol. 18, p. 132.

12 Bondurant, *op. cit.*, p. viii; Dalton, *op. cit.*, pp. 40–49.

13 Bondurant, *op. cit.*, p. 226.

14 From a letter dated February 24, 1939, reprinted in Peter Mayer, ed., *The Pacifist Conscience* (London: Penguin Books, 1966), pp. 270–82.

15 J.B. Kripalani, "Gandhian Thought and Its Effect on Indian Life," *Cahiers d'histoire mondiale* (Neuchâtel), vol. 5, no. 2 (1959), p. 419.

16 Laurence Housman in S. Radhakrishnan, ed., *Mahatma Gandhi: Essays and Reflections on His Life and Work* (London: George Allen & Unwin Ltd., 1949), p. 123.

17 See Peter Brock, *Studies in Peace History* (York [U.K.]: William Sessions Limited, 1991), chap. VIII: "Was Gandhi Ready to Become a Combatant in the Summer of 1918?" Also Jerald H. Richards, "Gandhi's Qualified Acceptance of Violence," *The Acorn: Journal of the Gandhi-King Society*, vol. 8, no. 2 (Fall, 1995), pp. 5, 6, 9–12, 14.

18 B. de Ligt, "Mahatma Gandhi on War: An Open Letter to Gandhi and His Reply," *The World Tomorrow* (New York), vol. 2, no. 11 (November, 1928), p. 446. De Ligt published an extremely critical study of Gandhi's attitude to

contemporary wars: *Een wereldomvattend vrangstuk – Gandhi en de oorlog* (Utrecht: Erven J. Bijleveld, 1930). See also Evert van der Tuin, ed., *Geweldloosheid: Een Briefwisselinq tussen Bart de Ligt en Mohandas K. Gandhi* (Amsterdam: Anarchistische Uitgaven, 1983).

19 *Young India* (13 September 1928); in *CWMG*, vol. 37, p. 270.

20 *Ibid.* (8 March 1928); in *CWMG*, vol. 36, p. 86.

21 *Ibid.* (17 September 1925); in *CWMG*, vol. 28, p. 186. Conducting a question-naire in the South Indian countryside fourteen years after Gandhi's death, the sociologist Johan Galtung (*op. cit.*, p. 15), found around 75 percent of those asked what they thought was the Mahatma's most important achievement replied – the winning of Indian independence. For these peo-ple he was, above all, "the father of the nation" – not the apostle of nonvio-lence or world unity.

22 *Young India* (29 December 1920); in *CWMG*, vol. 19, p. 174.

23 Under the leadership of the Gandhian Khan Abdul Gaffar Khan, the Mus-lim Pathans of the mountainous Northwest Frontier Province (now part of Pakistan) waged during the 1930s a heroic nonviolent struggle against the British to achieve social reform and national development. These Servants of God (Khudai Khidmatgar) belonged, we may note, to a people to whom traditional Hindu concepts like *ahimsa* or *tapasya* were entirely unfamiliar. They were not peace-loving sedentary peasants or effete urban dwellers, but hardy and pugnacious hillsmen. For a study of "Bacha" Khan, which emphasizes his Pathan identity and his idea of Pakhtunistan alongside his nonviolence, see M.S. Korejo, *The Frontier Gandhi: His Place in History* (Kar-achi: Oxford University Press, 1993). In 1941 he had declared: "With me, non-violence is not a policy but a permanent creed. To my mind ... it is the only path which will save the Pathan from servility and self-destruction" (p. 35). And he remained loyal to Gandhian nonviolence within the context of Paki-stan until his death in 1988, despite constant harassment by the authorities.

24 Speech, 10 December 1931, *CWMG*, vol. 48, p. 420.

25 The *Duce* was the only one of the European dictators whom Gandhi met personally. He did so in December 1931 during a three-day stay in Italy on his way home from the Round Table Conference in London; that is, before fascist Italy had embarked on the path of aggression. The visit is the subject of a detailed monograph in Italian by Gianni Sofri: *Gandhi in Italia* (Bologna: Il Mulino, 1988). See esp. pp. 59–61, 69–76, 87–95. Romain Rolland had tried to dissuade Gandhi from his visit maintaining – correctly – that the Fascists would exploit it for their own purposes. But Gandhi, brushing such fears aside, persisted. While he found, for instance, the armed bodyguard of fas-cist youths paraded in front of him "disgusting," he did succeed "on at least one occasion in speaking semi-publicly about nonviolence, even though the [Italian] papers failed to mention this" (pp. 81, 82).

26 *Harijan* (24 December 1938); in *CWMG*, vol. 68, p. 205.

27 *Saryodava* (June 1942); in *CWMG*, vol. 76, pp. 159, 160.

28 *Harijan* (13 April 1940); in *CWMG*, vol. 71, p. 412. Gandhi always regarded the inhabitants of India as a single nation; and the achievement of *swaraj* (self-rule) in the shape of a unitary nation-state became his eventual goal. He vigorously opposed all varieties of national separatism, whether on linguistic grounds, as in the case of the Tamils, or for reasons of religion, such as the protagonists of Pakistan asserted. Thus, his attitude in this regard conflicts with the cultural-linguistic nationalism we find in parts of modern Europe or with the religious nationalism that led to the creation of Israel. We should bear in mind, however, that the Indian situation, on this issue more akin perhaps to the one existing in the United States, differed fundamentally from that of contemporary Europe. Gandhi excluded Burma and Ceylon (as Sri Lanka was called at that time) from his concept of what formed India, even though for administrative purposes both formed part of British India.

29 *Ibid.* (4 August 1940); in *CWMG*, vol. 72, p. 334.

30 Letter to Lord Mountbatten, May 8, 1947, *CWMG*, vol. 87, p. 437.

31 Letter to William Q. Lash, January 25, 1945, *CWMG*, vol. 79, p. 62.

32 According to Galtung (*op. cit.*, p. 212), one of the reasons why the Nobel Committee never awarded Gandhi their Peace Prize was his often expressed view of violence being "preferable to cowardice." That could seem to contradict the Western "stereotype" of a genuine radical pacifist stance.

IV. Pacifism and War Resistance: The Interwar Years

The Community of War Resisters

In World War I the occurrence of conscientious objection had been confined mainly to the English-speaking world. In the interwar years pacifists attempted to implant their ideas in areas with a different political and cultural tradition. In India Anglo-American pacifism was grafted successfully onto the Hindu doctrine of *ahimsa* to produce Gandhi's philosophy of nonviolence (a process, however, which took place as the result of a reaching out from the Indian's side rather than from any direct Western initiative). Otherwise, pacifism in this period still remained largely an episode in the history of Great Britain and the United States.

Some progress was made in diffusing pacifist concepts beyond the Anglo-American cultural orbit. Expansion, however, was of limited dimension. Even though, for instance, Christian pacifism acquired a notable convert in Japan in the saintly Toyohiko Kagawa and a few others in both China and Japan came under the influence of Quaker or other pacifist missionaries from the West, the Far East was scarcely touched. In India the protagonists of nonviolence were at that date so involved in the nationalist movement that no indigenous pacifist organization emerged there either. In the countries of Latin America, the Near East, and among the peoples of Africa, pacifism aroused scarcely an echo. The same may be said of those parts of southern Europe, where deeply ingrained Catholicism provided an environment unpropitious to the spread of pacifism which drew its inspiration largely from Protestant dissent, as well as of the lands of Orthodox culture in the Balkans.

As a result of the Peace Settlement, however, Yugoslavia had become home for some 30–40 thousand Nazarenes, mostly of Serb nationality and located in the Voivodina. The central government regarded the sect with great suspicion, mistaking its otherworldliness for hostility to the régime. Thus, the "obstinate" Nazarenes now became victims of a persecution far exceeding what they had suffered earlier under the alien rule of the Magyars at any rate in peace-time. Until recently membership of the sect was confined almost exclusively to peasants or village craftsmen; now a small upper crust had formed, consisting of prosperous merchants and entrepreneurs as well as well-to-do farmers. But sectarian discipline still prevailed so that the wealthy minority obeyed the sect's ban on bearing arms with the same strictness as did the economically underprivileged majority. Throughout the interwar years there were usually several hundred Nazarenes in Yugoslav jails for refusing compulsory military service. The situation seems to have worsened in the 1930s. Sentences of ten years' imprisonment with hard labour recurred with surprising frequency; four to eight years was quite normal. Moreover, since Yugoslav conscripts remained liable to conscription until the age of fifty, they might well seem destined to spend a large portion of their youth and middle years in jail; this situation applied equally to those Nazarenes who had been conscripted under previous Magyar rule. As one middle-aged conscript (in 1927) remarked ironically: "I have been imprisoned by the Magyars and I shall be in prison again here. All this has passed before over my head." The prison experience often proved destructive of health; mistreatment was sporadic though by no means unknown, especially in military prisons. Accounts of harassment, and even torture, of Nazarene prisoners appeared from time to time in opposition Yugoslav newspapers.

All this happened despite the readiness of Nazarene conscripts to accept assignment to such noncombatant branches of the army as the medical corps or the pioneers, along with the arms drill that was obligatory for medical or other noncombatant draftees as for combatant soldiers. Nazarenes had done this in pre-war Hungary – on the understanding, of course, that the handling of weapons would never entail their actual use. "Thou shalt not kill" and "Resist not evil" remained obligatory for the Nazarene under all circumstances. Leaders of the sect, moreover, had even proposed to the Ministry of War a longer period of service for their conscripted members than the normal term if only some kind of noncombatant work would be guaranteed them. The government remained unwilling to make such a concession, arguing that to do so would constitute an invitation for shirkers to join the sect. Once or twice some imprisoned Nazarenes were amnestied as a result of international pressure but official indulgence went no further than that.

The Nazarenes in interwar Rumania were drawn mainly (though not exclusively) from the country's newly acquired Magyar minority. This fact made them doubly unpopular with Rumanian nationalists; and they suffered many hardships on this account from the country's increasingly authoritarian governments. Nazarene conscripts, along with other pacifist sectarians, all received rough handling from the army: two years in jail for a first refusal and then up to five more years on a second refusal to become soldiers. As in Yugoslavia, no provision existed for C.Os. to serve in a noncombatant capacity.

In Russia the existence of several million sectarians, who were hostile to the power structure of the state and rejected the authority of the Russian Orthodox Church, could have provided a potentially rich mission field for pacifist propaganda. Some of the sects, including the most numerous, the Baptists, already nurtured pacifist sympathies; they had provided some conscientious objectors during the recent war and the troubled times that immediately followed. There were also large Mennonite settlements in the south of the country.

At first, therefore, the outlook for pacifism in the new Soviet Union looked promising. As a result of representations from the C.Os.' defense organization known as the United Council of Religious Groups and Communities, which was led by Tolstoy's former secretary Vladimir Chertkov,[1] a decree was issued on 4 January 1919 that provided not merely alternative civilian service but unconditional exemption for those whose conscience forbade them to undertake such service. The machinery of exemption was placed almost entirely in the hands of the United Council. True, exemption was confined to religious applicants and the wording of the decree seemed to imply that membership in a pacifist denomination was needed, nevertheless, apart from the British provisions of 1916, the decree was more liberal than any legislation hitherto dealing with conscientious objection.

By subsequent amendments to the decree, however, the administrative functions of the United Council were whittled away and the Council was dissolved in 1921. The Soviet government may have been alarmed by the fact that by 1920 in the Moscow area alone some 30,000 persons had come forward as conscientious objectors. In November 1923 exemption was confined to members of certain specific pacifist sects (among which the Tolstoyans were not included) and in the following year further restriction took place when only birthright members were declared eligible for exemption. Many Mennonites were still able to serve as noncombatants in the Red Army.[2] Finally, in April 1929 the last of the pacifist organizations – the Tolstoyan Vegetarian Society in Moscow – was closed down. All open pacifist activity ceased. Although very limited provision for conscientious objectors was included in the Military Service Law of 1930, it had vanished altogether by 1939 on the pretext that such provision was no longer necessary; no applications for exemption, the government claimed, had been submitted during the previous two years.

Among members of Lenin's entourage there were some who had been sympathetic to the conscientious objector stand and had worked alongside Tolstoyans and nonresistant sectaries in defiance of the Tsarist government. The Marxist Vladimir Bonch-Bruevich, the Dukhobors' friend, was one of these; after the Bolshevik Revolution he became a prominent figure in Soviet political, cultural and academic life.[3] From the mid-twenties on, however, Stalin's destruction of the old Bolsheviks, his intensified campaign against all manifestations of religion as a counter-revolutionary element, the purges of the thirties, and the fervent Great Russian nationalism that eventually re-emerged under his leadership created an atmosphere hostile to the spread, even on a limited scale, of pacifist ideas. The Soviet inspired peace movement of the interwar years (like the post–World War II communist peace movement) was for export; home-grown pacifism was ruthlessly suppressed. That there were objectors to military service throughout the Stalinist era is certain; some evidently succeeded in getting themselves assigned to noncombatant duties, others were imprisoned or shot. A veil of silence still hangs over their fate; only one fact is certain, that they were increasingly fewer in number and utterly isolated.

We may mention here the presence in neighboring Finland, which until 1917 was attached to the Russian Empire, of Tolstoyans as well as of Protestant pacifists and nonreligious pacifist antimilitarists. The latter included socialists like Yrjö Kallinen, from 1907 an active member of the Social Democratic Party. (In the years 1946–1948 Kallinen was Minister of Defense, the only pacifist ever to hold that position; during his tenure of office he even promoted publicly the idea of Finland's unilateral disarmament as an example to the world.) However, even if they included an internationally known figure in the person of the prison reformer Mathilda Wrede, Finland's Elizabeth Fry, who was active in the Fellowship of Reconciliation in the 1920s, Finnish pacifists were few in number. They were drawn from members of the Swedish minority as well as from ethnic Finns. During the interwar years only strictly religious conscientious objection gained legal recognition; except in some "very delicate cases" objectors, who refused military service on ethical or political grounds, were normally jailed. Whereas the Military Service Act of 1922 allowed solely noncombatant army duties for C.Os., by the Act of 1931 those recognized as C.Os. could choose alternative civilian service. But they had to serve eight months longer than the regular conscripts. During World War II a few non-religious objectors were shot, including Arndt Pekurinen, a leader of the radical pacifist Antimilitarist Union, while a number of others, especially Jehovah's Witnesses and Pentecostals, underwent rigorous imprisonment.

In Italy, an overwhelmingly Catholic country, which like Russia succumbed early to totalitarian dictatorship, the interwar years saw little interest in pacifism *sensu stricto*. The priest politician, Don Luigi Sturzo, had espoused a liberal internationalism before the advent of Mussolini to power in 1922 and did so thereafter in exile. But the fascist dictatorship effectively closed the door to any organized manifestations in favor of peace, not to speak of absolute pacifism. All the more surprising, therefore, is the appearance in 1932 of an isolated conscientious objector, opposed to every kind of war, in the person of Claudio Baglietto, a promising young philosopher and literary historian attached to the prestigious Scuola Normale Superiore in Pisa.[4]

The twenty-four-year-old Baglietto had left Italy in June of that year on a scholarship for study abroad obtained for him by Giovanni Gentile, Italy's foremost philosopher and an ardent supporter of Fascism. It came as a shock to the latter when his young protégé not long afterwards wrote to tell him of his decision to refuse on religious grounds to serve in the army: "After much thought over the last few months and after deep consideration of all that could be argued on the other side, I have become convinced that to kill is not admissible at all even in self-defense, and therefore not in defense of the State either, because not to kill is always spiritually of greater advantage." After debating within himself whether to return home and face the consequences or remain abroad, Baglietto decided that the latter choice, if less heroic, was nevertheless a more reasonable one. Gentile did his best to shake Baglietto's resolve but without success. (The exiled Baglietto was to die prematurely in Geneva, in 1940.) For the fascist philosopher the young man's rejection of military service seemed inexplicable, indeed profoundly disturbing. He viewed it as a reflection of an "intellectual and moral disintegration," for which he could not account.[5] We would assess fascist Italy's lonely objector to military service differently.

In contrast to Italy antimilitarism in Spain spread during the interwar years among leftwing socialists and anarchosyndicalists, taking the form of draft evasion and in Catalunya, with the establishment of Spain's Second Republic in 1931, of open refusal of conscription. A group of absolutist war resisters (*Liga Español de Refractarios a la Guerra*) emerged in early 1936, under the leadership of two intrepid intellectuals, José Brocca and Amparo Poch y Gaston and after Popular Front government had replaced rightwing rule at the center. However, when civil war broke out in July of that year, most leftwing antimilitarists (like some former pacifists outside Spain) were to support armed resistance to General Franco's rebellion. The absolutists now faced a difficult situation. Numerically insignificant and moreover sympathizing deeply with the republican cause, they felt nevertheless that a nonviolent alternative existed to abject submission to injustice and that, therefore, they must remain loyal to their pacifist vision. As Brocca. wrote, "the people of Spain had no other way open to them but to fight"; in the existing situation antiwar propaganda was indeed inappropriate. Pacifists, in Spain and outside, must therefore express their total rejection of war through "humanitarian aid" to its victims. Franco's victory in March 1939 put an end for the time being to the existence of pacifist activity in Spain; its proponents went to jail or into exile. The movement of *insumisos*, which began in the 1970s and included both pacifist and nonpacifist objectors, long remained unaware of its predecessor in the 1930s.[6]

Interwar France remained largely, though by no means entirely immune to pacifism in its Anglo-Saxon form, for a minority of pacifist clergy and laymen existed within the small but intellectually vigorous Protestant Reformed Church. However, the hard-won respect of their church did not prevent the sentencing of pastors like Henri Roser or Philippe Vernier to long and repeated terms of imprisonment for their failure to answer the call to the colors.

More numerous than the religious pacifists were France's "integral pacifists," grouped during the 1930s chiefly in the *Ligue Internationale des Combatants de la Paix* (International League of Fighters for Peace). These people were all men and women of the left: Félicien Challaye, Camille Drevet, René Gerin, Victor Méric, Georges Pioch, Marianne Rauze, to mention the names of just a few prominent members of the movement. (The philosopher Alain [Emile-Auguste Chartier] and the novelist Jean Giono also shared most of the views of the integral pacifists on war and peace while not themselves advocating conscientious objection.) Their opposition to all forms of contemporary warfare was in essence humanitarian, though not derived from any religious creed; they believed that war in the twentieth century would destroy civilized life on the planet and leave only the vanquished at its conclusion, whichever side ostensibly won. They were also deeply concerned over such issues as alleged German war-guilt, colonialism, and conscientious objection to military service. They attacked bitterly those "conservative" peace advocates who supported collective security and the concept of a defensive war, and they split with their comrades on the left when the latter approved the idea of armed action against the fascist powers. According to Méric, "peace is only possible and lasting by total and rapid disarmament, without concerning oneself about the neighbour."[7] Even after Nazi Germany rearmed the integral pacifists continued to advocate *rapprochement* with that country, including treaty revision, as well as *détente* with Mussolini's Italy. On the Spanish Civil War, though, they divided. Gerin, for instance, considered that in Spain the Franco forces were "comparable to an individual enemy," whom only a Tolstoyan would fail to oppose by arms. He regarded the resistance of the Spanish government as equivalent to the action of a domestic police force engaged in the repression of crime. "It was the occasional duty of the citizen to aid his police force."[8] But a sizeable minority of members of the integralist *Ligue* strongly disagreed with Gerin and defended the absolute pacifist position rejecting all varieties of warfare, civil as well as international.

When Munich came, the integral pacifists supported the pact while still voicing their principled opposition to Fascism. And it was Gerin who in September 1938 wrote: "Courage, comrades! The treaties are being revised *without war*! This is indeed what we have been demanding in our propaganda. But we never dared to hope that we would be listened to so soon."[9] The outbreak of hostilities a year later brought the existence of the *Ligue* to an end. Its supporters were by now in complete disarray; the movement indeed never recovered from the blow dealt it by the collapse of all its political aspirations.[10]

In the Netherlands, until his premature death in 1938, the talented anarcho-pacifist writer, Bart de Ligt, developed in a series of books and articles the concept of revolutionary antimilitarism.[11] At the same time, a group of clergy and laity, drawn from the country's major Protestant denominations, espoused a radical pacifism – based on their Christian faith – that was close in spirit to the antiwar position of the agnostic de Ligt. They began their activities in 1924 with the founding of a society, which they called *Church and Peace* (*Kerk en Vrede*); it continued to function until suppressed by the Nazi invaders in 1941.[12]

Membership in *Church and Peace* reached its climax in 1933 falling gradually over the remaining prewar years.[13] The society possessed a lively journal run in an ecumenical spirit, which discussed world problems from a Christian pacifist viewpoint. Conscientious objectors were given support though more emphasis was laid on the positive aspects of nonviolence. It was largely due to the initiative of *Church and Peace* leaders that the International Union of Anti-Militarist Ministers and Clergymen came into existence in 1928. After Hitler gained power in Germany and with the impact in the Netherlands of Karl Barth's theology, strongly opposed to pacifism, some members left the organization in the course of the thirties – even though *Church and Peace* repeatedly emphasized its deep opposition to the Nazi ideology. At the same time, though, it never ceased to urge unilateral disarmament and nonviolent resistance as the proper Christian response to fascist aggression.

Small pacifist groups emerged in the interwar years in the Scandinavian countries as well as in Switzerland. But somewhat ironically, it was in Germany, a former enemy country, that Anglo-American pacifism made its greatest impact during the decade and a half following 1918, until Hitler's accession to power put a stop to all pacifist activity. The pre-1914 peace movement in Central Europe had possessed notable exponents in the German-Austrian, Alfred H. Fried, and the Bohemian Baroness von Suttner (née Kinská). But this traditional form of "pacificism," as everywhere on the European continent, remained rather academic, socially conservative, and opposed to political radicalism of any kind. It upheld the right of national states to wage defensive war and reacted coldly to the idea of individual resistance to military service. In Weimar Germany the radical pacifist societies were frowned on not merely by the political center and right but also by the social democrats who, like most socialists on the European continent, looked askance at individual war resistance. Pacifists like Carl von Ossietzky, editor of *Die Weltbühne*, who in the late thirties became both a prisoner in a Nazi concentration camp and a winner of the Nobel Peace Prize, were foremost in the campaign against German militarism and secret rearmament. They opposed the efforts of the right wing to cast exclusive blame for Germany's misfortunes on the Versailles peace treaty (at this point running counter to most pacifists in the victorious countries, who saw in Germany's treatment at Versailles an act of injustice that stood at the very root of the world's troubles). The energetic Fritz Küster, editor of the militantly pacifist *Das Andere Deutschland*, the circulation of which rose at one period to 15,000 copies, collected among his fellow countrymen pledges to refuse war service or support a belligerent government.[14] Among Küster's associates on his paper was a former commander in the Imperial navy now turned radical pacifist, Heinz Kraschutzki, who played an important role in the German section of the War Resisters International and, throughout the Weimar period, stood resolutely against resurgent militarism. He called repeatedly on the republican government to admit Imperial Germany's responsibility for unleashing war in 1914, incurring accusations of treason from the right-wing for this kind of activity. Societies arose dedicated to the furtherance of (potential) conscientious objection, whether humanist or religious in inspiration, and to propagating the slogan: "No More War." A lively *Linkspazifismus* (Left Pacifism), under the leadership of Kurt Hiller, advocated refusal of military service in all wars between capitalist states, while reserving the right to defend the workers' fatherland. Even among German Catholics, whose church hitherto had been everywhere hostile to the radical pacifist stand, a peace association embracing both priests and laity came into being with a program not unsympathetic to the position of the conscientious objector to twentieth-century war; its guiding spirit was a Dominican, Father Franziskus Stratmann. But time was to show that neither enthusiastic public meetings and crowded demonstrations on behalf of peace nor mass signatures to antiwar declarations signified much once the public mind and the machinery of state were bent toward war by an unscrupulous demagogue.

It was, of course, the absence of conscription, along with war disillusionment and the postwar experience in Germany and Austria – a result of these countries' defeat in World War I and the treaties imposed on them at its conclusion – that had provided an opportunity there for proselytizing for the cause of conscientious objection. Disenchantment with war and the return of the voluntary system, along with the legacy of endurance bequeathed by their objectors of 1914–18, were the main reasons why, in the United States and Great Britain, throughout the interwar years, pacifism – or war resistance, to use the term increasingly favored by those considering pacifism too negative – flourished even more freely than among their recent enemies.

In the United States the Fellowship of Reconciliation (FOR) soon showed itself to be the most vigorous and intellectually alive exponent of pacifism. Its political program will be discussed in greater detail later in this chapter. Apart from a very few small societies pledged also to war resistance, pacifists who wished to join an organization but could not accept the FOR's religious basis had only the War Resisters League (WRL), established in 1924, to choose from. Among its founders three pacifist women played a key role: Jessie Wallace Hughan, Tracy Mygatt, and Frances Witherspoon. All three had been active during the recent conflict in the antiwar movement; all three were convinced socialists and ardent campaigners for women's rights. In the WRL Christian pacifists worked harmoniously alongside the more numerous humanist war resisters. However, this body, which had less than a thousand members in 1928, grew very slowly, reaching a peak of 12,000 members in 1942 after the outbreak of World War II. Both the FOR and

WRL were predominantly middle-class: teachers, students, Protestant clergy, and housewives provided the bulk of their membership. In the thirties and early forties denominational pacifist fellowships were formed within the major Protestant churches: Methodists, Baptists, Episcopalians,[15] Lutherans,[16] Disciples of Christ, Unitarians, and Universalists. Once again, however, numbers here too remained small; it was the ministry rather than the laity which provided the backbone of these groups. Several leading pacifist clergy of this period belonged to churches that hitherto had produced few pacifists: John Nevin Sayre, for instance, was an Episcopalian while John Haynes Holmes was a Unitarian. Their influence in spreading the message of Christian pacifism extended, though, far beyond their own denominations.

The British FOR, unlike the American section, did not stand in the center of pacifist activities. But among its members it numbered such weighty churchmen and pillars of the establishment as Canon Charles Raven, chaplain to the King, and the Oxford theologian, Professor L.W. Grensted, as well as the eloquent Methodist preacher and popular Tower Hill orator, Donald (later Lord) Soper, and lay persons of the caliber of George M.L. Davies from Wales or the indefatigable social worker, Muriel Lester, Gandhi's host at Kingsley Hall in London's East End during the Mahatma's visit to England in 1931, or the Cambridge physicist, Alex Wood, who was equally active in the Peace Pledge Union from its foundation in 1936. The FOR in Britain continued to see its task as one of leavening society rather than leading the crusade for a new social order. In numbers much smaller than the American FOR, it concentrated primarily on the still by no means easy task of winning adherents within the Protestant churches to a pacifist interpretation of Christianity; in its efforts it was aided, too, by denominational affiliates.[17]

Just as during World War I conscientious objection in America had been in the main religiously motivated and in Britain both politically and religiously oriented, so in interwar Britain – in contrast to the Christian-based American FOR – its central pacifist organization united the religious and the nonreligious under one umbrella. After the dissolution of the No-Conscription Fellowship in November 1919, a new body had been set up early in 1921 to take its place. But this No More War Movement (NMWM), the leadership of which was provided by the pacifist radicals of the old NCF, lacked something of the drive of the wartime organization. Membership grew rapidly during the twenties but the NMWM did not succeed in mobilizing under its direction the mounting wave of antiwar feeling in the country, which manifested itself toward the end of the decade. In the 1924 parliament which saw the coming to power of the first Labour government, sixteen M.P.s (of whom three were in the government) had been conscientious objectors in the recent war. Many prominent members of the labor movement joined the NMWM, which had socialism as well as pacifism written into its program. Yet the NMWM was not able to draw into its activities the hundreds of thousands of labor supporters who voted for war resistance motions at conferences and congresses. It was only in the mid-thirties, after the deteriorating international situation had led organized labor to abandon its pacifist sympathies and thereby deprived the NMWM of most of its impetus, that anything approaching a pacifist mass movement was generated from the inchoate antimilitarism of the time. The Peace Pledge Union, with which the NMWM fused in 1937, had a membership of around 125,000 shortly before the outbreak of war in 1939. We shall have to return to the PPU for further discussion later in this chapter.[18]

Pacifist Internationals

The pacifist movement found institutional expression not only in national societies but in international organization. The twentieth century indeed has been an age of internationals. Socialist and cooperative internationals, communist "Red" and peasantist "Green" internationals do not exhaust their number. It was natural, therefore, that after the war the ex-conscientious objectors of Britain and America, along with a handful of sympathizers from the former allied, enemy and neutral lands, should band together in some form of fellowship, which would provide a basis, they hoped, for the expansion of the movement beyond its Anglo-American heartland.

Thus the International FOR dates back to a conference held at Bilthoven (Netherlands) in October 1919. There the fifty participants had solemnly acknowledged "each his own share in the sins of his own country in connection with the war and the making of so-called peace," and proclaimed their "shame for their part in the failure of their respective churches to maintain a universal spirit during war."[19] Although a few Roman Catholics collaborated in its work, sections affiliated with the International FOR drew supporters chiefly from Protestant clergy and laity. Its strongly emphasized Christ-centeredness remained a potential barrier to its spread to lands with a different religious tradition.

This religious exclusiveness did not feature in the program of the War Resisters' International (WRI), which was set up in 1921 – under the provisional name *Paco*, the Esperanto word for peace – with four affiliated sections located in Great Britain, the Netherlands, Germany and Austria. The WRI was prepared to accept into membership any group whose members individually assented to the International's pledge: "War is a crime against humanity. We therefore are determined not to support any kind of war and to strive for the removal of all causes of war."[20] This meant, however, that, whereas pacifists of any or no religious persuasion were free to join the WRI, organizations that did not require an individual pledge of war resistance were debarred from affiliating. Thus, if the international FOR would have had to refuse membership to Mahatma Gandhi (had he applied), the WRI could not enter into full communion with such bodies as the Women's International League for Peace and Freedom, the International Cooperative Women's Guild, the leftist International Anti-Militarist Bureau or even the peace committees of the Society of Friends, because they contained members who could not accept the full pacifist position. We must add to such dogmatic rigidity as a factor in slowing down expansion the fact that among the less socially committed pacifists there were many who felt unable to accept the nonviolent social revolution, to which both the International FOR and the WRI were explicitly committed in their programs, and that numerically large groups of potential conscientious objectors – the Seventh-day Adventists and the Jehovah's Witnesses, for instance, or most American Mennonite communities – remained aloof, if not actually hostile, to any collaboration with the pacifists outside their own fold. Though the WRI by 1939 could claim fifty-four sections in twenty-four separate countries, in fact it had failed so far to make much headway outside Great Britain and the United States. Elsewhere its affiliated groups mostly remained tiny conventicles alternatively ignored or suppressed by the powers that be.

By the early thirties civilian service schemes for conscientious objectors had been set up in all the Scandinavian countries as well as in the Netherlands. But apart from Austria and Weimar Germany compulsory military service remained the rule throughout the European continent. Even the Friends, whose name had become a byword for peaceableness in many countries on account of their postwar relief activities, failed anywhere to root Quakerism deeply, in part because of the difficulties involved in adjusting a pacifist religious ethic to a conscriptionist country. For some war resisters numbers of adherents were a matter of complete disinterest: what was important was the purity of the idea. The French novelist Romain Rolland, during the 1920s one of the most outstanding Western exponents of the Gandhian philosophy, spoke for these in his letter of greeting to a Ukranian conscientious objector imprisoned in the Soviet Union:

I want to tell you [he wrote] that I am never worrying about the near or future success of ideals which I know to be true, healthy and sacred. The success does not concern us. We are servants of our ideals. We have only to serve them bravely and faithfully. Whether we shall be victors or vanquished this matters little. It is a joy to serve the eternal and to sacrifice oneself for it. I do not love at all those who so ardently expect a sort of human paradise on earth, and I have no confidence in them. These are weak people who in order to act morally feel that they must be promised an earthly reward, either for themselves or for their own people. The reward lies in your own self – it does not come from outside. It lies in our faith, our struggles, our courage.[21]

But probably few pacifists, however dedicated, shared Rolland's seemingly complete indifference to earthly success or his contempt for numbers. They would have been happy to see pacifist movements arise on the European continent as broadly based as the American and British ones (they would likewise have been pleased if Anglo-American pacifism had been able to further extend its influence), and they were depressed at their inability to make any clearly perceptible impact in these politically important lands. "Regarded from the socio-logical standpoint we are today a sect," complained in 1928 a young pacifist scholar of Jewish background named Hans Kohn, who had recently emigrated from Prague to Palestine. "We must become a movement," he went on. "It is undoubtedly of great spiritual value that we have begun as a sect, a small group, a community of people united by one idea, who have gone out to seek to discover men who already belong inwardly to this sect." If pacifism was to prove an effective agent for creating a peaceable world, however, it must advance beyond the sectarian stage in its evolution to become a full fledged movement. Kohn pointed to the major obstacle to development: conscription. "If we wish to free the world from the compulsion to kill men," he concluded, "then we must strain every nerve against compulsory military service."[22]

But throughout most of the European continent, and especially in its central and eastern areas, conscription possessed an almost sacral quality; it formed part of the national myth. To refuse military service even on religious grounds appeared to most citizens of these countries to challenge not only their hard-won security but the very idea of the nation state. (Even in the United States immigrants, like Rosika Schwimmer the prominent peace advocate and feminist from Hungary in 1929, were refused citizenship because they were unwilling to promise to defend the Constitution by arms.) It was with the notion of providing for youth a substitute service – something along the lines of

William James's "moral equivalent of war" – which would be acceptable to those patriots still clinging to the older martial concepts that Pierre Ceresole, a Swiss convert to Quakerism, initiated in 1920 a *Service Civile Internationale* (International Voluntary Service for Peace – IVSP).[23] Its volunteers who were recruited on an international basis with any young person eligible, whether pacifist or not, undertook manual labor of the pick-and-shovel variety. They worked on land reclamation or afforestation; they helped in the reconstruction of towns and villages which had been devastated in earthquakes or floods; they participated in building projects for the needy. Ceresole always hoped that his IVSP would act as a prototype in conscriptionist lands for government-approved schemes of alternative national civilian service. In his native Switzerland there was no choice for a conscientious objector between noncombatant service in the army or prison, and until middle age he himself went regularly to jail for refusing to participate in the annual periods of military training. However, the British section of the IVSP, soon the largest and most active, in line with the British tradition of fighting conscription on libertarian grounds opposed this concept of IVSP's functions and wished to dissociate the organization from any compromise with the state. In the United States, on the other hand, in World War II the IVSP was taken as one of the models for the association of government and pacifists in running civilian public service camps for conscientious objectors. How that worked in practice will be discussed in a later chapter.

The postwar attempt to create an effective international pacifist movement failed. Pacifist societies, even in the two countries where the movement had roots going back before 1918, remained extremely small and weak when compared with the numbers and influence of other contemporary political movements. Yet in both the United States and Great Britain, as well as in most European countries, antiwar sentiment grew even after Hitler's accession to power presaged again the world's descent to war. Abhorrence of war was by no means equivalent to pacifism: the longing for a peaceable world was felt by millions who had no sympathy with war resistance. Even so, during the twenties and thirties, hundreds of thousands of men and women (especially young people) were vaguely attracted to the pacifist idea. In the English-speaking world many of them toyed with the idea of refusing to fight should another war occur. They were not, for the most part, associated with any pacifist organization; if they were, this often did not go beyond signing some pledge of war resistance. We must now consider more closely what pacifists were saying about war and peace during the years between the two wars.

The Pacifist Critique of War

The Moral Approach

The center of the pacifist argument against war, whether clothed in theological terms or urged on purely secular grounds, was moral protest. The liberal pacifist publicist Oswald Garrison Villard's description of war as "the sum of all villainies" is one with the Mennonite theologian Donovan E. Smucker's cry: "War is sin! War is hell! War is organized atrocity."[24] Christian antimilitarists called for the recovery of the pacifist vision of the early church, which had been obliterated with Constantine's conversion and the subsequent subservience of church to state. A Dutch theologian and leader of *Church and Peace*, G.J. Heering, wrote an influential book significantly entitled (in English) *The Fall of Christianity* (1930), in which he pleaded for a total renunciation of war by the churches.[25] Secular humanist pacifists, on the other hand, linked up with the eighteenth-century Enlightenment's vision of a world with reason enthroned, from which war would be forever banished.[26]

The killing of the innocent in modern war was a favorite theme of pacifist literature: women and children would be the first victims of air attack, poison gas, and economic blockade. This surely was a complete negation of both reason and Christian morality. But the waging of war entailed not only material destruction but the mutilation of the human personality; soldiers became mere killing machines obliged to obey the orders of their superior officers, even if they considered them wrong, or face death at the hands of a firing squad. The chief reason, for instance, why the American publicist Milton Mayer opposed war was "because it debases the man in men and exalts the animal." "And," as he wrote in an influential article he entitled "I Think I'll Sit This One Out" (*Saturday Evening Post*, 7 October 1939), "that is what I mean when I say that ... this will degrade humanity." In any case, war always penalized those bearing no responsibility for its outbreak; the really guilty ones might escape. Many pacifists believed that another war, whoever won, would bring the destruction of democracy and the imposition of some form of military dictatorship even in countries which till then had enjoyed parliamentary rule. Pacifists deplored the glamor of war, a relic of the barbaric past; its glorification in ceremonies and monuments was particularly harmful in that it helped to cloak the squalid realities of battle. Youth must be shown a better way in which to expend its energies and idealism than armed struggle. Workcamps on the IVSP model seemed a modest contribution to solving this problem.

In particular, pacifists in their writings pointed to the moral deception practiced by each side in the recent world conflict in order to maintain morale among their citizenry. Governments, including those of Great Britain and the United States, had resorted both to lies to cover up the true causes of the war and the real reasons for its prolongation, and to slandering the enemy with the object of whipping up hatred and the passion of revenge among their own peoples. Arthur Ponsonby, one of the promoters of the Union of Democratic Union and in the twenties and early thirties a chief adviser to the Labour Party on foreign policy, concluded a carefully documented study of the wartime press and propaganda by dramatically asking his readers: "Is further proof needed that international war is a monster born of hypocrisy, fed on falsehood, fattened on humbug, kept alive by superstition, directed to the death and torture of millions, succeeding in no high purpose, degrading to humanity, endangering civilization and bringing forth in its travail a hideous brood of strife, conflict and war, more war?"[27] Many people indeed, and not only pacifists, nursed a sense of having been tricked by the wartime politicians: they felt tricked both as to the war's origins and as to its outcome.

The Utilitarian Approach

The postwar world appeared neither a world fit for heroes to live in nor one in which liberal democracy had securely triumphed. Only in regard to the third battlecry of the victors – a war to end war – did there still remain the possibility of fulfillment. It, too, would prove a delusion, many argued, if militarism was not driven from the civilized world. Two methods were offered for achieving this result: the internationalist and the pacifist solution. During the twenties, allegiance to the League of Nations and advocacy of war resistance had not seemed incompatible. In the next decade the rise of the fascist dictatorships eventually forced a choice between the two. Both internationalists and pacifists, however, made use of roughly the same general case against war. Their opponents, too, were the same: protagonists of national power and prestige.

The enormous cost and wastefulness of modern war – one of the most frequently used arguments in the pacifist press – was one that could be expected to carry weight in an era of economic crisis and rising unemployment. Publicists tended to attribute to the aftermath of war much that was, in fact, due to other causes: increased taxation, for instance, or the depression itself. Villard wrote in 1934: "People are aware that our going to war ... was a useless crime against America, that we got nothing out of it but misery, and that it nearly ruined the Republic we love."[28] As evidence of the "futility" of war, publicists like Villard liked to cite not only the world's economic plight but the host of dictatorships, small and large, which had sprung up after the Paris peace settlement. The settlement itself – the *Versailles Diktat* – was a favorite target of pacifist (and other) writers. Its denial of the right of self-determination to millions was particularly painful to those who had taken the Wilsonian doctrine seriously. Aggressive tendencies on the part of countries like Germany and Italy, which claimed to have been victimized in varying degrees in the settlement, came to be explained as the psychological outcome of their treatment in 1919.

Political pacifism drew strength from the researches of the revisionist school of historians, who, correctly challenging the thesis of the exclusive war guilt of the Central Powers as contained in Article 231 of the Treaty of Versailles, on which the peace settlement seemed to rest, went on in some instances, more controversially, to absolve the ex-enemy countries of any major responsibility for bringing on the recent war. The leading revisionists – Sidney B. Fay and Harry Elmer Barnes in the United States; G.P. Gooch, G. Lowes Dickinson, and Raymond Beazley in Britain, to cite the most outstanding – were not pacifists, though some of the school's British representatives had been vocal wartime critics of allied diplomacy. (In postwar Germany, on the other hand, interest in the war guilt question, *Kriegsschuldfrage*, and the desire to minimize Imperial Germany's part in causing the outbreak of war were strongest on the right, with exponents of Germany's exclusive guilt located on the extreme left and in pacifist circles.) If, however, all the participants in the war had been more or less equally responsible – or equally innocent: it came to roughly the same thing – and if it was in the system of alliances, the ever-increasing armaments, the imperialist rivalries (as the more moderate revisionist historians were arguing with great cogency) that the blame for the war lay, then it was not illogical to conclude that, since even with the League of Nations, the system still remained basically almost intact, only a total repudiation of war would suffice to bring about the diplomatic revolution needed to establish peace on firm foundations.

Secret diplomacy, excessive nationalism, the struggle for overseas markets, and the arms race had, then, really been the responsible factors in bringing about the last war. If there were guilty men in addition to such impersonal forces driving to war, pacifist writers sought them not so much in the politicians, who were more often than not mere cat's-paws unable themselves to shape events, as in the armament manufacturers. These men, it was believed (not without justification in some cases), were ready to foment wars in various parts of the globe in pursuit of their private profit. Pacifists disagreed as to the exact extent of the war guilt that should be assigned to members of the "Bloody International." To many pacifists the nationalization of the arms industry, the solution proposed by such writers as the nonpacifist English Quaker Philip Noel-Baker, though a step in the right direction, would not in itself banish war from the globe. Militarism, as developments in the Soviet Union were proving, was not a capitalist monopoly. The sinister machinations of armaments manufacturers remained, however, a favorite theme in popular expositions of pacifism,[29] and it was also the subject of learned tomes and Congressional investigations.

The utilitarian case against war rested very largely on economic foundations. Liberal pacifists, like the American Villard, united with pacifist socialists, like the British Labour Party leader George Lansbury, in seeing the contemporary world divided into "have" and "have-not" powers. Among the latter were Germany, Italy, and Japan. France, Great Britain and, though to a lesser extent, the United States were regarded as sated powers clinging desperately to their imperial supremacy. The not unnatural claims of the "have-nots" for a greater share in the booty thus led to the possibility of renewed war – or at least to the perpetual military preparedness of the "have" powers against attempts at dispossessing them. Among the many pacifists who were also socialists, the belief prevailed that war was inherent in the capitalist system and could only be finally eliminated by the expropriation of the capitalists (a view that led some to abandon nonviolence in the class struggle).

Utilitarian pacifists – and religious and ethical-humanist pacifists when using utilitarian arguments against war, as they increasingly tended to do – were not so much relying on the basic goodness of humankind as on its essential teachability. The had faith "in the ultimate reasonableness of mankind."[30] If "man" could once be convinced that arms did not give a nation lasting security and that armed conflict in the modern world would ultimately be disastrous for all, he could ultimately be persuaded to abandon the war method in favor of other means of solving disputes. In the age of the bombing plane, bacteriological warfare, and poison gas, the individual could further the realization of the utilitarian principle of the greatest happiness of the greatest number only by an unequivocal renunciation of war. In the twentieth century, pacifism rather than militarism was the means for the survival of the fittest.

Basically, though, the utilitarian pacifism that emerged in strength after 1918 derived its inspiration from humanitarian sources. It expressed the deep moral repulsion felt by many at the inhumanity of modern war. It was not only, then, a utilitarian form of pacifism but essentially a humanitarian form of pacifism. As Martin Ceadel aptly comments: "Humanitarian pacifism [of this kind] was, in fact, to prove the major pacifist innovation of the inter-war years, though it was not to come into its own until the thirties when the imminence of aerial holocausts focused attention on the pain and suffering to be expected in the next war."[31]

Pacifist Proposals for Peace

There was no consensus among pacifists on methods for achieving peace, if we disregard their fundamental agreement on the moral imperative of war resistance. Many pacifists saw salvation in a reformed League of Nations which, no longer representing mainly the interests of the chief victors of 1918, would strive to act impartially in promoting the welfare of all (others put their faith in schemes for world government or federal union under which the nation states of the past would gradually wither away). The case for a reformed League, and the way to achieve it, was put cogently by Aldous Huxley in 1936 in a letter to Leonard Woolf, who had charged pacifists of acting "like ostriches" in the current international situation. Huxley told him:

What the pacifist suggests is ... eminently reasonable ... In the present circumstances this policy expresses itself in the ... proposal to call a conference at which the dissatisfied powers [would] be asked to express their grievances: [an] honest attempt on the part of the satisfied to find out how many of these grievances [could] be met and in what way [,] might have a chance of securing peace. Banding together in military alliances for collective security will certainly not achieve this end. The other, pacifist way may not succeed; but on the other hand it might. And if it succeeded only partially, the international atmosphere [would] be cleared and a chance given for the reconstruction of the League on a more satisfactory basis.[32]

In the United States the "outlawry of war," a slogan that became popular toward the end of the twenties, had its supporters too in the pacifist movement. Pacifists, however, were more inclined to dismiss it as a blind alley which would lead the movement away from its main tasks.

Disarmament gained the enthusiastic support of almost all pacifists for they believed that the very existence of armaments threatened peace; armaments entailed the danger of a renewed arms race and contributed indirectly to war by increasing the world's economic *malaise*. Unilateral disarmament, which would both act by force of example as a powerful factor in favor of peace and lessen the likelihood of invasion by removing any pretext for it, was certainly much preferable to no disarmament at all. Most pacifists, however, welcomed efforts to achieve multilateral disarmament by graduated stages. In the United States, for instance, they supported in large numbers the activities of the National Council for the Prevention of War which, under the able leadership of the Quaker Frederick J. Libby, worked for a step-by-step reduction of armaments. A few approved, as a compromise solution in a world where nonviolence hitherto had made little headway, the pooling of arms in an international police force, which would act only on the orders of an impartial international tribunal against those actually offending instead of against whole nations. Pacifists for the most part did not approve attempts merely to ban the most fearsome weapons of war – bombers, submarines, poison gas, etc. – while leaving more conventional weapons intact. The attack should be against war itself.

American pacifists called for the renunciation by their country of the alleged right to intervene in such areas as Central and South America in order to protect its citizens and their property rights. At a time when the achievement of international agreement to its abandonment seemed possible, British pacifists severely criticized the retention by their government of the bombing plane on the pretext that the bomber was essential for maintaining order in the outlying parts of the British Empire. In urging treaty revision in Europe and the abolition of tariff barriers, and the sharing of the world's raw materials and markets overseas on a basis equitable to all nations and by means of periodically held international conferences, British and American pacifists combined forces once again with the rest of the peace movement which did not share their belief in total war renunciation. They joined forces, too, in combating the various manifestations of militarism in national life – from the sale of military toys to army and navy appropriations.[33] Officers' training corps and cadet corps were denounced, for the military training of youth ran directly contrary to the pacifist desire to educate the young in a spirit free from narrow nationalism. Pacifists led the struggle against conscription in lands which retained compulsory military service.

However, the one aspect of pacifist tactics that was unique to their movement and not shared by any other nonpacifist political group was individual war resistance, a personal pledge to refuse participation in any future war. Many who gave this pledge, especially during the 1920s and early 1930s, believed that they were thereby giving their allegiance to a mass movement that could successfully sweep away any government that attempted to commit a country to war. Many pacifists, especially in the United States, were convinced that the man in the street was basically in favor of peace and had a natural inclination toward the war resistance movement – this, despite pacifists' belief in the need for extensive peace education to eradicate militarist preconceptions in the populace. The great scientist, Albert Einstein, argued that if no more than 2 percent of the male population of the globe refused to fight, this fact alone would stop all future wars, since there would not be prisons enough to hold so many conscientious objectors. No government, moreover, would dare to launch a war with so large a section of the men of military age in opposition.

Pacifists everywhere, whether regarding Einstein's proposal as feasible or not (and there were some like Romain Rolland who felt such a gesture ineffectual in the age of the bombing plane and bacteriological warfare and put their faith instead in a nonviolent social revolution), considered the organization of a war resistance movement as in itself an important, if not the decisive factor in preventing war. Governments, being uncertain of their citizens' readiness to fight, would be forced to pursue peaceable policies and to abandon war as a permissible method in the last resort; a renunciation that even the most peace-loving national administration had been most unwilling to make hitherto. In the second place, pacifists saw in public declarations of war resistance a valuable means for publicizing their cause and furthering its development. Only in this way could the state's control – directly or indirectly – of the major communications media be counteracted to some degree. Thirdly, they argued on the basis particularly of the 1914 experience that, at least in regard to modern war, it was impossible for the ordinary citizen to judge the pros and cons of the situation immediately prior to the outbreak of war. Each side emitted such a smoke barrage of propaganda that it was impossible at the time to see through to the truth; this alone served to destroy what the French antimilitarist writer Georges Demartial called "the myth of wars of legitimate defense." Lastly, of course, the case for war resistance rested on the moral objection. This objection was fundamental to it, whether the moral impulse derived from religion or from reason.

Adherence to pacifism did not necessarily entail allegiance to political or social reform, let alone nonviolent revolution. In England Quakers were by tradition supporters of the Liberal Party; in the United States they had been in many areas firmly Republican. Many religious pacifists eschewed all political activity; even among the nonreligious there were some who expressed disinterest in politics and felt that they could join effectively in the struggle against war without the need to wrestle with other social evils. In the interwar years, however, pacifists outside the sects mostly gave some degree of assent to the ideas of the left: we have already seen this pattern emerging in our survey of conscientious objection in World War I.

Capitalism is based on competition – thus ran the argument linking pacifism with the need to remold the social order – and its motive force is the exploitation of one human being by another. The competitive society merely reproduces the life of the jungle in more sophisticated terms. It is not sufficient for pacifists to say that they refuse to participate in war. They must go further and work for a classless society in which cooperation replaces competition as the goal of human actions. The struggle to win overseas markets for the surplus products of the developed capitalist countries had led to the recent war and would once again end in a similar holocaust if steps were not taken to counter this drive to war. Without tackling the roots of war in a faulty economic system, moral protest remained an empty gesture. "Only when countries adopt a Socialist form of government will the world be finally secure for peace." Pacifists like Lansbury argued that, just as a failure to eliminate capitalism would in the long run frustrate efforts to abolish war, so war and preparation for war would undermine the conditions for a socialist order both through the enormous waste of material resources for purposes of destruction and by the annihilation of the moral values for which socialism stood. Most socialist pacifists withheld assent from the Marxist prognosis of the inevitability of war under capitalism – or at least they believed that war might be indefinitely postponed, thus giving time for the transformation of the political structure in a socialist direction. Lansbury expressed this kind of revisionism when he wrote: "Just as capitalism had been compelled for its own safety to make concessions to the workers, so I believe it is not unreasonable to expect that the same system will be compelled to make concessions to the cause of world peace."[34] Such concessions would include a more equitable sharing of the world's economic resources by means of international control of colonies, removal of trade barriers, and periodic world conferences to discuss political and economic issues threatening the peace.

Pacifists remained suspicious, however, of the etatist tendencies in socialism. The decentralized cooperative commonwealth was their ideal and not the monolithic workers' state.[35] Nurtured in Britain on the traditions of guild socialism and based in the United States on the moral conscience as exemplified in the social gospel, the pacifist movement in these two countries tended to regard a society which retained a vital local democracy alongside a developed system of communal welfare as the best guarantee for a peaceable world. On the European continent pacifists were often drawn from circles influenced by the libertarian anarcho-syndicalist tradition. They stressed in even bolder form the role of the individual and of local self-government in maintaining a pacifist society.

Finally, mention must be made of the not inconsiderable number of pacifists who rejected political action of any kind in favor of what has aptly been called "the politics of the unpolitical." One of the most gifted spokesmen of this school of pacifist thought has defined it as "the politics of those who desire to be pure in heart: the politics of men without personal ambition; of those who have not desired wealth or an unequal share of worldly possessions; of those who have always striven, whatever their race or condition, for human values and not for national or sectional interests." "The Sermon on the Mount is the source of all the politics of the unpolitical."[36] This view derived much of its inspiration from Tolstoy; in the contemporary world Gandhi was its patron saint. It leaned toward a renunciation of this world, or at least of its materialism and its hedonistic culture. It did not usually follow Tolstoy or Gandhi, however, in their downgrading of artistic creativity. Indeed, for the artist and writer it provided a faith that expressed both their repugnance for a world that appeared to reject the aesthetic values they cherished most and their revulsion from the institution of war that threatened with destruction, and even total extinction, the creative impulses of humanity.

One variant in the pacifist politics of the unpolitical was provided in the second half of the thirties by the English novelist, Aldous Huxley, who, with his colleague the publicist Gerald Heard, then transplanted it just before World War II to the sunnier climate of California. The Huxley-Heard thesis was also an outgrowth of the Tolstoy-Gandhi symbiosis. For Huxley and Heard "non-attachment" should be the human ideal: non-attachment to worldly things, whether to persons (e.g., love) or to objects (e.g., greed or ambition) or to emotions (e.g., lust or anger or envy). It was not merely the goals people pursued which should be in consonance with this ideal, the means must be in line with it, too. For good ends can never emerge through the use of evil means. This proposition was argued by Huxley with considerable force and with an impressive wealth of illustrative documentation. He applied it in particular to war to prove war's incompatibility under any circumstances with the ends of a humane and democratic society (a society which he sought in the small community and the self-governing workshop). Huxley's theories were widely discussed at the time and undoubtedly exercised a considerable influence on pacifist thinking in Britain and America.[37] Yet there were few ready to swallow them whole: non-attachment for Huxley and his disciples entailed the practise of meditative union with the Ultimate Reality and the cultivation of asceticism along the lines laid down by Indian Yoga, with pacifists settled in small, self-contained communities, sealed off in this way against the inevitable doom of Western civilization, and the conversion of the pacifist movement into an ascetic – but not necessarily celibate – order of gurus and their followers. A movement that had in the past striven to bring the Kingdom of God down onto earth and to realize the Brotherhood of Man found it difficult to accept in its entirety so other-worldly a doctrine.

Nonviolent Resistance

There was indeed a certain contradiction in Huxley himself. Just as socialist pacifists appeared at times to believe war to be inevitable under capitalism and yet to advocate pacifism as a method of avoiding it even while capitalism remained intact, so Huxley posits a total reorientation of Western society toward a philosophy of non-attachment as the only method of eliminating the evil of war and at the same time preaches nonviolence as an effective resistant to war within a world order still given over to nationalism and "mechanomorphism." We have here perhaps just one further example of the tendency of a political philosophy dedicated to a radical transformation of society unconsciously to accept at times piecemeal reforms as a surrogate for total change.

In his exposition of nonviolent resistance as not only a moral equivalent of war but an effective instrument for preserving the values war was supposed to defend, should a nation decide to abandon its arms, Huxley emphasized the need for training nonviolent cadres. If, he argued, the making of an efficient soldier normally took some three or four years, then the creation of an equally efficient nonviolent resister would require no less a period. "Though mainly preventive," pacifism was also "a technique of conflict – a way of fighting without violence." Therefore, only "trained troops ... soldiers of peace" could successfully undertake nonviolent resistance.[38] Like Gandhi, Huxley was prepared to concede that these soldiers of peace did not have to be saints or mystics to wage successful nonviolent resistance; they did need, however, training in their technique of struggle.

Huxley's ideas on nonviolent resistance were derived in some measure directly from Gandhi. Even more, they were influenced by the writings of two Western exponents of nonviolence: the Dutch ex-pastor and convert to anarchism, Bart de Ligt, and the American ex-lawyer and convert to Quakerism, Richard B. Gregg. De Ligt strove to make from Gandhian nonviolence an instrument of revolutionary social change: the nonviolent equivalent of the class war. He developed a detailed program for mobilizing the antiwar forces behind a general strike in case war threatened, including a complete boycott of the functions of the warmaking government. De Ligt hoped that the general strike against war would quickly merge into a nonviolent social revolution.[39] In 1920, it is true that British workers had averted Britain's entry into the Russo-Polish war on the side of Poland by threatening a general strike and since then organized labor in several countries had toyed with the idea of a strike against war. The situation in the late thirties, however, was entirely different and Huxley himself was sceptical of the war resistance movement's ability to prevent war once any government had embarked on it.

Gregg, in his book *The Power of Nonviolence* (1934), interpreted Gandhi's *ahimsa* as a kind of "moral jiujitsu," which might be effectively substituted for armed violence in both domestic and international relations. He attempted to trace the practice of nonviolence in the history of modern Western civilization, pointing to such incidents as the Magyar struggle against Habsburg autocracy in the 1860s to back up his point that nonviolence was something more than a peculiarly Hindu custom. Though Gregg, like Gandhi, favored a decentralized, grass roots democracy and a society in which human needs and not technology set the tone, his writings lacked the revolutionary passion of de Ligt.

Most European and American pacifists looked for inspiration, if not always with complete agreement, to Gandhi's nonviolent struggle in British India, which covered – intermittently – the whole interwar period. They admired the moral superiority of nonviolence if used as a means of defense against external attack. In the domestic struggle for social justice it offered to left-wing pacifists a technique which appeared to avoid the danger of replacing capitalist oppression by Red totalitarianism. With the day of the barricades now over, nonviolence gave the workers a new weapon. Nevertheless, at this time pacifists seldom thought seriously of initiating nonviolent campaigns of their own. But the idea of a "Peace Army," recruited from volunteers ready to stand without weapons between the opposing forces, emerged in 1932 at the time of the Sino-Japanese conflict over Manchuria. The project, largely the brain child of two prominent British pacifists, A. Maude Royden and A. Herbert Gray, proved abortive. Looking back, Royden considered nevertheless:

It was an unparalled opportunity, for the fighting there was not guerrilla warfare nor in the air nor along a vast front of trenches ... Chinese and Japanese troops were facing each other and firing at each other across the streets of Shanghai and even a few thousand unarmed volunteers would have been seen, would have been effective, and could by their acceptance of death without resistance, have stirred the conscience of the human race.[40]

Many pacifists indeed, though sympathetic, felt that the time was not yet ripe for implementing Gandhi's technique on such an ambitious scale. To some religious pacifists, moreover, the Gandhian method seemed to be too like war with only the bloodshed left out. They felt that conciliation was the true task of the peacemaker and not the waging of nonviolent war. There were, too, nonreligious pacifists, like the popular English philosopher C.E.M. Joad, who were sceptical of the more far-reaching claims of the proponents of nonviolence. They felt that whereas nonviolent resistance had a role to play under the present conditions of international anarchy the best solution would be the creation of a genuine world authority backed by overwhelming force.

In general, there was much uncertainty within the pacifist movement concerning the relationship between nonviolence and a morally legitimate use of physical force. Might one, for instance, advocate the use of nonviolent means against external attack while supporting armed coercion in the internal arrangement of the state? Was there indeed a distinction in kind rather than merely in degree between loving persuasion and nonviolent coercion? In the idea of nonviolent resistance, it was widely felt, the pacifist movement now possessed a tool that might help to give positive content to what had previously seemed to outsiders a negative creed. The idea of nonviolence brought the pacifist philosophy down to earth, changing it from a counsel of perfection to a more perfect method of maintaining terrestrial values than the way of armed force. But when world war broke out again in 1939, for Western pacifists nonviolence still remained untried, still hung high in the realm of theory.

Pacifism and the Growth of Totalitarianism

The 1920s

During the decade and a half that followed the Armistice of 1918 the chances of eventually establishing a peaceable world looked promising. Germany was disarmed; the former Habsburg Empire lay in fragments; the United States and Soviet Russia had retreated into isolation; Italy and Japan had not yet clearly revealed expansionist designs. With Great Britain economizing radically on its armament expenditure, the only important power suspected of nurturing an aggressive militarism was France – and suspicions on this score were in fact considerably exaggerated. Moreover, that old dream of Europe and America's internationalists – a League of Nations – was in being: it needed reform and even reconstruction, many thought, but its very existence seemed to indicate that law was at last taking the place of anarchy in international relations. In 1932 the opening of the international disarmament conference momentarily raised hopes that a warless world was about to be brought into being. And for those who despaired of peace being established so long as economic exploitation held sway, the Soviet experiment in Russia combined with the seemingly imminent collapse of capitalism elsewhere offered the prospect of a new and more just international order in the not too distant future.

Pacifists shared in these various rosy dreams. Many indeed became pacifists in this period because war seemed unlikely and a pledge of war resistance, like an incantation against sickness, would itself remove the possibility of the occurrence of the evil. This did not mean that pacifism overnight became everywhere equally popular. In the conscriptionist countries of the European continent, as we have seen, the lot of the conscientious objector remained extremely hard; although in a few countries alternative civilian service now became permissible, the pacifist movement made little headway in this area. Even in the United States the intolerant wartime spirit persisted for several years. In November 1920, for instance, we find the editor of the *Christian Century* the near pacifist Charles Clayton Morrison, writing to the prolific pacifist publicist, Kirby Page: "Your book will be read by the esoteric few. The mood of the time is anything but congenial with pacifist doctrine."[41]

It was in Great Britain that postwar pacifism first gained momentum. It drew its adherents largely from the labor movement, the leaders of which had in many instances opposed the recent war, as well as from left-wing intellectuals. In October 1925 Arthur Ponsonby, a convert from Liberalism who had held the post of Under-Secretary of State for Foreign Affairs in the Labour government of 1924, wrote a letter to the press in which he called for signatures to a declaration of war resistance. Signatories were to pledge themselves to withhold support of any kind, including war service, to a belligerent government. In the civilized world, aggression was not the real cause of war, said Ponsonby: either direct negotiations or some form of arbitration could resolve all disputes between nations.[42] By the following December 40,000 pledges had been received. A year later Ponsonby and his associates organized a mammoth rally at the Albert Hall in London at which the trade union leader Ernest Bevin, among others, declared allegiance to pacifism.

The thinking behind the movement is best illustrated by quoting from an article entitled "The Prevention of War," which Bertrand Russell wrote in 1922 for the organ of the British No More War Movement. Russell did not envisage the abolition of war being reached "by the world in general adopting the pacifist theory." The role of pacifists was to be a leavening one, the influencing of opinion. They could do this best by pledging[43] themselves "to take no part" in any war as fought today.

Modern war, Russell implied, was fought mainly for prestige between contestants whose alleged reasons for going to war were equally fictitious and whose peoples could only be persuaded to fight if whipped up by war propaganda into a state of hysteria. As A.J.P. Taylor has remarked, "the principle of resistance to aggression was passed over so lightly in the twenties that the phrase 'collective security' was not used until 1932."[44] This attitude explains the fact that in this period many in Britain and America rallied to the pacifist movement without having fully considered the implications of their stand. In the pacifist ranks stood supporters of the class war and apologists for the military power of the Soviet Union as well as advocates of League sanctions and spokesmen for an armed international government, alongside believers in the gospel of reconciliation and in the practical power of nonviolence. Only during the thirties did the various positions become clearly demarcated from each other.

The end of the twenties saw a great upsurge of pacifistic feeling. A whole spate of popular antiwar novels, plays, poems, and memoirs appearing in the years 1928–30 illustrated rather than caused this tendency. Their authors were mostly former combatants, who shared the prevailing disillusionment with the course and outcome of the recent war: e. e. cummings ("i sing of Olaf glad and big / whose warmest heart recoiled at war: / a conscientious object-or / ... our president ... threw the yellowsonofabitch into a dungeon where he died") and Ernest Hemingway in the United States; Edmund Blunden, Robert Graves, Siegfried Sassoon, R.C. Sherriff and Richard Aldington in England; Erich Maria Remarque and Arnold Zweig in Germany. Several of these writers – Blunden and Sassoon, for instance – became for a time complete pacifists. Their works helped to bring new recruits into the pacifist movement, especially among the younger generation. Their moral in respect to war was the same: "Never again." In contrast to much literature in earlier periods that had glorified war, these writers stressed the darker side of war which the undoubted heroism of the ordinary soldier, often a conscript dragged unwillingly from his home and family, could not ameliorate. A similar impact was produced by a number of antiwar painters, of whom the Germans Käthe Kollwitz, Otto Dix, and George Grosz were perhaps the most outstanding.

Especially in English speaking countries, young people who grew to maturity in the years after 1918 were often drawn to pacifism. In part this trend reflected the perennial revolt of youth against an older generation, which in this case was held responsible for the recent holocaust and for creating the conditions for a new one. In the United States the student groups which pledged themselves to refuse to fight in another war were partly motivated by isolationist sentiment. However, while some of this antimilitarism was superficial, many young men and women saw in the pacifist movement an instrument through which they could work for a more decent world without resort to the degrading violence of modern war.

In the Oxford Union resolution of February 1933, youthful pacifism produced it *cause célèbre*. At the time, as well as later, much that was misleading was written concerning this incident. Winston Churchill, for instance, referred to it as an "ever-shameful resolution" passed by "foolish boys," an example of "the basest sentiments" receiving acceptance "in this dark time." "It was easy to laugh off such an episode in England," he goes on, "but in Germany, in Russia, in Japan, the idea of a decadent, degenerate Britain took root and swayed many calculations."[45] In fact, no evidence has ever been produced to show that it was taken abroad as a sign of England's degeneracy. It is true that the formal wording of the motion passed by this student debating society by a vote of 275 to 153 (and repassed by a number of such societies at other British universities) was pacifist: "That this House will in no circumstances fight for King and country." The guest speaker for the motion, Dr. C.E.M. Joad, certainly considered himself a pacifist. But the students who passed it were voting in most cases against imperialist wars, against obsolescent jingoism inherited from previous centuries and against the identification of patriotism with a declining military caste.[46] Armed sanctions under the League of Nations or resistance against totalitarian aggression were not points at issue in the debate. The last war in which Britain had been involved, it may be pointed out, was the war of intervention against Soviet Russia, the "nice new war" (to use the ironic phrase of the poet Osbert Sitwell), which Churchill himself had done so much to promote: this was in fact the kind of war against which his "foolish boys" were protesting.

The Great Divide

Two events in the 1930s contributed more than any others toward finally separating pacifism from its temporary allies among League of Nations internationalists and left-wing militants: the accession of Hitler to power in 1933 and the outbreak of the Spanish Civil War in 1936. The one raised the challenge of fascist aggression (together with the menace of antisemitism); the other presented a threat of extinction for all left-wing groups in a newly established democracy. Pacifists were forced to reconsider their position. The successive departure of all who now considered that in the last resort war might be justified in repelling expansionist dictatorships, in preserving democracy and social progress against their internal foes, or in maintaining humane values against an upsurge of barbarism, left the pacifist movement much weakened. Its political relevance appeared to have dwindled; by 1940 it had contracted once more within the confines of a quasi-religious sect. However, the increased cohesion that resulted from this ordeal may have proved ultimately of some advantage. It helped concentrate attention on developing the idea of nonviolence and its application to society. This might not have been possible if the movement had remained a mishmash of conflicting attitudes in regard to the central issue of violence.

We may take the case of Albert Einstein to illustrate the effect the Hitlerite challenge could have even on one who had only recently come out in favor of uncompromising war resistance. Einstein's commitment to pacifism, though its roots went back before 1914, became explicit in 1928. "I am convinced that the international movement to refuse participation in any kind of war service is one of the most encouraging developments of our time," he declared in that year. "Every thoughtful, well-meaning and conscientious human being should assume, in time of peace, the solemn and unconditional obligation not to participate in any war, for any reason." For the next five years he was actively associated in the work of the WRI and made many public statements in support of imprisoned conscientious objectors. He pleaded with conscriptionist governments to permit objectors to choose some form of civilian work in place of military service. His 1930 "Two-Percent Speech," as it became known, has already been mentioned in this chapter. In the early thirties Einstein was internationally the best known figure on the roster of the war resisters' movement.

The coming of the Nazi regime in Germany brought about a radical alteration in Einstein's thinking. As a liberal and a Jew, Einstein was forced into exile. After a few months we find him writing: "Conditions, unfortunately, have changed." Though he did not advocate a preventive war, he felt now that only "vigilance" on the part of strongly armed and united democracies would stem the expansion of Nazi Germany. Answering a plea to speak out on behalf of two conscientious objectors awaiting trial in Belgium, he said: "Were I a Belgian, I should not, in the present circumstances, refuse military service; rather I should enter such service cheerfully in the belief that I would thereby be helping to save European civilization." He continued to assert that a time might come again in the future when he would be ready to uphold the stand of the objector to war. But for the present only armed strength on the part of the democracies, however odious such means might still seem to him, could serve to maintain peace. To Arthur (now Lord) Ponsonby who, as chairman of the WRI, had tried to expostulate with Einstein, the latter replied: "I am sure, that if you were [a] responsible Minister in France, you would change your view [on] this point, as long as this threatening condition lasts."

Pacifist reaction to Einstein's renunciation of pacifism varied from angry outrage to pained disappointment. The Secretary of the WRI confided to the International's leading supporters: "I am afraid that this will do our Movement considerable harm. I think that the less publicity given to it, the better. You will notice that I have removed reference to Einstein in the *War Resister* which is about to be published and I shall drop the term "Einstein Fund" from our notepaper as soon as possible." To Einstein's old friend and fellow pacifist, Romain Rolland, the former's present stance smelled of apostasy. "Such weakness of spirit is indeed unimaginable in a great scientist." Rolland complained. "Had it never occurred to him that circumstances might develop, circumstances such as those that prevail today, which would make it dangerous to practice [the] conscientious objection which he espoused?" He accused Einstein of having been guilty of playing "a kind of intellectual game"; he had urged Europe's youth to refuse military service without considering responsibly the full implications and all the risks of such a stand. There was much force behind this critique, yet Rolland himself a few years later followed the same path as Einstein had done.[47]

In several ways Einstein's pacifism had been typical of much of the antiwar sentiment of the postwar era. In the first place it was largely an emotional response, a repulsion against the horrors of modern war and an expression of the disenchantment that had followed World War I.

Einstein did not hide this fact. "My pacifism is an instinctive feeling," he wrote in 1929. "My attitude is not the result of an intellectual theory." There was indeed nothing shameful in an emotional antipathy to the hatred and cruelty involved in war such as swept Einstein in these years. A purely intellectual pacifism based on a fine calculation of advantage and loss is likely to prove sterile in the long run. But, just as in 1914 the promptings of his heart had brought the American Clarence Darrow in the twinkling of an eye to exchange his belief in Tolstoyan nonresistance for an equally compulsive faith in the need to resist the German invasion of little Belgium, so Einstein and many others found that the same emotional impulse that had made them espouse war resistance now propelled them into the camp of those who urged armed resistance. For Einstein the path that conducted him away from pacifism led him (to his shocked horror, let it be added) toward the creation of the atom bomb.

A second point at which Einstein's pacifism coincided with that of many others among the movement's adherents was in his belief that arms could be dispensed with only in the civilized world. He was not prepared to urge unilateral disarmament on "a native African tribe" as a remedy for war, he had declared, "for the patient there would have died long before the cure could have been of any help to him." But what if in Europe itself a reversion to the law of the jungle should ensue and the painfully gained achievements of humanist culture were to be abandoned throughout large areas of that continent? Would not disarmament and conscientious objection be as out of place there as on the dark continent? That they were indeed no longer feasible was the understandable conclusion drawn from the state of Europe from 1933 on by Einstein, and by countless others who had previously sympathized with the war resistance movement.[48]

At first, however, many pacifists, as well as many politicians and ordinary citizens outside Germany, believed that negotiation combined with treaty revision would preserve the peace and satisfy the claims, some of them not unjustified, of the dictators. The English novelist, A.A. Milne, in one of the most popular expositions of utilitarian pacifism published in the interwar years, was typical of this way of thinking. In 1934 he wrote: "I shall assume that Germany is as amenable to reason as Italy (or any other nation), and that within certain limitations imposed on her by the Versailles Treaty, she is as anxious as any other nation for the security of peace."[49]

It was Italy's attack on Abyssinia (Ethiopia) in October 1935 that finally precipitated the division and brought subsequent hostility between the pacifists, on one hand, and those internationalists who were prepared to support collective security under the League of Nations' auspices to the point of military sanctions, on the other.[50] According to the privately organized Peace Ballot of the previous year, in which 11.5 million Britishers took part, an overwhelming majority had voted in favor of applying sanctions against any power found guilty of aggression. "The Peace Ballot," it has been pointed out, "was an appeal for militant resistance to aggression, not a manifesto of appeasement."[51] But the lines were still not yet clearly drawn. While a substantial minority of over two million came out against military sanctions, the vote in favor of economic sanctions was well over three million stronger than the vote for military sanctions. Among both non-pacifists and pacifists who participated in the balloting there was still a feeling that some measure of support for League action was not incompatible with an unwillingness to commit the country to full-scale war under the banner of the League.

There were pacifists who were not opposed to the application of an economic blockade when Italy began its conquest of Abyssinia. In the Quaker community, especially in the United States, opinion was divided on this issue with a vocal minority in favor of supporting League action. In Britain, Clifford Allen (now Lord Allen of Hurtwood) pleaded for pacifist support of even military sanctions, since the practical alternative then facing the world was not one between a nonviolent way to peace, however theoretically desirable, and collective security but between collective security and a reversion to the international anarchy of pre-League days. In his view, opposition to League action on the part of the pacifist movement meant lining up in practice with the believers in old-style power diplomacy and with the isolationists. While still reserving their personal renunciation of violence, war resisters could best further the cause of peace by supporting collective action for its preservation based on the rule of law, which, according to Allen, approximated more closely police action than the intra-national warfare of the past.[52] But Allen's agile balancing trick between personal repudiation of war and support for armed action by the League found few imitators. Those who approved the latter course inclined to lose their belief in the efficacy of nonviolence altogether.[53] On the other hand, pacifists tended to repudiate sanctions, especially military sanctions, as merely war under a new name.

At the beginning of October 1935, on the very eve of Mussolini's onslaught on Abyssinia, a showdown took place within the British Labour Party between Ernest Bevin, representing the majority which supported the League action against Italy even at the risk of war, and George Lansbury, till then the party leader and a convinced Christian pacifist. The scene of this confrontation was Brighton where the party was holding its annual conference. Lansbury, whom Taylor has well described as "the most lovable figure in modern politics," later admitted to having experienced increasing difficulty in "squaring my pacifist principles with the policy of my party" after he became its leader following Ramsay Macdonald's defection in 1931. At the conference, Bevin, alarmed by the impression rumors of a divided party leadership would create in the country just before a general election due in November and angry at what he considered Lansbury's prevarication hitherto on the issue of sanctions, attacked him in a harsh, even brutal speech. After appealing to the delegates to be influenced neither by sentiment nor personal attachment Bevin, posing "as a practical man dismissing the inconsequential musings of a saint" (as Jonathan Scheer aptly puts it), had turned to Lansbury and said: "It is placing the Executive and the [Labour] Movement in an absolutely wrong position to be hawking your conscience round from body to body to be told what you ought to do with it." Despite considerable personal sympathy for Lansbury the conference voted in favor of sanctions by an overwhelming majority.[54] With organized labor in Britain firmly committed to collective security (though not yet ready to back rearmament under the National Government), British pacifism's connection with official labor was severed. Though the two movements had never been identical, the post-1918 war resistance movement in Great Britain had derived, we have seen, considerable impetus and widespread support from the connection. After their ways had parted, British pacifism was left without representation in parliament, except for a solitary bishop, a Quaker independent, and a handful of Labour pacifists in the two Houses.

In the summer of 1935 Bertrand Russell, in answer to a prominent supporter of collective security who urged that armed action by the League would be equivalent *mutatis mutandis* to the beneficial measures taken by medieval kings to quell their turbulent barons, had replied: "I am against a League war in present circumstances because the anti-League powers are strong. The analogy is not King v. Barons, but the Wars of the Roses."[55] Whether collective security, if firmly applied, would have been successful in stemming the expansionist powers of the thirties without war is a question to which no conclusive answer can be given, since, in fact, that policy was never followed with any measure of consistency. Most pacifists by this time, however, believed that collective security meant war. It can well be argued that any practicable alternative involved equal risk of war, as well as the likelihood that war if it did come would be fought in much less advantageous circumstances for the antiaggressor powers. The policy, though, that large sections of the pacifist movement in Britain and America (rejecting not only collective security but also isolationism and national preparedness) promoted now was that of unilateral disarmament.

Unilateralism was urged in many cases not so much because its proponents put forward some form of nonviolent resistance as an alternative way of defending humane values – the question (to quote from Russell again) was considered to be "quantitative." For the unpleasantness which the possibility of enemy occupation might entail was found to be "infinitely less terrible than the consequences of a war, even if it ended in complete victory."[56] Like most of the military experts in the thirties, pacifists overestimated the effects of air warfare and underestimated the effectiveness of defense against the bomber which, it was believed, would always get through. Mass destruction of cities, millions killed by bombs and poison gas, largescale disorganization of the civilian population, and even the total extinction of civilized life and a reversion to barbarism in belligerent countries: this was the picture painted of the outcome of a future war. We cannot be sure today, in the age of nuclear warfare, if it was not the timetable rather than the prognostication itself, which was incorrect. Yet it certainly proved an exaggeration in respect to World War II, despite the terrible moral and material damage wrought by that conflict.

The mistake made by the pacifist movement in the half-decade before World War II was in trying to sell pacifism as an immediately viable political program without imparting sufficient insight into what its adoption would require or attempting to develop in any detail the positive aspects of nonviolent action as an alternative to military power. Fear of war was not by any means the only important factor leading to the rapid expansion of pacifism in the English-speaking world in the thirties (as some critics of pacifism have implied); it is true, however, that in its propaganda the movement did play unduly on the widely spread feelings of horror at the prospect of another world war. Understandably, pacifists, like most other people in the West, found it hard to comprehend the potentiality for evil of the Nazi and other totalitarian régimes and their capacity to dupe their own peoples by the mass communications media. Pacifists, with very few dishonorable exceptions, condemned both antisemitism and the repressive aspects of fascist ideology and practice. They rejected any suggestion of supporting Hitler and Mussolini as a bulwark against Communism. But they failed to consider properly the implications of pacifism and nonviolence in relation to a totalitarian dictatorship equipped with all the means of suppression provided by modern science.

If 1935 had at last sorted out the supporters of collective security from the pacifists proper, 1936 brought the beginning of the Civil War in Spain and a rift between pacifism and the antimilitarism of the radical left, which had been foreshadowed earlier in the debates within the peace movement following the Russian Revolution. What attitude should pacifists adopt if, as in Spain, right-wing elements supported by the military attempted to overthrow a democratically elected government by force? Was it possible to urge nonviolent resistance in these circumstances? Or might pacifists make a distinction (as, for instance, the American peace movement had done at the time of the war for the Union) between international war and civil war, maintaining a testimony against the one while regarding the other merely as an extension of the legitimate police functions of the state? Even the anarchists in Spain were supporting the Republican government. As the fighting ground on, however, it became increasingly hard to regard it as anything else but war.

As in the not dissimilar question of military action under the League, war resisters who actively supported the Loyalist war effort tended to abandon entirely their belief in pacifism: Fenner Brockway, the founder of the British Non-Conscription Fellowship in 1914, and the American socialist leader, Norman Thomas, who had played a leading role in the Fellowship of Reconciliation, are two such cases. Staff members of the now almost defunct No More War Movement in Britain (but not the members of its National Committee) took much the same line and argued in favor of modifying its pacifism so as to make the Spanish Civil War an exception to that organization's hitherto unconditional condemnation of war. The continuance of the war caused pacifists increasing uneasiness and generated a rising tension, which sought outlet in such activities as the relief of the victims of war, for pacifists' emotions were largely committed on the Loyalist side.

One of those whom the war in Spain presented with a severe dilemma was the English pacifist peer, Lord Ponsonby. He confided to Bertrand Russell in August 1936 that this conflict was proving "the very devil for the pacifists." He had indeed to admit that, were he a Spaniard, he would aid the government "by force of arms" if necessary.[57] But, despite his reservations concerning civil war, which in this case he saw as involving an act of rebellion on the part of the antigovernment side, Ponsonby, like the French integral pacifists of that period, never renounced his unconditional rejection of international war.

In regard to the Munich crisis of 1938 the pacifist dilemma expressed itself in different terms. A revision of the Versailles settlement and the claims of national self-determination had both long been planks in the pacifists' political platform. The demands of the Sudeten German minority in Czechoslovakia and Hitler's backing of these demands appeared at first sight by no means unreasonable. In themselves the demands provided no justification for unleashing another war, this time in defense of Czechoslovakia's integrity. These sentiments were widely held in Western countries: in fact they formed the intellectual superstructure erected by the architects of appeasement. For pacifists, Czechoslovakia (still less Poland in 1939) did not supply the emotional associations of Spain. Thus in the months before Munich, the pacifist press, as a perusal of the files of the English pacifist weekly *Peace News* for that period reveals, differed little in tone or in the nature of its comment on the Czechoslovak crisis from the organs of appeasement. Lacking much knowledge of the historical background of Central Europe, its publicists only too often served up the German viewpoint and pleaded for its acceptance on grounds of moral principle. In a not ignoble desire to avoid war they confused a principled pacifism with the politics of surrender.

The same weakness was exemplified across the Atlantic in many of the utterances and activities of American pacifists, especially among the more politically involved. The Emergency Peace Campaign, which was started in 1936 as a result of Quaker initiative and was led largely by pacifists, endeavored to find a middle way between isolationism and collective security. In striving to ensure American neutrality in case of European war, the Campaign was eventually driven into alliance, however unwillingly, with the isolationist forces, whose creed was basically opposed to the internationalism of the pacifist movement. This trend was accentuated after the outbreak of war in September 1939. Politically minded pacifists for the most part felt that the conflict was the inevitable outcome of the unrectified mistakes of the past, that essentially it was being fought to maintain an unjust *status quo*, that whatever the war's outcome, decency and democracy would disappear in Europe, and thus only a neutral, noncombatant America would be able to preserve the humanity and freedom for which the Western powers claimed to be fighting. "Somebody ought to be left the means to put the world together again if that is possible," wrote Villard. A desire to prevent at any cost America's entry into the war led Villard, the veteran liberal, who genuinely abhorred everything that smacked of Fascism or dictatorship, into virtual alliance with such right-wing, isolationist groups as the America First Committee. In 1941 we even find him praising the pro-Nazi and antisemitic Colonel Charles A. Lindbergh and calling his stand against American involvement in war "magnificent."[58] As in Britain, tactical collaboration with political elements basically hostile to everything for which pacifism stood, solely because of their opposition to the war in Europe, aroused intense misgiving and a strongly negative reaction in some sections of the pacifist movement. This was especially true of those pacifists who stressed the moral and religious case against war.

In neighboring Canada, where pacifism had always been much weaker than in the United States, its most prominent political spokesman during the 1930s, John Shaver Woodsworth, parliamentary leader of the democratic socialist Co-operative Commonwealth Federation (CCF), revealed in his arguments against war preparations a mixture of internationalism and isolationism similar to that displayed by pacifists south of the border. "As an individual," Woodsworth stated in the House of Commons in April 1935, "I refuse to participate or to assist in war, yet I am a citizen of a country that still relies upon force, and as a public representative I must vote on alternative military policies." He expressed qualified support for the League of Nations, for he felt it offered more hope for the future of humankind than any other realistic alternative. But he refused to back military sanctions while at the same time accepting the need to apply economic sanctions against an aggressor state like Italy in its war against Abyssinia – provided such a measure involved no risk of war.

In the spirit of the early Quaker, William Penn, in his plan for European peace, Woodsworth approved the idea of an international police force, controlled by a restructured League of Nations, preferring it – for all its violent concomitants – to the condition of international anarchy that had prevailed for most of history. But, as Allen Mills remarks, when Woodsworth used "the language of practicality and supported a vote for the league as a policeman, the clarity of his message was distorted by the undulations of his thinking on sanctions, collective security, the unreconstructed league, and the immorality of force." Sentimentally he was closely attached to the British connection, and he admired the British system of government, considering it as the model for Canadian democracy; but he feared that this connection could draw Canada once again into European quarrels and involve his country in a war to uphold an unjust *status quo*. On the other hand, he thought Canada had nothing to fear from the United States, even though the latter's political institutions and social mores were less attractive to him than British customs and institutions were. Thus, in his opinion, Canada could safely disarm – unilaterally and completely – and pursue confidently a policy of isolation from the armed disputes of the rest of the world. As he stated in 1936:

Let us consider realistically the defence of Canada. If we start with the assumption that Canada's first obligation is to her own citizens, our problem is: How can we save our next generation from annihilation? I submit ... that with our present military equipment or any which this country can support, Canada unassisted cannot defend herself against all comers. Fortunately she does not need to do so. The United States will not attack us, and under her Monroe Doctrine the United States would protect us, not because of her interest in our welfare, but because of her interest in her own affairs. At the moment, then, I have a good deal of sympathy with the isolationist position, though I quite agree that it cannot ultimately save us. We are a part not only of North America but of the world.

While under these circumstances believers in military force could rest assured in Canada's immunity from attack, Woodsworth did not feel that advocates of nonviolence like himself need feel disturbed at any moral incongruity about this situation. "If," he remarked somewhat disingenuously, "I live in an area of fireproof buildings why should I not be happy in enjoying immunity from fire hazards?"[59]

Woodsworth, though by no means entirely easy in the situation, seems to have experienced less of a dilemma over the Spanish Civil War than, we have seen, some European pacifists did. As a socialist and democrat, he sympathized with the Popular Front government and regarded Franco as a rebel. As a pacifist, however, he felt he could extend no more than "moral support" to the Loyalist cause. "May [the] struggle of [the] Spanish people soon end in victory and democracy triumph," he told the Spanish parliament, then removed to Barcelona, in February 1938. But he wanted Canada – and Canadians – to keep out of the mess: a sentiment reinforced both by his fears of communist dominance of the Loyalist government and its army and by his alarm at German and Italian intervention on Franco's side, which threatened to turn the civil war into an international conflict. So he urged his party colleagues: "Our work in the C.C.F. is not Russia or Spain or China, but here in Canada." By "educational and organizational work at home" they would do more to create "a better state of affairs in the world" than by sending arms, or volunteers, to Spain.[60] And Czechoslovakia in 1938, and even more Poland in 1939, were to reinforce Woodsworth in his isolationism. By this time, however, few members of his party shared his views on international issues. As shown by Thomas P. Socknat in his *Witness against War* (1987), a similar debate about war and peace – with a similar outcome – was taking place within the small Canadian pacifist movement as was going on among Canada's democratic socialists.

The Peace Pledge Union

The years which witnessed the exodus first of the League internationalists and then of the social militants from the pacifist movement saw
in Great Britain the genesis of a new organizational center for pacifist
activities: the Peace Pledge Union (PPU). For half a decade the PPU
infused new life into the British pacifist movement. The hundred thousand or more members whom it recruited within a short time were
mostly new to the movement; few of them had joined an antiwar society before, many were young people in their late teens or in their twenties. Never before had an organization pledged to complete pacifism
enlisted such enthusiastic support; never again were so many potential
conscientious objectors to war enrolled under one banner. Historians
of Britain in the 1930s have mostly either ignored the PPU altogether or
dismissed it as a front for appeasement – or at best a collection of naive
"do-gooders." Both verdicts are unjust. The PPU was a typical example
of the moral impulse of the time. For all its shortcomings, it represented a genuine and significant protest against the evils of modern
war.

The Union originated in a letter which Canon "Dick" Sheppard sent
to the press in October 1934 asking for the names of those ready to sign
a declaration renouncing war and expressing their determination not
to support another conflict. He modeled his pledge on one devised a
year earlier by the equally popular American pacifist preacher, Harry
Emerson Fosdick, for an Armistice Sunday sermon. At the beginning
Sheppard had not intended to found a new organization; the response
to his appeal, however, even though it was confined at first to men,
was so large that he soon took steps to set up a permanent body of war
resisters. The PPU came formally into existence in 1936.

Sheppard was a clergyman of the Church of England, a popular
preacher and broadcaster, and a talented organizer. One of his early
collaborators, the novelist Rose Macaulay, has written: "He had every
gift for running a mixed team, and a very mixed team his Peace Pledge
Union members were; ... he was probably the only person who understood all their various points of view and angles of approach. A Christian [pacifist] himself ... so far from regarding this as the only
creditable or genuine approach, he said that it made pacifism simple
and easy for him, as compared with that of his non-Christian friends.[61]
Anyone prepared to say no to modern war was welcome in the PPU.[62]
Indeed some who signed its absolutist peace pledge did not hide the
fact that they were really only "ninety-nine per cent" pacifists. Fred
Jowett of the Independent Labour Party, for instance, told Lord Pon-

sonby: "Yes, I have joined the Peace Pledge Union, not as a Non-Resister but as a War Resister." He supported both wars of national defense and the armed struggle of colonial peoples against imperialism as well as the right of legitimate governments to suppress a rebellion by force, as in the case of Spain at that moment. "I hope," he concluded, "you do not think that holding this point of view is inconsistent with membership of the Peace Pledge Union. After careful consideration before joining I felt sure it was not." Even a devoted Christian pacifist like the Labour Party M.P., Reginald Sorensen, considered that, as a democrat, he must approve rearmament, for almost all Britishers now fully supported this program. In the House of Commons he stated openly his belief "that a virile people must defend itself and that there are certainly worse things than war." It was, therefore, not for a tiny pacifist minority to oppose its decision (actually a not un-Gandhian position, as we know).[63]

The PPU had a formidable array of sponsors including a retired general ("a lifetime of professional soldiering has brought me, by painful ways, to the realization that all war is wrong, is senseless," he confessed[64]), a number of persons prominent in the literary and artistic worlds, an array of dignitaries from both the established church and the nonconformist bodies, and leading representatives of the World War I generation of war resisters alongside veterans of that conflict, like Dick Sheppard himself (an ex-army chaplain), who had subsequently become pacifists. The Union possessed not only well-known names, but was able to harness the enthusiasm of the unknown young to create a crusade of formidable dimensions. Local PPU groups sprang up throughout the country; there were as many as 800 functioning at the height of the campaign. A lively weekly newspaper, *Peace News*, commenced publication in 1936 under the editorship of a young Quaker journalist, Humphrey S. Moore. Bookshops and open-air meetings, study groups and travelling peace-caravans helped to spread the message.

The only snag was that, beyond a negative pledge of war renunciation, the message purveyed was exceedingly nebulous. We find a Tory pacifist (a very rare bird, it must be admitted) castigating the PPU for its left-wing sympathies.[65] Others criticized it for its alleged connection with extreme right-wing groups like the British People's Party and even for harboring crypto-Nazi tendencies. It is true that most PPU members belonged, often rather vaguely, to the left; but it is also true that many of them approved, with reservations, the Conservative-backed policies of appeasement that found their climax in Munich. And Stuart Morris, the PPU's general secretary, even went so far as to join The Link, an undercover Nazi organization (ostensibly working for international reconciliation).[66] Certainly "it is nonsense to charge the PPU with pro-Nazi sentiments. At the same time," a friendly critic goes on, "it is hard to escape the conclusion that there was too much sympathy for the German position, often the product of ignorance and superficial thinking. There was also a complete failure to grasp the nature of ... Germany's policies with regard to colonies, Austria, Czechoslovakia and Poland ... [and] the ... ruthless spirit ... of the Nazi state."[67]

The average PPU member probably felt that peace-pledging was the surest way to prevent war from again breaking out. After September 1939, since this hope proved to be an illusion, many at once abandoned pacifism for support of war. This fact alone would account for the decline in numbers that ensued after the declaration of hostilities. In addition, as in similar undertakings, many signatures to the peace pledge were purely nominal; in such cases those signing did not feel it incumbent on them to take any further part in the Union's activities.

The PPU faced the dilemma with which every mass movement of reform is confronted. Its promoters had to decide whether, on the one hand, to agitate on a broad platform and thus in all likelihood limit the number of its adherents through the difficulty of gaining agreement on such a wide number of issues or, on the other, to base their campaign on a single demand and risk reducing its program to meaninglessness by accommodating various – and possibly conflicting – views on other subjects. Even if in the past great moral crusades have sometimes prospered by a singleminded concentration on one issue – antislavery, for instance, or temperance, or women's rights – the PPU in its campaign against war had one great disadvantage: it had no control over time or circumstance. It could neither bring sufficient influence to bear on those in whose hands the issues of peace or war then lay, nor could it win time to slowly sway opinion toward the adoption of nonviolent techniques and attitudes. Despite its errors in tactics and in judgment, however, the prewar PPU expressed a sincere attempt to create from the widespread, but hitherto amorphous sentiment for peace, an unambiguously pacifist movement.

Politics and The Gospel of Reconciliation

Pacifism presents in most acute form perhaps the problem of the place of morality in political life. This is particularly true of Christian pacifism. Hans J. Morgenthau has spoken in this connection of "an element of tragedy," for "it is the very function of Christian ethics to call upon man to comply with a code of moral conduct with which, by virtue of his nature, he cannot comply."[68] True, in the twentieth century many religious pacifists have shared the tendency of liberal Christianity to regard humankind as perfectable; modern Quakerism also has frequently interpreted the Society of Friends' belief in "that of God in every man" as implying humanity's essential goodness. Yet, even outside the Mennonite communities, there have still been in this century many pacifists who have viewed war as the outcome of an inevitable human tendency to sin. For liberal Christians, too, both pacifist and nonpacifist, the problem remains of accounting for the continuing presence of violence in domestic and international life.

Have the injunctions of the Sermon on the Mount relevance outside the sphere of purely personal relations? The majority view within the Christian churches through the centuries has, of course, been that, in preserving order within the state and repelling attack from without, Christian authorities are not required to interpret the Beautitudes too literally. Many Christians have also maintained that when at the behest of the magistrate the Christian citizen is obliged to gird on his sword, the responsibility for bloodshed rests upon his rulers. In the interwar years two questions arising from this problem, above all others, exercised the minds of religious pacifists. In the first place, what was the relationship between violence as expressed in international war and violence as revealed in the existing capitalist economic order? Could the former be repudiated so long as the latter remained intact? And, secondly, was it possible for Christians to isolate one evil – war – if, as social beings, they were also implicated in an unchristian society, from which it was impossible to escape. Both questions revealed the increased interest in social affairs manifested throughout the Christian churches in the twentieth century.

In our discussion of the political program of the interwar pacifist movement we have drawn most heavily on Great Britain for illustrative material. Now the process will be reversed. It is to a consideration of the American section of the FOR that we must turn for insight into the political outreach and the political dilemmas of the gospel of reconciliation.

The American Fellowship of Reconciliation

The American FOR throughout the interwar period, although in 1930 it had opened it doors to all with "faith in love and nonviolence," nevertheless remained overwhelmingly Protestant in membership. What is more, it drew its main inspiration from one particular stream in modern American Protestantism: the "Social Gospel." The founder of the Social Gospel movement, Walter Rauschenbusch, had associated himself with the work of the FOR shortly before his death in July 1918. The three major denominations most strongly impregnated. with the ideas of the Social Gospel – Methodists, Disciples, and Congregationalists – were also those in which the pacifist minority was largest. From the outset most FOR members, and especially the leadership, which included such socially committed persons as Norman Thomas and Jane Addams, felt that objection to war must be buttressed by an effort to transform society. They shared the hopes of the protagonists of the Social Gospel to be able so to transform human society that it approximated the Kingdom of God. The coming of the Kingdom was for them no Utopian dream but a real possibility open to all men and women on this earth. The elimination of war between nations and the ending of economic exploitation within society were merely different aspects of one struggle: the struggle for the realization of Christ's Kingdom. Liberals in their theology, they based their pacifism not on Biblical texts but simply, as the national secretary of the Canadian FOR put it, on "the spirit of Jesus."[69]

Pacifism and the Social Gospel were not necessarily identical. In fact, before 1917 the Social Gospel movement was little, if at all, concerned with issues of war and peace, while religious pacifists had not been greatly interested in the labor question. After World War I, however, members of two of the three historic peace churches on which religious pacifism had hitherto been based, the Quaker Society of Friends and the Church of the Brethren, were influenced in considerable numbers by the Social Gospel. (Mennonites, on the other hand, were as yet almost entirely untouched by this movement.) Quakers and Brethren now began to advocate varying degrees of social reform as an integral part of their peace testimony. In addition, during the interwar years, members of nonpacifist denominations were drawn by their sympathy for the Social Gospel to repudiate war as an obstacle to the fulfillment of their social aspirations. By 1928, when it merged with the FOR, the Fellowship for a Christian Social Order, which Kirby Page and Sherwood Eddy started in 1921, had succeeded in winning over to pacifism many members whose first endeavor had been the changing of the social order. For both socialistically inclined Christian pacifists and antimilitaristic Christian socialists, the FOR acted as a fulcrum on which they could base their strategy for defeating both capitalism and war.

Since capitalism appeared as a primary cause of human conflict, pacifists affiliated to the FOR increasingly sought the seeds of war in the domestic scene. They detected them in the exploitation of labor by capital and in the brutal suppression of the workers' efforts to organize, a suppression carried out by capital backed by a state which it dominated. "Capitalism is based upon coercion and violence," wrote the theologian, John C. Bennett, in 1933, "it is destructive of human life and human values on a colossal scale ... a ruthless system which results in starvation, disease, death, warped bodies and souls for millions."[70] As the depression and its aftermath closed down on the country, it seemed clearer than ever to many FOR members, despite their middle-class origins and status, that the fight against war could, paradoxically, be pursued only by means of the class war. But could the class war be waged with the weapons of nonviolence alone? This was the question that continually haunted the FOR from the late twenties onward.

The FOR stand had thus ceased to be an inward-looking sectarian witness against war such as the historic peace churches had upheld for many centuries. For the FOR now, the rationale for the organization's pacifism, as a historian of the Social Gospel has well remarked, became "its effectiveness as a social technique adapted to every social problem ... the drive of energy was outward."[71] FOR members regarded themselves no longer as an elect minority leavening the world, but as the nonviolent vanguard of those political forces whose task it was to inaugurate the classless society. From this new Christian social order, capitalist exploitation would be banished along with international war. In the twenties and early thirties at least, the main dynamic of the FOR's thinking came to be directed, therefore, toward exploring the relationship between violence and an unjust domestic order. It was the use of physical force in the class war that aroused the most heated debates in the Fellowship. It was, therefore, not the problem of the magistrate's sword turned against a foreign aggressor that generated the first major schism in its ranks, but that of the policeman's baton raised against workers struggling to throw off the yoke of capitalism.

"I am determined to take the position of a conscientious objector in the labor movement, if the issue of a violent class war is ever clearly drawn, but I hope that this time may never come." So wrote a young minister Harold Rotzel, active at the time in labor organization, in the March 1926 issue of the FOR's lively unofficial journal, *The World Tomorrow*. A few years later came the depression accompanied by a steep rise in labor unrest and a heightened sense of class antagonism, even the threat of civil war. Many in the FOR had joined the organization in the belief that their ideal ends – social justice and a classless society – might best be achieved through peaceful means. The modern state in any case was in possession of such overwhelming physical power as to make the barricades appear an outmoded method of waging the social war. Violence appeared pragmatically a useless weapon in this struggle. "But," as the theologian H. Richard Niebuhr wrote, "the realistic purpose dominated. It was not the pacifism of non-resistance but the pacifism of nonviolent aggression."[72] Once the efficacy of nonviolent means in bringing the Kingdom appeared doubtful, hesitancy appeared, too, concerning continued adherence to an abstract nonviolence. And even before this, FOR members were already to be found on both sides of the Atlantic, who reserved the right of the Soviet Union, the worker's state, to use violence against the threat of capitalist aggression.

The Calvinist turned Quaker, A.J. Muste, who in 1919 had been Rotzel's colleague in leading a strike of textile mill workers at Lawrence, Massachusetts, was one of those whose attempt to face the dilemma led him temporarily to repudiate pacifism altogether and, in his case, to espouse the Trotskyite variant of Marxism.

I came to embrace the view [he wrote later] that only revolutionary action by the working class and other elements under the leadership of a vanguard party could bring in a new social order, and that revolutionary action did not in principle exclude violence. Violence in taking over power would almost certainly be necessary and hence justified ... For a time I tried to reconcile my Christian pacifism with involvement in the struggle as it was then taking place. Gradually ... I came to feel that I was more and more a caricature of a Christian pacifist and only a half-baked revolutionary, and that I had to choose. I chose revolution, recognizing that it might involve violence. I did not, having given up my pacifism, think that I could remain a Christian.[73]

In the late twenties and early thirties, many FOR activists were asking themselves the same questions as Muste was doing. They had already shown their readiness, indeed their anxiety, to join the picket line in industrial disputes and to act as labor organizers where worker leadership was still weak. They were prominent in the counsels of the Socialist Party; they took part in such lively experiments in working class education as the Brookwood Labor College.[74] But was this commitment sufficient? Could the Kingdom of God ever be ushered in, and righteousness established, if Christians relied only on conversion and persuasion vis-à-vis "a privileged class which ... may be described as the aggressor in the class-war."[75] Is there after all, as Reinhold Niebuhr enquired with increasing insistence, any real difference between nonviolent and violent means of coercion, which should lead one to exclude the latter under all circumstances as an instrument for changing society? If a Christian is presented in politics with a choice between justice and love, on which side should his choice lie? By the early 1930s Niebuhr, while still considering himself a pacifist and maintaining his membership of the FOR, now gave a somewhat ambiguous answer to such questions. "The difference," he wrote, "between violent and non-violent methods of coercion and resistance are not so absolute that it would be possible to regard violence as a morally impossible instrument of social change ... The advantages of non-violent methods are very great but they must be pragmatically considered in the light of circumstances." He gave his approval to Gandhi's *satyagraha* campaigns but qualified it; he saw nonviolent resistance as essentially a weapon of the dispossessed lacking other means of combating oppression. Nevertheless he urged fellow Christians to devote increased attention to "developing non-violent resistance" (he was thinking here, though, more of social oppression than aggression by an external enemy).[76]

Some FOR members, though, denied that Niebuhr's choices were in fact relevant; many were troubled. At last, in 1933, came a crisis within the organization on this issue.

When, in the last quarter of that year, a questionnaire was circulated among the membership, about 10 percent of those who answered (996 replying out of an active roll of 6,395) agreed – with varying degrees of enthusiasm – to the employment of violence by the workers to overthrow capitalism. In this number, moreover, were included three of the four secretaries of the FOR. But the statement which gained greatest assent was the fourth: that "in case the legal owners of the essential industries resort to armed force in an attempt to maintain or to regain control of their property, [members would] refuse to use violence against them, but offer to serve the workers as a social worker among their families, as a maintainer of food supplies, as a nurse or stretcher bearer, or in other nonviolent ways."[77] Despite the small percentage of members who participated in the poll it seemed clear that the Fellowship was still overwhelmingly in favor of nonviolence in class as well as in international war. In regard to the former, however, many members now took up a position of sympathetic nonbelligerency ready to support the proletarian side in every way short of combatant service. The Fellowship, then, was not against coercion, provided it were nonviolent coercion and exercised on behalf of the proletariat.

Publication of these results in December 1933 led to the resignation of the executive secretary, Joseph B. Matthews, who had been foremost in espousing militancy in the workers' cause. Matthews in fact was at this time collaborating closely with communist front organizations and wished to harness the FOR to the communist sponsored peace movement. He accused "the pure pacifists" within the FOR, despite their "political innocence" *vis-à-vis* "the class struggle," of rigging the questionnaire so as to produce the results they desired. "The larger   the unearned income, the greater the faith in love, moral suasion and education," he exclaimed sarcastically (without, however, producing evidence for this thesis). "An almost perfect demonstration," he called the results of the poll, "that those who have a vital stake in privilege are to be found arrayed against the only methods which, according to history, promise the slightest success in overthrowing the rulers of a parasitic order."[78]

Among those who soon followed Matthews out of the FOR was Reinhold Niebuhr. "I share, roughly speaking, the political position of Mr. Matthews," Niebuhr wrote at the beginning of 1934 in the *Christian Century*,[79] "as a Marxian and as a Christian" (though, we may add, without Matthews's bitterness against the pure pacifists or his unqualified ardor for Soviet Communism). For Niebuhr neutrality in the class struggle was impossible. Christians, who stood – as did most people in the FOR – for a more just social order than the existing capitalist one, could not reasonably stand aside if violence were needed to establish the new order. Violence indeed was implicit in capitalism: either negatively in the form of starvation and economic pressures on the working class or positively as in the case of police brutality. To maintain that one could escape implication in violence was a form of "ethical perfectionism." To refuse to choose between two inevitable species of violence was to shirk social responsibility. "There is no choice except between more and less violence. One cannot distinguish between violent and nonviolent coercion in our social system." Since love cannot be perfectly incarnated in human beings, Christians must recognize "the tragic character of man's social life" and, while still acknowledging a degree of imperfection in the course chosen, opt for "the devil of vengeance," which offered the chance of creating a more just society, in place of "the devil of hypocrisy," that is, a formal nonviolence cloaking the realities of class war. Reconciliation would come not from ignoring the violence endemic in capitalist society, but from so transforming society, if need be by violent means, that the seeds of violence would be removed from its midst.

With the departure from the FOR of the Christian Marxists, and the consequent cooling of relations between the main body representing American pacifism and the communist sponsored peace movement, the way was open for the FOR to explore the implications of a nonviolent alternative to class war, to which the majority was wedded. In fact, little was done in the period prior to America's entry into the war in

1941 to investigate the practical possibilities of nonviolent struggle on the domestic scene. The publication in 1934 of Gregg's book on the *Power of Nonviolence* certainly stimulated interest in the subject, which had already been awakened by Gandhi's civil disobedience campaigns in British India. In 1936, in the course of a strike, several FOR members active in the trade union movement, who had been studying Gregg's work, organized a "lie-down" in an effort to prevent strike-breakers from entering the plant. But this remained an isolated instance. Though many FOR members showed interest in Gandhian techniques, others cleaved to the older concept of the pacifist's role in society as one of mediation between two conflicting positions without actually taking sides.

In fact, from the mid-thirties the FOR's attention had begun to turn from the domestic to the international scene. Whereas the debate hitherto had been concerned primarily with the relationship between nonviolence and social revolution, interest moved over now to the problem of war itself. Here Christian pacifism's most trenchant critic was the FOR's one-time chairman, Reinhold Niebuhr, writing no longer in the role of a Marxian Christian anxious to greet the coming of the Kingdom but as the disciple of the pessimistic school of Neo-Orthodoxy associated in particular with the name of the Swiss theologian, Karl Barth.

For Niebuhr pacifism still retained a *raison d'être* within the church if it eschewed all attempts to claim political relevance. The other-worldly defenselessness of groups such as the Mennonites witnessed indeed to a legitimate striving for perfection in a fallen world; it represented "a genuine impulse in the heart of Christianity." Jesus himself had taught "an absolute and uncompromising ethic" of love and nonresistance: Niebuhr found the efforts of nonpacifist theologians to deny this "futile and pathetic." But the kind of pacifism represented by the FOR was a heresy. Rejecting "the Christian doctrine of original sin as an out-moded bit of pessimism," its protagonists had asserted the possibility of overcoming evil in this world by means of all-conquering love. This, in Niebuhr's view, was a dangerous illusion. It derived, as did liberal theology itself, not from the New Testament but from the humanist view of man which had emerged with the Renaissance. There was no such thing as "non-violent politics," for politics was the realm of sin. Political goals could never be pursued with wholly moral means, "It is because men are sinners that justice can be achieved only by a certain degree of coercion on the one hand, and by resistance to coercion and tyranny on the other hand." Where the objective situation presented only a choice between submission to injustice or war (both admitted evils from the Christian point of view), war might be less inconsistent with the law of love than not to fight. Why, asked Niebuhr, did pacifists isolate war from a number of social evils? Why did they pretend that by sacrificing justice to nonviolence they were absolving themselves from guilt?

The pacifist witness, Niebuhr thought, so long as it did not confine itself within the limits of a purely vocational framework, was usually "corrupted by self-righteousness." It failed to acknowledge the necessity of making imperfect choices in a sinful world, for while "man" might act morally "society" remained essentially immoral. Again, because to be human was to be a sinner, Christians were not thereby exempt from the obligation of resisting evil in others by armed force.

In answer to Niebuhr's critique, pacifists maintained that, despite the reality of human sin, his pessimism was out of tune with the New Testament. "Jesus," wrote the Scottish theologian Professor G.H.C. Macgregor, perhaps the most cogent spokesman on the FOR side, "saw the world always and everywhere as God's world." Christians, therefore, did have the obligation to strive to apply Jesus' ethic in politics as well as in personal relations. True, tension would always exist between the demands of the law of love and the exigencies of the political situation. But, wrote Macgregor cleverly paraphrasing Niebuhr's own words, an ethical ideal is not made politically irrelevant by the impossibility of its perfect fulfillment here and now. In the modern world, moreover, war presented the most pressing moral problem; it was "the test case" for Christianity, the most obvious denial of the redemptive means which Jesus had postulated and of the active outgoing love from which alone reconciliation could flow.[80]

Niebuhr once called the FOR "a kind of Quaker conventicle inside of the traditional church." And indeed the pacifism of the interwar FOR, like the traditional peace testimony of the Quakers, was at first an essay in moralizing politics. It aimed, as it were, at recreating the seventeenth-century Quaker experiment in Pennsylvania but on an extended scale. The United States, the whole world, must be molded into a Quaker-like peaceable kingdom because the Kingdom of God on earth was a realm of peace. But with the rise of the dictatorships and the deteriorating international situation of the late thirties and early forties, it became increasingly difficult to present pacifism as an immediately viable and responsible political policy. The peace witness of the FOR, which had originated in the Social Gospel's endeavor to realize the Kingdom of God on the international as well as the national plane, reverted more closely to an earlier type of pacifism and began increasingly to take on the coloring of a sectarian creed. In the years before

Pearl Harbor, with the exception of A.J. Muste who, after his return to the pacifist fold, had continued to argue for a national acceptance of pacifism as the sole realistic way out of the impasse and to plead for nonviolence as an empirical technique for achieving social objectives and for national defense, the FOR's leaders stood for a pacifism that judged more and more by standards other than political ones. The FOR now largely discarded the utilitarian arguments and the pragmatic justifications of earlier years. The Kingdom of God on earth remained its goal but the politics of the Kingdom might lead by way of the Cross.[81]

Notes

1 The extensive Chertkov Papers (Russian State Library, Moscow, *fond* 435) are, hopefully, now at last becoming accessible to scholars. They provide abundant materials for the history of conscientious objection in the inter-war Soviet Union, and especially for the vigorous Tolstoyan movement in the 1920s. This whole topic represents an important, and as yet unexploited, theme in twentieth-century pacifism. So far, apart from the work of Paul D. Steeves on the Baptists and the seriously biased writings of the Marxist expert on sectarianism, A.I. Klibanov, only "Russian" Mennonite pacifism, then recovering with difficulty from its temporary lapse into *Selbstschutz* (Self-defense), has received much attention – and almost exclusively from North American Mennonite historians. But for background and bibliography, see Steeves, "Tolstoyans in Russia and the USSR," in Joseph L. Wieczynski, ed., *The Modern Encyclopedia of Russian and Soviet History* (Gulf Breeze [Florida]: Academic International Press), vol. 39 (1985), pp. 114–21. The author deals *inter alia* with the military question in the Soviet Union.

2 See, for instance, Gerhard Penner, *Mennoniten dienen in der Roten Armee* (Winnipeg: published by the author, 1975), for the kind of tribulations Mennonite noncombatants underwent during this period.

3 Drawing on Bonch-Bruevich's papers in the Russian State Library, Alexei Zverev and Bruno Coppieters examine in their article, "V.D. Bonch-Bruevich and the Doukhobors: On the Conscientious Objection Policies of the Bolsheviks," *Canadian Ethnic Studies* (Calgary), vol. 27 (1995), no. 3, pp. 72–90, the early Soviet attitude toward C.Os. (among whom Dukhobors in fact formed only a very small percentage). Other early Soviet leaders not unfriendly to the Tolstoyans included Lenin's wife, N.K. Krupskaia, and A.V. Lunacharsky, who became People's Commisar for Education. See Alfred Erich Senn, "P.I. Biriukov: A Tolstoyan in War, Revolution, and

Peace," *The Russian Review* (Stanford, CA), vol. 32, no. 3 (July, 1973), pp. 283, 284. At first, too, many sectarian pacifists supported the Bolsheviks' seizure of power, while of course rejecting the latter's use of violent means to achieve their aim. Zverev and Coppleters (*op. cit.*, pp. 78, 79) give a good example of such support from a conversation in October 1917 between Lenin and Ivan Koloskov, leader of the pacifist Trezvenniki (Teetotallers).

4 The key to this enigma seems to lie in the presence as a philosophy teacher in the same institution of Aldo Capitini, a leading spokesman for nonviolence in post-1945 Italy and, already even before the war, a believer in pacifism. The two men became friends. Free religious spirits, they both felt drawn to Gandhi and his practice of *ahimsa*.

5 Sergio Romano, *Giovanni Gentile: La filosofia al potere* (Milan: Bompiani, 1984), pp. 260, 261.

6 Xabi Agirre Aranburu, "The Insumisos of '36: The Anti-militarist Movement and the Spanish Civil War," 2 pts, *Peace News* (London), no. 2400 (March, 1996), p. 11, and no. 2401 (April, 1996), p. 11.

7 Norman Ingram, *The Politics of Dissent: Pacifism in France 1919–1939* (Oxford: Clarendon Press, 1991), p. 136. Part two of Ingram's book, entitled *"Pacifisme nouveau style,"* surveys the movement from its roots in the 1920s down to the outbreak of war in 1939.

8 *Ibid.*, p. 219; Ingram's summary of Gerin's views.

9 Quoted in *ibid.*, p. 232. Italics in the original.

10 After the fall of France in June 1940 some of the integral pacifists became collaborationists and supporters of the Vichy régime, despite their leftwing past. Challaye, for instance, wrote for *Germinal*, "which preached outright collaboration with the occupier" and was financed by the Germans. They retained their hatred of war but were carried away by their antipathy toward the Soviet Union and desire for Franco-German reconciliation to support a Nazi victory. See Ingram, "Pacifism and the Liberation," chap. XIV in H.R. Kedword and Nancy Wood, eds., *The Liberation of France: Image and Event* (Oxford: Berg Publishers, 1995), pp. 210–16, 219, 220.

11 Bart de Ligt expounded such ideas in his book *The Conquest of Violence: An Essay on War and Revolution*, transl. from the French by Honor Tracy (London: Pluto Press, 1989). This edition contains a perceptive new introduction by Peter van den Dungen as well as Aldous Huxley's brief introduction to the 1937 edition. For the idea of anarcho-pacifism, see the pamphlet by Geoffrey Ostergaard, *Resisting the Nation-State: The Pacifist and Anarchist Traditions* (London: Peace Pledge Union, rev. edn., 1991).

12 Henk van den Berg and Ton Coppes, *Dominees in het geweer: Het christenantimilitarisme van Kerk en Vrede 1924–1950* (Nijmegen: Studium voor Vredesvraagstuken, 1982), chaps. II, IV, V.

13 *Ibid.*, p. 28.
14 The memoirs of his widow, Ingeborg Küster, *Politik – haben Sie das denn notig? Autobiographie einer Pazifistin* (Hamburg: Buntbuch-Verlag, 1983), throw light on Küster's antiwar activities. See also Johann Ortmann, *'Sind Kriege notwendig?': Lebenserinnerungen eines Pazifisten und Schulmannes*, ed. Gerda Brömel (Kiel: Malik Regional Verlagsgesellschaft, 1995), pp. 171, 172. Ortmann stresses Küster's gifts as an orator in addition to his talents as a journalist.
15 See Charles F. Howlett, "John Nevin Sayre and the International Fellowship of Reconciliation," *Peace & Change* (Newbury Park, CA), vol. 15, no. 2 (April, 1990), pp. 123–49, and "John Nevin Sayre and the American Fellowship of Reconciliation," *The Pennsylvania Magazine of History and Biography* (Philadelphia), vol. 114, no. 3 (July, 1990), pp. 399–421.
16 See the detailed monograph by Steven Schroeder, *A Community and a Perspective: Lutheran Peace Fellowship and the Edge of the Church, 1941–1991* (Lanham, MD: University Press of America, 1993).
17 A detailed account of FOR activity in interwar Britain is given in Jill Wallis, *Valiant for Peace* (London: Fellowship of Reconciliation, 1991), pt. 2. See also Martin Ceadel, "Christian Pacifism in the Era of the Two World Wars," pp. 391–408, in *Studies in Church History*, vol. 20: W.J. Sheils, ed., *The Church and War* (Basil Blackwell, 1983).
18 Ceadel, *Pacifism in Britain 1914–1945: The Defining of a Faith* (Oxford: Clarendon Press, 1980), the standard history of British pacifism during the thirty one years covered, is especially good for the 1930s.
19 *The Christian International* (London), no. 1 (April, 1920), p. 9.
20 Quoted in Grace M. Beaton, *Twenty Years' Work in the War Resisters' International* (Enfield, Middlesex: WRI, 1945), p. 5.
21 *Modern Martyrs: Documents Collected by the War Resisters' International* (Enfield: WRI, 1927), opposite p. 1. In East Central Europe conscientious objectors in the interwar years were drawn almost exclusively from such sects as the Nazarenes, Seventh-day Adventists or Jehovah's Witnesses or from isolated Tolstoyans. The influence Tolstoy's writings could still exert on religiously minded Slav peasants is shown in the following letter dictated by the illiterate mother of a young Belarusan peasant, imprisoned in Poland for refusing to undergo military training: "Five years ago there appeared what was at first a remarkable but joyful change in him. He was constantly reading. At my request he formed the habit of telling me what he had been reading, or he read it to me – and then I became convinced, to my great joy, that he was reading religious books. So that the name of Leo Tolstoy became known to me ... My son, who was then a lad of 17 or 18, began more to be sharply distinguished from others of his age. When he was 21 he appeared before the Recruiting Commission and explained

straightforwardly and plainly that he would not serve as a soldier because
he loved his neighbour and therefore could not learn to murder him." From
a leaflet (1937) in Archives, Swarthmore College Peace Collection: War
Resisters' International, DFG 39, Box 5. Eventually after spending some
time in jail, the young man consented to bear arms.

22 Hans Kohn in *War Resisters in Many Lands* (Enfield, WRI, 1928), pp. 34–36.
In the 1930s Kohn, later to become an outstanding historian of modern
nationalism, emerged as a severe critic of the political aspects of pacifism.
See for example his book *The Twentieth Century: A Mid-way Account of
the Western World* (New York: The Macmillan Company, 1949), pp. 204,
205.

23 Ethelwyn Best and Bernard Pike, *International Voluntary Service for Peace
1920–1946* (London: George Allen & Unwin Ltd., 1948), Appendix IV.

24 Quoted in John K. Nelson, *The Peace Prophets* (Chapel Hill: The University
of North Carolina Press, 1967), p. 45.

25 See van den Berg and Coppes, *op. cit.*, chap. III.

26 The key work here is of course Immanuel Kant's short treatise *On Eternal
Peace (Zum ewigen Frieden)*, published in 1795.

27 Arthur Ponsonby, *Falsehood in War-time* (London: George Allen & Unwin
Ltd., 1928), p. 192.

28 Quoted in Nelson, *op. cit.*, p. 55.

29 A good example is to be found in the bestseller by Beverley Nichols, *Cry
Havoc!* (London: Jonathan Cape, 1933).

30 C.E.M. Joad, *Why War?* (Harmondsworth, Middlesex: Penguin Books Limited, 1939), p. 231.

31 Ceadel, *op. cit.*, p. 81. The prominent economist and social scientist Barbara
(Baroness) Wootton, in her "autobiographical reflections" she entitled *In a
World I never made* (London: George Allen & Unwin, 1967), pp. 173–8, has
expressed admirably this kind of pacifism. Defining her mature view of life
as "equally well described as agnostic or atheistical" (p. 162), she declared
herself an absolute pacifist (though, like Quakers, not opposed to the use of
nonlethal means in law enforcement). "Except in a few extreme cases of
mercy killing," she wrote, "it is unthinkable to contemplate taking the life
of another human being ... nor, if I were liable to be conscripted for military
service, can I imagine the circumstances in which I should not resist on
grounds of conscience ... The doctrine that the end justifies the means is
widely held to be morally execrable. Yet what other possible justification
can be found to defend the wholesale sacrifice of innocent lives, including
those of young children, in war?" In Wootton's "secular morality," "first
and foremost" came "a profound sense of the value of human life and
human personality"; for "those who believe that this life is all that we can
expect to have naturally hold it dear."

32 Huxley to Woolf, March 2, 1936; from Grover Smith, ed., *Letters of Aldous Huxley* (London: Chatto & Windus, 1969), p. 401.
33 Nelson, *op. cit.*, p. 122.
34 George Lansbury, "Why Pacifists should be Socialists," *Fact*, no. 7 (October, 1937), pp. 37, 38.
35 Aldous Huxley, ed., *An Encyclopaedia of Pacifism* (London: Chatto & Windus, 1937), pp. 100, 101. Cf. p. 41: "Co-operation is applied pacifism."
36 See Herbert Read, *The Politics of the Unpolitical* (London: Routledge, 1943), pp. 1–12. Much the same thought is expressed in a letter from Aldous Huxley to Kingsley Martin, dated July 30, 1939 (printed in Martin's *Editor: A Second Volume of Autobiography 1931–45* [London: Hutchinson, 1968], p. 204): "Religion can have no politics except the creation of small-scale societies of chosen individuals outside and on the margin of the essentially unviable large-scale societies, whose nature dooms them to self-frustration and suicide."
37 Huxley's philosophical treatise *Ends and Means* (London: Chatto & Windus, 1937), along with his novel *Eyeless in Gaza* (London: Chatto & Windus, 1936), provided the main vehicles for spreading his version of pacifism.
38 Huxley, *What are you going to do about it? The Case for Constructive Peace* (London: Chatto & Windus, 1936), pp. 14, 17.
39 De Ligt, *op. cit.*, pp. 269–85.
40 Quoted, from MS. (1937) by Maude Royden, in Sybil Oldfield, *Women against the Iron Fist: Alternatives to Militarism 1900–1989* (Oxford: Basil Blackwell, 1989), p. 62. See also Sheila Fletcher, *Maude Royden: A Life* (Oxford: Basil Blackwell, 1989), pp. 258–61. We should note here the opposition to Japanese expansionism by the largely pacifist Mukyōkai movement of "non-church" Christians. At least one of them, we know, "refused to report for conscription" and suffered imprisonment along with Jehovah's Witnesses, Seventh-day Adventists, and members of Holiness groups. (Penalties for the handful of Japanese conscientious objectors increased in severity during World War II.) See Carlo Caldarola, *Christianity: The Japanese Way* (Leiden: E.J. Brill, 1979), pp. 159–63, 165–7, 171–6.
41 Letter quoted in Charles Chatfield, *For Peace and Justice: Pacifism in America 1914–1941* (Knoxville: The University of Tennessee Press, 1971), p. 91. Chatfield's is the most comprehensive history of American pacifism during this period.
42 Cf. Ponsonby, *Now is the Time: An Appeal for Peace* (London: Leonard Parson, 1925), pp. 109, 129.
43 *No More War* (London), vol. I, no. 5 (June, 1922), p. 5.
44 A.J.P. Taylor, *English History 1914–1945* (Oxford: The Clarendon Press, 1965), p. 299, n. 3.
45 Winston S. Churchill, *The Second World War*, vol. I: *The Gathering Storm* (London: Casell & Co. Ltd., 1948), pp. 66, 67.

46 Ceadel, "The 'King and Country' Debate, 1933: Student Politics, Pacifism
    and the Dictators,": *The Historical Journal* (Cambridge), vol. 22, no. 2 (June
    1979), pp. 397–422.

47 The various stages, through which Rolland's ideas on pacifism went during
    the interwar years, have been carefully traced by Ingram in his chapter enti-
    tled "Romain Rolland, Interwar Pacifism and the Problem of Peace," pp.
    143–164 in Chatfield and van den Dungen, eds., *Peace Movements and Politi-
    cal Cultures* (Knoxville: The University of Tennessee Press, 1988). For
    Rolland as a "Gandhian," see also David James Fisher, *Romain Rolland and
    the Politics of Intellectual Engagement* (Berkeley and Los Angeles: University
    of California Press, 1988), pp. 112–144, 323–331.

48 Discussion of Einstein's pacifism is based mainly on Otto Nathan and
    Heinz Norden, eds., *Einstein on Peace* (New York: Simon and Schuster,
    1960), esp. pp. 91, 98, 100, 101, 117–19, 124, 232, 233, 239, 246; WRI Interna-
    tional Council Communication No. 161 (5 September 1933), in Archives,
    Swarthmore College Peace Collection. See also Harold F. Bing, "Einstein
    and the WRI," *War Resistance* (London) , vol. 2, no. 23 (1967), pp. 10–15, 19,
    and Joseph Rotblat, "Einstein the Pacifist Warrior," pp. 99–116 in Maurice
    Goldsmith *et al.*, eds., *Einstein: The First Hundred Years* (Oxford: Pergamon
    Press, 1980).

49 A.A. Milne, *Peace with Honour: An Enquiry into the War Convention* (London:
    Methuen & Co., 1934), p. 144.

50 For the split between pacifists and internationalists, see two articles in the
    Historical Journal: J.A. Thompson, "Lord Cecil and the Pacifists in the
    League of Nations Union," vol. 20, no. 4 (December, 1977), pp. 949–59 and,
    on a broader background and with more questionable commentary,
    Michael Pugh, "Pacifism and Politics in Britain, 1931–1935," vol. 23, no. 3
    (September, 1980), pp. 641–56.

51 *The Role of the Peace Movements in the 1930's: Who Was for Munich?*, Pamphlet
    No. 1 (London: University Group in Defence Policy, 1959), p. 15.

52 For the ambiguities of Allen's peace position during the 1930s, see Tho-
    mas C. Kennedy, "'Peace in Our Time': The Personal Diplomacy of Lord
    Allen of Hurtwood, 1933–38," pp. 217–39 in Solomon Wank, ed., *Doves and
    Diplomats: Foreign Offices and Peace Movements in Europe and America in the
    Twentieth Century* (Westport, CT: Greenwood Press, 1978). In this period
    Allen shifted from absolute pacifism via collective security eventually to
    appeasement. Chamberlain called his defense of Munich "a masterly state-
    ment of the case" (p. 239 n. 76); Allen died five months later, so we shall
    never know how this leading opponent of conscription in World War I
    would have reacted to the Second World War. Another British peace advo-
    cate who urged pacifists to support League action, including military
    sanctions, was Sir Norman Angell (who at one moment had even claimed

to be "a non-resister" himself). See Louis Bisceglia, *Norman Angell and Liberal Internationalism in Britain. 1931–35* (New York and London: Garland Publishing, 1982), pp. 173, 174; Ceadel, *Pacifism*, p. 141–44. Unlike Allen, Angell opposed appeasement.

53 For one example of this tendency out of many, see Sherwood Eddy, *Eighty Adventurous Years: An Autobiography* (New York: Harper & Brothers, 1955), p. 104.

54 For this incident, see Taylor, *op. cit.*, p. 142; G. Lansbury, *My Pilgrimage for Peace* (New York: Henry Holt and Company, 1938), pp. 6, 7; Alan Bullock, *The Life and Times of Ernest Bevin*, vol. I (London: Heinemann, 1960), pp. 565–571; Bob Holman, *Good Old George: The Life of George Lansbury* (Oxford: Lion Publishing, 1990), pp. 143–45; Jonathan Schneer, *op. cit.*, pp. 130–195; see also Holman, *op. cit.*, pp. 76–78, 154–163. Lansbury's peace absolutism originated in World War I.

55 Letter dated August 7, 1935, in Martin, *op. cit.*, p. 194.

56 Bertrand Russell, *Which Way to Peace?* (London: Michael Joseph Ltd., 1936), p. 139.

57 Raymond A. Jones, *Arthur Ponsonby: The Politics of Life* (London: Christopher Helm, 1989), pp. 208, 209. See also Ceadel, *Pacifism*, p. 80.

58 Quotation from Nelson, *op. cit.*, p. 58; Michael Wreszin, *Oswald Garrison Villard: Pacifist at War* (Bloomington: Indiana University Press, 1965), p. 268.

59 Allen Mills, *Fool for Christ: The Political Thought of J.S. Woodsworth* (Toronto: University of Toronto Press, 1991), pp. 195, 198, 201 ff, 205–9, 213, 222–4. Woodsworth had once been a Methodist minister but by this date all that remained of his Christian faith was a vague belief in Jesus' ethical teachings, including pacifism (*ibid.*, p. 196). Pacifism in Canada at this time, though, was primarily religious with the Canadian Fellowship of Reconciliation as its chief interdenominational organization. Photographs of four Fellowship leaders are reproduced above. Other prominent members included James M. Finlay, a United Church minister, and Fred Haslam of the small Quaker Society of Friends, both in Toronto, and the independent Dukhobor, Peter Makaroff, in Saskatchewan. The groups which would produce most C.O.s in the coming war – like the Mennonites, communalist Dukhobors, and Jehovah's Witnesses – remained outside the organized pacifist movement.

60 *Ibid.*, pp. 220–2.

61 Quoted in R. Ellis Roberts, *H.R.L. Sheppard: Life and Letters* (London: John Murray, 1942), p. 277.

62 Sheppard was the author of *We Say "No": The Plain Man's Guide to Pacifism* (London: John Murray, 1935); not, however, one of the best expositions of Christian pacifism.

63 Ceadel, *op. cit.*, pp. 259, 260. Jowett's letter was dated September 4, 1936.

64 Brigadier General F.P. Crozier, *The Men I Killed* (London: Michael Joseph Ltd., 1937), p. 23. Crozier is not the only general to be converted to complete pacifism in the twentieth century. In France Percin and Verraux, in Germany von Deimling and von Schönaich, and in Austria Siegfried Popper, are other examples.

65 H.W.J. Edwards, *Young England* (London: Hutchinson & Co., 1938), chap. VII.

66 Ceadel, *Pacifism*, p. 282.

67 David C. Lukowitz, "British Pacifists and Appeasement: The Peace Pledge Union," *Journal of Contemporary History* (London), vol. 9, no. 1 (January, 1964), p. 126. See also Ceadel, *op. cit.*, pp. 274–81. Lukowitz is also the author of a series of perceptive articles on the PPU published in its not easily accessible house journal, *The Pacifist* (London), vol. 10, nos. 8–11 (June–September, 1971) and vol. 11, no. 4 (February, 1972).

68 In his Foreword to Robert O. Byrd, *Quaker Ways in Foreign Policy* (Toronto: University of Toronto Press, 1960), pp. vii–ix.

69 Cleo Mowers in May 1939; from Thomas P. Socknat, *Witness against War: Pacifism in Canada, 1900–1945* (Toronto: University of Toronto Press, 1987), p. 190.

70 Quoted in Nelson, *op. cit.*, p. 84.

71 Donald B. Meyer, *The Protestant Search for Political Realism, 1919–1941* (Berkeley and Los Angeles: University of California Press, 1961), p. 51.

72 Quotations from *ibid.*, pp. 95, 439.

73 Nat Hentoff, ed., *The Essays of A.J. Muste* (Indianapolis, New York, Kansas City: The Bobbs-Merrill Company, Inc., 1967), p. 75.

74 For the role of the College in the development of interwar American pacifism and Muste's contribution to its work, see Howlett, *Brookwood Labor College and the Struggle for Peace and Social Justice in America* (Lewiston/Queenston/Lampeter: The Edwin Mellen Press, 1993).

75 *Christ and the Class War* (London: International FOR, 1929), p. 2.

76 Reinhold Niebuhr, *Moral Man and Immoral Society* (New York and London: Charles Scribner's & Sons, 1932), pp. 251, 252, 254, 255. The book represents a transitional stage in Niebuhr's thinking between pacifism and antipacifism. The problem of war, though, is dealt with only peripherally, nonviolence being considered largely in a social setting.

77 Quoted in Nelson, *op. cit.*, p. 75.

78 J.B. Matthews, "Is Pacifism Counter-Revolutionary?" *New Masses* (New York), 2 January 1934. After travelling with the Communists for a time, Matthews ended up as Senator Joseph McCarthy's henchman for "exposing" Reds among the Protestant clergy (among whom he numbered his former left-pacifist colleague, Reinhold Niebuhr).

79 "Why I Leave the FOR," reprinted in D.R. Robertson, ed., *Love and Justice:*

Selections from the Shorter Writings of Reinhold Niebuhr (Philadelphia: The Westminster Press, 1957), pp. 254–9. See also Niebuhr's contribution in *Economic Justice* (New Haven, CT), vol. 1, no. 9 (November, 1933).

80 Niebuhr's polemics against pacifism are to be found scattered among his later writings. Perhaps his most succinct exposition is in *Why the Christian Church is not Pacifist* (London: Student Christian Movement Press, 1940). G.H.C. Macgregor's *The Relevance of the Impossible* was first published by the British Fellowship of Reconciliation (London, 1941). Most studies of Niebuhr's thought have something to say about the shifts in his views on pacifism. See, for instance, Ronald H. Stone, *Reinhold Niebuhr: Prophet to Politicians* (Nashville: Abingdon Press, 1972), pp. 40–43, 73–79, or his *Professor Reinhold Niebuhr: A Mentor to the Twentieth Century* (Louisville, Kentucky: Westminster/John Knox Press, 1992), pp. 84–86, 99–105, 119, 143, 144. Justus D. Doenecke, "Reinhold Niebuhr and His Critics: The Interventionist Controversy in World War II," *Anglican and Episcopal History* (Austin, TX), vol. 64, no. 4 (December, 1995), pp. 459–81, deals with the final stages in the clash between Niebuhr and the pacifists. See also Gerald L. Sittser, *A Cautious Patriotism: The American Churches and the Second World War* (Chapel Hill and London: The University of North Carolina Press, 1997), pp. 64–76, 97, 98. Sittser criticizes Niebuhr for "making his opponents mere caricatures of what they really were" (p. 72).

81 In biographies of two leading figures in the interwar FOR, Robert Moats Miller argues cogently in favor of the pacifist case against Niebuhr. "Not many scholars," he writes, "have troubled to listen carefully to what pacifists were [then] saying." In Miller's view it was "the idealists" of the FOR who proved to be "the true realists in their understanding of the demoniac nature of modern war." See his *How shall they hear without a Preacher? The Life of Ernest Fremont Tittle* (Chapel Hill: The University of North Carolina Press, 1971), pp. 451–6, and *Harry Emerson Fosdick: Preacher, Pastor, Prophet* (New York: Oxford University Press, 1985), pp. 525–31. The quotations are taken from *Tittle*, pages 453 and 456 respectively.

V. The Pattern of Conscientious Objection: World War II

On the outbreak of war in September 1939 a distinguished English Quaker theologian said of his two sons, both of military age: "They might feel they had to serve with the Friends Ambulance Unit or in any relief service Friends might organize; they might feel called to take the absolute position and suffer imprisonment if need be for conscience sake, or they might feel they had to serve with the armed forces. Whatever their decision, they would have my full support. But I told them however they might choose, they would never be entirely happy, and would always have a guilty conscience."[1] They would retain a sense of guilt, he said, because of their collective responsibility for the sin from which the war had sprung.

By no means all pacifists, either in Britain or America, shared in full this almost Niebuhrian view. In World War II, however, the pacifist movement in both countries shed something of its previous optimism and took on a quasi-vocational coloring to a much larger extent than had been the case in the First World War. In 1914–18 the pacifists who gave the movement its tone had looked forward, despite the discouraging present, to the speedy inauguration of a peaceable world in the years ahead. A quarter of a century later such confidence appeared to many of them to be misplaced. Endeavor slowly to infuse society with the pacifist ethic now largely replaced the earlier hopes. Pacifism had, as it were, become once again, as it had largely been in earlier centuries, the faith of a sect (a thesis which Martin Ceadel, in particular, has cogently argued).

In Great Britain during the so-called "phony" war, that is, until the rapid German advances of the spring and early summer of 1940 culminating in the battle of Dunkirk, the Peace Pledge Union (PPU) went on pleading the need for a negotiated peace. A slightly eccentric pacifist aristocrat, Hastings, Duke of Bedford, even undertook private efforts to this end. But after Dunkirk, as the PPU's chronicler wrote, "no-one who lived through those days would deny that to continue such a campaign [i.e., for a negotiated peace] was not only useless, but damaging to the pacifist cause."[2]

In beleaguered Britain there still existed a surprising degree of political freedom, even for pacifists. When in May 1940 the government prosecuted the PPU for circulating a poster displaying the slogan: "War will cease when men refuse to fight. What are *You* going to do about it?", the organization had immediately consented to withdraw it and the case was then dropped. A group of young PPU mavericks calling themselves the Forward Movement protested vehemently at what they considered to be the Union's pusillanimity. But they failed to carry many other PPU members along with them: the leadership was distinctly cold. In fact the Forward Movement soon fizzled out. Several months later, however, in the hectic summer of 1940, the PPU's journal *Peace News* experienced difficulty both in finding a printer and in circumventing an unofficial boycott of the wholesale news agents. Voices were raised demanding its suppression. But in the end *Peace News* continued to appear regularly – and legally – throughout the war, although for a time in a much reduced format. In 1940, too, a bulwark of English liberty, *habeas corpus*, was suspended by parliament. "Regulation 18B" of the Defence Regulations, whereby those suspected by the authorities of sympathy with the enemy could be confined for an indefinite period of time, was to be employed (with a few exceptions) against Sir Oswald Mosley's British Union of Fascists and allied groups rather than against pacifists. But among the exceptions was the Quaker pacifist Ben Greene, a former Labour Party parliamentary candidate who, however, had later moved over to the extreme right and become an apologist for Nazi Germany.[3]

This moderation, especially if we compare it with the situation either in Britain or the United States in World War I, is indeed striking. It was due in part to the realization by the authorities that the pacifist movement, despite the fears of alarmists, scarcely represented a threat to the security of the country: most pacifists disliked Nazism as much as anyone. It stemmed, too, from the liberal attitude of both administration and general public, which will also appear later from our discussion of the treatment of British conscientious objectors in World War II. The fact that ex-pacifists sat in the coalition government formed by Winston Churchill in May 1940 and that a small group of convinced pacifists (mostly members of the Labour Party) existed in the two houses of parliament guaranteed that this minority view would be granted at least some understanding.

At the end of the war, in 1945, the PPU still had nearly 100,000 names on its membership list. There had been of course a number of defections, including several among its sponsors; we find, for instance, the Rev. Leslie Weatherhead, a popular Methodist preacher, declaring after war broke out that his signing the PPU pledge had resulted from a failure to think his position through and not from any well grounded pacifist belief.[4] In the course of the war, as its younger and most active members were caught up in the draft, the Union's activities had slackened. Under the brilliant – and controversial – direction of John Middleton Murry, who took over as editor in July 1940, the Union's *Peace News* gave strong support to the growing movement among pacifists to form income-pooling communities.[5] According to Murry, these cells of a new society were to perform the same task in the contemporary war-ridden world as the Christian monastic orders had done in the dark days following the fall of the Roman Empire. By no means all pacifists, however, followed him in this plan, and the communitarian movement in fact proved a passing phase in the history of British pacifism. The well known Iona Community proved an exception here. Founded in 1938 by the aristocratic Rev. George Macleod, a decorated Great War veteran who subsequently converted to pacifism and a man prominent in the counsels of the Presbyterian Church of Scotland, this experiment in communal living survived the end of hostilities.

Equally debatable were other theses expounded by Murry on the pages of his weekly journal: his belief, for instance, that, although Nazism was *per se* a bad system, a *pax germanica* was preferable to the intra-national anarchy that had hitherto existed on the European continent, or his increasingly anti-Soviet stance and fear of Stalinist totalitarianism which eventually led him in 1947 to abandon pacifism altogether.[6] Despite his "philo-nazi discussion of the war" Murry, however, had quickly realized the terrifying implications of the Jewish holocaust and mass murders of Poles when these events reached the British public at the end of 1942. Such revelations of human bestiality became an additional factor in steadily diminishing Murry's faith in pacifism.[7] Meanwhile the PPU, whose organ Murry continued to edit – in defiance of mounting opposition from part of the membership – until October 1946, favored on the whole an unpolitical stance and threw most of its energies into the support of conscientious objectors. Some members were active in the movement to get food relief through the allied blockade to the starving population of occupied Europe. Others backed the Bishop of Chichester's courageous campaign to stop the saturation bombing of German cities (the senseless cruelty of which has since then been increasingly recognized). There were also members who participated vigorously in both crusades, like the uncompromising absolutist Roy Walker or the novelist and champion of women's rights, Vera Brittain. Brittain wrote in mid-1943: "I am not responsible for the cruel deeds done by the Nazis in the name of the Germans, and much as I deplore them I cannot prevent them. But so long as the breath is in me I shall protest against abominations done by my government in the name of the British ... The mercilessness of others does not release us from the obligation to control ourselves."[8]

For the United States, the Japanese attack on the American fleet at Pearl Harbor on 6 December 1941 played the same role as Dunkirk had done for the British in rallying the people behind war against the Axis powers. The prewar pacifist movement in America, as we have seen in an earlier chapter, had been organizationally weaker than its counterpart in Great Britain. Its orientation was in some respects more religious; its involvement in active politics – in the sense of party politics and not the struggle for the Kingdom of God on earth – had been less. Pearl Harbor found a single pacifist in Congress, the liberal Republican, Representative Jeannette Rankin, whose vote then was the only one cast against war. During the war years the American FOR concentrated its efforts on stating the case for Christian pacifism. The historic peace churches – Quakers, Mennonites and the Church of the Brethren – had their hands full in looking after the interests of conscientious objectors and in planning for the day when postwar relief activities would become possible. True, in 1942 the War Resisters League had published the socialist pacifist Jessie W. Hughan's pamphlet on *Pacifism and Invasion* outlining a plan for nonviolent resistance in case of enemy invasion of the United States, while in mid-1943 another leading member of the WRL, George W. Hartmann, together with the Quaker Dorothy Hutchinson, launched a Peace Now Movement. This venture, however, did not succeed in enlisting the support of more than a fraction of the country's pacifists. By a negotiated settlement, so its supporters hoped, the Nazi extermination of the Jews, news of which was beginning to percolate through, too, to the American populace, might have been averted. But most pacifists remained suspicious of Hartmann's movement, especially on account of the backing it sought to gain of extreme right-wing elements.[9]

In the United States, as in Great Britain, attempts to mount a political antiwar movement were regarded by most pacifists as mistaken. Pacifism remained for the duration an expression of private witness, however frustrating this might seem to some. In both countries, despite the greater threat from without, the violent antagonism aroused in the public mind by conscientious objectors and pacifists in World War I was largely absent. The attitude of the authorities, too, was more tolerant than it had been then; in the United States, freedom of the press remained intact. From the pacifist side there was a greater sense now of unity with their nonpacifist countrymen and a more widespread desire to witness to their faith by service to the community in its hour of need rather than by a merely negative protest.

In a letter from his Californian retreat at Pacific Palisades, the expatriate English novelist, Aldous Huxley, caught exactly this prevailing mood among a majority of World War II pacifists when he wrote:

The application of pacifist methods to international politics always seems to me to bear a close analogy to the application of curative treatments to cancer. If you deal with a cancer early enough ... there is a good chance of being able to get rid of it altogether, or for a long period at least. The longer it is neglected ... the smaller the chance of success. Finally, a point is reached when, whatever may be done, disaster is certain ... It is the same with international politics ... Thus, it is clear that to make peace now with the Germans on their terms will lead to catastrophic results. And to go on fighting until the Nazi regime is overthrown and the German armies are annihilated will lead, in all probability, to results hardly if at all less catastrophic ... In war time, it would seem, psychological conditions are such that the application of pacifism to politics is for all practical purposes impossible. There can only be the personal pacifism of individuals. That the existence of such personal pacifists cannot produce any large-scale amelioration ... is obvious. Nevertheless, they fulfill a real social function, particularly when their pacifism is based upon 'theocentric' religious experience. The world would be even more horrible than it actually is [without them] ... It is immensely to the credit of the English and American governments that they should have recognized the existence of personal pacifists, and provided for their functioning as integral parts of the democratic society.[10]

British Objectors: Service v. Witness

Legislative Provision for Conscientious Objection

In 1932 a popular novelist, temporarily in the pacifist camp, had envisaged his appearance before a tribunal in a future war as follows: "I am in the presence of General somebody, a bunch of Colonels and a clerk. My entrance coincides with the renewal of an air-raid outside. It is all rather dramatic, for the air-raid punctuates our arguments quite effectively."[11] In actual fact, although bombs did indeed fall on London and other cities in Britain, the reality was considerably more mundane. The administration of conscientious objection, too, was kept firmly under civilian control throughout the war.

Conscription was reintroduced a few months before the actual outbreak of war on 3 September 1939. In the previous May, a Military Training Act had been passed by Parliament, applying to males reaching the age of 20. In the debates that preceded its enactment both government and opposition spokesmen had talked of the need to avoid penalization of genuine scruples against war. Prime Minister Neville Chamberlain expressed a wish to respect even the absolutist stand. He had served himself on a tribunal during World War I and from his experience then, so he now assured the House, he felt "that it was both a useless and exasperating waste of time and effort to attempt to force such people to act in a manner which was contrary to their principles."[12]

On 3 September the previous act was replaced by a National Service (Armed Forces) Act, which made all men between the ages of 18 and 40 liable for military service for the duration of the war emergency. At the end of 1941 the age limit was raised to 51; in addition, single women between 20 and 30 were now made liable for some form of service.

Tribunals to deal with conscientious objectors were established under the conscription acts. These tribunals were bodies which, unlike their counterparts in World War I, were not required also to hear general cases of hardship: a duality of purpose which, we have seen, had not contributed to their efficient functioning in the earlier war. Tribunal members now were, on the whole, well chosen and they attempted to be courteous and fair in most instances. Some were moderately sympathetic to the pacifist case, while not themselves pacifists; a few Quakers and pacifists were even appointed to tribunals, but this was very rare. Every tribunal was required by law to include one trade union member, and the whole system was placed under the administration of the Ministry of Labour and National Service (whose head under Churchill's coalition government was the trade union leader, Ernest Bevin). If the application of a woman was being heard, the tribunal had to contain at least one woman member.

As in World War I, tribunals were entitled either to reject an application altogether, if they believed the applicant was insincere, or to give some form of exemption that would meet his conscientious scruples. This exemption might be unconditional, or it might be granted on condition that the applicant undertake some kind of alternative service under civilian control. A third possibility open to a tribunal was to require the applicant to do noncombatant service in the army: as in

World War I, a special Non-Combatant Corps (NCC) was set up within the army in April 1940, although a few objectors also served in the Royal Army Medical Corps (RAMC) or with Pioneer units. The duties of the NCC included trench digging, bomb disposal, construction of barracks and hospitals, and other tasks "not involving the handling of military material of an aggressive nature." The decision of the local tribunal might be appealed either by the applicant or by the Ministry of Labour's representative.

Although the administration of the tribunal system in World War II normally allowed a far fairer hearing to objectors than they had received in the previous war, the attempt to assess conscience did not fully succeed. In the first place, most tribunals in judging an applicant's sincerity put greatest reliance on supporting evidence: witnesses who would speak on the applicant's behalf, or letters of recommendation, or a past record of pacifist activity or of social work. Support from a minister of religion usually carried special weight. Those objectors, however sincere, who could not produce testimonials of some kind, were at a distinct disadvantage in presenting their case. Such persons were especially numerous among the youngest age groups called up. Again, many tribunal members experienced difficulty in understanding why most pacifists objected to noncombatant service. The former tended to regard such service as essentially humanitarian; while most objectors considered its basic aim, as with the rest of the army, to be the prosecution of war and not the saving of life. If an objector, asked whether he would help a wounded soldier, replied in the affirmative, he was quite likely to find himself directed by his tribunal to noncombatant duties, even if he had expressed his unwillingness to undertake them. (Objectors, usually through inexperience in argument, occasionally answered this question in the negative, and as a result were often given adverse publicity in the press.) Trouble would have been saved if tribunals had recognized that such applicants, whose objection to combatant service they had acknowledged to be sincere, also entertained genuine scruples concerning service in the NCC or RAMC. Rachel Barker, after examining the local tribunal records, has noted "the eagerness of Tribunal members to recommend applicants to the RAMC."[13] Finally, as the war dragged on and for several years the military situation continued to look extremely bleak, signs of strain began to appear among tribunal members as in the rest of the population. Less patience was shown toward unpopular attitudes; less understanding was displayed of the objectors' point of view.

About 60,000 men and 1,000 women applied for registration as conscientious objectors: roughly eight million were enrolled in the armed services. Of the applicants for C.O. status the local tribunals registered 4.7 percent unconditionally and 37.9 percent on condition that they did civilian alternative service; 27.7 percent were directed to noncombatant duties in the army and 29.7 percent were removed from the register altogether. About a third of these decisions were appealed; appellate tribunals then varied the terms of registration in about half the cases that came before them. Some tribunals were liberal in granting unconditional exemption; others gave it only infrequently. Agricultural work or forestry was the condition most favored by tribunals, followed closely by hospital work, civil defense and, toward the end of the war, coal mining. "Some Tribunals made frequent use of the condition of 'present occupation,' while others made a point of putting men to other work as a rough and ready means of preserving equality of sacrifice."[14]

The conscription of women, and the consequent appearance of women C.Os., had been a new development. "In practice the measure resembled industrial conscription rather than military conscription. There were Women's Services but women were free to choose between them, Civil Defence Services or work in industry. Additionally, no woman would have to use a 'lethal weapon' unless she gave her written permission."[15] The majority of women C.Os. eventually obtained a condition of service they could in good conscience accept, but often only after appeal. However, some unconditionalists, mostly Jehovah's witnesses, were sent to prison for rejecting the decision of their Appellate Tribunal. Magistrates, though, sometimes showed reluctance in sentencing "young women of good character" to a jail term.[16]

Conscience v. the Law

The clash between conscience and the law was less dramatic, and less painful, than in World War I. This stemmed from two main factors: on the one hand, the declining impulse toward an absolutist stand on the part of the objectors themselves and their greater willingness to accept some form of service as an acceptable witness and, on the other hand, the increased toleration and understanding of conscientious objection shown both by the authorities and the community at large. Nevertheless, despite the efforts of parliament to prevent the harrying of conscientious objectors that had taken place in World War I, and the genuine attempt made by most tribunals to reach a fair decision in the cases which appeared before them, some 5,500 objectors (of whom nearly 500 were women) were sentenced to terms in civil prison. In addition over 1,000 conscientious objectors were court-martialed and sentenced to detention in military prisons.

Not all the imprisoned objectors found themselves in jail for refusing to abide by their tribunal's judgment. A few were libertarian nonregistrants who objected to voluntary cooperation with the machinery of conscription; but in such instances the authorities usually registered the objector willy-nilly and his case was heard by a tribunal *in absentia*. There were objectors to service in the Home Guard, a part-time militia in which compulsory service was required in January 1942 for able-bodied males up to the age of 51. Conscientious objectors were automatically exempt – so long as they were registered as such either temporarily or permanently. However, objectors whose applications had been dismissed, or older pacifists whose age group had not yet been registered for military conscription, were sometimes prosecuted for refusing to serve in the Home Guard. There were objectors, too, to compulsion for various forms of civil defense, in particular for fire-watching in the cities which became obligatory in 1941 after Britain had experienced the *blitz*, as well as to industrial conscription introduced in April of the same year. In neither case was the character of the duties demanded usually regarded by pacifists as in itself objectionable; exception was taken to their ultimately military purpose and to the element of governmental compulsion.

Immediately prior to the war some pacifists had opposed Air Raid Precautions (ARP) as part of the machinery of war preparation. After raids had begun, however, pacifists along with the rest of the population shared in the measures taken to save life, care for the homeless, and prevent the destruction of property resulting from air bombardment. As the Minister of Labour, Ernest Bevin, told the House of Commons in December 1943: "There are thousands of cases in which conscientious objectors, although they have refused to take up arms, have shown as much courage as anyone else in Civil Defense"[17] – either in a part-time capacity or in the performance of their alternative service. Some pacifists, however, continued to regard civil defense as an integral part of the war effort and therefore objectionable for that reason. And absolutists, although some of them readily performed such duties voluntarily, were not prepared to accept civil defense or indeed any other condition in exchange for exemption. There were some 575 cases where men were prosecuted (one of them nine times!) for refusing compulsory fire-watching or other part-time civil defense duties; about 90 women were convicted for the same offense, the best known of whom was the Quaker scientist, Dr. (later Dame) Kathleen Lonsdale. A short term of imprisonment, usually of three months' duration, was the normal penalty imposed.

Those pacifists refusing directions imposed under industrial conscription, writes a historian of conscientious objection in World War II Britain, "were handled with circumspection and restraint."[18] The labor and trade movement, as in World War I, was itself disquieted by the possible implications of conscription of labor in regard to its own freedom of organization, for wartime regulations controlled in practice almost the whole industrial field: both wages and conditions of employment were frozen. The Ministry of Labour made no attempt to force an objector to go into munitions or other work directly connected with the prosecution of the war, but it did refuse to allow the same right to seek unconditional exemption as was permitted objectors to military service. Since most able-bodied male objectors were covered by the machinery of military conscription, and since conditions of alternative service prescribed by tribunals were not ordinarily subject to alteration by industrial direction (though this was legally permissible), those prosecuted were usually either young women, sometimes as young as 18 years of age, or respectable older citizens. Courts, therefore, were reluctant to convict in such cases. Some "industrial" objectors, however, were sentenced to short terms of imprisonment. A total of 610 men and 333 women were convicted for resisting industrial conscription.

The main body of objectors who clashed with the law were not the comparatively small number of nonregistrants and Home Guard, civil defense and "industrial" objectors, discussed just above, but draftees whose conscientious scruples had not been adequately dealt with at their tribunal hearings. Over 3,600 men were sent to prison for resisting induction into the army to which their tribunals had assigned them for either combatant or noncombatant services, and a further 355 persons (59 of them women) were jailed for noncompliance with their conditions of alternative civilian service, an offense which carried a maximum of twelve months' imprisonment if committed without "reasonable excuse." The latter were almost entirely of the absolutist persuasion; the former group included men who would willingly undertake some form of alternative service under civilian auspices but were prepared to go to jail rather than enter the army.

After an objector had had his application rejected successively by local and appellate tribunals, he was faced, if he wished to persevere in his stand, with two alternatives. One alternative was to submit to medical examination and subsequent induction into the army and thereafter refuse to obey military orders or in some other way make clear his objection to army service. Later, he might occasionally be the object of some sporadic, unorganized ill treatment of a none too serious nature if he declined to don an army uniform or was otherwise uncooperative. "The only organized savagery directed expressly at C.O.'s during the war took place at two army training centres . at Liverpool, during September and October, 1940."[19] This incident – usually known as the Dingle Vale case from the name of one of the two centers involved – became the subject of public protest and official enquiry. The maltreatment of objectors was then stopped and no further affairs of this kind occurred.

If the objector were sentenced by court-martial to a term of three or more months in a civil prison, he was entitled to apply for a review tribunal, which could then order his release. On the other hand, if the sentence, though a civil one, amounted to less than three months or if the court-martial decided that it should be served in a military detention barracks, the law did not permit the objector to renew his application to a tribunal. Despite recommendations from the War Office to the contrary, until the middle of 1941 nearly 50 percent of court-martial sentences were of the inadequate kind. In most instances this policy resulted not from ignorance of the law but from deliberate intention. For it permitted a species of "cat-and-mouse" treatment, to which objectors had been subjected in World War I. Repeated sentences could be inflicted on the objector in an effort to break down his resistance. One objector was court-martialed and sentenced as many as six times; two or three trials were quite usual. Sentences in detention barracks, where the regimen was extremely tough for all prisoners, might run up to two years (they were normally very much less). Eventually the worst abuses in regard to misplaced objectors in the army ceased, but the position still remained unsatisfactory.

A related problem which should be mentioned here was that of the "soldier C.Os.," men who had joined the army as volunteers or conscripts and later developed an objection to fighting. At first these were not eligible to apply for a tribunal after sentencing. The army authorities were apprehensive that, once the right to opt out of service was granted to serving soldiers, this concession might undermine discipline and cause a rush of the unconscientious to gain release in this way. In fact, though, these fears proved quite unfounded. In May 1940, soldiers who became objectors were permitted, under the same terms as other conscientious objectors under army control, to apply to an "Advisory Tribunal" for exemption and subsequent release from service according to the conditions laid down by the tribunal. Yet by the end of 1946 only 415 men had taken advantage of this provision.

The second alternative open to the civilian objector whose application had been dismissed by his tribunal was to refuse to undergo the prescribed medical examination. If he did this, there was no legal way of actually forcing him into the army. However, he could be – indeed he almost invariably was – haled before a civil court and sentenced to imprisonment for nonattendance at the statutory "medical." At the beginning, a small fine or a short prison term in lieu of a fine was all that the courts could impose. But, by the new National Service Act of April 1941, prison sentences of up to two years, or a fine of one hundred pounds, became the legal penalty for this offense. In fact, although there was considerable variation from place to place, courts usually sentenced objectors to terms of between six and twelve months. Only one objector, a Jehovah's Witness, received the maximum penalty of two years' imprisonment with hard labor.

Conditions in civil prisons, mostly fortress-like edifices dating back to the last century, differed from jail to jail though a monotonous régime prevailed throughout the system. While the violence found in the American prison system was almost totally absent, some amenities present there were lacking in wartime British jails, and scarcely any attempt was made to apply the findings of modern penology in the way this was done (with questionable success) in the federal prisons of the United States where almost all American C.Os., since they received sentences of over a year, were incarcerated. Imprisoned C.Os. in Britain received exactly the same treatment as other convicted prisoners, except that they were not fingerprinted at reception or photographed for criminal record or (normally) required to perform war work. They wore the gray prison uniform with its red star sewn on each sleeve to distinguish the "first offender" from the "old lag," or recidivist.[20] Prisoners spent a considerable part of their time locked in their cells, which contained no toilet facilities apart from a "baby-size" enamel chamber pot. A Quaker ex-inmate wrote of the insanitary daily routine of "slopping out" after fourteen hours locked up in one's cell: "Few prisoners will forget that revolting parade in the early morning when twenty or more men queue to empty their chamber-pots in a lavatory which as often as not is stopped up, and then rinse their chambers and fill their water jugs at the same sink." "The stench may be imagined," commented another Quaker ex-prisoner with reference to London's Wandsworth Prison.[21] But each C.O., at any rate, had his cell to himself – with an occasional bedbug or cockroach perhaps to keep him company. Due to the wartime shortage of manpower there were neither classes for prisoners nor recreational activities aside from the half hour or so walking in threes round the prison yard under close surveillance. However, after three months' incarceration prisoners came "on stage," i.e., they ate at least their midday dinner communally and no longer shut up in their cells. Food was perhaps adequate though usually badly cooked and unappetizingly served. And prisoners often complained of a "craving for food" which overtook them a week or two after entering prison. A Quaker C.O. wrote of this experience: "I well remember my joy, and the envy of others, when a bird dropped a half-eaten crust of bread at my feet on the exercise ground."[22]

Prisoners circulated within the prison only under escort provided by a prison guard (or warder), known in jail slang as a "screw"; they were subjected to repeated head counts as they were moved around as well as to the occasional frisking in search of forbidden articles concealed in the prisoners' clothing. C.Os. found the screws varied considerably in their attitude toward the prisoner of conscience: some were understanding and kindly (jailed Jehovah's Witnesses succeeded in making several converts among them), but others were hostile and hectoring. A slate with chalk was the only writing materials permitted, except when a pen was provided for the monthly letter out. As for reading matter, the inadequate resources of most prison libraries, with no personal choice permitted, could be supplemented by books sent in from outside, although of course literature considered to be undesirable would be confiscated before it reached the prisoner. Jehovah's Witnesses, though, succeeded in smuggling *The Watchtower* and a variety of Witness tracts into prison, and for a time C.Os. in Wormwood Scrubs Prison had their own clandestine house journal, which they christened *The Flowery*.[23] Some C.Os. found the monthly visits from relatives or friends of a half-hour duration to be somewhat painful, especially the first one when a pane of glass intervened between the prisoner and his visitors and communication had to be carried on, standing, through a wire mesh on either side of the glass pane. Still, even such contact with the outside world was generally appreciated.

Almost all C.Os. proved quite willing to cooperate while in prison,[24] performing the work to which they were assigned, however uncongenial, including the wearisome sewing of mailbags as an evening cell-task. They protested only on those rare occasions when they suspected such labor might be connected directly with the war effort. But a small minority of radical resisters, like the PPU activist Roy Walker,[25] consistently refused to work while in jail and were duly punished for this infringement of prison discipline, usually by the imposition of a restricted diet or solitary confinement, together with the withdrawal of any privileges accruing to the prisoner.

The jailed C.Os. of World War II, though they usually found the restraints of life in prison irksome and were glad to leave its walls and return to their wartime occupations, were well aware that their lot was now considerably better than that of their predecessors during the previous world conflict. The oppressive silence rule, for instance, endured by World War I C.Os., had gone and prisoners were free to converse with each other at exercise or in the workshops. Certainly British prisons still left ample room for improvement but the former iron régime, with its many brutalities, had passed away. In this difference in experience perhaps lies the explanation of the fact that no prison reformers of the caliber of Fenner Brockway or Stephen Hobhouse emerged from the ranks of the jailed objectors of World War II after the conflict was over.

At first it had looked as if the same species of "cat-and-mouse" treatment as we have discussed above in connection with objectors in the army would come into operation in regard to the larger number of objectors who had refused medical examination. But in December 1941 parliament permitted objectors in this last category, if their sentence amounted to a minimum of three months, to apply once again to an Appellate Tribunal for reconsideration of their case and for release from prison even before the expiry of their term. The concession was a wise one. There was indeed no sense, especially as most objectors were engaged outside in some kind of productive activity, in crowding the understaffed jails with prisoners whose reformation was extremely unlikely.[26]

There still continued to be, it is true, cases of reimprisonment for what was, in fact, essentially the same offense. Some objectors had received sentences too short to qualify them for a rehearing; others had their applications rejected again on appeal; yet others were unwilling to appear at all before a tribunal. But the Ministry of Labour soon adopted a policy of usually leaving such men alone (as well as those convicted for not observing their conditions of exemption), though use was sometimes made in this connection of the Ministry's powers of direction within the framework of industrial conscription. Otherwise a second prosecution became fairly rare, a third exceptional.

The Conscientious Objector

From what sections of the population were objectors in the Britain of World War II drawn? What kind of motives impelled them to take a minority and unpopular stand in a country that eventually became united behind its government to a degree that had scarcely been reached during World War I? What differences may be detected between the community of objectors in the First World War and that which took shape in the course of the second conflict?

"No class," writes Hayes, "had anything approaching a monopoly of 'conscience.' ... C.O.'s [before their call-up] could be found performing the hundred and one tasks that go to make up the wealth of the nation."[27] But we do see a preponderance among them of "white-collar" workers and a relative scarcity of manual laborers. Objectors from the lower income groups included a high proportion of members of the fundamentalist sects: Jehovah's Witnesses, Plymouth Brethren, Seventh-day Adventists, Christadelphians, etc. The Quakers, on the other hand, contributed a high percentage of professional men: university students and graduates played an important part in their Friends Ambulance Unit. The number of creative artists – painters, writers and musicians – who took the conscientious objector position is worth noting although naturally they formed a quantitatively insignificant element. The ugliness of modern war, its anarchic destructiveness, appeared to many of these men a denial of the values they stood for. We find major composers like Benjamin Britten, who returned from the United States to face a Tribunal, and Michael Tippett expressing in their music their detestation of war; the latter served a three-month sentence in Wormwood Scrubs Prison as a C.O.

The majority of objectors were church members, if not church-goers. Hayes is probably right in his view that statistics in this case are misleading, since the objector's religious affiliation, as with the rest of the population, might be nominal or his pacifism drawn primarily from nonreligious sources. "A good proportion of the applicants labelled 'religious' might properly have been included as 'general objectors,' typified by what one might call 'the Peace Pledge Union C.O.'."[28] Of the churches, the Methodists provided the highest percentage of conscientious objectors, followed by Anglicans (we find even as conservative a member of the established church as Dean Inge asserting: "As Christians we are bound to be pacifists"[29]), Baptists, and Congregationalists. There were also a few Catholic C.Os. inspired by the teachings of an older generation of Catholic pacifists like the artist, Eric Gill, or the theologian and preacher, W.E. Orchard (a founder member of the FOR who later exchanged Protestant nonconformity for Rome). The traditional bulwark of British pacifism, the Society of Friends, was a small body, numbering about 20,000 members. Though some of its young men, as in World War I, did combatant service, the majority of those who remained close to Quakerism became conscientious objectors.

Religious or religio-ethical motivation provided, then, the impulse for the overwhelming number of objectors. But there was, too, a small minority of political objectors who did not claim to be complete pacifists. A few of them were libertarians who objected to conscription and not to war (several men in this group even volunteered for the Home

Guard – a stand that does indeed seem curious but was in fact not illogical). There were also nationalist objectors: Welsh, Scottish, Irish and a handful of Indians, who were quite prepared to fight for their own country's independence and protection but not in a war they felt to be an alien cause.[30] Some Mosleyites claimed objector status as did a few persons of Italian origin who were unwilling to take up arms against their kin. Most political objectors, however, were drawn from the socialist "sects," i.e., from the Independent Labour Party, by now a mere shadow of its former self, and various smaller Marxist splinter bodies, as well as from anarchist groups of various kinds. There were, of course, objectors belonging to the Labour Party, but they were almost all thorough pacifists. Certainly not political, but perhaps not strictly pacifist, were the objectors belonging to such denominations as the Jehovah's Witnesses, who declared their willingness to support God's battalions at Armegeddon but who until then were unwilling to take part in the wars of this world. Whereas the Witnesses, as we have seen, carried on a militant propaganda for their beliefs and mostly claimed as ministers of religion (and were usually denied) unconditional exemption, other groups of this kind lived withdrawn from the world and readily accepted noncombatant service in the army.

Nonpacifist objectors – today we would call them "selective objectors" – were most often removed from the register by local tribunals. But the Appellate Tribunals adopted a much more liberal stand. They were prepared to accept the validity of such an objection if convinced of the sincerity of the applicant. Though some appellants were still unsuccessful and went to jail, the veteran antimilitarist, Fenner Brockway, was right in claiming the Appellate Tribunal's stand as a "notable victory for liberty." The Appellate Tribunals, in their search to give every sincerely held view its due, were even ready to recognize that employment on work connected with the manufacture of war materials did not in itself exclude the genuineness of an objection to fighting. This decision arose from the application for C.O. status of four Christadelphians engaged in such work, whose church based its noncombatancy on a literalist interpretation of the Biblical injunction: "Thou shalt not kill."

In comparing the pattern of conscientious objection in Britain in the two world wars of this century, several observations may be made. In the first place, there was general recognition among pacifists that the present liberal regulations concerning conscientious objection and the more understanding attitude adopted both by the authorities and a considerable section of public opinion were largely the result of the steadfast resistance to persecution put up by the objectors, and in par-

ticular the absolutists, of World War I. The rights now accorded to conscience were gratefully acknowledged, and many nonpacifists, too,
welcomed them as a significant achievement in the struggle for preserving individual liberty, even in wartime, against the increasingly
powerful modern state. At the same time – and this is the second point
that needs to be made here – the conscientious objectors of World War
II were less militantly crusading in spirit, less certain of being completely in the right, than their predecessors. A dilemma similar to that
presented by having to make a choice between the evil of war and the
evil of Hitlerism had been absent in the earlier struggle. The objectors
of World War II were also, we know, in many ways less politically
involved. In addition, in World War II the straight political objector
was no longer an important factor in the pattern of conscientious objection. Though the average objector might not be particularly religious in
the usual meaning of the word, his stand resulted from an ethical decision rather than a political choice.

Thirdly, in World War II it was no longer the absolutists – " the
logicians of conscience, the extremists of peace," as Hayes has called
them – who made the most vital contribution to the wartime pacifist
movement. For one thing the earlier absolutists by the uncompromising character of their war resistance had effectively made their point,
had won a fairly general, if sometimes grudging, recognition of conscientious objection. This did not really need to be done over again. In
addition, the complex organization of mid-twentieth-century war,
especially in a country so involved as Britain was, embraced the whole
community, including its conscientious objectors. To attempt to withdraw from society to the extent the absolutist position required
appeared now to many pacifists unrealistic. A desire to give a more
positive content to their witness against war seemed to them a more
appropriate response in the existing situation.

An academic philosopher with experience on a World War II tribunal, who was especially critical of the absolutist variety of objection,
once asserted that it was "chiefly to be found among the more extreme
members of the Society of Friends.,"[31] This judgment may well have
been correct, for a libertarian streak developed very early in the history
of the Quaker peace testimony. It found some confirmation at any rate
in the recollections of an objector jailed in the Second World War, who
wrote of the visiting Quaker chaplain (John P. Fletcher), a member of
the Quaker absolutist group of the 1914–18 era: "I remember a kind of
shy fervour with which he referred to the absolutist position; he would
... have been capable of staying in prison *indefinitely* for a reason of conscience – and that is a very rare quality – and I think he looked a little

disappointedly for signs of a similar quality in the C.O.'s of a generation later."[32]

Indeed in World War II one should not turn to its absolutists to find
the representative type of objector. One must look rather to those who
worked on the land as farm laborers or in forestry units or as market
gardeners, to those who served in the understaffed hospitals as porters, orderlies or ambulance drivers, to those who chose civil defense
or the Auxiliary Fire Service as the field of their alternative service, or
to those engaged in social work of the kind carried on, for instance, by
privately organized Pacifist Service Units among the depressed sections of the population in large industrial cities like London, Liverpool,
Manchester or Cardiff.[33] There is indeed some truth in Martin Ceadel's
assertion that "for most pacifists social service was a means of atoning
for being a tolerated sect without a political solution to offer."[34] Yet
many C.Os. found in such wartime occupations a source of genuine
satisfaction while a few discovered there a vocation for life.

In most cases the work done by objectors was undramatic; often it
was unskilled as well as monotonous. But it might occasionally allow
leisure for such activities as writing; for instance, the politically radical
Quaker Reginald Reynolds researched and wrote a large part of his
history of sanitation, intriguingly entitled *Cleanliness and Godliness*
(1943), during time-off from his Civil Defence duties in blitzed London. Alternative civilian service, though, rarely possessed any peculiarly pacifist flavor. Whereas objectors on the land frequently felt
isolated and ineffective in their witness, those employed in the cities
integrated more easily with the community. "The C.O. in the hospital,"
one of them wrote, "is in no way cut off from the world but rather constantly in touch with the fact of war. He works side by side with men
who support the war, yet his views are rarely held against him ... It is
by the way he does his job that he is judged."[35] Occasionally the nature
of the objectors' employment succeeded in attracting public attention –
and approval: the human "guinea-pigs," for instance, who assisted Dr.
Kenneth Mellanby in his researches on scabies at the Sorby Institute
(University of Sheffield), or the "conchies" in the Airborne Medical
Ambulance Unit who acted as medical orderlies with British para-
troopers at the battle of Arnhem, or the Anglican pacifists who ran the
Hungerford Club for vermin-ridden London tramps.

Though only a small percentage of the total number of objectors
served with the Friends Ambulance Unit (FAU), this body – like its predecessor in World War I – deserves brief notice. The FAU (pacifist "atheists not necessarily excluded" from membership) was not officially
sponsored by the Quakers but its association with the Society of Friends

was now closer than in the earlier war.[36] Part of its work was devoted to civilian relief in the blitzed cities of Britain and the devastated areas of western Europe as well as in India, China and the Near East. But it also continued its tradition of ambulance work with the Allied armies. The Unit remained a strange, though not disheartening, anomaly: a voluntary association of pacifists maintaining its identity and basic philosophy despite close integration into the army system. On a British troop ship, for instance, a Unit member *en route* to China once found himself asked to lecture on the work of the FAU. "I doubt," he later wrote with astonishment, "whether there are other armies in the world that would invite a man who refused to undergo military service to talk about other 'conchies' to a group of soldiers going overseas!"[37]

Honorable mention should be made, too, of a small group of pacifists of military age who, while not technically C.Os. and liable to appear before a tribunal, nevertheless gave up their regular jobs in order to share the lot of other pacifists in their age group. The scholarly Anglican clergyman, J.R.H. Moorman, provides a good example of this comradely spirit:

Moorman was Rector of Fallowfield, Manchester, when in 1942 refusing attractive offers of promotion, he resigned his living to become a farm worker. (His first book on St Francis had been published in 1940.) His decision was not a political protest, but a desire, as a pacifist, to share something of the hardship being asked of other men. He believed that the war was widening the gulf between the secure "little world" of the clergy and that of laypeople. The Bishop of Manchester ... was most sympathetic but could not quite follow his reasoning. Opinion in the parish was divided. During his two years as a farm labourer, at first he found it difficult to get used to tough manual work, primitive conditions and being ordered about. At weekends he helped the local vicar. In 1946 Bishop Bell asked Moorman to become Principal of Chichester [Theological College]. In 1959 he became Bishop of Ripon.[38]

Finally, we may note the absence in the Second World War of any organization comparable to the No-Conscription Fellowship (NCF). The PPU continued to function, of course, but it lacked the aggressive antimilitarism of the NCF. Moreover, the PPU included only the "pure" pacifists whereas the NCF had, in fact, embraced political opponents of war and many selective objectors as well. Its nearest equivalent in World War II was perhaps the Central Board for Conscientious Objectors, set up in 1939 soon after the re-introduction of conscription, with representation from some seventeen organizations sympathizing with the objectors' stand. The Board acted as a coordinating body to protect the interests of objectors of every variety (including, for instance, members of the Non-Combatant Corps refusing to do what they considered military work) and to make the objectors' case known to the public. It advised them concerning their legal rights and the consequences of the stand they had decided to take; despite occasional allegations in the press that the Board was attempting to coach conscience, it aimed not at manufacturing objectors but at clarifying their minds. Like the NCF in World War I, the Board lobbied parliament and supplied sympathetic M.P.'s with information which would be helpful to them in debate. It published periodically an information bulletin which included details of all legislative and executive rulings of concern to objectors, and it kept an accurate record of the wartime careers of almost all conscientious objectors. The Board performed its varied tasks with efficiency and zest. The establishment of a network of regional branches and local advisory panels helped, too, to make it effective in the provinces.

Associated with the Board, though an independent body, was the Pacifist Service Bureau, which acted as an employment exchange for objectors doing alternative service – with a license from the London County Council issued for this purpose! Calls to place objectors on the same pay as army privates had been strongly opposed by the powerful Trade Union Congress as a threat to the rights of labor; in any case there were serious practical difficulties in the way of implementing any such proposals. Especially at first, some discrimination existed as a result of private employers or local authorities refusing to employ objectors, but it was of limited occurrence. On the whole, though, the Bureau fulfilled a useful function in finding acceptable jobs for C.Os. who had received conditional exemption.

Britain's wartime objectors were gradually released from their obligations under conscription in 1946 and the first half of 1947, along with their contemporaries who had been serving in the armed forces. Some objectors continued in their wartime employment; in social service, in particular, there were those who found a lasting vocation. A few went on to take part in postwar relief in war-torn Europe. Others, especially in the youngest age groups, started to train for a future career in a university, teachers' training college or technical school. Most objectors, however, returned to their prewar jobs. In returning to peacetime conditions objectors met with little victimization and only infrequently with hostility. This had not been expected, for the intensity of the recent struggle, the losses in battle, and the destruction of the cities tested Britain perhaps as no other war had done. The tolerance shown toward a dissident minority, both during the struggle and after it was over, had its source not only in a long-standing respect for nonconformity, to which attention has already been drawn, but also to a growing feeling that in mid-twentieth-century war the traditional distinction between civilian and combatant had lost much of its meaning. This indeed posed a challenge, too, to pacifists. In such a situation where, if at all, could pacifism make a significant contribution? The question was given renewed urgency by the explosion of the first atomic bombs in August 1945.

American Objectors: Camp *v.* Prison

The Legislative Framework and Its Interpretation

As in Great Britain conscription in the United States was reintroduced before the country actually became involved in war. The Selective Training and Service Act of 16 September 1940, which called for the drafting of able-bodied males between the ages of 19 and 44, contained a section – 5(g) – outlining procedures for obtaining exemption as a conscientious objector. Exemption was allowed in the case of men who "by reason of religious training and belief" objected to participation in all warfare. It might cover only combatant service (1–A–O classification), or it might include exemption from noncombatant service as well (4–E classification). For those exempted from the latter, "work of national importance under civilian direction" was to be provided; the exact nature of such work, however, was not specified in the legislation. The task of assessing whether an application for exemption was genuine, a task which in practice also included that of deciding whether the objection was conscientious according to the definition laid down in the act, fell not as in Great Britain to specially constituted tribunals but to the local draft boards. If this Selective Service board decided positively on an application, it then had the obligation to assign the objector either to noncombatant duties in the armed forces or to civilian service, as it judged fitting. Appeal could be lodged against a local board decision through the Department of Justice, which would then refer the matter to a regional Board of Appeal.

If we compare these provisions with the legislation concerning conscientious objection passed by Congress in 1917, several improvements can be noticed. In the first place there was no requirement that the applicant belong to a pacifist denomination before his objection could fall within the meaning of the act. Secondly, alternative service outside the army was specifically provided for. Indeed, as we have seen, World War I experience had forced the administration in practice both to extend the categories of those entitled to exemption and to furlough men unwilling to accept noncombatant service for work in agriculture. The legislators in 1940 were wise to embody this experience in their conscription act. Yet there were serious deficiencies, too, in the new legislation. For one thing the sincere nonreligious objector, even when he was a complete pacifist, was left with no alternative except to submit or go to prison. And, of course, the same choice faced the selective objector. Again, the position of the absolutist received no consideration: no provision was made for unconditional exemption. A final shortcoming in the section of the act relating to conscientious objection may be mentioned: its failure to ensure that the work of national importance required of objectors as their alternative service would be not merely, as laid down, under civilian direction but would also, so far as possible, be unconnected with the war. Much, of course, would depend on the spirit in which this legislation was administered, whether it was interpreted formalistically or with a broader vision.

A registrant under the act who wished to apply for the status of conscientious objector was required to fill in a special form. (D.S.S. Form 47) giving details about his background and the reasons why he objected to participation in the war. His application was then considered by the local Selective Service board. These boards, each consisting usually of three or four members including one government-appointed lawyer, were made up largely of middle-class citizens: businessmen, members of the professions, substantial farmers in rural areas. There was rarely working class representation. Ex-servicemen and officers of the American Legion were numerous; this was not unnatural in view of the boards' main function in administering military conscription but scarcely conducive to an impartial consideration of conscientious objection to war.

Decisions were normally handed down without a hearing: only about 25 percent of objectors actually appeared before a board in person. However, if the applicant received a classification for which he did not ask, he had the right not only to lodge an appeal but also to demand a hearing first from the local board. Some boards treated objectors with courtesy and fairness; a few were clearly hostile (at Washita County, Oklahoma, for instance, the board referred to objectors as "un-American yellow dogs"). On the whole they tended, like the British tribunals, to put most reliance in reaching a decision on exterior criteria: membership in a church (especially in one of the peace sects) or in a pacifist society, or the length of time an applicant had been a pacifist. In some instances, especially in the rural Midwest where antipacifist feeling ran high and where communities of German-speaking Mennonites, Amish and Brethren aroused patriotic fears, boards, either through ignorance or prejudice – and certainly in contradiction both to the letter and the spirit of the law – refused altogether to grant IV-E (i.e., civilian service) classification. There were not infrequent cases, too, where local boards refused objectors the deferment to which they were legally entitled on grounds of hardship, age or nature of employment. Misclassification was of course often rectified on appeal.

A special problem was presented by the group of men, who may for convenience sake be called "humanitarian objectors." They did not belong to any church, though occasionally they might be members of an ethical society or secularist association. Many of them were affiliated to the War Resisters' League; some, though, had not participated in any organized pacifist activity. Their objection certainly did not stem from any religious training or belief. Yet these men opposed all war as contrary to their ethical code; they claimed a sanction for their stand as absolute as that of the religious objector. The local boards, understandably, were confused as to what to do. They could follow the letter of the law and reject such applications automatically; some boards did this. Or they might stretch its meaning a little and identify an ethical code with a religious belief. To add to the confusion – at least of those boards ready to take heed of government directions in the matter – the Selective Service administration was evidently itself perplexed how to proceed. Its first director, Clarence A. Dykstra, in December 1940 adopted an extremely liberal view. Membership in a religious body was not an essential qualification for classifying a man as a conscientious objector, he said. Any genuine conviction as to the ultimate purpose and value of life, which led a man to refuse participation in war, should be considered the outcome of "religious training and belief." Fifteen months later, in March 1942, General Lewis B. Hershey, who had succeeded Dykstra as director, considerably narrowed his predecessor's definition of religious belief. General Hershey now demanded "recognition of some source of all existence, which, whatever the type of conception, is Divine because it is the Source of all things." Thus belief is a transcendent deity now appeared essential. But the next year, 1943, the Second Circuit Court of Appeals in the case of Matthias Kauten provided a third interpretation. "A conscientious objection to participation in war under any circumstances," said the Court, "may justly be regarded as a response of the individual mentor, call it conscience or God, that is for many persons at the present time the equivalent of what has always been thought a religious impulse."[39] This almost Gandhian identification of God with truth was the farthest point reached in liberalizing the law on the subject until the decision in the Seeger case in 1965.

In regard to the selective objectors, the boards most often (though by no means invariably) rejected their applications. These men were usually, as in Great Britain, socialist or anarchist "sectarians," professedly antireligious men, who refused to fight in imperialist wars carried on by capitalist powers like Britain or U.S.A. or by renegades from socialism like Stalinist Russia. But there were borderline groups where a decision was extremely difficult. The objections to fighting of the Jehovah's Witnesses, for instance, were incontestably the result of religious training and belief. But should the Witnesses not still be considered ineligible for exemption since their refusal to participate in war did not appear to be absolute? They mostly had no theoretical compunction against taking human life; some Witnesses did not object to defending themselves or their families by arms or to employment in munitions or other war industry. They all approved the wars waged by the Jews in the Old Testament as a fulfillment of God's commandments (an approval incidentally that was shared by fundamentalist pacifists of the old school). They looked forward to the battle of Armageddon and God's victory over Satan's forces at some unspecified, but imminent date in the future, even though they might expect to take only a passive role there and leave the act of destruction to the Almighty. Like Alice faced by the White Queen through the looking-glass, members of the Selective Service boards were frequently puzzled how to interpret the Witnesses' program of war tomorrow, war yesterday, but never war today. Impressed by the patent sincerity of most Witnesses and their devotion to their church, some boards gave them exemption in one form or another. On the other hand, there were boards which were offended by the Witnesses' unyielding stance that neither Hitler's concentration camps nor other totalitarian régimes were to succeed in breaking down, and dismissed their applications.

A further complication ensued from most Witnesses claiming unconditional exemption under Section 5(d) of the 1940 act, which gave this status (4-D classification) to all theological students and accredited ministers of religion (a concession that had resulted, ironically, from pressure from the Roman Catholic hierarchy). Many Witnesses on being refused 4-D classification preferred – when given the choice – to go to prison rather than accept either noncombatant duties in the army or civilian public service. In 1942, however, General Hershey ruled that Witnesses putting in over 80 hours a month on work of a ministerial character had a justifiable claim for 4-D classification. Again, whether from ignorance or through prejudice against the Witnesses, boards in many instances continued to deny their claims for ministerial status.

A second group whose unwillingness to fight straddled the border-line between pacifist and selective objection was formed by the Roman Catholic opponents of war. American Catholics who took, or sup-ported, the conscientious objector position constituted only a very tiny fraction of the total active membership of the church. Some Catholic objectors were of the "evangelical" type arguing against war from its total incompatibility with the Christian spirit. They believed that Christians had an obligation to follow exactly the counsels of the Ser-mon on the Mount. There were also Catholic objectors who, without claiming to be unconditionally pacifist, refused to fight in modern wars because they considered the conditions under which such wars would be waged inevitably contravened the traditional Catholic teach-ing concerning a just war. Selective Service boards often failed to understand Catholic applicants and rejected them without more ado.

Appeals by conscientious objectors against decisions of the local boards were in fact successful in over 50 percent of cases. Recourse could be had from the judgment of the regional Board of Appeal, pro-vided this were not given unanimously, to a panel appointed by the Director of Selective Service at the President's request. Such panels were made up mainly of army officers, despite the protests of pacifist organizations. Sibley and Jacob, in their invaluable study of American conscientious objection in World War II (to which, on almost every page, our account is indebted), wrote of "military domination of the appellate system, particularly with respect to the presidential appeals committee."[40] This situation was indeed symptomatic of the control exercised by the army over the whole administration of conscientious objection, an authority which resulted in turn from the powerful influ-ence in such matters then exerted on Congress by the military.

No completely accurate figures exist of the number of men who became conscientious objectors to military service in World War II. The official Selective Service System estimate for the period 1940–47, totalled 72,354. But this is certainly too low. Sibley and Jacob, for instance, believe that the total number of conscientious objectors should probably be as high as 100,000, i.e., 0.30 percent of the 34 mil-lion registrants for military service, though they admit that this is merely an approximation. We should note, as this fact is not always realized, that over half of the C.Os. of World War II accepted noncom-batant service either in the army or (in very small numbers) in the navy.

Before moving on to discussion of how C.Os. fared at the hands of the American state we may briefly mention the emergence of a tiny group of war tax resisters, for whom – then as now – no provision existed in law. Most prominent of these was a young Methodist minister, Ernest Bromley, who in 1942 spent sixty days in jail for refusing to buy a compulsory "defense tax stamp" for his car; two years later Bromley began to withhold income tax because of its connection with war while at the same time filing an income-tax return. But nonpayment of war taxes of various kinds got under way only in the postwar period – and under the impact of the atomic bomb.

The Noncombatants

Of the men who accepted 1-A-O classification and served as noncombatants in the armed forces, somewhere between a quarter and a half were members of the by now world-wide Seventh-day Adventist Church (which still, however, drew its main strength from the United States where it had originated in the antebellum era). In July 1940 one of its leaders had stated: "We are not pacifists nor militarists nor conscientious objectors, but noncombatants ... as to the noncombatant [Adventist] he merely believes that he should not take human life. But he is willing to cooperate with his Government in any capacity that he can without having to violate his conscience in regard to taking a life."[41] Well before the outbreak of war Seventh-day Adventists had begun to train their young men as medical cadets in preparation for "man-made disaster," i.e., war.[42] They felt no hesitation, therefore, in entering upon noncombatant duties when called upon for service.

In World War II around 12,000 Seventh-day Adventists were inducted into the armed forces as noncombatants, a far larger number than that contributed by any other religious denomination. The prewar Adventist Medical Corps, which came into being in 1934, had been the creation of Everett Dick, a dynamic – and distinguished – history professor at Union College, an Adventist institution in Lincoln (Nebraska). Dick, though a lifelong member of the church, had served as a combatant in the U.S. Marines in the First World War; he continued to be at home in military circles, and he used these contacts to create a favorable atmosphere for Adventist draftees to undertake army medical work in a renewed global conflict he saw was approaching. "The training," Dick wrote later, "consisted of that given to medical department soldiers ... It was an orientation that would help the recruit, who would otherwise be entering the service of his country at a handicap, to fit into a place where he could serve God and his country conscientiously." Adventist draftees of 1917–18 had lacked such training. In a future war "it was hoped that the government would recognize this training by assigning ... trainees to the [army] medical department." Not all Adventists, however, approved the idea of quasi-military training for their youth. During the 1920s and the 1930s some members of the church, ministers as well as laity, became adherents of pacifism *sensu stricto* in contrast to the separatist, and more narrowly conceived, noncombatancy that had prevailed since the Civil War. Thus Dick and his associates in their plans to train future Adventist noncombatant soldiers – eventually of both sexes – consistently "emphasized the medical aspect." "We always spoke of it as medical corps rather than military training," he wrote. In their endeavors they seem soon to have won the support of the majority of church members.[43]

After war had broken out, the church leaders continued to insist that their draftees be considered conscientious cooperators – rather than conscientious objectors, except for purposes of exemption from combatant duties under the Selective Service Act. While in obedience to their Master they refused to kill or train to kill, they were ready in every other respect to assist their government in its time of need. Like most Mennonites at that date with their distinction between pacifism and nonresistance, the Adventist Church's leadership rejected the idea that it was a pacifist body. In September 1940, a few months before Pearl Harbor, its General Conference Committee had stated:

From the beginning of their existence, Seventh-day Adventists have called themselves noncombatants. ... This is not antimilitarism, it is not pacifism, it is not conscientious objection to war as that is ordinarily understood. ... The belief of the Seventh-day Adventist noncombatant does not require him to agitate against war, to oppose militarism, ... or to stand apart from the military establishment ... He recognizes that war is a natural, unavoidable consequence of ... a state of sin. ... He recognizes that war is an agency which God Himself has on occasion used to carry out divine objectives. He does not presume to sit in judgment upon civil governments for engaging in war. ... His belief in ... noncombatancy does not move the Seventh-day Adventist to refuse to wear a uniform, to salute his country's flag, to obey military orders. He will participate in any service, in the military service or out of it, ... which will contribute to the saving ... of human life ... [But] his discipleship to Jesus Christ prevents him from engaging in any act, ... which contributes to destroying or injuring human life, in the military service or out of it, in war or in peace ... As inconsistent with their noncombatant belief they avoid the bearing of arms in any capacity.[44]

In contrast to World War I, the church and its conscripts worked on the whole harmoniously with the military authorities in the Second World War. What friction there was usually concerned Sabbath observance.

"Is it proper to wash dishes in the Army on Sabbath?" figured, for instance, among ten questions the church proposed for prior discussion among potential draftees.[45] ("The instructor ... should eventually guide the discussion to proper conclusions" and be able to "outweigh the careless or extreme element in the group.")[46] Such difficulties eventually resolved themselves, though not always without court-martial proceedings; a satisfactory outcome was largely due to an understanding attitude on the part of the military on one hand, and to prompt action by such church officials as Carlyle Haynes, the energetic general secretary of its War Service Committee, on the other. Almost invariably Adventist draftees were granted 1-A-O classification. Refusal to carry a rifle, though, sometimes led to trouble after induction, especially from noncommissioned officers responsible for training recruits or from other G.Is., who resented what seemed preferential treatment of a fellow soldier. Such problems were quickly cleared up, often again due to the intervention of Elder Haynes; he put his numerous contacts in Congress or the military bureaucracy to good use in bringing relief to his afflicted brethren.

"Seventh-day Adventists," writes Cynthia Eller, "are especially proud of their record of [army] service [in World War II], which included at least two Legions of Merit, one Croix de Guerre, five silver stars, thirty bronze stars, twelve purple hearts, and one Congressional Medal of Honor, the highest award given to a soldier."[47] By their weaponless valor on the battlefield, these American Adventist soldiers deservedly gained respect for their position among many who had been unsympathetic hitherto toward those unwilling to fight in defense of their country. Their actions helped pave the way to an even smoother collaboration between Adventist noncombatants and the military during the Korean and the Vietnam Wars when again Adventist noncombatants gained awards for bravery. Perhaps, too, their meritorious military behavior even helped to improve the pacifist image generally among those who equated conscientious objection with cowardice and lack of patriotism, though this change of attitude could not have been entirely to the taste of the Adventist leaders who had proved so anxious to fence their people off in the public mind from other war resisters.

Two further comments are called for. In the first place, the Adventist position in World War II with regard to military service, despite appearances to the contrary, reflects a final abandonment of any kind of social isolation such as Mennonites, for instance, were still clinging to and a rapidly increasing acculturation to American society. Adventists now strove for respectability. They were keen to show that they

were good American patriots – indeed they *were* good American patriots – and they sought to demonstrate that only with respect to that
peculiar tenet of theirs of never taking human life did they differ on
war from their fellow citizens, including the top army "brass" and the
American Legion. Secondly, rejection of pacifism found expression in a
parochialism that hindered the cause of peace and in a lack of tolerance
for other pacifist approaches even when, basically, these were not far
removed from their own. Nevertheless, the Adventists bore a consistent wartime witness as noncombatant soldiers (and upholders of a
Saturday Sabbath), and they reaped the reward of their consistency as
noncombatants in growing respect for their sincerity and singlemind-
edness in the country at large as well as a genuine willingness in government circles to accommodate their position within any future
conscriptionist framework.

Apart from members of religious sects like the Adventists, whose
collective testimony against war stemmed from a literalist ban on taking life, noncombatant service appealed primarily to objectors who
sought in it an opportunity to relieve suffering humanity and to share
the hardships of the soldier. Such service, even if closely linked with
the war machine, appeared more directly useful than any alternative
civilian service. There were indeed members of most religious denominations among the noncombatants (be it noted, however, American
Christadelphians disowned members accepting noncombatant duties
as they had done in World War I while Mennonite leaders for the most
part sought to dissuade their C.Os. from entering the army). Some
men, especially those with heavy family commitments, accepted 1-A-O
status rather than 4-E because they felt they could not shoulder the
economic burdens entailed by the latter. "In Civilian Public Service one
had to pay one's own way or rely upon what one might regard as the
charitable contributions of others";[48] the authorities' steady refusal to
approve government pay for civilian service assignees stemmed in
part from a desire to push as many of them as possible to accept 1-A-O.
There were also objectors who, though they would have preferred
civilian work, did not turn down noncombatant service when assigned
it, since to do so would have entailed prosecution and imprisonment
and they did not feel strongly enough in the matter – or strong enough
– to face such consequences.

Although American noncombatants, unlike members of the British
army's Non-Combatant Corps, did not wear a distinctive badge, they
could not be required to carry arms or to train in their use. They might
nevertheless have to bear a club on guard duty, since the War Department did not define this as a weapon; they could, too, be given such

quasi-combatant duties as setting up targets for use in a rifle range (for refusal to do which one objector was in fact court-martialed).[49] From the beginning of 1943 objectors were assigned only to the Medical Corps. Even so, problems arose here too, for in 1944 in the Pacific theater of war medical units were armed. "The pressure on objectors to bear all types of 'arms' was great, and some 1-A-O's undoubtedly succumbed ... often a whole Medical Corps unit would be armed with the exception of the few objectors serving in it. It is not difficult to imagine how isolated and curious the objectors must have seemed, both to themselves and to the nonobjector members of their unit. But men like the [Adventist] Desmond Doss, who won the Congressional Medal of Honor, remained unarmed throughout the severe Pacific fighting, even though medical corpsmen were frequently fired upon."[50]

The army authorities in World War II were not confronted with the question, which had faced them in World War I, of what to do with large numbers of objectors unwilling to accept noncombatant status. A similar problem, however, did exist, though of much smaller proportions. There were, for instance, the misclassified objectors who, after induction, refused to take the military oath or to don uniform or obey military orders. They might have been classified as 1-A-O but object to army noncombatancy; or they might have been given straight combatant service (1–A classification) instead of the desired 1-A-O or 4-E, as the case might be. Such men, write Sibley and Jacob, "constituted in many instances the most difficult disciplinary problems from the viewpoint of the military and naval authorities."[51] Among them were those who, through inexperience or lack of education, did not properly understand the official procedure for registering conscientious objection and thus could easily find themselves in the army with 1-A status. Then there were soldiers who, while they had not claimed objector status either on registering or after induction, nevertheless developed a conscientious objection after having served for a short or long period in the forces.

At first these misclassified objectors along with the soldier objectors received short terms of up to six months' detention in guardhouses or camp stockades. If they persevered in their resistance, a court-martial normally followed with long prison terms usually ranging between five and ten years. One man, a socialist objector named Henry Weber, was condemned to death: the only sentence of its kind in World War II America, which was, however, on account of public protest, eventually whittled down in stages to five years' imprisonment.

After a while the army authorities devised procedures to try to eliminate its refractory objectors. In the first place, they became willing to assign a man, if he were ready to accept this, to noncombatant duties, even though he was not officially in possession of the 1-A-O status which only the local or various appellate boards were entitled to grant. But, of course, this sensible decision might be reversed arbitrarily at some later date and the man transferred back to a combatant unit. If this happened, court-martial and imprisonment followed automatically on refusal of a military order. A second way out of the impasse resulted from a decision handed down by the Supreme Court in 1944 in the Billings case. This made it possible for men who had not actually taken the military oath (many of course had done so) to obtain a writ of *habeas corpus* and receive trial and sentence in a civil court. A third possibility, though one that was open only if a court-martial had not yet taken place, lay in the objector obtaining his discharge through the army's own general administrative procedure. In this case, however, the initiative lay solely with the man's commanding officer; thus everything depended here on the latter's attitude, on whether he wished to get rid of the objector either because he found him a nuisance or because he was convinced of his genuineness. However, sincerity by itself was not grounds for a discharge. The officer had to urge this as a convenience to the army, or because of the man's inadaptability to life in the services, or on account of what were considered undesirable traits in his character. After discharge, the objector was reclassified by his Selective Service board.

For those misclassified objectors in the army's grip, who were neither prepared to accept unofficial noncombatancy nor eligible to apply for a writ of *habeas corpus* nor fortunate in having a commanding officer sympathetic enough – or irritated enough, as the case might be – to initiate the discharge procedure, court-martial and imprisonment continued to be the routine. Sentences were normally served in disciplinary barracks, though sometimes an objector was assigned to an army "rehabilitation center" (the sources are silent as to any cases where the treatment was successful). "It is fairly certain," write Sibley and Jacob, "that there was more actual physical brutality in military than in civil prisons – beatings of Jehovah's Witnesses, for example, and long periods in 'solitary' on bread and water." Such brutalities, however, were inflicted usually without the approval of higher authorities and were not comparable in either extent or intensity to those suffered in this sort of institution by objectors in World War I. Almost at the end of the war, in June 1945, an Advisory Board on Clemency, manned by civilians and not by military officers, was set up to review court-martial sentences imposed on conscientious objectors, something that religious and pacifist organizations had long been urging. "But ...

its performance was disappointing to civil-liberties and objector groups. ... In general, it seemed to give great weight to the opinion of Selective Service."[52] For instance, contrary to some official pronouncements cited above, the Advisory Board refused to recognize the objections of men like the socialist Henry Weber, however genuine, as being "conscientious" within the meaning of the act, and it therefore rejected their claims.

Civilian Public Service: The Sponsoring Agencies

In the 1930s the major Protestant churches had been influenced to a considerable degree by pacifist ideas, though none of them "went so far as to endorse the absolute pacifist position." When war came, while the fierce hostility shown by most clergy to their pacifist minority in World War I was now almost entirely absent, the pacifists still remained a minority, and a comparatively small one. The feeling that war was basically unchristian was general in the Protestant churches and was embraced by those supporting the war ("agonized participants," to adapt Edward LeRoy Long, Jr.'s telling phrase[53]) as well as by pacifist churchmen. Christian pacifists, from their side, admitted to "a mood of depression and frustration." Each party, therefore, felt a certain bond of unity in acknowledging their common inadequacy when faced by the challenge of war, despite the diversity of their responses to this challenge. Particularly clergy – on each side of the argument – shared a sense of shock and a "somber awareness" of the disaster the world was facing. The nonpacifist majority expressed sympathy and respect for the pacifist position and they called on legislators to give conscientious objectors from their midst the same rights as objectors from traditionally pacifist denominations would enjoy.[54]

Shortly after the passing of the Selective Training and Service Act the three historic peace churches – Quakers, Mennonites[55] and Brethren – joined in October 1940 with other churches and groups interested in the plight of conscientious objectors to form a National Service Board for Religious Objectors (NSBRO), which would both coordinate activities on behalf of the objectors and undertake combined negotiations with the government. A Quaker, Paul Comly French, was appointed secretary. Because of their long-standing concern for peace and the comparatively high percentage of objectors among their young men of military age, these three peace churches played the dominant role both in contacts with the administration and in shaping the policies that would govern the community of objectors.

In fact, the three churches had been active in the matter as early as

January 1940 when they presented personally to President Roosevelt a memorandum proposing, in view of the likelihood of conscription being introduced shortly, a scheme of alternative civilian service for objectors willing to accept it as well as provision for complete exemption for the absolutists. These efforts, which were backed by the pacifist movement in general, were only partially successful. The sponsors were able to broaden the original intention of the legislators to follow closely the pattern of World War I and give exemption only to members of pacifist sects, and then only from combatant service, so as to eventually get them to include all religious objection to war and to add the possibility of civilian alternative service. But, as we have seen, the September 1940 act, unlike its earlier British counterpart which was taken as a model by the pacifist lobbyists, gave no satisfaction either to the unconditionalist or to the nonreligious humanitarian pacifist (not to mention the selective objector). Although a few Congressmen were sympathetic, American pacifists lacked the support enjoyed by their British confrères at Westminster among the pacifist and ex–conscientious objector M.P.'s, who included several former absolutists in their ranks. Many Congressmen feared that if exemption were permitted in the case of nonreligious objectors, the door would be opened to Communist infiltration; there was little understanding, either, of the unconditional stand.

From the position of the historic peace churches and their pacifist colleagues (and from the vantage point of hindsight) it would probably have been ultimately better if they had turned down government proposals for their collaboration, however well meant, in view of the exclusion of part of the community of objectors from the benefit of the act and the privileged position this gave to the religious pacifist. Yet there were also cogent reasons for accepting the hand proffered them, despite the admitted shortcomings of the legislation. Some of the disadvantages of such cooperation were indeed difficult to foresee at the outset.

What the administration then proposed appeared to be a decided step forward from the position its predecessor had taken in 1917. It offered to the three historic peace churches – or rather to their service committees – representing, as it were, the community of religious objectors, the running of alternative civilian service. Thus, though prime responsibility for the scheme would still rest with the government, its day-to-day organization was to be in the hands of independent bodies staffed by pacifists. Assignees to Civilian Public Service (CPS) would be employed on soil conservation and in forestry, occupations clearly unconnected with the war and at the same time of obvious national importance; the model for this kind of project was drawn from the New Deal's Civilian Conservation Corps for the able-bodied unemployed of the depression period. The Selective Service System promised to provide camp sites and camp equipment with the technical supervision and work equipment coming from the Departments of Agriculture and the Interior. On the other hand, the administration of the camps and the men's maintenance were to be the responsibility of the historic peace churches; if, however, they became financially unable to carry out their obligations in this respect, the government promised to continue the program on its own. In any case Selective Service reserved to itself the right to exercise overall supervision of the camps and to lay down general lines of policy.

The peace churches, while ready all along to shoulder full responsibility for their own objectors, had urged the administration to open – for those not wishing to participate in the church units – a series of government-sponsored camps and to pay objectors for work done there. Selective Service was inclined to accept these proposals, but they were vetoed by the personal intervention of President Roosevelt, who felt they provided objectors with too soft an option to military service. The peace churches were then faced with the alternative of either rejecting collaboration altogether or accepting the government terms, which involved them in sole responsibility (that is, within the framework of Selective Service direction) for all conscientious objectors assigned to CPS. In December 1940 the three historic peace churches and their allies capitulated, agreeing to sponsor and finance the camps – at first, however, for a trial period of six months. The CPS program was officially inaugurated in February 1941 and the first camp opened on the following 15 May.

Objectors given 4-E classification and prepared, as at first most of them were, to accept its conditions, had no choice but to serve without pay in a church-organized camp; the sponsoring churches in their turn were obliged to receive all such men. This restricted freedom of action appeared the main drawback at first. However, as was later revealed, the full extent of the control exercised by Selective Service had also not been properly defined and serious misunderstanding and friction soon arose on this account.

Yet, "although the program fell short of the full desires of those concerned with the conscientious objector, Civilian Public Service was generally accepted as the best alternative which could be secured."[56] Even radicals like A.J. Muste approved the arrangement at the beginning; opposition voices like that of Dr. Evan Thomas, the socialist leader's brother and an ex-absolutist of World War I, who was then chairman of the War Resisters' League, were rare even if many pacifists did indeed have considerable misgivings. So far as one can judge, at first the rank-and-file objector also welcomed in outline a scheme that allowed him to perform his alternative service under pacifist auspices and in a sympathetic milieu. As for Selective Service, its leaders, and especially General Hershey, were enthusiastic. For them it appeared an experiment in vital democracy. They extolled it for promoting collaboration between the state and a nonconformist minority, even in a period of national emergency.

Before we move on to describe how the CPS experiment worked out in practice we should briefly discuss the wartime stands of the three sponsoring agencies, which helped to initiate CPS and later shared the major responsibility for administering it – and ultimately the blame for its shortcomings and failures.

Of the three historic peace churches the Quakers were probably the best known to the American public. "The Friends," wrote Sibley and · Jacob (themselves members of the Society), "were deeply divided in their attitudes toward the war. Only a minority in most meetings were pacifists, and many actually denounced the C.O.'s and opposed any action on their behalf."[57] This situation was especially true of the evangelical and, in places, fundamentalist Quaker meetings of the mid-West and Pacific coast. But even in the liberal meetings of the East, by World War II conscientious objection had become "a minority position." "75% is a conservative estimate of the members of the Society of military age who were in the armed forces."[58] Of course, some of these men were only nominally Quakers but the majority were members in good standing in their Society. The pacifist impulse in American Quakerism was centered in the American Friends Service Committee (AFSC), with its headquarters in Philadelphia – a body that was suspect with some Quakers on account of alleged theological liberalism and political radicalism. Tradition in the Society of Friends, however, was opposed to war and the antipacifist position was rarely given considered expression.[59] Many Quakers, especially among the older generation, eschewed any political implications to their renunciation of war and nurtured a purely vocational pacifism, which they claimed, not altogether without reason, as "the classic Quaker position." But there were also Quaker peace radicals and Quaker absolutists; at least one respected Friend resigned on joining the army because he believed the Society should maintain an uncompromising pacifist witness. The hallmark of wartime American Quakerism was thus one of very considerable diversity in regard to its peace testimony.

The Mennonites were more fragmented than the Quakers but the various bodies into which their church had separated in the course of the nineteenth century were more united than the Society of Friends in maintaining their traditional pacifist testimony. The majority of the sixteen branches of Mennonitism still disfellowshipped members who accepted military service; some did this even in the case of members who served as noncombatants. Where the barriers between the isolated sect and the world had largely broken down, there the enforcement of the discipline in regard to war service as in other aspects of life relaxed. In fact, where a Mennonite congregation had become largely acculturated there many of its draftees were likely to accept combatant service.[60]

The Mennonite Central Committee (MCC) collaborated with Quakers and Brethren and other pacifist bodies in promoting the scheme of alternative service for objectors; but Mennonites kept a little aloof, for they feared the influence which liberal pacifism of the FOR variety could exercise on their young men and the degree to which its proponents might undermine the Bible-centered nonresistance of Mennonite tradition. Since, however, they believed in rendering Caesar what in conscience they felt was his due, Mennonites welcomed the opportunity offered by CPS for amicable collaboration between their church and the state. CPS had had its prototype in their historical experience; from 1881 until 1918 Mennonites in Russia had performed alternative service in forestry camps under not dissimilar conditions from those now proposed by the government of the United States. In 1940–41, therefore, they once again entertained hopes of a harmonious relationship with the authorities, mixed with some apprehension concerning the impact of worldly ideas and values on the Mennonite conscripts.

The Church of the Brethren at this date stood halfway between Quakers and Mennonites. Like the latter, emerging, though more rapidly, from its rural isolation and sharing the same German background and a similar traditional Biblical nonresistance, the church reflected, on the other hand, something of the Quaker outreach on the subject of peace. During the interwar years the Brethren, or at least the church's most intellectually and spiritually aware members, had become increasingly concerned with the social and economic implications of pacifism. Disarmament, international reconciliation, and violence in labor relations were subjects which exercised their thought and attracted their study. But, as the war was to show, this social concern, this renovated witness for peace, was the demesne of a relatively small section of the total membership. There had been a failure to communicate the message so that, as the Brethren communities became integrated into the mainstream of American life, their members often shed pacifism along with their traditional peculiarities of speech, dress, and way of life (which many of the Mennonite denominations still retained virtually intact): a process that had been enacted a half century or more earlier in the case of the Quakers, though with less immediately alarming results for those concerned to preserve the peace testimony. In World War II the overwhelming majority of Brethren, it was discovered, accepted combatant service. Of 24,228 men from the church drafted up to March 1945, 21,481 accepted full military service, whereas only 1,382 entered noncombatant duties and slightly less – 1,365 – chose CPS.[61] This retreat from a clear pacifist witness came about despite the fact that Brethren leaders officially urged members of military age, who wished to follow the teachings of their church, against noncombatant as much as against combatant service.

The history of CPS reflects the interplay of a number of different human factors. Selective Service officials, from General Hershey down, were optimistic as to the outcome, viewing the inauguration of the program as a remarkable positive achievement for a country about to become involved in a gigantic war. The three peace churches and the groups associated with them shared something of these feelings, modified however by their disappointment at not actualizing a still more liberal plan and their regret at the restrictions now set to their freedom of action in the program's administration. But they were anxious at any rate to make a success of the scheme. The third factor, on which the ultimate fate of CPS depended, were the men themselves, those conscientious objectors who over the next half decade or so were to receive 4-E classification from the Selective Service System.

Civilian Public Service: Assignees or Inmates?

CPS, when compared with the pragmatic method of dealing with conscientious objectors practised in Britain, was a more grandiose, and at the same time a less elastic design. Its promoters among the pacifists hoped it would become, as it were, "a religious order whose members, though under legal compulsion, were moved primarily by their personal ideals to perform a sacrificial service."[62] It would reproduce, they hoped, the enthusiastic atmosphere and the devoted service of the voluntary work camps, which Quakers and other pacifists had been sponsoring before the war as twentieth-century youth's moral equivalent to fighting. It did not provide an easy option; the men received bare maintenance (and some even covered this themselves), did hard manual work and lived usually under conditions similar to those of an army camp. True, they were not subjected to the risks to life and limb that servicemen were but it would scarcely have been possible to devise a scheme of alternative civilian service where this would have been so.

The root cause of CPS's subsequent *malaise* lay, it would appear, in the fact that it is impossible to create a quasi-religious order of the kind envisaged by compulsion (as the whole experience, for example, of the Roman Catholic Church has shown). It was just this element of compulsion in CPS that finally eroded its idealism to a vanishing point.

Sibley and Jacob have summarized the work performed by CPS men, including the "detached service" units permitted from March 1942 onward, and have evaluated its significance in the following words:

They served in conservation and forestry camps, in hospitals and state training schools, at university laboratories and agricultural experiment stations, on individual farms and government survey crews. They made roads, cleared truck and foot trails, fought forest fires, dug irrigation ditches, constructed dams, built fences, planted trees, pulled weeds, conducted soil conservation experiments, acted as "guinea-pigs" for medical and scientific research, tended dairy cattle, tilled the soil, built sanitary facilities for hookworm-ridden communities, cared for the mentally ill, the feeble-minded, and the juvenile delinquent ... The conscientious objectors' record of service must also be measured in less tangible terms [than the millions of dollars saved by the government as a result of the objectors' unpaid labor]: the long-range values of the medical and scientific discoveries stemming from experiments performed with conscientious objectors; the demonstration of nonviolent techniques of treatment in the care of mental patients; a new care for the fate of the deranged as C.O.'s brought the appalling conditions in state institutions forcefully to public attention; the continuity of conservation experiments and programs which would have been broken by the war had it not been possible to staff them with C.O.'s.[63]

Yet, granted that both in camp and, even more, in the special projects much useful and creative work was done, there was a reverse side to the picture, too. "Much of Civilian Public Service was unworthy either of the caliber of men and convictions placed at its disposal or of the sacrifices of freedom and security which were imposed."[64] Much of the labor seemed to be just "made" work or lacking in any special urgency or importance. Selective Service was responsible for work assignment: it unaccountably (so it seemed at least to CPS men) rejected many requests for permission to take up special projects in hospitals or social welfare, which urgently needed personnel. Often little notice was taken in job assignment of a man's specialist skills. An outstanding botanist consigned to maintenance work in a mental hospital; an electrical engineer pulling weeds in a market garden; a leading research physicist clearing a swamp; a penicillin researcher sent to a wildlife reserve; such cases were by no means exceptional. A serious blow to CPS hopes came at the end of June 1943 when Congress by an amendment to the Army Appropriation Act refused permission for conscientious objectors to go overseas in relief work (a group of men seconded by AFSC for work with the British FAU in China had to turn back in mid-ocean) or even to train in colleges for this purpose. The motive underlying such restrictions was fear that these activities might help to glamorize the conscientious objector.

If the content of civilian public service often left the individual conscientious objector with a sense of unfulfillment and sometimes of concrete grievance, a lack of homogeneity among the campers often made it hard to create a feeling of group responsibility. Both these difficulties indeed stemmed from the fact that neither the sponsoring church bodies nor the men themselves were free agents. By the terms of their contract, as it were, they had delivered their freedom of action over into the hands of the Selective Service System.

Uniformity in background and belief was most apparent in the camps run by the Mennonite Central Committee. Mennonite objectors, who constituted almost 40 percent of the total number of CPS men, came mainly from farming communities; in CPS, therefore, their work did not greatly differ from their peacetime calling and they suffered, on the whole, from less frustration than city-bred CPS men. The strictly Bible-centered tone prevailing in the MCC camps did not attract outsiders to make them their choice, unless an objector shared a similar religious outlook; nor did the MCC seek recruits from elements whose way of thinking was markedly different from their own. The Mennonite leaders exercised, too, firm control over the intellectual life of their camps. They carefully vetted visiting speakers, not infrequently refusing permission to pacifists suspected of theological liberalism, political radicalism or a *penchant* toward the absolutist position. They also controlled the reception of literature from the outside, excluding those papers and books which they feared might cause unrest among their assignees. As a result, in cleaving to traditional ways of thought despite the potentially upsetting experience of CPS, Mennonite young men remained on the whole loyal to their church's position on war.

A similar harmony (or should one perhaps say a parallel intellectual aridity?) did not exist either in the Brethren or the Quaker camps. It was likewise impossible for these two groups to achieve the uniform composition of some Mennonite camps, where up to 90 percent of the assignees belonged to the Mennonite faith. Secondly, the fact that the three peace churches had agreed to administer CPS on behalf of any conscientious objectors whom Selective Service chose to assign to alternative civilian service meant that all CPS assignees had to find a place in a church-run camp. As explained above, comparatively few non-members selected a Mennonite camp. A considerable number chose the Brethren. But most objectors, who did not belong to the historic peace churches (and assignees of this kind amounted to as much as 40 percent of the CPS total), chose to join the Quakers. This was especially true of the religious liberals and the ethical objectors. Indeed, at least at first, they had really no alternative in most cases (just as the Quakers had no alternative but to accept them). True, several camps or detached service units were started by other bodies – e.g., Catholic objectors, the NSBRO or certain agencies attached to nonpacifist Protestant denominations – but these were either short-lived on account of lack of funds or very limited in numbers.

"Conscientious objection on a personal basis ... was found in most of the religious organizations of the United States," writes Colonel Wherry.[65] Most objectors who entered. CPS belonged to Protestant churches. But in addition there were humanists and spiritualists as well as Roman Catholics, Mormons, and practising Jews,[66] Moslems and Buddhists and Hopi Indians. The camps also contained a sprinkling of nonreligious socialist and anarchist objectors, whose claims to exemption their Selective Service boards – more generous than the legislators – had been ready to acknowledge. Many of the religious sects represented were small; they were often obscure and occasionally eccentric. However, some mainstream denominations, like the Methodists or the Baptists, were present in considerable numbers. The educational background of CPS men varied considerably, ranging from occasional illiteracy to the university professor level; however, the average intelligence, especially in the Quaker camps which contained a much larger proportion of students and professional men as well as of urban dwellers than those run Mennonites or Brethren, was considerably higher than among the CPS men's contemporaries who had been conscripted into the army.[67]

The proportion of Quakers in a Friends' camp or project was rarely more than a third; often it did not amount to more than a quarter. The diversity of belief and social background mirrored in the community of objectors at large was thus reflected in the Quaker camps to a greater degree than among the assignees under the care of the other two peace churches, and in particular of the Mennonites. Diversity can serve as a creative agent. There was no reason in theory why lack of homogeneity should necessarily act as an agent of disintegration. There was indeed every reason to hope that men united by a shared pacifist faith and dedicated to the resolution of conflict by loving means would be able to solve their problems to their mutual satisfaction. But this was, in fact, only partially the case. Tension, strain, and friction were soon generated, due primarily (that is, in so far as the internal composition of the Quaker camps was concerned) to the presence of two potentially explosive elements: a group with an intense concern for the further- ance of social justice and (often overlapping) a group which was opposed on principle to the presuppositions on which the whole CPS experiment was built. Let us call these two groups the "social action- ists" and the "crypto-absolutists."

Mennonite nonresistance, like that of the smaller fundamentalist sects represented in CPS, was still largely an inward-looking witness, an attempt to withdraw from contact with a warmaking world. The Quaker peace testimony in the twentieth century reached out to men in an attempt to transform domestic and international relations. "Because of the widespread peace program of AFSC," its secretary wrote, "we tended to draw into our camps those CPS men who were more aggres- sively concerned with social measures that might prevent war and make for creative living. When such men found themselves in a camp far removed from the mainstream of life, this social impulse often seemed completely thwarted."[68] Objectors of this kind, like the left- wing C.O.'s of World War I, derived their pacifism from a strong belief in human unity, a belief they might express in either religious or ethical or political terms. Most of these men had been involved in social action of some sort before entering CPS. But there were those, too, whose social conscience and drive to action were first aroused only as a result of experience in CPS: by witnessing perhaps the harsh treatment of patients in mental institutions, or through the first contact with racial discrimination in communities where they now worked, or from sym- pathy with fellow objectors imprisoned for their more radical stand. Especially in view of the presence in many camps of a small group of convinced social actionists, the very isolation of camp life could bring CPS men greater opportunity to ponder social problems than the rush of city life had provided. Even Mennonite men, as their directors feared, might not always be immune to such an awakening.

In constant camp discussions, as well as in mimeographed weekly newssheets, the social actionists pressed their views. Their demands for fargoing reforms in mental care were not likely to arouse hostility either among the church administrators of CPS or in the Selective Service administration; indeed they could expect to find sympathy in these quarters. But they also broached other and more controversial issues. They called for a more democratic organization of CPS and for increased autonomy *vis-à-vis* Selective Service. They criticized in particular the unpaid character of CPS work, as well as the failure of the government to provide the normal dependents' allowances and workmen's compensation, as an infringement of the rights of labor and human dignity. (General Hershey adamantly opposed CPS pay as likely to damage relations with the public and as an unmerited concession to men who were not being required to risk their lives on active service.) The social actionists protested vehemently, too, against Selective Service's refusal on occasion to assign black objectors for work in localities where segregationist feeling was strong. Selective Service claimed that it did this to avoid trouble and not from any racial discrimination. The sponsoring agencies, while stating their support for racial equality, refused to give a general undertaking that they would withdraw from sponsorship of any unit where such a practice had occurred. In the end AFSC went so far as to promise that it would not start any new project unless its interracial character were guaranteed. In the arguments in favor of caution put forward by the church agencies, whether in regard to internal camp organization or to the race question, the social actionists scented apostasy. They agitated in the camps; they organized intercamp conferences to plan a strategy of social activism. These conferences were frowned on both by the sponsoring agencies and by General Hershey, who attempted to ban them.

The question of camp democracy was a complicated one. Camp councils chosen from the men existed in every unit alongside the camp directors appointed by the sponsoring agency. The degree of responsibility in running the camp allotted to these councils varied. In Mennonite camps, where the councils were nominated by the directors, they were largely advisory; in Brethren and still more in Quaker camps, where the councils were elected, they exercised a considerable degree of authority. Quakers and Brethren also gave the men in CPS some representation on their service committees in an effort to disperse the resentment building up against them among the assignees. But camp administration was not simply a problem to be worked out between the men and their sponsoring church agency. Overall control lay in the hands of General Hershey and the Selective Service System, which claimed the right of inspection to see that its regulations were being observed and of taking disciplinary action in case of nonobservance. The System had its representative on the spot in the person of the project superintendent responsible for the work performed by the CPS men. Selective Service disliked the Quakers' way of running their camps (indeed this did have its disadvantages with sometimes too much talk and too little decision-making). Selective Service indeed seemed to regard the historic peace churches as its agents whose task it was to see that the men carried out the policies of Selective Service. Camp directors were answerable not only to their own service committee (and in practice often to the men in camp, too) but also to Selective Service, which demanded an array of reports showing how its orders had been fulfilled.

The stand of Selective Service – which in fact it was far from being able to enforce, as we shall soon see – is reflected in the following passage from a report drawn up by one of its officials, Colonel Franklin A. McLean:

From the time an assignee reports to camp until he is finally released he is under the control of the Director of Selective Service. He ceases to be a free agent and is accountable for all of his time, in camp and out, 24 hours a day. His movements, actions and conduct are subject to control and regulation. He ceases to have certain rights and is granted privileges instead. These privileges can be restricted or withdrawn without his consent as punishment, during emergency or as a matter of policy. He may be told when and how to work, what to wear and where to sleep ... He may be moved from place to place and from job to job, even to foreign countries, for the convenience of the government regardless of his personal feelings or desires.[69]

One did not need to be in basic disagreement with the concept of civilian public service to reject with indignation the views of CPS's role outlined here by Colonel McLean. And there were men in CPS who went much further than the majority of their colleagues in opposition to the system of conscription. For these "misplaced absolutists" (to use Sibley and Jacob's apt description) CPS was no better than a system of "slave labor." We may grant that there was much to criticize in the shape imposed on CPS by Congress and, equally, in the attitude subsequently adopted by Selective Service. In particular, the failure to provide sufficient outlet for the impulse toward community service was a serious shortcoming in the administration of CPS. But to speak of slavery, surely, was an exaggeration – if the word is to retain any significant content; indeed it manifested a certain lack of balanced judgment on the part of those who used it.

Slow-downs on the job or work strikes as well as demonstrative fasts were employed not merely to register protest against what the participants considered abuses in the system, but also to protest against conscription itself and the whole CPS system. What these men were in effect demanding as a minimum was a complete transformation of the pattern of administering conscientious objection so as to provide for unconditional exemption and a purely voluntary camp set-up freed from its connection via Selective Service with the military machine. There was really only one proper, though illegal, method of expressing such total protest: that was to walk out of camp altogether. Some men did this; the consequences for them of their action will be dealt with *inter alia* in the next section of this chapter. But to remain in camp and deliberately pursue there a policy of passive resistance and work sabotage, as others did, lacked straightforwardness.

As discontent grew, spreading from the social actionists and crypto-absolutists to embrace many who only partly shared their outlook but nurtured genuine grievances – mixed with some less conscientious, but not unnatural "gripes" – against the working of the civilian service system, camp administrators (especially in Quaker units) were faced with a dilemma. "Must they discipline men for taking conscientious action to express their disapproval of war and conscription?"[70] Selective Service regarded such action as virtually a crime. The religious agencies strove to establish "redemptive discipline," i.e., the remedying of any legitimate complaints (so far, of course, as this lay within their power) along with an acknowledgment of fault on the part of any camper guilty of a real delinquency. This appeal to the sensitized consciences of the men often worked but, as Sibley and Jacob admit, "some C.O.'s scorned redemption."[71] This was especially the case where church administration and assignees were divided by opposing views of what was right.

Apart from minor infractions of discipline, punishable by loss of privileges, problems which camp directors dealt with on the spot, the latter were required by law to report to Selective Service any assignee refusing to work ("R.T.W.") or absent from camp without leave for more than ten days ("A.W.O.L."). For these offenses CPS men were liable to prosecution in the civil courts. But courts were not always willing to sentence offenders; for example, in the case of work strikes there were federal courts which displayed considerable sympathy with the strikers and their struggle for more equitable conditions of labor. Selective Service also attempted reclassification, which would deprive delinquents of their 4-E status; but this was a lengthy and complicated procedure, which Selective Service found more effective as a threat than as an actual punishment. Reclassification was, moreover, strongly opposed by the religious agencies. They entertained qualms at taking any part, even a passive one, in a process which might end in depriving a man of his status as a conscientious objector and they were quite ready on such occasions to stand up, "sometimes quite vigorously," to Selective Service in defense of what they considered its arbitrary treatment of the objector. Finally, in its search for a realistic deterrent to employ against dissident CPS elements, Selective Service compiled a "black list" of men it considered trouble-makers, which it used in order to refuse them assignment to the more interesting and creative special projects. But none of these means of coercion, which represented the utmost Selective Service could do "within the constitutional limits of American democracy,"[72] proved particularly successful.

Whereas Selective Service and the Department of Justice advocated increasing the compulsory powers of the government to deal with infractions of CPS discipline, the three sponsoring church agencies, instead, urged as their remedy for the growing demoralization and rising discontent a relaxation of coercion together with a broadening of the outlets for more creative and useful service. In this way they hoped that the initial spiritual dynamism could be revived. They finally converted Attorney-General Francis Biddle to their standpoint; but in the meanwhile, as a result of their experiences in running the camps, they had subjected their own views on CPS to radical revision.

One last attempt was made to rescue CPS from the *impasse* in which it found itself when in July 1943 the first of several government-sponsored camps was opened: a step which the historic peace churches had urged on the administration from the beginning. Indeed, if at the outset the administration had heeded their advice, government camps might have helped to assuage the discontent of the nonreligious at being forced to serve under religious auspices and thus have removed at least one source of unrest. In fact, their inauguration now proved a disaster. They became, in the words of Sibley and Jacob, "the ultimate penal colonies of Civilian Public Service."[73]

The venture was ill-starred almost from the very beginning. Three major errors were committed by those who planned it. In the first place, a good proportion of those who were transferred from church-run camps – though, of course, by no means all, for campers who did not expressly opt for a church camp were so transferred – were noncooperators, extremists who were out to fight conscription by destroying CPS as a system of state slavery. Secondly, this mistake was compounded by the Selective Service System's habit of punishing men from church camps found guilty of indiscipline by banishing them to the government camps, thereby increasing the number of misfits there and underlining the penal character of such institutions. In the third place, the government's policy of stubbornly refusing to assignees in the camps directly under its control any say in their administration, which rested solely with outside officials, had the effect of turning even those inclined to collaborate into rebels against authority, for this policy appeared as a direct challenge to the often not unjustified demands of CPS men for greater internal democracy. The results of such mismanagement soon showed themselves in the obstructionist tactics pursued by a majority of government campers: work slow-downs, inflated sick-lists, and even failure to cooperate in keeping the camps clean and tidy. Thus, largely through the administration's inept-itude, and in part, of course, through the actions of the campers them-selves, assignees to the building of a cooperative society had indeed become inmates of a quasi-penal system.

But was not the general decline of CPS due at bottom neither to the attitude of Selective Service, for its leaders were only acting according to their light, nor to the CPS men, whose position was not altogether one of their own choosing, but to the stand of the three sponsoring churches and the pacifist organizations which had supported them? Had they not perhaps betrayed their mission, with however good intentions? If this were the case, was it not now their duty to acknowl-edge their mistake and free themselves, and thereby the men under their care, from the incubus of voluntary servitude to the military machine? Questions of this kind were being asked not only by the men in the camps but also fairly generally in pacifist and peace church cir-cles. Several smaller groups eventually withdrew from collaboration with the coordinating National Service Board for Religious Objectors. Finally, in March 1946, the Quaker AFSC itself withdrew from CPS administration, handing over its camps to the government. The Men-nonites and Brethren continued their cooperation with Selective Ser-vice until the government's decision in March 1947 to bring CPS to an end in view of the near completion of demobilization, which had been proceeding since October 1945, i.e., from a month after the surrender of Japan.

After CPS was over, those who had participated in it, whether as assignees or overseers, began the postmortem. No consensus emerged; no agreement was reached concerning the relative success or failure of the experiment. Both the government and the pacifists acknowledged that they had made mistakes, but they differed as to what these were and as to the remedies that should have been applied. On the whole, the Mennonites and those objectors who believed in going the second mile agreed with the government viewpoint that CPS had provided an opportunity for constructive service unconnected in any direct way with the prosecution of the war and performed in a relatively free and congenial environment. They regarded it not merely as the best possible alternative in view of the wartime state of public opinion and of Congress's attitude, they also believed it expressed American democracy's capacity for tolerating an unpopular minority opinion. At the same time they freely criticized certain aspects of the CPS program: its failure to recognize the nonreligious objector or to provide unconditional exemption for absolutists, its direct dependence on the military and denial of real autonomy to the sponsoring civilian agencies, and its semi-penal labor conditions.

Sibley (differing on this occasion in his assessment from his colleague Jacob, who believed that the historic peace churches were right to undertake the administration of CPS) has summed up the case against the churches' involvement as follows: "The pacifist churches, by their mere presence as administrators for a military agency, lent an air of religious sanction to a quasi-military treatment of conscientious objection." "While gaining incidental benefits for objectors in the process," he goes on, "they allowed themselves to be manipulated by the state for its own ends." Whereas the principle of alternative service for a wide variety of objectors was a definite advance on the position in World War I, the collaboration of pacifist bodies in running such service was a retrograde step. In exchange for the privilege of administering the CPS camps, an agreement for which the churches did not even insist on receiving a written contract defining their rights *vis-à-vis* Selective Service, thus leaving them dependent on the goodwill of the military men who ran the Service, these churches had ended up by acting as (unpaid) policemen for enforcing the Selective Service discipline on conscientious objectors. In this way, through the churches' collaboration with Selective Service, their men themselves eventually became partly alienated, while by their periodic and commendable resistance to the demands of Selective Service they failed to please the military men who ran the Service. The large sums expended on their camps by all three churches would, in Sibley's view, have been better spent on their postwar relief programs.[74]

CPS appears in retrospect as a classic example of what Lewis Mumford in another connection has described as "baroque planning": a style especially beloved by the military mind. Its principle was uniformity, regularity. Individual peculiarities must yield before the demands of the plan. Thus all objectors unwilling to accept noncombatant service were to be treated according to the same pattern. (Were not their contemporaries in the armed forces subjected to the same procedure?) But it was this planned freedom that proved CPS's undoing, for what would satisfy the conscience and vocational sense of a rural Mennonite nonresistant would not necessarily prove acceptable to the city-born Quaker or a war resister of the Social Gospel type. One camper from an intellectual background put the position thus: "The Bible pacifists, the ones who are simply against war because it's against the Bible, are in spite of their lovable qualities as persons, a bit pitiable from a conceptual standpoint. They miss so much."[75] For the literalist C.Os. ("the Holy Joes," "the Bible boys"), on the other hand, their more secular minded fellow campers remained objects of suspicion. In the pacifist community, too, there were conditionalists of every sort as well as a number of absolutist objectors. Unlike the British legislation, the American attempt at providing for conscientious objection – although in many respects well-intentioned and certainly generous in comparison with World War I or with most other belligerent countries in World War II – suffered from a proclivity to press conscience into a uniform mold.

Conscientious Objectors in Prison

We have seen that some objectors attempted to protest actively against conscription from within CPS – though often with rather unfortunate results. There were others who chose to become law violators and go to prison because they disagreed with the principle of CPS. There were also, it should be added, men who were sent to prison not on account of any objection to CPS but because they were refused 4-E classification.

In World War II America, nine times as many conscientious objectors were in jail as in World War I (or between two and three times as many if we take into consideration the greater number of objectors drafted in the later conflict). In all, some 6,000 objectors were given civilian prison sentences down to the end of March 1947, when the Selective Training and Service Act of 1940 expired. This, however, represented only a little over a third of the total number of prosecutions under the Act for draft evasion. Some at least of the remaining draft-evaders should undoubtedly be considered also as conscientious, for "sometimes the so-called evader had genuine objections but was not articulate about them."[76]

Over three quarters of the imprisoned objectors were Jehovah's Witnesses, whose Selective Service boards had rejected their claims for complete exemption as ministers of religion. In contrast, although Mennonites represented by far the largest group in CPS, very few of them – in fact less than fifty in all – were jailed. Their church's generally known pacifism and their own readiness in almost all cases to do alternative service led to their seldom being refused 4-E status by their draft boards. The average sentence for a Jehovah's Witness was four years; for other objectors the average was around three years (a much higher average, incidentally, than occurred with violators of narcotics or white-slave laws and much higher, too, than was the case with objectors in Great Britain, where prison sentences tended on the whole to be considerably shorter). The maximum sentence that could be imposed was five years and a $10,000 fine. Under 500 sentences ran to a year or less. The heaviest sentencing took place, as might be expected, in the period between Pearl Harbor and the surrender of Japan.

There were roughly 100 cases of "cat-and-mouse," i.e., repeated sentencing of an objector for what was in fact, if not in law, the same offense. There was a tendency, too, in some courts, as the number of cases began to accumulate, to hold mass trials of thirty to forty objectors at once. On the other hand, courts were often sympathetic to objectors and did their best, within the framework of the law they were duty-bound to administer, to respect conscience; one magistrate in Philadelphia, who was a Friend, expressed his dilemma at having to sentence young Quakers for doing what they believed the Inner Light told them to do. Some federal judges, especially those in the Los Angeles area, showed intelligence and understanding by imposing probation instead of prison on objectors appearing before them. The number of probationary sentences, however, remained small. For this three factors were responsible. First, the practice was discouraged by the Selective Service System. The System disliked, in particular, the fact that probationers worked for pay, even when directed to CPS, whereas (largely at the insistence of Selective Service) objectors assigned to CPS by reason of their 4-E classification labored without remuneration. In the second place, public pressure was often mobilized against the probationing of conscientious objectors, especially by groups like the American Legion. Thirdly, many sentenced objectors themselves felt unable to comply with the legal prerequisite for a probation order: a general promise to abide by the law. Yet, particularly for the misclassified objector anxious to perform alternative service if given the chance, probation, if more generally applied, would have provided a reasonable solution.

The prison community of objectors was quite a varied one. Apart from the Jehovah's Witnesses (unsuccessful candidates for ministerial status) who predominated, the misclassified alternativists, and the CPS delinquents prosecuted either on account of walk-outs or work strikes, most of the remaining objectors in prison may broadly be described as convinced absolutists. Some refused to collaborate with the conscription system at all and became nonregistrants in respect to the draft. Others registered but at some later stage made clear their opposition to alternative civilian service, at least of the kind that was offered by the existing legislation or as an enforced change from what they regarded as their vocation. They might balk at filling in their draft questionnaire, or they might refuse to go for induction into army or CPS as directed by a Selective Service board.

Among the nonregistrants (who did not total more than 300) were nonpacifist Black Muslims and Black Jews, whose consciences forbade them to fight in a struggle they believed was not a holy war. The group also included young Quakers as well as Christian pacifists like the "Union Eight," the eight students from Union Theological Seminary in New York then living in voluntary poverty in Harlem, who refused to register for the first draft in mid-October 1940.

A number of pacifists above the current draft age, including such veterans as A.J. Muste, Evan Thomas and Richard B. Gregg, also refused to register. Though they made a public declaration of their law violation – as indeed most nonregistrants did, for usually their position had to some extent the character of a public protest – the Department of Justice wisely decided not to prosecute. Indeed it slyly turned the tables by declaring that it accepted the men's statements as an effective registration! It did prosecute in 28 cases of "counseling and aiding evasion" of national service. But this number was small, especially when compared with the situation during and immediately after World War I. It illustrates both the Department of Justice's commendable caution in such matters and the fact that now "there was relatively little 'political' opposition to the war."[77]

Sentences imposed on conscientious objectors were served in federal prisons, except for a small number of men with terms of less than a year who went to county jails. These institutions were reported as being "for the most part dirty, badly managed and dominated by graft and corruption."[78] Concerning the various types of federal prison – penitentiaries, correctional institutions, reformatories, prison camps, and prison farms – in which some objectors were now to spend three or four or even more years, reports were on the whole a little more favorable. In contrast, for instance, to the mostly rather ancient jails in which British C.Os. served their sentences, they were usually clean and sometimes not unattractive in appearance. Yet the atmosphere was cold and repressive. The unchanging routine, combined with petty restrictions and irritating punishments for their infringement, produced an oppressive monotony and a feeling of intense constriction:

conditions, of course, that were as much the lot of the ordinary convict as of the prisoner of conscience. At the same time longer sentences allowed for a more creative use of labor than in British prisons. There was provision for sports as well as for recreational and educational activities, usually absent, we have seen, in the jails of wartime Britain. In American prisons, objectors were employed *inter alia* on farm work, truck driving, craft work, and the teaching of illiterate or under educated prisoners.

Most jailed objectors served out their terms without coming into conflict with the prison authorities. The Jehovah's Witnesses, for instance, who "possessed a high sense of group solidarity" and "tended in each prison to act as a group under the direction of a chosen leader," were cooperative. For the most part they kept to themselves, practising work slow-downs or other forms of protest only when prison authorities placed restrictions on their meetings or the reception of Witness literature from the outside.[79] On the other hand, many pacifists, Christian or secularist, with a strong social commitment (sometimes generated as a result of contact with the problems of prison society) found reason to oppose the prison system. In protest at injustices in the system they organized jail strikes or undertook individual work or hunger strikes. Racial segregation at meal tables or during recreation time,[80] arbitrary censorship of literature and correspondence, employment on tasks connected with war industry were among the matters at issue. Jailed C.Os. had also to learn how to cope with the latent violence among inmates – and sometimes prison guards too.[81]

Refusal to work, which was punishable by solitary confinement (sometimes in so-called "dark holes," officially abolished but in fact still retained in some prisons) as well as by dietary restrictions, was also practiced by libertarian objectors, who wished to register a total disengagement from conscription. Among work strikers of this kind were members of a sect of Russian origin, the Molokans, whose fathers had suffered severe manhandling in World War I for a similar stand. One of the most stubborn resisters was the absolutist, Corbett Bishop, who went on a hunger strike throughout the whole time of his incarceration.[82] He was forcibly fed by the prison authorities as were two other absolutists, Stanley Murphy and Louis Taylor (Krawczyk), whose case became something of a *cause célèbre*. They had walked out of CPS in October 1942 when they realized that they disagreed basically with the system it represented. Convicted and imprisoned, they embarked on a hunger strike in protest against conscription, which they kept up for 82 days. Despite incarceration in an institution for the criminally insane and attempts to get them certified as themselves insane, which were thwarted by the refusal to agree of the outside doctor required by law to confirm the verdict of the prison medical service, the two men continued to smuggle out reports of serious abuses in the treatment of other inmates, accusations that were eventually backed by the testimony of members of the prison staff. Many pacifists and socially concerned nonpacifists felt that "in dramatizing these facts ... Murphy and Taylor rendered the same kind of service to the community as those objectors who, with different tactics, exposed the conditions surrounding patients in mental hospitals."[83]

Conscientious objectors, like other prisoners, were eligible for various types of parole if they had been cooperative in the course of their incarceration and were prepared to abide by certain restrictions on their activities after release (for instance, Jehovah's Witnesses had to promise not to preach!). Failure to observe these conditions, which were quite unacceptable to many absolutists, could lead to a man's return to prison for completion of sentence. After the war was over the jails were gradually emptied of their wartime conscientious objectors either through paroling or by expiration of the latter's sentences. However, the widespread campaign organized by pacifist groups to obtain a blanket amnesty for all imprisoned objectors, which would remove the legal disqualifications incurred by persons convicted of federal crimes, was unsuccessful. The government granted amnesty on a purely individual basis, excluding thereby the overwhelming majority of objectors from its scope.

"Absolutism," wrote Sibley and Jacob of the group which provided the backbone, if not the numerical preponderance, of the prison C.O. community, "became something of a sect within the ranks of pacifists and conscientious objectors."[84] It had its own professional association, as it were, and its own press organ, with the War Resisters' League acting as its spokesman in regard to the wider public. Some friction existed between absolutists and alternativists. While the latter sometimes regarded the absolutists as fanatical and cranky, the absolutists tended to view pacifists in CPS (not to speak of noncombatant objectors) as compromisers and half-measuremen. In many cases the absolutists were strong individualists, for whom protest was almost a vocation. Their actions were often controversial, sometimes colorful, and occasionally a trifle bizarre. By their challenge to accepted norms, even while in prison, by their confrontation of pacifist orthodoxy as much as the presuppositions of militarism, by their refusal to cooperate where prudence indicated compromise, they contributed something of value to a society whose already existing tendency to conformism had been accentuated by the pressures of wartime. That they were able to make a protest of this kind at all, shows, however, that the libertarian impulse in American political life, if – at least for the time being – on the wane, still retained sufficient strength to absorb the shock of radical dissent.

Conscientious Objection outside Britain and the United States

In the three British dominions where wartime conscription was introduced – Australia, New Zealand, and Canada – the legislative pattern approximated in some respects more closely to the American than to the British one. In none of these countries was there provision for unconditional exemption, except for a brief period in Australia. However, in all three countries nonreligious claims, if based on pacifist grounds, were recognized in practice, if not always in law. Canada and New Zealand eventually instituted schemes of civilian alternative service, somewhat similar to the American CPS but entirely government-run.

Of these three Commonwealth countries Australia, after some hesitation, provided most generously for its conscientious objectors, even though (despite the efforts of a handful of dedicated peace activists like Eleanor May Moore) the prewar pacifist movement had been extremely small there as were pacifist sects like the Quakers. Moreover, there had been several prominent defections from a peace position, including that of the influential minister of the liberal Australian Church in Melbourne, Charles Strong, who now supported armed resistance to Nazi Germany.[85] It has been suggested that Australia's tolerance of conscientious objection reflected "values and traditions in society at large such as faith in the volunteer, a certain suspicion of governments and a degree of respect for individual rights."[86] Perhaps so; but earlier, government and society had certainly shown scant tolerance in the matter during the "boy conscription" of the immediate pre-1914 period.

At any rate, according to the Defence Act of September 1939, a man's conscientious objection to military service did not have to be "of a religious character" or "part of the doctrines of any religion." Sincerity alone should be the deciding factor in assessing whether an application for C.O. status was genuine or not. At first, exemption was granted only from combatant army service. But from July 1941 on, those objectors who could not conscientiously "perform naval, military or air force service (whether combatant or non-combatant)" were allowed to undertake "work of a civil character and under civilian control"; for a brief period unconditional exemption, as in Britain, was also available. These new regulations were carried through under the auspices of the ruling Labor government.[87]

In New Zealand, however, a different system prevailed, even though that country too was ruled at this time by a Labour government.[88] Here a severity existed in official policy toward the objector, which contrasted with his treatment in other English-speaking countries. "There was no recognition of objection that fell short of opposition to all war, no exemption from some form of national service, and no provision for appeals against the decisions" reached in the first instance. "The attack on civil rights extended to exclusion from government employment and, for defaulters [who refused to accept their allotted status], disfranchisement."[89] In addition, several respected pacifists, though over draft age, received prison sentences for their antiwar stand when this found expression in print or on the platform. The primary function of the Armed Forces Appeal Boards, which decided on applications for C.O. status, lay in dealing with applications for exemption from military service based on "private hardship and public interest." In fact less than 3 percent of cases heard involved conscientious objection. "These," writes a New Zealand historian, J.E. Cookson, "were conditions that militated against sensitive or even sensible handling of the issue. It is not too much to say that the New Zealand Boards, in comparison with the British tribunals, were too formal, too ignorant and too busy."[90] The Boards assigned those deemed to be "genuine" C.Os. (a category fairly narrowly defined) either to civilian work on soldier's pay or to noncombatant army service where this seemed appropriate. Applicants denied C.O. status were regarded as "defaulters" and despatched, for the duration of the war, to detention camps specially set up to accommodate such persons, who had in most cases already served "at least one prison term." "By 1945, 803 men had been sent to the camps,"[91] where they worked under semi-penal conditions. Any inmates who refused to cooperate were sentenced to imprisonment, but in a civil not a military jail.

Various explanations of the government's harshness in dealing with conscientious objection have been attempted. Cookson's appears to be the most plausible. Despite Labour's tradition of antimilitarism and its anticonscriptionist position in World War I, the party supported the present war with virtual unanimity, and thus, he explains, "in the wartime society of 1940–41 government and public broadly agreed that every individual could be called upon to meet the state's requirements ... Objectors should pay for the privilege of avoiding military service by some equivalent imposition."[92] Soldier's pay and defaulters' camps appeared then, to government and public alike, as a realization of the principle they were both agreed on. But viewed at a distance of half a century its harshness and severity appear more striking than the policy's equity.

In Canada, few objectors were jailed, at least for long, even when their applications had been rejected by the "Mobilization Boards," which were the equivalent of the U.S. Selective Service local boards. At first C.Os. were assigned to civilian service camps in remote rural areas where they worked chiefly on forestry and agricultural projects. But from 1943 onward this rigidity was abandoned in favor of the British model (though still without provision for unconditional exemption or for nonreligious types of objection). Work assignments on soldier's pay to "farms, factories, and hospitals" became increasingly frequent, while C.Os. were now permitted to enter the armed forces in a noncombatant capacity if this were their preferred form of service. In 1944 the government even permitted a small contingent of C.Os. to join the British-run Friends Ambulance Unit in their work in China. "Canadian pacifists," writes Thomas P. Socknat, "were especially proud of their role in this international relief effort"; indeed it "came to symbolize the rich possibilities of active pacifist service in assisting civilian populations in a time of war."[93] In Canada, too, blanket exemption deriving from earlier legislative guarantees had been granted at first to two religious groups: the Mennonites and Hutterites who had emigrated from Russia in the 1870s, and a sect of Russian ethnic origin, the Dukhobors. But this inherited exemption disappeared after the introduction of the draft in June 1940 had led to concrete measures to implement its C.O. clauses. One small section of the Dukhobors, the Sons of Freedom in British Columbia, whose spiritual anarchism led them on occasion to symbolic nudity and a certainly reprehensible display of arson, refused to register but remained untouched by the authorities, who clearly feared the consequences of strong measures in stirring up an ethnic hornets' nest.[94]

In New Zealand there were barely 3,000 objectors, with an even smaller figure recorded for the much larger population of Australia. Canada produced nearly 11,000 conscientious objectors; but of these almost three quarters were drawn from the various Mennonite sects. As in World War I, the sparseness of conscientious objection in these three countries reflected the previous weakness of their pacifist movements. In Canada, despite his general popularity the socialist CCF's parliamentary leader, J.S. Woodsworth, like British Labour's Lansbury four years earlier, failed to carry his party along with him in support of pacifism; in September 1939 Woodsworth's was indeed a lonely voice in the Canadian House of Commons when he spoke there in support of an unconditional rejection of war.[95] Though pacifist pockets existed in Canada's Protestant churches, a product to some extent of the same Social Gospel as motivated contemporary liberal religious pacifism across the border, Canadian conscientious objection remained largely a matter of the sects.

In Germany, as in Soviet Russia, the pacifist movement had been ruthlessly suppressed by the ruling dictatorship before the outbreak of war. Those leaders who were unable to flee the country were mostly imprisoned by the Nazis: indeed, among those prominent members who remained in Germany, only the pacifist general, Baron Paul von Schönaich, seems to have escaped comparatively unscathed, presumably because of his social position and military record. The movement's followers just melted away. Apart from Jehovah's Witnesses, whom Hitler either executed or put into a concentration camp, and a few individual C.Os. from the Catholic Church and from such Protestant denominations as the Seventh-day Adventists, who suffered a similar fate, conscientious objection scarcely existed in Nazi Germany.[96] As for the once nonresistant Mennonites, their church had formally abandoned pacifism after Hitler came to power and had renounced the noncombatant status its conscripts could claim in Imperial Germany if they wanted it. Still, a few continued to adhere to their traditional nonresistance and, if conscripted, sometimes succeeded – unofficially – in obtaining noncombatant duties of some kind.

Before 1939 the tiny Quaker Society of Friends, whose prestige stood high in Germany on account of the postwar Quaker relief action, had failed none the less to gain from the Nazi government the hoped-for exemption from bearing arms after conscription was reintroduced in March 1935. The Friends had at the time publicly confirmed their adherence to the Society's pacifism while assuring the government of their willingness "to serve their Fatherland with all means at their disposal." But, they added, "we do not wish to bind anyone whose conscience causes him to come to a different decision" with regard to military service. "We shall respect his decision in friendship ... Quakers ... have never obliged individual members to adopt a specific attitude" on this issue. During the war some Quaker conscripts were allowed to serve in the army medical corps; others, however, were unsuccessful in gaining this concession and, after induction into the army, had to do their best to avoid using their weapons to kill. One older Quaker, a war veteran, who was recalled to the colors as a former reserve officer in 1942, stated frankly his unwillingness "as a Christian pacifist" to undertake further military service. An army board, before whom he had been summoned, showed a remarkable understanding of his position and allowed him to return home.[97]

We do know, however, of another – pacifist – war veteran, Dr. Hermann Stöhr, the former secretary of the dissolved German branch of the Fellowship of Reconciliation, who adamantly refused reinduction into the army and was executed for this crime on 21 June 1940. Stöhr was a Protestant, as was a second FOR member executed by Hitler for antiwar activities, Elisabeth von Thadden (a sister, ironically, of the later leader of West Germany's extreme nationalist party, Adolf von Thadden). Mention should also be made of the pacifist Pastor Wilhelm Mensching, whose popularity with his congregation appears to have protected him from imprisonment, even though he never attempted to hide his distaste for Nazism, including its racist policies, or his love of peace. Constantly under suspicion, he continued to serve his country parish throughout the war years.

Only a handful of German (or Austrian) Catholics became C.Os., despite the many thousands of Catholics who had taken an antimilitarist stand during the Weimar Republic. Almost all these men suffered the death penalty on account of their refusal to fight. Some of them had adopted this stance because they believed Nazi Germany was engaged in an unjust war. In a book entitled *In Solitary Witness* the American sociologist, Gordon C. Zahn, has told the story of one of these courageous civilian resisters, the Austrian peasant Franz Jägerstätter. Others were inspired by a vision of evangelical pacifism and regarded Jesus' love commandment as their rule of life overriding the orders of the state and the military if these conflicted with gospel principles.

Catholic objectors, for the most part, received a cold, if not an actually hostile, response from their church. Several priests, however, took an absolute pacifist stand even after the outbreak of war. There was Max Josef Metzger, for instance, who was executed by the Nazis in 1944. The learned Austrian priest, Johannes Ude, possessor of four university doctorates, who proclaimed *Du sollst nicht toten* (Thou shalt not kill) in and out of season, narrowly escaped the same fate; arrested by the Gestapo and charged with treason, Ude escaped the death penalty only because the war ended before he could be executed. Another scholarly priest Hermann Hoffmann, a professor in the University of Breslau, who as a member of the FOR had worked zealously for Polish-German reconciliation throughout the Weimar period,[98] remained untouched by the authorities, perhaps because he was of a milder disposition than his fiery colleague, Ude.

In German-occupied Europe only Denmark, Norway, and the Netherlands had effective pacifist groups before invasion, the largest of these being the Dutch Christian pacifist society, *Church and Peace* (*Kerk en Vrede*). Each of these countries also had Quaker Yearly Meetings (the one in Norway with its roots in the early nineteenth century); but the Quaker presence, because of its small size, had made little impact.

The Nazis banned *Church and Peace* within a year of occupying the country and suppressed its journal, which hitherto had appeared regularly despite the German invasion. Its members, no longer able to meet openly, attempted nevertheless to keep alive a spirit of reconciliation while remaining adamantly opposed to the Nazi ethos and participating actively in aid to Jews. Several of its leaders were imprisoned, including J.B. Hugenholtz, its chief organizer, and J.J. Buskes, its most prolific publicist, and one – a Protestant clergyman of Jewish origin – perished in a German concentration camp.[99] After the war *Church and Peace* became the Dutch section of the FOR.

Denmark, where the reaction of government and populace approached passive resistance of the Gandhian variety (where, too, Nazi methods were rather less barbaric than elsewhere), the small pacifist movement continued to function openly, publishing regularly its monthly paper *Aldrig Mere Krig* (No More War) with articles protesting both against the Nazis' treatment of the Jews and their persecution of religion and culture in neighboring Norway.[100] In the latter country pacifists, steering clear – like their Danish colleagues – of the more violent manifestations of sabotage, participated in the largely nonviolent resistance of the civil population against attempts to nazify cultural life. Some of them were arrested and imprisoned by the Germans for such activities, including Olaf Kullman, co-founder in 1938 of Norway's WRI section and formerly a naval officer, who died during his incarceration in Germany. But they were too small a group either to initiate or to guide this passive resistance. In regard to such efforts, a Norwegian pacifist leader admitted: "It ... proved ... more difficult ... than our propaganda had led us to believe such resistance would be." But from his wartime experience he drew the same conclusion as Gandhi had done from his campaigns against the British, namely that "open uncompromising resistance" of this kind "produced the most effective results."[101]

Whether driven underground in Nazi-occupied Europe, or able to function openly as in Britain and the Commonwealth or in the United States or in certain neutral countries, pacifism in World War II appeared a small and seemingly ineffective sect. A war of hitherto unexampled destruction was raging throughout large parts of the globe. Under Nazi rule, atrocities that had not been seen since the days of Tamerlane were being committed daily. The Holocaust indeed witnessed to human barbarity on an unprecedented scale. On the allied side, Stalin's Russia enforced a system as despotic as that of the Pharoahs of Egypt, and the Anglo-American democracies carried out the incineration of tens of thousands of civilians because they lived in enemy cities. One might well ask whether, in the peace that would eventually succeed the turmoil of war, pacifism could ever regain political relevance or become anything more than a purely personal ethic or a counsel of withdrawal from an evil world.

Notes

1 Quoted in Richenda C. Scott, *Herbert G. Wood: A Memoir of His Life and Thought* (London: Friends Home Service Committee, 1967), p. 125. Cf. the attitude of another Christian pacifist theologian, the Congregationalist Cecil John Cadoux. "It would have shaken him badly if his [two] sons had accepted combatant service." In fact, both of them became C.Os. and joined the Friends Ambulance Unit. Cadoux's wartime defense of pacifism, which he entitled *Christian Pacifism Re-examined* (Oxford: Basil Blackwell, 1940), presents systematically, and with great restraint, the case for this position. See Elaine Kaye, *C.J. Cadoux: Theologian, Scholar and Pacifist* (Edinburgh: Edinburgh University Press, 1988), pp. 166–75. Curiously, as a young man Cadoux, for some half dozen years after becoming a convinced Christian pacifist, had continued to work as a civil servant at the Admiralty before resigning in 1911 to take up a teaching post in a theological college.
     Another curious father-son confrontation over the C.O. issue was that between the left-wing writer, Raymond Postgate, and his son Oliver. In 1916 Raymond, aged nineteen, had been jailed briefly as a pacifist–socialist C.O. – to the horror of his very conservative father. In 1944 he was now a happy Home Guardsman while his nineteen-year-old son was in Feltham boys' prison for refusing induction into the Household Cavalry. "Ray had been very discomposed – his own choice of word – by Oliver's decision to be a conscientious objector." A breach ensued for a time between the two. See John and Mary Postgate, *A Stomach for Dissent. The Life of Raymond Post-gate: 1896–1971* (Keele, Staffordshire: Keele University Press, 1994), pp. 41–69, 239, 240. Parents as tolerant as H.G. Wood are probably exceptional.

2 Sybil Morrison, *I renounce War: The Story of the Peace Pledge Union* (London: Sheppard Press, 1962), p. 45. The duke's chief supporter during the war years was the equally eccentric anarcho-pacifist, Guy A. Aldred, whose Strickland Press in Glasgow published most of the duke's antiwar pamphlets.

3 Yet Greene remained a pacifist. For the Greene case, see the discerning

treatment given it by A.W. Brian Simpson, *In the Highest Degree Odious: Detention without Trial in Wartime Britain* (Oxford: Clarendon Press, 1992), pp. 138, 139, 341–52, 356–62, 366–75. Greene was treasurer of the British People's Party, founded by the Duke of Bedford in association with Mosley's recent colleague, John Beckett.

4 For public recantations of pacifism, see, for example, the two Macmillan War Pamphlets, London, 1940: C.E.M. Joad, *For Civilization*, and A.A. Milne, *War with Honour*. See also *The Autobiography of Bertrand Russell*, vol. II (London: George Allen and Unwin Ltd., 1968), pp. 191, 192, 233.

5 See Andrew Rigby, "Pacifist Communities in Britain in the Second World War," *Peace & Change* (Newbury Park, CA), vol. 15, no. 2 (April, 1990), pp. 107–22. The Bruderhof represented a classic form of pacifist communitarianism. Founded in Germany in 1920 on a sixteenth-century model, it ceased activities there when its members had to emigrate to England in 1936–7. Though most of the brothers and sisters left for Paraguay between December 1940 and April 1941, the movement continued slowly to expand in Britain and later in the United States. See Benjamin David Zablocki, *The Joyful Community* (Baltimore, MD: Penguin Books, 1971), pp. 80–85; also Yaacov Oved, *The Witness of the Brothers: A History of the Bruderhof*, transl. from the Hebrew by Anthony Berris (New Brunswick, N.J.: Transaction Publishers, 1996), pp. 93, 97–100, 104–14.

6 See F.A. Lea, *The Life of John Middleton Murry* (London: Methuen & Co. Ltd., 1959), esp. chap. XXIII. Best of all, consult the files of *Peace News* during Murry's editorship, which lasted until October 1946. For intelligent analysis of Murry's role in the wartime PPU, see Richard A. Rempel, "The Dilemmas of British Pacifists during World War II," *Journal of Modern History* (Chicago), vol. 50, no. 4 (December, 1978), pp. D1223–D1225 (via Order No. IJ-00040). Unfortunately the text of this article is extremely hard to obtain.

7 Mark Gilbert, "Pacifist Attitudes to Nazi Germany, 1936–45," *Journal of Contemporary History* (London and Newbury Park, CA), vol. 27, no. 3 (July, 1992), pp. 503–06.

8 Her contribution to the food relief and bombing restriction campaigns is discussed in Paul Berry and Mark Bostridge, *Vera Brittain: A Life* (London: Chatto & Windus, 1995), pp. 425–32, 436–42. Some pacifists, we may note, regarded these campaigns as an attempt to "humanize war" by concentrating on merely two of its manifold evils. But this appears to have been a minority view. Yvonne Aleksandra Bennett has written extensively on Brittain as a pacifist; her "Vera Brittain and the Peace Pledge Union ... ," pp. 192–213 in Ruth Roach Pierson, ed., *Women and Peace: Theoretical, Historical and Practical Perspectives* (London: Croom Helm, 1987), is especially useful. For Brittain's linkage between feminism and pacifism, see Deborah Gorham, *Vera Brittain: A Feminist Life* (Oxford: Blackwell Publishers, 1996),

pp. 183, 250–59, 261. From the late 1930s on, peace rather than women's rights seems to have predominated among her interests.

9 Glen Zeitzer and Charles F. Howlett, "Political versus Religious Pacifism: The Peace Now Movement of 1943," *The Historian* (Toledo, OH), vol. 48, no. 3 (May, 1986), pp. 375–93.

10 Letter dated November 17, 1941; from Grover Smith, ed., *Letters of Aldous Huxley* (London: Chatto & Windus, 1969), pp. 469, 470. We find the same kind of sentiments expressed by that very "personal" pacifist, Evelyn Underhill. "Begin where you are," she wrote in beleaguered Britain in 1940, "by accepting one's place in a conflicted and sinful order and work to create an environment of love and peace. Establish a cell of tranquility in a world of war." Quoted in Dana Greene, "Evelyn Underhill and Her Response to War," *Historical Magazine of the Protestant Episcopal Church* (Austin, TX), vol. 55, no. 2 (June, 1986), p. 133.

11 Beverley Nichols, *"In the Next War I shall be a Conscientious Objector"* (London: Friends Peace Committee, 1932, reprinted from *Good Housekeeping*), p. 4. Nichols had ceased to be a pacifist by 1938.

12 Quoted in Denis Hayes, *Challenge of Conscience: The Story of the Conscientious Objectors of 1939–1949* (London: George Allen and Unwin Limited, 1949), p. 4. Reprinted in The Garland Library of War and Peace, 1972.

13 Rachel Barker, *Conscience, Government and War: Conscientious Objection in Great Britain 1939–45* (London: Routledge & Kegan Paul, 1982), p. 25. F.R. Davies, son of – the later – Quaker Lord Darwen, was one of those whom the Tribunal, this time at his own request, had assigned to the RAMC. He ended up, however, in the NCC (after a few years becoming a full combatant). See his autobiography, *Some Blessed Hope: Memoirs of a Next-to-Nobody* (Lewes, U.K.: The Book Guild Ltd., 1996), pp. 34, 35, 37–48, 75, 88. Some "conchies in battledress" took part as RAMC paratroops in the invasion of the continent, and several were killed in action while remaining noncombatant.

14 Hayes, *op. cit.*, p. 37.

15 Barker, *op. cit.*, p. 110.

16 Hayes, *op. cit.*, pp. 48–50, 255, 256.

17 Quoted in *ibid.*, p. 182.

18 *Ibid.*, p. 266.

19 *Ibid.*, p. 91.

20 Barker, *op. cit.*, p. 95, misunderstands the term "star prisoner." It does not imply any compliment to the C.Os., who simply wore these stars along with all other convicted prisoners who were in jail for the first time.

21 Charles F. Carter, *Snail's Progress* (London: Penal Reform Committee of the Society of Friends, 1948), pp. 12, 13.

22 *Ibid.*, pp. 11, 12, 20–22.

23 "Flowery dell": thieves' rhyming slang for "cell."

24 "This barren prison world of disciplined triviality" (Carter, *op. cit.*, p. 22). In that period at any rate, the punitive still prevailed over the reformatory in the treatment of Britain's convict population.

25 Hayes, *op. cit.*, pp. 173–6. By a work strike in prison, writes Hayes, Walker sought to show his "sense of vocation for pacifist and food-relief work" and protest against his incarceration, which was preventing him from fulfilling what he believed to be his wartime mission.

26 For C.Os. in civil prisons, see Barker, *op. cit.*, pp. 94–97; also Carter, *op. cit.*, pp. 9–13, 15–24. The reactions of C.Os. to prison life, as they reported on it later, varied considerably. We find, for instance, one C.O. writing in retrospect: "I quite enjoyed being in prison," while another comments: "Prison was shocking ... The idiocy of the work provided! ... The general futility of the prison system has remained with me." Quoted in Tim Evans, ed, *Standing up to be counted* (York, UK: William Sessions Limited, 1988), pp. 18, 23.

27 Hayes, *op. cit.*, p. 202.

28 *Ibid.*, p. 28.

29 William Ralph Inge, *A Pacifist in Trouble* (London: Putnam, 1939), p. 23. This position contrasted with that of World War I when pacifists formed a very small group within the Church of England.

30 We should note, though, the existence of Welsh nationalists who were also pacifists, e.g., Gwynfor Evans, leader of the nationalist party Plaid Cymru, and Iowerth Peate, a distinguished folklorist, who was dismissed from the National Museum for registering as a C.O. The erudite church historian and Congregationalist minister, Robert Tudur Jones, combined active membership in the Fellowship of Reconciliation with advocacy of an independent Wales and vigorous opposition to "expansionist English nationalism." In fact, a significant, though small, Welsh presence can be traced in British pacifism from the early nineteenth century to the present: at first of an exclusively cultural-linguistic character but later aiming, too, at the creation of a Welsh nation-state.

31 G.C. Field, *Pacifism and Conscientious Objection* (Cambridge: The University Press, 1945), p. 93. For a critique of Field's book, see E.L. Allen, Francis E. Pollard, and G.A. Sutherland, *The Case for Pacifism and Conscientious Objection: A Reply to Professor G.C. Field* (London: Central Board for Conscientious Objectors, 1946).

32 Stuart Smith, in Clifford Simmons, ed., *The Objectors* (London: Gibbs and Phillips, 1965), p. 65. Italics in the original.

33 These kinds of activities are dealt with by Pat Starkey, *I will not fight: Conscientious Objectors and Pacifists in the North West during the Second World War* (Liverpool: Liverpool Historical Essays No. 7, Liverpool University Press, 1992).

34 Martin Ceadel, *Pacifism in Britain 1914–1945: The Defining of a Faith* (Oxford: The Clarendon Press, 1980), p. 307.

35 Quoted in Hayes, *op. cit.*, p. 218.

36 See A. Tegla Davies, *Friends Ambulance Unit: The Story of the F.A.U. in the Second World War* (London: George Allen and Unwin Limited, 1947), and – for the activities of the official Quaker relief organization – Roger C. Wilson, *Quaker Relief: An Account of the Relief Work of the Society of Friends 1940–1948* (London: George Allen & Unwin Ltd., 1952).

37 David Morris, *China changed My Mind* (London: Cassell & Company Limited, 1948), p. 42. Morris's book tells how the questions raised by working in a country like China, where the framework of law and order was only tenuously maintained and where religious pacifism was only rarely comprehended, led eventually to the author's abandoning pacifism and joining the army. See esp. pp. 177–9, 191.

38 Alan Wilkinson, *Dissent or Conform? War, Peace and the English Churches 1900–1945* (London: SCM Press Ltd., 1986), p. 291. Moorman, who was the historian G.E. Trevelyan's son-in-law, besides becoming a bishop also wrote a number of important works on St. Francis and his order. We see a similar spirit of sacrifice in another Christian pacifist with very different theological opinions from Moorman's: Robert E.D. Clark was a lapsed Anglican who had "walked out of the established church because as a strong pacifist he could no longer accept its position on such issues as military service." Henceforward an unattached nonconformist close to the Plymouth Brethren, he eventually became "perhaps the most ... articulate creationist of his generation." After a brilliant career at Cambridge where he had gained a Ph.D in organic chemistry, Clark worked until the outbreak of war "as an industrial chemist, but quit to become a schoolmaster when he was assigned to military work." See Ronald L. Numbers, *The Creationists* (New York: Alfred A. Knopf, 1992), p. 154.

39 Quoted in Mulford Q. Sibley and Philip E. Jacob, *Conscription and Conscience* (Ithaca, N.Y.: Cornell University Press, 1952), pp. 68, 69. This volume is invaluable for the history of World War II C.Os. in the United States.

40 *Ibid.*, p. 81.

41 Quoted in Neal M. Wherry, *Conscientious Objection*, 2 vols. (Washington, D.C.: Selective Service System Special Monograph, no. 11, 1950), vol. I, p. 72. See Arthur Whitefield Spalding, *Origin and History of Seventh-day Adventists* (Washington, D.C.: Review and Herald Publishing Association), vol. IV (1962), chap. X ("Christian Servicemen").

42 David Mitchell, *Seventh-day Adventists: Faith in Action* (New York: Vantage Press, 1958), pp. 49–52, 65, 115–17.

43 Everett N. Dick, "The Adventist Medical Corps as seen by Its Founder," *Adventist Heritage: A Magazine of Adventist History* (Loma Linda, CA), vol. 1, no. 2 (July, 1974), pp. 19, 20. See also John D. Hicks, "Everett Dick: Teacher,

Scholar, Churchman" in Ray Allen Billington, ed., *People of the Plains and Mountains: Essays in the History of the West dedicated to Everett Dick* (Westport, CT: Greenwood Press, 1973), pp. 5, 15–19.

44 Carlyle B. Haynes, ed., *Studies in Denominational Principles of Noncombatancy and Governmental Relationships* (Washington, D.C.: Seventh-day Adventist War Service Commission, [1943]), pp. 22–24. See also pp. 25–29, 46–48.

45 *Ibid.*, p. 16.

46 *Ibid.*, p. 15. In a leaflet issued in September 1940, the General Conference Committee thus defined the "works of necessity and mercy" which Adventist soldiers could in good conscience perform on their Saturday Sabbaths: "Any service either direct or auxiliary which is immediately necessary for the alleviation of suffering and the maintenance of proper health and sanitation, and which cannot be cared for beforehand or postponed" (*ibid.*, pp. 13, 14).

47 Cynthia Eller, *Conscientious Objectors and the Second World War: Moral and Religious Arguments in Support of Pacifism* (New York: Praeger, 1991), p. 29.

48 Sibley and Jacob, *op. cit.*, p. 89.

49 A few noncombatants were ready to undergo weapon-training, even though the army did not require this from C.Os.; presumably they would refrain from actually using firearms in battle.

50 *Ibid.*, p. 97. See Booton Herndon, *The Unlikeliest Hero: The Story of Desmond T. Doss, Conscientious Objector who won His Nation's Highest Military Medal* (Mountain View, CA and Omaha, NE: Pacific Press Publishing Association, 1967), pp. 159, 160, 177, 178, for the War Department's account of Private Doss's "outstanding bravery and unflinching determination in aiding his wounded comrades in the fierce Okinawa campaign." No other C.O. has ever received this prestigious military award. Medical paratrooper Keith Argraves was another Adventist war hero. He consistently refused to carry a gun while in action behind the German lines; George W. Chambers, *Keith Argraves, Paratrooper* (Nashville, TN: The Southern Publishing Association, 1946), pp. 22, 41.

51 Sibley and Jacob, *op. cit.*, p. 87.

52 *Ibid.*, pp. 109 and 108.

53 Among these agonized participants were former pacifists who had abandoned their pacifism after the outbreak of war in Europe in face of mounting Nazi-Fascist aggression. We may cite as prominent examples such persons as Helen Keller, who would later regret her support of the war, the publisher William Allen White, and the Quaker scholar and WILPF activist, Emily Greene Balch. The latter wrote in a letter to Alice Hamilton, dated February 20, 1941: "I stop being non-resistant when it is a question of offering my neighbor's cheek for the blow ... I do not believe that there is *now*

'that' in Hitler et al. that responds with magnanimity to the non-resistant virtues ... they make a religion of force which makes them impervious along those lines." "At the same time," she went on, "I thank God for the Conscientious Objectors ... I am glad some have the vocation for this, though I have not." Quoted in Barbara Miller Solomon, "Dilemmas of Pacifist Women, Quakers and Others, in World Wars I and II," in Elisabeth Potts Brown and Susan Mosher Stuard, eds., *Witness for Change: Quaker Women over Three Centuries* (New Brunswick and London: Rutgers University Press, 1989), pp. 152–55. Italics in the original. In 1946 Balch shared the Nobel Peace Prize with another ex-Christian pacifist, John R. Mott, who had abandoned his pacifism during World War I.

54 W. Edward Orser, "World War III and the Pacifist Controversy in the Major Protestant Churches," *American Studies* (Lawrence, KS), vol. 14, no. 2 (Fall, 1973), pp. 6, 7, 20, 21. The denominations covered here are the Baptists, Congregational Christians, Episcopalians, Methodists, and Presbyterians: a list that is by no means exhaustive.

55 For the experience of Mennonite C.Os. in World War II, see especially the account in Paul Toews, *Mennonites in American Society, 1930–1970: Modernity and the Persistence of Religious Community* (vol. 4 in *The Mennonite Experience in America*) (Scottdale, PA and Waterloo, ON: Herald Press, 1996), pp. 129–83. Toews comments (p. 129): "Seldom if ever have Mennonites worked as closely with the state as during World War II. ... More than most religious pacifists, Mennonites brought to this partnership a theology that separated church from state. Yet Mennonites embraced the CPS system with fewer reservations than did other historic peace churches. Whatever the strains on their theology, Mennonites said little about compromises inherent in the new partnership."

56 Sibley and Jacob, *op. cit.*, p. 120.

57 *Ibid.*, p. 328.

58 Quoted in Bertram and Irene Pickard, *The Quaker Peace Testimony Today* (Philadelphia: Friends World Committee for Consultation, 1946), pp. 23, 26. For one American "birthright" Quaker's reasons for deciding to serve as a combatant in the war against Hitler, see Robert Lawrence Smith, *A Quaker Book of Wisdom: Life Lessons in Simplicity, Service, and Common Sense* (New York: Eagle Brook, 1998), pp. 65–77, 85–87, 95–97.

59 An exception here was the Quaker philosopher Brand Blanshard's forthright article "Non-Pacifist Quakerism," *Friends Intelligencer* (Philadelphia), vol. 99, no. 25 (20 June 1942), pp. 393, 394; no. 26 (27 June 1942), pp. 409, 410.

60 See Perry Bush, "Military Service, Religious Faith, and Acculturation: Mennonite GIs and Their Church, 1941–1945," *The Mennonite Quarterly Review* (Goshen, IN), vol. 67, no. 3 (July, 1993), pp. 261–82.

61 Wherry, *op. cit.*, vol. 1, p. 322. The figures which, it must be remembered,

include the unbaptized sons of Brethren as well as full members were those
supplied by the Brethren Service Committee.

62 Sibley and Jacob, *op. cit.*, p. 111.

63 *Ibid.*, pp. 124, 126. For the impact made by C.Os. working in mental hospitals, see Alex Sareyan, *The Turning Point: How Men of Conscience brought
about Major Changes in the Care of America's Mentally Ill* (Washington, D.C.:
American Psychiatric Press, 1994). The author, with a long career in mental
health education after the war was over, had himself been a C.O. volunteer
in a mental hospital during World War II.

64 Sibley and Jacob, *op. cit.*, p. 224.

65 Wherry, *op. cit.*, vol. I, p. 27. On pp. 24–7 the author lists 345 religious bodies
with members claiming registration as conscientious objectors between
1940 and 1947, and on pp. 318–320 he provides details concerning church
membership of CPS men during the same period.

66 The position of Jewish objectors was peculiarly difficult. In their own community they were frequently reviled because of their scruples concerning
an armed struggle against their people's Nazi persecutors; on the other
hand, patriots with antisemitic proclivities tended to view their stand as
treason to their country. Catholic and Jewish objectors, unlike objectors
coming from nonpacifist Protestant denominations, had this in common
that their spiritual leaders were often actively hostile to their position. See
below, chap. XI.

67 Sibley and Jacob, *op. cit.*, pp. 170, 171, 529.

68 Clarence E. Pickett, *For More than Bread* (Boston: Little, Brown and Company, 1953), p. 330.

69 Quoted in Sibley and Jacob, *op. cit.*, p. 202.

70 Pickett, *op. cit.*, p. 331.

71 Sibley and Jacob, *op. cit.*, p. 216.

72 *Ibid.*, p. 478.

73 *Ibid.*, p. 242.

74 *Ibid.*, pp. 471–5. Despite prolonged efforts by the historic peace churches,
the government adamantly refused to release for postwar relief the "Frozen
Fund," which had been formed out of the impounded wages paid for objectors' labor in off-camp assignments.

75 The poet William Everson, in William Everson and Lawrence Clark Powell,
Take Hold Upon the Future: Letters on Writers and Writing 1938–1946, ed., William R. Eshelman (Metuchen, NJ, and London: The Scarecrow Press, 1994),
p. 354. See also p. 408.

76 Sibley and Jacob, *op. cit.*, p. 334.

77 *Ibid.*, p. 339.

78 *Ibid.*, p. 352.

79 *Ibid.*, p. 356. According to the warden of the Medical Center for Federal
Prisoners at Springfield, Missouri, where many C.Os. were sent for exami-

nation: "There were no outstanding trouble makers among the Jehovah's Witnesses ... True, they did resent imprisonment, but they looked upon it as a religious trial by ordeal and not as a challenge to urge a concerted attack upon the federal prison system." He also confirmed that JWs usually received excessively severe sentences, "the median being ... almost 2 years higher than the median sentence imposed on psychopathic prisoners who are confirmed criminals." See M.J. Pescor, "A Study of Selective Service Law Violators," *The American Journal of Psychiatry* (Baltimore), vol. 105, no. 9 (March, 1949), pp. 643, 645–8.

80 Racial discrimination also surfaced sometimes in sentencing C.Os. For example, in 1942 a white judge in the South imposed an exceptionally severe sentence of four years on the African-American pacifist absolutist (and later civil rights activist), Bill Sutherland. In jail Sutherland was one of the first C.Os. to refuse to cooperate with prison segregation: others, white and black, followed.

81 A good example of this problem is given in the memoirs of one of the Union Theological seminary "eight"; see David Dellinger, *From Yale to Jail: The Life Story of a Moral Dissenter* (New York: Pantheon Books, 1993), pp. 128–30, 132–7.

82 When finally released on 12 March 1946 "Bishop had fasted and denied the state all cooperation for the incredible total of 426 days." Lawrence S. Wittner, *Rebels against War: The American Peace Movement 1933–1983* (Philadelphia: Temple University Press, 1984), p. 90.

83 Sibley and Jacob, *op. cit.*, p. 416. But even sympathetic relatives sometimes found it difficult to understand the rationale of a C.O.'s hunger strike. As the mother of John Kellam, jailed for five years, wrote to his wife: "He has an immediate duty to you and me and to his child ... I warned him about hunger strikes or other demonstrations of martyr complexes." From Judy Barrett Litoff and David C. Smith, eds., *Since you went away: World War II Letters from American Women on the Home Front* (New York: Oxford University Press, 1991), p. 227.

84 Sibley and Jacob, *op. cit.*, p. 400.

85 Malcolm Saunders, "The 'Pacifism' of the Reverend Dr. Charles Strong: 1844–1942," *Interdisciplinary Peace Research* (Bundoora, Victoria), vol. 5, no. 1 (May/June, 1993), pp. 24–31. In this article Saunders argues convincingly that, despite appearances to the contrary, Strong, who first became an advocate of peace during the Boer War, had never at any time really been an absolute pacifist.

86 Hugh Smith, "Conscience, Law and the State: Australia's Approach to Conscientious Objection since 1901," *Australian Journal of Politics and History* (St. Lucia, Queensland), vol. 35 (1989), no. 1, p. 26.

87 *Ibid.*, pp. 16–18, 23. See also Ian M. Macdonald, "Deviancy: The Experience of the Conscientious Objector in Melbourne, 1939–45," *La Trobe Historical*

Studies (Bundoora, Victoria), vol. 4 (1974): *Melbourne in the Second World War*, pp. 11–22. The study deals mainly with the Christadelphians.

88　See David Grant, *Out in the Cold: Pacifists and Conscientious Objectors in New Zealand during World War II* (Auckland: Reed Methuen, 1986), esp. chaps. V–VII.

89　J.E. Cookson, "Illiberal New Zealand: The Formation of Government Policy on Conscientious Objection, 1940–1," *The New Zealand Journal of History* (Auckland), vol. 17, no. 2 (October, 1983), p. 120.

90　*Ibid.*, p. 129. See also pp. 125–7.

91　*Ibid.*, p. 120. Cookson (*ibid.*, p. 142) comments: "Defaulters' detention, which saved men from long prison sentences and some from prison altogether, stands lonely witness to the fact that Labour felt some compassion for the conscientious objector."

92　*Ibid.*, pp. 133–41. "There was no doubt they were pretty vicious against the conchies all round in New Zealand," was how one of these "conchies" put it; Ian Hamilton, *Till Human Voices wake us* (Auckland: University of Auckland Press, 1984), p. 185. Hamilton, a humanist pacifist, took an absolutist stand; his prison memoirs reflect the anger and frustration he suffered during his long incarceration.

93　Thomas P. Socknat, *Witness against War: Pacifism in Canada, 1900–1945* (Toronto: University of Toronto Press, 1987), pp. 227–58. The quotations are from pages 251 and 254. See also Socknat's article, "The Canadian Contribution to the China Convoy," *Quaker History* (Harverford, PA), vol. 69, no. 2 (Autumn, 1980), pp. 69–89. Once again, the overwhelming majority of Canadian C.Os. were drawn from one or another of the Mennonite subsects. For the experiences of drafted Mennonites in World War II, see T.D. Regehr, *Mennonites in Canada, 1939–1970. A People Transformed*: vol. 3 of *Mennonites in Canada* (Toronto: University of Toronto Press, 1996), pp. 35–59, and for their womenfolk, see pp. 61–64. On the latter, see also Marlene Epp's article in *Mennonite Life* (North Newton KS), vol. 48, no. 3 (September, 1993), pp. 7–10. Epp has analysed perceptively the C.O. experience in British Columbia forestry camps where Mennonites formed the majority: "Alternative Service and Alternative Gender Roles: Conscientious Objectors in B.C. during World War II," *BC Studies* (Vancouver), nos. 105–106 (Spring/Summer, 1995), pp. 139–58. "Both men and women," she writes, "were carving out new gender space, which altered their self-definition, even as they and their communities simultaneously held on to proper, or normative, notions of their roles as husbands or wives." Mennonites, another writer comments, while differing among themselves as to exactly which alternatives to bearing arms were acceptable, won respect from the authorities "because, while non-conformist, they sought to accommodate the government as much as possible." David Fransen, " 'As far as Conscience will allow': Mennonites in Canada during the Second World War,"

p. 147, in Norman Hillmer *et al.*, eds., *On Guard for Thee: War, Ethnicity, and the Canadian State, 1939–1945* (Ottawa: Canadian Committee for the History of the Second World War, 1988). See also pp. 132–6, 138. A recent edition to the literature, Peter Lorenz Neufeld, *Mennonites at War: A Double-edged Sword – Canadian Mennonites in World War II* (Deloraine, MB: DTS Publishing, 1997), deals with those Mennonite young men who joined the armed forces, mostly in a combatant capacity. Three conclusions emerge from this rather chaotic compilation, which draws primarily on the experiences of Manitoba Mennonites. First, roughly the same number of draft-age Mennonites appear to have served with the military as took a C.O. stand. In the second place it is often difficult, especially in the case of the former, to distinguish between "ethnic" and religious identity. Thirdly, extreme hostility sometimes marked the response of the more conservative churches to members who accepted military service, even when they remained noncombatants.

94 The most comprehensive account of Canadian C.O. experience in World War II is given by William Janzen, *Limits on Liberty* (Toronto: University of Toronto Press, 1990), pp. 198–244. The well known philosopher of postwar Canadian "progressive" Conservatism, George Grant, became a convinced pacifist while studying at Oxford in the early period of the war. Though as a Canadian citizen not liable to British conscription, he trained for ambulance work over the tense summer of 1940 and then became a volunteer air-raid warden during the London blitz that followed. He wrote to his mother on June 4, 1940: "Perhaps when I get home I will try and join up – something *non-military* ... Not for a moment do I feel any differently towards the horror of this thing, or as to the evil that must come in its trail, but one cannot stand aside from it." George Grant, *Selected Letters*, ed., William Christian (Toronto: University of Toronto Press, 1996), pp. 56, 57. Italics in the original. Having developed tuberculosis Grant returned to Canada in 1942. After the conflict was over, while remaining firmly antiwar he abandoned absolute pacifism and the political left.

95 Kenneth McNaught, *A Prophet in Politics: A Biography of J.S. Woodsworth* (Toronto: University of Toronto Press, 1959), pp. 309–12.

96 Peter Brock, "Conscientious Objectors in Nazi Germany," *Reconciliation Quarterly* (London), Summer 1994, pp. 21–26. In a situation like that of wartime Germany it is often not easy to distinguish even now between unconditional and selective C.Os. or between C.Os. as a whole and deserters or refractory soldiers. This emerges, for instance, from Günter Saathoff *et al.*, eds., *Dem Tode entronnen. Zeitzeugeninterviews mit Überlebenden der NS-Militärjustiz: Das Schicksal der Kriegsdienstverweigerer und Deserteure unter dem Nationalsozialismus und ihre unwürdige Behandlung im Nachkriegsdeutschland* (Cologne: Heinrich-Böll-Stiftung, 1993). The German parliament, after finally in 1997 awarding at least token compensation to the families of

World War II deserters and C.Os. who were executed or sent to a concentration camp, took a further step in May 1998 when it removed the stigma
of being law-violators from such people. See *Fellowship* (Nyack, NY),
vol. 64, no. 7/8 (July/August 1998), p. 24.

97 Anna Sabine Halle, "The German Quakers and the Third Reich," *German
History* (Oxford) vol. 11, no. 2 (June, 1993), pp. 225, 226, and "Quäker, als
Deserteure damals, als Totalverweigerer heute?" *Der Quäker.*, vol. 67, no. 3
(March, 1993), p. 63.

98 See Hermann Hoffmann, *Im Dienste des Friedens: Lebenserinnerungen eines
katholischen Europäers* (Stuttgart and Aalen: Konrad Theiss Verlag, 1970),
pp. 219–41, for his endeavors to foster Polish-German understanding
before 1939. A positive view of these activities is found in Karol Fiedor,
Niemiecki ruch obrońców pokoju 1892–1933 (Wrocław: Wydawnictwo
Uniwersytetu Wrocławskiego, 1993), pp. 52, 155–8, 165, 166.

99 Henk van den Berg and Ton Coppes, *Dominees in het geweer: Het christenantimilitarisme van Kerk en Vrede 1924–1950.* (Nijmegen: Studium voor Vredesvraagstuken, 1982), pp. 171–203. For the wartime stance of the small
pacifist minority in the (once nonresistant) Dutch Mennonite church, see
Gerlof D. Homan, "'We must ... and can stand firmly': Dutch Mennonites
in World War II," *Mennonite Quarterly Review*, vol. 69, no. 1 (January, 1995),
pp. 24, 31.

100 See Peter Kragh Hansen, *Pacifister i krig* (Odense Universitetsforlag,
[1990]), esp. pp. 22–57, 65–68.

101 Diderich Lund, *Resistance in Norway*, translated from the Norwegian
(Enfield, Middlesex: War Resisters' International, 1954), p. 6. Lund's judgment is confirmed in the remarkable wartime experiences of André
Trocmé, the French pacifist pastor at the village of Le Chambon, and his
courageous wife, Magda. See Philip P. Hallie, *Lest Innocent Blood be shed*
(New York: Harper Torchbooks, 1985). Trocmé was a man of tempestuous
passions but fashioned from the stuff saints are made of. The Trocmés and
their parishioners were responsible for saving many persons, Jews and
non-Jews, who would otherwise have ended up in Vichy prisons or Nazi
concentration camps. It is also worth noting that the Jehovah's Witnesses
in northern France, where the sect was strongly represented among the
immigrant Polish miners, displayed the same kind of "uncompromising"
yet nonviolent "resistance" to the occupiers as the Trocmés showed –
despite the harsh treatment of conscientious objectors in interwar France.
See Régis Dericquebourg, "Note sur l'attitude des Témoins de jéhovah et
des Baptistes face à l'occupant pendant la seconde guerre mondiale,"
Revue du Nord (Lille), vol. 60, no. 237 (April–June, 1978), pp. 441, 442.

VI. Two Case Studies in Post-Gandhian Nonviolence

The influence of Gandhi's nonviolence, which he practised among his own people for four decades, was felt eventually in many countries outside India. While it made a significant impact on the West, it also affected some of the African nationalist leaders responsible for leading their countries into independence after 1945. Take, for example, the case of Kwame Nkrumah of Ghana. At first a Marxist sceptical of any talk of nonviolent action and placing reliance on armed revolution, he later began to study the history of Gandhi's campaigns against the British. But Nkrumah's support for a nonviolent political strategy was based, as Jawaharlal Nehru's had been in India, primarily on expediency. What for a time attracted Nkrumah and several of the other African nationalist leaders, like Kenneth Kaunda of Zambia, to Gandhian techniques of conflict was the successful use of such techniques against the British; they seldom experienced any affinity to the philosophical and religious concepts underlying Gandhi's cultivation of *satyagraha*. And they usually abandoned interest in such methods after their countries had gained independence.[1]

In this chapter we have chosen two case studies in the principled, rather than the expedient practise of nonviolence drawn from the period after Gandhi's death in January 1948. First we will examine briefly the nonviolent movement in India during the 1950s and 1960s, which was initiated by Gandhi's disciple Vinoba Bhave. Then we shall survey the nonviolent movement for racial equality, which had emerged in the United States in the mid-1950s under the leadership of Martin Luther King, Jr.. King, like Vinoba, derived his inspiration largely from the example of Gandhi's campaigns of *satyagraha* against social and political injustice; and he also shared much of the

Mahatma's nonviolent ethos, which matched his own belief in the Christian gospel of love.

India's Gentle Anarchists

After Gandhi's return to India in 1915 his practise of nonviolence had been directed primarily (though by no means exclusively) toward the achievement of self-government for his compatriots. Since the Mahatma's death the Gandhians have explored, in particular, two largely new dimensions of nonviolence. First they developed, under Vinoba's leadership, a practical program aimed at creating a nonviolent social order. "For Vinoba Bhave a violent revolution was not a true revolution." It meant only the exchange of one privileged class for another instead of the well-being of all: the achievement of the *sarvodaya* that was at the core of Gandhi's message for humankind.[2] In the second place the Gandhians have experimented with the idea of a peace corps – a peace army (*Shanti Sena*), the avowed object of whose members was to discover nonviolent solutions to conflict situations within their own country and, in the final resort, even to defend it from invasion by nonviolent means. In relating nonviolence to the problems of society and in stressing the urgent need in the nuclear age of devising a strategy of nonviolent conflict resolution, Gandhians found common ground with Western pacifists. That there still remained serious differences in approach between the two groups will emerge in the pages that follow.

Toward a Nonviolent Society

The Gandhians' positive program centered in the Indian village, just as Gandhi's thoughts on nonviolence had always returned to the idea of village reconstruction. Like Gandhi's, their position could be defined as "mildly anarchist."[3] They aimed essentially at creating – or at recreating, as they would prefer to say – a lively grass-roots democracy based on the village community, largely self-sufficient, simple in its needs and practising cooperation in all its undertakings. To achieve such a society, land reform was essential. Therefore, in April 1951, the hard core of convinced Gandhians, organised two years earlier in the *Sarva Seva Sangh* (Association for the Service of All), rallied to Vinoba's call to establish "a Land-Gifts Mission" (*Bhoodan Yajna*), which would work nonviolently toward this end. The first objective of Vinoba's mission was to persuade the country's well-to-do landowners to donate one sixth of their cultivable land for distribution among landless peasants. Vinoba and his disciples, walking from village to village and talking to landlords in an effort to persuade them to relinquish their sixth of the land, achieved at first a number of remarkable successes. They likewise made numerous converts to the crusade among both old and young; the most outstanding recruit to the movement being the ex-Marxist Jayaprakash Narayan, who in 1954 abandoned his leadership of India's democratic socialist party to follow Vinoba. Most of the movement's activists were Hindus by conviction as well as birth, but they also included humanists of various kinds and at least one militant atheist (G. Ramachandra Rao).

In Vinoba's concept *Bhoodan*, the landlords' voluntary gift of land to the landless, had to be followed by *Gramdan* whereby the villagers were themselves persuaded to renounce private property in land and to institute communal ownership – rather in the style of the prerevolutionary Russian *mir* beloved by the nineteenth-century *narodniki* (populists). But *Gramdan* would not, in Vinoba's view, "bring about a revolution by peaceful methods, unless the people also feel at the same time that our ideas offer them a powerful means of self-defense even in the present state of affairs (that is, even while unjust differences remain)." The nonviolent character of the quiet revolution envisaged by Vinoba and the Gandhians, the quest for a nonviolent social order, was thus to have a secure base in the masses. It was not to remain a middle-class movement passively imposed on the people; it had to put down roots in the countryside among the peasants.

Vinoba, on one occasion, described his land reform efforts as "nonviolent assistance" (in contrast to the resistance offered by Gandhi to British rule before independence).[4] "Bhoodan Yajna," he wrote, "is an application of non-violence, an experiment in transformation of life itself ... It is a phenomenon inspired by God. For how otherwise can people, who fight even for a foot of land, be inspired to give away hundreds of acres of land freely?"[5] But he warned recalcitrant landowners that if they remained stubbornly attached to their possessions, they and the whole society which supported them would be swept away in the not too distant future. His aim was indeed to transform society at its foundations but at the same time to keep within the limits of the existing legal system.

Vinoba was criticized, e.g., by the independent socialist Ram Manohar Lohia, for not using *satyagraha* as his method for achieving social justice and for combating economic exploitation, as Gandhi had used it in his civil disobedience campaigns. To such arguments Vinoba replied that in a democracy *satyagraha* was a last resort; civil disobedience should come only after every constitutional channel, every avenue of peaceful persuasion, had been explored and found to yield no result. In his view, *satyagraha* could not be regarded simply as a nonviolent substitute for the class war.[6]

A Peace Army

The Peace Army (*Shanti Sena*), which Vinoba set up in August 1957,[7] was indeed foreshadowed in Gandhi's thinking. But its purposes and its organization do not exactly correspond to those of his *satyagraha* campaigns. And, unlike the proposal by English pacifists in the early 1930s for a nonviolent army discussed in an earlier chapter, Vinoba's *Shanti Sena* was designed from the beginning primarily for employment within the state, especially during outbreaks of communal violence. It was intended as a means to promote "the welfare of all" (*sarvodaya*). In promoting a Peace Army, Vinoba wrote:

The goal which we have set before us is a society free from external government. When this "anarchist" society comes into being, it will need no *Shanti Sena* ... Everywhere, and in every house, there will be people ready to take upon themselves the task of withstanding wrong-doing. If a father does something wrong, the son will be prepared to withstand him. A father will be responsible for his son and the son for his father. A neighbour will feel responsible for his neighbour, and one village for the next. In some way or other the matter will be dealt with on the spot and there will be no need for anyone to go from a distance to make peace. That is the state of affairs which we ultimately want to bring about.

Until a system of "village states" was set up, however, there would be need for peacemakers "from a distance." It was to fill this role that Vinoba created his Peace Army. Its members should form a body of dedicated, disciplined men and women ready to go at a moment's notice to any part of the country where violence threatened. In the intervals between calls to active service of this kind they were to engage, either part-time or full-time, in the constructive work recommended by Gandhi for his *satyagrahis*.

Vinoba, like Gandhi, demanded strict discipline from his "peace volunteers" (*Shanti Sainiks*). He did not regard unquestioning submission to the orders of a commanding officer, if this were necessary, as inconsistent with his goal of an anarchist society or with freedom of thought, and he readily accepted the title of "Supreme Commander of the *Shanti Sena* for the whole of India." "*Ahimsa*," he wrote, "is not going to grow beyond its infancy until the two thousand *Shanti Sainiks* on our register report for duty at any given point as soon as the need is proclaimed." Volunteers should regard themselves as nonviolent soldiers (indeed we might well compare them to members of a rigorous religious order). They must drill regularly to keep themselves fit and capable of acting in unison and with effect in a situation of tension. They should train, too, "in the techniques of various kinds of useful work," taking care to keep in close touch with the people whom they strove to serve as social workers. In regard to politics, though, the Peace Army should remain strictly neutral; Vinoba frequently stressed the need for his volunteers to stand aloof from party politics if they were to fulfill their function of reconcilers and act as true servants of the people.

Two points may be made in regard to the Peace Army. First, although popular support is envisaged ("a hank of yarn" monthly from "every family of five persons") – as well as a form of associate membership drawing in "hundreds of thousands" whose aid could be called upon in an emergency – the organization remained a professional body of "picked people," a nonviolent elite corps. From the hoped-for total of 70,000, however, only about one sixth were actually recruited. The Peace Army, in the second place, was viewed by Vinoba and the Gandhians not as an alternative to the regular Indian Army and an armed police force – at least for the time being. "We do not refuse to cooperate with the present government," he declared. "On the contrary, we have got its full sympathy in this work. The great leaders of the nation have welcomed the concept of *Shanti Sena*." Vinoba did not contemplate his organization being directly serviceable as an international peace brigade, which *inter alia* could interpose itself between the sides in situations of conflict (though in 1961 Jayaprakash proposed this idea, with the support of some Western pacifists as well as of nonpacifist internationalist like Salvador de Madariaga). Vinoba did, however, believe that it should serve as witness to the possibility of a nonviolent solution to world conflict. "If," he wrote, "we can demonstrate that there is no need of the army to keep the peace within our own borders, the force of peace in India will be strengthened and the world will be shown a new path ... First ... let us try to cleanse the atmosphere which prevails within India itself – everything will flow from that." Thus successful employment of "non-violent power" at home would point the way ultimately toward using it with effect internationally.

The Gandhians and the Sino-Indian Conflict of 1962[8]

The border dispute between India and communist China, which in the summer and autumn of 1962 led to armed clashes between the troops of the two states and presented Indians with the possibility of a Chinese invasion, aroused a wave of patriotic feeling throughout the country. The Gandhians themselves did not prove immune to its infection. The incident showed that, while Vinoba and his followers might aim at building an anarchist society in the future, they were first and foremost nationalists in the present. They identified themselves wholeheartedly with the stand of their government. "We believe," stated the Sarva Seva Sangh, representing the Gandhian movement, "that this conflict has been forced upon India, for India has been working consistently for a peaceful solution of the border question." Their declaration, after branding China as the aggressor, expressed "our full sympathy ... with India."[9] Only as to the means of resistance did they differ from their government, for they continued to press for nonviolent defense as the most efficacious response to aggression and to advocate the "idea of the co-operative society"[10] as the positive answer to the challenge of Communism.

After the outbreak of hostilities the statement in the Peace Army's pledge denouncing war as a crime had even been softened so as not to cause offense. Some Gandhians felt that to retain the original wording would signify accusing their government of committing a crime in organizing armed resistance to the Chinese. "I cannot call Nehru a criminal," one of them explained.[11]

To many Western pacifists, especially those in the United States, the readiness with which the Gandhians had rallied to their government, their unwillingness to contemplate the possibility of their own side being to some extent at fault, and their placing blame for the quarrel, even as to its remoter origins, exclusively on the other party, were puzzling and even distressing phenomena. In the history of American pacifism there was indeed a close parallel in the last century: the non-resistance movement led by the abolitionist, William Lloyd Garrison, had given fervent support to the Lincoln administration in the Civil War (that is, while reserving, like the Gandhians, a personal conscientious objection to fighting). But in the twentieth century Western pacifists have, more often than not, been highly critical of their government's policies and suspicious of the motives behind patriotic slogans. Nonviolence in India, on the other hand, owed its origins to the nationalist struggle against the British: it was former colleagues of the Mahatma, in many cases the Gandhians' friends, who now occupied the top posts in independent India's administration.

In this moment of crisis there was considerable uncertainty as to the proper role of Vinoba's Peace Army, which had hitherto concentrated on the domestic situation; his followers were, however, united in opposing any attempt to hinder the nation's war effort. Unprovoked aggression, in their view, could only be met with some form of resistance (though, it is true, the Gandhians urged the need to find a negotiated solution to the dispute, if this were at all possible).

There was no military conscription operative in the country at that time: the Gandhians, however, stressed their personal allegiance to unconditional nonviolence. Two years earlier a leading Gandhian of the older generation, Kaka Kalelkar, had stated his belief that, in circumstances similar to the present crisis, a supporter of nonviolence, if conscripted, would allow himself to be inducted into the army, since he paid taxes used in part for military purposes and also took advantage of various services provided by the government. Once in the army he should inform the military authorities of his unwillingness to kill and of his readiness at the same time to undertake, as a demonstration of the power of nonviolence, some dangerous unarmed mission at the front or other perilous noncombatant service. Most Gandhians, however, felt such a stand was unrealistic and that it would most likely be misunderstood. They advocated the rejection of noncombatant duties in the army, should compulsion be introduced.[12]

The confusion was greatest in regard to what positive action, if any, should be taken in the existing emergency. An American Quaker observer recorded:

Some felt that a *Shanti Sena* (Peace Army) should proceed to the border to offer non-violent resistance to the Chinese. The question arose then as to whether they should fight beside the Indian Army, though nonviolently, and the additional question as to whether the Indian Army would ever let them reach the border. Doubts were also voiced as to how such a Peace Army would conduct itself in order to be effective. For example, if they were to stand quietly in the middle of a road down which the Chinese wished to proceed, placing their bodies in the path of the on-coming army, and then if the Chinese simply went off into the woods and later came back to the road, what would they do? How could non-violent resistance be effective in such a situation? There was also a realization that perhaps a *Shanti Sena* could function effectively only by placing itself in the territory between the two armies, thus not opposing one army more than another, but trying to bring an end to the operation of both military bodies. These questions, however, remained academic since no action was taken.[13]

The Gandhians were hampered by the smallness of their numbers. They did not see any way of winning over their fellow countrymen to their belief in a nonviolent solution to conflict, except by slow propaganda. They nursed a keen sense of disappointment that the latter had turned aside from the methods of resistance employed earlier by Gandhi against the British. Above all, the Gandhians' effectiveness in acting as an agent of conciliation was restricted by their strong commitment to their own nation's position. Many Gandhians were blind (or so at least they appeared to outsiders) to the element of power in India's policies, while remaining acutely aware of the aggressive factors in the policies of the Western world or of the Soviet bloc, or, especially, of communist China. For them Indian nationalism retained a special quality. "I have no fear," wrote Vinoba at this time, "that India will lose her soul and that war fever will take over ... because the whole spiritual background of a thousand saints will not allow India to go the violent way whole-hog."[14] Here we may detect the same Messianic note as Gandhi occasionally struck in some of his nationalistic utterances. Nonviolence, so both Gandhi and Vinoba believed, was India's gift to the world. For the Gandhians in the 1960s, even an India that was obviously unwilling for the foreseeable future to adopt nonviolence as national policy seemed to be peace-loving in comparison to its neighbors and its rivals on the international scene.

The dilemmas in which the Gandhians were plunged when hostilities erupted in October 1962 have been well summarized by Geoffrey Ostergaard, who stresses their practical ineffectiveness in the given situation.

Any idea that a group of Shanti Sainiks could physically get to the point of interposing themselves between the Chinese and Indian armies [was] out of the question. Nehru was prepared to permit and even encourage constructive peace work in the border areas, but no Indian government [was] likely to permit activity of the kind envisaged by those who wished to form the Shanti Dal [an abortive body, which included organized efforts at war resistance among its aims]. In addition, ... attempts to organize non-violent resistance by the Shanti Sena would arouse widespread public hostility and react on the movement's other activities. But it is not simply a question of the tactical expediency of deploying Shanti Sena forces in acts of non-violent resistance in situations such as that of October 1962. A much broader issue is also involved: the issue of 'negative' versus 'positive' satyagraha ... Symbolic acts of ['militant'] non-violent resistance ... may easily become no more than gestures to salve the conscience – a way of demonstrating that one's own hands are clean ... [On the other hand,] the 'moderate' approach may be interpreted as – and may in fact be – simply a rationalization for doing nothing that is likely to offend the government or the chauvinist public. The 'militants' ... feel that, unless the movement is prepared to risk offending the government and the chauvinists, it will be discredited as the vanguard of the non-violent revolution.[15]

Soon after these events Gandhian participation in the Delhi-Beijing

Friendship March (March 1963–January 1964) was to enjoy the support of both Vinoba and Jayaprakash. However, with the Indian press largely hostile, the venture, which was jointly sponsored by the World Peace Brigade (see below) and a group of Sarvodayites, soon ran into difficulties; "it ... was abandoned when the Chinese authorities refused it permission to enter China."[16]

In the next decade a split developed between the two leading figures in the Gandhian movement when Jayaprakash, disenchanted by what he saw as a failure of persuasion to achieve the goals of the Sarvodaya movement, developed his concept of nonviolent "total revolution." This eventually led him into a confrontation with the government of Nehru's daughter, Indira Gandhi. The imposition of emergency regulations curtailing civil liberties on a wide scale followed and then, two years later, the – unexpected – election of the coalition Janata Party government of oppositionists with an elderly Gandhian politician, Morarji Desai, as Prime Minister in place of Mrs. Gandhi – until her return to power in 1980. Vinoba, who had been in partial retirement since 1969, opposed Jayaprakash's "politicisation" of the Sarvodaya movement and refused to condemn Indira Gandhi's antidemocratic measures, calling them "an era of discipline," while at the same time striving – in vain – to bring about a reconciliation between her and Jayaprakash, whom she had meanwhile put in jail.[17] Jayaprakash himself, now seriously ill, did not live to see the eclipse of the Janata party, which he had been largely responsible for creating. "What had ... brought the party into being was the negative aim of opposing the institutionalization of Mrs. Gandhi's dictatorship;"[18] once that was achieved the fragile coalition out of which the Janata Party had emerged disintegrated quickly.

Since 1980 the nonviolent movement in India, though dormant for much of the time, has not become entirely extinct. But despite considerable achievements during the early decades after the Mahatma's death, the Gandhians never succeeded in resolving creatively the tensions, which he had also been forced to take into account, between persuasion as an aspect of nonviolence and nonviolence as an instrument of resistance and struggle.

The Civil Rights Movement in the United States

Precursors

The Congress of Racial Equality (CORE), for long the main institutional center of the civil rights movement, "came into being in 1942,"[19] when a small group of concerned people carried out the first sit-in against segregation in a Chicago restaurant. Next year a national organization – at first somewhat makeshift – was set up; it was not until 1944 that it received a permanent name.[20]

The founders of CORE and its earliest members were drawn mainly from radical members of the Fellowship of Reconciliation (FOR) and other social activists among the country's conscientious objectors. For instance, in June 1941 we find George M. Houser, one of the student nonregistrants from Union Theological Seminary whose stand was discussed in the last chapter, writing from Danbury Correctional Institution: "We must raise up a movement [for social justice and racial equality] based on non-violence as a method." Houser was shortly to become a co-founder of CORE. For pacifists like Houser, who was white, or James Farmer,[21] also a student of theology and black, or Bayard Rustin,[22] a black FOR worker and a Quaker who spent considerable periods in jail in World War II, race relations and international relations were part of one problem. Pacifism, if it were to have any relevance for the contemporary world, must measure up to the problems of society as fully as it sought to find a solution to the question of war. Thus these young men were following the dominant trend within the interwar American FOR with its concern for the resolution of domestic conflict and its sympathy for a revolutionary, albeit nonviolent, approach to social justice. Nevertheless they were somewhat impatient with many traditional pacifist approaches. In particular, they regretted the absence in pacifist programs of nonviolent techniques for achieving a just social order; the older generation of FOR leaders, with the exception of A.J. Muste, cleaved to democratic processes and remained suspicious of extra- parliamentary methods of rectifying abuses or resolving social conflict. The young FOR radicals, however, avidly read the interpretations of Gandhian nonviolence by Richard B. Gregg and Krishnalal Shridharani. They thirsted to be able to apply what they had read to the problems of their own country. Having girded themselves with the weapons of nonviolence, they wished to do battle for their ideas. They saw in the unequal status accorded within American democracy to its black citizens not merely a shameful injustice, a denial of Christianity and a gross contradiction of the country's declared ideals, but a direct challenge to pacifists. Their pacifist faith could only prove itself if it dared to face this problem squarely and find a solution. Gandhi's message to American blacks had been: "With right which is on their side and ... non-violence as their only weapon, if they will make it such, a bright future is assured."[23]

Some of the founding members of CORE, especially if they were themselves black, may have been impressed by the fact that hitherto pacifism had made scarcely any impact on America's racial minorities; these minorities had contributed very few conscientious objectors. CORE also drew support from young white pacifists who had been brought face to face with racial inequality when in prison or while working in CPS camps. The concern of most of the early nonviolent leaders for racial injustice, however, was already developed before they became conscientious objectors. Some had participated, too, in Gandhian-style *ashrams*, usually short-lived ventures, and in training-centers in nonviolence.

For some time the connection between CORE and FOR remained close. But by the end of the 1940s CORE had expanded in membership and support far beyond FOR circles. Soon it had succeeded in interesting such veteran campaigners for civil rights as the president of the Brotherhood of Sleeping Car Porters, A. Philip Randolph, a nonpacifist, in the idea of nonviolent civil disobedience. In 1947 CORE sponsored a "Journey of Reconciliation" to the Deep South, led by two secretaries of the FOR, George Houser and Bayard Rustin, with pairs of mixed black and white challenging the long established rule of segregation in this area.[24] Here indeed was an attempt to confront injustice directly, forcing its upholders either to yield to change or to face the consequences of enforcing the old conditions despite the mounting resistance to them.

The application of nonviolent techniques to race relations within the United States, as we have just seen, had had its origins among the radical social actionists of the conscientious objector community. This was perhaps the most promising development in World War II pacifism.

The Emergence of Martin Luther King Jr.[25]

Yet the nonviolent civil rights movement did not really gain momentum or mass support until the appearance of Martin Luther King, Jr. King was a southern black by birth and domicile. His leadership marks the transition from a northern-based movement carried along largely by the efforts of middle-class white sympathizers, which was typified in the activities of the early CORE, to one which, both in leadership and rank-and-file, was firmly centered in the South, where the main struggle was now located.

The event symbolizing this transition was the bus boycott organized by the black community of Montgomery (Alabama), in which King, while he did not initiate it, played a leading part. During the early weeks of the protest King relied particularly on Rustin's advice as well as that of Glenn Smiley, a white member of the FOR.

The boycott commenced in December 1955 and lasted about a year. Its immediate occasion was the arrest, trial and jailing of a rank-and-file black-activist seamstress named Rosa Parks[26], who, returning home after a long and tiring day, had refused to give up her seat to a white passenger when ordered to do so by the conductor. The incident aroused great indignation among the town's 50,000 blacks, who had long been subjected to similar treatment of an arbitrary nature. Black leaders, among them two young Baptist ministers, Martin Luther King and Ralph Abernathy[27], decided to call a one-day bus boycott which was almost a hundred percent effective, and then to extend its duration for an indefinite period, when a similarly high participation was still reached. The boycott was nonviolent throughout, an act of passive resistance but not one of civil disobedience, for no law was broken. It was rather noncooperation of the type practised by Gandhi in some of his campaigns.

Seventy percent of the passengers on Montgomery's municipal buses were blacks: a boycott of this kind, therefore, caused much disquiet among city officials. Yet it was not the bus boycott directly that in fact brought desegregation of the city's transport system (which became the boycott's objective) but the decision of the U.S. Supreme Court on 1 December 1956. The Court, on appeal being made to it by the boycotters' organization, the Montgomery Improvement Association, had ruled that segregation on city buses was indeed unconstitutional. Thus an element was introduced into the situation that scarcely existed in Gandhi's India under British rule. In the United States the nonviolent movement for racial equality worked within a constitutional framework, with appeal made by the passive resisters not solely to a higher righteousness than man-made law but also to the highest court of appeal in the land, from which support for civil rights might be expected.[28] Soon after the boycott began a sympathetic white librarian, Juliette Morgan, had written a letter which was published in the segregationist *Montgomery Advertiser*, comparing the boycott to Gandhi's famous Salt *Satyagraha* of 1930 (although in fact in the latter case the breaking of an unjust law was involved). In this way Gandhi's name became familiar for the first time to large numbers of the city's black inhabitants. And it was not long before a couple of staff members of the FOR, both of whom had been active in their organization's nonviolent quest for racial equality, arrived on the scene. In Montgomery the two men were able, as a result of their previous thought and experience in regard to nonviolence, to play an important role behind the scenes in directing the boycott movement into nonviolent channels. Yet the seminal influence lay elsewhere. It was the attachment to the idea of nonviolence of Martin Luther King, with his charismatic gift for leadership and his devotion to the cause of his people, that above all gave the movement its nonviolent direction.[29]

Whence did King derive his belief in nonviolence?[30] As a student in college he had read Thoreau's essay on civil disobedience several times; when the boycott began, he now pondered once again on the implications of Thoreau's message, with its appeal to refuse obedience to the demands of society, if unjust, in the name of a higher law. After graduating from college and entering divinity school he had become interested in Gandhi's nonviolent campaigns and read widely on the subject. He was impressed by what Gandhi had to offer to other oppressed peoples; yet at the same time, under the influence of Reinhold Niebuhr's critique, he rejected theoretical pacifism along with the optimistic liberal theology with which it was often associated in the West. When he moved on to Boston University, where he studied for his doctorate, he came under the influence of two pacifist professors then teaching in its School of Theology: Dean Walter Muelder and Allen Knight Chalmers. Both men were members of the FOR. Therefore, when he arrived in Montgomery in 1954 to take up a pastorate in the city, he was by now extremely sympathetic to the pacifist idea as well as open to the potentialities of Gandhian nonviolence as a technique for achieving political justice on the part of an oppressed segment of the population. For King, while gradually emancipating himself from the influence of Niebuhr's strictures on pacifism, had retained the latter's intensely social Christianity.

When I went to Montgomery as a pastor [he wrote], I had not the slightest idea that I would later become involved in a crisis in which nonviolent resistance would be applicable. I neither started the protest nor suggested it. I simply responded to the call of the people for a spokesman. When the protest began, my mind, consciously or unconsciously, was driven back to the Sermon on the Mount, with its sublime teachings on love, and the Gandhian method of nonviolent resistance. As the days unfolded, I came to see the power of nonviolence more and more. Living through the actual experience of the protest, nonviolence became more than a method to which I gave intellectual assent; it became a commitment to a way of life. Many of the things that I had not cleared up intellectually concerning nonviolence were now solved in the sphere of practical action."[31]

After the boycott started, King got rid of the gun he had kept for an emergency (in this respect closer to Gandhi than some of his colleagues in the movement, who did not repudiate the use of firearms where the law became inoperative and could not afford protection to citizens).[32] "Through nonviolent resistance," King now told his people, "the Negro will be able to rise to the noble height of opposing the unjust system while loving the perpetrators of the system." He thus pointed to an essential in the nonviolent technique of struggle: the appeal to the conscience of the opponent, the effort to win over sympathetic members of the opposing side. "Nonviolent resistance is not aimed against oppressors, but against oppression. Under its banner consciences, not racial groups, are enlisted." The struggle, said King, is "between justice and injustice."[33] Like Gandhi, he believed, too, that a nonviolent movement might recruit supporters among those who did not accept nonviolence as a principle of life, provided they were ready to stay nonviolent for as long as the campaign lasted. To the blacks of Montgomery, King and his fellow ministers presented nonviolence "as a simple expression of Christianity in action."[34]

Although their followers had no previous experience in the use of nonviolent techniques, these leaders were able to prevent the outbreak of violence, despite attempts at intimidation and at provocation by the segregationists. A newspaperman from Minneapolis reported their achievement of "the almost unbelievable by pulling the hoodlums out of the crap games and honky-tonks into the churches, where they sang hymns, gave money, shouted amen and wept over the powerful speeches."[35] The packed evening services in the churches, where King and his associates expounded the idea of nonviolence and its relation to the Christian ideal of love and instructed their followers not to hate or humiliate their white oppressors but instead to oppose only their oppressive acts, served the same purpose as the prayer meetings and singing sessions in Gandhian campaigns in sustaining the morale of the passive resisters. Workshops in Gandhian ideas and techniques were also held throughout the period of the boycott. And as an equivalent of Gandhi's constructive program, which the Mahatma always stressed was an essential component of successful *satyagraha*, King began to stress the role of such positive activities as the raising of education and cultural standards of Southern blacks, the fight against adult illiteracy and juvenile delinquency, and (later) the campaign for voter registration.

In the Montgomery bus boycott nonviolent resistance emerged for the first time in the United States as a mass movement. Henceforward the campaign for racial equality, for so long – and in so far – as it remained under the leadership of Martin Luther King, was to be one (to quote his own words) where "Christ furnished the spirit and motivation, while Gandhi furnished the method."[36]

Montgomery soon became a symbol. It helped to create a new self-image among black people and to destroy their traditional submissiveness dating back to the days of slavery. It started a chain reaction with similar nonviolent assertions of civil rights by the black communities of other southern cities; bus boycotts took place in Birmingham, Tallahassee and elsewhere. Several cities now took steps to desegregate their bus systems, often not waiting on a court order to do so. A Southern Christian Leadership Conference was set up under King's leadership to coordinate activities on a national scale; the nonviolent movement for civil equality ceased to be a merely local affair. It appeared, moreover, to most people that the desegregation which was now being accomplished was the result solely of a successful nonviolent boycott, although, as we have seen, this was in fact only partly true. "Here was a powerful legend that would inspire others to authentic victories based wholly or largely on nonviolence.[37]

James Farmer has described the civil rights movement during the decade after Montgomery as "a kind of wedding of two forces." Both went back to the war years: "the means-oriented idealists of a pacifistic turn of mind [like himself], for whom non-violence was a total philosophy, a way of life – we had founded CORE [he notes]; and the ends-oriented militants, the New Jacobins, disillusioned with America's rhetoric of equality, who saw in direct action a useful weapon and viewed non-violence only as a tactic."[38] Only by a fusion of these two forces, as Farmer points out, did the creation of a "revolutionary mass movement" become possible; just as, one may add, in India earlier it was an alliance between Gandhian idealists, devoted to the principle of *ahimsa*, and the nationalists prepared to adopt nonviolence as an expedient for winning their country's independence that made possible the creation of a broadly based freedom movement. In both cases the binding link was the charismatic leader endowed with the gift of harnessing the energies of the masses. That in both cases this leadership emerged from the side of the devotees of nonviolence was surely no coincidence. Only idealism of this kind was likely to generate the spiritual dynamism needed for such a task.

In the early years of the civil rights movement the Gandhian influence was strongly marked in most of its undertakings. Beginning in May 1961 CORE organized a series of "Freedom Rides" to test the state of desegregation – or, rather, lack of it – in the amenities on interstate bus routes; the project was modelled on the "Journey of Reconciliation" CORE had sponsored in 1947 with the testing done as before by mixed teams of blacks and whites. A black student from Howard University, who participated, reported: "The name Gandhi was constantly on the minds and lips of most of the imprisoned Riders. Anything Gandhi had said or done was interpreted and reinterpreted to be applied to the [present] situation." Different views often arose as to what was required of a consistent Gandhian by the existing circumstances. Some Riders felt called upon to embark on individual protest fasts; others argued that the Mahatma would have approved such a step only if it were more clearly a meaningful sacrifice.[39]

The *satyagraha* of the Freedom Riders was directed against a federal authority and not against a southern segregationist authority as it had been the case in Montgomery. This fact may have contributed to the fairly rapid success of the movement; on 1 November 1961, the Interstate Commerce Commission issued new regulations guaranteeing integration on interstate bus routes. On the other hand, unlike Montgomery where the protesting community could exercise considerable economic pressure by its boycott, the Freedom Riders possessed very little economic leverage to back their demonstration. It was mainly one of nonviolent witness to principle. The Riders' steady refusal to retaliate with counter-violence, despite repeated provocation and harassment on the part of segregationist mobs and police, made a big impression not only on wide sections of the American public but also abroad. A number of prominent white citizens took part in the Rides (including the chaplain of Yale University and a son-in-law of Governor Nelson A. Rockefeller).

In its clear presentation of the truth at the center of protest, in its fidelity to nonviolent means of struggle, and in its ability to win outside sympathy and support, the American blacks' movement for civil equality had achieved by the early sixties a considerable measure of success. An expansion of nonviolent protest took place in the Deep South during these years. Martin Luther King insisted on maintaining a nonviolent stance; he was indeed prepared, like Gandhi, to call off action where violence threatened to break out from the side of the demonstrators (violence, of course, was endemic on the part of the segregationists).

SNCC: From Nonviolence to Black Nationalism

Meanwhile, important developments were taking place among black college students in the South. The Fellowship of Reconciliation had recently published and distributed on the campuses of a number of Southern black colleges a picture-strip account of the Montgomery bus boycott under the title *Martin Luther King and the Montgomery Story*. A freshman as Shaw University in Greensboro (North Carolina) getting hold of a copy was inspired to follow the example of what had happened in Montgomery; he and three other students entered a café in the town and sat down at a lunch-counter segregated for the use of whites. On being refused service, they continued to sit at the counter. This incident occurred on 1 February 1960. The four students went on with their protest day after day and were joined by other black students, as well as a sprinkling of white sympathizers. As news of the Greensboro "sit-in" spread, the pattern was repeated in dozens of other college and university towns in the South; the movement eventually extended, too, to the black high schools. There were occasional disorders, for the demonstrators were young, and therefore high-spirited and utterly inexperienced in the practice of nonviolence, and in addition subjected to abuse and severe physical and psychological harassment by sections of the white community who opposed their action. Yet on the whole the protesters did not succumb to the temptation to retaliate violently. "Here and there the growing movement centered around groups that had attended seminars and workshops conducted [by FOR organizers]. Copies of Richard Gregg's *The Power of Nonviolence* were sought out and studied. Dozens of these had been given to Negro college libraries ... Thousands of copies of the FOR leaflet, *How to Practice Nonviolence*, and the leaflet *CORE Rules for Action*, found their way into the students' hands. Many of the students were not primed at all, however, and knew about nonviolence only by word of mouth."[40] The FOR sent a three-man team into the area to instruct students in nonviolent techniques and to prevent, if possible, the outbreak of violence among the uninitiated. Local leadership, however, soon developed. This crystallized around the many CORE groups which had sprung up in the South and, above all, around a new organization which emerged from among the students themselves, with some help from the Southern Christian Leadership Conference as well as from pacifist bodies in the North.

This new body, the Students Nonviolent Coordinating Committee (SNCC),[41] was set up in April 1960 at a conference in Raleigh (N.C.), attended mainly by black students who had taken part in the recent sit-ins. It concluded by adopting a "statement of purpose," written by James M. Lawson, a black civil-rights activist from Nashville (Tennessee) and FOR member then training for the Methodist ministry, which declared:

We affirm the philosophical or religious ideal of nonviolence as the foundation of our purpose, the presupposition of our faith, and the manner of our action. Nonviolence as it grows from Judaic-Christian traditions seeks a social order of justice permeated by love ... Through nonviolence, courage displaces fear; love transforms hate ... Peace dominates war ... Mutual regard cancels enmity. Justice for all overthrows injustice. The redemptive community supersedes systems of gross social immorality. Love is the central motif of nonviolence. Love is the force by which God binds man to Himself and man to man. Such love goes to the extreme; it remains loving and forgiving even in the midst of hostility. It matches the capacity of evil to inflict suffering with an even more enduring capacity to absorb evil all the while persisting in love. By appealing to conscience and standing on the moral nature of human existence, nonviolence nurtures the atmosphere in which reconciliation and justice become actual possibilities.[42]

In the following month SNCC's executive committee, assisted by King himself as well as by representatives of the Quaker AFSC, reiterated these principles.[43] Thus we can see clearly that SNCC's roots lie equally in FOR pacifism and its preaching of the Social Gospel and in the Gandhian ethic of nonviolence.

As the sit-in movement widened over the next year or two to include not only restaurants and lunch-counters but also the picketing or boycott of the stores which supplied them, and as clergy – both black and white – and other sympathizers from the older generation began to express support for the students' action, the white communities showed increasing nervousness at the consequences of a prolongation of the movement. Concerning its outcome, W.R. Miller in his study of nonviolence has made two points. In the first place, "settlement almost invariably occurred through direct negotiations rather than court rulings." Secondly, "opponents were seldom if ever won over to the side of justice as a result of voluntary suffering or Christian love on the part of the demonstrators." The decisive element in extracting concessions in this case was the fear of economic loss.[44]

The sit-ins, followed by the Freedom Rides, gave considerable impetus to the civil rights movement and an added prestige to King's nonviolent leadership. These protests highlighted the courage and determination of black demonstrators. Later, with the help of the federal government, they were able to show, too, a number of successes in extending the range of civil rights enjoyed by the black population in the South.

At the same time a note of uncertainty emerged concerning the direction in which the movement should travel in the future. Voices were raised demanding not piecemeal concessions, not just tinkering with the existing structure of southern society, but a thorough-going restructuring of this society: the achievement by nonviolent means of black power in the area where blacks were in a majority. For instance, in 1961 at the Southern Christian Leadership Conference's annual congress we find the FOR delegate, who was James Lawson, proposing the formation and training of a nonviolent "army" of up to 8,000 members. "Let us prepare these people," he said, "for mass nonviolent action in the Deep South. Let us recruit people who will be willing to go at a given moment and stay in jail indefinitely."[45] Community programs, voter registration and slum renovation would form, as with Vinoba Bhave's movement in contemporary India, the positive, constructive aspect of the nonviolent revolution. As the legal status of blacks improved in the course of the decade, through action taken by Federal courts to uphold their civil equality, some – but by no means all – black activists (e.g., Bayard Rustin), while still maintaining their adherence to nonviolence, came to feel that the movement should concentrate henceforward not so much on civil rights, the battle for which they considered virtually won, but on the struggle for economic and cultural equality by means of political pressure. For the economically retarded and culturally repressed black masses, even if they were to be endowed with full civil rights, would remain in practice outcasts in American society. Therefore, those who supported this way of thinking called now for a march of the poor toward economic and cultural prosperity in place of the old campaign for civil equality.

The most serious challenge to the leadership of Martin Luther King and to the nonviolent character of the black movement came from the gradual development within it in the course of the sixties of a militant Black Power faction. This group, led by Stokeley Carmichael and Malcolm-X, attracted support from black intellectuals of the younger generation; it drew off the interest of many who had adhered to nonviolence rather from expediency than from any belief in its inherent superiority to violent methods of social or national liberation.[46] Black nationalism represented to some extent, too, a return of the center of agitation to the North – but not to the predominantly white liberal and pacifist intellectuals, among whom the nonviolent movement had originated. Black nationalism began to make headway in the overcrowded and poverty-stricken ghettos of the great Northern industrial cities. Their inhabitants, more alienated and more isolated within a potentially hostile environment than their Southern brethren, were also less susceptible to the traditional Christian ethos, which had provided an effective background to the spread of nonviolence in the South. The messianic sects that flourished in the black quarters of cities like New York or Philadelphia provided a religious equivalent to the secular national separatism that now rejected nonviolence as both ineffective and actually destructive of the black's will to resist.

King was always aware of the difficulties he would encounter in keeping his people nonviolent. "The method of nonviolence," he wrote, "will not work miracles overnight."[47] There was little likelihood of an immediate and largescale change of heart on the part of white segregationists. Reconciliation and the way of love would be slow and fraught with suffering and travail for those who entered upon it. In his *Letter from Birmingham City Jail*[48] of 16 April 1963, in the course of the long, drawn out civil rights struggle in that city, King was to express his keen disappointment at the attitude of those white moderates who disapproved the employment of civil disobedience to fight segregation (though, of course, civil disobedience is essentially nonviolent[49]). King had indeed been under fire recently from black radicals for his alleged subservience to white opinion. In his letter now he endeavored to explain why blacks could not wait for the slow and uncertain working of the legal machine. "We know through painful experience," he said, "that freedom is never voluntarily given by the oppressor; it must be demanded by the oppressed." The awakening black will demand his rights ever more insistently. "If his oppressed emotions do not come out in ... nonviolent ways, they will come out in ominous expressions of violence. This is not a threat," King wrote, "it is a fact of history." If he were unsuccessful in his attempt to channel "this normal and healthy discontent ... through the creative outlet of nonviolent direct action," then violence would necessarily follow. Like Gandhi, King clearly believed a man should react to injustice, even by violence if he were unable to rise to a higher level of resistance, rather than meekly submit. In 1965, in answer to the question "Does your movement depend on violence?" he wrote: "When you give witness to an evil you do not cause that evil but you oppose it so it can be cured." He never attempted to hide from his followers the danger, even of death, which they had to face in their role of nonviolent resisters striving to end the evil of racial segregation.[50]

The nonviolent movement for desegregation in the South aimed primarily at assimilation of the blacks into American society. It strove to win the support, either active or passive, of the country's white majority for its assertion of the civil equality of the black minority, and it was indeed successful in achieving this goal. The Civil Rights Act of 1964 – the most far-reaching and comprehensive law in support of racial equality ever enacted by Congress"[51] – and the Voting Rights Act in the following year destroyed the legal framework of racial inequality in the United States. Thus, it became only a matter of time before the Black Revolution brought African Americans a measure of political power that would have seemed impossible a decade or two earlier.

Meanwhile Martin Luther King's assassination in April 1968 deprived the disciples of nonviolence within the black civil rights movement of their most effective and dedicated leader; he died at a moment when his forthright condemnation of the Vietnam War as "madness" reinforced his nonviolent message even at risk of losing support in government circles as well as among pro-war sections of the community. Both SNCC and CORE had already repudiated their nonviolent roots and transferred their allegiance to the ideology of militant Black Power.[52] But the contribution of Gandhian nonviolence to one of the most vital stages in the African-American's struggle for freedom is undeniable; it is securely anchored in the historical record.

Notes

1 Kaunda, though, is a partial exception here. For Kaunda's critique of unconditional nonviolence, see Colin M. Morris, ed., *Kaunda on Violence* (London: Collins, 1980). The book presents his arguments against absolute pacifism, while at the same time making clear its continued appeal to him as a convinced Christian as well as the influence which Gandhi's doctrine and practice of *satyagraha* exercised over him early in his political career.

2 Marcel Messing, *Buigzaam als riet: Beschouwingen over geweldloosheid* (Deventer: Ankh Hennes, 1994), pp. 124, 125.

3 Vishwanath Tandon, *The Social and Political Philosophy of Sarvodaya after Gandhiji* (Varanasi: Sarva Seva Sangh Prakashan, 1965), p. 123. The most stimulating work on the course of Indian nonviolence during the two decades following Gandhi's death is the sociological survey by Geoffrey Ostergaard and Melville Currell. *The Gentle Anarchists: A Study of the Leaders of the sSrvodaya Movement for Non-violent Revolution in India* (Oxford: Clarendon Press, 1971). Ostergaard, its principal author, later carried the story down to the deaths of the leading Gandhians, Jayaprakas Narayan in 1979 and. Vinoba Bhave in 1982, in a volume entitled *Nonviolent Revolution in India* (New Delhi: Gandhi Peace Foundation, 1985).

4 Ostergaard and Currell, *Gentle Anarchists*, p. 270.

5 D. MacKenzie Brown, ed., *The Nationalist Movement: Indian Political Thought from Ranade to Bhave* (Berkeley and Los Angeles: University of California Press, 1961), p. 198.

6 Tandon. *op. cit.*, pp. 194, 196–8. Geeta S. Mehta, in her *Philosophy of Vinoba Bhave (A New Perspective in Gandhian Thought)* (Bombay: Himalaya Publishing House, 1995), chaps. V, VI(i), VII, IX(vii), discusses in detail Vinoba's views on nonviolence. Her book is based on publications (many of them by the prolific Vinoba) in five Indian languages – in addition to English.

7 For the exposition which follows, see Vinoba's book translated from the Hindi, *Shanti Sena* (Varanasi: Sarva Seva Sangh Prakashan, 1961): also the pamphlet by Narayan Desai, *Shanti-Sena in India* (Varanasi: Sarva Seva Sangh Prakashan, 1962), Ostergaard and Currell, *op. cit.*, 59, 60, 163, 195. The recent work of an Australian scholar Thomas Weber, is particularly valuable, especially *Gandhi's Peace Army: The Shanti Sena and Unarmed Peace-keeping* (Syracuse: Syracuse University Press, 1996, chaps. V – VIII, and "'A Brief History of the Shanti Sena as seen through the Changing Pledges of the Shanti Sainik," *Gandhi Marg* (New Delhi), N.S., vol. 13, no. 3 (October–December 1991), pp. 316–26.

8 See James E. Bristol, *Non-violence and India Today* (Philadelphia: Peace Education Division of the American Friends Service Committee, 1963); Ostergaard and Currell, *op. cit.*, pp. 243–5, 253–7, and Weber, *Gandhi's Peace Army,* pp. 77–84.

9 Bristol, *op. cit.*, Appendix I.

10 Jayaprakash Narayan, *Saryodaya Answer to Chinese Aggression* (Thanjavur: Sarvodaya Prachuralaya, 1963), p. 36.

11 Bristol, *op. cit.*, p. 4. We may note that one of Vinobals followers, the prominent social worker Vimala Thakar, strongly opposed such extensive approval of government policy as almost all Gandhians gave at that time.

12 Tandon, *op. cit.*, p. 156.

13 Bristol, *op. cit.*, p. 3.

14 Quoted in *ibid.*, Appendix VI. Vinoba also stated that "when India maintains an army, it has to be used to repel an attack." He branded as "false" the view that, in the existing circumstances, "he was against the use of the Army for meeting Chinese aggression on Indian soil." Cited in Weber, *op. cit.*, p. 81. Jayaprakash Narayan however, while extremely critical of Chinese conduct, considered that Vinoba went too far in his support for the Indian government's use of armed force and he backed, at least in theory, the idea of interpositionary action on the part of the sainiks.

15 Ostergaard and Currell, *op. cit.*, p. 257. See also pp. 265–71. Another example of far-reaching Gandhian support of government policy occurred over the Kashmir issue in the mid-1960s. In September 1965 we find Jayaprakash Narayan expressing his "full support" for the Indian government in its stand against Pakistan's "aggression." See *ibid.*, pp. 239–43.

16 *Ibid.*, pp. 254 n.1, 256.

17 James D. Hunt's entry on Vinoba Bhave, in Harold Josephson, ed., *Biographical Dictionary of Modern Peace Leaders* (Westport: Greenwood Press, 1985), p. 78. For a perceptive discussion of Vinoba's and Jayaprakash's views of nonviolence and the impact their "ideological differences" continued to make, even posthumously, on the post-Gandhian movement in India, see Weber, *op. cit.*, pp. 138–60.

18 Ostergaard, *Nonviolent Revolution in India*, p. 286.

19 James Farmer, *Freedom – When?* (New York: Random House, 1965), p. 53. See pp. 53–65 for the Gandhian roots of CORE; also August Meier and Elliot Rudwick, *CORE: A Study in the Civil Rights Movement 1942–1968* (New York: Oxford University Press, 1973), pp. 3–39.

20 Then, "Congress" took the place of "Committee" in its title. A participant in the organization's first formal meeting in Chicago in June 1942 describes what happened there as follows: "Bob Chino – a [Chinese-American] University of Chicago student who had [earlier] been arrested for refusing induction – shouted: 'I've got it. Let's call it CORE, because it will be the center of things, the heart of the action.' We constructed a name from an acronym. RE easily stood for Racial Equality, CO, after much discussion, stood for Committee of. CORE became the Committee of Racial Equality." Homer A. Jack, *Homer's Odyssey: My Quest for Peace and Justice* (Becket, MA: One Peaceful World Press, 1996), pp. 117–19.

21 See his *Lay bare the Heart: An Autobiography of the Civil Rights Movement* (New York: Arbor House, 1985). Later Farmer ceased to be an absolute pacifist. In an interview by the then editor of the FOR's monthly journal, Robin Washington, Farmer described how in the 1950s, over the issue of apartheid, he had come to feel "there were things that were more evil than killing, than war. If ... war had erupted in South Africa between the blacks and the whites I would have wanted to volunteer." But, he added, "I don't know what they could have done with a fat, overage, bald man ..." From "James Farmer on the Beginnings and the End of the Congress of Racial Equality: 50 Years Later," *Fellowship*, vol. 58, no. 415 (April–May, 1992), pp. 8, 17.

22 See the recent biography of one of the most dynamic – and intelligent – of twentieth-century pacifists: Jervis Anderson, *Bayard Rustin: Troubles I've seen* (New York: Harper Collins, 1997).

23 M.K. Gandhi, *Non-violence in Peace and War*, 3rd edn., vol. I (Ahmedabad: Navajivan Publishing House, 1948), p. 127. The remark was made in 1937.

24 See James Peck, *Freedom Ride* (New York: Simon and Schuster, 1962), for an account by a participant of the movement which developed out of the 1947 ride.

25 See David Levering Lewis, *King: A Biography* (Urbana: University of Illinois Press, 1978); Stephen B. Oates, *Let the Trumpet sound* (New York: Harper and Row, 1982); James A. Colaiaco, *Martin Luther King Jr.: Apostle of Militant Nonviolence* (New York: St. Martin's Press, 1988); Taylor Branch, *Parting the Waters: America in the King Years 1954–63* (New York: Simon and Schuster, 1988); David J. Garrow, *Bearing the Cross: Martin Luther King Jr., and the Southern Christian Leadership Conference* (New York: Vintage Books, 1988); also James P. Hanigan, *Martin Luther King, Jr. and the Foundations of Nonviolence* (Lanhan, MD: University Press of America. 1984) and William D. Watley, *Roots of Resistance: The Nonviolent Ethic of Martin Luther King, Jr.* (Valley Forge, PA: Judson Press, 1985). King's major pacifist statements are gath-

ered as a pamphlet in *A.J. Muste Institute Series, No. 1* (New York, n.d.): 1. "Loving Your Enemies," 2. "Letter from Birmingharn Jail," 3. "Declaration of Independence from the War in Vietnam."

26 Parks had been active in the old established National Association for the Advancement of Colored People (NAACP) which, though not specifically pacifist, was certainly sympathetic to nonviolence and supportive of King's campaigns.

27 See Ralph David Abernathy, *And the Walls came tumbling down: An Autobiography* (New York: Harper & Row, 1989).

28 The question has been raised whether believers in nonviolence are morally entitled to appeal for federal protection in furthering civil rights, although obviously they have a legal right to do so. A.J. Muste, for example, felt that they were not; he pointed to the potential danger of a federal intervention turning into a full-scale civil war. See his article "Nonviolence and Mississippi," in G. Ramachandran and T.K. Mahadevan, eds., *Gandhi: His Relevance for Our Times* (New Delhi: Gandhi Peace Foundation, 1967), pp. 213–15, 217, 218.

29 One should not forget, either, the support given King by his wife, Coretta, a dedicated adherent of nonviolence.

30 The following account is derived mainly from autobiographical passages in King's *Stride toward Freedom: The Montgomery Story* (New York: Ballantine Books), first published in 1958.

31 *Ibid.*, p. 81.

32 But cf. Farmer, in *Fellowship*, p. 8: "King ... had armed bodyguards surrounding his house ... He must have seen the contradiction there." King's wife, however, states the exact opposite: "Martin could not reconcile a gun with his nonviolent principles." And she insists that he allowed no weapon in his home nor permitted any of his people to carry a gun even when keeping a watch outside the house. See Coretta Scott King, *My Life with Martin Luther King, Jr.* (New York-Chicago-San Francisco: Holt, Rinehart and Winston, 1969), p. 133. Possibly when things became really dangerous, King may sometimes have turned a blind eye to a follower with a hidden weapon while maintaining his general disapproval. See Branch, *op. cit.*, pp. 161, 162.

33 King, *op. cit.*, pp. 174, 175.

34 *Ibid.*, p. 71.

35 Quoted in William Robert Miller, *Nonviolence: A Christian Interpretation* (New York: Association Press, 1964), p. 301.

36 King, *Stride toward Freedom*, p. 67.

37 Miller, *op. cit.*, p. 305.

38 Farmer, *Freedom*, p. 77.

39 William Mahoney, "In Pursuit of Freedom," in Staughton Lynd, ed., *Nonviolence in America: A Documentary History* (Indianapolis: Bobbs-Merrill Co., Inc., 1966), pp. 427, 428.

40 Miller, *op. cit.*, p. 306.

41 See Clayborne Carson, *In Struggle: SNCC and the Black Awakening of the 1960s* (Cambridge, MA: Harvard University Press, 1981); also Jürgen Müller, *Die Geschichte des Student Non-Violent Coordinating Committee: Ein Kapitel der Bürgerrechisbewegung in den Vereinigten Staaten* (Stuttgart: F.B. Metzlersche Verlagsbuchhandlung, 1977).

42 Francis L. Broderick and August Meier, eds., *Negro Protest Thought in the Twentieth Century* (Indianapolis: The Bobbs-Merrill Company, 1965), pp. 273, 274; Carson, *op. cit.*, pp. 23, 24, 310.

43 Howard Zinn, *SNCC: The New Abolitionists* (Boston: Beacon Press, 1964), pp. 34, 220, 221.

44 Miller, *op. cit.*, p. 311. However, later on many opponents of racial equality did shift their attitudes, change their minds, and undergo almost conversionary experiences. Governor George Wallace of Alabama, for instance, begged the black community of his country to forgive him – indeed somewhat belatedly!

45 Quoted in *ibid.*, p. 83. For the role of Lawson. and the FOR in generating King's movement, see Aldon D. Morris, *The Origins of the Civil Rights Movement: Black Communities Organizing for Change* (New York: The Free Press, 1984), pp. 157–66.

46 "Since the founding of CORE in 1942 ... it [had] been a matter for more or less permanent debate whether nonviolence ... should be primarily a matter of *converting* or *coercing* the opponent." From Bo Wirmark, "Nonviolent Methods and the American Civil Rights Movement 1955–1965," *Journal of Peace Research* (Oslo), vol. 11 (1974), no. 2, p. 126. Italics in the original.

47 King, *op. cit.*, p. 178. Several otherwise sympathetic writers have pointed out a few ambiguities and inconsistencies in both King's view of pacifism and in his practice of nonviolence. See, for example, Colaiaco, *op. cit.*, chap. VIII, and Adam Fairclough, "Martin Luther King, Jr. and the War in Vietnam," *Phylon* (Atlanta GA), vol. 1 (March, 1984), pp. 21, 22, 38.

48 Reprinted in full in Lynd, ed., *op. cit.* The two passages cited here are on pp. 466, 474.

49 Hugo A. Bedau, "On Civil Disobedience," *The Journal of Philosophy* (Lancaster, PA), vol. 58, no. 21 (1961), p. 656.

50 Fairclough, "Martin Luther King, Jr. and the Quest for Nonviolent Social Change," *Phylon*, vol. 47, no. 1 (Spring, 1986), p. 11.

51 John Hope Franklin and Alfred A. Moss, Jr., *From Slavery to Freedom: A History of African Americans*, 7th rev. edn. (New York: McGraw-Hill, Inc., 1994), p. 508.

52 The two organizations soon disappeared in the ensuing reshuffles and crises of the black power phenomenon.

VII. Pacifism and War Resistance: The Cold War Years, Part 1

World War II, the victory of the "big battalions" and the exhaustion felt by those societies immersed in war and its aftermath, marked a traumatic caesura in the pacifist movement. Many turned to relief work, or utopian experiments, and there were a number who renounced pacifism.

Nevertheless, the core of the pacifist movement and the cause of conscientious objection emerged at the end of World War II still intact in their strongholds of Britain and North America but pacifism was decidedly shaken – even if not so severely as in the earlier conflict. In the second global conflict, conscientious objection had gained a degree of legitimacy absent earlier, and on the whole C.Os. were now less marginalized than their predecessors had been. The tens of thousands who had been recognized as C.Os. provided a much larger base for future pacifist activity in 1945 than had existed in 1918. It was, though, the coming of the atomic bomb, first exploded over Hiroshima on 6 August 1945, and the subsequent threatened proliferation of nuclear weapons that eventually brought renewed energy to, and a new context for, pacifism.

Gradually fresh impetus was derived from two considerations. First, the destructive powers of nuclear warfare, enlarged so tremendously that the ultimate annihilation of humanity thereby seemed not incredible to realistic minds, raised in more intensive form than even before the moral problem of war. Are such weapons consistent with a civilized ethic, not to speak of an advanced religious code? As a leading American newspaperman wrote: "For perhaps the first time in history reflective [persons] have had to grapple with the pacifists' question: Can rational interests and human values really be served by waging war with atomic and hydrogen weapons?"[1] Further, could the war-game in fact be played at all if resort to nuclear armaments were renounced? In the second place, people began, with increasing urgency to search for some alternative method of resolving the conflicts which appear to be an inevitable concomitant of humanity's functioning as a social animal. Was there possibly a nonviolent alternative in international relations to nuclear deterrence with its danger of spilling over into mutual destruction? Even the author of that futuristic nightmare *1984* could remark: "It seems doubtful whether civilization can stand another major war, and it is at least thinkable that the way out lies through nonviolence."[2]

The search for freedom from war, together with the parallel search for freedom from want, presented the mid-twentieth century world with its greatest challenge. The story of the (so far unsuccessful) efforts to bring about an agreed elimination of all nuclear, and a comprehensive planned reduction of conventional, weapons in the hands of national states does not lie within the framework of this book. Our purpose is to discuss attempts, by no means necessarily conflicting with the institutional and internationalist channels of conflict resolution, to develop a pacifist alternative to violence in the nuclear age.

For at least a decade after the conclusion of World War II the pacifist movement in both Great Britain and on the North American continent suffered from declining vigor: a condition already visible in the later years of the war. Adjustment to the new conditions of warfare came no more easily to most pacifists than to the bulk of military men. In the pacifist movement there was for some time little creative thinking on the problems of peace and war and generally a lack of dynamic action. The World Citizens movement, initiated in 1948 by Gary Davis, a former U.S. serviceman and postwar convert to pacifism, was welcomed by war resisters in Western Europe and the United States; but it soon petered out. There was much repetition of old slogans and shibboleths and a tendency to walk in the well-worn paths trodden already by two generations of war resisters. Older pacifist societies like the British Peace Pledge Union (PPU) or the American War Resisters' League (WRL) continued to function, but with diminished impetus, the former ceasing to be much interested in politics or political action.

With the coming of peace the wartime conscientious objectors in Britain and the United States returned to their prewar jobs or entered on a new career. Some former C.Os., including in the U.S. both Civilian Public Service (CPS) assignees and prison inmates, participated in postwar relief activities on the war-devastated European continent or in China, usually working under the auspices of one of the peace churches' service organizations. In China they worked in a society where pacifism of the Quaker kind was not easily comprehensible. In Germany and in Poland or France, the major European centers of post-war relief activities, they had to deal with the fierce hatred generated among the victims of Nazi oppression, on the one hand, and the difficulties many Germans experienced in facing responsibility for the crimes committed under German occupation, on the other. In a letter dated April 24, 1946, William B. Edgerton, the American Friends Service Committee's representative in Warsaw and himself an expert in Slavic cultures, presented starkly some of the problems with which this situation faced pacifists freshly arrived from countries that had not suffered from occupation. He wrote:

American Friends [arriving in] Germany ... will be appalled by the sight of most of the German cities in ruins. And they will find as they expected to find, being men of good will, that most Germans are friendly, pleasant, and of course quite human. Having seen destruction and suffering in Germany beyond anything they were prepared for, and not having seen with their own eyes the almost incomparably greater suffering and destruction in Poland, they will be filled with pity for all the Germans. ... This one-sided pity will correspond exactly to the one-sided pity the Germans already have for themselves, and therein lies the grave danger that Friends will do more harm than good. ... And if in our sympathy with the Germans, we in any way block the difficult road that would lead them to ... facing their moral responsibility, we shall fail at the very point where the Germans need help most and where we [Quakers], of all groups, might do our most effective work.

"Although forbidden to go abroad during the war, many CPS assignees [had] prepared for post-war relief work during their off-duty hours."[3] (No such wartime restriction, however, existed in Britain.) Among the various nonsectarian relief organizations operating in war-torn Europe the religiously motivated British and American Quakers had figured prominently alongside North American Mennonites and the Church of the Brethren, which now began an extensive Heifer Project, manned by "sea-going cowboys" (mostly C.Os.), in order to aid farmers in war devastated areas.

After 1945, in general C.Os. suffered now – in contrast to the position after World War I – from little discrimination on account of their refusal to fight. Some objectors remained active in the pacifist movement or in the peace programs of their churches; others ceased to take much interest in any positive way. In the United States, however, a small group of former C.Os., radicalized by their wartime prison or camp experiences, became pioneers in developing nonviolent direct action for peace and justice during the postwar decades.[4] Conscription continued for the time being in both countries; the number of conscientious objectors among young men reaching military age, however, was small. To members of the Anglo-American postwar generation, who had grown to manhood during the war years, compulsory military service now appeared a normal way of life, unless they happened to have been reared in a pacifist church or home. Conversely, conscientious objection had become "normal" in the Anglo-American context alongside conscription. On the European continent, which contributed several outstanding figures to the postwar pacifist and nonviolent movement (e.g., Danilo Dolci, the spokesman. of the Sicilian poor, or the Italian philosopher Aldo Capitini, or the indomitable anarcho-pacifist Louis Lecoin in France, or Pastor Martin Niemöller, one of Hitler's staunchest opponents), compulsory military service continued almost everywhere as the dominant pattern, with repeated imprisonment of war resisters.[5] In the United States, efforts to assert the unconstitutional character of peacetime conscription proved unsuccessful. Across the border in Canada, where peace brought an end to wartime conscription, devoted pacifists like the Vancouver-based Mildred Fahrni carried on a quiet witness against war, which was perhaps typical of Canadian pacifism as a whole.

Above all, the cold-war atmosphere of the time, which climaxed in the Korean War and in McCarthyism in the United States, proved uncongenial to the expansion of pacifist ideas, even in their Anglo-American homeland. In Britain we find men like Bertrand Russell and the ex-pacifist, ex-editor of *Peace News*, John Middleton Murry, advocating threat of war, even nuclear war, as a means of pressuring Stalin's Russia to accept cooperation with the West; while in the United States, for instance, a wartime convert to complete pacifism, like the able leftwing journalist Dwight Macdonald,[6] soon abandoned it as inadequate in face of Soviet totalitarianism and expansionism.[7] Indeed most pacifists remained suspicious of the communist-sponsored "world peace" movement of the 1950's, feeling it functioned essentially as a cloak for furthering the foreign policy of the Soviet Union, although a few participated in its activities.

Thus belief in armed preparedness and in negotiation from strength as the sole means of containing what was widely held to be the aggressive character of communist-bloc policies, combined with an absence of nonconformity and of political radicalism among the young, now caused a general isolation of pacifism. To the new *Realpolitik* the idea of nonviolence appeared to lack both moral strength and political validity.

Under such circumstances, pacifism, "as a significant social move-ment"[8] had to wait some years before renewal began. The rebirth did not occur until the mid-1950's. The account given here of this pacifist revival and subsequent developments must necessarily be selective. Three aspects – the ones the authors consider of primary importance – will be discussed in this and the next two chapters, namely: 1) the role of pacifists in the nuclear disarmament movement; 2) the relationship between pacifism and the antiwar movement of the Vietnam era; and 3) the emergence of the "new" conscientious objection.

Pacifists in Campaigns for Nuclear Disarmament: Britain 1957–65

Apart from brief consideration of continental Europe and the USA we shall confine our discussion of nuclear disarmament campaigns in their earlier phase to Britain: an appropriate example since the pacifist influence was particularly important there. Our discussion of the movement for nuclear disarmament is necessarily limited, as a case study, to the role of pacifists and pacifism in this new development in the peace movement.

For more than a decade after 1945 the British pacifist movement dis-played, as already shown, little vitality or original thought. It still stood for complete disarmament, unilaterally if that were necessary. It opposed German rearmament and was highly critical of American (but rarely of Soviet) foreign policy. It continued the fight against conscrip-tion and joined campaigns, as in the USA, against the utterly inade-quate measures of civil defense attempted in face of atomic warfare. By taking a "plague on both their houses" approach and opposing all war it helped foster (again as in the USA) the idea of a "third camp" of nations disengaged from, and standing between, the two opposing blocs. Moreover, renewed interest emerged in this period among some pacifists in Gandhian techniques of conflict resolution.

Within the PPU a small group had crystallized toward the end of the forties with an interest in exploring the possibilities of nonviolent action and its implications for the peace movement. At the beginning this interest was purely theoretical; it consisted entirely of study and discussion. A resolution was passed at the PPU's annual conference in 1947 calling for the organization of a campaign of noncooperation with peacetime conscription but was reversed shortly afterwards at a spe-cially convened meeting. Despite opposition a Non-Violence Commis-sion was set up by the PPU in 1949. In 1951 some members organized a "sit-down" in front of the Ministry of Defence, an action that was pro-phetic of the mass movement after 1958; and the following year they demonstrated outside the Atomic Weapons Research Establishment at Aldermaston, using the name "Operation Gandhi" for their work until 1953 when they changed it to "Non-Violent Resistance Group," and in 1957 to the "Direct Action Committee against Nuclear War." This group involved such figures as Pat Arrowsmith, Hugh Brock (then editor of *Peace News*), April Carter, and Michael Randle. During this period they staged a number of civil disobedience protests attracting little attention or support however, even from pacifists. Though most of the participants were members of the PPU, the PPU clung to its old policy of action as an umbrella organization embracing all varieties of pacifism and was therefore unwilling to sponsor activities which met with the disapproval of many members.

The explosion of Britain's first hydrogen bomb in November 1957 in the Pacific galvanized British pacifism into life. When news had appeared in the spring of 1957 of the projected explosion, two Quakers – Harold and Sheila Steele – with a group of pacifist direct actionists attempted to enter the area off Christmas Island in the Pacific Ocean where the test was to be conducted. The attempt proved abortive. But the publicity given to the venture in the press and the fears now rapidly emerging among the general public concerning the consequences of nuclear tests and nuclear warfare, together provided the initial impetus in the formation of the Campaign for Nuclear Disarmament (CND).[9] A leader of the new "nuclear pacifism," the Anglican Canon John Collins, criticized the older pacifist organizations for failing to realize the need for fresh techniques and approaches.[10] As CND emerged in Britain, it represented a fusion of the moral and individualistic urge of the old-school pacifists with the new impetus imparted by widening public protest against the use of nuclear weapons. The most striking fact about CND, something that came as a surprise at first to its initiators, was its ability to mobilize a younger generation in demonstrations and mass marches.

CND was officially founded at the end of January 1958. From the beginning it called for nuclear disarmament on the part of Britain and other nuclear powers, with Britain acting first, on its own if need be. It derived from groups established previously in the summer and autumn of 1957 as a result of the recent British nuclear testing. In this pacifists were active, as were left-wing intellectuals, like J.B. Priestley and Kingsley Martin of the *New Statesmian,* as well as figures from both the established church and the nonconformist denominations. From the outset CND was strong in the Labour Party, especially among its left-wing M.P.'s and among leftward leaning trade-unionists. CND also involved many nonpolitical scientists appalled at the destructive ends to which scientific discovery was being applied. After 1960 communists participated in the protest movement but only with some hesitation and after CND had become a substantial force. Unilateralism had some awkward implications *vis-à-vis* the Soviet Union's nuclear weapons; in fact communist influence on the direction taken by CND was very limited until the later sixties. Small leftist splinter groups also took part including a new wave of anarchists.

At first pacifists provided the moral fervor and those most active in local CND branches. New Left intellectuals also helped to shape the movement's ideas. The annual Easter protest march to the Atomic Weapons Research Establishment at Aldermaston, initiated in 1958, originated with the same group of pacifist direct actionists mentioned earlier, though civil disobedience did not become part of CND marchers' program. By the early 1960s hundreds of thousands of persons participated, marking an end of pacifist apathy in Britain, and the now famous peace symbol (ND) was adopted in 1958.

CND was essentially an educational campaign to influence public opinion in an extra parliamentary fashion. It expressed alienation from the official parties, which monopolized the political scene and helped sustain a "conspiracy of silence" on the nuclear issue. Critics of existing society as well as merely opponents of the bomb, CND supporters represented a new variant of English radical political dissent; its quasi-religious tone, strong moral enthusiasm, mass techniques yet predominantly "respectable" middle-class composition and leadership, and its anti-political tone paralleled nonconformist movements of the nineteenth century, as well as the new radical movements in the USA and elsewhere.

Partly as a result of CND pressure, the Labour Party voted for nuclear unilateralism in 1960; as it was to do again twenty years later, the resolution urged the UK to abandon nuclear bases and nuclear deterrence. The leader of the Labour Party, Hugh Gaitskell, accused the supporters of these proposals of being "pacifists, neutralists, and fellow travellers" (by implication communists), and the following year the decision was narrowly reversed. There had been genuine conversions of many in the labor movement to nuclear pacifism, but not in sufficient numbers to maintain the position.

Despite CND's focal policy, i.e., Britain's unilateral renunciation of nuclear weapons, the Campaign embraced a considerable diversity of views. Some campaigners did not disapprove of American retention of nuclear armaments; others looked favorably on the Soviet Union's nuclear arms (the "workers' bomb"). But from the pure pacifist point of view serious reservations were possible. Pacifist organizations like the Peace Pledge Union or the Fellowship of Reconciliation gave CND a cool welcome. And the PPU finally severed its ties with its weekly organ, *Peace News*, which had become an ardent supporter of nuclear disarmament. Pacifist "purists" felt that it was a betrayal of mission to single out one particular type of weapon from others instead of protesting as hitherto against all weapons of war. For many pacifists, however, the menace of nuclear warfare was so overwhelming that any movement organized to absolutely oppose nuclear weapons deserved pacifist support. In this view concern for nuclear disarmament could be the first step toward a total repudiation of war. Thus CND provided a mass movement in which pacifism could promote its message, and from which it could recruit a new generation for whom old-style pacifism was remote. One might see the role of pacifists within CND as keeping the campaign to its policy of unilateralism, and away from the compromises which would result if the movement converted itself into a merely political pressure group, or moved too far into Labour Party politics.

Although it had spawned many similar organisations throughout Europe and English speaking countries (even India) by 1965, by that date CND's influence and size at home were already waning. The nuclear arms race continued to threaten global destruction and indeed was to accelerate by the 1970's; nuclear proliferation continued, especially in Asia and the Middle East. CND had gradually informed the public on the facts as well as the moral implications of nuclear war and the dangers of escalation, and made these urgent issues in political life. (Pacifists, we may note, had done the same to war in general in the 1918–1940 period but with less effect.) Like the Anglo-American reform movements of the nineteenth century, CND presented basically a simple moral message: "Nuclear war is evil," (earlier movements had denounced drink or slavery as "sin"). Perhaps just because of its simplified appeal CND was able to inject a sense of urgency and of the wider dangers inherent in nuclear threats. It dispelled ignorance concerning the issue in a broader public which had previously displayed apathy: this was its lasting legacy. The same thing happened not only in Britain but also in Western Europe and North America where the movement was transplanted, though in less vigorous forms.

Since in all probability the resort to nuclear weapons would eventually be made if an East/West conventional war ever broke out, escalation of conventional weapons, which CND did not concern itself with directly, also contained a potential threat. Some CND supporters began to turn their attention increasingly toward the possibilities of "civilian defence," as they came to call their proposed policy alternative; this would involve total and unilateral disarmament based primarily, however, on expediency rather than on pacifist principle, but backed up by mass noncooperation. Stephen King-Hall, for example, a political commentator and retired naval commander, who did not consider himself a pacifist "in the accepted sense of the word," stated: "But I see no reason why opinions held by pacifists for moral causes are therefore necessarily to be ignored by non-pacifists if such opinions are useful for defence purposes."[11] In face of the threat posed by the unleashing of nuclear war, even if a state were intending the bomb only for defensive purposes, he urged it to disarm and develop a nonviolent strategy for defending the country physically in case of enemy occupation and for upholding democratic values. It would thus transfer the East/West conflict "between the two ways of life, from the sphere of violence to that of ideas."[12] If Britain were to give a lead of this kind, other countries might gradually move over from violent to nonviolent defense, a shift in strategic outlook which the commander considered essential if mankind was to avoid nuclear destruction.

King-Hall drew heavily on historical and other data provided by earlier pacifist literature dealing with nonviolent resistance. And it was among members of the more radical wing of the pacifist movement that his ideas found the readiest response rather than in government circles or among his former colleagues in the armed services where he had hoped to evoke interest, if hardly immediate assent. These ideas, developed among others by Adam Roberts, Gene Sharp, and Theodor Ebert (in West Germany), were disseminated in pamphlets and in *Peace News* and by other means. Pacifist radicals, influenced by Gandhian ideas, wished to advance beyond the hitherto essentially negative slogans of the peace movement: "No More War," or "Ban the Bomb." They sought to confront the new nuclear situation with a positive technique that could gain widespread support because it promised the preservation of a given society's values by means that did not threaten to destroy the values and the societies that upheld them.

For most pacifist radicals, the trend toward nuclear war must be first reversed by direct action rather than by the more conventional methods of protest pursued by CND, which seemed to be proving ineffective.

Nonviolent Direct Action for Peace

Nonviolent direct action has been defined as "a special form of ... resistance, in which the dissenter uses his own body as the lever with which to pry loose the government's policy."[13] We have discussed attempts to employ direct action of this kind for various purposes: to rectify economic or social abuses or to gain political concessions, as in some of Gandhi's earlier *satyagraha* campaigns; to win national independence and effect the withdrawal of a colonial power, as Gandhi tried to do in the 1930s and early 1940s and certain African nationalist leaders after World War II; or to achieve full civil equality for a politically depressed section of the population, as in the United States under Martin Luther King.

We have seen, too, that nonviolent direct action has usually, though by no means always, entailed civil disobedience. Civil disobedience can be direct and consist in refusing an objectionable law or, where a direct confrontation with wrong is impossible, it can be indirect and consist in the violation of laws that are in themselves unobjectionable. In the latter case, in particular, disobedience may act either as "a symbolic gesture," a form of witness, calling attention to an injustice and attempting in this way to mobilize opinion against it. Or, on the other hand, it may have almost revolutionary implications and be aimed at creating disruption so as to force an immediate change in official policy or even to overthrow the government altogether.

Direct Action in Britain

Among the diverse elements which preceded and went into the making of CND none proved more devoted and energetic than the direct action group – or at times more trying to the Campaign's less radically inclined leadership. Collins struggled with "direct action enthusiasts" – and their leaders, all young and mostly in their twenties. As has been seen, this group had first developed in the decade after 1949. They were as interested in the successful use of nonviolent techniques as in public persuasion. The loose non-membership organization of CND in its early days permitted the existence within it of such groups: engaged in obstruction of construction work at nuclear rocket bases, and influenced by syndicalist ideas, they attempted to persuade workers on these sites to strike or leave their jobs. The original nucleus of pacifist direct actionists soon expanded by drawing into its orbit some of the CND's young recruits, as well as older supporters of the campaign, of whom the octogenarian Bertrand Russell was among the most illustrious, and vigorous, examples. These new converts to direct action did not necessarily share their pacifist predecessors devotion to nonviolence as a matter of principle. Yet many of them now felt, as one of them wrote, that "in the twentieth century Gandhi is in fact a more relevant political thinker than Marx."[14]

The international crisis situation in 1960 raised the levels of antinuclear feeling in Britain and elsewhere. Russell was now persuaded by a young American graduate student at the London School of Economics, Ralph Schoenman, to inaugurate what both hoped could become a mass antinuclear civil disobedience campaign. In the early autumn of 1960 a "Committee of 100" was formed; its one hundred sponsors being drawn from sympathizers prominent in the political or cultural life of the country. "Russell and Schoenman ... set out to combine the mass support of the CND with the capacity for sensational civil disobedience of the Direct Action Committee."[15]

The setting up and actions of the Committee of 100 was accompanied by widespread publicity, and some accused its sponsors of planning subversion and sabotage. The leadership of CND, including Collins, feared that direct actions, leading to adverse publicity and the branding of the movement as ultra-leftist, would destroy CND's effectiveness as a political force, especially in the Labour Party. Bertrand Russell now resigned as president of CND, and the Campaign and the Committee henceforward pursued their separate ways, though sometimes overlapping (most Committee members were also in CND).

The opponents of direct action within CND, whether pacifist or nonpacifist, centered their case on the inappropriateness, indeed the dangers, of such methods in a democratic society. They supported the idea of individual civil disobedience if a law outraged an individual's moral values, as in the case of conscientious objection to military service, or its collective practice as an act of protest in a country where either the majority or a minority were deprived of their civil rights as occurred, for instance, in British India or with black Americans in the southern USA. But in a parliamentary democracy, critics of direct action claimed, there was – apart from the conscientious refusal of individual citizens to obey a thoroughly immoral law – rarely, if ever, room for such action. If engaged in on a wide scale, it might undermine parliamentary institutions; it might usher in an authoritarian régime as a consequence of bypassing the ordinary representative processes. Canon Collins complained of the Committee of 100's "deliberate breaking of laws, which in themselves cause no offence to conscience, in order to gain publicity and to bring pressure to bear upon governments."[16] Like others, he accused its members, while obviously still a clear minority, of attempting to enforce their policy on the government by a species of nonviolent blackmail instead of waiting until they had convinced a majority in the country of its correctness. Since tactics of this kind were anyhow unlikely to be successful, the final result would be to discredit the entire antinuclear cause and retard its further development.

In reply, spokesmen for civil disobedience pleaded the dangers and urgency of the situation in extenuation of their action. We cannot afford to wait, they said in effect. The nuclear threat and the extinction of the human race, which could result from prolonged competition in nuclear armaments, justified a shortcut in the democratic procedure. In their view civil disobedience, with the readiness of its practitioners to suffer arrest and imprisonment for their witness, would alone serve to arouse a still too apathetic public and to break through the wall of silence with which the British establishment attempted to surround the subject of nuclear disarmament. Nuclear policy was largely covert, and no amount of marchings and meetings would avail. They also argued that government and press had conspired to repress the nuclear issue. As one might employ radical measures to disarm a lunatic, so shock treatment in the form of direct action was needed to deal with the insane policies of the nuclear deterrent. To the charge that their tactics were essentially antidemocratic, the direct actionists countered both with the traditional appeal to a higher law and by the argument that nonviolent direct action provided a peaceable means for expressing radical dissent, which would prevent its deterioration otherwise into violent channels.

During the first two years of its existence the Committee of 100 organized a number of mass sit-downs and other acts of civil disobedience, which led to the jailing of Russell and other participants. By 1962, however, a change took place in the Committee's objectives. From an organization which, like the CND out of which it had sprung, aimed primarily at Britain's unilateral abandonment of the nuclear deterrent as a first step toward international nuclear disarmament, the Committee evolved toward ideas of nonviolent political revolution, which would eliminate nuclear weapons along with the social order generating them. The Committee of 100 had originally hoped to set going a mass movement of nonviolent protest and, by its cultivation of civil disobedience and its suffering of legal consequences, awaken tens of thousands to the nuclear danger. Schoenman argued that

demonstrations must not end with the sit-in. Otherwise after two days of headlines and a certain amount of inconvenience for the courts the authorities are in the clear. We must begin to pledge people in their thousands to carry the challenge further. If ten thousand have to be carried into court where they refuse to say a mumbling word: if ten thousand have to be jailed – then we shall realise the meaning of civil disobedience and I dare say so will the makers of [nuclear] bombs.[17]

Yet despite this vision, the Committee's support remained relatively small, and its acts of civil disobedience had fairly soon ceased to make much impact, especially after the jailing of its leaders (some for 18 months) and the suicide of its jailed treasurer. In addition to its failure to convince the whole of CND to commit itself to civil disobedience, the Committee's more revolutionary aims unnecessarily limited its appeal.

The Committee's decline seems attributable to two basic shortcomings. In the first place, there was the ambiguity (already noted), which developed concerning the Committee's ultimate objectives. Did it aim by means of mass civil disobedience to bear witness in the most dramatic way possible to the evil of nuclear war? Or was its purpose to generate something like a general strike against war, which (as syndicalists and anarchists had long been urging) could be used as a lever to carry out a far-reaching political and social revolution, even though the revolutionary situation, which the second alternative presumed, really did not then exist?

A second source of weakness lay in the Committee's inability (perhaps in part on account of this rapidly developing ambiguity as to its aims) to make its protest an effective symbol in the public mind of the truth it sought to convey. Success in this regard Gandhi had always emphasized as essential in a *satyagraha* campaign. The committee's failure here may also have derived from the difficulty of arranging a clear confrontation with the evil it opposed. Breaking the law by sitting down at the Ministry of Defence, or even by obstructing the entrance to a nuclear missile site or an aircraft runway, or trying to board a nuclear submarine, perhaps did not provide the same immediately obvious connection with nuclear war as Gandhi's illegal manufacture of salt had done with the evil of alien rule or a southern blacks' sit-in at a segregated lunch-counter with the shame of racial discrimination. Moreover it did not have a sympathetic press to report its actions.

Direct Action in the United States

A movement for nonviolent direct action to further peace developed in the United States at the same time as it was emerging, on a rather wider scale, in Britain. Apart from a short-lived revival immediately after World War II when the explosion of the first atomic bombs aroused some alarm concerning the future, the American pacifist movement had remained in the doldrums until its gradual reactivation toward the end of the fifties. The relaxation of East-West tensions which resulted in the Soviet Union after the death of Stalin, combined with a growing awareness throughout the United States of the threat presented by thermonuclear war, created a more receptive atmosphere for pacifist ideas than had existed during the early years of the Cold War and McCarthyism. In addition, a new generation, more susceptible to pacifist arguments, had by now arrived on the scene.

As in Britain, active interest in Gandhian techniques was confined at first to a small section only of the pacifist movement. The American Fellowship of Reconciliation, like the British PPU, decided early on that it could not sponsor civil disobedience as an instrument of pacifist policy, although members remained free to engage in such action as individuals. Official support, it was felt, would destroy the all-embracing character of the Fellowship. The secular War Resisters' League showed itself more sympathetic to the idea of nonviolent direct action. In 1948 a group of WRL members calling themselves the "Peacemakers" had enunciated a program which included nonregistration for the draft (some of them even burnt draft cards in symbolic protest against military conscription), refusal to pay taxes destined for military purposes, and the development of nonviolent techniques for achieving social change. The program represented a fusion of Gandhian and anarchist ideas and showed the influence, too, of the Marxist critique of capitalist society. But the Peacemakers did not flourish for long.

A fresh beginning came in 1956 when in March of that year a new journal of ideas appeared. *Liberation*, as it was named, was intended by its founders, among whom A.J. Muste was the *spiritus movens*, to serve as organ for a direct actionist variety of pacifism, which would be neither liberal-democratic, for it advocated a social revolution, nor Marxist, since it stood for antiauthoritarianism as well as nonviolent means to achieve the revolution. This new pacifist left was inclined toward a decentralized society. Some of its supporters had been interested in the communitarian movement, which survived the war here in a more flourishing state than its counterpart in Britain. (The historian Staughton Lynd, for example, one of the pacifist left's leading figures in the sixties, lived for a time in a Brüderhof settlement.) In any case the direct actionists were all profoundly disillusioned with the established political parties and utterly without hope of achieving social change or a peaceable revolution through orthodox political channels. One of the most creative thinkers among them was Barbara Deming, whose nonviolence was forged in the civil rights struggle and the peace protests of the sixties. A staunch feminist and protagonist of lesbian and gay rights, she perceived "the root violence in our society [in] the attempt by men to claim women and children as their property." At the same time, "if we can destroy a man's power to tyrannize, there is no need, of course, to destroy the man himself." "We ARE one kind – women and men." As Harriet Alonso writes: "The feminist peace movement lost a great voice when Barbara Deming died of cancer in 1984."[18]

For American pacifist radicals, Gandhi remained both teacher and guide for action (and Muste with his call for "holy disobedience" was his prophet[19]). "To understand the significance of Gandhi for American pacifists," one of the radicals has written, "it is necessary to look at the conflict between two fundamental ideas and orientations in the peace movement: the idea of *non-resistance* and the idea of *non-violent resistance.* ... The shift from one to the other represents a change from a conservative, individually-oriented pacifism to a radical, social action pacifism."[20] Moreover, whereas before 1939 Gandhi's influence in America was purely intellectual, in the decades after 1945 activists began to put Gandhian techniques into practice. These techniques were already known and influential at the outset of the Civil Rights movement (1956–7). But nonviolent direct action was also used in the United States against war preparation, and in particular in protest against nuclear armaments. Of course, American pacifists and peace-minded nonpacifists were no more united in regard to the value or justifiability of direct action than the contemporary British peace movement was. In fact no equivalent to CND emerged in the United States. SANE (National Committee for a Sane Nuclear Policy), set up in 1957 by a number of pacifists and nonpacifists concerned at the increasing threat posed by nuclear weapons and anxious to achieve nuclear disarmament, was officially more multilateralist, less clear in its unilateralist dimension and organizationally much less widely based than the British CND was. It also lacked the latter's mass appeal. SANE, too, proceeded from the beginning along entirely separate lines from the more clearly unilateralist direct actionists, who in June 1957 had established a Committee for Non-Violent Action (CNVA) to coordinate their hitherto dispersed efforts.

In some respects CNVA's activities paralleled those of the direct actionists in Britain. Like them its supporters sat down outside atomic plants and missile sites and "invaded" Polaris submarine bases, they conducted vigils before germ-warfare research stations. In New York City they disobeyed the order to take shelter in the annual civil defense drills. They distributed antiwar leaflets among workers engaged on projects connected with nuclear armament. Sometimes the demonstrators were arrested and fined or jailed. Sometimes they were received with hostility by local people, who might often be dependent for their livelihood on the arms industry.

An equally dramatic, innovative form of nonviolent direct action by CNVA in 1958 was an attempted sailing by the *Golden Rule* into the Americans' atomic test area around Entiwetok Atoll in the Marshall Islands. The boat had a four-man crew commanded by an ex-naval captain and convert to Quakerism, Albert S. Bigelow. Like the British Quaker couple, the Steeles, in the previous year, the *Golden Rule* was unsuccessful in reaching its destination; the crew being stopped and brought to Honolulu where they were tried and imprisoned. As convinced Gandhians, Bigelow and his colleagues had conducted their whole enterprise in the open, feeling that secrecy would have undermined the message they wished to convey.[21]

The sequel to the story is not uninstructive. An American anthropologist, Earle Reynolds, returning home across the Pacific with his family in their yacht, the *Phoenix*, after a long absence overseas, heard of the *Golden Rule* and thereupon determined to take over its uncompleted mission. Reynolds hitherto had been unconnected with the CNVA or the pacifist movement in general. His boat managed to enter the restricted zone but was subsequently halted, and its owner found his way into jail along with the crew of the *Golden Rule*.[22]

The forbidden voyages did not bring about a cessation of the nuclear testing. Indeed it is unlikely that the participants regarded immediate success in this regard as a probable outcome of their action. Like the later Greenpeace voyages, their purpose was to dramatize the evil of nuclear warfare by a direct confrontation, in which the crews incurred the risk not merely of a short prison term (which resulted) but of death by radiation or in the nuclear explosion. Their action was an exemplification of a basic principle in the Gandhian philosophy of nonviolence: *tapasya*, or self-sacrifice voluntarily undertaken in the name of a declared truth.

The two enterprises did in fact gain greater publicity and more sympathetic coverage for the antinuclear cause than any previous such demonstrations and marked a decisive stage in its development; the clouds of apathy hitherto covering public discussion of the nuclear deterrent in the United States were at last beginning to disperse.

Transnational Action[23]

During the first half of the sixties, CNVA, influenced by such ventures in nonviolent direct action as the Freedom Rides (and other marches), began to organize a series of international peace walks. In contrast to the British CND's annual Aldermaston marches, the example of which may also have been influential on CNVA's tactics now, the peace walkers were specially chosen and the number of participants restricted usually to two or three dozen.

In 1960–61 an international team carrying leaflets in each language used on the way made the journey from San Francisco to Moscow: the first and most effective of such enterprises. Their Russian hosts endeavored (unsuccessfully) to convince them that the Soviet Union, although armed with nuclear weapons, was entirely peaceable. Except for leafletting, and some difficult border crossings, the marchers did not practice civil disobedience *en route*; their object was to center attention – through the walk itself – on the nuclear threat to mankind and to demonstrate in favor of a nonviolent way to resolve conflict.[24]

In a later peace walk (Québec to Washington to Guantanamo, 1963–64) the marchers, however, did run into trouble in the South on account of the integrated character of the team and their determination to witness against the denial of human solidarity contained in racial discrimination. In Albany, Georgia, they were arrested and jailed. "The prolonged fast," wrote one of the participants in the walk, "is our chief weapon. We have others. A number of walkers practice kinds of civil disobedience other than fasting. Some refuse to walk into their cells. They oppose the prison system in principle. Others will not walk to court. They cannot recognize an apparatus created in the name of justice for the purpose of denying justice. By these acts they offset, indeed annihilate and make ridiculous, the mantle of power and authority that the Albany court has gathered about itself."[25]

By the second half of the 1960s the practice of nonviolence appeared to many in the West to be an instrument with as yet unmeasured potentialities, but one fraught with dangers and open to abuse. In certain circumstances it could obviously be wielded with effect by a subject people or an oppressed minority to demand concessions from the government, even without a total commitment to its use on the part of all participants in a nonviolent campaign. Past experience, however, could throw only an uncertain light on its possibilities as a substitute for armed defense.

In some universities in the West after 1959, "peace research," much of it directed toward the nonviolent resolution of conflict, had now been established. Once again pacifists such as Johan Galtung in Norway, Elise and Kenneth Boulding in the USA, Paul Smoker in Britain and Theodor Ebert in Germany, were centrally involved in this. Whether resulting from such scholarly research or from the urgings of the spirit, the adoption of nonviolence would seem to entail a fairly radical restructuring of society. A country, which pursued imperialist domination or tolerated far-going political or economic inequality, could scarcely expect to practice nonviolent resistance with success. Nonviolence, therefore, had indeed social revolutionary implications, as the direct actionists had argued.

Increasing participation of college students in the antiwar movement, especially in the USA, was a manifestation of growing campus-based action. Special forms of nonviolent protest developed by the American direct actionists in the 50s and 60s were, of course, by no means confined to students. They included refusal to pay taxes for war; "trespassing" within the area set aside for atomic testing; and the organization of the international peace walks. The first and second necessarily involved civil disobedience, while the third might do so in certain circumstances.

War and Conscientious Objection: USA in the Vietnam Era

Whereas in Britain conscription was phased out and finally abolished in 1961, in the United States compulsory military service, set at two years in 1951, continued on a selective basis almost without a break from the wartime system of conscription which came to an end in 1947. With increasing U.S. involvement in Vietnam the problem of conscientious objection began to take on new relevance and the idea of war resistance now spread from pacifist circles outwards to embrace many, for example in the New Left, who did not share pacifist principles.

"During World War II and the Korean War," a veteran antimilitarist has written, "there was little feeling among pacifists that *this* war must be stopped and we will do everything within our power to stop it. Not that any of them wanted war to continue, but the dominant psychology was one of personal nonparticipation in a catastrophe which had been sanctioned by the democratic process and, in any event, was beyond their power to shorten or stop."[26] The growing awareness of the dangers of nuclear war described in previous pages contributed of course to the subsequent extension of antiwar feelings in the population. Opposition to the Vietnam War proved an even more effective agent in creating such activist sentiment. Many Americans, who were far from considering themselves to be war resisters in the traditional meaning or even nuclear pacifists, regarded the war as unjust, even illegal. Thus not only a convinced pacifist such as Martin Luther King[27] but men like Dr. Benjamin Spock, who had supported America's participation in the Korean War, were prepared to risk imprisonment by urging all those who opposed the war to resist the draft if called upon for military service. Vietnam filled the streets of major American cities with thousands of demonstrators; sit-ins took place in front of army induction centers. Young men of military age burned draft cards in public or handed them back to the authorities. Others crossed the border into Canada.

Whilst draft "dodging" without principle certainly existed, draft "exile" may perhaps be considered a species of *hijrat*, a voluntary exile. Gandhi had commended *hijrat* as an alternative, neither dishonorable nor cowardly, to submission to wrong for those who did not feel able, if they stayed at home, to face the consequences of resistance (which in the existing circumstances might involve a five-year jail term) or for those who considered this kind of resistance was futile: many now, when in Canada, Sweden or the British Isles, continued actively to oppose the war.

A few opponents of the war, including the Catholic Roger LaPorte, the Quaker Norman Morrison, and the eighty-two-year-old Alice Herz, also a Quaker, following the example of Buddhist monks and nuns in South Vietnam, protested by setting fire to themselves and died. While other opponents of the war paid tribute to the self-sacrifice, few felt that such self-immolation, altruistic suicide, was an appropriate method in Western society.[28]

Conscientious objection, on the other hand, was part of the American political structure (in a way that was not yet true in many countries on the European continent). Most political objectors to the war in Vietnam took that stand because they condemned the United States's intervention in that country rather than from any desire to support the NLF (National Liberation Front) or North Vietnam. Yet, according to the letter of the law, only religious pacifists, with belief in "a Supreme Being" (until this phrase was omitted when the duration of military service was extended once again in 1967), continued to be eligible for exemption as conscientious objectors and subsequent assignment either to noncombatant or civilian alternative service. Nonreligious objectors to all wars as well as the various kinds of political objector, including "selective" objectors to the Vietnam War, were still excluded from the benefit of the act.

An advance occurred in 1965 with the U.S. Supreme Court's decision in the case of Daniel Seeger, a pacifist who, disclaiming belief in a personal God, appealed a sentence of imprisonment imposed after his application for exemption had been rejected.[29] The Supreme Court ruled in his favor, stating that "the test of belief 'in relation to a Supreme Being' is whether a given belief that is sincere and meaningful, occupies a place in the life of its possessor parallel to that filled by the orthodox belief in God of one who clearly qualifies for the exemption. Where such beliefs have parallel positions in the lives of their respective holders, we cannot say that one is 'in relation to a Supreme Being' and the other is not." At the same time, the Supreme Court stated its view that "essentially political, sociological, or philosophical views," however genuine, did not constitute a conscientious objection to war within the meaning of the act. Nonetheless it would seem that henceforward any fully pacifist objector qualified for exemption, unless he absolutely insisted that his objection was not religious even under the Supreme Court's broad definition of this term.[30]

But the problem of the selective objector remained. A not unrepresentative exposition of this viewpoint, and one more typical than the old-style socialist objection which predominated earlier in the century, may be found in the statement submitted by Benjamin Sherman explaining why he was resisting the draft. "I am not a pacifist," he wrote. He did not feel always able to be "completely and lovingly non-violent." Nevertheless, he did not believe violence or killing "for any reason" could be right. "I am trying to clean myself bit by bit," he went on. "I am seeking this status of conscientious objection to the war in Vietnam although I know objection to a particular war is not permitted in the C.O. statutes, because I believe our conscience is often the truest guide in achieving some sort of understanding, love, and compassion for our fellow human beings. And our conscience *must*, not the written statutes, be our guide if we are ever to achieve world peace, and, in a narrower sense, peace of mind."[31]

Serving soldiers who developed an objection to fighting in the war in Vietnam – but not to war in general – frequently had recourse to the concept of a higher code of international law, in addition to the same kind of appeal to a superior moral sanction which appears in Sherman's statement quoted above. Neither the civil courts nor military tribunals, however, were willing to admit such arguments.

Selective objectors, among whom were some whose scruples concerning participation in this particular war were religiously motivated, cited precedents such as the Nuremberg principle for refusing induction into an army engaged in a war they considered a crime against humanity. At Nuremberg obedience to the orders of one's superiors had been dismissed in extenuation of such deeds. In view of the alternatives facing selective objectors of long terms of imprisonment, voluntary exile (in this case without term), or going underground, some of them were prepared to play "semantic games with the Selective Service forms."[32] There was often indeed a quite genuine "situational" element in the objections of young draftees taking the C.O. stand, which was recognized by those in close contact with them. These men left the question of participation in a future war open, by no means wishing however to exclude the possibility of their further war resistance. At any rate, the burden of proving that a war was "just" lay, in their view, with the government. Some pacifists hoped this stance would form the prelude to a full conversion to pacifism.[33]

As the demands for manpower grew larger, concern spread at the continued refusal of the administration to give legal recognition to sincerely held objection to a particular war. This concern reached far beyond the limits of the peace movement. As in Germany in the 1960s, too, opponents of recognition here maintained that, if claims to political objection of this kind were sustained, they could eventually undermine a country's military security and destroy its effectiveness in prosecuting its war aims. Besides, was there really any more justification for admitting a selective objection to military service than for allowing a selective objection, let us say, to paying income tax? In response to these arguments it was urged by pacifists and civil libertarians that respect for the rights of religious conscience *vis-à-vis* participation in war had become a recognized part of the Western tradition, and more particularly of Anglo-American political practice. The extension of this same respect to embrace all conscientious opposition to military service was as valid as the recognition now extended in other areas to nonreligious conscience or situational ethics.[34] Moreover, from a more pragmatic standpoint experience had shown that the number of men ready to take the objector stand did not normally constitute a security threat – unless, of course, the antiwar movement outside the ranks of the objectors had already reached formidable dimensions. By the late sixties this had indeed become the case, by the early seventies the situation *vis-à-vis* C.Os. had become problematic for both the American and German governments – and by the eighties in Russia and Poland, too, as we shall see in a subsequent chapter.

Experiences of Pacifist Objectors

In conclusion we may ask, what were the experiences of drafted pacifists during the Vietnam era? There was no attempt to reconstitute Civilian Public Service camps. It is indeed unlikely that the historic peace churches would have been willing to sponsor such a program after what had happened during the last war, so that the government in all probability would have had to run them alone: a prospect that it scarcely relished. Final decision as to the sincerity of those claiming C.O. status still remained the prerogative of the local draft boards, though provision now existed for appeal to the C.O. Section of the Justice Department. "In nine out of ten cases the local board [then] followed the recommendations of the Justice Department."[35]

Pacifists were active in counseling potential objectors. In 1966 the Central Committee for Conscientious Objectors, a well established organization ably directed by a Quaker, Arlo Tatum, succeeded in selling within six months over eleven thousand copies of the eighth edition of its *Handbook for Conscientious Objectors* and then had to reprint it. Both the Fellowship of Reconciliation and the American Friends Service Committee were among the organizations participating in this work.[36] Such activities of course aimed not at impeding the war effort but at informing draftees of their legal rights if they decided to become C.Os.

Procedures differed little from the previous years of conscription. Those young men whom their draft boards recognized as genuine objectors continued to be given 1–0 status, which entitled them to perform civilian, in place of military service. A draft law expert wrote at the outset of the seventies:

Civilian assignments for alternate service have been very flexible. Most of this service is performed in hospitals, but assignments may be made to any public service operated by a political subdivision of a state, to a university clinic, a religious mission, or other humanitarian enterprise. Assignment to such civilian work of national importance may be made at a wage less than that prevailing in the country or area. If a board so chooses, it may assign work in an isolated place and without any compensation, but this is very rare. Current practise and selective service policy is that the C.O. drafted for civilian duty shall work the same hours, receive the same pay, and be subject to the same conditions as other employees on his job. The average C.O's. pay is lower than that of a drafted private, however. The C.O. must expect to forfeit all veterans' benefits ... Nor are there any dependency allowances or death or disability benefits for the person serving as a C.O.[37]

In addition to C.Os. exempted on condition of performing some type of alternative civilian service, there were those assigned to noncombatant duties in the armed forces, with 1-A-O status. While Seventh-day Adventists remained the most numerous group among the noncombatants, there were many others, though, like the rather confused but patently sincere college student unconnected with any peace group, Tom Bennett, who found this alternative the most satisfying way of combining their hatred of war with an anxiety to relieve the suffering of those involved in the fighting. (In Bennett's case it led to his death on the battlefield and subsequent transformation into a military hero.)

Lastly, we have the prison C.Os. Many of these men were either selective objectors, whose opposition to the existing conflict, however sincere, did not qualify them, we know, for C.O. status, or nonreligious pacifists whose qualifications for this – despite successive rulings on the issue by the Supreme Court, first in the Seeger case (1965) and then in the Welsh case (1970)[38] – remained ambiguous, or members of a church unwilling to support a pacifist stand. There were even a few libertarians who objected not so much to fighting as to the principle of conscription; politically, they might feel akin to Barry Goldwater's conservative republicanism. In addition, Black Muslims, who rejected fighting except in a war Allah himself had declared, and – as usual – Jehovah's Witnesses frequently ended up in jail; indeed most imprisoned objectors belonged to the latter sect. "Between 1965 and 1972, some ... 4,000 [young men] were imprisoned" for draft law violations, not always of course on grounds of conscience. Only a few of the jailed objectors, like the Quaker Richard Boardman, for instance, or the Mennonite David Rensberger, came from one of the historic peace churches.[39] And in such cases their incarceration often resulted either from refusal to register for the draft or an unwillingness, on grounds of conscience, to accept any conditions of exemption.

One of those who took this stand and was consequently jailed, summed up his motivation as follows:

I always considered that my views were a combination of ethical and moral, religious, social and philosophical – that I was not distinguishable in categories. They all coalesce in my personality, who I am. But the draft at that time was written in language that said you may be exempted by reason of religious training and belief, including belief in a Supreme Being with duties involving those superior to any human relationship. They specifically excluded moral, political, sociological, essentially philosophical objections. This seemed to me the worst kind of hair-splitting.[40]

As in World War II, apart from the loss of freedom for a prolonged period the main hardships of life in prison for C.Os., shared of course by other prisoners too, lay in the almost total lack of privacy and the widespread violence and brutality, including the danger of rape as well as that barbaric penal relic – "the hole." Such things, though, had long been present in the American penal system. In addition, boredom and mounting frustration remained the invariable accompaniments of prolonged incarceration in a federal penitentiary where many C.Os. served their sentences. "Being here," said another jailed C.O., "obviously is a painful waste, but waste doesn't necessarily mean failure. Because the reason I'm here is right, I have a certain amount of self-respect for myself. Basically, as long as I retain that I can endure imprisonment." Without condemning another's different decision, most of the jailed C.Os. felt that, at any rate for themselves, taking refuge in Canada, for instance, would have been "running away from the fight," a compromise they were unwilling to adopt.[41]

Baskir and Strauss, in their admirable study of the impact of the draft on the Vietnam generation of American males from 1964 to 1973,

view the stand of the jailed war resisters as, in the final analysis, a significant one, though perhaps not in the way they had themselves
envisaged – or would have wished. Behind prison walls or in prison
camps, and after release as well, they often felt themselves forgotten
and sensed failure in their years of involuntary exclusion from society.
"The public's attention was transfixed either on the POW's in North
Vietnam or the exiles in Canada." The authors continue:

In one sense, however, imprisoned draft offenders were very much on the
minds of millions of American youngsters. In living rooms across the country,
the choice was made clear for nineteen- and twenty-year olds who might have
had second thoughts about obeying their draft boards: Report for induction, or
you'll go to prison. Two million complied with induction orders, and two million others were pressured into enlisting by the threat of induction. If nobody
had been convicted, if nobody had been sent to prison, then many of these
people might have had second thoughts, and the draft system – and the war
effort – might well have collapsed.[42]

By 1973 the draft had indeed ended; it was replaced by all-volunteer
armed forces. In 1972, writes John Chambers, "more registrants [had
been] classified as C.Os. than were inducted into the army. Such a phenomenon was unprecedented in American history." Henceforward,
even during the Gulf War the C.O. "problem" was to be confined in
practice to those in the military. Yet subsequent events showed "that
war, conscription, and conscientious objection had not ended for
Americans with the Vietnam War."[43]

During the Vietnam era the C.O. – whether religious or secular, absolute pacifist or selective objector to a particular war – had enjoyed, in
marked contrast to the situation during previous conflicts from the
American Revolution onward, a fairly considerable degree of support
among the populace at large, alongside much hostility of course to
what many still considered an unpatriotic stand. This support
mounted as war weariness grew and the conflict dragged on with
increasing loss of life and threat of ultimate defeat. "Before the mid-
1960s," to quote Chambers again, "the federal judiciary had generally
been quite willing to sentence draft violators to stiff prison terms. But
in the late 1960s juries became increasingly unwilling to convict, and
judges imposed reduced sentences on those convicted."[44] True, selective conscientious objection remained unrecognized while unconditional exemption did not exist for any type of objector (these
concessions, however, had existed under British law). Nevertheless the
treatment of C.Os. during the Vietnam War, though sometimes harsh

especially if the objector's claims were not based on an accepted variety of religious pacifism, proved on the whole more liberal than during the two world wars of our century.

Notes

1 James Reston, as quoted in *Speak Truth to Power: A Quaker Search for an Alternative to Violence* (Philadelphia: American Friends Service Committee, 1955), p. viii.

2 George Orwell, *Shooting an Elephant and Other Essays* (London: Secker and Warburg, 1950), p. 111.

3 Mitchell L. Robinson, "'Healing the Bitterness of War and Destruction:' CPS and Foreign Service," *Quaker History* (Haverford, PA), vol. 85, no. 2 (Fall, 1996), p. 41. Especially the Quakers did their successful best to remove the "Starnes Rider" of 1943, which imposed this ban.

4 See Gretchen Lemke-Santangelo, "The Radical Conscientious Objectors of World War II: Wartime Experience and Postwar Activism," *Radical History Review* (New York), no. 45 (1989), pp. 5–29. The author selects Roy Kepler and James Peck as case studies for this development.

5 Conscription legislation was not reintroduced in West Germany until 1956, the year in which the draft began to be phased out in Britain.

6 For the vicissitudes of his influential, if unsystematic, anarcho-pacifism, see Stephen J. Whitfield, *A Critical American: The Politics of Dwight Macdonald* (Hamden, CT: Archon Books, 1984), pp. 73, 77, 84–90; Michael Wreszin, *A Rebel in Defense of Tradition: The Life and Politics of Dwight Macdonald* (New York: Basic Books, 1994), pp. 165, 192, 193, 196–8, 224, 234–7, 291–4, 519; Gregory D. Sumner, *Dwight Macdonald and the **politics** Circle: The Challenge of Cosmopolitan Democracy* (Ithaca and London: Cornell University Press. 1996), pp. 23, 87–99, 221, 222; and of course the files of his magazine *Politics* (New York, 1944–49). During the early years of the war Macdonald had not yet emerged from his Trotskyist phase. Cf. A.J. Muste's flirtation with Trotskyism. The two men, despite disagreements, continued to respect each other as they went their different ways. See also Penina Migdal Glazer, "From the Old Left to the New: Radical Criticism in the 1940s," *American Quarterly* (Philadelphia), esp. pp. 601, 602.

7 American pacifists condemned the Korean War almost unanimously. An exception was the distinguished Methodist theologian, Georgia Harkness, who felt her country was justified in taking military action in Korea as a police measure under United Nations auspices. Nevertheless she still retained a personal faith in pacifism; later she opposed the Vietnam war. See Rolaine Franz, "Georgia Harkness ... II. Theology and Ethics," p. 178 in

Paul Deats and Carol Robb, eds., *The Boston Personalist Tradition in Philoso-phy, Social Ethics, and Theology* (Macon, GA: Mercer University Press, 1986). Harkness's position in 1950 in many ways resembles that of Lord Allen of Hurtwood in Britain in the 1930s; see chap. IV above. Andrew Cordier is another example of this kind of thinking. Although previously active in the peace work of his Church of the Brethren, he held a highly responsible post in the United Nations Secretariat throughout the Korean War. See the *Breth-ren Encyclopedia* (Philadelphia and Oak Brook, IL), vol. 1 (1983), pp. 343, 344.

  8 Lawrence S. Wittner, *Rebels against War: The American Peace Movement, 1933–1983* (Philadelphia: Temple University Press, 1984), chaps. VI–VIII, deal competently with developments in the USA. The first volume, reaching through 1953, of Wittner's projected 3-volume history of the world nuclear disarmament movement, *The Struggle against the Bomb* (Stanford University Press, 1993), includes discussion of the part played in the movement by pacifists from various countries. The second volume covering the period from 1954 to 1970, entitled *Resisting the Bomb*, appeared at the end of 1997; it also discusses *inter alia* the pacifist role in the antinuclear movement. When completed, the trilogy is likely to remain for a long time the most compre-hensive study of the subject.

  9 Richard Taylor, in his *Against the Bomb: The British Peace Movement 1958–1963* (Oxford: Clarendon Press, 1988), has given an extremely thorough account of the British nuclear disarmament movement. However his focus is more on the relationship of CND to the Labour Party than on the role of pacifists, which perhaps he underestimates.

10 L. John Collins, *Faith under Fire* (London: Leslie Frewin, 1966), p. 268.

11 Stephen King-Hall, *Defence in the Nuclear Age* (London: Victor Gollancz, 1958), p. 14.

12 *Ibid.*, p. 173.

13 Hugo Adam Bedau, "On Civil Disobedience," *The Journal of Philosophy* (Lancaster, PA), vol. 58 (1961), no. 21, p. 657.

14 Alan Lovell, "Direct Action?" *New Left Review* (London), March–April 1961, p. 24.

15 Frank Earle Myers, "British Peace Politics: The Campaign for Nuclear Dis-armament and the Committee of 100, 1957–1962" (Ph.D. diss., Columbia University, 1965), p. 154.

16 Quoted in William Robert Miller, *Nonviolence: A Christian Interpretation* (New York: Association Press, 1964), p. 78.

17 Ralph Schoenman, "Mass Resistance in Mass Society," in David Boulton, ed., *Voices from the Crowd: Against the H-Bomb* (London: Peter Owen, 1964), p. 110.

18 Harriet Hyman Alonso, *Peace as a Women's Issue: A History of the U.S. Move-*

ment for World Peace and Women's Rights (Syracuse: Syracuse University Press, 1993), pp. 243, 244.

19 See Jo Ann Ooiman Robinson's perceptive biography of Muste, *Abraham Went Out* (Philadelphia: Temple University Press, 1981), pp. 93ff.

20 Roy Finch, "The New Peace Movement," *Dissent* (New York), vol. 10, no. 1 (Winter, 1963), p. 89. Italics in the original.

21 See Albert Bigelow, *The Voyage of the Golden Rule: An Experiment with Truth* (Garden City, NY: Doubleday & Company, 1959).

22 See Earle Reynolds, *The Forbidden Voyage* (New York: David McKay Company, 1961).

23 Michael Randle, in his excellent study of *Civil Resistance* (London: Fontana Press, 1994), pp. 80–86, 225, 226, surveys the course of this type of nonviolent action against war.

24 See Bradford Lyttle, *You come with Naked Hands: The Story of the San Francisco to Moscow March for Peace* (Raymond, NH: Greenleaf Books, n.d.).

25 From a report by Lyttle in Staughton Lynd, ed., *Nonviolence in America: A Documentary History* (Indianapolis: Bobbs-Merrill Co., 1966), p. 367.

26 David Dellinger in Paul Goodman, ed., *Seeds of Liberation* (New York: George Braziller, 1964), pp. 165, 166.

27 We should note that the black radical pacifist, Bayard Rustin, who at this date was moving toward a centrist position, advised King to keep the civil rights and the Vietnam War issues entirely separate. To criticize the Democratic administration and prowar liberal and labor leaders, Rustin argued, would seriously harm the cause of civil rights. But King did not follow this advice and in his last years spoke out decisively against the war. See James Tracy, *Direct Action: Radical Pacifism from the Union Eight to the Chicago Seven* (Chicago and London: University of Chicago Press, 1996), pp. 129–33.

28 For a discussion of the issues involved here, see Gordon C. Zahn, *War, Conscience and Dissent* (New York: Hawthorn Books, 1967), pp. 192–6: "The Martyr – Saint or Suicide?" Typical perhaps was the reaction of the radical WRL pacifist, David McReynolds: "While not agreeing with the action, I had profound respect for it." In Melvin Small and William D. Hoover, eds., *Give Peace a Chance: Exploring the Vietnam Antiwar Movement* (Syracuse: Syracuse University Press, 1992), p. 55.

29 *The Draft?* (New York: Hill and Wang for the Peace Education Division of the American Friends Service Committee, 1968), p. 27.

30 For the text of the Supreme Court's decision, see Robert T. Miller and Ronald B. Flowers, eds., *Toward Benevolent Neutrality: Church, State and the Supreme Court*, 3rd edn. (Waco, TX: The Markham Press Fund of Baylor University Press, 1992), pp. 124–32. Yet the decision was possibly not quite so liberal as that of the Second Circuit Court of Appeals in 1943 in the Kauten case; see chapter V above.

31 For a perceptive discussion of the subject, see especially Ralph Potter, "Conscientious Objection to Particular Wars," pp. 44–99 in Donald A. Gianella, ed., *Religion and the Public Order*, No. 4 (Ithaca, NY: Cornell University Press, 1968).

32 *The Draft?* (AFSC), p. 33.

33 They felt it sufficient, however, for the time being to say, as in the words attributed to the founder of Quakerism, George Fox, in conversation with the young William Penn: "Wear [thy sword] as long as thou canst."

34 The author of a recent historical survey of the subject concludes: "The concerns of the selective conscientious objector ought to be legally recognized, not because an exemption is granted to the pacifist, but because it is the right thing to do in a democratic society that is respectful of its members' religious commitments." Joseph E. Capizzi, "Selective Conscientious Objection in the United States," *Journal of Church and State* (Waco), vol. 38, no. 2 (Spring, 1996), p. 363. For the Vietnam era, see pp. 347–57.

35 Edward R. Cain, "Conscientious Objection in France, Britain, and the United States," *Comparative Politics* (Chicago), vol. 2, no. 2 (January 1970), pp. 301–3.

36 Charles DeBenedetti, *An American Ordeal: The Antiwar Movement: of the Vietnam Era* (Syracuse: Syracuse University Press, 1990), p. 166.

37 Cain, *op. cit.*, p. 303.

38 For the text of the decision in the Welsh case, see Miller and Flowers, eds., *op. cit.*, pp. 132–7.

39 Charles C. Moskos and John Whiteday Chambers II, eds., *The New Conscientious Objection: From Sacred to Secular Resistance* (New York: Oxford University Press, 1993), p. 41 (from essay by Chambers). For Boardman, see his "Letter to Local Board No. 114" (1967), pp. 178–86 in Bedau, ed., *Civil Disobedience: Theory and Practice* (New York: Pegasus, 1969), and for Rensberger, see below chap. X.

40 Willard Gaylin, *In the Service of Their Country: War Resisters in Prison* (New York: The Viking Press, 1970), pp. 41, 42. The core of this book by a sympathetic psychoanalyst comprises extended interviews with six anonymous prisoners of conscience, "gentle felons" as the author calls them. The quotation is from one of his interviews with "C-42893: Matthew [Morris]."

41 *Ibid.*, pp. 225–7. From an interview with "O-70296: John." For the experiences of imprisoned Vietnam War resisters – and their families who often endured hardship too – see Lawrence M. Baskir and William A. Strauss, *Chance and Circumstance: The Draft, the War, and the Vietnam Generation* (New York: Alfred A. Knopf, 1978), pp. 102–8. They point out that "a draft offender's prison experience depended largely on where he was sent" (p. 103), since treatment of inmates differed greatly from one category of penal institution to another.

42 Baskir and Strauss, op. cit., pp. 107, 108. "Almost every kid in this country
[was] either a draft evader, a potential draft evader, or a failed draft
evader" (from testimony by William Wick before the 1974 House Amnesty
Hearings, quoted in *ibid.*, p. 12).

43 Moskos and Chambers, *op. cit.*, pp. 42–45. See also DeBenedetti, *op. cit.*,
pp. 308, 309.

44 Moskos and Chambers, *op. cit.*, p. 41. Before that time three to five year sentences had been not infrequent. According to Baskir and Strauss, *op. cit.*, pp.
104, 105: "As a general rule, federal parole boards treated draft resisters
well. Most [spent] six to twelve months in prison, less than half their original terms. There were exceptions: Richard Duvall of New Orleans was
imprisoned for four years, most of it in maximum security at Terre Haute."
The authors note, too, that jailed draft resisters "were often denied participation in work-release or rehabilitation programs, the common excuse
being that they did not need rehabilitation" (p. 103).

VIII. Pacifism and War Resistance: The Cold War Years, Part 2

Pacifists and Wars of National Liberation: The Case of Vietnam

The war in Vietnam in some respects imparted renewed vitality to the American pacifist movement. Antimilitarist sentiments, especially among the young and on college campuses, became widespread. Interest in conscientious objection, antimilitarism's classic form of expression in the countries embraced by the Anglo-American political tradition, replaced previous apathy or disdain. Organizations like the FOR (Fellowship of Reconciliation) expanded both in numbers and in range of activities as well as in outreach to new sections of the population.[1] True, "most of those who marched in huge antiwar demonstrations, if they thought about the question at all, would have counted themselves opponents of that particular war rather than wars in general. Only a tiny minority of protesters understood the principles of nonviolent resistance." The vast majority just wished for an end to the war. But they were ready to accept "the leadership of pacifists and other radicals" without bothering too much about their political views.[2]

Cleavages were soon revealed, however, within the pacifist camp (as in the wider peace movement). Over against those pacifists who remained profoundly sceptical of communist aims and sympathetic to the values found in the tradition of representative democracy, others supported a revolutionary stance and felt a certain kinship with "heroic forces like the Cuban Fidelistas and the Viet Cong," despite disagreement with these latter over means.[3] They felt, as sections of the pacifist left had done in the interwar years, that the choice was not simply between violence and nonviolence, but a much more complex one between violence used to promote a desirable social revolution and to ward off external attack, on the one hand, and violence serving to uphold an outmoded and unjust social order and to quash the aspirations of those seeking to change it, on the other. They perceived the forces opposing the American presence in Vietnam as engaged in a war of national liberation against an imperialist aggressor and its satellites. As the Quaker Staughton Lynd, who became one of the prophets of the New Left, expressed it: "Although I may be a personal pacifist, I am by no means of the opinion that both sides [in the Vietnam War] are equally guilty or that it is a matter of indifference how the struggle ends."[4] What is interesting is that Lynd saw the struggle as one between only two sides; yet there were at least three – the pacifist, neutralist and nonviolent Buddhists were, however, sometimes forgotten!

Pacifism and National Liberation[5]

It is doubtful whether a cult of armed violence and iconography of the heroic guerilla would have come to dominate the New Left as it did, or have been sustained as long as it was, had not the radical pacifists' position on wars of liberation crumbled during the 1960s. One can trace this capitulation back to the early years of the decade with the disarray of European pacifists over the war in Algeria. The loneliness of figures like Albert Camus in his refusal to endorse the FLN (Front de Libération Nationale), an isolation and detachment in the constrained context of the Algerian crisis little different from that of A.J. Muste faced by the Cold War balance of-terror, has many parallels with the situation of those later confronted by similar choices in relation to Vietnam in the mid-1960s. In the case of both the Algerian and Vietnam wars, the attempts to avoid the roles of victim or executioner became an anguished one. Camus could not choose the military revolution that he had condemned in his work, even against an oppression that he fully acknowledged. Opposing the torture of the "paras" and the terror of the FLN, he drew hostility and slander from both sides. His call for a civilian truce, as a gradualist and nonviolent solution to the Algerian bloodbath, won him few allies, just as the call for ceasefire and reconciliation in Vietnam later isolated nonaligned pacifists.

Nevertheless, the intellectual foundations of the New Left's position lie more in the analyses of Cuba in its first years of revolution (1959–61), e.g., by C. Wright Mills's *Listen Yankee* and in the pages of *Liberation* than in pure pacifism.[6] Exemplifying the ambiguous tightrope walked by American pacifists on Cuba, that Muste and a majority of the *Liberation* editors should have given qualified support to the Cuban revolution was perhaps understandable. It had after all been achieved with minimal bloodshed; and despite the later military images of the revolution, it was its very lack of protracted warfare that could explain the relatively libertarian elements of its first years. Before the Bay of Pigs, the revolution was still mildly nationalist and socialist; though indications of its authoritarian character existed, thoroughgoing Marxist dictatorship developed only later, and largely in response to American encirclement. However, this pragmatic stance, while it kept *Liberation* close to the mainstream of American radicalism, was a thin end of a wedge. If a violent military coup and political executions were acceptable in Cuba, why not elsewhere? Moreover, *Liberation*'s tendency to give Cuba's questionable actions the benefit of the doubt (it published far less criticism than some more explicitly socialist journals) contributed to popularizing a blanket endorsement of Castroism.

Ironically, support for the Cuban régime increased at the same time as the revolution reverted into a more unrelenting authoritarian pattern; this support partly represented a reaction against U.S. military pressure, partly the growing radical identification by the young New Left. From 1959, Cuba was an essential part of the American New Left experience (no "liberation war" came as close in the British experience) – the proximity of Cuba and the initial independence of Castroism made it model, magnet, and inspiration for young mainland revolutionaries. As they were to do subsequently on Vietnam, pacifist spokesmen like David Dellinger, Staughton Lynd, A.J. Muste, and David McReynolds gave prestige to a position on Cuba that came close enough to endorsement of armed struggle; only if they held line at this point, might there have been fewer openings in the movement to crude anti-imperialist, promilitarist positions.

That these occurred had a great deal to do with changing leadership roles within the absolute pacifist *Liberation* (see below), its entanglement with Students for a Democratic Society (SDS), and the latter's influence on New Left attitudes to the Vietnam war. Of those associated with the magazine, Muste, Lynd, and Dellinger and later even McReynolds, drifted away from all but an individually held pacifism in the critical years after Cuba; of the four, only Lynd, the least absolute to begin with, maintained some elements of genuine pacifist critique. *Liberation* itself flirted with the cult of violence surrounding both the Cuban revolution and the National Liberation Front (NLF) in Vietnam; and those caught up in this process, like Dellinger and McReynolds – who had initially espoused unconditional pacifism – moved away from it; Dellinger, for example, in 1965 significantly refers to the "heroic forces" both of the Fidelistas and of the Viet Cong.

Reactionary or oppressive roles by others than the United States

were increasingly and flagrantly ignored, as the growing anti-imperialism of SDS in turn reinforced these double-standard tendencies. Young
Tom Hayden, bridging SDS and *Liberation*, had also been at the outset
an adherent of nonviolence opposed to "militarism and nationalism."[7]
But he quickly and easily came to terms with both the miltarism and
nationalism of the NLF; the visits to Cuba and North Vietnam of mem-
brs of the *Liberation* group and of Hayden himself appeared to affirm
and take this identification one stage further.

It is ironic that it was this very dilution of their pacifism that was a
factor in enabling such formerly staunch pacifists around *Liberation*
(Muste, Dellinger, Lynd and McReynolds) to take decisive leadership
roles in the American peace movement during the following years.[8]
Muste's concern with "neutralization" of potential world flash points
led him naturally to urge a unilateral U.S. ceasefire in Vietnam, negotiations and reunification, independent of his general "Third Camp"
politics. Lynd's appearance in the leadership of an alliance of SDS and
Liberation, forming in 1965 the first major anti-Vietnam war coalition,
was a significant early inclication of this new development. While
most older pacifist groupings and traditional peace groups tended to
keep aloof from this SDS-initiated coalition, some Old Left groups,
such as the Socialist Workers' Party (SWP) with their slogan "Bring the
Boys Home Now," as well as Muste and other radical pacifists around
Liberation, joined.

Muste, having been involved with this initial Vietnam coalition
cluring 1965, by 1966 – and right up to his cleath at eighty-two in 1967
– was to play a leading role in both the National Co-ordinating
Committee against the War, and the Spring Mobilization Committee –
a mantle that was to pass on to the shoulders of Dellinger, Muste's
chief lieutenant. But no one walked the knife-edge closer than Lynd;
calling himself, we have seen, a "personal" pacifist, he made distinctions enabling him to adopt positions on the Vietnam war in which this
personal pacifism became highly selective, since it was not derived
from any overall political analysis of war and militarism but from his
personal religious preference.

Lynd's equivocation on the Vietnam war stemmed primarily from
the common belief that the USA was altogether more culpable than the
NLF, the North Vietnamese Army, and their allies. Thus the outcome of
the struggle was "not a matter of indifference." As a result he took a
stretcher-bearer attitude to one of the armies, maintaining that his personal pacifism would have been compatible, for instance, with noncombatant participation in a "just war" in the ranks of the NLF or the
North Vietnamese Army.

This standpoint, also adopted by several *Liberation* editors, endorsing both the "just war" thesis and a noncombatant role in that war, signified a position previously rejected by radical pacifists. Thus it left any antimilitarist analysis in tatters, and a truly pacifist movement virtually leaderless. This subsequently had enormous implications both for the Vietnam war movement itself and the New Left generally.

However, unlike some of his colleagues, Lynd did not thereby abandon all his critical senses in relation to the armed solutions of the NLF/North Vietnam, and he showed this in dissociating himself from the bias and selectivity of the War Crimes Tribunal when it refused to entertain substantial evidence of terror and atrocities by the NLF and the North Vietnamese Army. Lynd also insisted on sending medical aid to *all* civilians and combatants (unlike the Medical Aid Committees) and condemned terror on both sides. Even though he wrote that one should not "*absolutely* condemn revolutionary terror" (no reasoning given), he expressed at the same time the hope that American opponents of the war would react to torture by the NLF "exactly as to torture by the other side."[9] Nevertheless, the same kind of ambiguity, if not contradiction, that characterized Muste's position, was also evident in many of Lynd's utterances.

Muste, like the others, expressed a surprisingly simplistic view of the relationship between a nonviolent revolution and the attempted military revolution by some sections of the Vietnamese people. He almost implied that he and they might only differ over means. Yet Muste had, over the years, consistently criticized various revolutionaries and political sectarians for separating means and ends, or believing that after a military victory or after "the revolution" "things" would be different.

The *démarche*, which began with the *Liberation* pacifists and later briefly included the pacifist Jesuit, Daniel Berrigan, now accelerated, each new convert finding some reason for identification with the NLF, and only a few taking note of the non-NLF, non-communist resistance groups in Vietnam, such as the Buddhists. By 1966, Muste had clearly qualified his previously nonaligned and fairly consistent pacifist position, now elaborating on the Vietnam issue an apparently contradictory stance. On the one hand, he claimed that he still "rejected all war and organized violence regardless of who or what movement resorts to it," and that he did "not accept and condone violence on the part of any people, any group." On the other hand, he believed that a "distinction between the violence of liberation movements" (i.e., the NLF) and "imperialist" violence had to be made, allowing the pacifist to "support some who are engaged in violent action" because their violence was morally superior. Moreover, as he told a journalist at this time, "I think you have to be for the defeat of the United States in this war. I just don't see how anybody can be for anything except withdrawal and defeat."[10] The elusive distinction, between refusal to condone violence and yet willingness to support those who used it, laid the fatal, if ambiguous, foundations for a shift from an antimilitarist analysis into an anti-imperialist one. It was a drift that moved not only *Liberation*, but substantial sections of the movement, across Camus's "tragic dividing line," from pacifism to militarism.

This change of position was reflected in the evolution of two distinct policy positions on how the war could be brought to an end (as distinct from a third calling for an unambiguous NLF military victory – which few in the New Left, at this stage, were prepared to do).

The first, more general position was to call for a ceasefire with the slogan "Stop the Killing Now" and implied an agreed or unilateral cessation of military activity by the USA, pending withdrawal. The second position, taken by Lynd, Dellinger and McReynolds (and also by some anarchists in Britain) was that since the USA had no right to be in Vietnam it should just unilaterally withdraw, even if this led to an eventual end to the war by communist victory. This latter position either did not call for a ceasefire *at all*, or called for it only after unconditional troop withdrawal or an agreement to so withdraw. Though these subtleties were generally lost on the larger peace movement, it became clear that those who held out for unilateral and unconditional withdrawal by the USA without ceasefire gave overwhelming political and military advantage to a specific armed formation in taking over South Vietnam, with heavy support continuing from its big-power allies. The argument among pacifists centered on whether genuine pacifists could take positions either way, which actually meant the continuation of killing and thus implicit support for a military solution.[11]

The parallel argument over "realism" revolved around the question whether, on the one hand, the USA would in any case accept a withdrawal *without* a prior ceasefire, and whether, on the other, the NLF and the North Vietnamese would ever accept a ceasefire without agreement on withdrawal. This was of course eventually the nub of the Paris peace negotiations, but even before that, it provided a sort of watershed for the peace movement both in the West and in Vietnam itself.

It was the Resistance, alone among the antiwar groups and tendencies, that retained its morale, unity and integrity in this period of movement crisis. That was largely because it was rooted in undramatic, morally based, personal action and a nonviolent ethic. It combined mutual aid with individual responsibility and organization on the local level. It is significant, too, that, from the start, it felt little need of identification with a foreign military force, such as the NLF or North Vietnamese, and did not in fact concern itself with supporting their violence.

Yet it is a tragic irony that, despite potentially common identity, the Resistance failed to make stronger transnational links with those resisters in Vietnam closest to them in spirit and action, e.g., the young, militant, and neutralist Buddhists, often monks, using nonviolent techniques against successive Saigon régimes. Calling for immediate cease-fire, the "Third Way" monks, nuns and social workers encouraged draft resistance against both armies, refusing to fight themselves and sheltering thousands of deserters. Their fearless opposition to the militarism of both Saigon and Hanoi led often to fatal results: the destruction of pagodas, assassination and execution or mass imprisonment of Buddhist workers, or else wounding or involuntary exile.

Yet even Resistance leaders like Lynd, with his Quaker background and his long record of civil disobedience, failed to publicly identify with this thoroughgoing and massive antimilitarism by ordinary Vietnamese, and instead juggled with inaccurate formulae that seemed to endorse the "just struggle" of "the Vietnamese." That the Western anti-war movements failed to identify with these forces until it was far too late[12] can only partly be explained by their ignorance of these groups' existence and activities, and the fact that the National establishments and the Left establishment both presented the war as a simple dichotomy between polar military formations. It was also a symptom of the tragedy of nonviolence in the late 1960s[13] that these Vietnamese of similar style and politics should actually have been consistently excluded or eliminated from peace movement platforms in the West, or even accused of CIA links. (It is also true that they did not seek allies in the West in the early years before Tet, the communist "New Year" offensive in February 1968.)

In the origins of the New Left, both in Britain and America, radical pacifists had occupied influential positions and played key roles, but during the 1960s they were faced with the choice of either retaining influence at the expense of their pacifism (the case in the United States) or retaining their pacifism with a consequent loss of influence (the case in Britain). Had a nonviolent critique of the expansion of national liberation movements been developed early enough, things might have gone differently, not only in the peace movement, but in the New Left as a whole, including the black movement and political groups like SDS. But such was not the case: this theoretical vacuum as well as the deep compassion felt by pacifists for those suffering the rigors of colonial rule, or American bombardment, and the lack of effective nonviolent strategies to alleviate these situations, led to the typical defensive double standard position of many pacifists in the later 1960s: nonviolence at home, but tacitly endorsed "just" violence abroad.[14]

Radical Pacifism and the Genesis of the New Left

Themes like unilateral disarmament, individual and collective war resistance, a positive policy of nonalignment, had played a major role in the development of the British and American peace movements in the early 1960s. We find them, for instance, in the program of the short-lived but influential Student Peace Union (SPU) in the United States. The Union was founded in 1959 by Kenneth Calkins, an AFSC worker and member of both the FOR and the Socialist Party, and it adopted a pacifistic Statement of Purpose, even though its membership included Marxists as well as radical pacifists (some of these anarcho-pacifists). Transitional between the Old and the New Left, the SPU was a direct forerunner of American campus New Left groups. With its Third Camp, antimilitarist position, it broke through various Cold War apologetics advocating international initiatives independent of existing power blocs.

In 1961, 3000 – 8000 SPU members and sympathizers demonstrated in Washington against resumed testing – at both the Pentagon and the Soviet Embassy. In February 1962, 8000 protested at the White House; the SPU also attacked the fall-out shelter program as making nuclear war more likely by creating illusions of reduced casualties. In the early 1960s, the SPU had several thousand members and was closely linked with the Young People's Socialist League, the youth wing of the Socialist Party. Never very cohesive, the SPU soon broke apart; the decision to dissolve was taken in mid-1964. Nevertheless, as George Vickers writes, "at its peak the SPU reached thousands of American students with a radical analysis of the cold war and its implications that they might otherwise never have heard."[15]

It is indeed arguable that, both intellectually and politically, the continuity of certain themes central to the growth of the New Left was linked to the theoretical and actual developments of radical pacifism after the Second World War. Besides pure antimilitarism or a Third Camp peace position, other major themes included communitarian utopianism, direct action, decentralist anarchism, and nonviolent revolution. It is notable that SDS's founders shared a number of the anarchist-pacifist views of *Liberation* magazine, and even the "Beats," or early hippies, have been termed "radical pacifists" at base.[16]

In bringing these elements together, the first mass protest against the war in Vietnam took on the broader overtones of a movement against war in general; the songs and speeches ("We are here to keep faith with those of all countries and all ages who have sought to beat swords into ploughshares and war no more," Lynd) gave a distinctively pacifist tone to the early climax of the anti-Vietnam war movement.[17] In SDS, the notion of building a peace movement to prevent the "seventh war from now," the politics of the long-haul in full awareness of the power of U.S. militarism, enabled close cooperation with pacifist groups like the War Resisters' League (WRL) and the Committee for Non-Violent Action, which supported SDS's March on Washington. Despite a growing existential appreciation of the possibility that, as Norman O. Brown argued, in one sense war might never be abolished,[18] pacifism as an opposition to brutalized, depersonalized or authoritarian killing represented a definite if inchoate strain of utopianism, which remained part of the New Left throughout its period of growth.

The attempt at democratizing another sector of life – replacing national "defense" by popular "civilian" resistance – was symptomatic of this strain. Whether at the level of state or community, nonmilitary action represented a more participatory, grassroots approach to the problem of war, making it attractive to liberals as well as libertarians. As the Prague Spring of 1968 later showed, it could put the emphasis on those democratic and decentralized actions which minimized systematic brutality and destruction. A nonviolent or civilian resistance force would clearly represent less of an internally repressive threat than a normal military force; it had already in a few cases been turned successfully against military coups, or attempts at totalitarian takeover. But its main political advantage, from the New Left point of view, was the wider popular base of decision-making inevitably involved in taking over and breaking down the monopoly of violence held by the state.

Paul Goodman's pacifism was typical of the early New Left rejection of violence and aggression. It advocated expression rather than repression of violent impulses, but it rejected *weapons* (the technological extension of personal aggression) and *armies*: the social organization of violence as bureaucratic negation of personal aggression. War seemed an unnatural extension of aggression, combining bureaucracy and technology in the service of an authoritarian state, contradicting and repressing any natural community, thwarting creativity. Such activity was not spontaneous, but coercive and hierarchical.

The main activist civil rights groups in the USA were each from the outset committed to nonviolent action.[19] But despite the part played by radical pacifists in developing the struggle, the influence of Muste and Gandhi on King, and the role of Christian ideas of love and brotherhood in the Southern movement, nonviolence was adopted by the desegregationists for practical as much as for moral reasons. The civil disobedience strategy arose naturally and directly from Southern black experience; as well as providing a notable advantage, nonviolence faced the realistic consideration that "the whites had the guns" (Ralph Abernathy).[20] But the working principle of King's nonviolence, as we have seen in an earlier chapter, was an active and creative "truth-force," not merely a disruptive or passive "resistance of the weak." Such nonviolence, adopted by the early New Left, was rooted in principles of interpersonal transaction: "If men cannot refer to a common value, recognized by all as existing in each other, then man is incomprehensible to man."[21] This sentiment, appearing in the founding statement of SDS, echoes Camus's plea that humankind reflect on species murder.

It was Camus's humanism and nonviolence, rather than Gandhi's, which were enormously influential on the first generation of movement activists (e.g. Mario Savio, Bob Moses or Tom Hayden). There is hardly a New Left spokesman or leader in the early 1960s who does not quote him; at one climax of the FSM (Free Speech Movement) a speech, quoting Camus's appeal against hate and murder, cooled a near riot. And in this phase the endorsement of such an appeal comprehended all organized violence: from war and revolutionary terror to state executions. Indeed in the early 1960s, nonviolence went largely unchallenged in the movement and a humane optimism was predominant. For several years it was still possible to use the word "love" in SDS without provoking catcalls: love is referred to in speeches and political pamphlets; what the antiwar psychologist, Erich Fromm, aptly described as a "taboo on tenderness" had far from captured the New Left in 1965. Indeed when Fromm developed his critique of violence he helped assist the import of such words as "love" into the language of the early New Left and the counterculture. For example, the phrase "love of man" and the word "love" appear in several places in the Port Huron Statement, the founding manifesto of the New Left in America. Equally, the Students Nonviolent Coordinating Committee's statement of principle had, two years earlier in 1960, affirmed SNCC's belief in the "ideal of nonviolence" with "love" as its "central motif."[22]

The founders and rank and file of SDS were at first deeply influenced by such ethics; as Carl Oglesby said in 1965, "our best concern comes from SNCC."[23] That "best concern" was "to make love more possible. We work to remove from society what threatens and prevents

it." But though SNCC's opening statement was unequivocally committed to nonviolence, there was, we know, a wide range of attitudes
within it; nevertheless SNCC added new dimensions of resourceful-
ness and courage to the nonviolent tradition, and its formal commitment to this nonviolence was to last for six years, or two-thirds of its
organizational life.

In October 1963 Tom Hayden, Todd Gitlin, and three others from the
SDS leadership met in New York with editors of the "Old Left" *Dissent*,
including Irving Howe. The major topic over which the two generations clashed on this occasion was Cuba. Exasperated in particular by
Hayden's arguments, Howe responded: "How can you be in favor of
Castro, who speaks of exporting revolution to South America, and
then also be in favor of nonviolence?" Gitlin, later, thought he could
resolve this seeming contradiction by supposing that "Hayden was
inspired by, and loyal to, the handfuls of students who had succeeded
in making history, whether through sitting-in at southern lunch
counters or storming the Moncada barracks in Cuba."

At the time however, Gitlin tells us:

The debate about Cuba left no imprint on me. What has stuck in my mind is
another moment: Hayden expounding the pure Gandhian theory of nonviolence – the idea that loving your enemy while suffering his violence not only
changes society but redeems the enemy himself. You had to love everyone,
Hayden insisted, in the voice of his southern experience. To me, this was Hayden at his most eloquent, the New Left at its most stirring. The question wasn't
academic; Hayden was wrestling with this question because around that time
his draft board was interrogating him about the absoluteness of his nonviolence. What I remember most vividly is Howe, the hard-nailed disbeliever,
sneering: "Could you love a fascist, Tom?" Backed into a corner, Tom insisted
he could indeed. Howe, aghast, declared that he couldn't love Hitler.[24]

In their acts of nonviolent resistance, early New Leftists claimed they
drew a line beyond which they refused to cooperate, affirming values,
beyond that line, which they endorsed. Like Camus's "man" in revolt,
by saying no, they were also saying yes. As a counterpart to the affirmative aspect of Goodman's anarchism, there was what he called
"drawing the line":[25] resisting the encroachments of technocracy and
the state on the individual, or the production of one-dimensional persons by a knowledge factory. In the often quoted words of one of
the FSM leaders (Mario Savio) before the final sit-in at Berkeley on
2 December 1964, in such an institution "the operation of the machine
becomes so odious ... that you've got to put your bodies upon the

gears, and upon the wheels, upon the levers, upon all the apparatus and you've got to make it stop. And you've got to indicate to the people who run it ... that unless you're free, the machine will be prevented from working at all."[26]

An outraged, often apolitical moralism was a fundamental characteristic of the early movement; Camus's appeal to choice, Muste's demand that the political and the normative be reunited; King's insistence that love be brought to bear on political institutions and struggles – all helped reinforce the movement's belief that what Buber had called "the ploughshare of the normative principle" must be "driven into the hard soil of political reality." In Britain, like Muste the political scientist, Ronald Sampson, contributed much the same uncompromising moral attack on the structures of power.[27]

That a political disillusionment with liberalism could take place demonstrated the immense idealism and moralism of the early New Left: "The best of the young take the proclaimed values of their elders with a seriousness which leads them to be appalled by their violation in practice."[28] The establishment's moral indifference, even cynicism, stood as a significant counterpoint to the idealism of the early protests and their calls for a moral opposition. Within the established version of politics, "ethics is subordinate to strategy" (Muste). It was therefore necessary to break out of the language and behavior pattern of a "corrupt political universe;" this "moral politics" demanded a refusal to acquiesce in violent structures, a persistent nonconformity with the state, a "holy disobedience" ranging from tax refusal to conscientious objection, or even to more assertive nonviolent acts.[29]

With the evolution of the peace and civil rights movements in the USA nationally, only the draft resistance movement developed the kind of character and integrity that typified localized, community-based responses to the war – as in the years of action against weapons shipments at Port Chicago in California.[30] The Resistance attempted, we know, with remarkable success, to combine local moral solidarity and example with practical noncooperation and mutual aid.

Theory and Practice

The widespread "existentialism" of the early New Left was filtered almost exclusively through such literary and political writings as those of Camus, whose most influential book, *The Rebel* (*L'homme révolté*, 1951), contains hints of a novel synthesis of anarchist politics, direct action, and existential revolt. Camus's emphasis was on personal choice (victim or executioner?) and decision, in a world in which choice and decision seemed the property of impersonal structures and administrative or technical processes; it lay at the base of the renewed determination to repossess such powers.

But the New Left read in Camus's "rebellion" a mystical stress on the act, rather than a presentation of personal and symbolic choice. Thus his lone literary and philosophical stance could be bent into service as justification for running battles with institutionalized power, continuous protest, and an individual confrontation with authority, that was the essence of the student revolt and the first movement projects. With a movement to identify with, Camus too might have been able to stand more clearly for a third way, and thus identify publicly and positively his "rebellion." As it was, his stance had appeared at the time a lone and anguished gesture of despair; unlike Muste, Camus was unable to accept or overcome political isolation and enforced detachment.[31] Only when linked to actions, however small or symbolic, do such stances and ideas seem to have any connection with reality. Thus it is such actions that are the preface to a theory, and are central to its identity. Subsequent debates about "praxis" led many to question whether the real breakthroughs that led to the birth of the New Left were in the realm of theory or rather in that of practice.

Most of the writers whose ideas first filtered through to the new activists, directly or indirectly, in leaflet, speech, quotation, slogan or conversation, stressed many common themes in relation to this synthesis; the need to reconnect the personal and the systemic, the moral and the political, is a concern running through the work of Mills the sociologist and Camus the political moralist,[32] the social psychology of Fromm, and the direct-action pacifism of Muste.

The stress on individual moral responsibility for action, uppermost in the early direct action against the bomb, in the freedom rides and later the draft resistance movement, provided the deep foundations of moral resource upon which much of the early opposition to the Vietnam war was constructed.[33]

The New Left's reaction to ideology was not merely existential rejection, it was located in a suspicion of theory divorced from fact; "if the facts do not support our theories so much the worse for the theories" (Savio). While a few broke through the ensuing consensus, which emphasized "praxis" and proof through action, with words and ideas alone,[34] others spoke almost exclusively by their deed.[35] Perhaps those who were most influential were leaders like Muste, King, Lynd, Dellinger or Hayden – also Russell in England – who merged words *with* deeds; for their own acts and ideas became fused with collective action.

Although this utopian activism of the American New Left was often tentative and experimental in character, it was generally more success-ful than its English counterpart in closing the gap between professed ideals and everyday activity. The litmus test of the quality of an ideo-logy became whether its proponents acted in terms of it, i.e., did they act it out *personally*? For, it was urged, the "truth we discover affects the lives we lead."[36] For the New Left, living one's beliefs became essen-tial, living like the poor, acting as "anarchistically as possible," or embodying the "new man" in one's action.[37]

Thus, moral authority in the movement rested not only in the ability to translate theory into easily understood formulae and proposals for political action, but also, as with Lynd, a personal unwillingness to allow oneself or others to separate this intellectualizing from practical activity. Lynd continually lived these theories whether in democratic participation, civil disobedience, or communitarianism. Such "Do-it-Yourself-Politics" was, in Paul Goodman's words, the "painfully American answer."

Goodman indeed was, in this tradition, a pragmatic utopian; the innovation of social hypotheses must become translated into social experiment – a form of theory-testing in a social context. As an exam-ple, Goodman threw himself into the draft-resistance movement in the last years of his life; the domineering state must be thwarted when it demanded its sacrifice of the young. At the center of his draft-resis-tance work was the idea of complicity – his own and that of others of his generation with the acts of the draft-card burners and the noncoop-erators with the draft.

This was an idea that deeply appealed to the university radicals who had experienced the action-distanced academicism of their more lib-eral heroes; Goodman was on the streets, his body on the line, mixing with the demonstrators. Yet he also contributed an element of rigorous thought and analysis to balance the cynicism bred of their rejection of academic withdrawal. He understood this rejection, which often amounted to anti-intellectualism, but opposed its renunciation of the worth of ideas. At the same time he opposed beaucratic centralization and mindless technology and refused to take much about the modern world for granted.

Most influential of all perhaps in this context was the Port Huron Statement, even though its ideas were borrowed. A synthesis of ideas from Mills, Fromm, Goodman, Camus, *Liberation*'s critique of society, and the democratic socialist Michael Harrington's recently revealed evidence about American poverty, it implied general support for the spreading revolution against injustice. In it the "civilized barbarism" of

America, invisible to the majority and protected from attack, is seen as beset by issues – war, militarism, racism, alienation and above all poverty, which the young founders of SDS saw liberalism as powerless to deal with.

Pacifism, the New Left, and the Vietnam War

In 1966, both SNCC and SDS had issued statements entirely uncritical of the "other side" (also referred to as "forces for liberation"). From then on, an increasingly one-sided view of the war developed, which concealed the deep contradiction between, for example, support for participatory democracy at home, and support of indisputably authoritarian régimes and movements abroad – formations that were quite clearly not dedicated to the principle of "let the people decide." In the long run, this identification helped not only to undermine the belief in participatory democracy, but also to tempt many to jump out of the frying pan of U.S. imperialism into the fire of a new oppositional Stalinism, even though, early on, the New Left had categorically rejected that ideology.

Thus almost from the start, criticism of the Vietnam war by the New Left almost always excluded critiques of authoritarian leftism. One of the left social democrats critical of SDS – Bayard Rustin – characterized prophetically the Lynd-SDS coalition of 1965 as being one between those giving covert, and those giving explicit, support to the NLF.

In 1965, SDS went so far as to vote to remove any antitotalitarian statements or criticism of the NLF from its constitution, and restrict its criticism to the policy of the USA. From this moment, SDS's attack on "anti-Communism," as Tom Kahn pointed out, failed to differentiate between criticism of, for example, the NLF by democratic libertarian socialists, and criticism by people in the establishment or on the far Right.[38]

The New Left failed in this context to create criteria by which to judge either the ideas or the methods of such movements and régimes. The very word or concept "totalitarianism" was rejected because of its previous deployment as a Cold War term. New Left leaders also argued, with some substance, that since Communism did not form an organized force in American politics, then domestically the question of pro- or anti-Communism was irrelevant. But while in domestic terms this was probably true, in international terms, particularly in relationship to Hanoi and the NLF, and to a lesser degree China and Cuba and Russia, it created deep ideological ambiguity.

The New Left's precipitate descent into propaganda, largely born out of compassion and frustration, was partly based on the felt need to counterbalance biased information with slanted material on the other side. The newspeak of "people's war" would probably have been challenged by the early New Left; however, by the later 1960s such formulae were not. Consideration of third or fourth choices in Vietnam (i.e., involving the millions of progressive Buddhists and others) was thus discounted. The majority disappeared, as in other wars, between two forces, two propaganda machines. Much of the New Left consequently became aligned with one of them as a lesser evil,[39] purveying images, symbols and slogans direct from Vietnamese materials, and making any balanced or accurate view of the war increasingly elusive.

The antiwar movement came to accept an imagery of the war drawn from the early 1960s, of a popular, spontaneous, and decentralized "struggle," in which the NLF and the "people of Vietnam" were synonymous, and preserved it long after the reality had become totally transformed. Indeed there was plenty of evidence around, even in the early 1960s, to suggest that Ho Chi Minh's régime (like the NLF) probably possessed one of the more brutalized and repressive, as well as highly bureaucratized, leaderships in the history of Communism. Its strong links to Stalin and Stalinism in the past, and its reproduction of Stalinist ideals and models in the present were beyond doubt.

Rather than allow the original illusion to be shattered, however, the "David and Goliath" imagery of the Vietnamese war was maintained, enabling Western radicals to identify with an Asian pygmy struggling against the imperialist giant. This version of the war, e.g., an ill-equipped peasantry brutally oppressed and spontaneously struggling against monstrous odds, documented by pictures of black pyjamas and old rifles pitted against long-range artillery and napalm, projected an "underdog" image which went down well with the New Left and liberals alike. At one point, significantly, Lynd used the extraordinary phrase "the oppression of Vietnamese guerrillas."

The myth springing from all this, that the struggle was a spontaneous, mass-based upsurge against Saigon and the USA, that half-a-million troops of the most advanced military-industrial power were stalemated by popular heroism, obscured the tragic reality of a North Vietnamese numerical superiority on the ground enabling an appallingly profligate use of life in combat (almost as careless as the communists in Korea); indeed it was essentially the *pattern of control* – over masses of men and resources – that had emerged North and South, which was able to meet and check American power on its own terms. Although at hideous cost, the growing political infrastructure and expanding industrial and armed strength of the North, together with substantial Eastern-bloc aid, reinforced the immense organizational effort in the South, and marked the increasingly "conventional" nature of the struggle. The guerrilla armies, far from the romantic image of decentralized spontaneity, turned out to be small versions of the military machines of the great empires, East and West – carefully wrought bureaucratic, military apparatuses.

Thus the image (never, even at the outset, the whole truth) was overtaken by the reality of the increasing conventionalization of the war. Imagery of this kind had depended on a notion of voluntary, majority support and sympathy for military struggle; after 1968, and probably a good deal earlier, evidence to sustain this was lacking. But many in the New Left seemed unwilling to relinquish an idealized image of the NLF.

Such a departure from reality would not have happened if pacifists and libertarians in the movement had not capitulated to propagandized versions of the war. The pronouncements by Dellinger, McReynolds, Hayden and Noam Chomsky in particular, made it possible (even Muste's early visit to North Vietnam was easy to misinterpret). Growing shame and anger over Vietnam provided the context for this but did not constitute an excuse.

The American Pacifist Impulse and Vietnam

American pacifists, opposed on principle to all wars, had united with nonpacifist opponents of this particular war, including the New Left, in condemning American intervention in Vietnam. They could scarcely have remained pacifists if they had not done so. They were appalled by the "horror of Vietnam" and the role of their country in bringing this about. In prosecuting a barbarous war the administration betrayed values that were deeply rooted in the American tradition; resisting it pacifists acted, they believed, "in the service of their country" (W. Gaylin). And if this was politics, it could not be helped; they had an obligation to raise their voices against the continuing bloodshed, including the de-struction of innocent civilians. As a Protestant theologian wrote some years later, "pacifism by its very nature is a form of politics, not ... merely the private expression of certain people's individual convictions." Pacifist witness, especially in wartime, may well lead to "tension with the surrounding political order."[40]

Looking back on his experiences as a war resister in World War I Britain, Bertrand Russell recalled how some of his fellow pacifists had "made out such a good case for the German Government that they embarrassed German pacifists, who were trying to persuade *their* public that the faults were not all on *our* side."[41] *Mutatis mutandis*, the same could unfortunately be said of the radical pacifist allies of the New Left we have discussed in the previous sections. Yet there were many pacifists who refused to justify violence whatever the pretext and upheld nonviolence unconditionally; some of them were unaffiliated, others held membership in the FOR, the country's major pacifist society, or in the smaller WRL.[42] While, like all mainstream pacifists they had roots in the Social Gospel tradition, even when they did not consider themselves religious, and were mostly sympathetic to socialist ideals and anti-imperialism, they remained sensitive to political persecution wherever this took place and even when it occurred under a régime which represented, its supporters claimed, an egalitarian and just society.

Alfred Hassler, jailed World War II objector and executive secretary of the FOR until mid-1974, presented their position in a memo dated August 1968:

We do not judge here the merits of the respective claims of the two sides. There are legitimate issues involved with which Christians and all those concerned for peace must deal: issues of land reform, exploitation, corruption in government, the right of a people to choose its own government without outside interference, the right of individuals to security in the free expression of opinion. We appeal to both sides, in the name of their common humanity, to stop the fighting. The negotiation of differences must take place sometime; let it take place now, before more lives are blotted out, more homes and villages destroyed, more communities embittered and impoverished.[43]

Hassler, while accepting "nonexclusionism" as a tactic provided pacifists made their total rejection of violence clear to the New Left participants in antiwar rallies and demonstrations, refused to mute protest against communist persecution of political, in this case neutralist, opponents when evidence became available.[44] The FOR organ. *Fellowship*, included articles expressing dismay at such developments and support for a Buddhist "Third Force" in Vietnam as a reconciling element in the divided country. As Hassler wrote in July 1968: "whatever the decency of their ultimate goals, the NLF, the North Vietnamese government, and their predecessor, the Viet Minh, have been ruthless in their suppression of dissent, ruthless in their destruction of nationalist political groupings, who were their allies against the French, ruthless in the use of terror and murder to achieve victory."[45]

Toward the end of the sixties and during the early seventies the FOR witnessed a prolonged, and at times bitter, debate between radical pacifists close to the New Left and moderates (purists one might perhaps call them), who feared that pacifism was being diluted as a result of the latter's qualified support of revolutionary violence and wars of liberation. Controversy, perhaps in the circumstances somewhat theoretical, revolved, in particular, around the question of how to end the war: by a negotiated settlement or by an immediate and unconditional withdrawal of U.S. forces. In 1971 the FOR National Council called for mutual toleration of contradictory viewpoints.[46]

One would obtain, however, a distorted view of the wartime FOR if one focused only on the policy debates, which occupied a prominent position in its paper *Fellowship* and among its staff and leading activists. The organization, along with other antiwar groups, spent much time and energy in draft counseling, for instance, helping both draftees with religious or ethical objections to fighting and "selective" war resisters; see chapter VII. Between July 1965 and July 1970 the organization sent three Study Teams to South Vietnam, fact-finding missions that included nonpacifists as well as pacifists. In a statement on reaching home, the first of these missions had deplored "the way in which major powers have used and are using the villages of Vietnam as a testing ground for ideological positions such as 'wars of national liberation' or 'containment of communism by military force.'"[47] This attempt to stand "above the battle" reflects the spirit which did not cease to animate the wartime Fellowship, despite the flirting with revolutionary violence while keeping a thin veneer of pacifist sentiment, which prevailed among some of its prominent members, and the New Left terminology that continued to find its way into many FOR statements.[48]

The Vietnam War was a traumatic experience for the FOR as it was for the country as a whole. The Fellowship emerged intact from this "American ordeal," still pledged to nonviolence though severely shaken by the years of internal controversy and external pressures through which it had passed. Tensions, however, did not disappear with the eventual coming of peace, for the underlying problems that had caused them continued. The FOR, all pacifists indeed inside America and outside, were condemned to walk a tight-rope between the demands of peace, social and economic justice, and human rights as well as of the newly emergent requirements for an ecologically balanced world: a feat, we have seen, they were not always able to perform with entire success. The problem of human rights, for instance, persisted in Vietnam, now united under communist rule, and even more acutely in neighboring Kampuchea (Cambodia), the scene of many atrocities committed by the Pol Pot régime, as well as in areas of

Latin America and the Caribbean, particularly Castro's Cuba and Nicaragua after the Sandinistas came to power there.

Among those pacifists protesting vehemently against human-rights
abuses perpetrated by the communist rulers of Vietnam was the folksinger, Joan Baez. In May 1979 she obtained the signatures, among a
number of others, of Bradford Lyttle, Staughton Lynd, and Daniel
Berrigan on an "Open Letter to the Socialist Republic of Vietnam,"
protesting such abuses, which she inserted as an ad in a number of
national newspapers. Dellinger and McReynolds were among those
refusing to sign; for this Baez branded them as "guilt-ridden stooges
of the Hanoi regime."[49] With respect to Latin America the FOR and
the WRL viewed with alarm signs of growing militarism in Cuba and
in Nicaragua after the Sandinista revolution as well as the failure of
these régimes to allow conscientious objection to military service even
in a noncombatant capacity; at the same time they strongly condemned American intervention in this area,[50] a phenomenon dating
back into the last century and, since then, the object of uninterrupted
criticism from the American left, including the pacifist societies. Once
again, pacifists, including the FOR, did not always succeed in preserving a balance between peace and social justice, on one hand, and
the requirements of freedom and human rights, on the other. Yet the
issues here were complex, the right and the wrong not easy to deter-
mine.

"In what Communist country are human rights not violated? Do
you know of any?" asked Charles Bloomstein of a fellow pacifist.[51]
American pacifism during the Vietnam War – and the continuing Cold
War – would have avoided at least some of the mistakes made by
adherents if all of them had asked themselves this question and
answered it honestly after examining the evidence available. What
they could not be required to do was to whitewash their own side, or
to refrain from condemnation of the violence and barbarism with
which the U.S. government pursued its policies in Vietnam – and elsewhere – and of that government's diplomatic and military support of a
corrupt régime in the South, or not to call for an end to hostilities at the
earliest feasible date. Opposition to the draft carried on in a spirit of
nonviolence, including the encouragement of all sincere draft resisters
and a call to end conscription of any sort, belonged indubitably in the
tradition of liberal pacifism. There was indeed no logical reason, either,
to ask pacifists to abandon their support for social goals because the
communist "enemy" was attempting to realize these in practice (or at
any rate claimed to be doing so). None of these things constituted a
"betrayal" of pacifism, an illegitimate politicization of what some

claimed was properly an unpolitical – and politically innocuous – faith. Where the radical pacifists, who followed the revolutionary program of the New Left in everything except an acceptance of violence on the personal level, went astray was surely in their whitewashing of the violence of the "other side", including unrestricted forms of warfare and the suppression of civil liberties, and human rights in general, even for those, like the progressive Vietnamese Buddhists, who strove – in vain – to stand above the battle lines and bring about a negotiated settlement in their country.

But American pacifism survived. The conflict in Vietnam, of course, affected pacifists and the whole transnational peace movement with analogous effects everywhere. In the United States, we have seen, the older religious-ethical conscientious objection, which rejected wars of every sort, became submerged in a different type of conscientious objection, more secular in its inspiration and "selective" rather than absolutist in its premises. We must now turn to the "new" conscientious objection as it manifested itself cluring this period in other parts of the world.

Notes

1 The FOR, for example, reported that a third of the monthly intake of new members were Catholics, "including many priests and nuns": elements that hitherto had been largely unreceptive to the pacifist message. See chap. XI below.

2 Maurice Isserman, "The Irony of American Pacifism," *Peace and Change* (Kent, OH) vol. 11, no 3/4 (1986), p. 60. Isserman's essay reappeared in chap. IV of his book on the origins of the New Left, *If I had a Hammer ... : The Death of the Old Left and the New Left* (New York: Basic Books, 1987).

3 David Dellinger, quoted in James Finn, *Protest: Pacifism and Politics* (New York: Random House, 1967), p. 214.

4 *Ibid.*, p. 225. Italics in the original. Lynd went on to say that, if he were a citizen of a country whose cause he deemed just, he would participate in the struggle, though as a noncombatant.

5 This and the two following sections are drawn almost entirely from Nigel Young, *An Infantile Disorder? The Crisis and Decline of the New Left* (London and Henley: Routledge and Kegan Paul, 1977).

6 See Dellinger in Paul Goodman, ed., *Seeds of Liberation* (New York: George Braziller, 1964), pp. 201 ff.

7 E.g., in the Port Huron Statement; see below, note 21.

8 As well as A.J. Muste, Dellinger, Lynd and McReynolds, the *Liberation*

group also included Paul Goodman, Barbara Deming, Sidney Lens, Nat Hentoff, Mulford Sibley and (until 1966) Bayard Rustin, who were all more sceptical of the Cuban and Vietnamese revolutions. It also maintained contact with older socialists like Erich Fromm, Norman Thomas, and Irving Howe; as well as with the younger Leftists from SDS, like Tom Hayden. McReynolds, initially critical of Communism and totalitarianism, was pragmatic and even reformist (he once lined up with Rustin); yet he seems to have shifted the most sharply on these issues.

 9 See Lynd in Finn, ed., *op. cit.*, pp. 223 ff. Presumably Lynd meant here that he would not "absolutely" condemn either side.

10 Quoted in Jo Ann Ooiman Robinson's biography of Muste, *Abraham Went Out* (Philadelphia: Temple University Press, 1981), p. 172. Robinson comments: "the care with which Muste avoided censuring the violence practised by the victims of U.S. actions was striking."

11 Since 1945, pacifism had undoubtedly found itself profoundly compromised by successive wars of liberation; faced by the armed strategies of the FLN in Algeria, of Fidel Castro and Che Guevara, the Biafran and other African military struggles, Bangladesh, the Palestinian guerrillas, and the IRA in Northern Ireland, etc., pacifists did not always give a clearly nonviolent response. In this last case the arguments around the "British Withdrawal" campaign ran somewhat parallel to those on the Vietnam issue, i.e., simple withdrawal *vs.* ceasefire and negotiated withdrawal.

12 Daniel Berrigan and the FOR both strongly identified with the Buddhists (see below). But only at a late stage did such identification become widespread in the peace movement. (Adam Roberts, though, had advocated this even in the early 1960s in the pages of the British *Peace News.*)

13 See Thich Nhât Hanh and other Buddhist writers on this exclusion in *Peace News, Fellowship,* and also *Le Lotus* (their overseas peace newsletter). McReynolds both supported their exclusion and opposed even a temporary ceasefire to enable humanitarian tasks to be performed.

14 See N. Young "Wars of Liberation and the State," *Peace News* (London), 1969. The most common justification was that armed methods were only used when all other channels had been tried and found blocked, justifying support for violent methods and goals for the Third World (tacitly or more directly by practical help) that would be rejected outright in working for changes in advanced industrial societies.

15 James O'Brien, "Beyond Reminiscence: The New Left in History," *Radical America* (Cambridge, MS), vol. 6, no. 4 (July–August, 1972), pp. 17, 19; George R. Vickers, *The Formation of the New Left: The Early Years* (Lexington, Mass.: Lexington Books, 1975), pp. 51–61. The quotation from Vickers is from p. 61.

16 During the later 1960s *Peace News*, formerly the organ of the Peace Pledge

Union, also came close to the counter culture and alternative society approaches.

17 Joan Baez's "With God on Our Side" and Bob Dylan's "Blowing in the Wind" soon took their place alongside the repertoire of civil rights songs.

18 Norman O. Brown's reply to Herbert Marcuse in *Commentary* (New York), vol. 43, no. 3 (March, 1967), pp. 83, 84.

19 See above, chap. VI. Even the more conservative NAACP (National Association for the Advancement of Colored People) came to accept nonviolence and direct action; and the Urban League, reformist and nonactivist, had some of its leaders arrested. See Langston Hughes, *Fight for Freedom: The Story of the NAACP* (New York: Norton, 1962), chap. VI.

20 See also Lerone Bennett Jr., *Confrontation: Black and White* (Baltimore: Penguin Books, 1966), chap. V and subsequent discussion of this ambivalent and problematic stance.

21 Port Huron Statement," 1962; reprinted in Massimo Teodori, ed., *The New Left: A Documentary History* (Indianapolis and New York: The Bobbs-Merrill Company, 1969), pp. 163–72.

22 See above, chap. VI.

23 Oglesby was then president of SDS.

24 Todd Gitlin, *The Sixties: Years of Hope, Days of Rage* (New York: Bantam Books, 1987), pp. 171–3. Hayden, several decades after the event, explained to Gitlin that his profound irritation with Howe had provoked him to speak in this way of loving Hitler. He did not, however, deny he had thus spoken.

25 The title of one of his most significant essays, reprinted in *Drawing the Line* (New York: Random House, 1962).

26 Quoted in Gitlin, *op. cit.*, p. 291. For Savio's nonviolence see "The Free Speech and Civil Rights Movement" (*News and Letters Pamphlet*, July 1965). Savio was chairman of the SNCC group at Berkeley at the time of FSM.

27 Advocating nonviolent noncooperation, from a Tolstoyan anarchist standpoint, the radical moralism of Sampson's work was probably more in tune with the early mainstream of the New Left than most of its commentators or critics would admit.

28 Irving Howe's contribution to the debate on "Is There A New Radicalism?" in *Partisan Review* (New Brunswick, NJ), vol. 32, no. 3 (Summer, 1965), pp. 341–5. See also his "New Styles in Leftism," *Dissent* (New York), vol. 12, no. 2 (Summer, 1965), p. 299.

29 *The Essays of A.J. Muste*, ed. Nat Hentoff (New York: Simon and Schuster, 1970) includes most of Muste's important pieces on war and social justice, including those from the 1950s and 1960s.

30 A naval weapons station, north of Berkeley, supplying Southeast Asia.

31 He failed even to ally with the "New Left" groups (e.g. Bourdet's) or the antiwar resistance of French youth, finding both deeply compromised in

their relationship to the authoritarian violence of the Algerian Left. Ultimately, capitalism was a lesser evil for Camus than totalitarian rule and
that was the main reason for critics calling him a liberal. For Camus's support during the 1950s and early 1960s for the legalization of conscientious
objection, not then recognized in France, and for a scheme of alternative
civilian service for C.Os., see Michel Auvray, *Objecteurs, insoumis, déserteurs:
Histoire des réfractaires en France*, pp. 211, 230, 231. Though perhaps not quite
a pacifist in the Anglo-American sense, Camus believed deeply in the value
of nonviolence; he collaborated with the anarchist C.O. leader, Louis
Lecoin, in pressing the claims of conscientious objection, Auvray deals with
the various types of French war resistance during the Algerian War in chap.
IX ("Des oppositions très differentes à la guerre d'Algérie").

32 It is central as well to writers like Ronald Sampson in Britain.

33 For example, drawing in part on the Quaker notion of the inner light and
on American tradition of several centuries, Muste's thought and action
were rooted, like King's, in a notion of the inward search, which linked
them to militant young activists.

34 Among some influential theorists (Mills and Camus, and subsequently
Marcuse and Sartre), political participation did not take publicly activist
forms.

35 Individual nonviolent acts like those of Rosa Parks, James Meredith,
Jim Peck, Medgar Evers, Mario Savio, Bob Parris, Harold Steele, Albert
Bigelow, Pat Arrowsmith and Michael Scott, put a stamp on these years in
Britain and the USA.

36 See Noam Chomsky, "The Responsibility of Intellectuals," pp. 254–98 in
Theodore Roszak, ed., *The Dissenting Academy* (New York: Pantheon Books,
1968), p. 227.

37 The phrase "new man" suggests the lack of any consciousness of sexism in
language at this state of the movement and was widely employed in movement literature. Other examples occur in this chapter.

38 Tom Kahn, "The Problem of the New Left," *Commentary*, vol. 42, no. 1 (July,
1966), pp. 30–38.

39 In understanding the emergence of this Manichean choice, it is worth recognizing that most New Left activists do not seem to have known that
other popular options even existed, because of the degree to which the
establishment and the Old Left alike presented the war as a simple military
struggle between two sides. But one of the more sinister elements in the
Vietnam tragedy was that this essentially *third force* option was not even
allowed to enter radical debate between 1965 and 1968. Here, again those
libertarian pacifists, who were aware of the Buddhist struggle against Ngo
Dinh Diem and of the continuing size of the Buddhist movement, have
something to explain.

40 Stanley Hauerwas in Michael Cromartie, ed., *Peace Betrayed? Essays on Pacifism and Politics* (Washington, D.C.: Ethics and Public Policy Center, 1990), pp. 135, 137. Cf. Guenter Lewy, *Peace & Revolution: The Moral Crisis of American Pacifism* (Grand Rapids, MI: William B. Eerdmans Publishing Co., 1988), pp. 240, 248: "at the moment that pacifists enter the political arena to seek to influence the policies of their nation, they cease to speak as pacifists ... When the pacifist's conscience does not allow him to support policies that utilize force or the threat of force, the proper course for him is to remain silent." Should pacifists, one may then ask, have remained silent and not tried "to influence the policies of" Hitler's Germany, if they had been given an opportunity to do so? The contention that "pacifist silence" is only appropriate in a democracy does not appear to be entirely valid, at least on a theoretical level.

41 Bertrand Russell, "Some Psychological Difficulties of Pacifism in Wartime" in Julian Bell, ed., *We did not fight: 1914–18. Experiences of War Resisters* (London: Cobden-Sanderson, 1935), p. 332. Italics in the original.

42 As well as in the *pacificist* Women's International League for Peace and Freedom (e.g., the Quaker Dorothy Hutchinson or the well known Congress lobbyist Dorothy Detzer). As Lewy (*op. cit.*, pp. 76–88) has shown, the WILPF, however, succumbed more thoroughly to the New Left view of the war than did either the FOR or even the WRL. It is worth noting that membership of pacifist organizations was often overlapping.

43 Quoted in Charles Howlett, "Fellowship and Reconciliation: A Pacifist Organization confronts the War in Southeast Asia," *The Maryland Historian* (College Park MD), vol. 25, no. 1 (Spring/Summer, 1994), p. 6.

44 The WRL's vice-chairman, Charles Bloomstein, had supported a similar position within that organization. He told its executive committee in June 1967: "The extremism with which the 'new left' castigates American society is the reverse of pacifism, which seeks to reconcile not to polarize." Quoted in Lewy, *op. cit.*, p. 95. Though others in WRL shared Bloomstein's views, the Muste-McReynolds-Dellinger position came to predominate there; Bloomstein soon gave up the struggle and in October 1967 withdrew from active membership of the League.

45 Quoted in Howlett, *op. cit.*, p. 16. See also Lewy, *op. cit.*, chap. III.

46 Howlett, *op. cit.*, p. 20.

47 *Ibid.*, pp. 9–16.

48 As an instance of this Howlett points to the "New Left vocabulary" in the FOR National Council's statement of May 1970 entitled "Violence and the United States." Still, emphasis is placed there on the struggle against social exploitation being strictly nonviolent. *Ibid.*, p. 23. And, after all, the American FOR had been saying more or less the same kind of things since at least the 1920s. However Lewy, in his discussion of this document (*op. cit.*, pp.

66, 67), dismisses its plea for nonviolence as mere window-dressing and presents the text as substantially a justification for the revolutionary violence then being advocated by "the radical antiwar movement of which the FOR had become an integral part." This style of interpretation is not unusual in Lewy's book. We may note that Lewy's critique of the pacifist New Leftists in the United States was preceded, in outline, by Nigel Young in his volume on the New Left, which came out over a decade before Lewy's. The two authors, of course, were writing on the basis of very different premises. Lewy does not appear to have been aware of Young's work; at any rate he does not refer to it.

49 Lewy, *op. cit.*, pp. 138–40. For Hassler's immediate successor as editor of *Fellowship*, James Forest's defense of human rights in Vietnam as well as the Soviet Union, see *ibid.*, pp. 73–75, 112, 113, 115–23, 130–7. Also see chap. XI below.

50 *Ibid.*, pp. 158, 159, 161–4, 171, 172.

51 Letter to Louis Schneider (executive secretary of the American Friends Service Committee), December 3, 1976, quoted in *ibid.*, p. 117.

IX. Pacifism and the "New" Conscientious Objection

In what Moskos and Chambers have recently defined as "the new conscientious objection" three features predominate, they claim, distinguishing it from the older form which emerged in the second quarter of the sixteenth century, if not earlier. These features are "the augmenting, indeed, near supplanting, of the old religious and communal grounds for objection by a new secular and often privatized base; the proliferation of C.Os. in uniform; and the recognition and acceptance of these trends by the state."[1] Moreover, compulsory military service is itself under a question mark in some – formerly – staunchly conscriptionist states. In the Nuclear Age, and with the aid of modern technology, a state can now wage war without summoning its citizens to arms. This was starkly confirmed in the Gulf War. Certainly the state still needs money but, while conventional warfare continues in some parts of the world, conscript armies seem no longer essential for the warmaking potential of the major military powers.[2]

Before the present century, the state, where it offered conscientious objectors to military service a possibility of gaining exemption from bearing arms, had given this privilege only to Christian pacifists (in fact virtually the only kind of pacifists there were in those days), and Christian pacifists alone sought this way of escaping armed service. Others conscientiously opposed to a war in progress, if they did not possess the means – or the wish – to purchase the exemption usually open to the non-conscientious before the era of universal military service, had gone into hiding or emigrated – or deserted if the army had already got its hands on them. But in World War I, Britain (alone) had permitted "secular" objection in principle as a qualification for registration as a C.O.; the British law did not exclude political – or, as we would say, today, selective – grounds, provided these were regarded as sincere. Pacifism, based on ethical and humanitarian reasons rather than religion, was likewise not deprived of the benefits of the law. True, the passions of wartime often led tribunals, especially on the local level, to refuse exemption to selective objectors and nonreligious, ethical pacifists. But this did not alter the principle now established. The situation in Britain during the Second World War remained unchanged.

During the Cold War period, in the United States as well as in Britain and the British Commonwealth, the traditional homelands of conscientious objection, and also even in some countries on the European continent with a less firm C.O. tradition, the religious – "communal" component of conscientious objection remained strong. In Vietnam War America, for instance, while the "historic peace churches" were not as visible perhaps as other elements in the draft resistance movement, still, they made a contribution to it;[3] and there is no reason to believe they would not do so again were the draft to be reimposed in the United States. Nevertheless, secular draft resistance became in this period predominant in both the USA and Europe, and especially in Germany.

Thus the concept of "newness" in the C.O. situation of recent decades appears to reside, for Moskos and Chambers, primarily in its increasingly secular character, the more positive attitude to conscientious objection on the part of at least some states, especially those no longer so much reliant on conscript armies as in the past, and lastly – though this perhaps is of secondary importance – an extension in the incidence of conscientious objection within the ranks of the military, and particularly of conscript armies (e.g., in the USA and in Israel).

At this point in our narrative, from the perspective of the history of pacifism we may make two remarks. First, the idea of conscientious objection to compulsory military duties of various kinds[4] is historically rooted in the pacifist tradition and states' corresponding attempts to grapple with this phenomenon in ways that would not damage their interests. In the second place, whereas "privatized" objections to military service may scarcely be regarded as conscientious in the usual meaning of that word (they reflect perhaps what Martin Ceadel has called "vocational pacifism"), "secular resistance" to war, whether selective or "integral," derives in essence from the same moral roots as religious or ethical pacifism, the basic factor being conscience which some may regard as "sacred" and others of nontheistic origin.[5]

Conscientious Objectors in Selected Countries, 1960s to Early 1990s: Western Europe

The countries we have selected here are indeed all European (or peopled by fairly recent European settlers), which is inevitable in view of the weakness of the pacifist impulse in conscriptionist countries elsewhere and the absence of conscription in the United States since 1973. As Moskos and Chambers comment, "In 1991 among some forty-three countries outside Europe where conscription existed, virtually none recognized conscientious objection."[6]

After intensive lobbying and prolonged transnational campaigning for public support by pacifist and antimilitarist groups as well as by human-rights organizations like Amnesty International, in 1989 both the United Nations and the European Parliament passed resolutions calling on member states, which required their young men to perform military service, to recognize conscientious objection as a human right and to give C.Os. the possibility of substituting civilian service for service in the army. These resolutions did not possess binding force but, by that date, all member states at any rate of the European Community (EEC) had their C.O. law, except for Greece (for our purposes included in "Western" Europe).[7]

Greece indeed has continued in this respect to lag far behind other EEC members, a reflection perhaps of a deep feeling of political insecurity – "strategic vulnerability" – on the part of both public opinion and successive right and left-wing governments. For whatever cause, treatment of C.Os. in Greece has remained extremely harsh. Although from 1977 on, religious objectors could serve as noncombatants in the army for double the normal length of conscript service, i.e., for four and a half years, nonreligious objectors as well as those religious objectors who refused noncombatant duties, as Jehovah's Witnesses (JWs) did, continued to be sentenced to long terms of imprisonment, usually of as much as four years' duration – and this despite widespread international protest.

Moreover, "cat-and-mouse" treatment prevailed, and as a result there were Jehovah's Witnesses who, accordingly to a Greek expert on national security, Dimitrios Smokovitis, had in total "served sentences of ten, fifteen, or even twenty years."[8] In 1988 the option of noncombatant army service was extended to nonreligious objectors. This happened after an imprisoned political objector, Mihalis Maragarakis, embarked on a series of hunger strikes that obtained widespread publicity abroad. However, Greece still remains without any legal provision for alternative civilian service.*

---

*The position has changed for the better since our manuscript was completed. On 5 June 1997 the Greek parliament passed a law (to come into effect on

West Germany and Alternative Civilian Service

From Greece we may turn to the C.O. situation in West Germany (Federal Republic of Germany, BRD) where, since the reimposition of compulsory military service (for males) in 1959, more favorable conditions have existed for conscientious objectors than in any other conscriptionist country of the contemporary world. The number of conscripts opting to become C.Os. soon rose steeply there as a result.

The shadow of Nazi militarism undoubtedly proved a major factor in creating this situation; for the authorities, military as well as civil, strove to create a pacific image for the new Germany. Conscientious objection had indeed been specified as a citizen right in the state's Constitution. Article 4 of the Basic Law of 1949 declared: "No one shall be forced to do war service with arms against his conscience."[9]

The clauses of the Military Service Act of 1959 relating to C.Os. provided for exemption of every sincere objector whether to all or only to particular wars, including any whose grounds of objection were nonreligious. Originally the intention had been to include the possibility of C.Os. serving as noncombatants in the *Bundeswehr* if they wished to do so, but only very exceptionally did this prove feasible.[10]

Until 1984 all applications were carefully scrutinized.[11] The procedure also included an appeals mechanism. How liberal examining boards could be in granting C.O. status to political objectors can be seen in the following example: that of a student whose application was successful on appeal. "I cannot," the man explained, "say for certain whether the whole policy of our government and army is based on stupidity or cool calculation. But I am convinced that it does not contribute to peace; rather it threatens peace. To work against this threat and contribute to international peace is why I became a C.O."[12]

Successful applicants for C.O. status were required to report for

---

1 January 1998) allowing C.Os. in peacetime to perform alternative civilian service. However, they will be required to serve 18 months longer than the regular conscript, i.e., for 42 months instead of 24 months. See Amnesty International, *Concerns in Europe January–June 1997*, AI Index: EUR 01/06/97, pp. 36, 37. Alas, in the spring of 1998 comes the news that Greece's socialist government is planning to introduce military conscription for able-bodied women between the ages of 18 and 50 – apart from mothers of children under 12. This decision, however, has aroused widespread opposition.

civilian service known at first *as zivil Ersatzdienst* (civilian alternative service) and then as *Zivildienst*. Until 1984 "the procedure of recognition ... did not provide for a free choice with regard to one of the enforceable duties to serve." In the early years, too, there was sometimes a waiting period before a suitable job was available but latterly the number of job openings exceeded the number of civilian servicemen (*Zivildienstleistende*) at the government's disposal. Most C.Os. were assigned to work either as hospital orderlies or nursing aides or in old people's homes or in care for the seriously handicapped. Since 1969 the Third World also became a permissible field of service. Assignments were always unconnected with the military and the work had to be of use to the community.

"Nineteen eighty-four was a watershed year in conscientious objection" in Germany. Starting with that year responsibility for administering *Zivildienst* was transferred from the Ministry of Defense to a civilian ministry,[13] while the previous, sometimes rather intimidating procedure of recognition was done way with. True, some checking of applications continued but "without there being any possibility of rejecting an application for reasons relating to its content"; that is, a letter outlining why the applicant was requesting C.O. status sufficed for obtaining it.

Thus, since 1984, and on into the postreunification period, "men liable to do military service have [enjoyed] a *de facto* choice between military service and civilian service."[14]

For conscripts with no prior service, there no longer is a formal examination procedure in which individuals, decisions to object to military service for reasons of conscience are put to the test. The Federal Office for Civilian Service is required to accept applications for recognition as conscientious objector, if they are complete and conclusive. They are not allowed to check whether the reasons of the applicant are credible and serious. If a young man gives detailed reasons for his conscientious objection, provides a curriculum vitae, and submits a police clearance, he will be exempted from military service, and instead, will have to do civilian service. As a result, for all practical purposes, it is no longer possible to force eligible persons to do military service against their will.

In an attempt to see that the plea of conscience was not abused, the Federal Constitutional Court now increased the term of civilian service making it one-third longer than that of soldier conscripts; previously there had been only one month extra. 'According to the court's argument, it can be assumed that anyone who accepts the "tedious alternative of serving a comparatively longer period of time" is carrying out honestly "his constitutional right to make a free decision based on reasons of conscience."[15] In reality, it would seem that we have here one of the few examples of a legal opening for what Moskos and Chambers have called "a privatized base" for objection to military service, that is, alongside *conscientious* objection which still remains, even here, in theory the only type of objection officially qualifying for recognition.

How have the civilian servicemen reacted to their period of service? No clear picture emerges from the fragmentary evidence available. On the whole, however, most of the men seem to have responded positively to their experiences; despite some negative features – boredom, for instance, or a feeling of time wasted – they evidently felt they had received an opportunity to carry into action their desire to be of service to humanity in place of learning how to kill other human beings.[16]

Some C.Os. as well as representatives of the pacifist movement and war-resister organizations have protested against what they consider to have been discrimination against C.Os.: for instance, the lengthened period of service since 1984; fewer possibilities of further education than those enjoyed by soldier conscripts; obstacles in obtaining certain types of employment after release from the *Zivildienst*.[17] More serious reservations against the functioning of the system have also been made by critics from outside the pacifist–C.O. community. Chief among these is the charge that in fact the civilian servicemen are being exploited by the state as cheap labor. In other words, *Zivildienst* had been transformed into "underpaid social work": a charge, if correct, not likely to make it popular with the trade unions. True, the intention was to employ C.Os. only "in positions where private provision for assistance in distress [could not or would] not be applied." But this did not always seem to work out in practice, as the following frank statement by the Evangelical Church, issued in 1989, shows:

Civilian service participants are cheap labor for the social sector. All the work that cannot be handled by specialized employees, perhaps because they are too expensive, is done by civilian service participants. Depending on need and suitability, they can be employed anywhere without having to observe the inhibitory restrictions of labor laws and they have to function at will. Civilian service participants can be employed very quickly to handle any activities that have become unattractive and for which employees cannot be found any longer.[18]

On the positive side, Kuhlmann has noted in recent years the growth of a more favorable attitude toward civilian servicemen among older persons. On the other hand, "among young men aged sixteen to twenty-four, conscientious objection always had a good image." In 1988 the Federal Ministry of Defense reported – with surprise – that among young Germans, especially those who had finished secondary school, "the standing of a conscientious objector ... [was higher] ... than that of a young man who had decided to volunteer for service in the armed forces."

The reverse side of the favorable attitudes now displayed by many of the old as well as the young lies in the fact that some dilution of the earlier idealism is observable among C.Os. themselves, especially since 1984. Of course many objectors are still led, as before, by religious and humanitarian principles or by strong political motivation to choose the *Zivildienst* option. Yet, to quote Kuhlmann once again: "In view of the *de facto* free choice between military and civilian service ... [it] can be supposed that pragmatic considerations are given equal status in the young man's calculations and, thus, the idea of standing up for one's convictions, which caused conscientious objection to be viewed as a kind of symbolic protest, no longer applies to a large extent."[19]

Following reunification, "the number of COs. ... reached an unprecedented 151,000 in 1991. Put in another way, about half of potential draftees were conscientious objectors," calling to mind the statistics on non-induction of U.S. draftees in the early 1970s; see chapter VII. There has been some speculation that, unless the present trend is reversed, e.g., by reinstituting a more stringent procedure of inquiry such as existed before 1984, eventually draftees opting to serve in the Bundeswehr could find themselves in a minority compared to those choosing *Zivildienst* and C.O. status. On the other hand, were conscription to be abolished in Germany, as recently its neighbors, France and the Netherlands, have both announced they would do, then "ironically ... German society may miss its conscientious objectors more than its drafted soldiers. The civilian servers have become an inexpensive part of a delivery system of social services for which there is no readily available replacement."[20]

Soldiers on the reserve in West Germany, too, both "career" and "non-career," could seek exemption as C.Os. on being recalled to the colors.[21] If, after inquiry by the authorities, they were deemed sincere in their objection to further handling of weapons, they were transferred from the Bundeswehr to the *Zivildienst* register. For the present no further turns of duty were required; in case of a national emergency they would be treated as civilian servicemen on the same footing as other recognized C.Os.[22] The flow of reservists into the C.O. ranks has continued steadily. In 1982, for instance, more than 6,000 reservists had applied for C.O. status. The law in this regard provides another example of the liberal character of the country's C.O. legislation.

Equally liberal has been its attitude to serving soldiers who have wished to make the same transfer from soldier to C.O. A request for such a transfer, forwarded through the man's regimental commander, had to be processed in the same way as that of an ordinary C.O., regardless of the length of previous service in the army. If, meanwhile, the man were to refuse any longer to handle a weapon, he could be tried and punished for disobeying military orders. But patient waiting usually brought a successful outcome to an application and subsequent transfer to the *Zivildienst* register. In the case of conscripts, time served in the Bundeswehr was deducted from their period of civilian service, while career soldiers who became C.Os., like reservists, were freed from further duties.[23]

The picture of the C.O. situation in West, and later reunified, Germany would not be complete if we did not devote a few paragraphs to the so-called total draft resisters (*Totalverweigerer*), i.e., absolutist or unconditionalist C.Os., for whom Germany, unlike Britain during both world wars, has so far failed to grant recognition.[24] This is not the place to enter into a discussion of the absolutist case against military conscription, which we find already had the support of eighteenth-century British and colonial Quakers; the argument is essentially libertarian rather than strictly pacifist. German total draft resisters, however, while utilizing libertarian arguments, have generally been more concerned with what they see as a close linkage between *Zivildienst* and the country's capacity to wage war.[25]

At first JWs were virtually the only absolutists; in West Germany, as elsewhere, they claimed unconditional exemption on the grounds of being ministers of religion dedicated entirely to the spread of their faith, a claim that was seldom allowed. Most of them paid the penalty for not collaborating with the draft – jail. But from the mid-seventies the number of total draft resisters increased: a phenomenon observable in certain other west European conscriptionist countries; West German supporters of this stand, no longer exclusively JWs, engaged actively in propaganda and the issue became the subject of public debate. Total resisters now organized transnationally under the auspices of the radical War Resisters' International; Amnesty International, while unwilling to take a position with respect to the relative merits of acceptance versus rejection of alternative service, was usually ready to acknowledge jailed "total resisters" as prisoners of conscience.

In West Germany these people had two choices as to how to proceed. First they could ignore their call-up altogether; that, we know, was the position of C.O. nonregistrants in the U.S. in World War II and during the postwar era (until the draft ended in 1973). In this case they faced seizure by the military police and then a couple of months of "disciplinary arrest." After that came trial by an army tribunal for draft evasion, followed by a fairly stiff jail sentence – sometimes of a year or even longer – which was served in a military prison, where conditions of course were more severe than in a civilian jail. The penalty imposed corresponded indeed to that handed out to a disobedient soldier; legally, the resister did not count as a C.O. and was not covered by the article of the constitution guaranteeing that no one could be forced to bear arms if this went against his conscience.

Secondly the total resister could choose to apply for C.O. status and then, on being assigned to civilian service, refuse any further collaboration with the system. This was the form of protest adopted by most of these men. It ensured that the "refuser" would continue to be treated as a civilian when brought to trial (for, we know, there was no exemption from *Zivildienst* for C.Os. unless on grounds of health), thus preserving him from the clutches of the *Bundeswehr* while at the same time giving him perhaps an even better opportunity for publicizing the absolutist cause. Although procedures differed considerably from district to district, prison sentences, too, were lighter for the civilian-service refuser, with the possibility of his being put on probation or simply being let off with a fine, alternatives to jail not offered to the nonregistrant.[26] Moreover, the "cat-and-mouse" treatment, endured by JWs and other nonregistrants, did not apply to those whose point of refusal came only when the time arrived to report for *Zivildienst*.[27]

Estimates differ as to the number of West German C.Os. who have become absolutists, though everyone is agreed on their forming only a very small – if clearly visible – section of the C.O. community. Official statistics are confusing. In fact, "only the criminal proceedings, which often are in various states of appeal, give us some inkling of this phenomenon." Whereas Günter Werner from the C.O. side, writing in 1991, supposes that annually around 200–300 draftees had become nonregistrants of one or another variety, Kuhlmann and Lippert at the German Armed Forces Institute for Social Research have given a much higher figure. Writing a couple of years later, they state: "We estimate that, at the upper limits, there are [up to] 2,000 potential absolutists each year."[28]

A study of the C.O. situation in West Germany from the emergence of compulsory military service in the late 1950s to the postreunification era appears to confirm, at any rate more clearly than elsewhere, the Moskos-Chambers theses concerning the "new" conscientious objection. Here the state, and to some extent society too, has come to recognize conscientious objection, in the form of *Zivildienst*, as an acceptable way of performing compulsory national service; here, too, nonreligious motives now predominate over traditionally religious ones in leading draftees to choose the C.O. option, and, we have seen, a "privatized base" for such decisions is found among a minority of potential C.Os.; and finally we see the emergence, though still on a comparatively small scale, of career soldiers and reservists seeking C.O. status in accordance with the law. Yet these considerations do not in fact present the full picture. In the first place the German state has failed to recognize absolutist objectors and continues to jail these men; despite such procedure, this type of C.O. has not vanished. Secondly, it is unclear how far we are in fact justified in considering most nonreligious C.Os. as "secular" objectors; rather, they carry on the tradition of humanitarian-moral protest against war, whose impulse derives from ethical beliefs akin to religious faith. In the third place, up to now at any rate, conscientious objection among servicemen – in the shape it presented itself, for instance, in Gulf War America – has really not put in an appearance in Germany, at least to any significant degree; moreover, we may also note, reservist-into-C.O. is a slightly different phenomenon in Germany from the way this took shape, for instance, in Israel (see below).

Whether, as some have argued, Germany's *Zivildienst* represents a successful realization of William James's vision of a civilian alternative to compulsory military training (as part of his moral equivalent of war) remains doubtful. *Zivildienst* bears witness certainly to the present German state's liberal attitude toward its conscientious objectors and postwar German society's repugnance to war. But the experiment is fraught with practical difficulties and encompassed with ethical dilemmas. Whether or not they can be resolved, only the future will show.

France and Spain

Whereas throughout Germany pacifism and conscientious objection represented an attitude diametrically opposed to Nazi ideology, in postwar France they were generally seen as reflecting defeatism and collaborationism. Despite the heroic anti-Nazi stance of Protestant pacifists like Pastor André Trocmé, the pro-Vichy sympathies of many of the prewar "integral" pacifists inevitably soiled the reputation of pacifism in the eyes of the French public. Although a bill to give C.Os. the right to perform alternative civilian service was introduced in the National Assembly as early as 1949, it took several decades – and the rise of the counterculture – for the situation to improve. Meanwhile C.Os., including the handful of Christian pacifists who were drafted, continued as before to be repeatedly jailed. It was not in fact until December 1964, after General de Gaulle had been won over to the idea of allowing alternative civilian service, that the National Assembly finally passed a C.O. law. It was, it is true, of a somewhat restricted character; civilian service lasted twice as long as the service of the regular conscript, and there were legal obstacles in the way of making draftees aware of the fact that they could apply for civilian service. Still, as Auvray observes, "the age of the martyrs had at last come to an end."[29]

Some of the restrictive features of this first C.O. legislation were later removed, especially by a new law passed in 1983, and an increasing, if still small, number of draftees now chose C.O. status in lieu of serving in the army. "Conscientious objection was recognized as a right ... But [it] was certainly not seen as normal conduct, and the terms of alternative service – especially the extended duty period – were designed to discourage significant interference with conscription in France." The "citizen soldier" remained the country's model.[30]

Spain was a country in which until recently pacifism possessed even fewer adherents than France. Pacifism and the phenomenon of conscientious objection were not present in the Spanish past as they had been in France's, if there still only on a very modest scale.[31] The first Spanish conscientious objectors emerged in 1958 while General Franco was still in power; they were all Jehovah's Witnesses whom the army proceeded to sentence to long terms of imprisonment. Then in 1971, four years before Franco's death, the first nonsectarian objector appeared: Pepe Beunza, too, disappeared into prison. But at his trial Beunza had called on the state to allow C.Os. to perform their compulsory service outside the army framework. He told the court:

Every man is my brother, including you who are going to sentence me; I have indeed nothing whatsoever personal against you who are now judging me ... I am a Catholic but I would not be acting honestly were I, in stating my conscientious objection, to give this as my motive for it. ... Rather, I believe I should cite ethical reasons. I am a believer in nonviolence and consider that history has shown enough of the disastrous consequences of violence to oblige us to try other ways of social change ... But my action is by no means negative. I am quite ready to accept civilian service of double the length of military service ... There are at present in Spain a million children without schools, 20 per cent of the population illiterate, ... a shortage of some 4,300,000 houses as well as various other deficiencies with respect to culture, health, agriculture, and forestry.

The 200 C.Os. now in jail could be freed to help supply some of these needs. In this way they would be struggling to remove the causes of war since, as [Pope] Paul VI has said, the existing excessive economic, social and cultural inequalities among peoples provoke tensions and discord, thus endangering [international] peace.[32]

From this time on, the C.O. movement in Spain expanded rapidly. As it did so, it grew in radicalism, especially after Basque and Catalan nationalist components entered it and a strong political emphasis became increasingly apparent. The Movement of Conscientious Objectors (Movimiento de Objetores de Conciencia, MOC), established in 1977, strove with increasing difficulty to function as an umbrella organization for all those, whether secular or religious, pacifists or pacificists, who were determined to refuse service in the army on grounds of conscience.[33] Its task, it declared, was to achieve "the coexistence of three different strategies": to obtain cooperation between (1) supporters of a government-sponsored scheme of civilian alternative service, (2) advocates of service for C.Os. independent of government control and oriented directly toward the creation of a peaceful world, and (3) unconditionalists, *insumisos*, who rejected all compromise with the state on this issue and the imposition of any alternative for those unwilling to bear arms.[34] In any event, at its second conference in 1986 the MOC, now ready to embark on civil disobedience to end conscription altogether, pledged itself to employ only nonviolent means when resisting the state. Even so, its base of support by this date had narrowed to include only those whose opposition to compulsory military service was total.[35]

In 1978 the new democratic régime had guaranteed C.Os. the right to perform civilian service but a C.O. law was not fully implemented until 1989. In fact, the majority of objectors, including JWs, rejected the alternative it provided; and total resistance to conscription continued to mount, especially in 1989 after the authorities refused any longer to approve the tactic adopted by the MOC of presenting them with "collective statements of the grounds for [C.O. applications] to obviate personal investigation." To date there appear to have been among Spain's C.Os. more unconditionalists, corresponding to Germany's *Totalverweigerer*, than in any other conscriptionist country in Europe.[36] According to Spain's new Penal Code, promulgated in May 1996, total resisters to military service will no longer be jailed, unless *insumisión* occurs after their commencement of conscript service. Otherwise punishment will consist in deprivation, for eight to fourteen years, of public sector employment and of the right to receive government funds.[37]

Conscientious Objectors in Selected Countries, 1960s to Early 1990s: Eastern Europe

Nearly all the non-communist countries of continental Europe imposed conscription on their male citizens; in the degree of liberalism with regard to C.Os. they ranged, we have seen, from West Germany at one end of the spectrum to Greece at the other.[38] In most countries of communist Eastern Europe, during the early decades of the Cold War the C.O. situation approximated that of Greece but by the end of the era it had changed so far that, almost everywhere, legal provision for alternative civilian service existed.[39]

Before World War II conscientious objection had made an appearance in the area[40] but, except for the Soviet Union, objectors were few in numbers; a pacifist tradition indeed scarcely existed there outside Russia. In the Soviet Union, as we have shown in an earlier chapter, the Stalinist régime had eventually suppressed ruthlessly the once flourishing pacifist movement and declared that there were no longer any C.Os. in the workers' fatherland. And in fact, in the postwar communist bloc as well as breakaway Yugoslavia, before the mid-1970s only Jehovah's Witnesses and an occasional dissident Baptist or other sectarian refused to do his conscript service, or at least rejected training in weapons. "Almost no one attempted deliberately and openly to challenge the regular call-ups to military service. Then this general acceptance of such obligations began to crack in a number of places."[41]

East Germany (German Democratic Republic, DDR), which at the beginning of its existence had deployed antimilitarist slogans for political purposes, became the first communist state to make some provision for C.Os., though this proved unsatisfactory to most objectors.[42] The country's largest religious denomination (Evangelical Lutheran Church of Germany) was by no means pacifist. But, while it gave moral support to members accepting service after military conscription was introduced in 1962, it recognized conscientious objection at the same time as a valid response to conscription; and it continued to champion the rights of C.Os. so long as East Germany existed as a separate state. In 1964, as a response to the Evangelical Church's call for legal provision for conscientious objection, the government established noncombatant "construction units" (*Baueinheiten*) within the armed forces (*Nationale Volksarmee*).[43]

As Klippenstein writes:

Recruits for the *Baueinheiten* (also referred to as *Bausoldaten*, that is, literally "construction soldiers") were given a distinctive uniform carrying the design of a spade as a shoulder emblem. This insignia gave rise to the designation, *Spatensoldaten*, meaning "soldiers with a spade." Their regular work excluded the carrying of arms, although the units remained under military administration. The specified eighteen-month term of service equaled that of regular soldiers. Construction projects were primarily related to military sites and installations ... All units were still fully controlled by the army, the construction of military sites ... seemed to involve them directly in military-related activity, and the required oath of commitment to service differed little in substance ... from that required of regular servicemen.[44]

Obviously these construction units served military, and not humanitarian, needs. Only a very narrowly based pacifism, an objection solely to handling weapons, would find this sort of work satisfactory. We need not be surprised, therefore, if there were cases from the outset of *Bausoldaten* refusing the military oath. Others objected to a given piece of work on account of its specially close connection with war making. Indeed among the first batch of *Bausoldaten* drafted in 1964, five of them did just this when they found the timber from the trees they were felling would be used to construct a rifle range. Prison sentences of eighteen months resulted from their act of insubordination.[45]

Well over 50 per cent of the *Bausoldaten* came from the Evangelical Church while around 15 per cent were Seventh-day Adventists. But we have no means of knowing exactly how many "construction soldiers" served during the years of conscription in the DDR since, late in 1989, the Communist authorities deliberately destroyed the records containing this information as well as related statistical data concerning *Totalverweigerer* and those jailed for individual acts of disobedience to military orders on grounds of conscience.[46]

Many objectors, some of whom (but not JWs of course)would willingly have accepted a civilian alternative, went to jail rather than become in effect an integral part of the military machine. An example of unconditional resistance was provided by 26-year-old Michael Frenzel, drafted for service in 1982. Frenzel was a convinced Christian pacifist employed by the Evangelical Church as a youth worker (*Sozialdiakon*) in East Berlin. He had taken an absolutist stand from the beginning, and this brought him a 20-month jail term, which he served in various penal institutions. His account of these experiences, later published, provides insight into prison conditions in the DDR and reflects the attitude of a radical war resister to that state's conscription law.[47]

In neighboring East Central Europe the growth of conscientious objection was slower; neither in Poland, nor Czechoslovakia, nor Hungary[48] was the Catholic church sympathetic to pacifist ideas. Thus the situation in some ways remained less favorable in these three countries than in East Germany since they possessed only small mainstream Protestant denominations, and these anyway were little concerned either with C.Os. or with pacifism. In Czechoslovakia the Prague Spring of 1968 and the subsequent Soviet invasion led during the seventies to some conscripts refusing to serve in the army. A few of these young men were motivated in their stand by pacifism as well as by patriotism, especially when they were members of the Evangelical Church of the Czech Brethren, the major Protestant denomination in the Czech lands which derived its name – but little more – from a fifteenth-century pacifist sect, inspired by the radical separatist Petr Chelčický. As in the DDR and some other East European countries, Czech C.Os. were often associated, too, with the dissident human-rights movement, in their case Charter 77. The government responded by sentencing such men to lengthy terms of imprisonment, even when they expressed readiness to perform alternative civilian service: a request the authorities adamantly refused. As one of the C.Os. put it at his trial in June 1981 when he was sentenced to two and a half years in jail: "a legal alternative to military service would enable many of our citizens to live according to their consciences and beliefs, and would ensure ... tolerance of [varying] attitudes [to] life and personal conviction."[49]

Among the Czechs the struggle for C.O. rights had been closely lined with the wider campaign for human rights and support for the Helsinki Accords. On the other hand, in Poland the "new" conscientious objection (new, that is, in distinction from that of JWs and other small sects that went back many decades), when it emerged there around 1980, often took on a distinctly patriotic, anti-Russian coloring prompted by the suppression of the Solidarity movement and imposition of martial law in December 1981. In many cases protest centered on a conscript's refusal of the military oath, which many found objectionable,[50] rather than on army service in itself. A new organization *Freedom and Peace* (*Wolność i Pokój*), founded in 1985, provided a focus for supporters of the burgeoning Polish peace movement. It was anti-militarist and supported C.O. rights but it was not exclusively pacifist, despite the prominent role of pacifists within it. The government of General Jaruzelski responded in the same way as other communist governments by imposing heavy prison sentences on C.Os. of every kind: patriots (some of them practising Catholics) indignant at Soviet domination, ethical and nonsectarian religious pacifists (still a very small group), a few anarchists and libertarians as well as Jehovah's Witnesses and members of other traditionally pacifist sects.

Somewhat the same pattern as in East Central Europe can be seen in the C.O. situation in the Balkans, including Yugoslavia. At first objectors there came almost exclusively from antimilitarist sects like the Nazarenes or the JWs. If anything, the penalties suffered by these men, including "cat-and-mouse" treatment, exceeded those imposed under Communism elsewhere. While Rumania and Bulgaria, it is true, sometimes granted C.Os. exemption, such cases were irregular and confined to the grant of noncombatant army duties.[51] The government of Yugoslavia, though, steadily resisted mounting pressure during the seventies and eighties to give at least a measure of exemption to its C.Os., who indeed were not a large group and were still drawn almost exclusively from JWs and other small pacifist sects. But to do so, according to a ruling of the Federal Constitutional Court issued in November 1987, would mean that certain religious groups were receiving more favorable treatment than others; no exceptions could, therefore, be made with regard to the obligation of all citizens to participate actively in defending their country.[52]

The dominant partner among the members of the Warsaw Pact was of course the Soviet Union. There, from the 1970s, two types of conscientious objection mingled. First, the old sectarian pacifist witness was undergoing renewal as a result of schisms within some of the major sects hitherto fettered by membership in the state-controlled All-Union Council of Evangelical Christians-Baptists; among a number of similar actions, unregistered Baptists, independent Pentecostals, True and Free Seventh-day Adventists now asserted their newly discovered spiritual freedom by returning to their pacifist roots in the 1920s. Jehovah's Witnesses, absent from the Soviet scene earlier on, conducted missionary work with increased zeal in (illegal) contact with their coreligionists abroad. Through *samizdat*, which was smuggled across the frontiers, the outside world became aware of the existence of C.Os. in the Soviet Union; now, when a C.O. was sent to a labor camp for three or four years for refusing induction into the army, consignment to Gulag for this, as for other offences, could no longer be kept a secret.

Some C.Os. began their protest by refusing to take the military oath: to the army such an act was tantamount to rejecting military service altogether. This was perhaps a not unreasonable conclusion. "I am a believer," stated one such objector, "and from purely religious conviction, I cannot take the military oath, or bear arms. [Otherwise] I do not refuse to serve in the ranks of the Soviet army, and am prepared to fulfill conscientiously all that my service demands."[53]

Religious C.Os. in the Soviet Union were almost all either JWs or Seventh-day Adventists, or evangelicals of one kind or another; the latter based their arguments on Biblical texts like "Thou shalt not kill" and the Sermon on the Mount. But the second type of Soviet objector (a new phenomenon in the Union) sought a rationale for his position elsewhere. The number of political objectors and deserters from the army on grounds of conscience increased during the Gorbachev era and as the dissolution of the Soviet empire approached. The prolonged and bloody Afghanistan war had proved a catalyst in this respect. In the three Baltic republics nationalists were led to openly reject conscription into the Soviet army, which they regarded as any army of occupation. As one such nationalist C.O. declared in May 1989: "As a Lithuanian I regard service in the Soviet Army as immoral and illegal ... I refuse categorically ever to serve in that army under any conditions, whether with weapons or as a noncombatant."[54] Here indeed we have a genuine conscientious objector to military service. But such objection clearly had nothing to do with pacifism, for there is no reason to believe the man would not willingly have fought in defense of an independent Lithuania. The widespread revulsion from the military felt throughout the Union, and particularly in the Baltic republics, led to demands for the introduction of alternative civilian service for C.Os. both from nonpacifist opponents of the existing régime and from the small band of convinced war resisters. Such demands met at first with stubborn opposition from the authorities.

The Dawn of a New Era for East European C.Os.

In July 1989 Amnesty International reported that of roughly a hundred Soviet political prisoners whose cases were known directly to them almost all were conscientious objectors.[55] But, as Klippenstein puts it, the curtain was rising throughout communist Eastern Europe, and a new era dawning for pacifists and conscientious objectors as well as for the rest of its inhabitants.[56]

Poland was the first to introduce alternative civilian service for C.Os.; the Polish *Sejm* passed a law to this effect on 3 July 1988. Difficulties of course did not end there. Whereas most JWs refused to accept alternative service none were jailed after 1990 whereas Catholic C.Os., few in number but quite ready to accept such service even though it was a year longer than the normal two-year term of duty, were often rejected by the conscription commissions whose task it was to judge applicants' sincerity – on the grounds that a Catholic could not be a conscientious objector (a position denied by the Episcopate despite that body's unanimous support for military conscription). Thus, ironically Catholic C.Os. now found themselves in jail while the state granted the JWs unconditional exemption! The majority of Polish C.O. applicants, however, derived their pacifism from ethical – or "moral" – principles of various kinds ranging from undenominational Christianity through humanism to anarchist antimilitarism.[57]

Hungary had followed Poland in making alternative civilian service available for C.Os. in January 1989. It was to be twice as long as the ordinary conscript service then lasting eighteen months. The 73 C.Os. then in jail were now released. Czechoslovakia, for its part, introduced a C.O. law in March 1990 shortly after the "Velvet Revolution" of the previous December; the new democratic government also took steps to release all imprisoned C.Os.

Before the Federal Republic of Yugoslavia finally dissolved in the spring of 1991 the same process just described had taken place there, too. In fact, C.Os. were scarce in former Yugoslavia, apart from the JWs and the Nazarenes, a small multiethnic pacifist sect which had emerged in the mid-nineteenth century; see above, chapter IV. Hitherto C.Os. belonging to these and other religious groups had suffered prolonged and repeated imprisonment for refusing to bear arms, even though the Nazarenes at least had always been ready to serve in the army as noncombatants.

Antimilitarist sentiment was strongest in Slovenia in the north-west of the country.[58] Here, from the early eighties on, the Slovene Peace Group in Ljubljana represented a coalition between left-wing Slovene nationalists, adherents of the youth counterculture, and a few ethical pacifists, like the dynamic young Marko Hren, who in particular gave the group an antimilitarist thrust. Opposition to conscription and defense of C.Os., combined with advocacy of democratic pluralism and far-reaching autonomy for Slovenia (and the other Yugoslav republics), formed the core of the Ljubljana Group's program. Its members, largely students and younger academics, soon established contact with human-rights groups abroad as well as with radical pacifist organizations like the War Resisters' International. After the collapse of communist rule and the establishment of Slovenia's independence, the Peace Group disintegrated. Whereas one of its prominent sympathizers, Janez Janša, became the new state's Minister of Defense, Hren remained active in the War Resisters' International until, somewhat disillusioned, he finally turned his energies to other activities. Although independent Slovenia re-tained an army, it did establish a liberal system of alternative civilian service for its C.Os., who continued, however, to be drawn mainly from the sects.[59] Nationalism once again seemed to have won out against the antimilitarist impulse.

In the new Russia that began its separate existence at the end of 1991, at the time of writing no C.O. law has yet been passed, although such legislation was announced in early 1991, i.e., before communist rule had ended.[60] This curious situation stems, at least indirectly, from the prolonged power struggle going on in that country. The Russian pacifist impulse, once strong, has indeed revived while remaining weak in comparison with defensist sentiments of right, center, and left and the nonpacifist – and ardently patriotic – stance of the Russian Orthodox Church. Pacifism and conscientious objection today draw support from a variety of sources: in addition to neo-Tolstoyism (the old Tolstoyans are nearly all dead) and the sects with a resurgent pacifist tradition, there are nonviolent anarchists and antimilitarists of various sorts, whose ideas often remain inchoate though they reflect pacifist ideals leading to the rejection of military service even should that still entail a spell in jail. Outside support for C.Os. and for isolated pacifist groups has come from Quakers as well as North American Mennonites and Canadian Dukhobors: this has been helpful, in particular in providing pacifist literature, in Russian translation as well as in English. Pacifist women have been active both before and after the fall of Communism; the Committee of Soldiers' Mothers, for instance, whose original purpose was to improve the deplorable conditions in which Soviet conscripts had to serve their period of military duty, while not abandoning their concern for the young men drafted into the forces, has moved over to an attack on war itself, and some of the mothers, avowedly pacifists, now support the C.O. position on principle.

Ironically, it was East Germany, once one of the most rigid communist régimes (though the only one we have seen that had early on made – inadequate – legal provision for C.Os.), which eight months before its demise on 3 October 1990, had introduced a C.O. law exceeding even West Germany's C.O. legislation in its liberalism. Henceforward, "recruits would be allowed to choose their own field of service. The term of service would be twelve months whether in the army or in alternative service. Total resisters [i.e., unconditionalists] would not be imprisoned, but asked to pay a fine."[61] In view of these uniquely favorable conditions we need not be surprised at the official announcement "that half of the recruits who had just started their basic training in the army (about 80,000 men) would be opting for conscientious objection."[62] At least with respect to the DDR's conscientious objectors, reunification of the two Germanies was not an exchange for the better.[63]

The "New" Conscientious Objector in Uniform: The Case of Israel

For several centuries soldiers from time to time have opted to become conscientious objectors as a result of their conversion to pacifism. Corporal James Hastie or private Thomas Watson, British soldiers during the American Revolution, are just two of the early cases of this transformation; we could cite more. "The thought of taking away a man's life [had become] distressing to James," a Quaker sympathizer wrote of Hastie's motivation for refusing any longer to bear arms. But the soldier C.Os. we shall deal with briefly in this section were prompted by different motives; their military disobedience was relativist not absolute. Its scope was somewhat narrower than that of the selective objection we have dealt with hitherto, e.g., in the case of the antiwar socialists gathered in World War I Britain's No-Conscription Fellowship or of the nonpacifist war resisters in Vietnam War America. For in the case of these Israeli "refusers," their conscientious objection centered not on the total effort of a war in progress, but on individual acts of war considered to be immoral.

Like selective objection as a whole, these acts of resistance reflect "just-war" theory in one or another variant. But formerly, when similar acts occurred those who carried them out rarely, if ever, claimed the classic pacifist status of conscientious objection recognized in some Western countries. A precedent can perhaps be seen in the case of William Douglas Home a British army officer who, toward the end of the last war, refused to carry out military orders he regarded as immoral.[64] And there have been others. But for the most part, such refusers if they succeeded in escaping punishment, simply deserted, sometimes going abroad for greater security.

This is not the place to give an account of the activities of the Israeli peace movement or of the resistance mounted by Israeli soldiers to what they regarded as unjust treatment of Palestinian Arabs or other Arabs in the occupied territories (in chapter XI, though, we shall deal with the small, specifically pacifist section of the country's peace movement). A psychologist from Haifa University has summarized as follows the mental attitude of these Israeli soldier selective objectors (SCOs) during the Lebanon War of 1982–1985 and the Intifada:

The position of an SCO was not the mere action of disobedience but the need to undergo some process of external suffering on top of the internal moral pain: legal punishment, personal humiliation, being regarded as unpatriotic, financial loss ... For the Israeli SCO, however, it seems that the (perceived) separate position of criticism that he assumed also entailed the pain of detachment as a form of punishment: an exclusion from the unit and/or the subjective feeling of exclusion from the community.

She concludes by stressing the SCO's "desire to return to the same [army] unit" after he had served his – usually brief – prison sentence.[65]

We find among the Israeli soldier-SCOs points of resemblance – as well as dissimilar traits to those displayed by traditional pacifist C.Os. The readiness to plead conscience for the act of military disobedience (a plea the state also was willing to consider) and at the same time the feeling of isolation from a community unlikely to approve of such disobedience, the readiness to accept punishment as part of the protest witnessing to a moral truth and at the same time an insistence that protest and witness rather than compliance were the correct response to a wrong – all this was shared by the C.O. and the SCO. On the other hand, on a closer look the Israeli SCO, though he had adopted some of the forms of the pacifist mode of war resistance, was not in fact a war resister, not even a resister to a particular war as the selective objectors of Vietnam-era America, for instance, had been. His quarrel with the Israeli army did not revolve around the question of bearing arms but around the problem of how the weapons he carried would be used.

This, of course, in no way detracts from the validity of his moral protest nor the courage he displayed in carrying it through: indeed he needed considerably more guts for his "act" than did the average pacifist C.O. or selective objector. The refusers, moreover, displayed a sensitivity to injustice rarely, if ever before, displayed within army ranks: the result perhaps of the knowledge that their forefathers had been so long the victims of oppression culminating in the Holocaust and a reflection, too, of the liberal conscience strong among many Israeli intellectuals. The distinction here is, therefore, made solely for the purposes of typology.[66]

War Tax Objectors

Refusal to pay war taxes is an old technique employed by pacifists and proponents of nonviolence, though seldom used before the nuclear era when danger of an atomic conflict brought increasing numbers of war resisters to consider this kind of action. However, the saintly New Jersey Quaker, John Woolman, had practised it as early as the 1750s, while nearly a century later the famous American essayist, Henry David Thoreau in 1845, in his classic act of civil disobedience which led to a night in the Concord jail, was refusing to pay a tax he felt gave support to slavery and war. Where the whole tax, or at any rate the greater part of it, went to cover military purposes war resisters have found it comparatively easy to refuse payment; the issue was then clear-cut and the witness consistent with a potential impact on the environing society. The matter was less clear, however, when the government allocated only an undefined – even though by the twentieth century usually a considerable – portion toward war or its preparation.[67]

Most pacifists have continued to pay their taxes, appreciative of the need to support financially the beneficial activities of government and not seeing a way to subtract, effectively and with any degree of accuracy, the amount devoted to war purposes. In addition, if they were Christians they could fall back on the – possibly ambiguous – Biblical text: "Render to Caesar the things that are Caesar's and to God the things that are God's" (Mark 12:17). But, as the Cold War continued, war tax resistance of one kind or another increased until support for this position among pacifists, though still small, could be found in most countries of the industrialized world outside the communist bloc. In the United States, the Vietnam War gave it a powerful boost; it gained the enthusiastic backing of absolute pacifists, like Joan Baez and the Presbyterian minister, Maurice McCrackin, as well as of some nonpacifist opponents of the war.

A few war resisters so reduced their income as to fall below the taxable level. Others refused payment of the sum they calculated the government would assign to warlike uses. Such persons, like Thoreau, were ready to go to prison if the authorities chose to jail them. (The government of course might take other measures to extract unpaid taxes.) Civil disobedience of this kind was conceived both as witness to the truth and as a challenge to military power. Where "collection at the source," i.e., tax deduction by the employer, was the current procedure, the situation became more complicated – with a further dilemma when the employer was a pacifist organization sympathizing with at least the aims of the tax resisters.

Another form of protest, less radical in character and thus enjoying the support of those unwilling to break the law over this issue, lay in organizing a public campaign to gain the government's consent for establishing a peace tax fund, which would be used exclusively for nonmilitary purposes. Conscientious objectors to war could then pay into such a fund the money that would otherwise have been assigned to the military just as, in the case of conscription, genuine C.Os. could undertake alternative civilian service where the law allowed a conscience clause. In Canada Dr. Jerilynn Prior, an assistant professor of medicine at the University of British Columbia, took the matter to the courts claiming that the Canadian Charter of Rights and Freedoms gave each citizen a legal right not to have to pay for war if this ran counter to her or his conscience. But Prior finally lost on appeal to the

Supreme Court of Canada. So far, despite continuous pacifist campaigning, no government has sanctioned the right to object on grounds of conscience to payment of such taxes as the objector claims will be used for military purposes. In this relatively "new" area of conscientious objection the future remains unclear. One thing, though, is certain: that pacifists are not likely to give up on this issue and cease pressuring the state to concede at least the most essential – and least controversial – points of their program.

Notes

1 Charles C. Moskos and John Whiteclay Chambers II, eds., *The New Conscientious Objection, From Sacred to Secular Resistance* (New York and Oxford: Oxford University Press, 1993), p. 196. By "communal" the writers mean an objection to military service stemming from membership of a pacifist religious group like the Quakers or Mennonites. They do not, of course, imply that this type of C.O. is not sincere because he is following the pattern of behavior accepted in his family background.

2 This point was made effectively by the Canadian Quaker scientist and peace activist, Ursula Franklin, in her 1989 Massey Lectures, *The Real World of Technology* (Toronto: CBC Enterprises, 1990), p. 80. "Abandoning compulsory military service," she writes, "is not so much a sign of peaceful intentions as it is a sign of galloping automation."

3 The considerable space Lewy devotes in his *Peace & Revolution* to attacking the wartime role of the American Quaker service organization (AFSC) could be perceived as a backhanded tribute to the continuing importance of the Society of Friends with respect to war resistance, or at any rate of the sections of that body remaining loyal to pacifism.

4 Use of the term "conscientious objection" with respect to military service dates back at least to 1820 when it was used (in the plural) in an antipacifist pamphlet by John Sheppard. See Martin Ceadel, *The Origins of War Prevention: The British Peace Movement and International Relations 1730–1854* (Oxford: Clarendon Press, 1996), p. 37. Conscientious objection can of course apply to other compulsory activities besides military service (e.g., vaccination or religious instruction in schools), as has been amply demonstrated in the recently published study by Constance Braithwaite with reference to British law.

5 Cf. Hellmuth Hecker in his introduction to the volume of documents, *Die Kriegsdienstverweigerung im deutschen und auslandischen Recht: Dokumente ... XIII* (Frankfurt am Main and Berlin: Alfred Metzner Verlag, 1954), p. 3: "The distinction often made between ethical and religious grounds is really

invalid. It is of no significance for the depth of the conviction (*Gewissens-entscheidung*) that rejects killing whether this position is defined in the usual religious terms, or whether it refers back to idealist, humanist, Stoic, Confucian or other moral teachings, or whether it is drawn from no particular dogmas or doctrines. A creedless (*frei*) motivation for the refusal to kill can indeed be more profound and more genuine than one based on religion. Everything depends on the sincerity and completeness of the call of conscience."

6 Moskos and Chambers, *op. cit.*, pp. 15, 233 n. 44. Cf. the comment of a German peace researcher (possibly a little exaggerated): "in the countries of the Third World ... conscientious objection is not a matter of discussion." Heinz Janning *et al.*, eds. *Kriegs-/Ersatzdienst-Verweigerung in Ost und West* (Essen: Klartext Verlag, 1990), p. 354. Of course India, in which the idea of nonviolence (*ahimsa*) has long been widely known, has never had conscription, whether before or after independence, while Japan, another Asian country though in no way belonging to the "Third World," while it possesses a comparatively strong peace movement including pacifists of various kinds, has not had conscription since 1945. However, in Vietnam, where all sides conscripted, the call for conscientious objection was strongly voiced by the Buddhist peace movement, despite continuing repression. Perhaps these facts modify, to some degree at any rate, the bleak situation referred to by the American and German authors. One only has to read current issues of the press organs of the War Resisters' International and the International Fellowship of Reconciliation to perceive the growth of pacifist groups, still small of course, in areas of Africa and Asia (and Latin America, too) that were scarcely touched hitherto by pacifist outreach.

7 April Carter, *Peace Movements: International Protest and World Politics since 1945* (London and New York: Longman, 1992), pp. 231, 232; Moskos and Chambers, eds., *op. cit.*, pp. 205, 270. See also the useful survey of civilian service for C.Os. in EEC countries outside Germany by Sam Biesemann and Gerd Greune, pp. 346–51 in Janning *et al.*, eds., *op. cit.* We may note that the European Parliament's resolution of October 1989 laid down that C.O. civilian service should not last more than six months longer than the regular military conscript service.

8 The Greek government's treatment of JW conscientious objectors certainly displays more savagery than that of any other state in the post-1945 world, not excluding the countries of the Communist bloc. But that does not mean that harsh treatment did not emerge elsewhere, especially in countries of the so called "Third World" where pacifism lacked a firm base. In the Dominican Republic, for instance, young JWs like the Glass brothers, Leon and Enrique, might spend as much as nine years in jail for repeated refusal to serve in the army. In dealing with the situation in this area the Watch

Tower Society in Brooklyn (New York), acting as the governing body of the worldwide Witness movement, could adopt a surprising degree of *Realpolitik*, considering the Witnesses' uncompromising rejection of earthly rulership. In Mexico, beginning in 1960, the JW leadership approved of JWs bribing army officers to furnish draftees with certificates stating – falsely of course – that they had performed their conscript service and placing them on the army reserve. The "double standard" here, and the contrast with the sufferings expected of young JWs in the neighboring Dominican Republic, derived from the Watch Tower leaders' desire to avoid a clash over military service with the government of Mexico. That, they feared, might endanger the sect's precarious legal status in that country and seriously impede its expansion there. See M. James Penton, *Apocalypse Delayed: The Story of Jehovah's Witnesses* (Toronto: University of Toronto Press, 1985), pp. 149–51.

9 Essentially the Basic Law was West Germany's constitution. Quotation from Jürgen Kuhlmann, "West Germany: The Right not to bear Arms" in Donald Eberly and Michael Sherraden, eds., *The Moral Equivalent of War? A Study of Nonmilitary Service in Nine Nations* (Westport CT: Greenwood Press, 1990), p. 133. Kuhlmann has summarized, and updated, this useful essay in a chapter, co-authored with Ekkehard Lippert and entitled "The Federal Republic of Germany: Conscientious Objection as Social Welfare," in Moskos and Chambers, eds., *op. cit.*, pp. 98–105. Both writers are senior research scholars at the German Armed Forces Institute for Social Research in Munich.

10 Kuhlmann, "West Germany," p. 134. "In individual cases, conscientious objectors were drafted to serve in the medical service, orderly rooms, or mess Halls."

11 Volker Möhle and Christian Rabe, *Kriegsdienstverweigerer in der BRD: Eine empirisch-analytische Studie zur Motivation der Kriegsdienstverweigerer in den Jahren 1957–1971* (Opladen: Westdeutscher Verlag, 1972), pp. 35–42, 53–61, 89–94, describe in detail and analyze the procedures of inquiry leading to the granting – or in a few cases rejection – of C.O. status. A final rejection came only if those judging the case considered the application simply "a form of protest or a matter of expedience" and not the result of a sincerely held belief it was wrong to bear arms. Kuhlmann, *op. cit.*, p. 135. See also Winfried Schwamborn, *Handbuch für Kriegsdienstverweiger*, 8th rev. edn. (Cologne: Pahl-Rugenstein Verlag, 1982), pp. 40, 41, 65–93, 142–8, 154, 155 ("Die Gewissensprüfung").

12 Herbert Kloss, "Warum ich den Kriegsdienst verweigert habe" in Wilfried von Bredow, ed., *Entscheidung des Gewissens: Kriegsdienstverweigerer heute* (Cologne: Pahl-Rugenstein Verlag, 1969), p. 80.

13 The Ministry of Youth, Family Affairs, Women and Health.

14 Kuhlmann, *op. cit.*, p. 137.

15 *Ibid.*, p. 136.

16 See the recollections by ten *Zivildienstleistende* of their sixteen months of enforced social work. " 'Unser soziales Ding': Zivildienstleistende berichten von ihrer Arbeit," pp. 46–116 in Klaus Pokatzky, ed., *Zivildienst: Friedensdienst im Inneren* (Reinbek: Rowohlt Taschenbuch Verlag, 1983). The editor was himself a former C.O.

17 See, for instance, Peter Tobiassen, "Diskriminierung," pp. 176–93 in Janning *et al.*, eds., *op. cit.*

18 Quoted in Kuhlmann, *op. cit.*, p. 148.

19 *Ibid.*, pp. 145–7. In recent years less than a fifth of the C.Os. have given religious grounds for refusing military service; the rest cited nonreligious reasons of one kind or another.

20 Kuhlmann and Lippert, *op. cit.*, pp. 100, 104, 105. However, if compulsory nonmilitary service for the country's youth were retained, this situation would not necessarily arise although other problems, connected with finding employment for a greatly increased number of civilian servicemen, might have to be faced.

21 See Bernd Müllender and Peter Vermeulen, *Nicht mehr mit uns! Reservisten verweigern* (Cologne: Pahl-Rugenstein Verlag, 1984). The authors, both former reservist C.Os., include extensive materials designed to assist reservists in applying for C.O. status.

22 *Ibid.*, pp. 48, 49.

23 Schamborn, *op. cit.*, pp. 149–51.

24 Kalle Seng, "Weder Bundeswehr noch Zivildienst; Totale Kriegsdienstverweigerung," pp. 211–19 in Pokatzky, ed., *op. cit.*, and Günter Werner, "Radikale Positionen werden radikal geahndet: Totale Kriegsdienstverweigerung und die Rechtsprechung," pp. 218–29 in Janning *et al.*, *op. cit.*, are both useful in exploring the emergence of *Totalkriegsverweigerung* in West Germany. See also Dieter Maas, *Materialen zur Kriegsdienstverweigerung* (Koblenz: ZinFü, 1989), pp. 41–45.

25 Cf. Kuhlmann, "West Germany," p. 140: "conscripts in West Germany have the right *not* to bear arms. However, the Bundeswehr is not willing to let conscripts complete their military service within the armed forces without arms, which gives rise to the necessity and existence of the Zivildienst. Consequently the Zivildienst has no official political goals of its own. Its legal purpose is to ensure equity in drafting. Commitment to social welfare is legally a subordinate objective." Italics in the original.

26 Werner, *op. cit.*, pp. 218–20.

27 *Ibid.*, pp. 223, 224. Whereas a decision of the Federal Constitutional Court in March 1968 had put a stop to the repeated jailing of JWs, which at the end of the first decade of conscription had reached a figure of over one thousand, the practise continued with respect to other nonregistrant C.Os. so

that, writing at the end of the eighties, Werner calls "these Draconian penalties" "up to now ... the most serious problem" facing the C.O. movement.
See also *ibid.*, pp. 226–8.

28 *Ibid.*, p. 229; Kuhlmann and Lippert, *op. cit.*, p. 100.

29 Michel Auvray, *Objecteurs, insoumis, déserteurs: Histoire des réfractaires en
France* (Paris: Stock, 1983), p. 255. In his detailed history of war resistance in
France from prerevolutionary times, Auvray includes among the *réfractaires*
both absolute pacifists, an extremely small group until recently at any rate,
and selective objectors of different kinds and with various methods of resistance to conscription. Traditionally, a large number of French C.Os. were
anarchists, like Louis Lecoin who spent long periods of his life in prison as
a result of his war resistance. Lecoin commented as follows on C.O. legalization: "A breach has been opened in the ramparts of militarism, a breach
we shall easily be able to widen in the years to come."

30 Michel Martin in Moskos and Chambers, eds., *op. cit.*, p. 92.

31 The same point could be made about Italy where, after the collapse of Fascism, the draft was reimposed in 1947 – without any provision for conscientious objection. In the following year, with the case of Pietro Pinna, who
based his refusal to serve on an amalgam of political, philosophical and
broadly religious motives, a steady, though still small, stream of C.Os.
emerged – until in 1972 the government felt obliged to pass a law permitting alternative civilian service for genuine objectors. Space does not allow
us to do more than refer to the excellent survey of the subject by Sergio
Albesano, *Storia dell'obiezione di coscienza in Italia* (Treviso: Editrice Santi
Quaranta, 1993). See chap. II for Pinna's path-breaking case.

32 Rafael Ajangiz *et al.*, eds., *Objectores, insumisos: La juventud basca ante la mili
y el ejército* (Vitoria; Servicio Central de Publicaciones del Gobierno Vasco,
1991), pp. 46, 47. Though this book is concerned primarily with Basque
C.Os. it includes a chapter by Ajangiz outlining the development of the
C.O. movement in Spain as a whole since the late sixties ("La objeción de
conciencia en el estado españo: Evolución de un concepto," pp. 39–89), followed by a chapter by Rafael Sainz de Rozas on the Spanish state's reaction
to the expanding C.O. movement and the resulting C.O. legislation ("La
respuesta a la desobediencia: Las leyes reguladores de la objeción de conciencia," pp. 91–100).

33 *Ibid.*, pp. 49–65, 68–81, 84–89.

34 *Ibid.*, p. 51.

35 *Ibid.*, pp. 69–71.

36 See Ajangiz *et al.*, eds., *op. cit.*, *passim*; Andreas Brandhorst, "Kriegsdienstverweigerung in Spanien,," in Janning *et al.*, eds., *op. cit.*, pp. 351–6; Carter,
op. cit., pp. 227, 228, 232.

37 *Peace News* (London), no. 2408 (December, 1996), pp. 10, 14.

38 The case of Switzerland – the country that repeatedly jailed the Quaker champion of *Service civile*, Pierre Ceresole, for failing to carry out the annual turn of military duty he was unwilling to perform as a noncombatant – illustrates the fact that political liberalism has not necessarily led a state to treat its C.Os. generously: a thesis worked out more fully in Peter Brock's *Pacifism in Europe to 1914* (Princeton NJ: Princeton University Press, 1972). For, as a Swiss sociologist commented of his fellow citizens: "Conscientious objectors ... have traditionally been considered state-objectors. This rejection of COs has softened only gradually in the course of the twentieth century" (in Moskos and Chambers, eds., *op. cit.*, p. 144). A good insight into Swiss thinking on the subject can be obtained from the 21 essays in Marc Häring and Max Gmür, eds., *Soldat in Zivil? Militärdienst – Militärdienstverweigerung – Zivildienst – Militärjustiz* (Zürich: EVZ Verlag, 1970). The contributors include theologians (Catholic as well as Protestant), lawyers, philosophers, politicians, C.Os., and an army officer.

39 The most useful overview of pacifism and conscientious objection in the communist states of Eastern Europe during the Cold War era is Lawrance Klippenstein, "Conscientious Objectors in Eastern Europe: The Quest for Free Choice and Alternative Service," pp. 276–309, 393–404 in Sabrina Petra Ramet, ed., *Protestantism and Politics in Eastern Europe and Russia: The Communist and Postcommunist Eras* (Durham and London: Duke University Press, 1992). This study is richly documented; though of course the author at that date lacked access to archives, eleven pages of footnotes provide a lead into the extensive printed literature on the subject. See also for the Soviet Union, Seng "Kriegsdienstverweigerung in der Sowjetunion," pp. 372–81 in Janning *et al.*, eds., *op. cit.*; and for Poland, Wojciech Modzelewski, "Pacifism, Anti-Militarism and Conscientious Objection in Poland," *Polish Sociological Review* (Warsaw), no. 1 (106), 1994, pp. 59–67. This article, though, concentrates on the postcommunist era.

40 Except for Albania, traditionally a predominantly Muslim country. The idea of pacifism reached it only after the collapse of communism. For the other countries, see Peter Brock, "The Small-sect Antimilitarists of Interwar East Central Europe," *Reconciliation Quarterly* (London), Autumn 1955, pp. 6–16. (The printers made havoc of page 12.)

41 Klippenstein, *op. cit.*, p. 278.

42 The fullest treatment of conscientious objection in the DDR is Bernd Eisenfeld, *Kriegsdienstverweigerung in der DDR – ein Friedensdienst? Genesis – Befragung – Analyse – Dokumente* (Frankfurt am Main: Haag und Herchen Verlag, 1978). The book contains 87 pages of documentary appendices.

43 The decree of 7 September 1964 establishing *Baueinheiten* as well as the oath the *Bausoldaten* were required to take are reproduced in Uwe Kock and Stephan Eschler, eds., *Zähne hoch – Kopf zusammenbeissen: Dokumente zur*

Kriegsdienstverweigerung in der DDR 1962–1990 (Kuckenshagen: Scheunen-Verlag, 1994), pp. 35, 36. We may note that political instruction was obligatory and that the oath included such extremely ambiguous requirements as "unconditional obedience" to military orders and readiness to do everything to raise "the defensive capability" of the Fatherland.

44 Klippenstein, *op. cit.*, pp. 282, 283. Eisenfeld's assessment of the post-1960s role of the Evangelical Church *vis-à-vis* C.Os. is less positive than Klippenstein's; see, for instance, his conclusions on p. 138. At any rate the Evangelical Church in the DDR certainly did not possess such outstanding champions of pacifism as West German Evangelicals did in Niemöller, Mensching and *Oberkirchenrat* Heinz Klippenburg (to cite only three examples).

45 Koch and Eschler, eds., *op. cit.*, pp. 37–39. One of these "refusers" was Gottfried Arlt, then a theological student and later a Protestant clergyman, whose account is printed by Koch and Eschler.

46 Eisenfeld, *op. cit.*, p. 79; Koch and Eschler, eds., *op. cit.*, p. 39.

47 Michael Frenzel, "Und dann zuruck in den Verwahrraum," pp. 255–61 in Janning *et al.*, eds., *op. cit.* See also p. 395. After reunification absolutists from the former DDR faced prison sentences, as happened for instance in the case of the anarchist objector Ralf Morwinsky from Rostock. Andreas Ciesielski, *... und er sagt NEIN* (Kuckenshagen: Scheunen-Verlag, 1993).

48 Here the evangelical pacifism of Father Bulányi and his followers aroused stiff opposition among the hierarchy. See chap. XI below.

49 Klippenstein, *op. cit.*, pp. 291–4. Cf. p. 401 n. 83: "Noncombatant service was available in the army, with three years of working on underground construction regarded as fulfilling military obligations." These conditions certainly compare adversely even with those in East Germany's *Bauein-heiten*.

50 Introduced in 1976, it called on Polish soldiers "to safeguard peace in fraternal alliance with the Soviet Army and other allied armies."

51 Klippenstein (*op. cit.*, p. 295) cites the case of a Bulgarian Pentecostal, Emil Kalmakov, who was jailed five times between 1979 and December 1988 for his refusal to serve in the army. When the army authorities finally let him go, Kalmakov had spent a total of seven years in prison. Moreover his father, when he had protested the harsh treatment of his son and other C.Os., was himself sentenced to what eventually amounted to a five-year term. See *ibid.*, p. 401 n. 93.

52 *Ibid.*, p. 294.

53 Quoted in *ibid.*, p. 285. A commanding officer could assign a C.O. to noncombatant duties if he wished. But if he was unwilling to do so – or if a C.O. was unwilling, to serve as a noncombatant – then imprisonment inevitably followed.

54 Quoted in Seng, *op. cit.*, p. 377.

55 *Ibid.*, p. 380.

56 See Klippenstein, *op. cit.*, pp. 298–307.

57 Modzelewski, *op. cit.*, pp. 62–64. Apart from the JWs, Seventh-day Adventists formed the most numerous religious C.O. group in Poland.

58 See Carter, *op. cit.*, pp. 197–200 ("Anti-militarism in Slovenia").

59 It is interesting to note that in neighboring Croatia shortly before independence, a drafted Catholic priest, Father Andrija Ursić, had been jailed as a C.O. He was, writes Klippenstein (*op. cit.*, p. 295), "the first Yugoslav Catholic and priest to have refused military duties on grounds of conscience." Thus, as we might expect, in the successor states of Yugoslavia Catholics as well as ethical objectors have figured among the small minority of conscripts who have applied for C.O. status. Orthodox C.Os. have not come to our notice, though they probably exist.

60 See "Russian Court rules No Alternative to Army Service," *Peace Magazine* (Toronto), vol. 13, no. 1 (January/February 1997), pp. 14, 15. For the latest situation, see Amnesty International, *Russian Federation: The Right to Conscientious Objection to Military Service*, AI EUR 46/05/97, esp. pp. i, 3, 4.

61 Klippenstein, *op. cit.*, p. 303.

62 *Ibid.*

63 The Minister of Defense and Disarmament in the government which affected the epoch-making transition, Rainer Eppelmann, was a Protestant pastor who had been jailed as a C.O. under the communist régime. See Carter, *op. cit.*, p. 186. Pastor Eppelmann, even though he was not an absolute pacifist, from his own experiences certainly understood the viewpoint of the conscientious objector.

64 Home was the brother of a future conservative Prime Minister and himself later to become a popular playwright. For his act of defiance, he was naturally sentenced to a term in jail.

65 Ruth Linn, *Conscience at War: The Israeli Soldier as a Moral Critic* (Albany: State University of New York Press, 1996), pp. 201, 202. Refusers were drawn from officers as well as men; while most of them were reservists there were some current draftees, too. The Arab Intifada represented a largely, though by no means entirely, nonviolent resistance movement in Israeli occupied territories; see chapter XI below.

66 Conscription was introduced in South Africa in 1960: it applied only to males legally defined as white and it allowed – religious – C.Os. exemption solely from combatant duties. Until the end of apartheid the C.O. situation in the Republic of South Africa bore a fairly close resemblance to that existing in Israel during roughly the same period. In South Africa, alongside a small number of absolute pacifists who, if drafted, objected to bearing arms on religious or religio-ethical grounds, there existed from the 1970s an

increasing – though still small – number of draft resisters, who refused to serve in the South African Defence Force because they viewed it as an instrument of racial discrimination and oppression. While the state in 1983 had for the first time granted a civilian alternative for C.Os. who were religious pacifists, such exemption was not open to those objectors – of whatever white "ethnie" – for whom "apartheid, not war, was the issue." The latter might be religious or nonreligious: as in Israel, that was not the point. But unlike the Israeli situation, in South Africa most SCOs made their protest outside and not inside the army framework. Whereas in Israeli penalties for SCOs were comparatively mild, in South Africa, on the other hand, they tended to be harsh until the growing anti-apartheid movement finally put a brake on such excesses. Before that happened, in mid-1988, for instance, we find David Bruce, an SCO, being sentenced to six years' jail for ignoring his call-up; he was unwilling to help maintain apartheid by armed force. For a competent survey, see Annette Seegers, "South Africa: From Laager to Anti-Apartheid," pp. 127–34 in Moskos and Chambers, eds., *op. cit.*; also Carter, *op. cit.*, pp. 233–5. Carter (p. 235) calls attention to the Israel-South Africa SCO parallel and its perception by both sides.

67 Radical Quaker war-tax objectors included Nathaniel Morgan in England early in the nineteenth century and Joshua Maule during the American Civil War. Just prior to World War II an English schoolteacher (F.C. Ade at Eltham College) was sentenced to 21 days' imprisonment for refusing to pay that portion of his income tax he considered went to pay for armaments. See *The War Resister* (Enfield, Middlesex), no. 44 (July, 1938), p. 27. His stance, though, was still an exceptional one among pacifists in general.

X. The Historic Peace Churches since 1945

During the Cold War and its aftermath the prolonged struggle against nuclear weapons and the widespread draft resistance, slowly growing larger during this period, drew support predominantly from people who did not share the pacifist faith *sensu stricto*. Yet, as the previous chapters have shown, in the international peace movement of the Cold War era, pacifists, religious and secular, still played a significant role, that of a prophetic minority; they had frequently provided inspiration for peace activists both in states where conscription was already a permanent institution and where it had been introduced – or, as in the case of West Germany, reintroduced – after the war. Pacifists, working within a context of "nuclear pacifism," also took an active, and sometimes initiatory, role in the nuclear disarmament movements that emerged after 1955. Of equal value was the part they played, beginning in the early 1950s, in introducing and developing nonviolent direct action for peace. Other aspects of the broad peace movement in which pacifists were prominent included opposition to militarism and the encouragement of war resistance. On many occasions they supported those refusing the draft in the case of specific wars and upheld, as part of their total pacifist rejection of war, the principle of conscientious objection for all who sincerely refused to fight. They stood up for the rights of the "selective objector" alongside those of the absolute pacifist war resister. For, we know, there now existed on a wide scale new non- pacifist forms of conscientious objection, no longer confined mainly to the traditional and strictly pacifist minorities but involving a majority of non-pacifists.[1]

Christian pacifism continued to form an important component of the pacifist community, with liberal Protestants predominating, at any rate at first, in such organizations as the International Fellowship of Reconciliation (IFOR), which began to expand again once the war was over. The largest, and most active, fellowship was the American, to which a number of denominational societies were affiliated. In postwar Britain the FOR, though not large, included some distinguished members ranging from high-church Anglicans to Unitarians. Elsewhere, except for the Dutch fellowship which had merged in 1946 with the revived *Church and Peace* of the interwar years (see above), the other fellowships scattered over the globe remained small and usually made little impact on society. Theirs was an isolated witness; they did what they could for the cause of peace – and went on in faith.

Compared to the interwar period Christian pacifism after 1945 has so far produced no expository work to compare in its wide impact and broad scholarship to the Dutch Remonstrant theologian G.J. Heering's book entitled, in English translation, *The Fall of Christianity* (1930). Nevertheless there have been some notable contributions in the postwar era to the theology of Christian pacifism. In Protestant Germany, for instance, Luise Schottroff and Dorothee Sölle have explored *inter alia* the relationship between Jesus' love commandment and feminist theology, while Hans Werner Bartsch examined again the New Testament bases of pacifism.[2] In France, the small pacifist minority in the Reformed Church continued its prewar peace witness in word and deed.[3] In Britain we may mention the classical scholar, John Ferguson, who, in addition to his work on behalf of the Fellowship of Reconciliation, wrote eloquently in support of Christian pacifism as did the research chemist and lay theologian R.E.D. Clark in his *Does the Bible teach Pacifism?* (1976), which was designed for popular consumption. Pacifist expositors in the United States have included both evangelical and liberal Protestants[4] as well as Mennonites and Catholics whose work will be dealt with below.

This chapter centers attention on the three historic peace churches: Quakers, Mennonites, and Brethren.[5] But we should remember that, even in the United States, where the peace churches were strongest, the majority of active religious pacifists belonged to nonpacifist denominations. By now they had, for the most part, gained toleration – and often respect – from their fellow members. But pacifism remained a minority position in these bodies; that could sometimes cause a certain alienation, especially in time of war or during an international crisis. Some religious pacifists outside the peace churches, moreover, remained only loosely connected denominationally. From time to time such people moved into the Quaker orbit if diversity of view and a pacifist *ambiance* prevailed there.

Developing Quaker Peacemaking

The peace witness of the Quakers (Society of Friends) over the last half century has continued on the whole along the course already embarked upon in an earlier period. Within the religious pacifist community, it was the Society of Friends that made the most striking – and at times perhaps the most controversial – contribution to the peace movement of the Cold War era: repetition of a role they had played for at least a century.

No outstanding exposition of the foundations of Quaker pacifism has emerged, it is true, from a Quaker pen for a very long time. If "in their 300-year history Friends have rarely produced first-rate theologians, ... in virtually every generation those grappling with the implications of the peace testimony have been truly creative."[6] Quakers indeed have shown a persistence in the enterprise of peace unequalled by any other religious body. Thus we find today the two most significant communities of Friends, the Quakers of Britain and of the United States, both active in the peacemaking process of our dangerous contemporary world. Not all Quakers in these countries, of course; for some Friends, especially in the United States, have abandoned pacifism and given unconditional support to military preparedness. (After all, the late Richard Nixon could lay claim to membership in the Society of Friends as well as to having been twice elected president of the United States.) Yet the widespread identification of Quakerism with pacifism is certainly not unjustified. Pacifism continues to be the faith of most Friends who have remained closest to Quaker essentials, whether belonging to the liberal or evangelical branches of their Society, and these people have continued to work diligently for a more peaceful world.

Usually post-1945 Quaker peacemaking, like wartime and postwar Quaker humanitarian relief work, has not been specifically pacifist, that is, these activities have been such as nonpacifists could support and participate in. (Indeed nonpacifists, whether members of the Society of Friends or outside it, have often done so.) What has been specifically Quaker and pacifist has been the spirit in which such work has been carried on, and the ethos underlying it that has prompted Friends to undertake action either as a body or as individuals acting under a religious concern.

Quakers as Conciliators

This is not the place to give anything approaching a comprehensive history of the Quakers' peacemaking efforts since 1945.[7] Let us just select several of their more significant endeavors so that the reader may gain a reasonably clear picture of their contribution to recent pacifist history. As Sydney Bailey has written: "peace is a process to engage in, not a goal to be reached."[8] The success of contemporary nonviolent conflict resolution, whether by Quakers or by others, can be judged only in the light of the ongoing character of world events.

Efforts to ease tensions between the Eastern and Western power blocs and with China figured of course during the Cold War among the Quakers' major concerns. More limited conflicts where Quakers attempted a mediating role included the India-Pakistan War over Kashmir in 1965 and the Nigerian Civil War of 1967–70[9] as well as the more prolonged Arab-Israeli confrontation in the Near East and the Catholic-Protestant conflict in Northern Ireland where in particular two Quakers, Denis P. Barritt from Ulster and Will Warren from England, worked indefatigably for a peaceful resolution of the conflict. In all their mediation efforts Friends have tried to keep an open mind.[10] "Our sympathies," a Quaker has said, "are for *all* the people in conflict, not for one side or the other." True, "one cannot be impartial when faced with gross injustice or aggression but one can try to be fair."[11] The path of the reconciler is strewn with pitfalls, as in the case of the American Friends Service Committee (AFSC), which has been charged with bias in favor of communist countries and liberation movements in the Third World over a twenty-year period from the late 1960's to the late 1980s. (We shall discuss this controversial issue below.) Such bias, in so far as it has in fact existed, certainly runs contrary to the basic principles on which the fabric of Quaker conciliation rests, principles that have been operative since such early projects as the three-man peace mission which English Quakers sent to Russia in 1854 on the eve of the Crimean war. But even then, as in similar episodes later, their acting under religious and humanitarian concern, and not for political motives, did not shield Quakers from attack.

In our own day the residential conferences for mid-career diplomats held since 1952 represent one of the most interesting developments in Quaker international work. Participants came from around one hundred countries; "many of them [subsequently] reached positions of distinction in the diplomatic field." These conferences were started in the belief that, although "diplomats are agents of the governments they represent, ... within these constraints they could play a key role in relieving international tension." The conferences have had four major objectives:

1. To reinforce the commitment of diplomats to ethical principles and values ...

2. To open up for discussion the findings of social science, peace and conflict research, and other disciplines bearing on contemporary diplomacy.
3. To raise issues of special Quaker concern (e.g. refugee problems, disarmament, mediation, human rights).
4. To facilitate human contact across political barriers.[12]

In administering this program British Friends worked in close cooperation with the AFSC. Other – often jointly sponsored – Quaker international efforts have included: a Quaker presence in Geneva and at the United Nations headquarters in New York; the appointment of loosely Quaker-attached International Affairs Representatives (QIAR); a project, representing an adaptation of the idea first conceived by the English Quaker Carl Heath after World War I, of "Quaker embassies" in the major world capitals to further world peace and understanding; and the continuation from the interwar period of Quaker centers in various key cities, including post-Soviet Moscow, as bases for supporting various Quaker concerns, and especially that of promoting international understanding.[13] American Friends have attempted to influence Congress decision-making on such issues as disarmament, or at least reduction in armaments, East-West reconciliation, etc.; and for many years E. Raymond Wilson, as executive secretary of the Friends Committee on National Legislation, kept a close watch on Capitol Hill (a task earlier performed by that indefatigable pacifist lobbyist, Dorothy Detzer, of the Women's International League for Peace and Freedom).[14] British Friends, together with the small and scattered Quaker Yearly Meetings on the European continent, were particularly active in pressing for international recognition of conscientious objection as a human right, including selective, i.e. nonpacifist, objection.

Individual Friends, too, have been pioneers in the scholarly study of peace, beginning with the Englishman Lewis Fry Richardson, meteorologist and statistician, who died in 1953,[15] and including outstanding peace researchers like the economist (and sonneteer) Kenneth E. Boulding and Adam Curle, who has been active in peace work on both sides of the Atlantic. These scholars, along with non-Quaker colleagues, have investigated *inter alia* the workings of the international system, examined the causes of violence, and enquired into ways and means of resolving nonviolently both conflicts within society and those between states.

A characteristic feature of post-1945 Quaker peacemaking has been (to quote Cecil Evans) "the emphasis or linkage between peace and justice: thus there can be no real peace without justice." That idea indeed does not represent a totally new dimension in Quaker – or pacifist –

thinking; we find it, for instance, clearly expressed by members of the Quaker Socialist Society, founded in Britain back in 1898. But since 1945 it has come for the first time to the fore.

Quakers today number world-wide a little over two hundred thousand members. Since many of these are not in sympathy with mainstream. Quakerism's activities for peace, resources for such activities, both as to personnel and to funds (in this case partly provided by non-Quakers), are obviously limited. So Friends have needed to select carefully the issues where they believed they might be able to intervene successfully in helping to resolve a conflict and to choose only those occasions where there appeared to be some chance of making a worthwhile contribution in a situation of impending or actual violence. Necessarily, as Mike Yarrow points out, "many conflict situations [occur] ... in which the Quaker organizations [do] not feel called to intervene." For intervention to happen there must, above all, be a deep sense of concern among Friends that action in the matter is right, arising not so much from "an objective assessment" as from "a subjective interest" on the part of individuals whose past or present involvement has led them to feel strongly moved to action. Such a pattern of procedure can be traced back in Quaker history by way of John Woolman, "the supremely conscientious eighteenth-century Quaker," to Quaker beginnings at the time of Fox and Penn.[16] Considerations of this kind explain why, for instance, Quakers attempted to act as conciliators in the India-Pakistan War of 1965, the mission they then sent to South Asia for this purpose achieving a limited success "by aiding the cooling-off process" at the end of hostilities, whereas no Quaker action materialized during the civil war in East Pakistan in 1971 and India's armed intervention in what soon emerged as Bangladesh. In this case Friends nearest the problem judged that a Quaker "visitation" of the kind undertaken six years earlier would be inappropriate and lead at best to the restoration of an unjust status quo. Therefore, "Quakers sent no conciliatory mission."[17]

The design of Quaker peacemaking after World War II, continuing the tradition of "integrational pacifism" inherited from the Society's past,[18] was set on a background of sovereign states loosely bound by the United Nations organization, but with this international structure shaken by periodic outbreaks of violence or the threat of such. Quaker peacemakers have sought to create a more peaceable world within the existing international system. With their will to achieve greater peace generated by their Society's absolute pacifism, they nevertheless accept working for intermediate goals in collaboration with men and women who, even though they may not accept even conditional nonviolence, Friends still hope may be amenable to persuasion in reaching a nonviolent resolution of a given conflict. This outlook is anchored deep in the Quaker past. For instance, in 1692 we find William Penn writing: "Our present condition in Europe ... needs an olive branch, the doctrine of peace, as much as ever."[19] Next year he was to publish a brief essay on *The Peace of Europe*,[20] which would lay the foundations for Quaker efforts to strengthen international organization and lessen the incidence of conflict – in a belief that "the advantages of peace and mischiefs of war are so many and sensible to every capacity under all governments."[21] The Quaker peacemakers, whose activities we have referred to above, are in their endeavors today clearly Penn's heirs.

There is, it is true, a certain elitism in these Quaker intrusions into the realm of high politics. Participants in such projects have usually been specialists of one kind or another or Quaker bureaucrats (if one may use this word in a non-pejorative sense). But Quaker pacifists have often sought "to speak truth to power"[22] in other, perhaps more egalitarian ways. Some have chosen to act as prophets rather than re-concilers and exercise their prophetic mission in acts of civil disobedi-ence, including war tax resistance. Others have engaged in various forms of legal protest against war, including street demonstrations against the atomic bomb, or have worked on such schemes as the insti-tution of a peace tax, recognized by governments, for those who do not wish to see their tax money go toward preparation for war.[23]

Quakers have rarely hesitated to follow conscience when this clashed with the decrees of governments. Breaking the law in obedi-ence to conscience is an even more ancient Quaker tradition than the kind of peacemaking inaugurated by William Penn. After World War II, where governments still imposed conscription young Quakers have sometimes gone to jail as draft resisters, or they have performed alter-native service as part of their witness as conscientious objectors when the laws of their country allowed this. In the United States, we may note, the consensus among Friends went against resuscitation of Civil-ian Public Service, at any rate in so far as Quaker participation in run-ning CPS camps was concerned. Both Quaker draftees and Quaker administrators have indeed had second thoughts concerning this expe-rience, despite the optimism with which CPS was inaugurated in 1941.

Controversy over the American Friends Service Committee

In recent decades the chief Quaker service organization in the United States, AFSC, has come under attack for its cold-war-era activities beginning with the 1960s. Critics have accused it of undergoing secularization; they have claimed that its originally religious message of peace was replaced during this period by a political program supporting communist-dominated régimes and movements throughout the world. Paying only lip-service to the idea of nonviolence, the AFSC, say the critics, now abandoned pacifism in practice and actively supported wars of liberation from political and social oppression as well as armed resistance to what it considered to be U.S. aggression. And as the Vietnam War developed, the organization "joined" the New Left in all but name, along with other leading pacifist societies.[24] Since criticism of this kind has been voiced not only by antipacifists of various kinds but also – usually in more moderate fashion – by both Quaker and non-Quaker pacifists, it is appropriate that we should deal with this issue, however briefly.

In 1947 the AFSC, jointly with its sister organization the Friends Service Council in Britain, had been awarded the prestigious Nobel Peace Prize for its humanitarian efforts and its endeavors on behalf of international peace.[25] Over the next decade and a half it continued to stress its faith in the "relevance" of pacifism and in "the effectiveness of love in human relations," including relations between states. It argued the case for unilateral disarmament and urged "in terms of common sense" (since "in the nuclear age ... we are constrained to make peace" in order to avoid universal destruction) the adoption of nonviolent resistance as national policy in case of invasion. But at the same time it took care to restate carefully the religious bases of its pacifist absolutism.[26]

From the 1960s on, however, the AFSC began indeed to take up a rather more clearly political stance. This development, which was not entirely novel since Quaker pacifism had never excluded politics from its purview, took place on a background of rising radicalization, especially of American youth, and mounting U.S. intervention in Vietnam. In addition liberation struggles in the Third World, and especially in Latin America, and the explosive situation in the Near East, where endemic warfare existed between Arabs and Israelis, threatened to involve the United States in an escalating conflict.

In this situation Quakers could scarcely stand aloof nursing their pacifist purity in isolation from the environing society. The trouble, however, was that the Society of Friends in the United States, though numerically small, contained within its membership "a complex mixture of subcultures, from the evangelicals through to the closet Marxists,"[27] so that consensus on peace issues was difficult to achieve. The fact that a considerable number of American Quakers, we know, were not pacifists, or at best very lukewarm ones, added a further complication. On the other hand, AFSC staff tended toward the political left, whether they belonged to the Society of Friends or not;[28] and most of the staff, too, were religious liberals, in many cases influenced by the Social Gospel tradition. This alone was sufficient to create a sense of alienation from AFSC among evangelical and fundamentalist Friends, especially in the West, and among the large number of Quakers with Republican sympathies (sympathies dating back to Lincoln's time). With some justification indeed, these sections of the Society of Friends felt themselves underrepresented on the AFSC's governing bodies and excluded from an effective role in determining its policies.[29]

The AFSC, as did most other pacifists, viewed the American presence in Vietnam as an act of aggression by the United States, and they condemned it as such in no uncertain terms. They blamed the U.S. administration for supporting a corrupt and undemocratic régime and for the wholesale destruction of innocent civilians and their property, especially through massive aerial attacks and the use of napalm bombs. Earlier Quakers had adopted a similar line during the Mexican War of 1846–8 branding the armed intervention by their country then as a "horrid affair," an "iniquitous" reversion to savagery by a hitherto civilized nation.[30] Once again, therefore, there was nothing novel in the AFSC stance, however reprehensible such an attitude might seem to some American patriots. The appropriateness of AFSC participation in mass demonstrations against the war and in "inclusive" coalitions of antiwar organizations was more questionable; but there were rational arguments pro as well as con.[31] The same might be said of such issues as the proper strategy for ending hostilities in Vietnam, whether by an immediate withdrawal of U.S. forces, for instance, or by a negotiated cease-fire between the two sides. In the existing situation, however, every step toward establishing peace was fraught with danger. The AFSC was also divided on the issue of civil disobedience in a war situation, including the destruction of draft board records and other government property.[32]

But the flaw in AFSC thinking on the war resided elsewhere. It lay in a tendency among some influential staff members to romanticize the other side; such persons failed to apply to the National Liberation Front (NLF) and North Vietnam the rigorous critique to which they invariably submitted the actions of their own government. Thus they succumbed to "the typical defensive pacifist double-standard position of the later 1960s: nonviolence at home, but tacitly endorsed 'just' violence abroad."[33] True, the AFSC never abandoned its traditional policy of bringing aid to the victims of war regardless of their religious or national affiliation; the AFSC relief program at Quang Ngai in South Vietnam, together with the aid it was able to get to the civilian population in the North, witnesses to this. It is also true that, despite assertions by critics to the contrary, the organization maintained friendly contacts with the Buddhist "third force," though possibly these were not as close as they could have been. Guenter Lewy, its major critic, cites several statements in support of revolutionary violence, made by top AFSC staff and especially by members of its Peace Education Division; qualified though such statements were by an assertion of personal pacifism and a preference for nonviolent revolution where that was possible, they departed startlingly from traditional expressions of the Quaker peace testimony.[34] The key to this palliation of violence and leaning toward the idea of just war is not far to seek. The impulse here was not indeed an ignoble one and, *mutatis mutandis*, the position adopted resembled, for instance, that taken up during the Civil War by the nonresistant and abolitionist, William Lloyd Garrison,[35] or at the outset of Indian independence by Mahatma Gandhi: one party in an international conflict or internal confrontation had right on its side and, unless prepared to undertake nonviolent resistance, would be cowardly if it did not resist the aggressor or oppressor by arms. In World War II also, Quakers and the other pacifists, while remaining by no means uncritical of the Allies, usually made a distinction to the latter's advantage when comparing them to the Axis powers. During the Vietnam War, however, some responsible persons in the AFSC certainly went very far in identifying themselves with the "enemy"; they failed to speak truth to the latter's power when this was clearly the proper Quakerly response.[36]

Such failures of Quakerly critical acumen and sensitivity to wrong became particularly apparent after hostilities came to an end in the spring of 1975. We find, for example, the head of the AFSC's Indochina program, John McAuliff, who was then visiting Hanoi, extending his stay so as to be able to participate in the North Vietnam's victory celebrations and, as McAuliff's *Indochina Program Newsletter* of 5 May put it, the defeat of "the combined power of the Pentagon, CIA, FBI and five successive Administrations."[37] True, Garrison had taken part in analogous celebrations at the conclusion of the Civil War. That was certainly a precedent but hardly a justification. In fact the idea of pacifists celebrating a military victory at once elicited a sharp response from the ASFC's New England regional office, whose peace education secretary, Ed Lazar, published an article in its house journal entitled "Military Victories Are Not Cause for Celebration." Elaborating on his argument in a later issue, Lazar wrote:

Those 'just' bullets in wars of liberation kill – and they kill civilian women, men and children as well as other combatants; and the combatants are victims as well ... I do not believe that we should support wars of liberation ... The public and the media have every reason to be sceptical about a peace movement that opposes war only when the war is going the wrong way.

In Lazar's view Quakers and other pacifists should only "actively support peaceful struggles for radical change and liberation."[38]

In the aftermath of war AFSC strove to achieve a normalization of relations between the former belligerents and to contribute materially to the reconstruction of the devastated – but at last reunited – country. They appealed for a spirit of reconciliation in place of the enmity that had prevailed hitherto between the U.S. and the communists who now ruled all Vietnam. This, anathema to some of America's hawks, was in line with the Quaker spirit as it had manifested itself in the aftermath of previous wars. However, when evidence soon reached the outside world of persecution inflicted by the new régime on non-conformists, including the imprisonment of pacifist Buddhists and the suppression of their activities, the AFSC refused to join with those antiwar activists like Richard Neuhaus and the Catholic Worker James Forest when they mounted an appeal to the new régime asking it to observe basic human rights. The AFSC justified its refusal on the grounds that insufficient evidence of abuse of human rights was then available and that, moreover, protests of this kind would only hinder the essential task of postwar reconstruction being undertaken by the Vietnam government.[39] McAuliff of the AFSC was among those misguided members of the peace movement who "helped spread the slander that [the poet] Thich Nhât Hanh, a member of the Unified Buddhist Church and an international vice-president of the FOR, was a CIA agent."[40]

In January 1977 the AFSC sent a delegation of six to Vietnam. It included Stewart Meacham, head of its Peace Education Division, and Wallace Collett, a businessman and chairman of its board of directors. On returning home members of the delegation painted a rosy picture of political conditions in that country and virtually denied the existence of repression there. Collett before he left Hanoi spoke of "the decency, the sincerity, and the *humaneness* of Vietnam." This proved too much for Kenneth Boulding and John P. Powelson, colleagues in the Department of Economics at the University of Colorado and for long active and influential members of the Society of Friends. Powelson charged the AFSC with having become an apologist "for third-world repression"; he feared its attitude "might even be construed as a

Quaker endorsement of it." He deeply regretted that the delegation had deemed it "inappropriate" to make any serious inquiries into the plight of political detainees. Boulding, equally disturbed by the position taken by the AFSC toward the communist government of Vietnam over the last few years, went so far as to carry out a two-hour silent vigil in the lobby of the AFSC's Philadelphia office on the morning of 31 March 1977. He did this, he declared, to express his distress "that the AFSC is departing from the light of the Gospel ... and is following an ideology that is ... secular and untrue." For Boulding, the whole experience proved indeed extremely painful; for he perceived it "as betrayal by someone whom we considered part of the 'we' and turned out not to be."[41]

This sense of alienation *vis-à-vis* AFSC, which Boulding now felt, was shared by many other Quaker pacifists, if not always so acutely. It took many years before the wounds were healed, for causes for dissatisfaction with the organization continued to occur. The AFSC, for instance, was to lag behind in its awareness of the widespread atrocities committed by the Khmer Rouge in Cambodia (Kampuchea).[42] It did, however, publicly condemn the subsequent Vietnamese invasion of Cambodia and extend humanitarian aid to the refugees who fled from repression in this area.[43]

Other issues over which AFSC policies generated controversy during this period include its Latin American programs and its role in the ongoing Arab-Israeli conflict. In each case wrong judgments or decisions were made (as was only natural in view of the complicated nature of such issues); on the other hand, there were also achievements in these areas reflecting the Quaker impulse toward peace and justice.

Life and its problems can look very different when viewed from a shanty town of a Latin American metropolis rather than from a well-to-do Washington suburb. The AFSC, to its credit, has endeavored not only to bring relief to the victims of war but also to the many millions suffering from poverty, itself a producer of conflict; it has sought to understand the causes of such major evils afflicting humankind and not merely alleviate their results. In this connection the Quaker sociologist, Elise Boulding, has written perceptively:

The AFSC ... had gone [far] in acknowledging kinship with and staying in relationship with groups whose lifeways differ sharply from those of middle class pacifists, groups that sometimes seek more far-reaching changes than the average pacifist feels called upon to support. This has led the AFSC into uncomfortable situations that many of us have never had to confront. Keeping a steady and loving spirit in those situations, and upholding the commitment to nonviolence, requires great inner strength ... Certainly the AFSC has made mistakes. But they have been the mistakes of love and concern ... We can choose to stay in risk-free spaces where the purity of our pacifism is never questioned, or we can choose to move into those spaces where humanity's growing pains are most acutely on display.[44]

With respect to Latin America and its liberation struggles there were indeed AFSC staff members who flirted with the idea of a qualitative justification for revolutionary violence. But the organization as a whole stood firmly by its peaceable principles and refused to compromise on this issue, "however extreme the provocation." "Although we yearn for and work for an end to galling exploitation," the Board of Directors declared in a policy statement issued in January 1981, "we cannot endorse the use of violence," even when used against the "violence of the powerful" by "those seeking to end their own oppression." Therefore, for Quakers there could be no "theory of 'acceptable' revolutionary violence."[45]

As regards Castro's Cuba (where a Quaker Yearly Meeting existed) and Sandinista-ruled Nicaragua AFSC supported the principle of self-determination and opposed the kind of undercover intervention practised in Nicaragua by the U.S. administration through support of the "Contras." In the case of both governments the AFSC stressed, perhaps unduly, the social achievements of these régimes and pointed out that neither of them constituted a genuine threat to U.S. security. On the other hand, the warlike atmosphere prevailing in both countries alarmed Quakers. As AFSC reported about Cuba in 1969, society there seemed "to be a mixture of warm humanitarianism and domestic militarism."[46]

Turning now to the AFSC's role in the Arab-Israeli conflict we scarcely need be surprised at the organization coming under attack when we learn what were its objectives in that area: "Peace *and* justice ... Negotiations between present enemies instead of war."[47] Thus, contacts established by AFSC with the Palestine Liberation Organization (PLO) were sometimes interpreted as support of "unbridled terror" and promotion of violence, while the presence of staff members of Jewish background in key positions in AFSC's Middle East program as well as AFSC collaboration with "the other Israel," composed of doves of various hues, appeared in a sinister light to certain American Zionists.[48] In fact the AFSC, while urging what it considered to be the rights of the Palestinians, including recognition of the PLO as a negotiating partner, never ceased to express support for "the legitimacy of the state of Israel," alongside a still nonexistent Palestinian state. In the late

1990s what the AFSC strove to achieve over previous decades appears near realization – to the mutual advantage of both peoples.

The AFSC emerged from the Cold War era intact but not unscathed. It had attempted to combat the excesses of anticommunism as well as unreasoning hostility to the Soviet Union on the part of both the American public and the administration and to build bridges, and establish dialogue, between East and West so as to create détente before both sides were swallowed up in a global nuclear holocaust. In doing this it had sometimes fallen into the opposite error of minimizing oppression and painting an idealized picture of conditions in the communist world. In the mid-1980s, for instance, we find Friend John Powelson (see above) complaining about this in connection with recent reports on the Soviet Union published by the AFSC.[49] Nevertheless, despite these shortcomings the AFSC had helped to keep communications open between the peoples of the rival blocs in a period of prolonged international tension.

With the dissolution of the Soviet empire and the ending of the Cold War the AFSC has entered a new phase of activity. At its outset the Gulf War presented it with an immediate challenge: how to counter "the myths propagated to convince the American public the war was just and necessary." In the long run the task of the AFSC remains today what it had been since at least mid-century: to create "a vision of the future which does not rely on massive military force and sophisticated technology, but on strengthened mechanisms for international conflict resolution and on pursuit of justice within and between nations."[50]

Pacifist Renewal among Mennonites and Brethren

The Quakers' peacemaking after 1945 was sometimes innovative. But, on the whole, we have seen that it did not represent a startling break with their traditional patterns of action. On the other hand a far-reaching transformation occurred over the last half-century with respect to the peace witness of the two other "historic peace churches" of North America – the Mennonites and the Church of the Brethren. These bodies now abandoned much of their former quietism, replacing it by a more active form of peacemaking situated alongside the peace efforts of all those who strove for a warless world.

This process had already begun in the Church of the Brethren before the outbreak of World War II; with the Mennonites it came really only after 1945. In both denominations there remained several small other-worldly – and largely rural – sects which were affected scarcely, if at all, by these changes. Such groups continued to nurse their separateness and uphold a doctrine of nonresistance little altered throughout the centuries. But they represented only a small percentage of their respective religious communities.[51]

The Mennonites

On the European continent acculturation of the Dutch and German Mennonites, the largest communities outside Russia, had led finally to an unconditional rejection of nonresistance in favor of members accepting full military service in defense of the *patria*. This adaptation was completed in the Netherlands in 1795 and in Germany in 1934. Would the same thing happen eventually in the case of the Mennonites of North America as – socially and educationally – their once largely isolated congregations integrated gradually with the environing society? Around mid-twentieth-century many competent observers considered that process was indeed only a matter of time. But subsequent developments have shown such pessimism to have been mistaken.

The modernization of the Mennonite peace witness in the United States and Canada[52] took place on a background of the overall modernization of large sections of the North American Mennonite community. As a result of industrialization and "the jolt of World War II," Mennonites began to emerge in considerable numbers from "their rural shelters." Thus, "uprooted from rural homesteads, seeking higher education, entering professions and engaging in worldwide service activities, many Mennonites joined the mainstream of social [and cultural] life in the last half of the twentieth century."[53] Hitherto, their opposition to war had gone hand in hand with a determination to keep themselves as separate as possible from the affairs of the world. For the most part they avoided close association with the Christian pacifist movement, dominated as it had long been by the Social Gospel and by Gandhian concepts of nonviolent struggle and often caught up in political issues and international problems. For Guy F. Hershberger,[54] a leading exponent of Mennonite nonresistance in that period, Gandhi's *satyagraha* represented a form of coercion incompatible with the Christian ideal. Hershberger and his colleagues distinguished carefully between pacifism and nonresistance, which in their view was apolitical and ready to go the second mile rather than resist even nonviolently and for the most justifiable of causes. Understandably, Hershberger's intense biblicism led him to reject the idea of Mennonite collaboration with non-Christian pacifists even more strongly than collaboration with liberal Christian pacifists.

"The transformation of passive peasants into active peacemakers was," as Driedger and Kraybill point out, "a gradual metamorphosis" with its roots stretching back to the end of the last century.[55] But from 1950 on change became fairly rapid. Three issues, successively, dominated church discussions of peace and war and led in turn to a radical restructuring of the North American Mennonite peace witness: the question of political responsibility, the draft especially during the Vietnam War, and the liberation of the socially oppressed, particularly in Latin America where missionary activity had led to the emergence of indigenous Mennonite churches in virtually every country there.

The "separational" nonresistance that had prevailed among North American Mennonites hitherto, while it enjoined obedience to the powers that be (Romans 13: 1–7), frowned on most forms of political activity. Now some younger Mennonites began to ask if this attitude did not entail a dereliction of Christian duty. Could – and should – Mennonites stand aside in face of injustices of various kinds and take no political action to counteract them? "The charge of irresponsibility ... tormented their souls."[56] Various experiences had pushed these younger church members toward a more positive attitude to society and the state. They did not advocate abandoning nonresistance; but they sought a reinterpretation preserving what they believed was its essence while permitting action that would bring Mennonites into the pacifist mainstream.

Participation in postwar relief as well as various ecumenical contacts, especially the series of meetings known as the Puidoux theological conferences, held in Europe between 1955 and 1962 with the participation of the three "historic" peace churches and nonpacifist European Protestant churches as well,[57] all helped to strengthen these trends. Both Mennonite leaders of the older generation like Hershberger or Harold S. Bender, the scholarly rediscover of the "Anabaptist Vision," and younger men like Gordon Kaufman and J. Lawrence Burkholder, each of whom was to contribute significantly to the restructuring of their church's peace witness, agreed that Christian discipleship led along the way of love and that, moreover, a "prophetic witness" was called for that might eventually bring a collision with the state as it had done in the past.[58] But Kaufman and Burkholder went further and argued that Mennonites must now shoulder responsibility by entering the world and there engaging actively in the quest for peace and justice. If they failed to do this, they would have to plead guilty to the charges made against them of social irresponsibility. They could no longer shelter behind a perfectionist ethic which shielded them from reality, even if the new course they proposed entailed a measure of compromise that conflicted with the teaching of a basic document of their church like the Schleitheim Confession of 1527 or with Bender's recent interpretation of the Anabaptist vision. "Politics is a presupposition of life," Burkholder asserted; and if Mennonites wished to bear a meaningful peace witness in the contemporary world, they must somehow or other come to terms with this fact. They had to grapple with the problem of power in the international arena – and even in their own church community."[59]

The civil rights movement of the 1960s, led by Martin Luther King and inspired by Gandhi's practice of nonviolent resistance made, a strong impact on many Mennonites. A black Mennonite pastor, Victor Harding, who had worked closely with King in his campaigns against racial segregation, helped to popularize the idea of nonviolent resistance in the Mennonite community.[60]

The Vietnam War proved an equally powerful factor in pushing concerned American Mennonites toward a more active role in the peace movement and a more assertive stand against war. We find a Kansas Mennonite, James C. Juhnke, running – unsuccessfully – for Congress as a peace candidate; indeed over a long period some mid-West Mennonites, descendants of immigrants from Russia in the previous century, had participated in state politics. A few Mennonites felt unable conscientiously to pay taxes they believed were being used to finance the on-going war. More – especially urban – Mennonites participated in various forms of antiwar protest: street demonstrations, vigils and sit-ins at military bases and nuclear sites, and public draft-card burnings. Some of these actions involved breaking the law and brought the risk of jail sentences. All this was indeed new and was "quite different from passing virtuous resolutions at church conferences on pleasant summer days in the company of friends."

The most dramatic contrast with patterns of the past lay in the presence among Mennonite males of military age of a small group of radical draft resisters.[61] Mennonite conscientious objectors of World War II had sometimes been called, ironically, "the good boys of CPS."[62] And after 1945 Mennonites had not at first envisaged, if war were again to break out, any clash occurring with the state over the issue of conscription. Conscientious objection of their kind appeared now almost "respectable."[63] But attitudes were soon to change, at least among a small section of Mennonite youth who were liable to the draft.

Various motives prompted the young Mennonites who now adopted a nonregistrant position. Most of these young men were college students. Like their peers, they were influenced by the youth counterculture; they had in many cases read Thoreau or one or another exposition of the Gandhian way of nonviolent struggle; and they followed closely King's nonviolent campaign for civil rights for American blacks. Some of them were in contact with radical Quaker or Catholic – as well as secular – war resisters, who regarded registration for the draft as an unjustifiable degree of cooperation with military conscription and the war machine. Above all, these boys felt guilt at the favored treatment the administration accorded to Mennonite C.Os. as a matter of course. That seemed unfair. They perceived their coreligionists as a kind of pacifist elite, privileged by government, and they did not like it. They thought Mennonite draftees should take their stand on an equality with others who opposed war and refused to fight; and they tended to see their own stance, though it brought them into conflict with the law, as a "prophetic witness" to the excessive demands of the state.[64]

However, "draft resisters were anomalies among Mennonites."[65] Almost all the church's young men, if conscripted, still accepted the alternative service offered them by the government. The noncooperators, on the other hand, either went to jail or, in a few instances, escaped to Canada;[66] several of those who stayed at home were not prosecuted after all. Church leaders continued to give wholehearted support to alternative civilian service and express gratitude to the U.S. government for allowing their young men to fulfill their national service in this way. Nevertheless the two major Mennonite bodies both gave a cautious measure of recognition to the "conscientious noncooperators" in their midst. The first to do this was the Mennonite Church, which declared in August 1969: "We recognize the validity of noncooperation [with the military draft] as a legitimate witness and pledge the offices of our brotherhood to minister to young men in any eventuality they incur in costly discipleship." A similar recognition came two years later, in August 1971, from the General Conference Mennonite Church, which in its turn offered "a supportive ministry" to its nonregistrants.[67] Miller and Shenk, in their study of Mennonite draft resistance, doubt whether such sentiments were shared by most members of these two groups. "Some congregations did give at least tacit approval to the consciences of the noncooperators, most did not. Likewise, some church leaders understood and supported the noncooperators, many did not."[68] Still, the very fact of resolutions like these being passed indicated the depth of the transformation within American Mennonitism being effected on the issue of peace. They also testified to the spirit of toleration among church administrators, which had replaced the rather rigid doctrinal dogmatism prevailing in the leadership hitherto.

The period from the nineteen-seventies up into the nineteen-eighties brought an escalation in the rate of restructuring Mennonite nonresistance and its ultimate transformation into the concept of "peacemaking,"[69] a term which best reflects current Mennonite concerns with regard to peace and war issues. Mention should be made at this point of a seminal work by the theologian and ethicist, John Howard Yoder, first published in 1972 with the provocative title *The Politics of Jesus*. For hitherto, "to link the word *politics* with the name of Jesus was virtually an outrage to meek, apolitical Mennonites ... To suggest that Jesus so much as even cared about politics was to turn the tradition of passive resistance on its conceptual head." Yet Yoder's book came at an opportune moment. While it foreshadowed a more aggressive, if more politically responsible, witness for peace, it did not break the link with the Anabaptist-Mennonite vision of a loving and suffering discipleship even when this also entailed confrontation with the powers that be.[70]

It is impossible to summarize here the extremely complex argument of Yoder's book. Its kernel, though, lies in his statement that "Jesus is, according to the biblical witness, a model of radical political action."[71] At the same time such action is of an entirely different character from traditional power politics. It results from "an ethic marked by the cross, a cross identified as the punishment of a man who threatens society" by the very fact of his instructing his followers to adopt "a radically new kind of life." The gospels, Yoder asserts, showed Jesus preaching – and practising – a nonviolent form of resistance in contrast to the "Zealot option," which urged the use of violence to achieve Jewish liberation. Jesus' stance constituted "a social, political, *structural* fact" challenging "the Powers." The New Testament proclamation (*kerygma*) called for "the creation of a new community and the rejection of violence of any kind."[72] Though Yoder's arguments may have appeared at first sight startling to traditionally minded Mennonites (while at the same time, we should note, proving acceptable to his coreligionists seeking to "politicize" their church's peace witness), he retained enough of the essence of the traditional Anabaptist-Mennonite doctrine of nonresistance to win a – perhaps grudging – acceptance even among the more conservative sections of the denomination.[73] Thus, the book helped in a way to bridge the widening gap in the church fellowship between activists and quietists.

During the seventies and eighties, and especially after an end came at last to the Vietnam War in 1975, the antiwar impulse among Mennonites centered on protest against the nuclear arms race, which might even include breaking the law in the name of a higher righteousness. As one of their activists put it: "I felt more 'Anabaptist' sitting in a jail cell outside the Nevada nuclear test site with Dan Berrigan ... than I ever did sitting around a committee table at MCC [Mennonite Central

Committee]."[74] In Canada, where the pressures were less acute than among that country's southern neighbors, we find Conrad Grebel College, a Mennonite institution affiliated to the University of Waterloo (Ontario), sponsoring – as a result of the initiative of a Mennonite publicist Ernie Regehr – a conflict-resolution body, known as Project Ploughshares. The project soon gained wider support in Canada among mainstream Protestant churches. "It [now] serves as research and publicity arm of the largest churches of Canada on matters of peace ... placing it de facto both at the center of the peace movement in Canada and at the conference table with government."[75] Indeed everywhere in North America Mennonites were beginning to reach out toward a peace witness that, while still religious in inspiration, was not merely a personal ethic but one projecting into the contemporary international scene and grappling with ways of resolving its problems in a nonviolent manner.[76]

In this period, too, Mennonites became increasingly concerned with the issue of justice. As an illustration of this trend we may take a small volume published in a popular series in 1988. Entitled *The Good News of Justice*, it was written by Hugo Zorrilla, a Mennonite theologian from Colombia. As a result of missionary and relief work in Latin America, members of the Mennonite fellowship became acutely aware of the economic exploitation and social injustice prevailing in the Third World; thus they began to show increasing understanding of the efforts of liberation theology, especially strong in the Catholic church, to find a Christian solution of Third World social problems by the path of resistance – armed if necessary. Was Mennonite nonviolence "relevant" in this situation? After working in Nicaragua subsequent to the Sandinista revolution of 1979, with that country threatened by the U.S.-backed "Contras" one young Mennonite wrote: "silence and passivity are actually complicity in violence." He went on to call for a "totally engaged Anabaptism" involving nonviolent "discipleship [that] will not shrink from acting on behalf of the powerless and violated, as we know Christ himself did when he was among us." Without this, pacifism would prove "irrelevant" to the world's poor and oppressed.[77] And another former Mennonite worker in Nicaragua wrote: "We must seek more ... solidarity with nonviolent movements in Latin America, but without a judgmental spirit toward those who in tragic circumstances turn finally to armed resistance." While an endeavor of this kind might prove "existentially" a painful one for a church built upon the foundation of *Wehrlosigkeit*, the "defenselessness" forming an integral part of the Anabaptist-Mennonite heritage, the tension thus generated could not fail in the end to be creative.[78]

Of course such concerns as these were shared by only a relatively small minority of the fellowship, for they did not enjoy the widespread interest engendered, among Mennonites as among the rest of the population in North America, by nuclear protest, for instance, or by the draft. Such concerns are nevertheless indicative of the expanded vision of nonviolence making itself apparent, at any rate among the Mennonite intelligentsia.

At the outset of 1991 the Persian Gulf War, brief as it was, presented a new problem for Mennonites as for other pacifists: that of "a massive technological war which lasts only a few weeks," with the government making few "direct claims ... for service or money" compared with those made in previous wars. Thereby conscientious objection was, as it were, "neutralized."[79] Yet a war bringing within six weeks an overwhelming victory to one side does not yet appear to have replaced the late twentieth-century pattern of prolonged and often inconclusive warfare as displayed in Bosnia or in various parts of Asia and Africa. Moreover, though dormant since the conclusion of the cold war and the collapse of East European communism, the threat of nuclear destruction has by no means disappeared.

In the nineties, therefore, Mennonite peacemaking continues to be actively pursued. How far ordinary members have fully accepted their sect's peace witness as restructured by its "intellectual elite" over the last half century is not entirely apparent.[80] But clearly, without this thorough rethinking of fundamentals, traditional "separatist" nonresistance might have taken the same course among North American Mennonites as it had done earlier among the acculturating Dutch and German Mennonite communities and eventually vanish altogether.[81] "Mennonites are well known as the quiet folks in the land," comments David Rensberger.[82] "There is something very good and true about that. But when the land is filled with evil, then it is not necessarily good and faithful to remain quiet." Justice, nonviolent resistance, and civil disobedience have become components of contemporary Mennonite peacemaking; in place of apartness close cooperation with other peacemakers characterizes the witness of a growing number of Mennonites today. "Old enemies (Catholics, mainline Protestants, radical Anabaptists) are finding each other in the practice of peace."[83]

Before concluding this section we may take a brief look at Mennonites in France where, since 1945, interest has re-emerged in nonresistance, including conscientious objection to military service which ceased altogether, at least in the church's Francophone congregations, over a century ago. This development resulted in part from personal contacts, through the mediacy of the Mennonite Central Committee

then active in postwar relief work in Europe, with American protago-
nists of the Anabaptist Vision like Harold Bender and John H. Yoder.
Even more decisive was the influence of an indigenous leader, Pierre
Widmer, who in 1945 became editor of the church's paper *Christ Seul*
and the driving spirit behind a new phase of evangelical renewal (*Le
Réveil dans le Réveil*).[84]

Widmer had fought as an officer in World War II, spending most of
the war in a German P.O.W. camp, and was awarded the *croix de guerre*
for his war service. Yet despite this impeccable military record Widmer,
when conscripted in 1935, had been on the verge of seeking some form
of noncombatant status; he was finally persuaded to alter his intentions and train to become an officer. Subsequently, though, his wartime
experiences as well as meditations as a prisoner of war had led him
back to pacifism,[85] which he proceeded to promote with vigor among
his coreligionists after his return to civilian life. Widmer now urged
Mennonite conscripts on call-up at least to apply for noncombatant
duties, and he supported the postwar campaign, ultimately successful,
to legalize civilian alternative service for conscientious objectors.[86]
After a decade of effort his influence led the Mennonite congregations
to reinstate nonresistance, at least in theory, as the church's official doctrine. The declaration ran as follows:

Defenseless ... Christians! It was under this name that our forefathers, the
Anabaptist-Mennonites of the heroic centuries who suffered valiantly for their
faith, were known. This is what we ought to be ourselves ... Submission to
earthly authorities has no validity for a Christian unless he be first of all obedi-
ent to God. ... And God must be obeyed, above all, in cases where human law
is in contradiction to divine law. ... With respect to military service and war,
which is a result of sin, we believe that God forbids the Christian to kill, or to
cause harm to, a fellow creature but, on the contrary, requires that he love and
cherish him, even if he be an enemy. A child of God, though he is necessarily
attached closely to his nation, ought therefore to refuse combatant service,
choosing instead to serve in the medical corps or in alternative civilian service,
where he would seek to ... practise the love of his neighbor. On account of conscience (*Par scruple de conscience*), a Christian may even be led to refuse any
kind of participation in military organization.[87]

Widmer found support for his position on war among some of his
church's elders, especially in the still predominantly German-speaking
congregations of Alsace where attachment to the traditional *Wehrlosigkeit* had continued even though their young men had not been able
to escape induction into combatant service first in the interwar French

army and then from 1942 to 1945 into Hitler's *Wehrmacht*. But among postwar Francophone Mennonites the military question has remained "a delicate one." There were even conservative church members who favored noncombatant army service but rejected the idea of Mennonite conscripts performing alternative civilian service, seemingly on the grounds that the latter option would exercise a more worldly influence on their young men than the former. In fact, since 1945 few young Mennonites have refused induction into the army, the handful who did so being regarded with some suspicion by the majority of church members, especially if, as happened occasionally, the objector ended up in jail. Indeed acceptance of full army service continued to be the communally approved line of conduct while conscientious objection existed in the church merely as a tolerated minority position.[88]

Even during the Algerian War when revulsion against the employment of torture by the French army became widespread in the Mennonite community as in many other sections of French society,[89] "a large majority of French Mennonites who had been drafted ... accepted military service without apparent hesitation." And today, while the church now possesses its peace committee and publishes fairly extensively on peace theology, "for many French Mennonites peace concerns are marginal to church life."[90] The general emphasis has remained on evangelism and personal piety.

The Church of the Brethren

The Brethren throughout their history have always stood close to the Mennonites on the sectarian spectrum. Since the foundation of their sect in Germany at the beginning of the eighteenth century and their emigration not long afterward to the New World, they have shared with the Mennonites a belief in nonresistance. Before the twentieth century the norm had been for Brethren who bore arms to be expelled from the church, at any rate unless they expressed regret for their conduct. In this century acculturation has proceeded rapidly, with abandonment of pacifism on the part of the majority of church members, so that in World War II only a small percentage of its draftees became C.Os. either in Civilian Public Service or noncombatant service in the army.[91] Many Brethren congregations gave enthusiastic – and virtually unanimous – support to the war effort.[92] In fact, "the wholesale involvement of Brethren in the military mobilization of the 1940s, as well as the doctrinal revisions that accompanied it, indicated that individual conscience had in fact displaced the church as the final custodian of personal behavior."[93] At the same time the church has continued to uphold nonresistance as its official position with the general, though by no means unanimous, concurrence of the Brethren leadership. There have indeed been pastors who did not accept pacifism but most have regarded all war as unchristian.

In comparison with the major Mennonite denominations, the Church of the Brethren at mid-century would seem to have been in a more advantageous position with regard to modernizing its peace witness. For already in the interwar years and under the influence of the Social Gospel and Gandhian nonviolence, Brethren had begun to add the dimension of social responsibility to their church's peace testimony and coordinate its efforts more closely with other liberal Christian pacifist groups, shifting the emphasis explicitly from nonresistance to nonviolence and the obligation to challenge the warmaking state by political action.[94]

Since 1945 the pattern of Brethren peace efforts has in most respects paralleled that of the Mennonites, with the same concern for problems of social and economic justice and for international order. In the latter sphere, for instance, the writings of the Brethren ethicist, Dale Aukerman, matches the work of Mennonites like J.H. Yoder or D.K. Friesen. The threat of global destruction posed by the atom bomb "impels us," Aukerman has written, "beyond the Anabaptist view" so as to bring about "some degree of *public* readiness ... to face enemies without violence as Jesus did, and thus risk the worst that they might do."[95] There have been young Brethren radical draft resisters and Brethren, both young and old, who have participated in various forms of civil disobedience and nonviolent direct action alongside other peace activists. In its official statements the Church of the Brethren has been perhaps even more supportive of such modes of peacemaking than its Mennonite counterparts. And unofficially some of its spokesmen, especially during the Vietnam War era, went much further in promoting radical activity in support of peace and justice. Thus we find one of the founders of the Brethren Action Movement, and himself a pastor of a midwest Brethren church, writing around 1970:

The violence of the oppressed is qualitatively different from that of the oppressor. Who are we to tell the Vietnamese people to lay down their arms in face of the American destruction of their homes? It is one thing to tell the oppressor to stop fighting, but something quite different to tell the oppressed to accept defeat ... We must be able to understand why the oppressed go the way of violence, but at the same time realize that violence is self-defeating. While we can support the aim of the revolutionary, we cannot support his violent means ... We need to recognize that the violent people in our society are not those struggling for liberation, but rather the leaders of our government, business executives, and university presidents; those who use their power to suppress change and who devise new and more efficient methods of killing and controlling people. These are the ones who are most violent and the ones the pacifist should oppose.[96]

Yet one gains the impression that the restructuring of the Brethren peace witness has not been accomplished so securely as in the case of the Mennonites; nor would it seem that the dominant trend in the church membership at large toward a "defensist" position has been stemmed successfully. For the leadership all war remains "sin," yet among the rank-and-file – of what, after all, has now become politically a fairly conservative community – many Brethren appear quite ready, if called upon, to undertake combatant service.

A Brethren sociologist has referred to present-day responses to war within the church as "the Brethren peace puzzle." He goes on to talk about "the chasm separating official Brethren condemnations of war from the attitudes of the general membership," which since the 1930s at least has given a steadily diminishing adherence to pacifism. His data, too, confirm "that the bulk of today's Brethren would support" another war if it came.[97] The key to an understanding of why the Brethren have failed to restructure their peace witness as effectively as the Mennonites have done seems to lie in their having gone further than the Mennonites did in acculturation before the process of restructuring their nonresistance and transforming it into a largely new pattern of peacemaking got under way. It has so far proved impossible for the Brethren to regain the ground once lost, though the final outcome is not yet certain.[98]

Notes

1 See above, chaps. VII and VIII.

2 For the attitude to conscientious objection of the Evangelical Church in Western Germany (EKD), with its small but vocal pacifist minority, see Bernd W. Kubbig, *Kirche und Kriegsdienstverweigerung in der BRD* (Stuttgart: Verlag W. Kohlhammer, 1974).

3 For instance, Jean-Michel Hornus, Jean Lasserre, and André Trocmé. We may also note the names of French Catholic theologians, like Pierre Lorson and Pie-Raymond Régamey, who have ably defended the idea of nonviolence as well as the stand of the conscientious objector.

4 For instance, among evangelicals the Baptist Culbert G. Rutenber, the

Methodist Stanley Hauerwas, and Ronald J. Sider from the Brethren in Christ; among liberals John M. Swomley, Jr., also a Methodist.

5 The term 'historic peace churches' was first applied to these three denominations in 1935. It soon became current, at any rate in the United States.

6 Hugh Barbour and J. William Frost, *The Quakers* (Westport, CT: Greenwood Press, 1988), p. 258.

7 In fact no such history has yet been written. In the meantime see C.H. Mike Yarrow, *Quaker Experiences in International Conciliation* (New Haven and London: Yale University Press, 1978) and Sydney D. Bailey, *Peace is a Process* (London: Swarthmore Lecture Committee, 1993), pp. 93–173. Two other Swarthmore Lectures also contain useful materials: J. Duncan Wood, *Building the Institutions of Peace* (London: George Allen & Unwin Ltd., 1962) and Wolf Mendl, *Prophets and Reconcilers: Reflections on the Quaker Peace Testimony* (London: Friends Home Service Committee, 1974), pp. 86–94.

8 Bailey, *op. cit.*, p. 173.

9 Yarrow, *op. cit.*, chaps. III and IV. See also Cynthia Sampson, "'To make real the Bond between us all': Quaker Conciliation during the Nigerian Civil War," pp. 88–118 in Douglas Johnston and C. Sampson, eds., *Religion, the Missing Dimension of Statecraft* (New York and Oxford: Oxford University Press, 1994). Sampson writes (p. 111): "The Quaker team was the sole third party that won the complete trust of both parties in the conflict, and they sustained that trust for the duration of the war ... By their presence and availability at critical moments, the Quakers succeeded in opening lines of communication that would otherwise have remained closed."

10 For literature on recent Quaker mediation-reconciliation, see Bailey, *op. cit.*, p. 184 n. 211.

11 *Ibid.*, pp. 143, 145. Italics in the original.

12 Yarrow, *op. cit.*, p. 46; Bailey, *op. cit.*, pp. 118–22.

13 Yarrow, *op. cit.*, pp. 23–9, 40–9.

14 See E. Raymond Wilson, *Uphill for Peace: Quaker Impact on Congress* (Richmond, Indiana: Friends United Press, 1975); Dorothy Detzer, *Appointment on the Hill* (New York: Henry Holt and Company, 1948). Detzer, a humanist by conviction, never joined Friends although she had been closely associated with the AFSC in post-World War I relief work.

15 See Oliver M. Ashford, *Prophet – or Professor? The Life and Work of Lewis Fry Richardson* (Bristol and Boston: Adam Hilger Ltd, 1985). During his lifetime Richardson's peace research was largely ignored; he failed to find a publisher for the books in which he developed a mathematical theory of war, and editors sometimes rejected his articles too. But since his death his reputation has steadily grown, and he is generally regarded now as a seminal influence on the quantitative study of international conflict.

16 Yarrow, *op. cit.*, pp. 261–6.

17 *Ibid.*, pp. 177, 178, 295, 296. A leading American Quaker historian has warned against overestimating the international impact of Quaker peace-making since 1945; despite "Friends' hard work" and devotion to "service," in his view the effect of such efforts was "minuscule." In fact they have "neither prevented nor stopped any war." See Frost, "The Christian Religion and War: An Evaluation," in Chuck Fager, ed., *A Continuing Journey: Papers from the Quaker Peace Roundtable ... 1995* (Wallingford, PA: The Issues Program of Pendle Hill, 1996), p. 181.

18 See Peter Brock, *Pacifism in Europe to 1914* (Princeton, NJ: Princeton University Press, 1972), p. 475.

19 Quoted in Margaret E. Hirst, *The Quakers in Peace and War: An Account of Their Peace Principles and Practice* (London: The Swarthmore Press, 1923), p. 158.

20 William Penn, *The Peace of Europe, the Fruits of Solitude and Other Writings*, ed. Edwin B. Bronner (London: Everyman's Library, 1993), pp. 5–22.

21 *Ibid.*, p. 6.

22 *Speak Truth to Power* was the title of a seminal report prepared by AFSC and published in 1955. With the descriptive subtitle: "A Quaker Search for an Alternative to Violence," it argued in favor of nonviolent resistance as much on pragmatic and rational as on religious grounds. For the background and significance of this publication, see Elizabeth Walker Mechling and Jay Mechling, "Hot Pacifism and Cold War: The American Friends Service Committee's Witness for Peace in 1950s America," *The Quarterly Journal of Speech* (New York), vol. 78, no. 2 (May, 1992), pp. 175, 177–87, 193–5. In a challenging essay Allen Smith dates the start of a movement by "the peace testimony's most ardent backers" to revitalize – and radicalize – Quaker pacifism in the United States to 1955, the year of the publication of this report; "The Renewal Movement: The Peace Testimony and Modem Quakerism," *Quaker History* (Haverford, PA), vol. 85, no. 2 (Fall, 1996), pp. 1, 6–8. By the 1970s, however, "disagreements, seemingly small in the beginning, divided and eventually helped end the renewal movement."

23 See, for instance, Nicholas Grief, "British Quakers, the Peace Tax and International Law," pp. 243–60 in Mark W. Janis, *The Influence of Religion on the Development of International Law* (Dordrecht: Martinus Nijhoff, 1991). According to Grief (p. 255), "if ever the right of conscientious objection is extended [in Britain] to the payment of tax for military purposes, this will in no small measure be due to [the Quakers'] witness." The most recent treatment of this subject is by Cecil Evans, *The Claims of Conscience: Quakers and Conscientious Objection to Taxation for Military Purposes* (London: Quaker Home Service, 1996).

24 Specifically the FOR, WRL, and WILPF. These charges occur most forcefully in Guenter Lewy, *Peace & Revolution: The Moral Crisis of American*

Pacifism (Grand Rapids, Michigan: William B. Eerdmans, 1988), *passim.* Cf. Michael Cromartie, ed., *Peace Betrayed? Selected Essays on Pacifism and Politics* (Washington, D.C.: Ethics and Public Policy Center, 1990), pp. 111–22, 151–61, 169–84; also Charles (Chuck) Fager, ed., *Quaker Service at the Crossroads* (Falls Church, VA: Kimo Press, 1988).

25 Irwin Abrams, *The Nobel Peace Prize and the Laureates* (Boston: G.K. Hall, 1988), pp. 148–50.

26 *Speak Truth to Power* (Philadelphia: AFSC, 1955), pp. v, vi, 63–68.

27 Kenneth Boulding in Fager, ed., *op. cit.*, p. 181.

28 The percentage of actual Quakers working for the AFSC was on the decline; Lewy, *op. cit.*, pp. 227, 231. But we should note it was understood that all staff members accepted a commitment to nonviolence, at any rate for so long as they worked for AFSC. Also of course, the non-Quaker staff were usually much closer at any rate to pacifism than the nonpacifist sections of the Society of Friends.

29 See Fager, ed., *op. cit.*, pp. 23, 24, 162–8.

30 Brock, *Pioneers of the Peaceable Kingdom* (Princeton, N.J.: Princeton University Press, 1970), pp. 252–4.

31 See Fager, ed., *op. cit.*, pp. 162, 188, 189; Cromartie, ed., p. 117; Lewy, *op. cit.*, pp. 33–7, 40–4.

32 Lewy, *op. cit.*, pp. 37–40.

33 Nigel Young, *An Infantile Disorder? The Crisis and Decline of the New Left* (London and Henley: Routledge & Kegan Paul, 1977), p. 174.

34 Lewy, *op. cit.*, pp. 28, 29, 46, 47.

35 See Brock, *Radical Pacifists in Antebellum America* (Princeton: Princeton University Press, 1968), pp. 248–52.

36 What was wrong with the Quakers (and other pacifists), according to Marvin Maurer, was that they had "supported the wrong side during the Vietnam War" (letter to *Midstream* [New York], vol. 26 [1980], no. 6, p. 64); whereas another critic implied that, if such people had been so misguided as not to have supported the right side, they should at least have kept quiet about it (Lewy, *op. cit.*, pp. 20–22, 247–9). But from a pacifist viewpoint at any rate such arguments could hardly sound convincing. The account by the AFSC's Vietnam War era's executive secretary, Bronson P. Clark, *Not by Might: A Viet Nam Memoir* (Glastonbury, CT: Chapel Rock Publishers, 1997), reached us too late for use in our book. Clark served in this capacity from 1968 to 1974.

37 Quoted in Lewy, *op. cit.*, p. 109.

38 *Ibid.*, pp. 110–12. Our italics.

39 *Ibid.*, pp. 115–19; Fager, ed., *op. cit.*, pp. 180, 181, 186, 187, 193. In fact the Vietnamese communists had pursued a policy of repression toward the Buddhists since the mid-1950s. After 1968 the accusation that the latter

were CIA agents became a full-scale propaganda exercise; henceforward it was difficult for Buddhists in North Vietnam to obtain permission from their government to speak at "peace" gatherings in the West.

40 Ed Lazar in Fager, ed., *op. cit.*, p. 186. Lazar rightly brands such conduct as "disgraceful."

41 *Ibid.*, pp. 117, 118 (Powelson); p. 179 (Boulding). See also Lewy, *op. cit.*, pp. 123–30. Our italics.

42 Lewy, *op. cit.*, pp. 141–4.

43 Letter from John A. Sullivan, *Midstream*, vol. 26, no. 6 (June/July, 1980), p. 59.

44 E. Boulding in Fager, ed., *op. cit.*, p. 104.

45 Quoted by Sullivan in *ibid.*, pp. 76, 77. See also James Matlack in Cromartie, ed., *op. cit.*, pp. 178, 179. Lewy's claim (*op. cit.*, pp. 173–5) that this declaration was merely window-dressing, and that "it left the door open to ... cooperation with and encouragement of Marxist-Leninist guerrillas," appears to be entirely without foundation. Certainly some AFSC staff members earlier had supported a more ambiguous position on nonviolence. But they met with opposition from other staff members, and the former's qualified approval of revolutionary violence as being "qualitatively different from the violence of the oppressor" (while nevertheless still not the Quaker way of opposing evil) was decisively rejected by the Board of Directors when that body came to consider the matter.

46 Quoted in Maurer, "Quakers in Politics ...," *Midstream*, vol. 23, no. 9 (November, 1977), p. 42 n. 65.

47 Letter from Sullivan, *Midstream*, cited above. Our italics.

48 For examples of such views, see *Midstream*, vol. 25, no. 9 (November, 1979): Rael Jean Isaac, "The Seduction of the Quakers: From Friendly Persuasion to PLO Support," pp. 23–29, and Maurer, "Quakers and Communists – Vietnam and Israel," pp. 30–35. Both writers regard AFSC insistence on nonviolence as merely a camouflage for complicity with terrorism and unlimited support of the PLO. As Rael Isaac put it: "The AFSC pastes fig-leaves over the nakedness of its anti-Israel bias" (letter to *Midstream*, vol. 26, no. 6, p. 60). Lewy, *op. cit.*, pp. 175–7, reflects some of these attitudes, too.

49 Lewy, *op. cit.*, p. 186. But cf. William B. Edgerton, "Adventures of an American Slavist in Soviet Russia," pp. 8–10 (English text of his article published in *Tynyanovskie Chteniya*, vol. 5 [1994], pp. 343–5) for an account of the furor created by his frank speaking at an international youth seminar in Leningrad, which was co-sponsored by AFSC in 1960. Edgerton had been a co-author of the AFSC pamphlet *Speaking Truth to Power*; and that was exactly what the Quaker professor did on this occasion. Irwin Abrams, in his article "The Dilemma of not speaking Truth to Power," *Friends Journal* (Philadelphia), vol. 40, no. 9 (September, 1994), p. 12, poses some troublesome ques-

tions, "Should Quakers have spoken truth in the spirit of [George] Fox to Soviet and East German communists ...?" he asks. "Because we spoke only 'partial truth,' some good was done. Did we do right?" We may note that Fox's contemporary, William Penn, once remarked: "We must creep where we cannot go, and it is necessary for us, in the things of life, to be wise as to be innocent." But many Quakers – and others – have rejected this view as incompatible with a consistent adherence to the   Truth.

50 *Lessons of the Gulf War* (Philadelphia: Peace Education Division, AFSC, 1991), pp. 2, 3. The first quotation is from David Gracie, peace education secretary, and the second from Asia Bennett, AFSC executive secretary.

51 We may also note here the (still) tentative renewal of pacifism within Russian sectarianism in the postcommunist era. For the background, see Bruno Coppieters, "Die pazifistischen Sekten, die Bolschewiki und das Recht auf Wehrdienstverweigerung," pp. 308–60 in Reiner Steinweg, *Lehren aus der Geschichte? Historische Friedensforschung* (Frankfurt am Main: Suhrkamp, 1990).

52 This section deals mainly with the modernization of the Mennonite peace witness in the United States; here the process was highlighted especially by the Vietnam War. For parallel developments in Canada, which was not involved directly in that conflict, see T.D. Regehr, *Mennonites in Canada, 1939–1970: A People Transformed*: vol. 3 of *Mennonites in Canada* (Toronto: University of Toronto Press, 1996), pp. 382, 383, 394–404, 407, 408. Many of the same economic and social factors affected the process of Mennonite modernization in both countries, continuing during the quarter of a century since the closing date of Regehr's volume.

53 Leo Driedger and Donald B. Kraybill, *Mennonite Peacemaking: From Quietism to Activism* (Scottdale, PA, and Waterloo, ON: Herald Press, 1994), p. 14; this study is invaluable as a guide to the evolution of the North American Mennonite peace witness since 1945. See also Beulah Stauffer Hostetler, "Nonresistance and Social Responsibility: Mennonites and Mainline Peace Emphasis, ca. 1950 to 1985," *The Mennonite Quarterly Review* (Goshen, IN – cited below as MQR), vol. 64, no. 1 (January, 1990), pp. 49–73, and Tom Yoder Neufeld, "Varieties of Contemporary Mennonite Peace Witness: From Passivism to Pacifism, From Nonresistance to Resistance," *The Conrad Grebel Review* (Waterloo), vol. 10, no. 3 (Fall, 1992), pp. 243–57.

54 See especially his *War, Peace, and Nonresistance* (Scottdale: Herald Press, 1944). Revised editions of this influential work were published in 1953 and 1969.

55 Driedger and Kraybill, *op. cit.*, p. 79.

56 *Ibid.*, p. 88.

57 Selected documents prepared for these conferences are included in Donald F. Durnbaugh, ed., *On Earth Peace: Discussions on War/Peace Issues between Friends, Mennonites, Brethren, and European Churches, 1935–75* (Elgin, IL:

Brethren Press, 1978). The initiative for holding these meetings came from the Brethren peace leader, M.R. Zigler, while from the Mennonite side John Howard Yoder was particularly active in successive conferences.

58 As argued, for instance, by Guy F. Hershberger, *The Way of the Cross in Human Relations* (Scottdale: Herald Press, 1958), p. 202.

59 Rodney J. Sawatsky and Scott Holland, eds., *The Limits of Perfection: Conversations with J. Lawrence Burkholder* (Waterloo: Institute of Anabaptist-Mennonite Studies, Conrad Grebel College, 1993), pp. 44, 53. From Burkholder's autobiographical reflections contained in the volume (pp. 1–54), we learn how his experiences as a relief worker in wartorn China led him to formulate a number of probing questions as to how Jesus' disciples today should apply his "perfectionist" teachings, including the love commandment (pp. 18–21). At first such questioning seldom found a welcome response in his church community, especially among the older generation. But by the 1990s that situation had largely changed.

60 Driedger and Kraybill, *op. cit.*, chap. IV: "Ferment in the Fifties" and chap. V: "The Strident Sixties and Seventies."

61 See Melissa Miller and Phil M. Shenk, *The Path of Most Resistance: Stories of Mennonite Objectors who did not cooperate with the Vietnam War Draft* (Scottdale and Ktichener: Herald Press, 1982). The authors present ten case "stories" of Mennonite nonregistrants out of over sixty known cases. See also Paul Toews, *Mennonites in American Society, 1930–1970: Modernity and the Persistence of Religious Community* (vol. 4 in *The Mennonite Experience in America*) (Scottdale and Waterloo: Herald Press, 1996), pp. 324–9.

62 *MQR*, vol. 66, no. 5 (October, 1992), was devoted to reappraising the experience of North American Mennonites in alternative service during World War II.

63 This was the word used by Hershberger (*ibid.*) in 1958. In the following year, however, a writer in the *Gospel Herald* suggested "another alternative for draft-age youth" (the title of his article), namely refusal to register with Selective Service. Cited in Driedger and Kraybill, *op. cit.*, pp. 125, 126. We may note, for the record, that from World War II onward we find a handful of Mennonites of draft age refusing to register. However, the very small numbers involved meant that their stand passed virtually unnoticed. See Miller and Shenk, *op. cit.*, pp. 227–9.

64 Miller and Shenk, *op. cit.*, pp. 22, 233, 234.

65 *Ibid.*, p. 13.

66 The emigration of some eighteen thousand Mennonites from Russia to escape universal military service, introduced in that country in 1874, may be seen as a precedent for the draft-emigration movement of the Vietnam War period. Of course the overwhelming majority of those involved in the latter were non-Mennonites and were unaware of such a precedent.

67 *Ibid.*, pp. 234, 237.

68 *Ibid.*, p. 222.

69 See Driedger and Kraybill, *op. cit.*, chap. VI: "New Patterns of Peacemaking."

70 *Ibid.*, p. 148, 149.

71 John H. Yoder, *The Politics of Jesus: Vicit Agnus Noster* (Grand Rapids, MI: William B. Eerdmans Publishing Company, 1972), p. 12.

72 *Ibid.*, pp. 62, 63, 90ff, 115, 160–2, 214, 250. Italics in the original.

73 Yoder's writings proved a major influence in bringing the distinguished theologian, Stanley Hauerwas, into the pacifist fold. Describing himself as "a Mennonite camp follower" located in "the Protestant mainstream," Hauerwas writes: "Part of what Yoder ... taught me was ... not that our commitment to the way of non-violence promised to rid the world of war, but rather that God had given the world an alternative to war *through the kind of politics present in the church*, where reconciliation triumphs over envy and hate." From his essay "Pacifism: A Form of Politics," in Michael Cromartie, ed., *op. cit.*, pp. 134, 135. Our italics.

74 Edgar Metzler, quoted in Driedger and Kraybill, *op. cit.*, p. 141. War tax objection emerged, too, during this period among Mennonites as among other religious and secular pacifists. See *Mennonite Encyclopedia*, vol. 5, pp. 873–5.

75 Neufeld, *op. cit.*, p. 251.

76 One might almost call such an attitude a "Quakerization" of the Mennonite peace witness. Typical of this new direction in Mennonite thought is Duane K. Friesen's *Christian Peacemaking & International Conflict: A Realist Pacifist Perspective* (Scottdale and Kitchener: Herald Press, 1986). Organizationally, this new direction found expression in the establishment by the MCC in 1968 of an office in Washington for the purpose of religious lobbying, especially on peace issues. Since then, "Mennonites have been learning a new language – that of public discourse ... hoping to bring to bear a vision of nonviolent alternatives while acknowledging political realities." Such endeavors naturally did not meet with the approval of all the brethren. Keith Graber Miller, *Wise as Serpents, Innocent as Doves: American Mennonites engage Washington* (Knoxville: The University of Tennessee Press, 1996), pp. 187, 188. See also Hope Nisly, "Witness to the Way of Peace: The Vietnam War and the Evolving Mennonite View of Their Relationship to the State," *The Maryland Historian* (College Park), vol. 20, no. 1 (Spring/Summer, 1989), pp. 16–23. "The Mennonites," writes Nisly, "wanted to take a step toward a new role and also to maintain the core of their identity as a peace church. They understood that with the opening of the doors of the Washington office, they were, in effect, opening the door to a new era for the Mennonite Church" (pp. 21, 22).

77 C. Arnold Snynder, "The Relevance of Anabaptist Nonviolence for Nicara-

gua Today," pp. 112–27 in Daniel S. Schipani, ed., *Freedom and Discipleship: Liberation in an Anabaptist Perspective* (Maryknoll, NY: Orbis Books, 1989), esp. pp. 119–22. See also Ronald J. Sider's essay entitled "Mennonites and the Poor: Toward an Anabaptist Theology of Liberation," *ibid.*, pp. 85–100, and John Driver, "The Anabaptist Vision and Social Justice," *ibid.*, pp. 101–11. Sider writes (p. 99): "Unless the Mennonite leadership ... revamps our church organizations ... so they reflect the same concern for the poor and oppressed described in the Bible, Third World theologians will have every right to charge that our proud claim to follow the Scriptures is dishonest."

78 Philip McManus and Gerald Schlabach, eds., *Relentless Persistence: Nonviolent Action in Latin America* (Philadelphia and Santa Cruz, CA: New Society Publishers, 1991), pp. 263, 264. The quotation comes from the Epilogue by Schlabach subtitled "North American Nonviolence and Latin American Liberation Struggle." (We may recall here that in 1539 the peaceable Menno Simons had referred to the violent Münsterite Anabaptists as "dear brethren" despite their differences with respect to the sword.)

79 J.C. Juhnke, "Limited War in a Century of Total War," in D.K. Friesen, ed. *Weathering the Storm: Christian Pacifist Responses to War* (Newton, KS: Faith and Life Press, 1991), pp. 58, 59.

80 Driedger and Kraybill, *op. cit.*, pp. 158, 272.

81 From the interwar years onward a small, though active, group of Dutch Mennonites once more adhered to pacifism. Today the *Doopsgezinde Vredesgroep* (Mennonite Peace Association) supports conscientious objection and works with other pacifist groups for such objectives as nuclear disarmament. See *Mennonite Encyclopedia*, vol. V, pp. 243, 686. In Germany, as well as among the remnants of the once numerous Mennonite congregations of the former Soviet Union ruthlessly suppressed during the Stalinist terror, the idea of nonresistance remains dormant though by no means entirely absent.

82 Jailed Vietnam War draft resister and later New Testament scholar; quoted in Miller and Shenk, *op. cit.*, p. 208.

83 Neufeld, *op. cit.*, p. 255 n. 42.

84 Widmer was also son-in-law of Pierre Sommer (1874–1952), the leading figure in the first Mennonite *Réveil*. Sommer was himself not unsympathetic to pacifism and his church's lost tradition of nonresistance; only he thought it was not realistic at that time to expect more than that Mennonite conscripts should refrain from ever using their weapons to kill. He believed that God would help them to keep a resolve never to shed human blood. He also accepted without protest the fact that the majority of his coreligionists rejected even a modified noncombatancy of this kind.

85 For a translation of Widmer's own account of his "conversion" to pacifism, see "From Military Service to Christian Nonresistance: The Testimony of a

Former French Army Officer," *MQR*, vol. 23, no. 4 (October, 1949), pp. 246–56.

86 Jean Séguy, *Les assemblées anabaptistes-mennonites de France* (Paris and The Hague: Mouton, 1977), pp. 721, 722. The first French law permitting conscientious objection and including a civilian service option came into force in December 1963.

87 From the *Nouveau manuel d'instruction*, issued on 1 May 1956 with the approval of the elders of all the church's congregations. Quoted in *ibid.*, pp. 679, 682.

88 *Ibid.*, pp. 674–9, 719, 722, 784–6, 823.

89 *Ibid.*, pp. 678, 679, 722, 723.

90 Neal Blough, "The Anabaptist Vision and Its Impact among French Mennonites," *MQR*, vol. 69, no. 3 (July, 1995), p. 386.

91 Durnbaugh in the *Brethren Encyclopedia*, vol. II, p. 1372: "thus ... fully 80% of its young men had rejected the peace position." Among Mennonites, on the other hand, over 60 percent of World War II draftees became conscientious objectors.

92 Carl F. Bowman, *Brethren Society: The Cultural Transformation of a "Peculiar People"* (Baltimore and London: The Johns Hopkins University Press, 1995), pp. 351–6, 467.

93 *Ibid.*, p. 355.

94 See *Brethren Life and Thought*: Robert McFadden, "Perspective in Pacifism," vol. 6 (Spring, 1961), pp. 39–41, and Richard B. Gardner, "Brethren and Pacifism: An Analysis of Contemporary Brethren Approaches to Peace and War," vol. 8 (Autumn, 1963), p. 39.

95 Dale Aukerman, *Darkening Valley: A Biblical Perspective on Nuclear War* (New York: The Seabury Press, 1981), p. 161. Our italics. See also Aukerman's articles in the *Brethren Encyclopedia*, vol. I ("Conscientious Objection") and vol. II ("Peace"), esp. pp. 336, 337, 1000.

96 Arthur G. Gish, *The New Left and Christian Radicalism* (Grand Rapids, MI: William B. Eerdmans, 1970), pp. 141, 142. One wonders whether the author included among "the violent ... university presidents" his fellow Brethren minister, Andrew Cordier, who was at that time president of strife-torn Columbia University.

97 Bowman, *A Profile of the Church of the Brethren* (Elgin: Brethren Press, [1987]), pp. 8, 12, 30; *Brethren Society*, pp. 389–91.

98 For a recent example of Brethren pacifist outreach in Brazil, see Durnbaugh, *Fruit of the Vine: A History of the Brethren, 1708–1995* (Elgin: Brethren Press, 1997), pp. 563, 564.

XI. Religious Pacifist Outreach since 1945

Until around mid-century pacifism *sensu stricto* remained largely a product of Protestantism, and especially, though by that date by no means exclusively, of sectarian Protestantism. The emergence of Gandhian nonviolence in the interwar years scarcely disproves this statement, since the Mahatma drew his pacifist inspiration from Christianity, filtered through Protestant sources, as much perhaps as from his own Hindu religious tradition. (In exactly what proportions he drew on each tradition remains of course a matter for discussion.) Nor does the fact that since World War I nonreligious pacifists have existed within the pacifist fold in considerable number disprove it, either, since in this case humanist pacifism has often possessed a quasi-religious quality and sometimes, too, has drawn its inspiration from the ethic of the Sermon on the Mount. Today, with non-theists accepted within such religious denominations as the Quakers or the Unitarians, belief in a Supreme Being has long ceased in this connection to be a *sine qua non* of religious conviction.[1]

Pacifist outreach in fact got under way really only after World War II. We have chosen two such developments for discussion here – first in Catholicism and then in a non-Christian religion, Judaism. This does not indeed exhaust the list. We could have included the emergence of absolute pacifism within Eastern Orthodoxy or, beyond the frontiers of Christianity, in Islam (generally regarded in the West as a militaristic faith). At the moment, though, these both remain fragile growths.[2] At least mention should also be made here of the pacificist universalism of the Bahai's, ruthlessly persecuted in Iran, the country of their origin, but expanding in many other parts of the globe.

The peacemaking impulse has, moreover, made itself felt during the last half century within socially engaged Buddhism. Its doctrine of nonviolence of course is as old as the Buddhist religion itself; for non-violence flourished in ancient India already in the pre-Christian era among Buddhists as well as among the kindred Jains (whose faith remained confined until recently to the South Asian subcontinent). Although, as in the case of Christianity too, the original message of nonviolence became blurred in the course of the centuries, it was never entirely lost. Over the last few decades Buddhist nonviolence has displayed itself more actively than in the past. During the 1960s, for instance, the Vietnamese poet and monk, Thich Nhât Hanh, led a powerful nonviolent movement in favor of peace in his native land; after being driven into exile by the communists, he joined the Fellowship of Reconciliation (FOR) as a gesture of solidarity with the pacifist cause in the West. During the war a select few of the members of his Unified Buddhist Church, including lay persons as well as monks and nuns, displayed a heroic antiwar witness when they immolated themselves in protest against the continued fighting.[3] In Thailand, to cite another example of contemporary Buddhist pacifism, Sulak Sivaraksa has promoted a specifically Buddhist vision of resolving international and domestic conflict, while in the United States a Buddhist Peace Fellowship was established in 1978 and is now affiliated to the FOR.[4]

Buddhist rulers waging war, as Sivaraksa points out, "could not quote any saying of the Buddha to support them however just their war might have been."[5] Still, so far proponents of Buddhist nonviolence seem never to have had to grapple directly with the question of conscientious objection as Western pacifists have had to do. (A possible exception is the draft resistance movement in South Vietnam during the war; it was especially strong among university students.) To sum up, Buddhist pacifism has apparently not yet emerged completely from the chrysalis of monastic vocational pacifism in which, early on, it became enclosed. Such a transformation, however, appears to be already on the way.

Catholicism

Before this century absolute pacifism was virtually unknown within the Catholic Church. During the First World War a handful of Catholic conscientious objectors in Britain and the United States had claimed exemption from military service when conscripted; but practically no Catholic C.Os. appeared elsewhere. After the war was over a flourishing Catholic peace organization arose in Weimar Germany but Hitler suppressed it as soon as he came into power. Its members, even when they condemned modern warfare *in toto*, usually did so on the grounds that waging modern war inevitably conflicted with the conditions laid down by classical Catholic just-war theory. The same was generally true of Catholic peace advocates in Britain as well as elsewhere on the European continent, even if here and there we find an isolated evangelical Catholic pacifist, who, like the Austrian Kaspar Mayr, often joined the ranks of the International Fellowship of Reconciliation, though that organization was still an overwhelmingly Protestant body.

The upsurge of Catholic pacifism that took place after World War II had its roots in the United States of the 1930s. There the dynamic Dorothy Day, a convert from Communism to Catholicism, founded the Catholic Worker movement in New York City in 1933.[6] The movement soon spread to other large American cities. Day, who was a talented journalist as her *Catholic Worker* newspaper soon testified, sought through her movement to relieve the sufferings of the people hardest hit by the depression. She opened houses of hospitality, ran soup kitchens for the destitute, and gathered around her a group of concerned young men and women, who accepted voluntary poverty and strove to achieve a decentralised society as their ultimate goal. Hers was "fundamentally a movement of Catholic lay people," a phenomenon "unique in the history of American Catholicism."[7] Day had been strongly influenced in her activities by the "personalist" philosophy[8] of a French immigrant Pierre Maurin, a self-educated peasant who collaborated closely with her in the early years of the movement. Maurin was not explicitly a pacifist but Day was from the very beginning; and it was Day who was responsible for making pacifism one of the movement's core beliefs.

From the outset she had declared her adherence to a gospel-based rejection of war for whatever cause. When the Spanish Civil War came in 1936, she spoke out against it as a pacifist – and this at a time when most Catholics regarded General Franco as a crusader for the faith. In her absolutism she was influenced at the beginning by the arguments of Father (later Monsignor) Paul Hanly Furfey, then a professor at the Catholic University of America, who based the Catholic case against all war "on the Gospel counsel of perfection."[9] She always stressed that her absolutism remained a "Catholic pacifism." She would, she once said, have obeyed if her church had ordered her to stop proclaiming pacifism; for the church authorities, even so, could not have prevented her from spreading pacifism by means of the New Testament message of peace as well as the long chain of Catholic witness for peace down the centuries!

Some Catholic Workers left the movement because of their disagreement with Day's pacifist stand during World War II. But the movement remained intact. Although the number of Catholic C.Os., by no means all of whom were connected with the Catholic Worker movement, was extremely small, that signified a considerable increase over the four known American Catholic .C.Os. of the First World War.[10] Expansion began only in the 1950s; "the Catholic Worker movement, though subdued, was not intimidated by the Cold War." Now, under the influence of two newcomers – both to Catholicism and the Catholic Worker movement – the movement broadened the range of its peace witness. It was Robert Ludlow, an ex-C.O. and for a time associate editor of the *Catholic Worker,* who in the first postwar decade introduced Gandhian nonviolence to its readers as a potential substitute for war and as "a new Christian way of social change." And it was the colorful Ammon Hennacy, a World-War-I socialist C.O. and a lifelong political radical, who now as a self-styled "Catholic anarchist" galvanized the Worker movement in the course of the 1950s into becoming a mainspring of antiwar activity (and also provoked Ludlow into leaving it in protest against Hennacy's flamboyant tactics).

Beginning in 1954 some Catholic Workers in New York, including Day and Hennacy, refused to enter an air raid shelter during compulsory drill; they were soon joined by other pacifists from organizations like the War Resisters' League and the Fellowship of Reconciliation. These striking acts were widely publicized in the media, and their practitioners often underwent short jail sentences for breaking the law. Thus began the Catholic pacifist connection with civil disobedience; "the air raid drill demonstration also marked a new spirit of cooperation among [pacifist] Catholics with other peace groups in the United States." More acts of civil disobedience in protest against war preparations followed over the next decade until the escalation of the Vietnam War in the mid-sixties brought a new dimension to the antiwar movement and expanding resistance to the draft."[11]

"Ludlow," writes Patricia McNeal, "had said that Gandhian nonviolence and Catholic Worker pacifism were compatible, but Hennacy had demonstrated how to join the two together and how to apply these nonviolent tactics to the issue of peace in America."[12] The sense this brought of fresh possibilities and of expanding horizons led to the establishment first of PAX in 1962, uniting under one umbrella both pacifists and nonpacifists, and then, two years later, of a Catholic Peace Fellowship (CPF) on an unambiguously pacifist basis and affiliated to the FOR. Hitherto many Catholic peace advocates had been somewhat suspicious of organized Protestant pacifism.[13] Now these barriers began to break down and old misunderstandings dissolve.

Hennacy's ties with Catholicism and the Catholic Worker movement soon began to loosen. But fortunately there were young recruits, like James H. Forest and Thomas Cornell, to provide the energy, enthusiasm, and ability necessary to make the new Fellowship a success. Thus American Catholic pacifism now possessed a firm, if narrow, base from which to operate during the troubled decade that ensued. At the same time the atmosphere created by the epoch-making Second Vatican Council and by the strong condemnation of war, though still in general terms, in Pope John XXIII's encyclical *Pacem in Terris* (1963) opened the way for wider recognition of the pacifist position within the Catholic Church. Among those lobbying at the Council in favor of pacifism and conscientious objection were two Americans, the Trappist monk and mystic Thomas Merton and the lay theologian James Douglass. Both men helped to shape the further development of American Catholic pacifism.

Merton, though he never considered himself an unconditional pacifist, became an eloquent exponent of Gandhian nonviolence as well as a harsh critic of American policy in Vietnam. He was a prolific writer on peace and war; his views on these topics sometimes brought him into conflict with his monastic superiors. Merton, in fact, became (in the words of one who knew him well) "really more of a pacifist than his frequent and earnest disclaimers would lead one to believe." True, "his was a relative pacifism, a position which always left room, in theory at least, for even a defensive nuclear war."[14] But he felt himself enough of an absolutist to join the FOR, and he also became a sponsor of the recently formed Catholic Peace Fellowship.[15] Right up to his untimely death in 1968 Merton's concept of peacemaking continued to evolve, but he held fast to his belief in the essentially nonviolent character of the Christian message. For him, as for Gandhi, nonviolence if properly understood remained the best way to resist evil and oppression. As he wrote, echoing the thought of the Hindu Mahatma but in Christian terms:

Has nonviolence been found wanting? Yes and no. It has been found wanting wherever it has been the nonviolence of the weak. It has not been found so when it has been the nonviolence of the strong ... Nonviolence ... is not pragmatic but prophetic. It is not aimed at immediate political results, but at the manifestation of fundamental and crucially important truth. Nonviolence is not primarily the language of efficacy ... It does not say "We shall overcome" so much as "This is the day of the Lord, and whatever may happen to us, *He* shall overcome.[16]

In the years ahead Catholic pacifist activists drew inspiration from

Merton's kind of "prophetic" nonviolence, even though Merton himself remained sceptical with regard to direct action against war as well as the more extreme forms of civil disobedience. A believer in personal nonresistance and a supporter of conscientious objection, he refused nevertheless to exclude altogether the possibility of a Christian participating in the unlikely event of a just war. But it was not by his reservations and hesitations that Merton made his mark on American Catholic thinking on war but by the skillful manner in which he blended Gandhian *satyagraha* with the Sermon on the Mount and made the former an acceptable component of Catholic peacemaking. He left to others to draw the practical consequences of this linkage.

Douglass, on the other hand, strode boldly onto territory where Merton carefully avoided treading. Despite his academic background, which might have impeded such behavior, he took part as an antiwar activist in a number of acts of civil disobedience, including those initiated by his Ground Zero Center for Nonviolent Action near Seattle in the seventies and eighties. But his contribution to Catholic pacifism lay primarily as an exponent of Catholic nonviolence. In 1968 he had published *The Non-violent Cross*, the first of a series of strongly polemical books on this theme that lie on the borderline between theological treatises and politico-moral tracts. Here he presents Jesus dying on the Cross as a nonviolent revolutionary with a message to humankind under the imminent threat of nuclear holocaust. This message, Douglass explained, the Hindu Gandhi had clothed with life during a long series of experiments with Truth; even though the Mahatma had rejected Christianity, he had done so with full recognition of "the suffering, loving Christ," who had chosen the cross rather than resort to the violence he had renounced in the Sermon on the Mount. Today "a non-violent ethic" was "in ... process of being formulated," which rejected war in all its forms. Thus Douglass, unlike Merton, moved decisively beyond just-war theory and nuclear pacifism while remaining for all his ecumenism a devout son of his Church. "The Truth," he wrote, "is man's end. But the Truth is also the way, and the way is Love. That the God of Truth and the God of Suffering Love are one is the meaning of the cross."[17]

Douglass's first book, "which became a kind of primer for Catholic pacifists," had appeared as the conflict in Vietnam intensified and its opponents, including Catholic pacifists, adopted increasingly radical techniques to express their detestation of the war being waged by the U.S. administration. Already in October 1965 a young Catholic Worker, David Miller, had publicly burnt his draft card, for which he was sentenced to two-and-a-half years in prison. This symbolic act soon spread. For war resisters to destroy their draft cards was not something entirely new. But Miller gave it a new twist when he proclaimed just prior to burning his card: "I believe the napalming of villages is an immoral act; I hope this will be a significant act. So here goes."[18] We should remember, though, that most Catholic conscientious objectors, like most other C.Os., registered for the draft, going to jail only if their objection was dismissed.[19] Catholic nonregistrants and practitioners of civil disobedience remained a minority, though the more visible one.

The antiwar activities of the most radical section of this minority became known as the Ultra-Resistance; it soon came to include non-Catholics as well as Catholics. The name itself derived from a series of sensational actions beginning with that of the Catonsville Nine on 17 May 1968.[20] Foremost among these ultra-resisters were the Berrigan brothers, Philip the Josephite priest and Daniel the Jesuit – and poet. The Berrigans worked closely with Dorothy Day and the Catholic Worker movement and participated in the activities of the FOR as well the Catholic Peace Fellowship. Early on they had rejected "just-war pacifism" and, under the influence of the *Catholic Worker* and Thomas Merton's writings, they now espoused an evangelical doctrine of peace based on Jesus' love commandment and the Sermon on the Mount. But the brothers were to give this a radical turn into paths where not all their colleagues could follow them.[21] The stumbling block here lay in their campaigns to destroy government property, carried out as a gesture of total repugnance for the massive destruction that the U.S. administration was bringing to an innocent and far-away people. When the Berrigans and their associates seized files from local draft board offices and burnt them or when draft board files were deluged with blood drawn from the veins of the demonstrators, those taking part regarded this as nonviolent. They were ready to become "criminals for peace."

Others in the peace movement – as well as outside it – saw things differently, however. True, during India's nonviolent struggle for freedom Gandhi's followers had burnt foreign-made cloth, but such materials had usually been the property of those who destroyed them. That was not the case now. So, had not these actions of the Berrigans and their colleagues in the Catholic Resistance overstepped the thin line dividing a nonviolent from a violent action? Dorothy Day was among those Catholic pacifists who were troubled by the implications of the ultraresistance, which she feared might eventually lead to the loss of innocent lives. She was also disturbed when the Berrigans, in order to delay sentencing, went temporarily underground – an un-Gandhian practice in her view. She certainly admired the Berrigans' courage and devotion to the common cause, and she understood the frustration they felt with the seeming ineffectiveness of antiwar protest hitherto. She remained cautious in expressing her misgivings so as not to provide fuel for hostile critics or cause a split in the pacifist ranks. But her final decision was to recommend "that the peace movement refrain from such provocative actions, even if property, rather than human life, were the object of destruction.[22]

Under the Berrigan brothers' inspiration the Catholic Resistance continued throughout the seventies and eighties and on into the nineties, albeit with declining momentum. Even though the Vietnam War had ended in 1975, the threat of nuclear war continued, and those involved in resistance were prepared to face heavy, and repeated, jail sentences for breaking their country's laws – in obedience to what they believed was a higher law, which they were bound by if they wished to remain loyal to their faith.[23] "The Berrigan brothers," writes Patricia McNeal, "emerged from the American Catholic pacifist tradition ... they, together with the Catholic Resistance, came out of the Catholic Worker tradition of pacifism and nonviolence ... The combination of Philip's and Daniel's unique strengths and talents enabled them to bring forth the message of peace to their church and country in a way never before experienced in the history of American Catholicism."[24]

"We are Catholics who are trying to be Christians" is how Philip Berrigan describes the Plowshares activists in his autobiography.[25] Married to a former nun, Philip now became the *spiritus movens* behind the antiwar civil disobedience campaigns inaugurated in September 1980 and continuing until the present. These men and women formed, as it were, a religious pacifist order devoted to keeping radical protest against nuclear – and other – weaponry alive even after the Cold War ended. Philip writes:

During our 26-year marriage, Liz [his wife, Elizabeth McAlister] and I have often been separated. Altogether, we've spent ten years apart while one of us was in jail. I've spent over seven years in jail, Liz about four ... Our [three] children grew up in a resistance community. Their parents and friends poured blood at the Pentagon, attempted to disarm airplanes and submarines, attacked missile sites with hammers ... Were we to live our lives again, we would do very little differently.[26]

In its pastoral letter of May 1983 entitled *The Challenge of Peace: God's Promise and Our Response*, the National Conference of Catholic Bishops acknowledged for the first time the right of Catholics to profess pacifism and become conscientious objectors. The letter now placed non-violence alongside just-war theory as acceptable Catholic attitudes; henceforward. the faithful were free to differ on matters of peace and war. Absolute pacifism made several notable converts among the hierarchy, including Archbishop Raymond G. Hunthausen of Seattle and Auxiliary Bishop Thomas Gumbleton of Detroit, who was active in the Fellowship of Reconciliation from the early eighties on. The former, whose pacifism included war tax resistance, was profoundly influenced by the teaching and example of James Douglass. The archbishop as a result of their impact on his thinking had declared his adherence to pacifism in unambiguous terms:

As followers of Christ [he stated] we need to take up our cross in the nuclear age. I believe that one obvious meaning of the cross is unilateral disarmament. Jesus' acceptance of the cross rather than the sword raised in his defense is the Gospel's statement of unilateral disarmament. We are called to follow. Our security as people of faith lies not in demonic weapons which threaten all life on earth. Our security is in a loving, caring God. We must dismantle our weapons of terror and place our reliance on God.[27]

Dorothy Day had died in 1980. But others continued her work for peace either in the Catholic Peace Fellowship or in a new transnational organization, Pax Christi International, that included nonpacifists alongside those who condemned war *in toto*. The Catholic component, too, was now strong in the equally transnational International Fellowship of Reconciliation, including the American FOR, which in May 1998 for the first time appointed a Catholic as its executive director in the person of the Jesuit priest, John Dear, author of a number of books on nonviolence and an antiwar activist in the style of the Berrigan brothers. Of course Catholic pacifists differed from time to time from some of their Protestant, Jewish, or humanist confrères on various issues – abortion, for instance,[28] or human rights in North Vietnam. During the early seventies to their credit Catholic pacifists, including the Berrigans, had insisted on raising the question of the torture of Buddhist and other political prisoners there; and they persisted in protesting such infringements of human dignity wherever they occurred, even though some sections of the peace movement, we know, felt they were not always right in doing so.[29] In general, by the last decade of this century American Catholic pacifism, despite limited support, had come to occupy a significant position on the pacifist spectrum as well as in the counsels of the Catholic Church on matters of peace and war.

In other areas of the world where pacifism surfaced among Catholics, the situation did not look as promising as in the United States. In Britain, Catholic pacifists remained a tiny group; most of them continued, as before, to adhere in principle to just-war theory while rejecting modern warfare as essentially inconsistent with its criteria. In Catholic countries on the European continent several interesting experiments in cooperative pacifist living emerged, like the *Communauté de L'Arche* (Community of the Ark) in France, organized by Lanza del Vasto, a disciple of Gandhi and of "the gentle anarchist" and Gandhian, Vinoba Bhave. Del Vasto, a dedicated Catholic of Italian origin, accepted non-Catholics into his community provided they accepted its nonviolent life-style.[30] More decisively Catholic in its inspiration was the community founded by the scholarly Father György Bulányi in Hungary some years before the collapse of Communism. Intensive study of the Sermon on the Mount during the years immediately after the end of the war had made Bulányi a pacifist. Then followed a sentence of life imprisonment, imposed by the communist authorities in 1952, and the beginnings of a prolonged conflict with his own conservatively minded church superiors when he tried to spread among the Hungarian youth this perception he had gained of the meaning of the gospels. Released from prison in 1961 he eventually succeeded in reviving the earlier movement, suppressed by the communists, to set up small "base" communities throughout the country. These communities accepted nonviolence as an essential element of their life-style. As Bulányi himself put it:

There is no worse contradiction than the Christian soldier: the gospel under the arm, a grenade in the hand. This scandal that mocks Christ has endured for nearly one thousand seven hundred years. However fine the words we use to describe it, as long as a Christian swears a military oath, i.e., promises to destroy the enemy – his fellow man – we bring shame upon Jesus ... There is no Christianity without nonviolence. The "enemy" is of necessity son, father, husband of fellow human beings – a person ... And if the state puts us into prison or executes us for this [love of enemies], we must simply accept it. Without it we cannot be disciples of Jesus.[31]

Bulányi and a handful of fellow priests who shared his views also encouraged young Catholics to refuse to bear arms when conscripted: a position at that date equally obnoxious to the church hierarchy as to the communist government. In Hungary and elsewhere on the European continent, Catholic conscientious objectors have been comparatively few, even after 1945 when their numbers began slowly to grow.[32] Indeed, Catholic pacifism in this area lacked an institutional base such as the Catholic Worker movement provided in the United States. Since the end of the last war the International Fellowship of Reconciliation, and more recently Pax Christi International, have gone some way toward giving it support; still, that has not been sufficient to counter the effects of deeply rooted conscriptionist traditions and of hostile or indifferent church hierarchies. In addition, in countries like Poland and Hungary or Spain and Italy, Catholicism and nationalism have down the centuries fused inextricably so as to make it extremely difficult to detach religion from defense of the *patria* (a situation that has occurred of course in Protestant and Orthodox lands as well).[33]

If European Catholicism so far has lacked a pacifist Catholic Worker movement, a European Dorothy Day may perhaps be seen (*mutatis mutandis*) in Hildegard Goss-Mayr. Daughter of an Austrian Catholic pacifist and pioneer of Polish-German reconciliation (Kaspar Mayr) and wife of a French Catholic trade unionist Jean Goss (a decorated World-War-II warrior subsequently converted to pacifism), Hildegard, along with her husband, have played a key role in the history of pacifism in the nuclear age. Indeed from their marriage in 1958 onward, the Goss-Mayrs made it their life-mission, among other tasks, to spread the message of nonviolence in areas where pacifism was little, if at all known before: a mission carried on by Hildegard alone after Jean's death in 1991. As Catholics the Goss-Mayrs felt a special concern for Catholics in the Third World, especially those in Latin America which the couple first visited in 1962. In 1984 and 1985 their work for nonviolence among Catholics in the Philippines assisted in keeping the forthcoming revolution, which succeeded in overthrowing the Marcos régime, a nonviolent one.[34] They travelled on their peace missions as field secretaries of the International Fellowship of Reconciliation, formerly as we know a predominantly Protestant organization but accessible to pacifists of other faiths since the 1970s. What the Mennonite Doug Hostetter wrote of Jean Goss at the time of his death could be applied equally to Hildegard: "Jean is truly present in hundreds of communities around the world where oppressed people join together in the nonviolent struggle for a better life."[35]

The Goss-Mayrs based their faith in nonviolence on the Sermon on the Mount; they believed this entailed a radical discipleship. Christ's words on that occasion constituted a "revolutionary manifesto of love"; for those words adumbrated a nonviolent strategy for achieving a just and peaceful world order. Nonviolence represented "a form of struggle which aims at overcoming injustice by the power of love and reconciliation." Christians, in the Goss-Mayrs' view, must learn from Gandhi the way to make this love a reality.[36]

Two of the leading exponents of active nonviolence in Latin America

have acknowledged the debt they owed to the Goss-Mayrs for introducing them to the idea of nonviolence as a consistent method of
resisting social oppression and the abuse of human rights: we refer to
the Brazilian Archbishop Hélder Câmara of Recife and the Argentinian
1980 Nobel Peace Prize winner and co-founder in 1974 of Servicio Paz
y Justicia (SERPAJ – Service for Peace and Justice), Adolfo Pérez
Esquivel.[37] The latter writes of this influence and the network of
groups and personalities that came into being as a consequence of the
Goss-Mayrs' efforts:

They were the first who began the work that eventually resulted in what is
now the Service for Peace and Justice in Latin America ... They began from a
gospel perspective even as they delved into the methodology of the Gandhian
struggle ... Dom Hélder Câmara is like a son of theirs. When he was auxiliary
bishop in Rio de Janeiro in the 1960s, they began to explain to him what the
strength of nonviolence is all about. Before that he had used nonviolence
almost intuitively. What Hildegard and Jean did was give him a clearer understanding of nonviolence and its history, showing him the possibilities and the
capacity of nonviolence and its power in ... society and in individuals.[38]

Hitherto the few scattered pacifists in Latin America had belonged to
the Protestant minority of the population, nearly 90 percent of which
was Catholic – at any rate in name. The IFOR, although it had succeeded
in organizing groups in Mexico, Argentina, and Uruguay, remained
extremely weak throughout this area, largely because of "the scarcity of
Roman Catholic pacifists."[39] From the 1960s onward the situation
changed radically as active nonviolence gained support among those
struggling against political and social oppression and seeking to make
Catholicism "the church of the poor."[40] SERPAJ adopted as its slogan the
words: "La paz es fruto de la justicia (Peace is the fruit of justice)," and
it sought to promote a specifically "Latin American" form of communitarianism that would eventually replace the existing structures of social
oppression and militarism. Like Gandhi and King, though, its adherents
rejected decisively the idea of nonviolence being merely a weapon of the
weak. They insisted, too, that liberation theology was correct in believing injustice must be resisted – but, in their view, nonviolently and not
with lethal weapons. "I respect those who have felt obliged in conscience to opt for violence," Câmara has said, "who have proved their
sincerity by the sacrifice of their lives. It seems to me the memory of
Camilo Torres and Che Guevara deserves as much respect as that of Dr.
Martin Luther King, Jr.".[41] And the Goss-Mayrs have also recorded their
esteem for Torres, the Colombian guerrilla-priest killed in combat with

the security forces in 1966. They had met him shortly after their arrival on the continent four years earlier. Like Câmara, they admired his readiness to sacrifice his life in the struggle for justice, and they later paid tribute to "his great integrity and his idealism" in pursuit of the people's welfare. At the same time they regretted his unwillingness, for he had been reared on just-war theory, to follow Jesus' love command and pursue just aims by the methods of evangelical nonviolence. From his side Torres appreciated the Goss-Mayrs' sincerity and the passion for social justice they shared with him. He even suggested they should remain in Colombia to work alongside the revolutionaries – but in a spirit of nonviolence. The couple's prior commitments, however, prevented them from considering this proposal.[42]

The struggle for the rights of the poor and disinherited throughout Central and South America has engaged the efforts of indigenous nonviolent actionists. Whereas the rank-and-file practitioners of nonviolence, ordinary workers or peasants, often acted to right a local wrong "quite spontaneously scarcely realizing how [rooted in their past was] their strategy," the leaders and organizers drew for inspiration on Catholic social teaching as well as on the experiences of Gandhi and King and the direct impact of reading the Sermon on the Mount. (Jailed in 1977 by Argentine's military dictatorship, Pérez Esquivel ironically was refused access to a Bible by these "defenders of ... Christian civilization" on the grounds of its being "subversive material".)

Participants in the various nonviolent actions and demonstrations pledged themselves to nonviolence, on the Gandhian model, for as long as the action lasted but without necessarily promising a more permanent adherence to it as a principle. Yet many of the leaders saw their activities as a first stage in the creation of a nonviolent society. Like Gandhi in India, they built a "myth" of their peoples' past. The indigenous population, in Pérez Esquivel's words, "have long known the methods of nonviolent struggle. It is just that they have used it as a way to survive, not to try to overturn a whole system." "Their social structure is nonviolent too." So now, with growing "conscientization (*conscientización*)" of the hitherto marginalized and the rapid spread throughout the continent of Christian base communities, and with "a great chain" of nonviolent struggles emerging everywhere, surely the transformation could not be long in coming? Such was the vision which kept hope alive among the adherents of nonviolence in a continent dominated for so long by military dictatorships and by reactionary religious and social structures.[43]

The thrust of Latin American nonviolence has lain in the area of social struggle. Latin American pacifists, as Gerald Schlabach has pointed out, have been concerned so far primarily with justice whereas international peace has remained the major preoccupation of pacifists in North America and Europe.[44] This is quite natural. The two concerns are indeed complementary and, as Gandhi came to recognize, closely interlocked with each other.

That was clear, too, to Dorothy Day when she wrote of the leader of the United Farm Workers Union in California and his nonviolent struggle to win justice for the Mexican-American grapepickers: "Cesar Chavez and the Farm Workers' movement [are] also part of the peace movement, committed to nonviolence, even where they resist." And she pointed out how in their boycott against the grape growers they were fighting – nonviolently – for their own and their families' livelihood.[45] Chavez the labor leader and Câmara the people's archbishop shared the same nonviolent ethos.

From Day and the Berrigans via the Goss-Mayrs and nonviolent liberationists of Latin America to the marginalized *chicanos* in sunny California, we have followed in outline the network of Catholic pacifism that has been forming since the end of World War II. The vision of some Catholic pacifists to see their church transformed into a peace church embracing a large part of humankind is still far from realization. Though it may always remain a dream, a century ago there was scarcely anyone in the Church who could even have dreamt it.

Judaism

The roots of Jewish pacifism lie in a different religious tradition from those of Christian – or humanist – pacifism. The difference is perhaps not so decisive as in the case of Buddhist, Hindu or Muslim nonviolence, since it was Judaism from which Christianity emerged two millennia ago in the heterodox teachings of the rabbi Jeshua; still, that difference is often sufficient to impede understanding on the part of those belonging to the pacifist mainstream, a lack of understanding due primarily to unfamiliarity with Jewish religion in its later stages.

An explicitly Jewish pacifism of the absolutist variety appears, seemingly for the first time, during the First World War when in Britain and the United States a small number of Jewish conscientious objectors emerged who based their refusal to fight on their understanding of Judaism. Though in both countries the official spokesmen of the Jewish communities claimed almost unanimously that a Jew could not be a pacifist, isolated figures like the American Reform rabbi, Judah Magnes, or the Englishman John Harris, a minister at a Liverpool synagogue, had denied this while at the same time proclaiming their own belief in the wrongness of war and their support, as Jews, for the position of the conscientious objector.[46]

We must distinguish at the outset between, on the one hand, pacifists of Jewish extraction, who, though they might have been influenced in their rejection of war by their Jewish background, nevertheless drew their major inspiration for doing this from non-Jewish sources, and on the other hand Jewish pacifists, whose major inspiration lay in Judaism itself, though non-Jewish influences may also have helped shape their pacifism. Naturally it is impossible to draw a precise line dividing these two positions; they often overlap.

As a good example of the first position we can take the case of the American Max Kampelman, a Jewish C.O. of World War II and afterwards a Cold War "warrior."[47] In his autobiography he testifies to the influence in making him a pacifist of his Jewish home and neighborhood background and of his early Jewish religious training in a New York yeshiva. Later, as a law student he came into touch with two outstanding pacifist rabbis – the saintly Abraham Cronbach and the scholarly Isidor Hoffman, whose unconditional rejection of war derived from "the idea of brotherhood and its implications for nonviolence," which they had both discovered in the Talmud. But a more direct impulse leading young Kampelman to declare himself a C.O. came from his avid reading of Tolstoy and Gandhi and the writings of "the American Christian pacifist community." "What I learned" from these sources, he writes, fitted "easily into the Jewish pacifist vision of brotherhood that Rabbis Hoffman and Cronbach enunciated." He joined not only the War Resisters' League, which included a number of secular Jewish pacifists like its executive secretary, Abraham Kaufman, but also the then overwhelmingly Christian FOR.[48] A summer spent at a Quaker work camp under the direction of a charismatic Friend named David Richie, together with his initiation around that time into the labor movement, provided a suitable background to Kampelman's years in CPS when he helped to edit a newspaper "unambiguously" entitled *The Conscientious Objector.*[49]

Bernard Gross, a co-founder of the Jewish Pacifist Fellowship (JPF) in 1942, was typical of the second position. He indeed wrote of himself: "I am a Jew ... but I am also a Quaker, and perhaps a few other things besides." Yet, unlike Kaufman or Kampelman he still sought, for all his interdenominationalism, to maintain a Jewish content in his pacifism while at the same time preserving and expanding the nonviolent ethic he had learnt in his early religious training. It was this content that was basic. Men like Gross felt the need to create a wartime pacifist fellowship in which Jews could feel entirely at home.[50] Despite discouragingly small numbers the JPF managed to survive into the postwar era. Nazi persecution had brought about defections from the ranks of prewar Jewish pacifism: both prominent figures like Rabbi Stephen S. Wise and obscure draftees like Moshe Kallner, a strictly orthodox Jewish refugee from Nazi Germany, who finally gave up his CPS status to join the army.[51] It is true that the dilemma experienced here existed, at any rate in theory, for all pacifists but emotionally its effects were likely of course to be more traumatic for Jews.[52]

This situation, however, would no longer hold in the case of the Vietnam War when secular and religious Jews figured both as selective objectors and absolute pacifists. Some Jewish C.Os., especially if they chose to be nonregistrants, went to prison as had happened in the two world wars; others accepted alternative service or took refuge in Canada. The pattern resembled that which held for other conscripts who now refused to fight. By this time the JPF, though still small, had increased considerably in numbers; in December 1965 it affiliated to the now interfaith Fellowship of Reconciliation. In addition, within American Jewry a more tolerant atmosphere prevailed with respect to pacifism (indeed from the interwar years onward pacifism had been generally recognized as being at any rate a possible Jewish position). Peace-minded rabbis became active in draft counselling; they saw to it that those who came to them for advice not only knew their rights but were made aware of the case for a specifically Jewish pacifism of the unconditional sort as well as of the restrictions placed upon warfare in Jewish tradition rooted in the Talmud, which could justify selective objection at the present day.

The JPF in its statement of aims had proclaimed that "nonviolence and conscientious objection stem directly from the loftiest motives of Judaism" and that its members united in the belief "that Jewish ideals and experience provide inspiration for a nonviolent commitment to life and the remaking of society."[53] Jewish pacifists could not deny of course that the Hebrew Bible permitted wars of various kinds any more than Christian pacifists could claim that down the centuries their religion had not often supported the sword. They asserted, instead, that "Judaism developed from the Bible and [was] not limited to it," that it was a religion in process of evolving with room in it "for many points of view,"[54] and that the idea of nonviolence had been present in Judaism from early on in its history.

American Jewish pacifism was greatly strengthened by the accession of the philosopher Steven S. Schwarzchild, a powerful mind and also a widely respected figure in world Jewry. Two years before his death in 1989, Schwarzchild had written: "I believe, on the basis of intense lifelong and professional studies, that pacifism is the best, the most authentic interpretation of classical Judaism."[55] Despite the Holocaust and the other horrors of the twentieth century, perhaps indeed because of them, he confessed: "I am deeply tired of and sickened by killing." A man must die only once; his own wish was that he would not die "with human blood on my hands." For Schwarzchild Judaism was essentially a religion of nonviolence; in his view, Jewish law (*halakha*) , Jewish doctrine (*agada*), and Jewish history all confirmed this, even if there were texts and actions that appeared to contradict such a belief.[56]

The fact that expositions of Jewish pacifism have so far appeared almost exclusively in the English language stems from absolute pacifism based on the Jewish religious tradition having hitherto been largely confined to English-speaking Jewry. What about pacifists in the beleaguered state of Israel? World pacifist opinion, before as well as after the creation of the state of Israel in 1948, has been divided in its attitude to Jewish settlement in that area. Some pacifists, like the black radical war resister Bayard Rustin, who presided over a Black Americans in Support of Israel Committee (BASIC), gave warm support to the existence of the new state[57] (though not to its military policies) but there were others who did not, like the Englishwoman Dr. Maude Royden on the eve of World War II, or the prominent Canadian Mennonite educator, Frank H. Epp. Epp in the 1970s pleaded the case for the Palestinians in several well documented studies of Near Eastern politics (a case supported also by a number of Israeli "doves" despite its general unpopularity among their fellow citizens). On the other hand, even within the U.S. Jewish Peace Fellowship there were members who believed that Israel was justified in defending itself by arms if its existence were at stake.[58]

Thus Israeli pacifists, with their country either at war or threatened with attack, faced a far more difficult situation than Jews in the United States whose dilemmas (except during the Vietnam War) were mainly of a theoretical nature. An Israeli political scientist writes:

The conditions of an entire nation mobilized in the effort to establish a strong, independent nation-state are incompatible with the growth of a refusal [to bear arms]. In fact, against such a background, conscientious objection is perceived to be antithetical to the prevailing value system. To recoil from the use of power becomes a form of dissociation from the collective effort ... Further, the military and the civilian sectors intrude upon each other. There is a civilianization of the military and a militarization of society ... Taking this background into consideration, one understands why it was so difficult for a pacifist movement to grow and develop during the first twenty years of Israel's existence.[59]

Though most Israeli C.Os. have been selective objectors, especially during recent decades, Jewish pacifism has existed in Palestine/Israel since the 1920s. The rise of Hitlerism drove such convinced pacifist immigrants as Judah Magnes, the protagonist of a bi-national Jewish-Arab Palestine to replace the British mandate, and the more secular Hans Kohn (from Prague) to abandon their belief in nonviolence. But there were a handful who remained steadfast in their adherence to pacifism rallying around the tiny war resisters' (WRI) section in Jerusalem. These people were pacifists and at the same time Zionists. We may call them cultural Zionists, like many other Jews who before World War I had escaped from the pogroms and antisemitism often prevailing in their countries of birth and had settled in Palestine, where they worked the land living peaceably beside the Arab population they already found there. Some who had emigrated from Russia remained under the spell of Tolstoy's populism; most professed some form of agrarian socialism, in which the establishment of income-pooling rural communes figured prominently. However, with the growth of a militantly political Zionism began the alienation of many of these early cultural Zionists, against whom the tide had now turned irrevocably. It was from this background that the pioneer pacifist, Natan Hofshi, emerged; he continued to preside over the WRI group into his old age.[60]

Hofshi was born in Russian Poland in 1889 into a devout Jewish family. In his youth he learnt Hebrew (his mother tongue was Yiddish) and studied the Hebrew Bible so thoroughly that he came to know large parts of it by heart. In 1909 he emigrated to Palestine (*Eretz Israel*), forming part of a movement of highly idealistic Zionists known as the second *aliyah* (immigration). Working at first as an agricultural laborer, Hofshi experienced no difficulties in his relationship with his Arab coworkers. He had come to Palestine as an adherent of revolutionary socialism. But as a result of intensive reading of the later prophets – especially Isaiah, Hosea, and Amos – he eventually became convinced of the essentially pacifist message of Judaism. Isaiah's peaceable vision of a time when "nation shall not lift up sword against nation, neither shall they learn war any more" (AV Isaiah 2:4) constituted only one among many passages that buttressed Hofshi's belief. As he explained:

The [Hebrew] Bible is neither a legislator nor a pedagogue ... violence [often] is dominant ... But in the part of the Bible we call the late prophets, one finds a true world of purity, and it is there that there is an ethical Judaism at once Jewish and universal ... and there we hear time and again the vision of peace between individuals, between one nation and another, between men and women and every thing that lives.[61]

He linked up with others who had begun to think along these lines. When in the 1920s Hofshi came into contact with the newly formed War Resisters' International these people formed the core of its small Palestine section. They remained confident that they could somehow break down the distrust the Arabs felt toward Jewish settlers and that "confidence and friendliness" would slowly grow between neighbors in place of the existing hatred. While Hofshi, "as a farmer," condemned "the Effendis" for exploiting the "poor Arabian peasants and land-workers," he denounced "Jewish Chauvinism" with equal vigor. "I know it so well," he wrote, "being a Jew ... I am deeply offended by it. I should like to root it out from the hearts of my fellow- countrymen."[62]

After World War II, with the creation of the state of Israel, the situation for pacifists changed radically. Hofshi himself was over age but younger men now became liable to compulsory service in the army. No legal provision existed for conscientious objection, even on grounds of religion. But, anxious to avoid creating martyrs, the army wisely avoided jailing the few who refused the draft. Some kind of compromise, some form of *modus vivendi*, was usually reached. The military did not even try to touch members of the dissident Hasidic group known as the Guardians of the City (*Neturei Karta*) who, rather like the Christian sect of Jehovah's Witnesses, reject bearing arms except in the unlikely situation of being ordered to do so by the Messiah.[63] The handful of pacifist C.Os. scarcely presented a problem, either. They could be assigned some civilian task – or, on some technicality, just left alone, as happened in the case of the musician Joseph Abileah.

Pacifists might also be persuaded to undertake noncombatant military duties when drafted. Amos Gvirtz, for instance, tells us that he "wanted to do civilian not military service. The army compromised but I still had to do my service within the army." What the army conceded in its bargain with the objector was, as Gvirtz relates, "that I didn't handle weapons, that I didn't wear a uniform and that I didn't have to serve in the occupied territories."[64] Yehezka Landau, an American born and Harvard trained psychologist who had emigrated to Israel in 1978, met with a somewhat similar fate when he declared himself a C.O. On receiving his call-up papers in 1982 he wrote very politely to General Ariel Sharon, then Minister of Defense, asking for exemption from the draft. He had been, he explained, an objector on religious grounds during the Vietnam War when he had joined both the JPF and the FOR. As he told General Sharon:

I am a religious Zionist who has made *aliyah* from the United States out of an identification with Israel and the Jewish People ... I have always been, and still am, a conscientious objector to military service in *any* army. Being a Zionist and a C.O. creates an obvious inner conflict of loyalties ... I am prepared to serve in any social or educational field where I am needed. And in wartime I would certainly do whatever task I am assigned to help the civilian population, or wounded soldiers in a hospital, within any framework outside *Zahal* [the Israeli Defense Forces] ... My C.O. convictions ... do not derive from the policies of this or any other Israeli government ... Clearly it is more difficult to be a C.O. in Israel than it is anywhere else, since we are confronted by adversaries who seek Israel's destruction ... I deeply respect the sense of duty which most Israelis feel in fulfilling their national service through *Zahal*. And I realize that, without our army, Israel would not exist as a free and independent nation.

His objection to bearing arms, then, remained a very personal one – quasi-vocational, we might even call it. In the end the military authorities, taking advantage perhaps of Landau's compliant spirit, refused to budge beyond allowing him to perform his annual spell of duty in a noncombatant branch of the army.[65]

During the 1960s, and especially after the Six-Day War in June 1967, a rift developed among Israel's small band of pacifists. On the one hand were the old timers like Hofshi, whose pacifism stemmed from their Judaic faith and was inextricably linked with their belief in a cultural, peaceable, religious Zionism, and on the other a younger generation, often born in Palestine unlike their elders who were all immigrants who had made *aliyah* in their early years. The younger men now rejected the policies of the Zionist state and took their stand alongside their fellow Palestinians of Arab origin. In a letter to the then secretary of the Israeli section of the WRI, Hofshi exclaimed bitterly: "You are alien to this Jewish pacifist Zionism, which has instilled in me and my fellows the fire of faith and yearning for Zion of 'the end of days' ... My Zionism and my resistance to war and violence – both are grounded on religion and conscience." The old man, now in his eighties, complained he had been effectually driven out of "our movement" as a result of the new attitude adopted by these young pacifists. For the latter shrank "from the spiritual Jewish sentiment, which had been the soul of our movement in its early years."[66]

The new stance, personified in particular by Uri Davis (who eventually emigrated to the U.S.), signified a trend toward the "politicization" of the WRI in Israel and its alignment with the growing movement of selective – and nonpacifist – conscientious objection and with the swelling protest against the policies adopted by the government both toward the Palestinians and toward Israel's Arab neighbors. For Davis and his friends, a "Zionist frame of reference" for the WRI, prevailing hitherto, had come to seem increasingly "incompatible with [secular] conscientious objection and draft resistance," with the kind of war resistance now beginning to pose a serious problem for government and military alike.[67] In the 1960s, Davis had even proposed that the WRI should omit the word 'conscientious' from its sectional name (in Hebrew), "The Movement for Conscientious War Resistance," and pledge full support to selective objectors and their struggle. This proved too much for the majority of members, however; they rejected Davis's proposal "indignantly," arguing that the change would undermine the essentially pacifist and nonpolitical character that the founders had given their movement at the outset.[68] The section survived the crisis; eventually a few Palestinians joined it to strive together against seemingly overwhelming odds for a common political destiny.

Nonviolence and the Palestinian Arabs

With the growth of the *intifada*, the – in practice – largely nonviolent movement for Palestinian liberation in the West Bank and Gaza Strip inaugurated in December 1987, and with rising pressures from within and outside Israel to reach some kind of *modus vivendi* between the country's two nationalities, the outlook for peace in this troubled area began slowly to improve, though conflicts still abounded on every side. Nonviolent nuclei existed now among the Arabs; and these, though extremely small, began to show signs of increased activity.

There had always been the ethnically Arab Quakers, located at Brummana in Lebanon and at Ramallah in the West Bank and dating back to Quaker missionary activity there toward the end of last century. But they formed a tiny group. Of wider significance was the establishment in Jerusalem in 1985 of the Palestinian Center for the Study of Nonviolence. Its founder was Mubarak Awad, a youth counsellor whose father had been killed in the Arab-Israeli War of 1948. Reared by his mother in Jerusalem as a Palestinian nationalist but also in a spirit of reconciliation (his background was Christian), he remained receptive to this spirit after he had reached manhood. Of his mother he writes: "She said that we should dedicate our lives to finding solutions so that others would not suffer as we did." His fulfillment of her wish began only much later as a result of attending Bluffton College, a Mennonite institution in the United States. Awad tells us how his stay there transformed him into a pioneer of nonviolence among his own people after his return home in 1983:

I was introduced [at Bluffton] to the writings of Martin Luther King and Gandhi. I started to wonder, "Why don't the Palestinians try nonviolence?" ... In college, I came in contact with Mennonites, Quakers and other members of the historic peace churches. The people I met didn't just believe in nonviolence; they put their ideas into practice in their daily lives. I had trouble understanding this but I was inspired.

The Center, which he brought into existence two years later, with its workshops and seminars on nonviolence, its publication program in this area, and its organization of nonviolent direct actions among the Palestinian villagers, formed Awad's response to the challenge he had received at Bluffton.[69] Shortly before the Center opened Awad had formulated in outline the principles and strategy of a genuinely nonviolent campaign of resistance in the occupied territories. His ultimate aims coincided with those of the Palestine Liberation Organization (PLO) but the means he urged on his fellow patriots resembled those employed by Mahatma Gandhi in British-ruled India. First published in English,[70] Awad's text was then translated into Arabic and widely distributed. In his article Awad expounded "many of the classic methods and techniques of nonviolent struggle that since have been utilized by the *intifada*."[71] He called for the Palestinians to remain nonviolent in face even of extreme provocation; he used the Arabic word *sabr*, meaning "enduring patience," to describe the resistance they should mount against the occupying forces, reflecting the persistence of the cactus of that name "that remains where Palestinian villages have been destroyed" and stubbornly "refuses to die."[72]

After the outbreak of the *intifada*, as before the uprising, Awad and his group continued to advocate an unconditional acceptance of nonviolence as the basis of struggle. They regarded it "as superior to the use of arms on ethical and practical grounds."[73] Awad stressed the importance of providing an example of nonviolent behavior, so that, "hopefully, looking at you [others] will say, 'I want to be like that.'"[74] Like Gandhi, these people were themselves committed to nonviolence as a life principle; and like the Mahatma, they expected all who participated in the protest to accept this principle at any rate for as long as they were engaged in action. Awad failed however to reach unanimous agreement with his compatriots in the *intifada* on this issue. Indeed, even after the coming of Palestinian autonomy in the formerly occupied territories, something more still seems to be needed than a formal, merely external, acceptance of nonviolence on the part of the Palestinians alongside concessions from the government of Israel. According to an expert on the area, "without the alchemy that comes through daily acts of reconciliation between Arab and Jew it is doubtful that increased Palestinian autonomy in the territories will bring true peace to the most violent region of the world."[75]

Adherents of Jewish *shalom* and Arab nonviolence working together – along with other persons of goodwill – in such organizations as the IFOR branch, "Palestinians and Israelis for Nonviolence," in continuous efforts to find a solution to the conflicts long afflicting the Near East: this may provide an uncertain perspective. But at any rate the appearance of this vision gives further proof that, by the last decade of the twentieth century, the pacifist impulse and the idea of nonviolence, closely related to it, are no longer wholly alien even to the thought patterns in an area hitherto unreceptive to them.[76]

Notes

1 In the United States, despite its clumsy phrasing the Supreme Court's decision in the Seeger case (380 U.S. 163 [1965]) proved epoch-making, at any rate for that country. Henceforward any opponent of war was entitled to exemption as a C.O., if this opposition were based on "a sincere belief, which in his life fills the same place as a belief in God fills in the life of an orthodox religionist." See above, chap. VII. We may note here that even that paragon of rationalism, Bertrand Russell, claimed that the emergence of his otherwise utilitarian pacifism had come during "a sort of mystical illumination," which he underwent in 1901. See *The Autobiography of Bertrand Russell 1872–1914* (London: George Allen and Unwin Ltd., 1967), p. 146.

2 For pacifist "adumbrations" in the past and present of the Orthodox church, see Alexander F.C. Webster, "The Pacifist Option: An Eastern Orthodox Perspective on War in the Nuclear Age" (Ph.D. diss., University of Pittsburgh, 1988: University Microfilms, No. 8817619), an informative, if somewhat discursive work. The essays in Glen D. Paige *et al.*, eds., *Islam and Nonviolence* (Honolulu: Center for Global Nonviolence Planning Project, 1993) examine elements of nonviolence in the Muslim tradition. The American Fellowship of Reconciliation now has Orthodox and Muslim affiliates.

3 See James H. Forest, *The Unified Buddhist Church of Vietnam: Fifteen Years of Reconciliation* (Alkmaar: International Fellowship of Reconciliation, 1978). "Do not shoot your own brother: use love to resist hatred" were among the pacifist slogans employed by the Unified Buddhist Church in South Vietnam. Continuing its antimilitarist witness even after the communists' military victory in 1975, it suffered severe persecution from both sides on account of this witness. No provision for conscientious objection existed

during or after the war; objectors who failed to evade military service were jailed while successive governments continually harassed church leaders for encouraging conscripts not to bear arms. Forest, *op. cit.*, pp. 15, 16, 18–20, 22–31.

4 Kenneth Kraft, ed., *Inner Peace, World Peace: Essays on Buddhism and Nonviolence* (Albany: State University of New York Press, 1992), pp. 14, 15, 23, 24.

5 Fred Eppsteiner, edn., *The Path of Compassion: Writings on Socially Engaged Buddhism*, 2nd rev. edn. (Berkeley, CA: Parallax Press, 1988), pp. 17, 18. Even the pacifistic Buddhist Emperor Aśoka had occasionally engaged in punitive campaigns against the forest tribes of ancient India.

6 See William D. Miller, *Dorothy Day: A Biography* (San Francisco: Harper & Row, 1982); Mel Piehl, *Breaking Bread: The Catholic Worker and the Origin of Catholic Radicalism in America* (Philadelphia: Temple University Press, 1982), chap. VI: "The Catholic Worker and Peace"; Nancy Roberts, *Dorothy Day and the Catholic Worker* (Albany: State University of New York Press, 1984); and Eileen Egan, "Dorothy Day, Pilgrim of Peace," pp. 69–114 in Patrick G. Coy, ed., *A Revolution of the Heart: Essays on the Catholic Worker* (Philadelphia: Temple University Press, 1988).

7 Patricia McNeal, *Harder than War: Catholic Peacemaking in Twentieth-Century America* (New Brunswick, NJ: Rutgers University Press, 1992), p. 21. McNeal's monograph is the best guide to the history of American Catholic pacifism.

8 Defined in the *Catholic Worker* (May 1987) as a philosophy replacing "self-centered individualism" by "the good of the other" while "taking personal responsibility for changing conditions, rather than looking to the state ... to provide impersonal 'charity'." Quoted in Coy, ed. *op. cit.*, p. 354. Maurin's personalist democracy was a distillation of his reading – chiefly of Aquinas, Berdyaev, Maritain, Mounier, and the English distributists.

9 McNeal, *op. cit.*, p. 38. Later, during World War II Day found confirmation of her pacifism in the writings of another Catholic theologian, Father John J. Hugo.

10 *Ibid.*, pp. 55, 56, 269. "The highest estimate of the number of Catholic COs was 135," that is, apart from a few – unrecorded – Catholics who accepted noncombatant service in the army. The fact that almost half the known Catholic C.Os. served prison sentences reflects the widely held view (even among the Catholic clergy) that it was impossible to be both a Catholic and a conscientious objector. A handful of the Catholic C.Os. had been followers of the extreme rightist Father Coughlin but the overwhelming majority were genuine pacifists of one kind or another.

11 *Ibid.*, pp. 75–79, 86–93. See also Coy's essay on "The One-Person Revolution of Ammon Hennacy," pp. 134–73 in Coy, ed., *op. cit.* The historian of libertarianism, George Woodcock, has described Hennacy as "spreading as

much fire and brimstone antigovernmentalism as any two ordinary anarchists I know" (*ibid.*, p. 171 n. 51).

12 McNeal, *op. cit.*, p. 93.

13 Conversely deep hostility toward Catholicism sometimes surfaced among Protestant pacifists well into the present century. The eminent British theologian, the late C.J. Cadoux, provides a good example of this phenomenon.

14 From Gordon C. Zahn's introduction to his selections from Merton's writings on peace *The Nonviolent Alternative* (New York: Farrar, Straus, Giroux, 1980), p. xix. Zahn's anthology fomis an excellent introduction to Merton's views on nonviolence. See also David W. Givey, *The Social Thought of Thomas Merton: The Way of Nonviolence and Peace for the Future* (Chicago: Franciscan Herald Press, 1983) and McNeal, *op. cit.*, chap. VI: "Thomas Merton at the Crossroads of Peace."

15 McNeal. *op. cit.*, p. 122.

16 Merton, *Nonviolent Alternative*, p. 75. Italics in the original.

17 James W. Douglass, *The Non-violent Cross: Theology of Revolution and Peace* (New York: The Macmillan Company, 1968), pp. 54, 76, 157, 182, 292. See also Charles E. Curran, *American Catholic Social Ethics: Twentieth-Century Approaches* (Notre Dame, IN: University of Notre Dame Press, 1982), chap. VI: "The Catholic Peace Movement and James W. Douglass." There are both parallels and differences between the Catholic Douglass's and the Mennonite Hershberger's approach to the Cross as a symbol of Christian rejection of war and other forms of violence.

18 McNeal, *op. cit.*, pp. 146, 147.

19 *Ibid.*, p. 170.

20 See in particular *ibid.*, chap. VII: "The Berrigan Brothers and the Catholic Resistance," and Anne Klejment, "War Resistance and Property Destruction: The Catonsville Nine Draft Board Raid and Catholic Worker Pacifism," pp. 272–309 in Coy, ed. *op. cit.*

21 Klejment, *op. cit.*, pp. 278–300.

22 *Ibid.*, p. 295. Day also disapproved of the self-immolation, on the model of anti-war Buddhist monks and nuns in South Vietnam, of the young Catholic worker, Roger LaPorte.

23 See Arthur J. Laffin and Anne Montgomery, eds., *Swords into Plowshares: Nonviolent Direct Action for Disarmament* (San Francisco: Harper & Row, 1987). Participants in the actions discussed here included priests and nuns as well as lay persons. For brief descriptions of actions taking place between September 1980 and September 1986 and the trials and jailings of those participating, see pp. 32–45. For Philip Berrigan's account, see his autobiography, with Fred A. Wilcox, *Fighting the Lamb's War: Skirmishes with the American Empire* (Monroe, ME: Common Courage Press, 1996), pp. 183–205.

24 McNeal, *op. cit.*, pp. 209, 210.

25 Berrigan, *op. cit.*, pp. 215.

26 *Ibid.*, p. 199.

27 Quoted in George Weigel, *Tranquillitas Ordinis: The Present Failure and Future Promise of American Catholic Thought on War and Peace* (Oxford and New York: Oxford University Press, 1987), p. 172. On pages 148–73, 242–8, Weigel gives a neoconservative – but not wholly unsympathetic – critique of post-1945 American Catholic pacifism and its leading exponents.

28 Cf. Gordon Zahn's view: "No one who publicly mourns the senseless burning of a napalmed child should be indifferent to the intentional killing of a living fetus in the womb." Quoted in Weigel, *op. cit.*, p. 155.

29 McNeal, *op. cit.*, pp. 218–22.

30 Del Vasto, along with two other prominent proponents of nonviolence, General Jacques de Bollardière and Abbé Jean Toulat, exercised a major influence on the "Gandhian-style" struggle during the 1970s of French sheep farmers at Le Larzac in Occitania (Languedoc) with the object of preventing the seizure of their land for use as an army camp. The peasants' nonviolent contest reached a successful conclusion in 1981. See Roger Raulinson, *Larzac – A Popular Nonviolent Campaign in Southern France* (York, U.K.: William Sessions Limited, 1996), pp. 34–43, 92, 97, 98.

31 György Bulányi, "God does not lord it over us," *The Plough* (Rifton, NY), no. 28 (February/March, 1991), pp. 18–20. Bulányi's movement was often known as "The Bush" – from the burning bush in the Book of Genesis, out of which God spoke to Moses. See also Hans-H. Hücking, "Ruf nach der Alternative: Kriegsdienstverweigerung in Ungam," in Heinz Janning *et al.*, eds., *Kriegs-/Erstasdienst-Verweigerung in Ost und West* (Essen: Klartext Verlag, 1990). pp. 367–71.

32 For Bulányi, see Lawrence Klippenstein, "Conscientious Objectors in Eastern Europe: The Quest for Free Choice and Alternative Service," pp. 286–8, 299–301, 398, 402 in Sabrina Petra Ramet, ed., *Protestantism and Politics in Eastern Europe and Russia: The Communist and Postcommunist Eras* (Durham, NC: Duke University Press, 1992). See also B. Welling Hall, "The Church and the Independent Peace Movement in Eastern Europe," *Journal of Peace Research* (Oslo), vol. 23 (1986), no. 2, p. 198, for a striking appeal by one of Bulányi's group, Father László Kovács, in 1981 to young Hungarian Catholics, urging them to refuse "military training for licensed murder" and "suffer ... jail if need be" rather than kill. In neighboring Germany some sections of the postwar Catholic Church have become more receptive to a pacifist interpretation of the New Testament and the early-church experience; see, for example, Egon Spiegel, *Gewaltverzicht: Grundlagen einer biblischen Friedenstheologie* (Kassel: Verlag Weber, Zucht & Co., 1987); also Josef Blank, "Gewaitlosigkeit-Krieg-Militärdienst: I. Im Urteil des Neun Testaments;

II. Im frühen Christentum; III. Im Urteil und Praxis der Alten Kirche," *Orientierung* (Zürich), vol. 46 (1982), pp. 157–63, 213–16, 220–3, and above all the pacifist exegesis found in the massive volumes of the New Testament scholar and student of comparative religion, Eugen Drewermann. Bernd W. Kubbig, *Kirche und Kriegsdienstverweigerung in der BRD* (Stuttgart: Verlag W. Kohlhammer, 1974), pp. 90–100, 120, deals briefly with the attitude to conscientious objection of the postwar German Catholic Church, which became "seriously" concerned with the problem only from the late sixties. See also Alice Holmes Cooper, *Paradoxes of Peace: German Peace Movements since 1945* (Ann Arbor: The University of Michigan Press, 1996), pp. 170, 171 and for the role of pacifists in general in West Germany, pp. 98–104, 111, 112, 181, 182, 189, 190.

33 We should note, however, a dramatic increase in the number of conscientious objectors in these four traditionally Catholic countries from the 1970s to the 1990s.

34 See Jim and Nancy Forest, *Fours Days in February: The Story of the Nonviolent Overthrow of the Marcos Regime* (Basingstoke, UK: Marshall Pickering, 1988), pp. 39–45, 59, 132–7. The authors also show the important role played by the Jesuit Father José Blanco, who led the newly established Philippine branch of the FOR (known by its acronym AKKAPKA), as well as the inspiration provided by the American Methodist minister and FOR leader, Richard Deats, especially among the country's Protestant minority.

35 *Fellowship* (Nyack, NY), vol. 57, no. 6 (June, 1991), p. 3.

36 Hildegard Goss-Mayr, *Die Macht der Gewaltlosen: Der Christ und die Revolution am Beispiel Brasiliens* (Graz: Verlag Styria, 1968), 149–51, 153–9. See also her *Der Mensch vor dem Unrecht: Spiritualität und Praxis gewaltloser Befreiung* (Vienna: Europaverlag, 1976), pp. 69–84, for the methods of active nonviolence. Hildegard had gained a Ph.D. at the University of Vienna in 1953; while Jean's talents lay primarily in organization, hers were more exclusively intellectual. Gérard Houver, *A Non-Violent Lifestyle: Conversations with Jean and Hildegard Goss-Mayr*, translated from the French by Richard Bateman (London: Lamp Press, 1989), gives a clear insight into the Goss-Mayrs' thinking on peace and nonviolence.

37 See Jean Toulat, *Dom Helder Camara* (Paris: Éditions de Centurion, 1989)), chap. IX: "L'arme de la non-violence." Also Ronald G. Musto, *The Catholic Peace Tradition* (Maryknoll, NY: Orbis Books, 1986), pp. 224–31. In the 1930s Câmara had been attracted to corporatism as exemplified in Salazar's authoritarian régime in Portugal; later he acknowledged this to have been a serious mistake which he deeply regretted (Toulat, *op. cit.*, p. 19).

38 McManus and Schlabach, eds., *op. cit.*, pp. 242, 243. "The Goss-Mayrs especially wanted to recruit the clergy to the creed of active nonviolence, believing their leadership was uniquely important in Latin America. Once

recruited, this cadre of priests and ministers would be able to reach people at all levels of society." Quoted from Ronald Pagnucco and John D. McCarthy, "Advocating Nonviolent Direct Action in Latin America: The Anteced-ents and Emergence of SERPAJ," in Bronislaw Misztal and Anson Shupe, eds., *Religion and Politics in Comparative Perspective* (Westport, CT: Praeger, 1992), p. 131.

39 Vera Brittain, *The Rebel Passion* (Nyack, New York: Fellowship Publications, 1964), pp. 100–3; Pagnucco and McCarthy, *op. cit.*, pp. 130, 131, 133. In Montevideo Earl Smith, an ecumenically minded American Methodist pas-tor, had been active in FOR work since 1924; later, he became one of those responsible for bringing the largely Catholic SERPAJ into being during the 1970s. See Carlos Muñoz *et al.*, *Reseña historica del SERPAJ-AL*, pt. 1; *Una alternativa revolucionaria?* (Rio de Janeiro: SERPAJ-AL, 1986), p. 5–7, 25, 35, 36, 50, 54.

40 Quoted in McManus and Schlabach, eds., *op. cit.*, p. 246. Our italics.

41 Quoted in *ibid.*, p. 9. According to the Brazilian liberation theologian, Leonardo Boff, "the theology of liberation is not an alternative to active nonviolence, nor vice versa. On the contrary they are born of the same inspiration." Quoted in *ibid.*, p. ix. But cf. the American Catholic pacifist Gordon Zahn's view (in 1977) that even qualified pacifist approval of liber-ation theology signified a revival of just-war theory in a new form and could lead on to an extenuation of guerrilla tactics and terrorism as "*coun-ter*violence" and to disregard of the potentiality of nonviolence as an alter-native to political and social oppression. See Lewy, *op. cit.*, pp. 231–3.

42 Goss-Mayr, *Macht der Gewaltlosen*, pp. 131–6. In any case it is probable they would have decided that acceptance of such a proposal would lead to com-promise of their nonviolence and, therefore, would have turned it down.

43 McManus and Schlabach, eds., *op. cit.*, pp. 239–44, 249.

44 *Ibid.*, p. 262.

45 Quoted in Egan, *op. cit.*, p. 106. For a brief summary of Chavez's non-violent struggle for social justice, see John Dean, "Cesar Chavez, Prophet of Nonviolence," *Fellowship*, vol. 69, no. 6 (June, 1993), pp. 10, 17. Chavez, a practising Catholic influenced in his trade union activities by Catholic social teaching and in his principled adoption of nonviolence by the Catholic Worker movement (in addition to the examples of Gandhi and King), died in April 1993. In 1968 he had undertaken a 25–day fast to strengthen his Union's resolution to remain nonviolent. "For us," he said, "nonviolence is more than academic theory; it is the very lifeblood of our movement."

46 See Evelyn Wilcock, *Pacifism and the Jews* (Stroud, U.K.: Hawthorn Press, 1994), chaps. I and II.

47 In Britain the publisher Victor Gollancz, who became an absolute pacifist

after 1945, is another example of that position. Before this date he had supported first the loyalists in the Spanish Civil War and then the war against Hitler. Gollancz's evolution, therefore, was the reverse of Kampelman's.

48 We may note, though, that in the 1930s the American Maurice N. Eisendrath, who was then rabbi of Holy Blossom Temple in Toronto, had been extremely active in the Canadian Fellowship of Reconciliation. "Although his pacifism was not derived solely from Judaism neither was it entirely alien to Jewish teaching ... He argued [that] pacifism was not exclusively Christian." See Thomas P. Socknat, *Witness against War: Pacifism in Canada, 1900–1945* (Toronto: Toronto University Press, 1987), pp. 125–7.

49 Max M. Kampelman, *Entering New Worlds: The Memoirs of a Private Man in Public Life* (New York: Harper-Collins Publishers, 1991), pp. x, 27, 30–55, 102, 377, 378. After the war was over Kampelman abandoned his pacifism and in 1955 joined the Marine Corps reserve; subsequently he became a high ranking U.S. diplomat. His memoirs, however, display a certain lingering respect for his lost pacifism. Michael Young, "Facing a Test of Faith: Jewish Pacifists during the Second World War," *Peace & Change* (Sonoma, CA), vol 3., no. 2/3 (Summer/Fall, 1975), pp. 34–40, gives an insightful account of the dilemmas of American Jewish pacifists during the war against Hitler. See also above, chap V, n. 61.

50 Young, *op. cit.*, pp. 34, 35, 37.

51 *Ibid.*, p. 34. Kallner wrote to Evan Thomas of the WRL about his dilemma: while continuing to detest war, "I find myself torn between the desire to refuse to cooperate with conscription and ... my remorse which tells me that refusing to participate in war means not to take a stand on the basic problem" of the Nazi massacre of his people (letter dated July 24, 1943).

52 *Ibid.*, p. 38; also Wilcock, *op. cit.*, pp. 118, 131.

53 Albert S. Axelrad, *Call to Conscience: Jews, Judaism, and Conscientious Objection* (Hoboken, NJ, and Nyack, NY: KTAV Publishing House and Jewish Peace Fellowship, 1986), p. 33.

54 *Ibid.*, pp. 63, 80.

55 Wilcock, *op. cit.*, pp. 186–91.

56 From Schwarzschild's introduction to Allan Solomonow, ed., *Roots of Jewish Nonviolence* (Nyack, NY: Jewish Peace Fellowship, 1981), p. 5. For discussion of the bases of Jewish pacifism, see Abraham Cronbach, "War and Peace in Jewish Tradition," pp. 198–221 in *Central Conference of American Rabbis Yearbook*, vol. 46 (1936); André Neher, "Rabbinic Adumbrations of Non-violence: Israel and Canaan," pp. 169–96 in Raphael Loewe, ed., *Studies in Rationalism, Judaism & Universalism in Memory of Leon Roth* (London: Routledge and Kegan Paul, 1966); Everett E. Gendler, "War and the Jewish Tradition," pp. 78–102 in James Finn, ed., *A Conflict of Loyalties: The Case for Selective Conscientious Objection* (New York: Pegasus, 1968); Reuven Kimel-

man, "Non-violence in the Talmud," *The Religious Situation*, vol. 2 (Boston: Beacon Press, 1969), pp. 441–63 (reprinted with more extensive annotation in *Roots of Nonviolence*, pp. 24–49) ; and Nahum N. Glatzer, "The Concept of Peace in Classical Judaism," pp. 36–47 in his *Essays in Jewish Thought* (University: The University of Alabama Press, 1978).

57 Kampelman, *op. cit.*, p. 43.

58 Wilcock, *op. cit.*, pp. 183–5, 197, 198.

59 Yoram Peri, "Israel: Conscientious Objection in a Democracy under Siege," in Charles C. Moskos and John Whiteclay Chambers II, eds., *The New Conscientious Objection: From Sacred to Secular Resistance* (New York: Oxford University Press, 1993), pp. 147, 148, 156.

60 See Martin Blatt, Uri Davis, and Paul Kleinbaum, eds., *Dissent & Ideology in Israel: Resistance to the Draft 1948–1973* (London: Ithaca Press, 1975), pp. 22–34, 124–6; Wilcock, *op. cit.*, chap. IX: "Nathan Hofshi and Pacifism in Israel"; Murray Polner and Naomi Goodman, eds., *The Challenge of Shalom: The Jewish Tradition of Peace and Justice* (Philadelphia: New Society Publishers, 1994), pp. 91–93. Hofshi died in 1980.

61 Letter written in 1969, quoted in Anthony G. Bing, *Israeli Pacifist: The Life of Joseph Abileah* (Syracuse: Syracuse University Press, 1990), pp. 168, 169. This biography gives a valuable picture of the conditions under which Israeli pacifists have had to exist. Abileah's pacifism, though as absolute as Hofshi's, was less Bible centered and more universalist; he was greatly influenced by Gandhi as well as by the Quakers. See also Blatt *et al.*, *op. cit.*, pp. 48–52.

62 *The War Resister* (Enfield, Middlesex), no. 23 (Summer, 1929), pp. 25, 26.

63 Wilcock, *op. cit.*, pp. 2, 82–92.

64 *Ibid.*, pp. 208–10.

65 Axelrad, *op. cit.*, pp. 104–7. Italics in the original.

66 Letter to Yeshaahayu Schick, dated June 28, 1972, printed in Blatt *et al.*, *op. cit.*, p. 30.

67 *Ibid.*, pp. 13, 17, 124–6. See Peri, *op. cit.*, pp. 146–57, 261, 262, for an overview of selective conscientious objection in Israel from 1948 to the end of the 1980s. According to Peri (p. 156), "the opposition to military service by Israeli conscientious objectors has always been couched in secular terms, *moral* or political, rather than a convoluted harking back to a Judaic tradition of absolute pacifism" (my italics). But we have seen there have been exceptions to this generally correct statement.

68 Blatt *et al.*, *op. cit.*, pp. 129–32.

69 Mubarak E. Awad, "Nonviolence in Action," *Fellowship*, vol. 53, no. 6 (June, 1987), pp. 14, 15.

70 Awad, "Non-violent Resistance: A Strategy for the Occupied Territories," *Journal of Palestine Studies* (Washington, D.C.), vol. 13, no. 4 (Summer, 1984), pp. 22–36. Awad's article shows the influence of Gene Sharp's study *The*

Politics of Nonviolent Action (1973); like Sharp, Awad argues (p. 36) that non-violence can be adopted with success also "by individuals who are not necessarily committed to non-violence and who may choose, at a different stage, to engage in armed struggle."

71 Philip Grant, "Nonviolent Political Struggle in the Occupied Territories," in Robert E. Crow *et al.*, *Arab Nonviolent Political Struggle in the Middle East* (Boulder and London: Lynne Rienner, 1990), p. 61.

72 Awad, *op. cit.*, p. 15.

73 Grant, *op. cit.*, pp. 61, 62, 69.

74 Awad, "Nonviolence and the Intifada," in Graeme MacQueen, ed., *Unarmed Forces: Nonviolent Action in Central America and the Middle East* (Toronto: Science for Peace / Samuel Stevens & Co., 1992), p. 87.

75 Grant, *op. cit.*, p. 71. In June 1988 the government of Israel expelled Awad, who meanwhile was training as a clinical psychologist and he them went into exile in the United States. There he set up in Washington, D.C., an organization for the further promotion of his ideals, which he named Nonviolence International.

76 Around the time of the signing of the Declaration of Principles between Israel and the PLO on 13 September 1993, Mubarak Awad was permitted to return temporarily to Israel to take part in a conference held in Jerusalem and organized by "Palestinians and Israelis for Nonviolence." Muslims, Jews, and Christians participated, including the veteran Israeli pacifist, Amos Gvirtz, and the stalwart protagonist of unconditional nonviolence, Mary Khass, from the Arab side. See Amos Gvirtz, ed., *Nonviolent Possibilities for the Palestinian–Israeli Conflict* (Jerusalem: Palestinians and Israelis for Nonviolence, 1998), pp. 7–9, 13, 52.

Conclusion

During the late seventies and the eighties, down to the end of the Cold War and the collapse of Communism in Eastern Europe, pacifists participated in a number of antiwar activities alongside others who opposed nuclear war without accepting the full pacifist position. April Carter has written of this "second wave of the nuclear disarmament movement" as involving "more countries than the first" and evoking "more intensive support within these countries."[1] National sections of the War Resisters' International and the International Fellowship of Reconciliation as well as the Quakers, particularly in Britain and North America where Friends were numerically strongest, continued to play a role in these new antiwar campaigns, though not a dominant one. Opposition to the arms trade and protests against the production of war toys remained on the agenda of many pacifist groups, while the American Fellowship of Reconciliation made work for disarmament one of its chief concerns after the Vietnam War was over. In Britain there were many pacifists among the Greenham women who kept up a prolonged nonviolent blockade of the Cruise missile base at Greenham Common. Their campaign gained worldwide publicity; "the Greenham Common peace camp in the 1980s [became] the central symbol of radical feminist campaigning for peace."[2] In strife-torn Northern Ireland the Peace People strove untiringly to find an acceptable *modus vivendi* between Catholics and Protestants;[3] in both communities ordinary folk were sick of the seemingly endless violence and the continuance of ancient hatreds. In 1981, on the other side of the Atlantic, a group of concerned Canadians, including the Quaker Murray Thomson, established a Peace Brigades International (PBI). The new organisation has continued on a transnational basis earlier experiments in nonviolent action; PBI teams, who receive previous training in nonviolent techniques, have worked in areas of conflict like Guatemala and El Salvador. Their work has so far been on a small scale but shows promise of expansion.[4]

In this period most mainstream pacifists felt, more than ever, that the struggle against war and the setting in motion of nonviolent methods of conflict resolution were linked to a series of cognate issues awaiting solution: poverty; political, social, gender, and racial injustice; overpopulation; and the many environmental and ecological problems threatening disaster to humankind unless dealt with in the near future. While it has become increasingly difficult to disentangle the practical activity of individual pacifists and pacifist organizations from that of the peace and allied nonviolent movements as a whole, yet pacifism remains distinct from *pacificism* (to once more use Martin Ceadel's term for the ideology of nonpacifist peace advocates).

The ending of cold war at the outset of the 1990s relaxed the nuclear threat, though by no means did this eliminate altogether the danger of atomic warfare. Moreover, large portions of the globe continue to be the scene of war and domestic conflicts fought out by conventional weapons. Strife has arisen between the peoples of former Yugoslavia and as a result of the dissolution of the Soviet Union; parts of Africa and South Asia find themselves in a continuous state of turmoil, even though the creation of a multiracial South Africa provides encouragement for future peace in the world; the Near East, where the emergent Arab-Israeli reconciliation is offset by other continuing foci of violence, often under the cloak of religion, remains, too, a powder-keg. The danger of an explosion in that area was demonstrated in 1991 with the outbreak of the Gulf War.

Looking backwards from the viewpoint of the later 1990s, it is important to see twentieth-century pacifism within the wider context of the history of social movements and the history of ideas. Pacifism, like all ideas and movements, has waxed and waned in periodic and cyclical developments.[5] Moreover, its history is intertwined with the history of war and revolution and with the development of states and societies as well as with cultural shifts toward modernism and modernity. At certain points it appeared as if its history was virtually ended; its reappearance was often associated with the rise of other social movements such as feminism, ecologism, movements of emancipation in the Soviet bloc, and the cultural revolt of the young. It was pacifism's relationship with the opposition to the threat of nuclear war and the existence of the East/West conflict that was of particular salience during the second half of the century. The anti-nuclear movements went through two phases in the Western World (with somewhat different dates in Japan and the Pacific rim): 1957–64 and 1979–86. The second phase was marked by greater transnationalism, greater acceptance of nonviolence and nonalignment, along with less deference to the communist peace claims and a greater focus on local action and community-based activism. And it is certainly arguable that this reflects the influence of pacifism. Carter has suggested a definition of the contemporary peace movement which shares much with pacifism, *sensu stricto*, her three criteria being 1) autonomy, 2) nonalignment, and 3) nonuse of violence. In her view a true peace movement is aligned with no state or ideology; it is autonomous, that is, free to criticize other organizations, parties or governments; and it is committed to nonviolence as a means (though not necessarily on pacifist grounds).[6]

Pacifist influence is clearly visible in the transnational nuclear disarmament movement in Europe in the 1980s, which sprang out of such nonviolent campaigns as those against nuclear energy of the 1970s and the Greenpeace protests against nuclear testing in the Pacific. By 1979 the influence of ecopacifism, ecofeminism and the Greens was strong; training in nonviolent civil disobedience at nuclear power plants in the USA and the UK was, too, an important ingredient in recommending such methods as models for the actions of the 1980s when they aroused much less controversy. What indeed did divide the movement now were such issues as feminist separatism (practised in the women's peace movement as at Greenham Common) and whether to ostracize the official peace committees of the Eastern bloc countries and build links, instead, with the dissident movements of all kinds which had sprung up in that area (whether they were pacifist or not and indeed whether they were antimilitarist or not). More traditional groups in the British Campaign for Nuclear Disarmament (CND) and elsewhere, including at first some Quakers, wished to continue the dialogue with the old communist front organizations rather than open up dialogue with the new grassroots independents, even though the former were largely discredited. The traditional groups feared that building links with unofficial groups could undermine traditional peace movement strategy; some tried to speak to both the official and the dissident groups in Eastern Europe. In the case of END,[7] that new and vigorous organisation emphasized the need to find a symmetric link between citizens' peace groups, however small, in Eastern and Western Europe respectively. It also supported *inter alia* the idea of conscientious objection as a human right, which continued to gain support generally. Finally even the traditional groups, like CND, were to adopt most of END's strategy; and most pacifists concurred.

The main area within the wider peace movement in which Cold War era pacifists exercised an independent influence, lay in stressing the issues of war resistance and the rights of imprisoned C.Os. as well as in furthering the practical application of nonviolent techniques. They were also influential on the theoretical side with regard to "non-offensive defense" and in reviving earlier civilian resistance ideas. By the late eighties a new emphasis had appeared on mediation and reconciliation projects where groups would visit war-torn regions to help build trust and pre-empt conflict by "accompaniment," by bringing groups together and developing a local infrastructure so as to help resolve – or mediate – conflicts. Centers of such activities appeared in Sri Lanka, in Israel and the occupied territories, and in areas of the former republics of Yugoslavia and the Soviet Union where fighting occurred.

Pacifism in the twentieth century can also be usefully surveyed in terms of such typologies of means and goals as have been developed by writers like April Carter and especially Bob Overy.[8] Overy classifies pacifism as part of a larger peace movement, as does Carter. And in his typology Overy includes movements against all war (which pacifists clearly have supported), movements against specific weapons or use of weapons, and movements to stop specific wars. (The two latter types of movement historically are not specifically pacifist, but have included pacifists among their participants.) Overy, however, does not include in his typology movements to prevent wars or resistance to military service, or opposition to an arms race (all of these activities in which pacifists have participated). On the other hand, though resistance to war, it seems, can be the litmus test of pacifism, yet some pacifists have been passive and retreatist. Thus Overy's category of movements "against all war" clearly begs the question of participation in wars, insofar as war may be opposed but not personally resisted.

Overy introduces certain categories from political sociology, e.g., pressure groups, mass movements, etc., and refines concepts such as the prophetic or permanent minority and the nonviolent revolutionary group or movement. These indeed are not discrete categories but are overlapping ones; nor, we may note, are they exhaustive. But we may attempt here to situate pacifism in them.

Pacifism certainly has never been as such a mass movement; rather, it has inspired and guided larger movements. It has never been solely a peace pressure group or lobby either, though its adherents have been part of pressure groups (e.g., on arms sales) and have at times acted on specific pacifist issues (the rights of C.Os., for example). Pacifists have also acted as a pressure group *on* and *within* the larger peace movement.

Pacifism has also constituted the principled part of the movement for change by means of nonviolent revolution. However, not all pacifists have been committed to nonviolent action, let alone nonviolent revolution. Equally, such movements have included supporters; of pragmatic rather than principled nonviolence, and thus they may have had a nonpacifist majority. The most pertinent category, therefore, into which pacifism and its adherents fall is that of the "prophetic minority," a permanent gadfly in the body politic, a ginger group within the peace movements, and an element that survives, even thrives, in times of crisis in which the larger peace movements collapse. Such continuing minorities may be crucial in sustaining linkages between movements, despite cyclical decline. Yet pacifism, we may note, has been much less cyclical in character than the larger, mass peace movements; in the twentieth century undoubtedly its major trough occurred after 1945 when pacifists tended generally to turn to other (if related) activities.

By the 1990s, in no country had either legal political demonstrations, or symbolic civil disobedience of an individual character, or attempts to obstruct the nuclear effort, succeeded in persuading a nuclear government either to abandon its reliance on a nuclear deterrent or to take serious steps toward implementing a nonviolent strategy of civilian defense. Nevertheless, the peace movement had certainly spread awareness of the nuclear threat. True, in no nuclear state did the citizenry come near to approving the relinquishment of nuclear, let alone conventional, weapons. Yet in the early 1990s, in a referendum the nonnuclear Swiss showed a substantial minority (30 per cent) willing to abolish the army. Though not all who voted in favor did so on pacifist grounds, this surely may be taken as a significant achievement for pacifists and antimilitarists.

The pursuit of peace in the modern world is too complex an activity to be comprised within the old pacifist slogan, "wars will cease when men refuse to fight." Conscientious objection still retains validity as a moral stand and pacifism as an individual ethic, but the world in the nuclear age stands in pressing need of collective alternatives to violence if its conflicts, whether domestic or international, are not to bring it sooner or later to extinction. Ultimately, the gospel of reconciliation, the Gandhian approach, may prove sounder politics than a philosophy of violent deterrence. Meanwhile, since modern wars are likely to require smaller armies and thus fewer soldiers[9] and to be highly technological, pacifism must necessarily adapt to new strategies – away from the focus on war resistance and conscientious objection toward creative cultural change and collective political noncooperation with the state's war-making activities.

Notes

1 April Carter, *Peace Movements: International Protest and World Politics since 1945* (London and New York: Longman, 1992), chaps. V and VI. The passages cited are from p. 108. Carter's book provides the best account of the international peace movement during the Cold War era.

2 *Ibid.*, p. 22. See also p. 115.

3 In 1976 two young women, Mairead Corrigan and Betty Williams, both of them recent converts to pacifism, were jointly awarded the Nobel Peace Prize for their role in organizing the Peace People movement. See Irwin Abrams, *The Nobel Peace Prize and the Laureates* (Boston: G.K. Hall, 1988), pp. 216–19. As this book finally goes to press, the chances of ending the long years of civil strife at last look promising.

4 For Canada's Assembly of First Nations then Chief, Ovide Mercredi's espousal of Gandhian nonviolence as a strategy to promote native rights, see Metta Spencer, "Nonviolence and Aboriginal Rights," *Peace Magazine* (Toronto), vol. 12, no. 6 (November/December, 1996), pp. 8–13. In another, and hitherto more troubled, part of the world – among the Albanians of Kosovo (Kosova) in what is left of Yugoslavia – we find the concept of Gandhian nonviolence inspiring resistance to outside oppression in an area where such ideas until now have been virtually unknown. Of course, in neither case has struggle without weapons met with universal acceptance in the given community (as happened, too, with Gandhi in India).

5 Nigel Young has attempted in his work to develop the idea of peace cycles and link these to the unfolding of a cumulative series of peace traditions, of which he has identified nine: three clearly pacifist and three clearly not pacifist, and three more a mixture. The relationship of these nine traditions to pacifism is of considerable interest and deserves much greater attention in , the future. Cf. the classification of peace traditions that provides the framework of James Turner Johnson's study, *The Quest for Peace* (Princeton, NJ, 1987).

6 We may note, though, that in her book Carter does not analyze the ambiguities, which we have seen emerged during the 1960s and 1970s from pacifist efforts to relate to violent liberation movements. These ambiguities split the pacifist movement and still remain unresolved in the 1990s. They are not entirely covered by Carter's definition.

7 European Nuclear Disarmament, which in its initial Appeal in 1980 had called for a nuclear-free Europe. The organization went on to develop contacts with independent minded individuals and groups in Eastern bloc countries.

8 In his *How Effective are Peace Movements?* (Montreal: Harvest House, 1982).

Both Carter and Overy are former peace activists and, while writing as scholars, they remain personally sympathetic to pacifism.

9 According to the *Friend* (London), vol. 154, no. 44 (1 November 1996): "Several European nations are moving towards an end to conscription: in 1992, Belgium announced that it had such plans in place, in January 1996 the Netherlands took its last draft and in February France announced that its armed forces will be entirely professional by 2001. Germany and Italy are both reducing the proportion of conscripts in their armed forces." For a survey of the C.O. situation in Europe around the time our book was completed, see Amnesty International, *Out of the Margins: The Right to Conscientious Objection to Military Service in Europe*, AI Index EUR 01/02/97. The report was released in April 1997. In addition, the War Resisters' International (London) has announced for publication at the end of 1998, "in loose-leaf format for easy updating," a detailed handbook, *Refusing to bear Arms: A Worldwide Survey of Conscription and Conscientious Objection to Military Service*, which will cover "key issues related to compulsory military service in 177 countries."

Further Reading and Reference: Books and Pamphlets

Abrams, Irwin. *The Nobel Peace Prize and the Laureates: An Illustrated Biographical History, 1901–1987*. Boston: G.K. Hall, 1988.

Adams, Judith Porter, ed. *Peacework: Oral Histories of Women Peace Activists*. Boston: Twayne Publishers, 1991.

Albesano, Sergio. *Storia dell'obiezione di coscienza in Italia*. Treviso: Editrice Santi Quaranta. 1993.

Alonso, Harriet Hyman. *Peace as a Women's Issue: A History of the U.S. Movement for World Peace and Women's Rights*. Syracuse: Syracuse University Press, 1993.

Anderson, Richard C. *Peace was in Their Hearts: Conscientious Objectors in World War II*. Watsonville (California): Correlan Publications, 1994.

Anet, Daniel. *Pierre Ceresole: La passion de paix*. Neuchâtel: Les Editions de la Baconnière, 1969.

Auvray, Michel. *Objecteurs, insoumis, déserteurs: Histoire de réfractaires en France*. Paris: Stock, 1983.

Bacon, Margaret Hope. *One Woman's Passion for Peace: The Life of Mildred Scott Olmsted*. Syracuse: Syracuse University Press, 1992.

Bagwell, Philip S., and Joan Lawley. *From Prison Cell to Council Chamber: The Life of Philip William Bagwell 1885–1958*. York (U.K.): William Sessions Limited, 1994.

Barber, Chris, ed. *FAU Postscript: Some Reflections of Former FAU Members on what Their Unit Experience of 40 Years Earlier has meant to them*. Oxford: Oxfam, 1984.

Barker, Rachel. *Conscience, Government and War: Conscientious Objection in Great Britain 1939–45*. London: Routledge & Kegan Paul, 1982.

Bäuerle, Dietrich. *Totalverweigerung als Widerstand: Motivationen, Hilfen, Perspektiven*. Frankfurt am Main: Fischer Taschenbuch Verlag, 1988.

Beale, Albert. *Against All War: Fifty Years of Peace News 1936–1986*. London: Peace News, 1986.

Beaman, Jay. *Pentecostal Pacifism: The Origin, Development, and Rejection of Pacific Beliefs among the Pentecostals*. Hillsboro (Kansas): Center for Mennonite Brethren Studies, 1989.

Bechtel, Judith A., and Robert M. Couglin. *Building the Beloved Community: Maurice McCrackin's Life for Peace and Civil Rights*. Philadelphia: Temple University Press, 1991.

Bell, Julian, ed. *We did not fight: 1914–18 Experiences of War Resisters*. London, Cobden-Sanderson, 1915.

Beyer, Wolfram, ed. *Widerstand gegen den Krieg: Beiträge zur Geschichte der War Resisters' International*. Kassel: Verlag Weber, Zucht & Co., 1989.

Blackwell, Michael Dwayne. *Pacifism in the Social Ethics of Walter George Muelder*. Lewiston/Queenston/Lampeter: Mellen University Press, 1995.

Blatt, Martin, *et al.*, eds. *Dissent & Ideology in Israel: Resistance to the Draft 1948–1973*. London: Ithaca Press, 1975.

Blishen, Edward. *A Cackhanded War*. London: Thames and Hudson, 1972.

Bockel, Rolf von. *Kurt Hiller und die Gruppe Revolutionärer Pazifisten (1926–1933)*. Hamburg: Bormann-Verlag, 1990.

Bondurant, Joan V. *Conquest of Violence: The Gandhian Philosophy of Conflict*. Berkeley and Los Angeles: University of California Press, 1965.

Boulton, David. *Objection Overruled*. London: McGibbon & Kee, 1967.

Bowman, Rufus D. *The Church of the Brethren and War 1708–1941*. Ed. Donald F. Durnbaugh. New York and London: Garland Publishing, 1971.

Boyle, Beth Ellen, ed. *Words of Conscience: Religious Statements on Conscientious Objection*. Washington, D.C.: National Interreligious Service Board for Conscientious Objectors, 1983.

Braithwaite, Constance. *Conscientious Objection to Various Compulsions under British Law*. York: William Sessions Limited, 1995.

Bredemeier, Karsten. *Kriegsdienstverweigerung im Dritten Reich*. Baden-Baden: Nomos Verlagsgesellschaft, 1991.

Brinton, Henry. *The Peace Army*. London: Williams & Norgate, 1932.

Brittain, Vera. *Diary 1939–1945: Wartime Chronicle*. Eds. Alan Bishop and Y. Aleksandra Bennett. London: Victor Gollancz Ltd., 1989.

– *The Rebel Passion: A Short History of Some Pioneer Peace-makers*. Nyack (New York): Fellowship Publications, 1964.

– *Testament of a Peace Lover: Letters from Vera Brittain*. Eds. Winifred and Alan Eden-Green. London: Virago Press, 1988.

Brock, Peter. *The Mahatma and Mother India (Essays on Gandhi's Non-violence and Nationalism)*. Ahmedabad: Navajivan Publishing House, 1983.

–, and Thomas P. Socknat, eds. *Challenge to Mars: Essays on Pacifism from 1918 to 1945*. Toronto: University of Toronto Press, 1999.

Burkholder, John Richard, and Barbara Nelson Gingerich, eds. *Mennonite Peace*

Theology: A Panorama of Types. Akron (Pennsylvania): Mennonite Central Committee Peace Office, 1991.

Burns, J. Patout, ed. *War and Its Discontents: Pacifism and Quietism in the Abrahamic Traditions*. Washington, D.C.: Georgetown University Press, 1996.

Burtchaell, James Tunstead, ed. *A Just War no longer exists: The Teaching and Trial of Don Lorenzo Milani*. Notre Dame (Indiana): University of Notre Dame Press, 1988.

Bush, Roger, ed. *FAU: The Third Generation – Friends Ambulance Unit Post-War Service and International Service 1945–1959*. York: William Sessions Limited, 1998.

Byrne, Paul. *The Campaign for Nuclear Disarmament*. London: Croom Helm, 1988.

Cameron, Caitriona. *Go anywhere do anything: New Zealanders in the Friends Ambulance Unit in China 1945–1951*. Wellington (N.Z.): The Beechtree Press, 1996.

Cantine, Holley, and Dachine Rainer, eds. *Prison Etiquette: The Convict's Compendium of Useful Information*. Bearsville (New York): Retort Press, 1950.

Carsten, F. L. *War against War: British and German Radical Movements in the First World War*. London: Batsford Academic and Educational, 1982.

Carter, April. *Direct Action and Liberal Democracy*. London: Routledge & Kegan Paul, 1973.

– *Peace Movements: International Protest and World Politics since 1945*. London and New York: Longman, 1992.

–, ed. *Mahatma Gandhi: A Selected Bibliography*. Westport (Connecticut) and London: Greenwood Press, 1995.

Carter, Charles F. *Snail's Progress: The English Local Prison. Edited from the Experiences of Quaker Prisoners, 1939–48*. London: Penal Reform Committee of the Society of Friends, 1948.

Case, Clarence Marsh. *Non-violent Coercion: A Study in Methods of Social Pressure*. Ed. A. Paul Hare. New York and London: Garland Publishers, 1972.

Catchpool. T. Corder. *Letters of a Prisoner: For Conscience Sake*. London: George Allen & Unwin Ltd., 1941.

– *On Two Fronts*. London: Headley Bros., 1918.

Cattelain, Jean-Pierre. *L'objection de conscience*. Paris: Presses universitaires de France, 1975.

Ceadel, Martin: *Pacifism in Britain 1914–1945: The Defining of a Faith*. Oxford: Clarendon Press, 1980.

Chambers, John Whiteclay II, ed. *Draftees or Volunteers: A Documentary History of the Debate over Military Conscription in the United States, 1787–1973*. New York and London: Garland Publishing, 1975.

–, ed. *The Eagle and the Dove: The American Peace Movement and United States Foreign Policy 1900–1922*. Syracuse: Syracuse University Press, 1991.

Chatfield, Charles. *The American Peace Movement: Ideals and Activism*. New York: Twayne Publishers, 1992.

– *For Peace and Justice: Pacifism in America, 1914–1941*. Knoxville: The University of Tennessee Press, 1971.

–, ed. *The Americanization of Gandhi: Images of the Mahatma*. New York: Garland Publishing, 1976.

–, ed. *International War Resistance through World War II*. New York and London: Garland Publishing, 1975.

–, ed. *The Radical "No": The Correspondence and Writings of Evan Thomas on War*. New York and London: Garland Publishing, 1974.

–, and Peter van den Dungen, eds. *Peace Movements and Political Cultures*. Knoxville: University of Tennessee Press, 1988.

–, and Ruzanna Ilukhina, eds. *Peace/Mir: An Anthology of Historic Alternatives to War*. Syracuse: Syracuse University Press, 1994.

Chester, Gail, and Andrew Rigby, eds. *Articles of Peace: Celebrating Fifty Years of Peace News*. Bridport (U.K.): Prism Press, 1986.

Chrisp, Peter, ed. *Conscientious Objectors: 1916 to the Present Day – A Study in Evidence and Empathy* (with Pupils' Study Notes). Brighton (U.K.): Tessell Publications, 1988.

Coffin, Linda B., ed. *Handbook on Military Taxes & Conscience*. Philadelphia: Friends Committee on War Tax Concerns, 1988.

Cooney, Robert, and Helen Michalowski, eds. *The Power of the People: Active Nonviolence in the United States*. Philadelphia: New Society Publishers, 1987.

Cornell, Julien. *Conscience and the Slate: Legal and Administrative Problems of Conscientious Objectors, 1943–1944*, printed with *The Conscientious Objector and the Law*. Ed. John O'Sullivan. New York and London: Garland Publishing, Inc., 1973.

Cromartie, Michael, ed. *Peace Betrayed? Essays on Pacifism and Politics*. Washington, D.C.: Ethics and Public Policy Center, 1990.

Dalton, Dennis. *Mahatma Gandhi: Nonviolent Power in Action*. New York: Columbia University Press, 1993.

Dasenbrock, J. Henry. *To the Beat of a Different Drummer: A Decade in the Life of a World War II Conscientious Objector*. Winona (Minnesota): Northland Press of Winona, 1989.

Davies, George M. L. *Essays towards Peace*. London: Sheppard Press, 1946.

– *Pilgrimage of Peace*. London: The Fellowship of Reconciliation, 1950.

DeBenedetti, Charles. *The Peace Reform in American History*. Bloomington: Indiana University Press, 1980.

–, with Charles Chatfield. *An American Ordeal: The Antiwar Movement of the Vietnam Era*. Syracuse: Syracuse University Press, 1990.

–, ed. *Peace Heroes in Twentieth-Century America*. Bloornington and Indianapolis: Indiana University Press, 1988.

Defrasne, Jean. *Le Pacifisme*. Paris: Presses universitaires de France, 1983.

– *Le pacifisme en France*. Paris: Presses universitaires de France, 1994.

Dellinger, David. *Revolutionary Nonviolence*. Indianapolis and New York: The Bobbs-Merrill Company, 1970.

Deming, Barbara. *Revolution & Equilibrium*. New York: Grossman Publishers, 1971.

Donat, Helmut, and Karl Holl, eds. *Die Friedensbewegung: Organisierter Pazifismus in Deutschland, Österreich und in der Schweiz*. Düsseldorf. ECON Taschenbuch Verlag, 1983.

Drewermann, Eugen. *Reden gegen den Krieg*. Ed. Bernd Marz. Düsseldorf: Patmos Verlag, 1991.

Driedger, Leo, and Donald B. Kraybill. *Mennonite Peacemaking: From Quietism to Activism*. Scottsdale (Pennsylvania) and Waterloo (Ontario): Herald Press, 1994.

Duckers, James Scott. *"Handed Over."* London: C.W. Daniel, 1917.

Durnbaugh, Donald F. *Pragmatic Prophet: The Life of M.R. Zigler*. Elgin (Illinois): Brethren Press, 1989.

Dyck, Harvey L., ed. *The Pacifist Impulse in Historical Perspective*. Toronto: University of Toronto Press, 1996.

Dyck, John M., ed. *Faith under Test: Alternative Service during World War II in the U.S. and Canada – Over Forty Personal Experiences* ... Moundridge (Kansas) and Ste. Anne (Manitoba): Gospel Publishers, 1997.

Early, Frances H. *A World without War: How U.S. Feminists and Pacifists resisted World War I*. Syracuse: Syracuse University Press, 1997.

Easwaran, Eknath. *A Man to match His Mountains: Badshah Khan, Nonviolent Soldier of Islam*. Petalurna (California): Nilgiri Press, 1984.

Eide, Ashbjorn, and Chama Mubanga-Chipoya, eds. *Conscientious Objection to Military Service. A United Nations Report prepared in Pursuance of Resolutions 14 (XXXIV) and 1982/30 of the UNESCO Commission on Human Rights, Sub-Commission on Prevention of Discrimination and Protection of Minorities* ... New York: United Nations, 1985.

Ein Christ verweigert den Kriegsdienst: Hermann Stöhr zum Gedächtnis. Zwiefalten (Württemberg): Sonderheft der *Versöhnung*, 1951.

Eller, Cynthia. *Conscientious Objectors and the Second World War: Moral and Religious Arguments in Support of Pacifism*. New York: Praeger, 1991.

Epstein, Barbara. *Political Protest and Cultural Revolution: Nonviolent Direct Action in the 1970s and 1980s*. Berkeley: University of California Press, 1991.

Evans, Gwynfor. *Nonviolent Nationalism*. New Malden (U.K.): Fellowship of Reconciliation, 1973.

Farrugia, Peter. *Religious Pacifism in Britain: A Case Study from the 1930s*. Occasional Papers Series (Loyola Jesuit Institute for Studies in International Peace): 2. Montreal, 1993.

Ferber, Michael, and Staughton Lynd, eds. *The Resistance*. Boston: Beacon Press, 1971.

Finn, James. *Protest, Pacifism and Politics: Some Passionate Views on War and Non-violence*. New York: Vintage Books, 1968.

Finney, Torin R.T. *Unsung Hero of the Great War: The Life and Witness of Ben Salmon*. New York and Mahwah (New Jersey): Paulist Press, 1989.

Forest, James H. *Thomas Merton's Struggle with Peacemaking*. Erie (Pennsylvania): Pax Christi USA, 1983.

— *The United Buddhist Church of Vietnam: Fifteen Years of Reconciliation*. Alkmaar (Netherlands): International Fellowship of Reconciliation, 1978.

Foster, Carrie A. *The Women and the Warriors: The U.S. Section of the Women's International League for Peace and Freedom, 1915–1946*. Syracuse: Syracuse University Press, 1995.

Foster, Catherine. *Women for All Seasons: The Story of the Women's International League for Peace and Freedom*. Athens and London: The University of Georgia Press, 1989.

Frazer, Heather T., and John O'Sullivan, eds. *"We have just begun to not fight": An Oral History of Conscientious Objectors in Civilian Public Service during World War II*. New York: Twayne Publishers, 1996.

Friends in Civilian Public Service: Quaker Conscientious Objectors in World War II look back and look ahead. Wallingford (Pennsylvania): Pendle Hill, 1998.

Gandhi, M.K. *An Autobiography or The Story of My Experiments with Truth*. Translated from the Gujarati by Mahadev Desai. Harmondsworth (Middlesex): Penguin Books, 1982.

— *Non-violent Revolution (Satyagraha)*. Ed. Bharatan Kumarappa. New York: Schocken Books, 1961.

Gestrich, Andreas, *et al.*, eds. *Gewaltfreiheit: Pazifistische Konzepte im 19. und 20. Jahrhundert (Jahrbuch für Historische Friedensforschung – 5)*. Münster: Lit Verlag, 1996.

Giannini, Giorgio. *L'obiezione di coscienza al servizio militare: Saggio storico-giuridico*. Naples: Edizioni Dehoniane, 1987.

Goodall, Felicity, ed. *A Question of Conscience: Conscientious Objection in the Two World Wars*. Stroud (U.K.): Sutton Publishing, 1997.

Goodman, Paul, ed. *Seeds of Liberation*. New York: George Braziller, 1964.

Goossen, Rachel Waltner. *Women against the Good War: Conscientious Objection and Gender on the American Home Front, 1941–1947*. Chapel Hill: The University of North Carolina Press, 1997.

Gordillo, José Luis. *La objeción de conciencia: Ejército, individuo y responsabilidad moral*. Barcelona: Ediciones Paidós, 1993.

Goss-Mayr, Hildegard. *Wie Feinde Freunde werden: Mein Leben mit Jean Goss für Gewaltlosigkeit, Gerechtigkeit und Versöhnung*. Freiburg: Herder, 1996.

Graham, John W. *Conscription and Conscience: A History 1916–1919*. London: George Allen & Unwin Ltd., 1922.

Grant, David. *Out in the Cold: Pacifists and Conscientious Objectors in New Zealand during World War II*. Auckland: Reed Methuen, 1986.

Gray, Harold Studley. *Character "Bad": The Story of a Conscientious Objector – As told in the Letters of Harold Studley Gray.* Ed. Kenneth Irving Brown. New York and London: Harper & Brothers, 1934.

Gregg, Richard B. *The Power of Nonviolence.* Nyack: Fellowship Publications, 1959.

Gressel, Hans. *Der internationale Versöhnungsbund: Ein Modell des christlichen Pazifismus.* Uetersen: Internationaler Versöhnungsbund-Deutscher Zweig, 1993.

Griffith, Reva, ed. *One Man's Story: A Conscientious Objector in World War I – As told through Letters Written by Arthur C. Standing and His Family July 1918 to September 1919.* Kansas City: John and Reva Griffith, 1997.

Griffiths, E.H. *Heddychwr mawr Cymru: George M. Ll. Davies.* Caernarvon: Llyfrfa'r Methodistiaid Calfinaidd. 2 vols., 1967–68.

Gronowicz, Anthony, ed. *Oswald Garrison Villard: The Dilemma of the Absolute Pacifist in Two World Wars.* New York and London: Garland Publishing, 1983.

Grudo, Cynthia Lee, ed. *Conscientious Objection: From Religious Pacifism to Political Protest.* Zikhron Ya'akov: The Israeli Institute for Military Studies, [1992].

Grünewald, Guido, ed. *Nieder die Waffen! Hundert Jahre Deutsche Friedensgesellschaft 1892–1992.* Bremen: Donat Verlag, 1992.

–, and Peter van Dungen, eds. *Twentieth-Century Peace Movements: Successes and Failures.* Lewiston (New York): The Edwin Mellen Press, 1995.

Guenther, Waldemar, *et al.*, eds. *"Our Guys": Alternate Service for Mennonites in Russia under the Romanows.* Transl. from the German by Peter H. Friesen. Winnipeg: Bethania Mennonite Personal Care Home, n.d.

Guide to the Swarthmore College Peace Collection. Swarthmore (Pennsylvania): Swarthmore College, 1981.

Habenstreit, Barbara. *Men against War.* Garden City (New York): Doubleday & Company, 1973.

Hassler, Alfred. *Diary of a Self-Made Convict.* Chicago: Henry Regnery Company, 1954.

Hayes, Denis. *Challenge of Conscience: The Story of the Conscientious Objectors of 1939–1949.* Ed. John W. Chambers. New York and London: Garland Publishing, 1972.

Hedemann, Ed. *War Tax Resistance: A Guide to withholding Your Support from the Military.* Ed. Ruth Benn. New York and Philadelphia: War Resisters' League and New Society Publishers, 1992.

Hershberger, Guy Franklin. *War, Peace, and Nonresistance.* Scottdale: Herald Press, 1969.

Heynis, Hans. *De Christelijk Democratische Unie, Kerk en Vrede en het pacifisme (1924–1940).* Zwolle: Stichting Voorlichting Aktieve Geweldloosheid (SVAG), 1981.

Hinton, James. *Protests and Visions: Peace Politics in Twentieth-Century Britain.* London: Hutchinson Radius, 1989.

Hoare, Richard J., ed. *John Hoare: A Pacifist's Progress – Papers from the First World War.* York: Sessions Book Trust, 1998.

Holl, Karl. *Pazifismus in Deutschland*. Frankfurt am Main: Suhrkamp Verlag, 1988.

–, and Wolfgram Wette, eds. *Pazifismus in der Weimarer Repbulik: Beiträge zur historischen Friedensforschung*. Paderborn: F. Schöningh, 1981.

Holmes, Robert L., ed. *Nonviolence in Theory and Practice*. Belmont (California): Wadsworth Publishing Company, 1990.

Homan, Gerlof D. *American Mennonites and the Great War 1914–1918*. Scottdale and Waterloo: Herald Press, 1994.

Home, William Douglas. *Sins of Commission*. Wilton (U.K.): Michael Russell, 1985.

Hope, Marjorie, and James Young. *The Struggle for Humanity: Agents of Nonviolent Change in a Violent World*. Maryknoll (New York): Orbis Books, 1977.

Horsburgh, H.J.N. *Non-violence and Aggression: A Study of Gandhi's Moral Equivalent of War*. London: Oxford University Press, 1968.

Howlett, Charles F., ed. *The American Peace Movement: References and Resources*. Boston: G.K. Hall & Co., 1991.

Hurvitz, Deena, and Craig Simpson, eds. *Against the Tide: Pacifist Resistance in the Second World War – An Oral History*. New York: War Resisters' League, 1984.

Huxley, Aldous. *Eyeless in Gaza*. London: Chatto & Windus, 1936.

– *Pacifism and Philosophy: An Aldous Huxley Reader*. London: Peace Pledge Union, 1994.

Ibarra, Pedro, *et al.*, eds. *Objeción e insumisión: Claves ideologicas y sociales*. Madrid: Editorial fundamentos, 1992.

Ingram, Norman. *The Politics of Dissent: Pacifism in France 1919–1939*. Oxford: Clarendon Press, 1991.

Jacobs, Clyde E., and John F. Gallagher, eds. *The Selective Service Act: A Case Study of the Governmental Process*. New York: Dodd, Mead & Company, 1967.

Jahn, Beate. *Politik und Moral: Gandhis Herausforderung für die Weimarer Republik*. Kassel: Verlag Weber, Zucht & Co., 1993.

Jannaway, Frank G. *Without the Camp: Being the Story of why and how the Christadelphians were exempted from Military Service*. London: published by author, 1917.

Janzen, Rod. A. *Terry Miller: The Pacifist Politician – From Hutterite Colony to State Capitol*. Freeman (South Dakota): Pine Hill Press, 1986.

Janzen, William, and Frances Greaser. *Sam Martin Went to Prison: The Story of Conscientious Objection and Canadian Military Service*. Winnipeg: Kindred Press, 1990.

Josephson, Harold, ed. *Biographical Dictionary of Modern Peace Leaders*. Westport: Greenwood Press, 1985.

Kapur, Sudarshan. *Raising up a Prophet: The African-American Encounter with Gandhi*. Boston: Beacon Press, 1992.

Katsuya, Kodama, and Unto Vesa, eds. *Towards a Comparative Analysis of Peace Movements*. Aldershot (U.K.): Dartmouth Publishing Company, 1990.

Keim, Albert N. *The CPS Story: An Illustrated History of Civilian Public Service*. Intercourse (Pennsylvania): Good Books, 1990.

–, and Grant M. Stoltzfus. *The Politics of Conscience: The Historic Peace Churches and America at War 1917–1955*. Scottdale: Herald Press, 1988.

Kennedy, Thomas C. *The Hound of Conscience: A History of the No-Conscription Fellowship 1914–1919*. Fayetteville: The University of Arkansas Press, 1981.

Kerans, Marion Douglas. *Muriel Duckworth: A Very Active Pacifist*. Halifax, Nova Scotia: Fernwood Publishing, 1996.

Kiljunen, Kimmo, and Jouko Väänänen, eds. *Youth and Conscription*. Helsinki: Peace Union of Finland, 1987.

King, Martin Luther, Jr. *Stride toward Freedom: The Montgomery Story*. New York: Harper & Row, 1958.

Klassen, A.J. ed. *Alternative Service for Peace in Canada during World War II 1941–1946*. Abbotsford (British Columbia): MCC (B.C.) Seniors for Peace, 1998.

Klejment, Anne, and Nancy Roberts, eds. *American Catholic Pacifism: The Influence of Dorothy Day and the Catholic Worker Movement*. Westport: Praeger, 1996.

Klippenstein, Lawrence, ed. *That there be Peace: Mennonites in Canada and World War II*. Winnipeg: The Manitoba CO Reunion Committee, 1979.

Kobler, Franz, ed. *Gewalt und Gewaltlosigkeit: Handbuch des aktiven Pazifismus*. Ed. Přemysl Pitter. New York: Garland Publishing, 1971.

Kohn, Stephen M. *Jailed for Peace: The History of American Draft Law Violators, 1658–1985*. Westport: Greenwood Press, 1986.

Krücken, Wolfgang. *Kriegsdienstverweigerung: Politisch-ethisch-theologische Erinnerungen und Erwägungen zu einem unbewaltigten Problem*. St. Ottilien: EOS Verlag, 1987.

Krueger, Jake, *et al.*, eds. *ASM: Alternative Service Memoirs*. Altona (Manitoba): privately printed, 1995.

Kubbig, Bernd W. *Kirche und Kriegsdienstverweigerung in der BRD*. Stuttgart: Verlag W. Kohlhammer, 1974.

Lakey, George. *Strategy for a Living Revolution*. New York: Grossman Publishers, 1973.

Lester, Muriel. *Ambassador of Reconciliation: A Muriel Lester Reader*. Ed. Richard Deats. Philadelphia and Santa Cruz: New Society Publishers, 1991.

Lewis, John, with Michael D'Orso. *Walking with the Wind: A Memoir of the Movement*. New York: Simon & Schuster, 1998.

Lewy, Guenter. *Peace & Revolution: The Moral Crisis of American Pacifism*. Grand Rapids (Michigan): William B. Eerdmans Publishing Company, 1988.

Liddington, Jill. *The Road to Greenham Common: Feminism and Anti-Militarism in Britain since 1820*. Syracuse: Syracuse University Press, 1991.

Ligt, Bart de. *The Conquest of Violence: An Essay on War and Violence*. Transl. from the French by Honor Tracy. London: The Pluto Press, 1989.

Lipp, Karlheinz. *Religiöser Sozialismus und Pazifismus: Der Friedenskampf des Bundes der Religiösen Sozialisten Deutschlands in der Weimarer Republik*. Pfaffenweiler: Centaurus-Verlagsgesellschaft, 1995.

Locke, Elsie. *Peace People: A History of Peace Activities in New Zealand*. Christchurch and Melbourne: Hazard Press, 1992.

Lofland, John. *Polite Protesters: The American Peace Movement of the 1980s*. Syracuse: Syracuse University Press, 1993.

Lütgemeier-Davin. Reinhold. *Hakenkreuz und Friedenstaube: "Der Fall Hein Herbers" (1895–1968)*. Frankfurt am Main: Dipa-Verlag, 1988.

Lynd, Staughton, ed. *Nonviolence in America: A Documentary History*. Indianapolis: Bobbs-Merrill Co., 1966.

Lyttle, Bradford. *You come with Naked Hands: The Story of the San Francisco to Moscow March for Peace*. Raymond (New Hampshire): Greenleaf Books, 1966.

Maar, Dieter. *Materialen zur Kriegsdienstverweigerung* ... Koblenz: Zentrum innere Führung (Zifü), 1989.

Maclachlan, Lewis. *C.P.F.L.U.: A History of the Christian Pacifist Forestry and Land Units*. London: The Fellowship of Reconciliation, 1952.

Martin, David A. *Pacifism: An Historical and Sociological Study*. London: Routledge & Kegan Paul, 1965.

Martin, J.B., and N.M. Bearinger, eds. *Laws affecting Historic Peace Churches*. N.p.p.: Conference of Historic Peace Churches [in Canada], 1941.

Mayer, Peter, ed. *The Pacifist Conscience*. London: Penguin Books, 1966.

Mayr, Kaspar. *Der andere Weg*. Ed. Hildegard Goss-Mayr. New York and London: Garland Publishing, 1972.

McKeown, Bonni. *Peaceful Patriot: The Story of Tom Bennett*. Charleston (West Virginia): Mountain State Press, 1980.

McNeal, Patricia. *Harder than War: Catholic Peacemaking in Twentieth-Century America*. New Brunswick (New Jersey): Rutgers University Press, 1992.

McSorley, Richard. *It's a Sin to build a Nuclear Weapon: The Collected Works on War and Peacemaking of Richard McSorley, S.J.* Ed. John Dear. Baltimore: Fortkamp Publishing Company, 1991.

– *New Testament Basis of Peacemaking*. Scottdale and Kitchener: Herald Press, 1985.

Mellanby, Kenneth. *Human Guinea Pigs*. London: Merlin Press, 1973.

The Mennonite Quarterly Review (Goshen, Indiana), Vol. LXVI, No. 4 (October 1992): *Mennonites and Alternative Service in World War II*.

Metzger, Max Josef. *Für Frieden und Einheit: Briefe aus der Gefangenschaft*. Meitingen: Kyrios-Verlag, 1964.

– *Max Josef Metzger: Priest and Martyr 1887–1944*. Ed. Lilian Stevenson. London: S.P.C.K., 1952.

Meyer, Ernest L. *"Hey! Yellowbacks!" The War Diary of a Conscientious Objector.* New York: The John Day Company, 1930.

Mitchell, Hobart. *We would not kill.* Richmond (Indiana): Friends United Press, 1983.

Moore, Howard W. *Plowing My Own Furrow.* Syracuse: Syracuse University Press, 1993.

Moorehead, Caroline. *Troublesome People: Enemies of War 1916–1986.* London: Hamish Hamilton, 1987.

Morrisey, Will. *A Political Approach to Pacifism.* 2 vols. Lewiston/Queenston/Lampeter: The Edwin Mellen Press, 1996.

Morrison, Sybil. *I renounce War: The Story of the Peace Pledge Union.* London: Sheppard Press, 1962.

Moskos, Charles C., and John Whiteclay Chambers II, eds. *The New Conscientious Objection: From Sacred to Secular Resistance.* New York: Oxford University Press, 1993.

Müller-Bohn, Jost, ed. *Letze Briefe eines Wehrdienstverweigerers 1943.* Lahr-Dinglingen: Verlag der St. Johannis-Druckerei, C. Schweickhardt, 1984.

Musto, Ronald G., ed. *Catholic Peacemakers: A Documentary History.* Vol. II, 2 pts. New York and London: Garland Publishing, 1996.

Naess, Arne. *Gandhi and Group Conflict: An Exploration of Satyagraha – Theoretical Background.* Oslo: Universitetsforlaget, 1974.

Naeve, Lowell. *A Field of Broken Stones.* Glen Gardner (New Jersey): Libertarian Press, 1950.

Nelson, John K. *The Peace Prophets: American Pacifist Thought, 1919–1941.* Chapel Hill: The University of North Carolina Press, 1950.

Noone, Michael F., Jr., ed. *Selective Conscientious Objection: Accommodating Conscience and Security.* Boulder (Colorado): Westview Press, 1989.

O'Gorman, Angie, ed. *The Universe bends toward Justice: A Reader on Christian Nonviolence in the U.S.* Philadelphia and Santa Cruz: New Society Publishers, 1990.

Oldfield, Sybil. *Women against the Iron Fist: Alternatives to Militarism, 1900–1989.* Oxford: Basil Blackwell, 1989.

Olinger, John C. *Place of Conscience: Camp Downey.* Pocatello: Idaho State University Press, 1991.

Oliver, Bobbie. *Peacemongers: Conscientious Objectors to Military Service in Australia, 1911–1945.* South Fremanatle (Western Australia): Fremantle Arts Centre Press, 1997.

Orr, E.W. *Quakers in Peace and War, 1920–1967.* Eastbourne (U.K.): W.J. Offord, 1974.

Osborne, J.K. *I refuse.* Philadelphia: The Westminster Press, 1971.

Ostergaard, Geoffrey. *Resisting the Nation State: The Pacifist and Anarchist Traditions.* London: Peace Pledge Union, 1991.

–, and Melville Currell. *The Gentle Anarchists: A Study of the Leaders of the Sarvodaya*

Movement for Non-violent Revolution in India. Oxford: Clarendon Press, 1971.

Out of Step: War Resistance in South Africa. London: Catholic Institute for International Relations, 1989.

Overy, Bob. *How Effective are Peace Movements?* Montreal: Harvest House, 1982.

Pacifica Views: A Weekly Newspaper of Conscientious Objectors. Ed. William L. Neumann. New York and London: Garland Publishing, 1972.

Parker, Malcolm. *Prison Privilege!* Kaslo (British Columbia): KLC Publications, 1984.

Partridge, Frances. *A Pacifist's War*. New York: Universe Books, 1978.

Paying for Peace: Conscientious Objection to Military Taxation. Brussels: Quaker Council for European Affairs, [1982].

Pchelintsev, A.V. *Pravo ne streliat': Alternativnaia grazhdanskaia sluzhba*. Moscow: Institut religii i prava – "Pallada," 1997.

Peck, Jim. *We who would not kill*. New York: Lyle Stuart, 1958.

Peterson, H.C., and Gilbert C. Fite. *Opponents of War 1917–1918*. Madison: The University of Wisconsin Press, 1957.

Pierce, Nathaniel W., and Paul L. Ward. *The Voice of Conscience: A Loud and Unusual Noise? The Episcopal Peace Fellowship 1939–1989*. Charlestown, Massachusetts: Charles River Publishing, 1989.

Pierson, Ruth Roach, ed. *Women and Peace: Theoretical, Historical and Practical Perspectives*. London: Croom Helm, 1987.

Poindexter, Beverly M., ed. *Selective Service: The Attorney's View*. Ann Arbor (Michigan): The Institute of Continuing Legal Education, 1969.

Polner, Murray, and Naomi Goodman, eds. *The Challenge of Shalom: The Jewish Tradition of Peace and Justice*. New Society Publishers: Philadelphia and Gabriola Island (British Columbia), 1994.

–, and Jim O'Grady. *Disarmed and Dangerous: The Radical Lives and Times of Daniel and Philip Berrigan*. New York: Basic Books, 1997.

Posset, Franz. *Krieg und Christentum: Katolische Friedensbewegung zwischen dem Ersten und Zweiten Weltkrieg unter besonderer Berücksichtigung des Werkes von Max Josef Metzger*. Freising: Kyrios-Verlag, 1978.

Power, Paul F. *Gandhi on World Affairs*. Washington, D.C.: Public Affairs Press, 1960.

Powers, Roger S., and William B. Vogele, eds. *Protest, Power, and Change: An Encyclopedia of Nonviolent Action from ACT-UP to Women's Suffrage*. New York and London: Garland Publishing, 1997.

Prasad, Devi, and Tony Smythe, eds. *Conscription: A World Survey – Compulsory Military Service and Resistance to It*. London: War Resisters' International, 1968.

Puri, Rashmi-Sudha. *Gandhi on War and Peace*. New York: Praeger, 1987.

Pyarelal. *Mahatma Gandhi: The Last Phase*. 2 Vols; Ahmedabad: Navajivan Publishing House, 1956–58.

Rae, John. *Conscience and Politics: The British Government and the Conscientious Objector to Military Service 1916–1919*. London: Oxford University Press, 1970.

Randle, Michael. *Civil Resistance*. London: Fontana Press, 1994.

Rani, Asha. *Gandhian Non-violence and India's Freedom Struggle*. Delhi: Shree Publishing House. 1981.

Ratz, Albert. *Jean Gauchon: Le roman d'un pacifiste*. Paris: Le cherche midi éditeur, 1994.

Rempel, Hans, ed. *Waffen der Wehrlosen: Ersatzdienst der Mennoniten in der USSR*. Winnipeg: Canadian Mennonite Bible College Publications, 1980.

Riesenberger, Dieter. *Geschichte der Friedensbewegung in Deutschland: Von den Anfängen bis 1933*. Göttingen: Vandenhoeck und Ruprecht, 1985.

– *Die katholische Friedensbewegung in der Weimarer Republik*. Düsseldorf: Droste Verlag, 1976.

Rigby, Andrew. *A Life in Peace: A Biography of Wilfred Wellock*. Bridport: Prism Press, 1988.

Robbins, Keith. *The Abolition of War: The 'Peace Movement' in Britain, 1914–1919*. Cardiff: University of Wales Press, 1976.

Roberts, Nancy L., ed. *American Peace Writers, Editors, and Periodicals: A Dictionary*. Westport: Greenwood Press, 1991.

Robinson, Jo Ann Ooiman. *Abraham went out: A Biography of A.J. Muste*. Philadelphia: Temple University Press, 1981.

Rodger, Donald and Betty. *Dear Heart: Letters to and from Two Conscientious Objectors*. Ed. Faith Rodger and Margaret Lawson. Sheffield (U.K.): ALD Design & Print, 1997.

Rohr, John Anthony. *Prophets without Honor: Public Policy and the Selective Conscientious Objector*. Nashville: Ablingdon Press, 1971.

Russell, Bertrand. *Justice in War Time*. London: George Allen & Unwin Ltd., 1924.

– *Which Way to Peace?* London: Michael Joseph Ltd., 1936.

Sampson, Ronald V. *The Anarchist Basis of Pacifism*. London: Peace Pledge Union, 1965.

– *Equality and Power*. London: Heinemann, 1965.

Saunders, Malcolm. *Quiet Dissenter: The Life and Thought of an Australian Pacifist Eleanor May Moore, 1875–1949*. Canberra: Peace Research Centre (Australian National University), 1993.

–, and Ralph Summy. *The Australian Peace Movement: A Short History*. Canberra: Peace Research Centre (Australian National University), 1986.

Scheer, Friedrich-Karl. *Die Deutsche Friedensgesellschaft (1892–1933): Organisation, Ideologie, politische Ziele – Ein Beitrag zur Geschichte des Pazifismus in Deutschland*. Frankfurt am Main: Haag und Herchen Verlag, 1981.

Schlabach, Gerald, ed. *Bibliografia en español sobre la no-violencia*. Tegucigalpa (Honduras): Comité Central Menonita, n.d.

Schlabach, Theron F., and Richard T. Hughes, eds. *Proclaim Peace: Christian Pacifism from Unexpected Quarters*. Urbana and Chicago: University of Illinois Press, 1997.

Schlissel, Lillian, ed. *Conscience in America: A Documentary History of Conscientious Objection in America, 1757–1967*. New York: E.P. Dutton, 1968.

Schmid, Gerhard. *Wehr- und Zivildienst in europäischen Ländern: Informationen, Anaylsen, Unterrichtsbausteine*. Schwalbach: Wochenschau Verlag, 1994.

Schöll, Guus van. *Dienstweigering in Nederland voor de Tweede Wereldoorlog*. Zwolle: Stichting Voorlichting Aktieve Geweldloosheid (SVAG), 1981.

Schott, Linda. K. *Reconstructing Women's Thoughts: The Women's International League for Peace and Freedom before World War II*. Stanford: Stanford University Press, 1997.

Sharp, Gene. *The Politics of Nonviolent Action*. Boston: Porter Sargent Publishers, 1973.

Shepard, Mark. *Gandhi Today: The Story of Mahatma Gandhi's Successors*. Cabin John (Maryland): Seven Locks Press, 1987.

Sibley, Mulford Q., and Philip E. Jacob. *Conscription of Conscience: The American State and the Conscientious Objector, 1940–1947*. Ithaca (New York): Cornell University Press, 1952.

–, and Ada Wardlaw. *Conscientious Objectors in Prison, 1940–1945*. Philadelphia: Pacifist Research Bureau, 1945.

Simmons, Clifford, ed. *The Objectors*. London: Gibbs and Phillips, 1965.

Simons, Donald L. *I refuse: Memories of a Vietnam Objector*. Trenton (New Jersey): The Broken Rifle Press, 1952.

Small, Melvin, ed. *Give Peace a Chance: Exploring the Vietnam Antiwar Movement*. Syracuse: Syracuse University Press, 1992.

Smith, Lyn. *Pacifists in Action: The Experience of the Friends Ambulance Unit in the Second World War*. York: William Sessions Limited, 1998.

Smock, David R. *Perspectives on Pacifism: Christian, Jewish, and Muslim Views on Nonviolence and International Conflict*. Washington, D.C.: United States Institute of Peace Press, 1995.

Socknat, Thomas P. *Witness Against War: Pacifism in Canada, 1900–1945*. Toronto: University of Toronto Press, 1987.

Stafford, William E. *Down in My Heart*. Elgin (Illinois): Brethren Publishing House, 1947.

Stockdale, William. *The Government is the Criminal*. Putnam (Connecticut): The Wilda Press, 1947.

– *Jehovah's Witnesses in American Prisons*. Putnam: The Wilda Press, 1946.

Swalm, E.J., ed. *Nonresistance under Test: A Compilation of Experiences of Conscientious Objectors as encountered in Two World Wars*. Nappanee (Indiana): E.V. Publishing House, 1949.

Tatum, Lyle. *Vignettes of an Anti-War Vet*. Westmont, New Jersey: published by the author, 1997.

Taylor, Richard. *Against the Bomb: The British Peace Movement 1958–1965*. Oxford: Clarendon Press, 1988.

–, and Nigel Young, eds. *Campaigns for Peace: British Peace Movements in the Twentieth Century*. Manchester: Manchester University Press, 1987.

Thomas, Norman. *Is Conscience a Crime?* New York: Vanguard Press, 1927.

– *Norman Thomas on War: An Anthology*. Ed. Bernard K. Johnpoll. New York and London: Garland Publishing, 1974.

Tollefson, James W. *The Strength not to fight: An Oral History of Conscientious Objectors of the Vietnam War*. Boston: Little, Brown and Company, 1993.

Tracy, James. *Direct Action: Radical Pacifism from the Union Eight to the Chicago Seven*. Chicago and London: University of Chicago Press, 1996.

The Tribunal. Ed. John G. Slater. New York: Kraus Reprint Co., 1970.

True, Michael. *An Energy Field more Intense than War: The Nonviolent Tradition and American Literature*. Syracuse: Syracuse University Press, 1995.

Van Dyck, Harry R. *Exercise of Conscience: A World War II Objector remembers*. Buffalo: Prometheus Books, 1990.

Van Kirk, Walter W. *Religion renounces War*. Chicago and New York: Willett, Clark & Company, 1934.

Vaux, Kenneth L. *Ethics and the Gulf War: Religion, Rhetoric, and Righteousness*. Boulder: Westview Press, 1992.

Vellacott, Jo. *Bertrand Russell and the Pacifists in the First World War*. Brighton: Harvester Press, 1990.

Vinoba Bhave. *Moved by Love: The Memoirs of Vinoba Bhave*. Translated from the Hindi by Marjorie Sykes, Totnes (U.K.): A Resurgence Book, 1994.

Wallenberg, Harry A., Jr. *Whither Freedom? A Study of the Treatment of Conscientious Objectors in the United States during World Wars I and II and Its Relation to the Concept of Freedom*. Glen Gardner: Libertarian Press, 1954.

Wallis, Jill. *Mother of World Peace: The Life of Muriel Lester*. Enfield Lock (Middlesex): Hisarlik Press, 1993.

– *Valiant for Peace: A History of the Fellowship of Reconciliation 1914 to 1989*. London: Fellowship of Reconciliation, 1991.

Washington, James Melvin, ed. *A Testament of Hope: The Essential Writings of Martin Luther King, Jr.* San Francisco: Harper & Row, 1986.

Weber, Thomas. *Conflict Resolution and Gandhian Ethics*. New Delhi: The Gandhi Peace Foundation, 1991.

– *Gandhi's Peace Army. The Shanti Sena and Unarmed Peacekeeping*. Syracuse: Syracuse University Press, 1996.

Wells, Tom. *The War within: America's Battle over Vietnam*. Berkeley and Los Angeles: University of California Press, 1994.

Wetzel, Donald. *Pacifist: Or, My War and Louis Lepke*. Sag Harbor (New York): The Permanent Press, 1986.

Wilcock, Evelyn. *Pacifism and the Jews: Studies of Twentieth Century Jewish Pacifists*. Stroud: Hawthorn Press, 1994.

Wilhelm, Paul A. *Civilian Public Servants: A Report on 210 World War II Conscientious Objectors*. Washington, D.C.: National Interreligious Service Board for Conscientious Objectors, 1990.

Williams, Eryl Hall, *A Page of History in Relief ... Quaker Relief: 1944–1946*. York: Sessions Book Trust, 1993.

Williams, Juan. *Eyes on the Prize: America's Civil Rights Years, 1954–1965*. New York: Viking Penguin, Inc., 1987.

Williamson, Janice, and Deborah Gorham, eds. *Up and Doing: Canadian Women and Peace*. Toronto: The Women's Press, 1989.

Wilson, Adrian. *Two against the Tide: A Conscientious Objector in World War II. Selected Letters, 1941–1948*. Ed. Joyce Lancaster Wilson. Austin: W. Thomas Taylor, 1990.

Wirmark, Bo. *The Buddhists in Vietnam: An Alternative View of the War*. Brussels: War Resisters' International, 1974.

Wittner, Lawrence S. *Rebels Against War: The American Peace Movement, 1933–1983*. Philadelphia: Temple University Press, 1984.

– *The Struggle Against the Bomb*. Vol. 1: *One World or None – A History of the World Nuclear Disarmament Movement through 1953*. Stanford (California): Stanford University Press, 1993.

Young, Nigel. *An Infantile Disorder? The Crisis and Decline of the New Left*. London and Henley: Routledge & Kegan Paul, 1977.

– *On War, National Liberation & the State*. London: Peace News, 1971.

Zahn, Gordon C. *Another Part of the War: The Camp Simon Story*. Amherst: University of Massachusetts Press, 1979.

– *In Solitary Witness: The Life and Death of Franz Jägerstätter*. New York: Holt, Rinehart and Winston, 1964.

– *War, Conscience and Dissent*. New York: Hawthorn Books, 1967.

Zaroulis, Nancy, and Gerald Sullivan. *Who spoke up? American Protest against the War in Vietnam 1963–1975*. Garden City (New York): Doubleday, 1984.

Zimmer, Timothy W.L. *Letters of a C.O. from Prison*. Valley Forge (Pennsylvania): The Judson Press, 1969.

Appendix

The Cold War era produced one outstanding antiwar artist: FRITZ EICHENBERG (1901–1990). We conclude our study with a small sampling of his work.

Born into an assimilated German Jewish family, Eichenberg began his artistic career in the Weimar Republic. Emigrating in 1933 to the United States where he continued his career as an artist, he became a Quaker in 1940 – and a committed pacifist as well. "If," he once wrote, "you see Christ in every living [human] being, how can you kill? It's impossible." He drew inspiration, in particular, from the vision of the Peaceable Kingdom depicted by an early nineteenth-century primitive painter, the Pennsylvania Quaker Edward Hicks. Eichenberg's art witnessed unremittingly to his belief in noviolence as well as in social justice and racial equality. He found these beliefs exemplified among his fellow Americans most clearly in Dorthy Day and her Catholic Worker movement. While remaining a Quaker, Eichenberg collaborated closely with the Catholic Workers from his first meeting with Day in 1949 until his death thirty one years later.

A master of the wood engraving and lithograph and an accomplished book illustrator, "Eichenberg achieved the synthesis of artistic vision, social conscience, and undogmatic faith that epitomized his own personal stance" (Robert Ellsberg). In the artist's own words describing this stance: "It has been my hope that in a small way I have been able to contribute to peace through compassion and also to the recognition, as George Fox said three centuries ago, 'that there is that of God in everyone,' a conception of the sanctity of human life which precludes all wars and violence."

FURTHER READING AND REFERENCE

Eichenberg, Fritz. *The Wood and the Graver: The Work of Fritz Eichenberg.* New York: Clarkson N. Potter, Inc., 1977.
Ellsberg, Robert, ed. *Fritz Eichenberg – Works of Mercy: The Catholic Worker.* Maryknoll, NY: Orbis Books, 1992.

STALEMATE *from* DANCE OF DEATH (*1980*)

THE PEACEABLE KINGDOM (*1950*)

*For more than half a century, at
Christmas time, I have sent a print
to my friends everywhere, usually a
commentary on the state of the
world – and incidentally on my
own condition. There are many
ways of spreading our message of
peace, hope and faith among the
peoples of this earth. We are all
blessed with different gifts, witnesses
ready to be counted.
The debt we owe great art,
accumulated over the centuries, is
immesurable. Let's try to pay it off
by listening to its immortal voice,
reviving our own creative spirit for
the sake of the Peaceable Kingdom.*

FRITZ EICHENBERG, 1984

BLACK CRUCIFIXION (*1963*)

To our bitterest opponents we say: we shall match your capacity to inflict suffering by our capacity to endure suffering. We shall meet your physical force with soul force. Do to us what you will, we shall continue to love you. We cannot in all good conscience obey your unjust laws, because noncooperation with evil is as much a moral obligation as is cooperation with good. Throw us in jail, we shall still love you. Bomb our homes and threaten our children, we shall still love you. Send your hooded perpetrators of violence into our community at the midnight hour and beat us and leave us half dead, and we shall still love you. But be assured that we will wear you down by our capacity to suffer. One day we shall win freedom, but not only for ourselves. We shall so appeal to your heart and conscience that we shall win you in the process and our victory will be a double victory.

MARTIN LUTHER KING, JR.

Drawing by Fritz Eichenberg for his wood engraving printed in the *Catholic Worker*, vol. 28, no. 10 (May, 1962)

Index

About the Authors

PETER BROCK is Professor Emeritus of History, University of Toronto

NIGEL YOUNG is Professor of Peace Studies and Sociology, Colgate University

VARIETIES OF PACIFISM:
A Survey from Antiquity to the Outset of the Twentieth Century

by
PETER BROCK

This survey of pacifist history begins with the idea of nonviolence among the Jains and Buddhists of ancient India and its reemergence in the teaching of Yeshua (Jesus) of Nazareth and the early Christian church. Varieties of medieval sectarian pacifism are considered next. Subsequent sections deal with Anabaptist and Mennonite nonresistance and the Quaker peace testimony as well as with the role played by conscientious objection in the American Revolution and the American Civil War. The author pays special attention to the period from 1815 to 1914 when an international peace movement came into existence, with absolute pacifists active in the peace societies of Britain and the United States; and he highlights the powerful impact of Tolstoy's radical writings on peace and war from the 1880s on. A short list of books and pamphlets for further reading and reference is included at the end of the book with additional bibliographical details in the notes.

Also obtainable from
SYRACUSE UNIVERSITY PRESS
1600 Jamesville Avenue
Syracuse, New York 13244-5160